American Higher Education in the Twenty-First Century

American Higher Education in the Twenty-First Century

Social, Political, and Economic Challenges

THIRD EDITION

Edited by

Philip G. Altbach, Patricia J. Gumport, and Robert O. Berdahl

The Johns Hopkins University Press

Baltimore

The Johns Hopkins University Press
2715 North Charles Street
Baltimore, Maryland 21218-4363
www.press.jhu.edu

Library of Congress Cataloging-in-Publication Data

American higher education in the twenty-first century : social, political, and
economic challenges / edited by Philip G. Altbach, Patricia J. Gumport, and
Robert O. Berdahl. — 3rd ed.
     p. cm.
     Includes bibliographical references and index.
     ISBN-13: 978-0-8018-9905-8 (hardcover : alk. paper)
     ISBN-10: 0-8018-9905-2 (hardcover : alk. paper)
     ISBN-13: 978-0-8018-9906-5 (pbk. : alk. paper)
     ISBN-10: 0-8018-9906-0 (pbk. : alk. paper)
     1. Education, Higher—Aims and objectives—United States.   2. Education,
Higher—Social aspects—United States.   3. Education, Higher—Political
aspects—United States.   I. Altbach, Philip G.   II. Gumport, Patricia J.
III. Berdahl, Robert Oliver.
     LA227.4.A45   2011
     378.73'0905—dc22   2010026156

A catalog record for this book is available from the British Library.

*Special discounts are available for bulk purchases of this book. For more
information, please contact Special Sales at 410-516-6936 or
specialsales@press.jhu.edu.*

The Johns Hopkins University Press uses environmentally friendly book
materials, including recycled text paper that is composed of at least
30 percent post-consumer waste, whenever possible. All of our book papers
are acid-free, and our jackets and covers are printed on paper with recycled
content.

Contents

American Higher Education in the
Twenty-First Century

The Contexts of American Higher Education

Robert O. Berdahl, Philip G. Altbach, and
Patricia J. Gumport

This volume seeks to capture several crucial dynamics in the nexus of higher education and society. Many aspects of the relationship between colleges and universities and their external environments are being critically analyzed as the importance of higher education to the nation's future in a global economy becomes increasingly visible. This is the third edition of this book, and those issues considered current have changed considerably over the past ten years (to go back no further than the date of our first edition). For instance, in 1999 we listed multiculturalism in the curriculum, racially based admissions procedures, violence and hate crimes on campus, grade strikes waged by graduate student teaching assistants, accountability to the state, assessment of student learning, monitoring of faculty productivity, scientific misconduct and fraud, university-industry partnerships, technology transfer, university mismanagement of indirect cost funds, and budget cuts and downsizing mandates from state legislatures. In contrast, in the second edition in 2005, we noted the emphasis on the values of the free market. From society and the broader economy in general to the halls of academe in particular, we were assured that the correct path to improvement and prosperity was that of deregulation, decentralization, privatization, globalization, information technology (IT), reinventing government, and total quality improvement (TQI). We noted the emergence of for-profit providers, in part due to technological capabilities for distance education. Participants in these new ventures, and even some observers, advocated new organizational forms that prioritized efficiency and expanded revenue-generating capacities. While the discourse about the issues reflects some change in what's most urgent, the many topics previously discussed remain relevant concerns for many in higher education, albeit for some readers more in the background than in the foreground.

Today one senses that the major public agenda in the United States has become one of the Four A's: Access, Attrition, Affordability, and Accountability. As later chapters will explain, in American federalism the primary responsibility for systems (note the plural) of higher education rests with the states, but since 1945 the U.S. national government has come to play an increasingly powerful role. The eight years of the George W. Bush administration included many activities affecting the public and private institutions of higher education in this country. Primary among them was the 2006 report of the Spellings Commission (*Charting the Future of U.S. Higher Education*), established by Secretary of Education Margaret Spellings, which pushed institutions to be more affordable and accessible, and accrediting agencies to produce more information relevant to accountability for student learning. Supplementing these efforts, there was also a National Commission of Student Financial Assistance report, *Access Denied* (February 2001); a Lumina Foundation report, *Making Opportunity Affordable* (2007); and a joint report by the National Association of State Universities and Land-Grant Colleges (NASULGC) and the American Association of State Colleges and Universities (AASCU), *A Voluntary System of Accountability* (2008). Again, later chapters will analyze in much more detail the dilemmas of our student aid programs, inadequate access patterns, overly high attrition rates, and spiraling college tuition costs.

Such urgent concerns dominate the state level as well. Nor are things better at this level. In the current economic crisis, when most states are struggling with the already heavy burdens from Medicare, Medicaid, state prison costs, and K–12 mandatory expenses, it is unrealistic to expect many states to find sufficient upturns in their economy to support the increasing costs of higher education, particularly with an enrollment growth projected in the near future for most states. Thus, when the National Center for Public Policy and Higher Education issued its most recent periodic analysis of the states, *Measuring Up 2008: The National Re-*

port Card on Higher Education, it was no surprise to find it giving a grade of F in Affordability to every state in the union except California (which received a C). While some of the states did much better on the other dimensions of the report (Preparation, Participation, Completion, and Benefits), the document continued its earlier practice of giving all the states an incomplete on Learning, as it noted that the data are still inadequate for cross-state comparisons. Again, later chapters will elaborate on some of these palpable frustrations and problems.

Clearly, American higher education is in a state of ferment! Of course, this is nothing new. In a system of higher education as large and decentralized as that in the United States, it is difficult to analyze the cumulative record of twentieth-century strains and transitions comprehensively, much less reassess priorities so that higher education will survive and prosper. However, there is analytical utility in examining the affairs of colleges and universities within their changing social, political, and economic contexts. Accordingly, the editors of this volume and its contributors share a common view of colleges and universities as social institutions embedded in the wider society and subject to society's constraining forces. We stress that in view of the obviously changing agenda of issues, the importance of the policy process becomes magnified. In trying to assess the validity of criticisms of American higher education, it is helpful to bring a broader perspective to the process.

That is why this volume begins in Part One, "The Setting," with chapters on American higher education in world comparisons (which helps to show that other countries are also wrestling with at least some of our current problems) and on American higher education in historical dimensions (which helps to show that our universities and colleges have long been in some degree of tension with their surrounding societies). Part One also includes chapters on such fundamental issues as autonomy and accountability and academic freedom.

Part Two, "External Forces," includes chapters analyzing the roles of the major external constituencies: the federal government, state governments, the court system, and nongovernmental elements.

Part Three, "The Academic Community," provides coverage of the internal constituencies: faculty, students, and the presidency.

Part Four, "Central Issues for the Twenty-First Century," offers a more detailed analysis of several key issues: finance, technology, graduate education, the curriculum, race, and what Derek Bok has termed the "commercialization of higher education."[1]

We have, in effect, posed macro questions such as the following to ourselves and our contributors: Given our casting of universities and colleges as social institutions, what are they like today? What forces, either unique to our era or continuing from the past, are shaping higher education? What is the future of higher education in the context of twenty-first-century America?

Universities as Social Institutions

Universities—and by extension many four-year and two-year postsecondary institutions—have generally had ambivalent relations with their surrounding societies: both involved and withdrawn, both servicing and criticizing, both needing and being needed. Eric Ashby identifies the central dilemma of this ambivalence: a university "must be sufficiently stable to sustain the ideal which gave it birth and sufficiently responsive to remain relevant to the society which supports it."[2]

The medieval universities of Europe developed as supranational institutions under the jurisdiction of a distant pope and operated in a uniform cultural milieu, which allowed them to combine practical learning for the "higher" vocations or professions with a search for universal truths. Later, when nation-states replaced the Catholic Church as the dominant authority over universities, the latter were often able to retain significant autonomy. Clark Kerr notes how remarkably stable many of these medieval universities have proven: "About eighty-five institutions in the Western world established by 1520 still exist in recognizable forms, with similar functions and with unbroken histories, including the Catholic Church, the Parliaments of the Isle of Man, of Iceland and of Great Britain, several Swiss Cantons, and seventy universities."[3]

Of course, it was easier for a nation to grant its universities autonomy when only a small proportion of its youth were attending, when students were not going much beyond the trivium and the quadrivium in their curriculum, and when few, if any, state funds were involved. In the nineteenth century, however, three developments were to occur that would increase tension between autonomy and accountability. First, beginning in German universities and spreading to universities in other Western countries, was the notion of the importance of science and research in higher education. Governments began to see the links among universities, economic growth, and military strength. Second, the Morrill Land Grant Act of 1862 in the United States broadened the curriculum to include the agricultural and mechanical arts. This led to the diversification of higher education institutions, a larger and more heterogeneous student body, higher state costs, and the notion of university public service. The American pattern, like the German, eventually spread to other countries. Third, the public and governments grew reluctant to increase public spending, which led to increased accountability on the part of higher education institutions and to a constraint on their unbridled growth.

Martin Trow shows how the autonomy-accountability dichotomy has changed as higher education has moved from an "elite" system to a "mass" system—that is, from educating less than 15 percent of the college-age cohort to educating between 15 and 50 percent of it.[4] Trow also examines the probable consequences of another transition, to "universal access," which has been tried in only a few states.[5]

In the present era, questions have arisen about the usefulness of mass access and about whether higher education is a public good, which primarily benefits society and which, therefore, merits public expenditure, or whether it is a private good, which directly benefits the individual, who should therefore bear the cost.[6] Some have come to see higher education as a "mature industry" in which expansion will be slow; basic assumptions about the nature of the academic enterprise will focus on stability rather than on growth.[7]

In this new context, some see community colleges coming to play even more important roles in keeping access open and in training and retraining the American workforce in an increasingly globalized economy.

A Matter of Definitions

At first glance, the terms *autonomy* and *accountability* do not seem to present semantic problems. Taken most simply, *autonomy* means the power to govern without outside controls, and *accountability* means the requirement to demonstrate responsible actions to external constituencies. In theory, between being both highly autonomous and rigorously accountable are not necessarily incompatible. In practice, in cases in which more accountability is required, less autonomy remains. The ideal would seem to be a balance of both. Too much autonomy might render universities unresponsive to society, while too much accountability might destroy the academic ethos.

The dilemma, however, is more complicated. For example, given academic complaints about "intrusions" into institutional autonomy, one would like to know what the action in question is; academic freedom and institutional autonomy are not the same, and the academy's reactions should reflect this distinction. We need to distinguish among the several dimensions of autonomy:

—*Academic freedom* is the freedom of the individual scholar to pursue truth wherever it leads in his/her teaching and research, without fear of punishment or termination of employment for having offended some political, methodological, religious, or social orthodoxy.

—*Substantive autonomy* is the power of the university or college in its corporate form to determine its own goals and programs (the *what* of academe).

—*Procedural autonomy* is the power of the university or college in its corporate form to determine the means by which its goals and programs will be pursued (the *how* of academe).

These three concepts are obviously interrelated; for example, a college enjoying substantive and procedural autonomy would normally be better able to protect the academic freedom of its faculty (although autonomous Oxford and Cambridge universities in the early nineteenth century denied academic freedom to their faculty, whereas nonautonomous Berlin University became known for its *Lehrfreiheit,* or academic freedom). Along another dimension, onerous governmental procedural controls would seriously hinder a college's ability to achieve its chosen goals. Notwithstanding such blurring of categories in real life, an examination of relations between higher education and government will be helped by distinguishing these three concepts.

Ashby envisions academic freedom as an "internationally recognized and unambiguous privilege of university teachers, which must be protected whenever and however challenged," even though "the question as to what constitutes autonomy in universities is anything but unambiguous, and the patterns of autonomy which satisfy academics in different countries are very diverse."[8] Therefore, in exploring autonomy issues, it is helpful to clarify whether the intervention is in *procedural* or *substantive* matters. Intervention in procedural matters (preaudits and controls over purchasing, personnel, and some aspects of capital construction) can be an enormous bother to academe and often even run counter to efficiency, but it does not usually prevent colleges or universities from achieving their goals. In contrast, governmental actions that affect substantive goals compromise the very essence of academe. What is needed in this sensitive area is negotiation of the roles of government and universities, leading to a division of powers and a decision on which one will make which decisions relating to academe. For Ashby, the real safeguard for autonomy lies in ensuring that the following "essential ingredients" of autonomy "are widely understood among the public, politicians, and civil servants":[9]

—the freedom of universities to select staff and students and determine the conditions under which they remain in the university
—the freedom of universities to determine curriculum content and degree standards
—the freedom of universities to allocate funds (within the amounts available) across different categories of expenditures

The definition of accountability must also be examined. To speak of demonstrating "responsible actions" begs the following questions: What constitutes such actions? Who determines the form and content of the reporting process? What are the sanctions for inadequate performance? In addition to furnishing information on planning, programs, and budgets to justify public tax funds before the fact, colleges and universities are also held accountable after the fact. There are at least three ways in which postaudits can be conducted (for legality, for efficiency, and for effectiveness), with varying consequences. Traditionally, governmental postaudits have focused on legality and efficiency and, through such concerns, have exerted considerable pressure on colleges and universities to tighten their operational procedures. Normally, such pressures have not forced institutions to alter their substantive goals; however, a performance-audit aspect of the accountability movement has arisen at the state level, one that focuses on the effectiveness of the policy area being examined. If extended more deeply into academe, this development could greatly affect its substantive dimensions.[10]

Lessons can be learned from this discussion. First, governments ought to stay away from issues that threaten the academic freedom of persons undertaking teaching and research at colleges and universities. Second, governmental procedural controls are probably counterproductive, and certainly irritating, but they do not justify the same academic outrage as legitimate threats to academic freedom. Third, in the crucial domain of substantive autonomy, government and universities must form a partnership wherein—while force majeure obviously lies with the former—sensitive mechanisms reconcile state concerns about accountability and academic concerns about autonomy. In the U.S. federal system, the primary governmental interface for most public-sector institutions—and some private-sector ones as well—lies at the level of state government.

Cooperation, Coordination, and Consolidation

Various modes of resolution of government-university conflict can be envisaged: bottom-up voluntary cooperation, top-down consolidated governance, or an intermediate form of statutory coordination that goes beyond cooperation but stops short of consolidated governance.

Comparative experience suggests that voluntary cooperation normally does not lead to tough decisions being made, because a voluntary association usually operates on the principle of near unanimity, and objection from a threatened party usually halts the association's progress. A later chapter illustrates the many valuable ends that may be accomplished when universities and colleges cooperate, but such collaborative ventures have not usually included making difficult decisions. The consortium movement in the United States and the history of the British Committee of Vice-Chancellors and Principals (now Universities UK) bear witness to the limits of interinstitutional cooperation. Certain goals can be accomplished, but disagreements over serious issues cannot usually be overcome.

While the authority to resolve differences between academic and governmental perspectives could be obtained through a political decision to merge all universities into one consolidated university, comparative perspectives again suggest that this response could lead to too much accountability and too little autonomy. Those states in which such consolidation has occurred do exhibit top-down retrenchment, and this retrenchment often appeals to those who yearn for a simple method of accountability. But these states also often exhibit excessive centralization of power and a preoccupation with details of governance at the expense of careful planning and coordination.

Having revealed both voluntary cooperation and consolidated governance as ineffective in taking into account the legitimate perspectives of both academe and government in the area of substantive autonomy, we are left with coordination as the most desirable (or least undesirable) means of accomplishing this vital process.

Coordination: Political, Bureaucratic, Academic, and Market

A state that honors academic freedom and resists inappropriate procedural controls may nevertheless harm its system of higher education by intervening in substantive matters. The structure, function, membership, and staffing of the mediating agency thus become crucial. In discussing the role of such an agency as a potentially "suitably sensitive mechanism" in its responsibilities for coordination, we must heed Burton Clark's warning against treating the coordination process too narrowly, as only a function of a bilateral government-institutional relationship. Clark urges that, in addition to the traditional political and bureaucratic modes of coordination, we include those modes emanating from the academic profession and the market. The market and privatization, after being ignored by political analysts as major factors in the development of U.S. universities and colleges, are now being so aggressively pushed that excessive claims are being advanced on their behalf. What may be desirable for the economies of Central and Eastern European countries after decades of communist control may not be desirable for U.S. universities and colleges, which operate in a very different social, political, and economic context:

> The special function of political coordination is to articulate a variety of public interests . . . as these are defined by prevailing groups within and outside of government. The special function of bureaucratic coordination is to compose a formal system out of fragmented parts and to provide fair administration. The function of academic oligarchy is to protect professional self-rule, to lodge the control of academic work, including its standards, in the hands of those permanently involved and most intimately connected with it. And the special function of the market is to enhance and protect freedom of choice, for personnel, clientele, and institutions and thereby indirectly promote system flexibility and adaptability.[11]

The proportions of each mode of coordination vary markedly from one system to another. For example, earlier in Britain, British academics had a pervasive role in making the system function behind the formal facade of the secretary of state for the Department of Education and Science, the civil servants in that department, and the University Grants Committee. Similarly, in the United States, a fundamental role was played by market forces based on student choice and fortified by institutional, state, and national student financial aid programs.

The simplified arguments connected with each of these modes of coordination run as follows:

—Political and bureaucratic coordination tends to overdo accountability and to be insensitive to academe's needs for flexibility and creativity.
—Collegial or academic coordination may be preoccupied with the protection of autonomy and unresponsive to the public interest.

—Coordination by market forces may promote responsiveness to social demand while relieving public authority of the burden and blame for deciding which programs and which institutions may survive during a period of retrenchment, but it may compromise the integrity of the university as the purveyor of truth and knowledge.

Thus, one is left with Clark's observation that most systems partake of the elements of coordination in varying degrees. What may be a correct balance for one system may not be appropriate for another system; and, indeed, what may be optimal for one system at one stage in its development may not be right for that same system at another stage. There is no theoretical model for the correct balance at a given time, so we are left with making subjective judgments based on common sense and both conscious and unconscious biases.

We are concerned in this book not only with how specific governmental actions affect the administration of postsecondary education, but also with how broader societal forces impact the entire academic community. Unraveling the web of relationships between higher education and society is paramount to understanding the academic enterprise and all that goes on within it. The perennial dynamism evident at all levels of American higher education provides fodder for analysts of all inclinations. We hope that the following chapters will help readers make up their own minds about many of the pressing issues covered in them.

NOTES

1. Derek Bok, *Universities in the Marketplace: The Commercialization of Higher Education* (Princeton, NJ: Princeton University Press, 2003).

2. Eric Ashby, *Universities: British, Indian, African* (Cambridge, MA: Harvard University Press, 1966), 3.

3. Clark Kerr, *The Uses of the University* (Cambridge, MA: Harvard University Press, 1982), 152.

4. Martin Trow, "Problems in the Transition from Elite to Mass Higher Education," in *Policies for Higher Education* (Paris: Organisation for Economic Co-operation and Development, 1974).

5. Universal access means that no one is prevented from going to college for lack of resources or institutions; in some states, more than 50 percent of high school graduates go on to postsecondary institutions.

6. David W. Breneman, "The 'Privatization' of Public Universities: A Mistake or a Model for the Future?" *Chronicle of Higher Education*, Mar. 7, 1997.

7. Arthur Levine, "Higher Education's New Status as a Mature Industry," *Chronicle of Higher Education*, Jan. 31, 1997.

8. Ashby, *Universities*, 292.

9. Ibid., 296.

10. John K. Folger and Robert O. Berdahl, *Patterns in Evaluating Systems of Higher Education: Making a Virtue Out of Necessity* (College Park, MD: National Center for Postsecondary Governance and Finance, 1987).

11. Burton R. Clark, "The Many Pathways of Academic Coordination," *Higher Education* 8 (1979): 251–68.

PART I / The Setting

CHAPTER ONE

Patterns of Higher Education Development

Philip G. Altbach

U niversities are singular institutions. They have common historical roots yet are deeply embedded in their societies. Established in the medieval period to transmit knowledge and provide training for a few key professions, in the nineteenth century universities became creators of new knowledge through basic research.[1] The contemporary university is the most important institution in the complex process of knowledge creation and distribution, serving as home not only to most of the basic sciences, but also to the complex system of journals, books, and databases that communicate knowledge worldwide.[2] Universities are key providers of training in an ever-growing number of specializations. Universities have also taken on a political and cultural function in society, serving as centers for civil society. At the same time, academe is faced with unprecedented challenges, stemming in large part from a decline in resources. After almost a half century of dramatic expansion worldwide, universities in many countries are being forced to cut back on expenditures and, in some cases, to downsize. The unwritten pact between society and higher education that provided expanding resources in return for greater access for students, as well as research and service to society, has broken down, with significant implications for both higher education and society.

This chapter is concerned with the patterns of higher education development evident in the post–World War II period throughout the world, analyzing some of the reasons for these trends and pointing to likely directions for universities in the coming decades. Issues such as autonomy and accountability, research and teaching, reform and the curriculum, and the implications of the massive expansion of universities in most countries are of primary concern.

A Common Heritage

There is only one common academic model worldwide. The basic European university model, established first in Italy and France at the end of the twelfth century, has been significantly modified but remains the universal pattern for higher education. The Paris model placed the professor at the center of the institution and enshrined autonomy as an important part of the academic ethos. It is significant that the major competing idea of the period, the student-dominated University of Bologna, did not gain a major foothold in Europe, although it had some impact in Spain and later in Latin America.[3] The university rapidly expanded to other parts of Europe—Oxford and Cambridge in England, Salamanca in Spain, Prague and Krakow in Central Europe—and a variety of institutions in the German states were established in the following century.

Later, the European imperialist nations brought universities to their colonies, along with other accoutrements of colonialism. The British, for example, exported academic models first to the American colonies and later to India, Africa, and Southeast Asia.[4] The French in Vietnam and West Africa, the Spanish and the Portuguese throughout Latin America, the Dutch in Indonesia, the Americans in the Philippines, and other colonial powers also exported academic institutions.[5] Colonial universities were patterned directly on institutions in the metropole but often without the traditions of autonomy and academic freedom in the mother country.[6]

The university has by no means been a static institution; it has changed and adapted to new circumstances. With the rise of nationalism and the Protestant Reformation in Europe, the universal language of higher education, Latin, was replaced by national languages. Academic institutions became less international and more local in their student bodies and orientations and were affected by their national circumstances, Protestant Amsterdam differing, for example, from Catholic Salamanca. Harvard University, although patterned on British models, slowly developed its own traditions and orientations, reflecting the realities of colonial North America. Academic institutions have not always flourished. Oxford and Cambridge, strongly linked to the Church of England and the aristocracy, played only a minor role in the industrial revolution and the tremendous scientific expansion of the late eighteenth and nineteenth centuries.[7] In France, universities were abolished in 1793, after the initial phase of the revolution; gradually, they were reestablished, and the Napoleonic model became a powerful force not only in France but also in Spain and Latin America.[8] German universities, which were severely damaged during the Nazi period by the destruction of autonomy and the departure of many professors, lost their scientific preeminence.[9]

For the purposes of this chapter, two more recent modifications of the Western academic model are relevant. In the mid-nineteenth century, a newly united Germany harnessed the university for nation building. Under the leadership of Wilhelm von Humboldt, German higher education was given significant resources by the state, took on the responsibility for research aimed at national development and industrialization, and played a key role in defining the ideology of the new German nation.[10] German universities also established graduate education and the doctoral degree. For the first time, research became an integral function of the university, and the university was reorganized as a hierarchy based on the newly emerging scientific disciplines. American reformers further transformed higher education by stressing the relationship between the university and society through the concept of service and direct links with industry and agriculture. They also democratized the German chair system, through the establishment of academic departments, and developed the land-grant concept for both research and expanded access to higher education.[11] Thus, even institutions that seem deeply embedded in national soil have in fact been influenced by international ideas and models.

Virtually without exception, the institutional pattern followed by the world's universities derives from these Western models. Significantly, in one of the few remaining fully non-Western institutions, Al-Azhar University in Cairo, which focuses mainly on traditional Islamic law and theology, science faculties are now organized along European lines.[12] There are many variations of the Western model—open universities, two-year vocational institutions, teacher-training colleges, polytechnics—but while the functions of these institutions differ from those of traditional universities, their basic organization, pattern of governance, and ethos remain remarkably close to the Western academic ideal.[13]

Networks of Knowledge and Higher Education

There are many explanations for the dominance of the Western academic model. The institutionalization of the study of science and, later, scientific research are central elements. The link between universities and the dominant world economic systems no doubt is an important reason for Western hegemony. In many parts of the world, academic institutions were imposed by colonizers, and there were few possibilities to develop independent alternatives. Indigenous institutional forms were destroyed, as in nineteenth-century India with the British imposition of European patterns.[14] None of the formerly colonized nations have shifted from their basically European academic model; the contemporary Indian university, for example, resembles its preindependence predecessor.

Japan, which was never colonized, recognized after 1868 that it had to develop scientific and industrial capacity and jettisoned its traditional academic institutions in favor of Western university traditions, importing ideas and models from Germany, the United States, and other countries. Other noncolonized nations, such as China and Thailand, also imported Western models and adapted them to local needs and conditions.[15]

The harnessing of higher education to the broader needs of national economic and social development was perhaps the most important innovation of this era. Western universities were seen as successful in providing advanced education, fostering research and scientific development, and assisting their societies in the increasingly complex task of development. Universities in both the United States and Germany fostered industrial and agricultural development. The ideas that higher education should be supported by public funds, that the university should participate in the creation as well as the transmission of knowledge, and that academic institutions should, at the same time, be permitted a degree of autonomy were behind much of the growth of universities in the nineteenth century. Further, Western universities were at the center of a knowledge network that included research institutions, the means of knowledge dissemination (such as journals and scientific publishers), and an "invisible college" of scientists. As science became more international, a common scientific language emerged, first German and then, since the mid-twentieth century, English. Even scholars in such industrialized nations as Sweden and the Netherlands often communicate their research findings in English. The large Dutch multinational publishers Elsevier and Kluwer publish virtually all of their scholarly and scientific books and journals in English.

The circulation of scholars and students worldwide—even the so-called brain drain—is an element of the international knowledge system, helping to circulate ideas and also maintaining the research hegemony of the major host countries. More than one and one-half million students study outside their home countries, the large majority of them from Third World nations and the newly industrializing countries of the Pacific Rim. India and China send the largest numbers of students abroad to study in the industrialized nations, especially the United States, Britain, Australia, France, and Germany. Japan is both a major sending and major receiving country.[16]

As a result of their sojourns abroad, students gain expertise in their studies but also learn the norms and values of the Western academic system, often returning home with a zeal to reform their local universities. Frequently, foreign graduates have difficulty readjusting to their home countries, in part because the advanced training they acquire abroad may not be easily assimilated into less-industrialized economies. Such frustrations, along with significantly better remuneration in industrialized countries, lead to brain drain. However, in the contemporary world, brain drain is often not permanent. Members of the Third World scientific diaspora maintain contact with their colleagues at home, contributing advanced knowledge and ideas.[17] They often return home for periods of time to work with local academics and, increasingly, return home permanently when conditions are favorable. These returning students bring considerable expertise with them to their native countries and often assume leadership positions in local scientific and academic communities. With few exceptions, knowledge and institutional patterns are transferred from the major industrialized nations to the Third World—or even to more peripheral industrial countries—with very little traffic in the other direction.[18]

The English language and the Internet have become key elements in the contemporary knowledge network. English is now the unquestioned medium of scientific research and communication—with the major journals published in English, and international conferences and Web sites conducted in English. This places English-speaking academic systems, such as those in the United States, in a privileged position. The Internet has also greatly impacted knowledge networks. More journals are now published electronically, and scientific communication is increasingly conducted virtually. Paradoxically, while the Internet has permitted most of the world's scientific communities to participate in the global network, it has, in some ways, strengthened the major academic systems (especially the United States), which are most influential on the Web.

The knowledge network is complex and multifaceted; while its centers remain extraordinarily powerful, there is a movement toward greater equalization of research production and use. Japan, for example, already has a powerful and increasingly research-oriented university system, and some of the newly industrializing countries of East and Southeast Asia are building research capacity in their universities, with China playing a particularly important role.[19] But while hegemony may be slowly dissipating, inequality remains endemic in the world knowledge system.

Expansion: Hallmark of the Postwar Era

Postsecondary education has expanded since World War II in virtually every country in the world. This growth has, in proportional terms, been more dramatic than that of primary and secondary education. Writing in 1975, Martin Trow spoke of the transition from *elite* to *mass* and then to *universal* higher education in the context of the industrialized nations.[20] The United States enrolled some 30 percent of the relevant age cohort (eighteen- to twenty-two-year-olds) in higher education in the immediate postwar period, while European nations generally maintained an elite higher education system, with fewer than 5 percent attending postsecondary institutions. By the 1960s, many European nations were educating 15 percent or more of this age group; in 1970, Sweden enrolled 24 percent, and France 17 percent. That year, the United States increased its proportion to more than 50 percent and was approaching universal access. By the end of the twentieth century, most Western European countries had increased their enrollment rates to about half, reaching close to what is considered "universal" access. Thus, while American patterns of access have stabilized, those in Europe and many newly industrializing countries continue to expand. A number of countries, including South Korea and Finland, now enroll more than 70 percent of this age group.

In the Third World, expansion has been even more dramatic. Building on tiny and extraordinarily elitist universities, Third World higher education expanded rapidly in the immediate postindependence period. In India, enrollment grew from approximately 100,000 at the time of independence, in 1947, to more than 11 million by 2008. Expansion in sub-Saharan Africa has also been rapid, with the postsecondary student population growing from 181,000 in 1975 to more than 1.7 million two decades later. Expansion continues despite economic crises and the AIDS epidemic. There has been a decline in per capita student expenditure, and this has contributed to a decline in academic standards.[21] China now has the world's largest higher education enrollment, with more than 20 million in postsecondary education.

Similar trends can be seen among other non-Western countries. In a few instances, such as the Philippines, where more than one-third of the relevant age cohort enters postsecondary education, enrollment ratios have reached those of industrialized nations, although in general the Third World lags far behind in terms of the proportion of the population attending higher education institutions. Even China, with more than 14 million students in postsecondary education (approximately the same number as the United States) enrolls only 15 percent of this age group. Expansion in the Third World has, in general, exceeded that in the industrialized nations, at least in proportional terms. Among those with the highest rates of expansion and participation are Asia's newly industrializing countries, such as South Korea and Taiwan, and, recently, Latin America.

Regardless of political system, level of economic development, or educational ideology, the expansion of higher education has been the single-most-important trend worldwide. About 7 percent of the relevant age cohort attends postsecondary educational institutions, a statistic that has increased each decade since World War II. Higher education expanded first in the United States, then in Europe, and later in the Third World and the newly industrializing countries. Women now constitute approximately 40 percent of university enrollments, with considerable variation by country. The industrialized nations, with a few exceptions, have a higher proportion of the age cohort in postsecondary education than Third World countries. Generalized statistics concerning enrollments in postsecondary education mask many key differences. For example, industrialized nations have, in general, a higher proportion of students in technological and scientific fields than in liberal arts, which tend to predominate in the developing nations—although even here there are exceptions, such as China.

There are many reasons for the expansion of higher education, a central one being the increasing complexity of modern societies and economies, which demands a more highly trained workforce. Almost without exception, postsecondary institutions have been called upon to provide the required training. Indeed, training in many fields that was once imparted on the job has become formalized in institutions of higher education. Whole new fields, such as computer science, have come into existence and rely on universities as a source of research and training. Nations now developing scientific and industrial capacity, such as South Korea and Taiwan, as well as emerging agents China and India, depend on academic institutions to provide high-level training as well as research expertise.[22]

Not only do academic institutions provide training, they also test and provide certification for many occupations in contemporary society. These roles have been central to universities since the medieval period, but they have been vastly expanded in recent years. A university degree is a prerequisite for an increasing number of occupations in most societies. Indeed, academic certification is necessary for most positions of power, authority, and prestige in modern societies, which places immense power in the hands of universities. Tests to gain admission to higher education are rites of passage in many societies and are important determinants of future success.[23] Competition within academe varies from country to country, but in most cases stress is also placed on high academic performance and tests. There are often further examinations to permit entry into specific professions.

The role of the university as an examining body has grown for a number of reasons. As industrial and economic expansion has taken place, more sorting mechanisms have been needed. The older, more informal, and often more ascriptive means of controlling access to prestigious occupations no longer provide the controls needed, nor are they perceived as fair. Universities are seen as meritocratic institutions, which can be trusted to provide impartial tests to measure accomplishment and, therefore, to determine access. When such mechanisms break down (as they did in China during the Cultural Revolution), or when they are perceived as subject to corrupt influences (as in India), universities are significantly weakened. Furthermore, entirely new fields have developed for which no sorting mechanisms exist, and academic institutions are frequently called upon to provide not only training, but also examination and certification.

Expansion has also occurred because growing segments of the population of modern societies demand it. The middle classes, seeing that academic qualifications are necessary for success, demand access to higher education, and governments generally respond by increasing enrollment.[24] When governments do not move quickly enough, private initiative frequently establishes academic institutions to meet the demand. In countries such as India, the Philippines, and Bangladesh, as well as in many Latin American nations, a majority of the students are educated in private colleges and universities.[25] At present, there are powerful worldwide trends toward imposing user fees in the form of higher tuition charges, thus increasing the stress on private higher education, and in general considering higher education, in economic terms, as a private good. These changes are intended to reduce the cost of postsecondary education for governments while maintaining access, although the long-term implications for the quality of, access to, and control over higher education remain unclear.

In most societies, higher education is heavily subsidized by the government, and most, if not all, academic institutions are in the public sector. While there is a growing trend toward private initiative and management-sharing responsibility with public institutions, governments will likely continue to be a central source of funding for postsecondary education. The dramatic expansion of academic institutions in the postwar period has proven very expensive for governments. Nonetheless, the demand for access has been extraordinarily powerful.[26]

Many analysts writing in the 1960s assumed that the world, and particularly Western industrialized nations, would move from elite to mass and finally to universal access to higher education, generally following the American pattern. But the path to universal access has proved to be circuitous.[27] For a period in the 1970s, expansion slowed, only picking up again in the late 1980s. The nations of the European Union are, in general, moving toward U.S. levels of access. The causes for the slowdowns were in part economic, given the problems in Western economies that followed the oil shocks of the 1970s; in part demographic, result-ing from a significant drop in the birth rate and a smaller cohort of young people; and in part philosophical, as countries became less sympathetic to the growth of public institutions, including universities. Generally, the proportion of the rele-vant age cohort going on to higher education in Western Europe stabilized at under 20 percent in the 1970s; it began to increase again in the late 1980s, and it continues to expand.[28] This expansion has taken place in a context of steady population trends and has been impelled by changes in European economies, which have moved to the postindustrial stage. By 2003, most Western European countries were sending half of their people in this age group on to postsecondary education.

In sharp contrast to Western industrialized countries, Third World universi-ties have, in general, continued to expand without interruption. With only a very few exceptions, such as the Philippines, Third World enrollment ratios remain significantly lower than those in the industrialized nations, but there continues to be a strong commitment to continued expansion and access. This is the case even in countries like India, where there is severe unemployment of graduates and a brain drain of university graduates. In many Third World countries, it re-mains impossible for local universities to absorb all of those qualified to attend, creating an exodus of students abroad. This is the case in, for example, Malaysia.[29]

As in the industrialized nations, there is a notable trend toward shifting the burden of funding for higher education from the state to the individual.

The Third World presents a special set of circumstances. Unmet demand, an expanding middle class, and continuing population growth in many countries mean that the bulk of the world's higher education growth in the coming decades will be in developing countries. Many of these countries are building more complex economies that require more skilled workers, and this, too, contributes to expansion. Even if political authorities wanted to slow expansion, they would find it impossible to do.

General agreement that postindustrial economies need large numbers of university graduates means that participation rates in the industrialized world will continue to expand. At the same time, the retirement of the large cohort of people hired in the 1960s will open additional highly skilled jobs, and demographic trends will limit the need for more university places.[30]

Change and Reform: The Legacy of the Sixties

The demands placed on institutions of higher education to accommodate larger numbers of students and expand their functions resulted in reforms in higher education in many countries. Much debate has taken place concerning higher education reform in the 1960s, and a significant amount of change did take place.[31] Without question, the student unrest of the period contributed to disarray in higher education. This unrest was in part precipitated by deteriorating academic conditions, which were the result of rapid expansion. In a few instances, students demanded far-reaching reforms in higher education, especially an end to the rigid, hierarchical organization of the traditional European university.[32] The chair system was modified or eliminated, and the responsibility for academic decision making, formerly a monopoly of full professors, was expanded—in some countries, even to include students. At the same time, the walls of the traditional academic disciplines were broken down by interdisciplinary teaching and research.

Reform was greatest in several traditional Western European academic systems. Sweden's universities were completely transformed: decision making was democratized, universities were decentralized, educational access was expanded to previously under-served parts of the country, interdisciplinary teaching and research was instituted, and the curriculum was expanded to include vocational courses.[33] Reforms also took place in France and the Netherlands, where reformers stressed interdisciplinary studies and the democratization of academic decision making. In Germany, the universities in states dominated by the Social Democratic Party were also reformed, with the traditional structures of the university giving way to more democratic governance patterns.

In many industrialized nations, structural change was modest. In the United States, for example, despite considerable debate during the 1960s, there was very limited change in the structure or governance of higher education.[34] Japan, where unrest disrupted higher education and spawned a number of reports on university reform, experienced virtually no basic change in its higher education system, although several "new model" interdisciplinary institutions were established, such as the science-oriented Tsukuba University near Tokyo. Britain, less affected by student protest and with a plan for expansion in operation, also experienced few reforms during the 1960s.[35]

Many of the structural reforms of the 1960s were abandoned after a decade of experimentation or were replaced by other administrative arrangements. By the end of the twentieth century, there was a second wave of reforms evident worldwide. These reforms can be characterized as a "managerial revolution" in higher education, where the overall goal was to ensure more accountability and efficiency in the management of academic institutions. These reforms generally increased the power of administrators and reduced faculty authority; students, too, had less power. In Germany, for example, reforms in governance that gave students and junior staff a dominant position in some university functions were ruled unconstitutional by German courts.[36] Outside authorities, such as government (particularly in the public sector)—but also including business, industry, and labor organizations—came to play a more important role in academic governance. These changes were stimulated both by the growing size and complexity of many academic institutions and systems and by a desire to rein in expenditures. Efforts were made to privatize elements of public institutions and, in some countries, to stimulate the private sector in higher education. Curricular innovations, however, have proved more durable; interdisciplinary programs and initiatives and the introduction of new fields, such as gender studies, remain.

Vocationalization has been an important trend in the past two decades. Throughout the world, there is a conviction that the university curriculum must provide relevant training for a variety of increasingly complex jobs. Students, worried about obtaining remunerative employment, have pressed universities to focus more on job preparation. Employers have also demanded that the curriculum become more relevant to their needs. Enrollment in the social sciences and humanities, at least in industrialized nations, has declined.

Curricular vocationalism is linked to another worldwide trend in higher education: the increasingly close relationship between universities and industry.[37] Industrial firms have sought to ensure that the skills they need are incorporated into the curriculum. This trend also has implications for academic research, since many university-industry relations are focused largely on research. Industries have established formal linkages and research partnerships with universities to obtain help with research of interest to them. In countries such as Sweden, representatives from industry have been added to the governing councils of higher education institutions. In the United States, formal contractual arrangements have been made between universities and major corporations to share research results. In many industrialized nations, corporations provide educational programs for their employees, sometimes with the assistance of universities.

Technical arrangements with regard to patents, the confidentiality of research findings, and other fiscal matters have assumed importance as university-industry relations have become crucial. Critics also point out that the nature of research in higher education may be altered by this relationship, as industrial firms are not usually interested in basic research. University-based research, which has traditionally been oriented toward basic research, may be increasingly skewed to applied and profit-making topics. There has also been some discussion of research orientation in fields such as biotechnology, in which broader public policy matters may conflict with the needs of corporations. Specific funding arrangements have also been questioned. Pressure to serve the training and research requirements of industry has implications for the organization of the curriculum, the nature and scope of research, and the traditional relationship between the university and society.[38]

The traditional idea of academic governance stresses autonomy, and universities have tried to insulate themselves from direct control by external agencies. However, as universities expand and become more expensive, there is immense pressure by those providing funds for higher education—mainly governments—to expect accountability. The conflict between autonomy and accountability has been a flashpoint for controversy in recent years. Without exception, university autonomy has shrunk, and administrative structures have been put into place in such countries as Britain and the Netherlands to ensure greater accountability.[39] The issue takes on different implications in different parts of the world. In the Third World, traditions of autonomy have not been strong, and demands for accountability, both political and economic, sometimes mean government domination of academe.[40] In the industrialized nations, accountability pressures are usually more fiscal in nature.

Despite the varied pressures on higher educational institutions for change and the significant reforms that have taken place in the past two decades, there have not been many structural alterations in universities. One of the few places where this has occurred is in Sweden. Elsewhere, curricula have been altered, expansion has taken place, and there have been continuing debates concerning accountability and autonomy, but universities as institutions have not changed significantly. As Edward Shils has argued, the "academic ethos" has been under strain, and while in some ways it has been weakened, it has so far survived.[41]

The Millennium

The university is a durable institution. The modern university retains key elements of the historical models from which it sprang, even while evolving to serve the needs of societies during a period of tremendous change.[42] There has been a convergence of ideas and institutional patterns and practices in higher education, due in part to the implantation of European-style universities in developing areas during and after the colonial era, and in part to universities having been crucial to the development and internationalization of science and scholarship. Many of the changes discussed here are the result of great external pressure and were instituted despite opposition from within academe. Some scholars argue that the university has lost its soul.[43] Others claim that the university is irresponsible because it uses public funds without meeting the needs of industry and government. Pressure from governmental authorities, militant students, and external constituencies have all placed great strains on academic institutions.

The period since World War II has been one of unprecedented growth in universities, and higher education has assumed an increasingly central role in virtually all modern societies. While growth may continue, the dramatic expansion of recent decades is at an end, at least in the industrialized countries. It is unlikely that the position of the university as the most important training institution for virtually all of the top-level occupations in modern society will be weakened, although other institutions have become involved in training. The university's research role is more problematical, because of the fiscal pressures of recent years. There is no other institution that can undertake basic research, but the consensus that has supported university-based basic research has weakened.[44]

The challenges facing universities are, nonetheless, significant. The following issues are among those that will be of concern in the coming decade and beyond.

Access

Access remains a controversial issue in most countries. Worldwide, higher education is more readily available to wealthier segments of the population. With expansion, the demand has broadened, and providing access to lower-income groups is a challenge, especially in the context of fiscal constraints in higher education. Even in the United States, where access is relatively open regardless of social class, because of a highly differentiated higher education system and government-sponsored loan and grant programs, some racial and ethnic minorities remain underrepresented in the student population. There is greater inequality of access in Western Europe, although there is widespread commitment there to broaden participation. In much of the rest of the world, the lack of participation of those with low incomes, rural youths, and, in some countries, women remains a central issue. Access remains a challenge of both concern and controversy.

Administration, Accountability, and Governance

As academic institutions become larger and more complex, there is increasing pressure for professional administration, as in the United States. At the same time, the traditional forms of academic governance are increasingly criticized for being unwieldy and, in large and bureaucratic institutions, inefficient. As the administration of higher education increasingly becomes a profession, an "administrative estate" will be established. Growing demands for accountability will cause academic institutions considerable difficulty. And as academic budgets expand, there will be inevitable demands to monitor and control expenditures. At present, no general agreement exists concerning the appropriate level of governmental involvement in higher education. The challenge will be to ensure that the traditional—and valuable—patterns of faculty control over governance and basic academic decisions are maintained in a complex and bureaucratic environment. Worldwide, the rise of "managerialism" and ever-more-complex bureaucratic arrangements is part of the academic landscape. So far, the trend is for traditional governance to lose authority and power.

Knowledge Creation and Dissemination

Research is a central part of the mission of many universities and of the academic system generally. Decisions that will be in contention in the future will concern the control and funding of research, the relationship of research to the broader curriculum and teaching, the uses made of university-based research, and related issues. Further, the system of knowledge dissemination, including journals and books and computer-based data systems, is rapidly changing. Who should control the new data networks? How will traditional means of communication, such as journals, survive in this new climate? How will the scientific system avoid being overwhelmed by the proliferation of data?[45] Who will pay for the costs of knowledge dissemination? The needs of peripheral scientific systems, including both the Third World and smaller academic systems in the industrialized world, have been largely ignored but are, nonetheless, important.[46]

Information technology, or IT, has become a central element of the knowledge distribution network. Individual scientists and scholars use the Internet for direct communication. Databases accessible on the World Wide Web are increasingly important. Libraries use a greater number of electronic resources to access journals and other kinds of information and data. Issues such as the ownership of knowledge, the cost of access to electronic networks, and the influence of new electronic journals and other publications, among others, remain to be determined. At present, publishers and other data providers in the United States and other English-speaking countries stand to gain the most from the new technologies. The effect on academic institutions, especially in developing countries, remains unclear in terms of access and cost.

Major Western knowledge producers currently constitute a kind of cartel of information, dominating not only the creation of knowledge but also most of the major channels of distribution. Simply increasing the amount of research and creating new databases will not ensure a more equal and accessible knowledge system. Academic institutions are at the center, but publishers, copyright authorities, funders of research, and others are also necessarily involved.

The Academic Profession

In most countries, the professoriate has been under great pressure in recent years. Demands for accountability, the increased bureaucratization of institutions, fiscal constraints in many countries, and an increasingly diverse student body have all challenged the professoriate. In most industrialized nations, a combination of fiscal problems and demographic factors led to a stagnating profession.[47]

Circumstances vary by region, but some factors are evident worldwide. Fiscal problems create multiple difficulties. Remuneration has not kept up with either the cost of living or salaries offered elsewhere in the economy, and it is now difficult to lure the "best and brightest" to academe. The terms of academic appointments have deteriorated in many places—tenure has been abolished in Britain, for example, and in many countries a larger proportion of the profession is part time. Traditional career ladders have been modified. Class sizes have increased and academic autonomy has been limited. Pressures on the professoriate, not only to teach and do research but also to attract external grants, do consulting, and earn additional income for themselves and for their universities have grown. The difficulties faced by the academic profession in developing countries are perhaps the greatest—to maintain a viable academic culture under deteriorating conditions and without the protection of established norms.

Private Resources and Public Responsibility

In almost all countries there has been a growing emphasis on increasing the role of the private sector in higher education. One of the most direct manifestations of this trend is the role of the private sector in funding and directing university research. In many countries, private academic institutions have expanded or new ones have been established. Students are paying an increasing share of the cost of their education as a result of tuition and fee increases and through loan programs. Governments try to limit their expenditures on postsecondary education. Privatization has been the means of achieving this broad policy goal.[48] Inevitably, decisions concerning academic developments will move increasingly to the private sector, with the possibility that broader public goals may be ignored. Whether private interests will support the traditional functions of universities—including academic freedom, basic research, and a pattern of governance that leaves the professoriate in control—is unclear. Some of the most interesting developments in private higher education can be found in such countries as Vietnam, China, and Hungary. Private initiatives in higher education will bring a change in values and orientation, but it is not clear that these values will be in the long-term best interests of the university. At the beginning of the twenty-first century, the major expansion of higher education worldwide is taking place in the private sector.

Diversification and Stratification

While diversification—establishing new postsecondary institutions to meet diverse needs—is not new, it is of primary importance and will continue to reshape the academic system. In recent years, the establishment of research institutions, community colleges, polytechnics, and other academic institutions designed to meet specialized needs and serve specific populations has been a primary char-

acteristic of growth. At the same time, the academic system has becom
stratified—individuals in one sector of the system find it difficult to move
different sector. There is often a high correlation between social class (and othe
variables) and participation in a particular sector. To some extent, the reluctance
of traditional universities to change is responsible for some of the diversification.
Perhaps more important is the belief that limited-function institutions are more
efficient and less expensive. An element of diversification is the inclusion of larger
numbers of women and other previously disenfranchised segments of the population. Women now constitute 40 percent of the student population worldwide and
more than half in many industrialized countries.[49] In many countries, students
from lower socioeconomic groups and racial and ethnic minorities have entered
postsecondary institutions in significant numbers.

Economic Disparities

The substantial inequalities among the world's universities and academic systems are likely to grow. Major universities in industrialized nations generally
have the resources to play a leading role in scientific research, in a context in
which it is increasingly expensive to keep up with the expansion of knowledge.[50]
Universities in much of the Third World, however, simply cannot cope with the
increased enrollments, budgetary constraints, and, in some cases, fiscal disas-
ters. Universities in much of sub-Saharan Africa, for example, have experienced
dramatic budget cuts and find it difficult to function, not to mention improve
quality and compete in the international knowledge system.[51] Academic institutions in the newly industrializing Asian countries, where significant academic
progress has taken place, will continue to improve. Thus the economic prospects
for postsecondary education worldwide are mixed.

Globalization and Internationalization

Universities throughout the world are necessarily engaged in a ever-more-
globalized environment. Student and faculty mobility, a global job market, the
internationalization of science and scholarship, and global competition for status
are all part of contemporary globalization. Universities everywhere must now
cope with the influence of branch campuses, academic programs that are fran-
chised internationally, and dual-degree initiatives. A recognition that internationalization is central to the academic mission of higher education is universal,
as exemplified by growing numbers of mobile students. The United States, as the
most powerful academic system, has significant advantages in the international

...enges of the new globalized environment create new

...mon culture and a common reality: in many basic ways, there is a convergence ... institutional models and norms. At the same time, there are significant national differences that will continue to affect the development of academic systems and institutions. It is unlikely that the basic structures of academic institutions will change dramatically: the Humboldtian academic model will survive, although administrative structures will grow stronger and the traditional power and autonomy of the faculty will diminish. Open universities and other distance-education institutions may provide new institutional arrangements, and efforts to save money may yield further organizational changes. Unanticipated change is also possible; while the emergence of significant student movements, at least in industrialized nations, do not seem likely, circumstances may change.[53] The situation for universities in the first part of the twenty-first century is not, in general, favorable. The realities of higher education as a "mature industry" in industrialized countries, with stable rather than growing resources, will affect not only the funds available for postsecondary education, but also academic practices. Accountability, the impact of technologies, and the other forces discussed in this chapter will all affect colleges and universities, although patterns will vary. Some academic systems, especially those in the newly industrializing countries, will continue to grow. In parts of the world affected by significant political and economic change, the coming decades will be ones of reconstruction. Worldwide, the coming period is one of major challenge for higher education.

NOTES

I am indebted to Robert Arnove, the late Gail P. Kelly, and Lionel Lewis for their comments on an early version of this chapter and to Lalita Subramanyan and Patricia Murphy for their help with editing.

1. For a historical perspective, see Charles Haskins, *The Rise of Universities* (Ithaca, NY: Cornell University Press, 1957).

2. Philip G. Altbach, *The Knowledge Context: Comparative Perspectives on the Distribution of Knowledge* (Albany: State University of New York Press, 1987).

3. For further discussion of this point, see Alan B. Cobban, *The Medieval Universities: Their Development and Organization* (London: Methuen, 1975).

4. The history of British higher education expansion in India and Africa is described in Eric Ashby, *Universities: British, Indian, African* (Cambridge, MA: Harvard University Press, 1976).

5. See Philip G. Altbach and Viswanathan Selvaratnam, eds., *From Dependence to Autonomy: The Development of Asian Universities* (Dordrecht, Netherlands: Kluwer, 1989).

6. Irene Gilbert, "The Indian Academic Profession: The Origins of a Tradition of Subordination," *Minerva* 10 (1972): 384–411.

7. For a broader consideration of these themes, see Lawrence Stone, ed., *The University in Society*, 2 vols. (Princeton, NJ: Princeton University Press, 1974).

8. Joseph Ben-David, *Centers of Learning: Britain, France, Germany, the United States* (New York: McGraw-Hill, 1977), 16–17.

9. Friedrich Lilge, *The Abuse of Learning: The Failure of the German University* (New York: Macmillan, 1948).

10. Charles E. McClelland, *State, Society, and University in Germany, 1700–1914* (Cambridge: Cambridge University Press, 1980). See also Joseph Ben-David and Awraham Zloczower, "Universities and Academic Systems in Modern Societies," *European Journal of Sociology* 3 (1962): 45–84.

11. In the German system, a full professor was appointed as head (chair) of each discipline, and all other academic staff served under his direction; the position was permanent. Many other countries, including Japan, Russia, and most of Eastern Europe, adopted this system. On developments in America, see Laurence Veysey, *The Emergence of the American University* (Chicago: University of Chicago Press, 1965); Edward T. Silva and Sheila A. Slaughter, *Serving Power: The Making of the Academic Social Science Expert* (Westport, CT: Greenwood, 1984).

12. For a discussion of the contemporary Islamic university, see Hamed H. Bilgrami and Syed A. Ashraf, *The Concept of an Islamic University* (London: Hodder and Stoughton, 1985).

13. Philip G. Altbach, "The American Academic Model in Comparative Perspective," in *Comparative Higher Education*, ed. Philip G. Altbach (Greenwich, CT: Ablex, 1998), 55–74.

14. See David Lelyveld, *Aligarh's First Generation: Muslim Solidarity in British India* (Princeton, NJ: Princeton University Press, 1978).

15. Michio Nagai, *Higher Education in Japan: Its Take-Off and Crash* (Tokyo: University of Tokyo Press, 1971). See Altbach and Selvaratnam, *From Dependence to Autonomy*, for case studies of Asian universities.

16. See Philip G. Altbach, David H. Kelly, and Y. G-M. Lulat, *Research on Foreign Students and International Study: Bibliography and Analysis* (New York: Praeger, 1985).

17. Hyaeweol Choi, *An International Scientific Community: Asian Scholars in the United States* (Westport, CT: Praeger, 1995).

18. The number of American students studying abroad is only a small proportion of the number of foreign students studying in the United States, and the large majority of Americans who do study in other countries go to Canada and Western Europe. See Robert Arnove, "Foundations and the Transfer of Knowledge," in *Philanthropy and Cultural Imperialism*, ed. Robert Arnove (Boston: Hall, 1980).

19. For a discussion of higher education development in the newly industrializing countries, see Philip G. Altbach, Charles H. Davis, Thomas O. Eisemon, S. Gopinathan, Steve H. Hsieh, Sungho Lee, Pang Eng Fong, and Jasbir Sarjit Singh, *Scientific Development and Higher Education: The Case of Newly Industrializing Countries* (New York: Praeger, 1989).

20. Martin Trow, "Reflections on the Transition from Elite to Mass to Universal Access: Forms and Phases of Higher Education in Societies since WWII," in *International Handbook of Higher Education*, ed. James J. F. Forest and Philip G. Altbach, 243–80. (Dordrecht, Netherlands: Springer, 2006).

21. See Task Force on Higher Education and Society, *Higher Education in Developing Countries: Peril and Promise* (Washington, DC: World Bank, 2000).

22. Altbach et al., *Scientific Development and Higher Education.*

23. Max A. Eckstein and Harold J. Noah, "Forms and Functions of Secondary School Leaving Examinations," *Comparative Education Review* 33 (1989): 295–316.

24. Academic institutions serve as important sorting institutions, sometimes diverting students from highly competitive fields. See, for example, Steven Brint and Jerome Karabel, *The Diverted Dream: Community Colleges and the Promise of Educational Opportunity in America, 1900–1985* (New York: Oxford University Press, 1989).

25. Roger L. Geiger, *Private Sectors in Higher Education: Structure, Function, and Change in Eight Countries* (Ann Arbor: University of Michigan Press, 1986). For a focus on Latin America, see Daniel C. Levy, *Higher Education and the State in Latin America: Private Challenges to Public Dominance* (Chicago: University of Chicago Press, 1986). See also Philip G. Altbach, ed. *Private Prometheus: Private Higher Education and Development in the 21st Century* (Westport, CT: Greenwood, 2000).

26. The World Bank, in *Education in Sub-Saharan Africa* (Washington, DC: World Bank, 1988), strongly argues against the continued expansion of higher education, believing that scarce educational expenditures could be much more effectively spent on primary and secondary education. See also D. Bruce Johnstone, *Sharing the Costs of Higher Education: Student Financial Assistance in the United Kingdom, the Federal Republic of Germany, France, Sweden, and the United States* (Washington, DC: College Board, 1986).

27. Trow, "Reflections on the Transition."

28. See Ladislav Cerych and Paul Sabatier, *Great Expectations and Mixed Performance: The Implementation of Higher Education Reforms in Europe*, pt. 2 (Trentham, England: Trentham Books, 1986).

29. Jasbir Sarjit Singh, "Malaysia," in *International Higher Education: An Encyclopedia*, ed. Philip G. Altbach (New York: Garland, 1991).

30. There are also significant national variations. For example, Britain under Margaret Thatcher's leadership consistently reduced expenditures for postsecondary education, with significant negative consequences for higher education. See, for example, Sir Claus Moser, "The *Robbins Report* 25 Years After: And the Future of the Universities," *Oxford Journal of Education* 14 (1988): 5–20.

31. For broader considerations of the reforms of the 1960s, see Cerych and Sabatier, *Great Expectations*; Ulrich Teichler, *Changing Patterns of the Higher Education System* (London: Kingsley, 1989); Philip G. Altbach, ed., *University Reform: Comparative Perspectives for the Seventies* (Cambridge, MA: Schenkman, 1974).

32. For an example of an influential student proposal for higher education reform, see Wolfgang Nitsch, Uta Gerhardt, Claus Offe, and Ulrich K. Preuß, *Hochschule in der Demokratie* (Berlin: Luchterhand, 1965).

33. Jan Erik Lane and Mac Murray, "The Significance of Decentralization in Swedish Education," *European Journal of Education* 20 (1985): 163–72.

34. See Alexander W. Astin, Helen Astin, Alan Bayer, and Ann Bisconti, *The Power of Protest* (San Francisco: Jossey-Bass, 1975), for an overview of the results of the ferment of the 1960s on American higher education.

35. "The Legacy of *Robbins*," *European Journal of Education* 14 (1988): 3–112.

36. For a critical viewpoint, see Hans Daalder and Edward Shils, eds., *Universities, Politicians, and Bureaucrats: Europe and the United States* (Cambridge: Cambridge University Press, 1982).

37. See, for example, "Universities and Industry," *European Journal of Education* 20 (1985): 5–66.

38. Of course, this is not a new concern for higher education. See Thorstein Veblen, *The Higher Learning in America: A Memorandum on the Conduct of Universities by Business Men* (New York: Viking, 1918).

39. See Klaus Hufner, "Accountability," in Altbach, *International Higher Education*.

40. Philip G. Altbach, "Academic Freedom in Asia: Learning the Limitations," *Far Eastern Economic Review*, June 16, 1988.

41. Edward Shils, *The Academic Ethic* (Chicago: University of Chicago Press, 1983).

42. See Ben-David and Zloczower, "Universities and Academic Systems."

43. See, for example, Robert Nisbet, *The Degradation of the Academic Dogma: The University in America, 1945–1970* (New York: Basic Books, 1971). Allan Bloom, in his *The Closing of the American Mind: How Higher Education Has Failed Democracy and Impoverished the Souls of Today's Students* (New York: Simon and Schuster, 1987), echoes many of Nisbet's sentiments.

44. In those countries that have located much of their research in nonuniversity institutions, such as the academies of sciences in Russia and some Central and Eastern European nations, there has been some rethinking of this organizational model, and a sense that universities may be more effective locations for major research. Since the collapse of the Soviet Union, there have been some moves to abolish the

academy model. See Alexander Vucinich, *Empire of Knowledge: The Academy of Sciences of the USSR, 1917–1970* (Berkeley: University of California Press, 1984).

45. See Thomas W. Shaughnessy et al., "Scholarly Communication: The Need for an Agenda for Action—a Symposium," *Journal of Academic Librarianship* 15 (1989): 68–78. See also National Enquiry into Scholarly Communication and American Council of Learned Societies, *Scholarly Communication: The Report of the National Enquiry* (Baltimore: Johns Hopkins University Press, 1979).

46. These issues are discussed in Altbach, *Knowledge Context*. For a different perspective, see Irving Louis Horowitz, *Communicating Ideas: The Crisis of Publishing in a Post-Industrial Society* (New York: Oxford University Press, 1986).

47. For an American perspective, see Martin Finkelstein, Robert Seal, and Jack H. Schuster, *The New Academic Generation: A Profession in Transformation* (Baltimore: Johns Hopkins University Press, 1998).

48. Levy, *Higher Education*. See also Geiger, *Private Sectors in Higher Education*.

49. Gail P. Kelly, "Women in Higher Education," in Altbach, *International Higher Education*.

50. A possible exception to this situation are universities in Britain, where a decade of financial cuts by the Thatcher government sapped the morale of the universities and made it difficult for even such distinguished institutions as Oxford and Cambridge to continue top-quality research. See Geoffrey Walford, "The Privatization of British Higher Education," *European Journal of Education* 23 (1988): 47–64.

51. World Bank, *Education in Sub-Saharan Africa*, 68–81.

52. See Philip G. Altbach, *Tradition and Transition: The International Imperative in Higher Education* (Rotterdam, Netherlands: Sense, 2007).

53. For a survey of student movements, see Philip G. Altbach, ed., *Student Political Activism: An International Reference Handbook* (Westport, CT: Greenwood, 1989).

CHAPTER TWO

The Ten Generations of American Higher Education

Roger L. Geiger

We study the history of higher education because things change and because some things do not change. Continuity is evident in individual institutions in which circumstances or self-images of origin and development continue to influence current conditions. Basic forms persist as well, perhaps most notably in the centrality of the American college. Issues also recur, particularly those concerned with curriculum, institutional mission, and student development. But change also is an irreducible reality and must, by its nature, be analyzed in a temporal dimension. The key elements here are understanding the processes of change and aggregating such changes to discern fundamental transformations in the entire system of higher education. This last element forms the premise of the analysis that follows: that the character of American higher education has perceptibly shifted in each generation, or approximately every thirty years. The exploration of these successive generations is intended to illuminate these historical dynamics, as well as the underlying processes of which they are composed.

The ten generations of American higher education, from the founding of Harvard to the current era, are characterized here in terms of what was taught, the experience of students, and the array of institutions. Existing knowledge was and is screened by institutions and their faculty for certified acceptance into the curriculum. That curriculum, in turn, has an implied relationship with subsequent uses. Next, the place of higher education in the lives of students can be captured in the phrase "origins and destinations." The expansive nature of American higher education has meant that student origins have tended to be broad and diverse. Yet expectations about career destinations have largely motivated college attendance, and these same expectations have inspired crucial interventions by third parties—whether governments, churches, foundations, or individuals. Between origins and destinations lies the college experience itself, certainly one of the most critical variables. Finally, there is institutional order—all the institutions offering higher education and their internal makeup. This chapter's organizational scheme is intended to be heuristic, highlighting central features for monitoring change over time without excluding any factors impinging on higher education.

Generation 1: Reformation Beginnings, 1636–1740s

Each of the first three colleges in the British colonies of America was unique, but all may be described as "schools of the Reformation."[1] Harvard College, the College of William and Mary, and Yale College were established as adjuncts of their respective churches, which in turn were integrally related to the colonies' civil governments. The long head start enjoyed by Harvard gave it a special, settled character. A true product of the Wars of Religion when it was chartered in 1636, it evolved in the eighteenth century into a more cosmopolitan and tolerant institution. This evolution away from strict Calvinism reflected the spreading heterodoxy of Puritan society and the support of the more secular and mercantile elements in that community. The College of William and Mary was formally linked with the Church of England. Its founder, James Blair, and his successors were titular heads of the church in Virginia. Originally operated as a grammar school, William and Mary did not offer collegiate instruction until the 1730s. It then embodied the relative tolerance of official Anglicanism, a stance congenial to the planter families who governed the colony.[2] Only Yale preserved and cultivated the sectarian zeal of the Reformation era into the middle of the eighteenth century.

Some original features persisted long after the Reformation era. External governance was a natural outgrowth of viewing the colleges as an emanation of the polity. Both Harvard and William and Mary had dual structures, consisting of corporations and boards of overseers or visitors. Yale was guided by a single board, originally consisting of ten Congregational ministers, but it looked to the General Assembly of Connecticut for financial support and legal backing.[3] This combination of provincial authority external to the college and the clerical authority lodged within it generated recurring conflicts. Control of Harvard was contested among old-line Puritans and more liberal Congregationalists. Yale's minister-trustees, left to themselves, disagreed over where to locate the college. And at William and Mary, the inability of the board of visitors to control the faculty was a perpetual problem. All three colleges nevertheless received financial support from their respective colonies.

A relatively powerful college president eventually emerged as the natural complement to lay authority. A circumscribed role remained to be played by the faculty of tutors, who were usually recent graduates preparing for the ministry. The curriculum of the colleges in this era was adapted from the Arts course of medieval universities. Its aim was to provide students with a liberal education, which meant facility with classical languages, grounding in the three basic philosophies of Aristotle—ethics, metaphysics, and natural philosophy or science—and a grounding in logic. In order to be admitted, students had to show knowledge of Latin, the language of instruction, and a bit of Greek. The first two years were devoted for the most part to polishing linguistic skills and then learning logic in order to engage in disputations. Philosophy and general subjects were taught in the final two years. The education offered was a practical one for the seventeenth and early eighteenth centuries, when most learned texts were in Latin. The process of education was undoubtedly as valuable as the content. The collegiate way of living and the constant presence of tutors gave students complete immersion in both religion and learning. Delivering declamations and engaging in disputations inculcated a facility with language that was indispensable to the oral public culture they would enter.

The founding documents of all three schools speak to the aim of educating ministers. Indeed, except at William and Mary, this was the chief expectation associated with college matriculation. Actual ministerial training, nevertheless, followed upon a liberal education. Nearly two-thirds of the graduates of seventeenth-century Harvard entered the ministry, but nonministerial students were both welcomed and expected. William and Mary sought to make youths "piously educated in good Letters and Manners"; the founders of Yale intended to provide education "for Publick employment both in Church & Civil State."[4]

The nexus between college and the ministry would erode slowly during the eighteenth century. Under president John Leverett (1708–24), Harvard already possessed a clientele of young gentlemen who took scant interest in studies or piety. At William and Mary, where a ministerial career required a journey to England for ordination, most sons of the Virginia gentry sought only a patina of liberal education, and almost none graduated.

By the third decade of the eighteenth century, Harvard surmounted the narrow role of a Reformation college in another way. Gifts from Thomas Hollis created two professorships, in divinity (1721) and in mathematics and natural philosophy (1727). The hiring of individuals who could specialize over the years in a single field of knowledge overcame an inherent curricular limitation. By the next generation, learned professors, in addition to young tutors, would be sought by the colonial colleges.[5]

Generation 2: Colonial Colleges, 1745–1775

The mold of Reformation colleges was broken with the founding of the College of New Jersey (Princeton University) in 1746. A compromise between Presbyterians and the colony of New Jersey produced a board of trustees having twelve ministers, ten laymen, and the governor of the colony as ex officio presiding officer. The college was rooted in the colony yet served a far wider constituency of Presbyterians; it was denominational in nature yet tolerant of other Protestant sects. The next four colleges to be founded followed this same pattern of "toleration with preferment," although for somewhat different reasons. King's College (Columbia University, 1754), as an Anglican founding, had to assuage fears of institutionalizing a state religion. The College of Philadelphia (University of Pennsylvania, 1755), successor to the academy that Benjamin Franklin had helped to found, continued the tradition of toleration in a context of considerable religious diversity. Baptists, too, believed in toleration, even while insisting on control over the College of Rhode Island (Brown University, 1765). New Hampshire's eagerness to have, above all, a provincial college prompted it to entice Eleazer Wheelock to found Dartmouth College (1769). Only the creation of Queen's College (Rutgers University, 1771), by and for the Dutch Reformed community, introduced an exclusive (and unsuccessful) model at the end of this period.[6]

Harvard and William and Mary also conformed to the new model of provincial colleges. Yale under Thomas Clap (1740–66), however, resisted this form in the name of doctrinal purity but, in doing so, demonstrated that the theocratic ideal of the Reformation was no longer tenable. Clap's rearguard action to defend Yale against the doctrines of the Great Awakening, against an Anglican presence in Connecticut, and, finally, against the Connecticut General Assembly ironically ended when he lost control of the college to rebellious students.

On the eve of the Revolution, the colonial colleges enrolled nearly 750 students, but three-quarters of them attended the four oldest colleges.[7] The latter, in particular, exemplified instruction that had become more secular in its curriculum and purpose. Fewer than half of the graduates of Princeton pursued careers in the ministry. In the small but vital urban centers of the colonies, a sizable class of gentlemen now existed, consisting of professional men and successful merchants. At King's College perhaps 40 percent of the students originated from that milieu, and the proportion at Harvard may well have been higher. Still, many students clearly came from more humble circumstances, chiefly the sons of farmers. They, no doubt, were more likely to be destined for the ministry, while gentlemen's sons more typically followed the path that led to law and public life.[8]

At the outset of this period, the curriculum was an incoherent amalgam of works predicated on both the old, theocentric universe and the new, enlightened views reflecting the writings of John Locke and Sir Isaac Newton. The doctrines of the "Moderate Enlightenment" gradually prevailed.[9] The enlightened spirit also included a more thorough teaching and appreciation of classical authors. Latin and Greek thus remained at the heart of the curriculum, but Latin ceased to be a language of instruction. Classical authors introduced the generation of the Founding Fathers to the political forms and lessons of the ancient world. Scottish "common-sense philosophy," as taught by John Witherspoon (1768–95) at Princeton, reconciled Christian doctrines and the new knowledge. Students also received more competent instruction in these decades, as college teaching became a settled occupation, attracting men of genuine learning.[10]

In sum, during the colonial generation the colleges balanced duties to both church and province, offered a richer and more secular intellectual fare, and served, among others, a constituency of aspiring gentlemen. The new nation soon called upon them to make a still larger contribution.

Generation 3: Republican Education, 1776–1800

The revolution against England was clearly a spark for igniting political feelings in the colleges. However, college life was disrupted for much of the War for Independence and then developed slowly before the nation was united under the

Constitution in 1788. Despite this triumph of federalism, political passions rose to a crescendo at the end of the century.

The ideal for collegiate education in this period sought a harmonious joining of disparate elements. First was the notion of republican education—instilling selflessness, patriotism, and virtue in the citizens and leaders of the new republic. Such an outlook was conveyed through the choice of texts, topics for student oratory, and the widely touted (though unsuccessful) introduction of the study of law. Second, Enlightenment learning was welcomed as never before, although the fiscal limitations of colleges made realization fall far short of aspirations. Indeed, these years mark the zenith of Enlightenment influence in American colleges, a time in which theology sought to accommodate the truths of science and reason. Samuel Stanhope Smith (1795–1812), who succeeded Witherspoon at Princeton, epitomized both the ascendancy and the fragility of this "republican Christian Enlightenment": learning was valued in the colleges, and higher education was valued in the polity.[11]

After independence, the newly sovereign states made provision for collegiate education for their citizens. States that had no colleges chartered new institutions— Maryland (1782 and 1784), Georgia (1785), South Carolina (1785), North Carolina (1789), and Vermont (1791)—although some years passed before most of these institutions were able to open. Elsewhere, this same impulse sometimes became entwined with controversial changes in existing colleges. The board of visitors of William and Mary imposed a reorganization of the faculty in 1779. That same year, Pennsylvania supplanted the College of Philadelphia with a "public" institution (the two were merged in 1791 to form the University of Pennsylvania). The superstructure of the University of the State of New York was erected in the 1780s to counter the conservative influence of Columbia. Where continuity was the rule, state officials were made ex officio trustees of colleges (Massachusetts, Connecticut, New Hampshire, and New Jersey), and financial support was sporadically provided. Denominationally sponsored colleges found few students and little influence in these years. The new colleges founded near the frontier often reflected close-knit denominational communities, but they, too, assumed a public outlook.

The vision of republican higher education was undermined considerably by the material weakness of the colleges. The nation's most solid institution, Harvard, had just three professors at the turn of the century, but that was two more than Yale or Princeton could manage. Collegiate enrollments for the last quarter of the century did not keep pace with population growth, despite the proliferation of new institutions. Where roughly 1 percent of a four-year male cohort attended college in 1775, the corresponding figure for 1800 was 0.75 percent. In some new colleges, like North Carolina, the absence of experienced teachers for a time fomented chaotic conditions. Student unruliness was a particular blight at institutions associated with Jeffersonian republicanism, such as William and Mary and Dickinson College. Public subsidies for state-sponsored colleges were soon terminated, leaving these institutions in an exceedingly weak state. At the end of the eighteenth century, there was no functioning model of a state college.[12]

Ironically, popular sentiment now began to turn decisively in support of religion, but the religion of the heart, not the head. In this respect, as in others, the consequences of the dissolution of republican education were realized after 1800.

Generation 4: The Passing of Republican Education, 1800–1820s

The first generation of the nineteenth century is perhaps the least understood in American history. It has largely been associated with negative developments. Indeed, the most widely known historiographical treatment interprets it as the beginning of a "great retrogression."[13] Signs of trouble are not hard to find. The underpinnings of republican education were dislodged by the election of Thomas Jefferson, to the horror of the Federalists who dominated most colleges, and by the upsurge of religious spirit known as the Second Great Awakening, to the detriment of denominations with learned ministers. In addition, many institutions were in a parlous state. In a plea some other colleges might have echoed, Columbia trustees described the college's sorry state as "mortifying to its friends, [and] humiliating to the city."[14] The universities of Maryland and of North Carolina lost their state support; and such major institutions as Princeton and William and Mary began prolonged declines.

Such a picture, however, portrays only misfortunes. Harvard, Yale, Brown, and Union College all strengthened notably, and even Columbia was much improved by the 1820s. Moreover, an important group of institutions opened their doors shortly after 1800—Transylvania University, Bowdoin College, and the state colleges of Georgia and South Carolina. College enrollments outpaced the rapid population growth, except during the depression caused by the War of 1812, bringing male participation back to 1 percent by the end of the 1820s. Underlying the fortunes of individual institutions, nevertheless, lay fundamental questions stemming in large measure from the obsolescence of the putative republican model: Who owned the colleges? What was their mission? What should students be taught? And how could they be controlled?

In the first three decades of the century, colleges experienced the worst student violence of their histories. Unruliness had long been endemic in all-male residential colleges, but these years were distinguished by episodes of collective resistance to college authority.[15] They invariably began with some relatively minor transgression of college rules, but what followed was the key. In certain cases, students deemed disciplinary action, based on measured degrees of public disgrace, to be unjustly severe. Believing their rights and dignity to have been violated, they would either remonstrate or commit further acts of insubordination. The colleges invariably won these contests of will, but at considerable cost. Numerous unrepentant students were expelled, and the college's reputation was besmirched. Such riots at Princeton and William and Mary were factors in precipitating their declines; Harvard endured its periodic riots more stoically; North Carolina forfeited public support.

Steven Novak interpreted student riots as the stimulus for college leaders to shift the emphasis of the curriculum back toward ancient languages. Latin and Greek were considered safe, and their difficult study promoted behavioral as well as mental discipline. However, "having embraced [this] curriculum for the wrong reasons—as a bulwark against dangerous ideas—academics were never able to bring it to life."[16] Other factors played a role here as well. Most conspicuous was the collapse of efforts to construct a republican curriculum of scientific and professional subjects, due to the lack of suitable teachers or interested students. Moreover, attempts to deemphasize classical languages threatened to undermine the entire enterprise. At Transylvania, the college course without Latin and Greek lasted just two years; and Dickinson students in 1800 demanded and were granted a reduction of the course to a single year. Socially, some knowledge of the classical languages was a badge of cultural distinction appropriate to gentlemen. As a practical matter, lax entrance requirements brought immature and poorly prepared students to campus. Most established colleges thus made concerted efforts to raise their entrance requirements, impose a minimum age, and strengthen instruction in Latin and Greek.

This restandardization of the classical curriculum corresponded to a refocusing of institutions on their collegiate missions. In a reciprocal development, the links between professional education and the colleges were dissolving. This trend has seldom been noted. Yale and other colleges sprouted professional schools during these years and appeared to become fledgling universities. Few institutions followed this path, however, and in those that did, professional schools were largely proprietary undertakings with little organic connection to the parent college. They resembled, in fact, the independent professional schools that began to flourish in this era.

The most vigorous law school after 1800 operated independently—in Litchfield, Connecticut. Unlike earlier attempts to teach law in the colleges, which were intended for civic education, Litchfield Law School prepared students for professional practice. In medicine, the dominant institution was the University of Pennsylvania. With enrollments exceeding four hundred, this medical school was the largest higher education unit in the country. But its students paid the professors directly for lectures, making the school virtually independent of the university. Other medical schools either sought similar arrangements or else they collapsed. The Columbia medical school faltered and was absorbed by another school; Harvard's medical school achieved greater autonomy by moving to Boston; and Brown's medical school folded when the college sought to control its faculty.[17] The most consequential change for the colleges, nevertheless, concerned the training of ministers.

The preparation of ministers was an integral mission of the colleges, even though ministerial training had always followed the undergraduate course. When New England Congregationalists reacted to the Unitarian capture of Harvard by establishing Andover Theological Seminary (1808), a new alternative became available. During the next two decades, more schools for ministerial training were opened than new colleges. These institutions were, in a sense, alternatives to collegiate education and, as in the case of the Princeton Theological Seminary (1812), were votes of no confidence in the colleges. Seminaries became the locus for serious scholars of language and philology (and, hence, German academic scholarship), and they attracted gifts that might have gone to colleges.[18] Most seriously, they distanced colleges from the function of ministerial preparation because, like future lawyers and medical doctors, aspiring ministers increasingly dispensed with collegiate degrees.

The final issue hanging over the colleges was the ambiguous mix of public function and private control. Controversies arising from this situation had plagued the colleges since the Revolution. What proved to be a definitive resolution had to await the justly celebrated Dartmouth College case (*Dartmouth College v. Woodward*, 1819). When the Supreme Court ruled that New Hampshire could not without cause alter the charter of an "eleemosynary corporation" like Dartmouth

College, it effectively provided colleges with a shield against unwanted intrusions of democratic legislatures. More significantly, it resolved an implicit question of ownership that had plagued virtually every college. In Massachusetts, for example, the composition of the board of overseers had been altered by the legislature three times in the 1810s. Justice Joseph Story, a member of that board, was undoubtedly as concerned with the autonomy of Harvard as with that of Dartmouth when he supported the trustees. Years passed before the import of the Dartmouth College case became fully apparent; the colleges continued to present both public and private personae, but an agenda of privatization clearly triumphed. Not only did the eastern provincial colleges become fully private institutions, but the way was also cleared for the establishment of a new type of unambiguously private denominational college.[19]

Generation 5: The Classical Denominational Colleges, 1820s–1850s

Generation 5 began in the 1820s, with widespread challenges to the classical college, and was superseded in the 1850s by new waves of reform. The first efforts largely failed, but the second produced permanent change. In between, the private denominational college emerged as the characteristic institution of American higher education. Its success drove a rapid expansion in both the number of colleges and total enrollments. At the same time, sectional differences created distinctive patterns for higher education in the Northeast, the South, and the trans-Appalachian West.[20]

Criticism of the classical college in the 1820s in part reflected the success of efforts to bolster the curriculum. Now colleges were attacked for their obsession with dead languages, for neglecting practical subjects and science, and for the continued unruliness of apparently disgruntled students. A flurry of specific reforms occurred in the middle of the decade.[21] George Ticknor, after a student insurrection at Harvard, managed to reform his own modern languages department, offering advanced courses outside the rigid boundaries of the separate classes. Thomas Jefferson's University of Virginia (1824) provided an entirely new departure, aimed at achieving the nation's first true university. And Eliphalet Nott created a parallel course for a bachelor of science degree at Union College (1827). Little lasting change resulted from this ferment of reform. The efforts of Ticknor and Nott remained isolated achievements, and the University of Virginia proved an incongruous setting for the sons of southern planters. Instead, the reforms provoked a magisterial defense of the classical college—the Yale Report of 1828.

In defending the classical curriculum, the report defined the purpose of college as "to lay the foundation of a superior education."[22] The object, above all, was to discipline the mind and only secondarily to provide content, or "furniture." The classical languages were championed as the ideal vehicle for instilling mental discipline as well as culture and "balance." From these premises, the report could argue that all other forms of education—for practical training or advanced learning—should be relegated to other kinds of institutions. This position rationalized the de facto undergraduate focus of the colleges. The cogency of the Yale Report, moreover, seemed to grow over time and became the principal defense of the classical course for the next sixty years.

The classical college drew on deeper strengths than the arguments of the Yale Report. Furthermore, it had rather different histories on the eastern and western sides of the Appalachians. In the Northeast, generally the colleges preserved their narrow focus on preprofessional liberal education and were content to serve the relatively limited clientele who valued such an expensive badge of cultural distinction. Student life in these institutions changed profoundly during this era and served to fortify this sense of distinction. As the colleges relaxed their oppressive discipline, the students themselves developed a rich extracurriculum of their own. Student life was transformed into a self-contained world of activities and social ceremony that engendered deep loyalties instead of intense hostility.[23] In the West, the most salient development of this era was the proliferation of denominational colleges in territories that had, only short years before, been considered the frontier.

The prototypical denominational college nevertheless emerged in the East in the 1820s. The definition given by the Lutherans of Pennsylvania College (Gettysburg College, 1832) cut to the heart of the matter: noting that its students, teachers, trustees, and benefactors all were church members, they concluded that the college "may then with truth be said to belong to that Church." The denominational college was thus consciously established as an alternative to the mixed ownership of "provincial colleges." These colleges were established by religious minorities (some of whom had previously disdained advanced education for their ministers) so that they might have educational institutions that fully belonged to their church. Regional church organizations generally played an important role in their founding as well as in their governance. Thus, Baptists established Waterville College (Colby College, 1820) and Columbian College (George

Washington University, 1821). Episcopalians finally broke the Yale monopoly in Connecticut in 1826 (Trinity College). And Methodists joined the collegiate movement by founding Randolph-Macon College (1830) and Wesleyan University (1831). State legislators required that the charters of these colleges impose no religious tests. The conditions described by the Gettysburg Lutherans nevertheless defined the foremost reality of the denominational colleges.

On the western side of the Appalachians, where colleges were virtually nonexistent in 1820, denominational colleges soon proliferated. The earliest exemplars were founded by Congregational or Presbyterian missionaries almost as soon as the frontiers were settled. Later foundings tended to be sponsored by regional church organizations. In both cases, a crucial role was played by local boosters, who believed that a college would enhance the cultural and economic standing of their towns.[24] The western colleges were capable of notable experiments, especially where student access was concerned. Manual labor schemes were tried repeatedly in the 1830s and 1840s, and Oberlin College became the first college to admit women. Pedagogically, though, they initially replicated the classical curriculum. Given denominational sponsorship and clerical leadership (often from graduates of Yale or Princeton), this path was a natural course to follow. Colin Burke argues that these institutions need to be viewed in a different framework from the established colleges of the East: they served the basic need for educational upgrading for their localities. Nearly all found it necessary to establish preparatory departments, for example. Over time, they tended to add diverse educational programs to the classical core in spite of limited means. The average size of western colleges in 1860 was about fifty-six students (compared with 174 in New England), and costs were kept low for their far-from-wealthy students. By 1860 the Southwest and Midwest contained 59 percent of colleges and 43 percent of students.[25]

A somewhat different institutional pattern, characterized by dominant state universities, emerged in the South during this era. The College of South Carolina (1803) and the University of Virginia (1824) were the region's strongest institutions and the only universities in the country to receive regular state appropriations before the Civil War. Both institutions catered to sons of the planter aristocracy, who dominated their states politically and socially. Such students, with exaggerated notions of personal honor, made student unrest endemic in southern universities. Denominational colleges in such milieus developed later and attracted a more humble clientele. The pattern of strong state universities spread throughout the Cotton Belt but conspicuously failed in states like Kentucky and Tennessee, where social and religious fragmentation favored denominational colleges.

The 1820s and 1830s were two of the most expansive decades for higher education. Enrollments jumped by roughly 80 percent in each decade, fueled by the establishment of denominational colleges. The 1840s, however, were years of comparative stagnation: they were no doubt hampered by the severe economic downturn that followed the crash of 1837 and by the limited appeal of the classical college. Exasperation with these conditions prompted one last spasm of reform. Brown president Francis Wayland (1827–56) diagnosed the weakness of the eastern colleges: they catered solely to the professional class and furnished students with only a preprofessional education—precisely the narrow focus advocated in the Yale Report. Entirely neglected were practitioners of industry and commerce, who were responsible for the transformation taking place in the American economy.[26] However, these were the polemics of the 1820s in a more sophisticated guise. Wayland's attempt to restructure Brown in order to appeal to this new class proved disastrous. Ironically, his failure occurred at the opening of one of the most dynamic eras of American higher education. The ensuing generation, rather than displacing the classical college, created new institutions and studies to complement it.

Generation 6: New Departures, 1850s–1890

The Civil War has long been the conventional dividing line for the history of American higher education. However, most of the new departures associated with the postbellum years emerged in preliminary form in the 1850s, if not earlier. German-style universities, offering graduate education, are associated with the opening of Johns Hopkins University in 1876, but Henry Tappan (1853–63) transformed the University of Michigan in these same directions. The Morrill Land Grant Act of 1862 can lay exclusive claim to neither "schools of science" nor agricultural colleges. Daniel Coit Gilman estimated that twenty such institutions existed before 1860, including Yale's Sheffield Scientific School, which had evolved from a few extracurricular courses into a department in which both practical and advanced subjects could be studied.[27] In addition, at least four agricultural colleges were chartered in the 1850s, in Pennsylvania, Michigan, Maryland, and Ohio.

In the same decade, collegiate education was broadened to include other than white males. More than forty women's institutions were chartered to offer collegiate degrees before Matthew Vassar presumed to give women "a college in the proper sense of the word."[28] Ashmun Institute (Lincoln University, 1854) in Pennsylvania and Wilberforce University (1856) in Ohio provided college education for free African Americans.

Perhaps the greatest continuity from antebellum to postbellum years existed for denominational colleges. They began a second period of proliferation in the 1850s, which carried through to the early 1870s. The dynamics of this expansion derived from a dual process of extension and elaboration. Through extension, colleges followed close behind the ever-moving frontier into the trans-Mississippi West. Once again, the agents of these initial foundings were largely missionaries from the principal denominations. In the wake of this movement, and indeed throughout the Midwest, a second process of elaboration occurred as denominations without colleges made provision for the education of their church members. These colleges differed from their earlier counterparts in being multipurpose in nature. They still preserved the classical core, but added degree courses in English and science as well as practical courses in business and teaching. In keeping with this impulse to serve their denominations broadly, these multipurpose colleges were usually coeducational, except for denominations opposed to this in principle (Roman Catholics, Presbyterians, German Lutherans). This great expansion of denominational colleges proceeded unfazed by the dawning age of the university, until conditions changed radically after 1890.[29]

The Morrill Land Grant Act still largely determined the character of the new utilitarian education. Enthusiasm among the industrial classes for education in agriculture or the mechanical arts turned out to be sparse. True, well-publicized Cornell University attracted the nation's largest entering class in 1868, but these initial students were mixed in their aspirations and qualifications. Only 10 percent eventually graduated. Outside of New England, preparatory departments overshadowed collegiate ones in the new land-grant colleges. After a slow start, enrollment in the mechanical arts (engineering) grew in the 1880s and then accelerated after 1890. Matriculants in agriculture, however, remained few and far between. Reformers simply misjudged the nexus between farming and advanced education.

Contrary to the conventional view, land-grant colleges did not meet an exigent popular demand, nor did they appreciably democratize higher education. Had they been dependent on enrollment, many undoubtedly would have failed. However, the circumstances of their beginnings gave them an assured, if meager, income as well as an implicit relationship with their respective states. They were thus sustained long enough through their sickly infancy for social and economic conditions to catch up to the expectations that had prompted their somewhat premature founding. In 1890, after intensive lobbying by land-grant presidents, the Second Morrill Act gave these institutions direct annual infusions of federal funds, a crucial advantage at a time when universities were entering their most dynamic era of growth.[30]

The first Morrill Act nevertheless set the most important precondition for utilitarian education when it stipulated the establishment of "at least one *college*" in which these subjects would be taught "without excluding other scientific and classical studies."[31] Unlike continental Europe, where modern languages and useful subjects were taught in less-prestigious institutions than those offering classical and theoretical studies, in the United States the progeny of the industrial classes would eventually study in the same institutions as those from the professional classes.

Despite the salience of the Morrill Act, these years were characterized far more by private initiatives and, particularly, single acts of philanthropy. Gifts of hitherto unprecedented size sought to fill lacunae in American higher education. Matthew Vassar, Henry Wells, Sophia Smith, and Henry Durant (Wellesley College) created colleges for women between 1861 and 1875 that were intended to equal the best men's colleges.[32] Ezra Cornell and John Purdue enhanced the effectiveness of land-grant colleges. Trustees of estates were responsible for establishing the Stevens Institute of Technology and the Johns Hopkins University. This era culminated with the most spectacular new institutions (after Hopkins)— Clark and Stanford universities and the University of Chicago.

The American university is the most enduring legacy of these developments, even though its ascendancy over American higher education would have to await the next generation. Charles Eliot said in 1869 that no university yet existed in the United States, and prior to 1890 it was uncertain what form an American university would assume. Indeed, Daniel Coit Gilman, G. Stanley Hall, David Starr Jordan, and William Rainey Harper each independently attempted to invent such an institution (at Johns Hopkins, Clark, Stanford, and Chicago, respectively). The chief conundrum was the relationship between advanced learning, or graduate education, and the American college.

The true paradigm of the American university evolved instead at the country's paramount institution. Charles W. Eliot assumed the presidency of Harvard in 1869 with a clear sense of the changes that were needed in both college and professional schools. For the college, he sought to replace recitations and the classical curriculum with an elective system that could accommodate true learning. This reform took a decade and a half, but by then the old regime was vanquished at Harvard and in retreat at other eastern colleges. Eliot also attacked the decadence of the professional schools at the outset of his presidency. A learned, full-time faculty replaced practitioner-teachers; a mandatory curriculum was put in place; and professional education was eventually defined as requiring a bachelor's degree. Eliot's instincts were by no means as sure when it came to graduate education. But as the elective system allowed him to appoint many more learned professors, a distinguished faculty emerged, capable of scholarship, research, and advanced instruction. In 1890 the scientific school and the college faculty were merged into the faculty of arts and sciences. The Graduate School of Arts and Sciences was its other face. Finally, Eliot felt that Harvard was "now well on the way to the complete organization of a university in a true sense." The American university would be an institution in which the instruction of large numbers of undergraduates would support a numerous, specialized faculty who would also teach graduate students. Not even the ingenious William Rainey Harper could devise anything better. Moreover, this model was a natural one for the more vigorous state universities, whose growth was about to explode. The next generation of American higher education would see the efflorescence of this powerful combination of mixed purposes.[33]

Generation 7: Growth and Standardization, 1890 to World War I

The character of growth in American higher education changed profoundly around 1890. During the previous generation, enrollment growth had been absorbed into an increasing number of institutions, but during generation 7 the net number of institutions remained fairly stable, while enrollments swelled. The average institution in 1870 had 10 faculty and 98 students; in 1890, these figures had grown to just 16 faculty and 157 students; but in 1910, they were up to 38 faculty and 374 students. Moreover, the largest institutions led this growth: in 1895 the ten largest universities averaged nearly 2,000 students; in 1910 they approximated 4,000; and in 1915, 5,000.[34]

At the other end of the spectrum, colleges that failed to grow were threatened with extinction. The institutional order was anything but stable; the founding of new colleges continued unabated into the 1890s, but many institutions expired during these years.

One important source of growth was the assimilation of women into higher education. In 1890 the majority of female students were found in single-sex colleges, most of which were regarded by contemporaries as inferior. This situation changed abruptly with the opening of the elective curriculum and the expansion of universities. The proportion of women students grew slowly, from 32 to 37 percent (1890–1913), but the proportion of women in coeducational institutions nearly doubled, to 68 percent. The gulf between the educational experiences of women and men narrowed much further in the next generation.[35]

The standardization of the universities after 1890 is the central theme of Laurence Veysey's classic study. His deliberate emphasis on the cerebral aspects of this subject, however, may slight some of the more mundane features, largely caused by similar adaptations to a common environment. The rapid growth of universities resulted from the growth of their several parts. Most added units in engineering, business, and education, plus different combinations of other smaller specialties (e.g., mining, forestry, dentistry, pharmacy, veterinary medicine, art, architecture, and music), in addition to schools for graduate study, medicine, and law. Universities became compartmentalized institutions, whose parts shared little common intellectual ground. Administrative structures were necessary to serve these autonomous compartments and especially to secure ever more resources to fulfill their needs.[36]

By 1908 it was possible to define the standard American university. It admitted only bona fide high school graduates. It provided them with two years of general education followed by two years of advanced or specialized courses. It offered doctoral training in at least five departments, appropriately led by PhDs, and had at least one professional school. A sizable list of possible options might be added: summer sessions, extension work, correspondence courses, a university press, and the publication of learned journals. Idiosyncrasies faded away in this environment, such as Eliot's unconstrained elective system and proposed three-year bachelor's degree. Outliers moved closer to the norm: Johns Hopkins enrolled more undergraduates and lengthened the bachelor of arts course to four years; the Massachusetts Institute of Technology established units for research and graduate education.

The universities, in turn, were the most powerful force in generating standards for the rest of higher education, chiefly by defining academic knowledge and the academic profession. From about 1890 to 1905, all of the major disciplinary associations assumed their modern form. In a parallel development, the departmental structure of colleges and universities replicated these contours. Academic disciplines henceforth possessed a dual structure, whereby scientific recognition was embodied in disciplinary organizations while the most consequential positions, those commanding the means to advance these fields, were in university departments. As teaching positions were increasingly reserved for faculty who contributed to the knowledge base of disciplines, the universities imposed a definition on the academic profession. University faculty then took this definition a step further by organizing the American Association of University Professors (1915) to champion their professional rights, particularly academic freedom.[37]

Probably much more apparent to contemporaries was the spread of a set of practices that can best be called the collegiate ideal. Church ties were weak threads for sustaining liberal arts colleges. An alternative emerged from younger alumni with business careers in urban centers. They appreciated the social qualities that were instilled by extracurricular activities, including athletics. Their ability to contribute badly needed funds gave their wishes weight among college trustees and eventually influenced the selection of modernizing presidents. Denominational doctrines were soon deemphasized in favor of broad, middle-of-the-road Protestantism, epitomized in the soaring popularity of the campus YMCA. New kinds of students began to matriculate, eager to throw themselves into campus activities and consciously destined for careers in the business world. Intercollegiate athletics tended to be the catalyst in this process, galvanizing the enthusiasm of students and the loyalties of alumni.[38]

The collegiate ideal developed first out of the unique traditions of the Ivy League schools, especially Harvard and Yale. It quickly captured imaginations among the principal eastern colleges and spread to include state universities. The older generation of university leaders, such as Charles Eliot, had scant regard for such activities, but the next generation—Eliot's successor, Abbott Lawrence Lowell (1909–33), and above all Woodrow Wilson (1902–10) at Princeton—sought to amalgamate the collegiate ideal with their own concern for undergraduate learning. The collegiate ideal projected clear normative standards about the nature of the college experience, while another form of standardization found champions after 1900.

In 1905 the Carnegie Foundation for the Advancement of Teaching was chartered to provide pensions for college teachers. That same year, the General Education Board reoriented its activities toward promoting "a comprehensive system of higher education in the United States." Both foundations sought to alleviate the "chaos" and "confusion" they perceived in American higher education. The former promulgated stringent criteria of eligibility for its pensions, and institutions scrambled to conform. The latter worked more subtly by providing matching endowment grants that forced colleges to turn to their alumni.[39] Neither required an institution to have a football team, but they validated the types of schools that did: residential colleges with strong alumni support.

Following the model of the Land-Grant College Association (1887), successive associations were formed in this era, and their efforts also furthered standardization. The National Association of State Universities formulated the definition of the "standard American university." The Association of American Universities, formed to set standards for graduate education, soon became, in effect, an accrediting agency for colleges.[40]

A generation of standardizing activities gave much greater definition to the American system of higher education, even if it left the system still highly diverse and decentralized. By World War I, American colleges and universities by and large conformed to a single pattern in terms of admissions, credit hours, offerings, majors, and so on. The large divergence among institutions pertained chiefly to the level of resources each commanded for the fulfillment of this pattern. Differences in resources would henceforth produce an increasingly steeper hierarchy among American institutions of higher education.

Generation 8: Hierarchical Differentiation between the Wars

Enrollments in higher education approximately doubled during the 1920s, and this expansion triggered qualitative changes analogous to what Martin Trow would later identify as the transition from elite to mass higher education.[41] Elite patterns are characterized by full-time residential students, by cultural ideals of liberal learning and character formation, and by destinations in high-status professions. In contrast, mass forms of higher education cater to part-time or commuting students, convey applicable knowledge, and prepare students for employment in technical or semiprofessional positions. American higher education had always been somewhat hierarchical in terms of resource levels and admissions requirements. Between the two world wars, however, it became much more explicitly so. Emergent forms of higher education fulfilled "mass" roles, and educational leaders directly addressed the issue of offering qualitatively different kinds of instruction for different levels of students.

The growth of a mass sector in American higher education was apparent in the burgeoning junior colleges, teachers colleges, and urban, service-oriented

universities.[42] Teachers colleges resulted from the process of continuously upgrading normal schools. This process began in the 1900s, although the majority
of normal schools were converted in the 1920s. For years, many teachers colleges
remained confined to education degrees. In addition, they faced competition in
this sphere from traditional universities. But as heirs to the normal schools, they
provided access to higher education for a broad segment of the population, especially women.

The expansion of higher education to serve city dwellers included both new
and existing institutions. The free municipal university established in Akron
(1913) exemplified the former. It aimed to produce employable graduates for the
region, typically with programs in engineering, home economics, commerce, and
teaching. The College of the City of New York was perhaps the most spectacular
exemplar of this phenomenon, growing to more than 24,000 students during the
1920s. Private municipal universities shared in this growth, largely by creating
special programs for part-time students. In 1930, for example, part-time and summer students exceeded full-time students at New York, Northwestern, Southern
California, Boston, and Western Reserve universities. By that date, the biggest
American institutions were no longer research universities, but municipal universities with large, irregular enrollments.

True junior colleges first appeared in the decade of the 1900s but multiplied in
the 1920s. They provided local access to higher education for both sparsely popu-
lated areas of the West and cities. By 1940, 11 percent of college students were
enrolled in junior colleges, many of which were still attached to local high schools.
The emergence of junior colleges nevertheless profoundly affected thinking
about the structure and purpose of American higher education.

The waves of mass higher education lapping the shores of traditional institutions produced largely defensive reactions. President Ernest Hopkins of Dartmouth caused a stir by declaring that "too many young men are going to college."
Probably the most vehement critic was Abraham Flexner, who charged that universities had become " 'service' stations for the general public."[43] A number of educators took inspiration from the apparent success of junior colleges and concluded
that democratic access should extend through the sophomore year of college. The
University of Minnesota created a two-year, terminal General College for students deemed unfit for its regular programs. Another clear rationalization of hierarchical differentiation was the Carnegie Foundation's 1932 report, *State Higher
Education in California*, which defined separate roles for the university in Berkeley, regional state colleges, and largely vocational junior colleges. This document

was representative of a crystallization of opinion that sought to redefine the most open sector of higher education—the junior colleges—as terminal programs.

Determined efforts by the leaders of higher education had the effect of hardening the outlines of the mass sector of higher education, which had emerged almost spontaneously. Similarly, purposeful actions were required to define the upper reaches of American higher education. As with the mass sector, this was a matter combining, all at the same time, social origins and destinations, manner or style of attendance, and links with higher learning.

Three general criteria could be used to claim elite status. The *collegiate ideal*, especially popular in the 1920s, was determined by the peer society of students, by extracurricular activities, and by expectations of subsequent careers in the business world. *Quality of undergraduate learning* was a persistent concern; not only did colleges attempt to raise their standards, but many educators also sought to re-create the elusive ideal of liberal education. In universities, the imperative of *advancing knowledge* was an end in itself, the touchstone of research and graduate education, but also a distinguishing feature of only a handful of institutions.

At the leading private institutions, financial constraints and rising applications prompted limits on the number of students after World War I. At the same time, these institutions became more sensitive to the social composition of their students and the implications it had for their collegiate image. Columbia pioneered a form of selective admissions in which social criteria were used to limit the proportion of Jewish students, and the same discriminatory procedures were soon copied by Princeton, Yale, and Harvard.[44] Selective admissions were part of a larger pattern of fashioning elite status. These institutions shaped the peer society and collegiate environment not only by excluding supposedly nonconforming social types, but also by widening their recruitment pool to encompass the entire country. They simultaneously became national rather than regional institutions, culling the weakest academic performers from among their traditional clientele and raising the level of study, at least slightly. As these institutions prospered in the 1920s, they vastly increased educational spending on each student. When Yale launched higher education's largest endowment drive in 1927, it promised "to make a finer, not a bigger Yale."[45]

For elite universities, additional wealth was invested in more and better faculty—in scientists and scholars actively engaged in the advancement of knowledge. This phase of development was strongly assisted by philanthropic foundations, particularly the Rockefeller trusts. Participation in research also conferred prestige and elite status. Recognition in this dimension lay outside of universities, in international communities of scholars. It thus created an altogether different set of imperatives, which universities could scarcely ignore. It was no paradox, then, that a Jew could be a physics professor at Princeton but not an undergraduate: universalism prevailed in the former sphere but not in the latter.

Probably the most difficult course for sculpting an elite status was to excel in only undergraduate education. However, Swarthmore, under president Frank Aydelotte (1921–39), was a notable success in this regard. Inspired by his Oxford experience as a Rhodes scholar, Aydelotte established an honors program to provide a rigorous course of study for able and motivated students. At the same time, he progressively deemphasized the underpinnings of the collegiate ideal— sororities, fraternities, and big-time football. The honors program was used to attract academically ambitious students and soon made Swarthmore one of the most selective colleges in the country. The high cost of this education was met with help from supporters of elitism, Abraham Flexner and the General Education Board.[46]

The hierarchical differentiation of the institutional order between the wars simultaneously moved American higher education in several different directions with respect to elite and mass sectors, access, and the curriculum. American higher education became open to virtually all high school graduates, a category that grew from 9 to 51 percent of age cohorts between 1910 and 1940. Yet social exclusiveness among many elite institutions increased, too, as nativist prejudice strengthened. The system was only weakly meritocratic and largely mirrored the social biases prevailing in the workplace. In curricular matters, the expanding mass sector was dominated by vocationally oriented programs, including attempts to define terminal tracks. A preoccupation of the era was nevertheless the persistent desire to fashion a true liberal education. At the same time, the implacable advancement of the academic disciplines weighed ever more heavily on the structure of college courses. Which trends predominated? The answer would become apparent during the next generation of American higher education: democratic access triumphed over social exclusiveness; academic development raised the stature of mass institutions, even as elite ones became strongly meritocratic; and an academic revolution confirmed the ascendancy of the academic curriculum.

Generation 9: The Academic Revolution, 1945–1975

The thirty years following the end of World War II were possibly the most tumultuous in the history of American higher education. Two fundamental movements

nevertheless underlie these myriad developments: expansion and academic standardization. Beginning with the flood of returning soldiers, supported by the
Servicemen's Readjustment Act of 1944 (the GI Bill), and concluding with the
tidal wave of community college students in the early 1970s, this period was
the most expansive in the American experience. The proportion of young people
attending college tripled, from 15 to 45 percent; from 1940 to 1970, undergraduates grew almost fivefold, and graduate students almost ninefold; and the 1960s
alone registered the largest percentage growth of any decade.[47]

While previous growth spurts, like the 1920s, were associated with new types
of institutions reaching new clienteles, the postwar period was characterized by
an implacable movement toward common academic standards. Not only did institutions become more alike in terms of curricular offerings, faculty training,
and administrative practices, but students migrated toward studies in the arts
and sciences. The principal dynamics of this era fortified these developments.

Most generally, an excess demand for college places existed through most of
the era. This phenomenon arose when returning veterans took advantage of the
GI Bill in unprecedented and unanticipated numbers. In 1947, 1.1 million ex-GIs
were enrolled, compared with 1.5 million total students before the war. This surge
did little to raise standards, though, as overcrowded institutions were forced to
run year round, shorten courses, and curtail requirements. This interlude nevertheless rebuilt depleted institutional treasuries and boosted morale as well. In the
wake of this experience, most institutions sought to consolidate and bolster their
programs.

Enrollment backtracked only slightly in the early 1950s, before larger cohorts
began coming of age and seeking college places. Student numbers grew by approximately 50 percent in the 1950s. By the end of the decade, however, the baby-
boom generation had already filled the high schools. The 1960s experienced a
double effect: participation rates increased by half (from 30% to 45%), and the
eighteen- to twenty-one-year-old age cohort grew even more (from 9 million to 15
million). This flood of students flowed into flagship state universities, which expanded to their limits and then became increasingly selective. Private institutions, without generous appropriations to fund expansion, largely sought to opti-
mize their efforts by building stronger academic programs for a more select
student body. A large portion of the new students found places at burgeoning
regional state institutions. Formerly teachers colleges, these institutions eagerly
expanded academic programs, ventured into graduate education, and became regional universities. The final component of this growth came from new public

community colleges, which, from 1965 to 1972, were opened at a rate exceeding one per week.

Higher education expanded in another way by opening to previously excluded minorities, most dramatically African Americans. The 1954 *Brown v. Board of Education* decision outlawing segregation had little impact on southern colleges and universities. Instead, often violent confrontations achieved no more than token integration. Only the 1964 Civil Rights Act overcame the obstruction of southern politicians and allowed a genuine process of desegregation to begin. At the same time, northern colleges and universities began to undertake proactive efforts to reverse the grievous underrepresentation of African American students.

The idealism suffusing higher education after the war lent support for the basic arts and sciences. Institutions emphasizing these subjects had assumed preponderant prestige in the interwar years. Now, a consensus formed endorsing the *Harvard Report on General Education*, which pronounced that a judicious sampling of the basic disciplines would compose the foundation for a liberal education.[48] The pattern of institutional expansion also supported this trend toward arts and sciences. Service institutions that had embraced vocational-professional programs (or were confined to teacher education) in the interwar years gradually fortified disciplinary departments. A shift in student majors ensued in the 1960s, when bachelor's degrees awarded in the arts and sciences rose to a peak of 47 percent.[49]

These trends were powerfully fortified by a prodigious expansion of research and graduate education, largely due to federal support.[50] Federal sponsorship of research initially extended, under different organizational headings, the channels established for the wartime emergency. For more than a decade after World War II, the bulk of the increased funding for academic research came from the defense establishment and was skewed toward the physical sciences. However, a new federal relationship with higher education emerged from the Sputnik crisis of 1957. For about a decade after Sputnik, funding growth for academic science came from the civilian side of the federal government: the National Science Foundation, the National Aeronautical and Space Administration, and, most prolifically, the National Institutes of Health. Moreover, this bounteous support was accompanied by assistance for universities to support graduate students, build laboratories, and develop new science programs. Sputnik also provoked Washington to support higher education directly, first through the National Defense Education Act and later through direct aid for buildings and students. The federal largess, superimposed on mushrooming enrollments and state support, produced an ephemeral golden age in American higher education.

Christopher Jencks and David Riesman characterized the transformation that occurred during this era as "the academic revolution."[51] They meant the process by which the theoretical and specialized academic outlook of graduate schools was conveyed throughout the institutional order. It was a process that transcended the sciences, ultimately affecting virtually every school and department. The agents were the new PhDs, trained in burgeoning graduate programs, who staffed the expanding universities. Their teaching and their writings brought the most current and specialized academic knowledge into the classrooms of all types of institutions. Ultimately, however, the expectations and idealism of the academic revolution set the stage for a backlash that arose in the late 1960s. Its chief manifestation was the great student rebellion.

The student movement crystallized from the Free Speech Movement at the University of California at Berkeley and Students for a Democratic Society. The national issues of the war in Vietnam and racial injustice largely propelled its evolution toward increasing radicalism and militancy. Although the major campuses suffered their greatest disruption from 1967 to 1969, the enduring impact was to alter the prevailing atmosphere of higher education. The momentum of the academic revolution was checked. The university's relation to its students was profoundly altered, from paternalism to exaggerated permissiveness. And universities retreated for a time to a heightened aloofness. The student rebellion was the crescendo to the tumultuous postwar generation, but it only partially foreshadowed the dawning new era.

Generation 10: Privatization and the Current Era, 1975–2010

To extend historical analysis beyond the point in which documentation is available and ensuing consequences can be known is perilous. Nonetheless, it is now apparent that the 1970s represented a transitional decade for higher education, and that since 1980 significant developments have altered the demographics, politics, and social relations of American higher education.

In 1975, enrollments in higher education topped 11 million for the first time, but then an unprecedented change occurred: student numbers, also for the first time, ceased to grow. In the ensuing years there was an upward creep, but twenty years later the number of full-time students had grown by just 20 percent. Never before had enrollments been so stagnant for so long. One important dynamic was nevertheless at work: whereas 55 percent of students were male in 1975, 55 percent were female in 1995.

Higher education's relationship with the federal government changed in these years. Federal investment in higher education increased significantly in the 1970s, with the new funds being used to support access through student financial aid. The 1972 amendments to the Higher Education Act were a watershed in two respects. First, they formalized a major commitment to provide aid to students on the basis of financial need. Second, the 1972 amendments extended the government's regulatory control over higher education. The student rebellion of the 1960s had, in effect, staked the claim for a greater presence in higher education for minorities and women. Title IX now provided the means for legal enforcement. It was perhaps the most significant of a number of measures by which federal regulation became an inescapable presence in higher education.

One clarion call of the student rebellion was for greater relevance in university studies. Relevance indeed became a hallmark of the new era, but in ways not anticipated by student activists. They had advocated a tendentious relevance predicated on the university's role as an aloof critic of society. Thus they urged universities to study and seek to ameliorate problems stemming from the Vietnam War, racial inequality, poverty, and the environment. These topics long remained preoccupations on campuses, but students sought a more tangible form of relevance by turning away from the arts and sciences toward more vocational or professional majors. Bachelor's degrees in arts and sciences plummeted to just over one-quarter of the total, barely more than the number awarded in business alone. Beginning around 1980, American higher education entered a new era of privatization. Whereas the previous generation had been characterized by increasing government investments, higher education now began to extract a growing proportion of revenues from the private sector. The most prominent manifestation was rising absolute and relative levels of tuition. From the 1950s to 1980, average tuition in both the public and private sectors had been stable, as a percentage of median family income. These figures doubled in both sectors by the late 1990s and then rose steeply again after 2001.[52] These increases made possible higher levels of spending in colleges and universities, but they also shifted the burden for these expenditures to students and parents. Several conditions made this feasible.

Private colleges and universities adopted a strategy of "high tuition–high aid," whereby large tuition increases were accompanied by financial aid for students with financial need. The increasing availability of federal student loans after the

Middle Income Student Assistance Act (1978) touched off the development of a loan culture that has grown ever since. However, private schools amplified the impact of federal student aid by offering additional institutional aid—tuition discounts—to help students to meet escalating prices. Differential pricing and loans thus prevented demand from falling due to lack of affordability. Private schools also benefited from a soaring demand for high-priced, high-quality education at selective colleges and universities. Rising monetary returns to a college education and media publicity for college rankings encouraged this "selectivity sweepstakes." Some of these same factors affected the public sector, although not tuition discounting. However, public institutions had to adapt to the stagnation of state appropriations. Real spending per student peaked in the late 1970s and fluctuated at somewhat lower levels since then. Rising tuition had thus compensated for the relative shrinkage of public support.[53]

The consequences of this financial aid revolution have been mixed. Private colleges and universities have enjoyed unparalleled prosperity, with the wealthiest institutions receiving the greatest bounty from burgeoning student demand, rising tuition revenue, large donations, and outsized investment returns. At the same time, despite programs to recruit diverse students and provide greater student aid, the wealthiest institutions predominantly enroll wealthy students, and in fact depend on them to pay the high tuition that is necessary for high financial aid. For American higher education as a whole, rising prices have been accompanied by increasing social stratification. In the public sector, regional campuses and community colleges have, on the whole, been weakened by declining appropriations. Public research universities have been better able to adapt by raising tuition and performing an ever-increasing volume of research.

Privatization in university research began decisively in 1980, with a succession of federal actions designed to encourage the transfer of university technology to private industry and the commercialization of university inventions. During the current era, the expectation that university research can or should contribute to economic development has become an article of faith in many circles. This rationale, in turn, has justified a healthy growth of private, state, but mostly federal investments in academic research. On campuses, research has grown far more rapidly than instruction or faculty, thus increasing its relative weight in the balance of university activities. Controversy over university involvement in commercial pursuits has accompanied these developments. But, undeniably, the current era has seen an enormous expansion of university research, a corresponding strengthening of most research universities, and greater contributions to society.[54]

The economic turmoil of 2008–10 almost certainly signaled the passing of generation 10 and the probable inception of new trends as yet too inchoate to identify. Nonetheless, the experience of generation 10 will no doubt shape the nature of future developments. The achievements of American research universities first excited the envy of the world and now have stimulated growing competition. The United States has long been the most educated society in the world, but due to enrollment stagnation, our college graduation rates now trail more than a dozen countries. National commitments to rectify this situation will need to overcome the high price of tuition and an excessive reliance on student loans. Yet the demand for places in public four-year and community colleges is growing, even while public investment is declining. The next generation will be challenged to sustain the immeasurable contributions that colleges and universities make to American society, let alone to improve on them.

NOTES

References have been limited to principal secondary works and quotation sources. For a general history, see John R. Thelin, A History of American Higher Education *(Baltimore: Johns Hopkins University Press, 2004). For a bibliography, see Christine A. Ogren, "Sites, Students, Scholarship, and Structure: The Historiography of American Higher Education in the Post-Revisionist Era," in* Rethinking the History of American Education, *ed. William J. Reese and John L. Rury (New York: Palgrave Macmillan, 2008). Additional material has been drawn from Roger L. Geiger, ed.,* The American College in the Nineteenth Century *(Nashville, TN: Vanderbilt University Press, 2000).*

1. Jurgen Herbst, *From Crisis to Crisis: American College Government, 1636–1819* (Cambridge, MA: Harvard University Press, 1982), 1–61.

2. Samuel Eliot Morison, *Three Centuries of Harvard, 1636–1936* (Cambridge, MA: Harvard University Press, 1936), 53–82; Richard Hofstadter, *Academic Freedom in the Age of the College* (New Brunswick, NJ: Transaction, 1996 [1955]), 98–113; Susan H. Godson, Ludwell H. Johnson, Richard B. Sherman, Thad W. Tate, and Helen C. Walker, *The College of William and Mary: A History*, 2 vols. (Williamsburg, VA: King and Queen Press, 1993), vol. 1, 3–80; J. David Hoeveler, *Creating the American Mind: Intellect and Politics in the Colonial Colleges* (Lanham, MD: Rowman and Littlefield, 2002).

3. Herbst, *From Crisis to Crisis*, 38–47; Richard Warch, *School of the Prophets: Yale College, 1701–1740* (New Haven, CT: Yale University Press, 1973).

4. Bruce A. Kimball, *The "True Professional Ideal" in America: A History* (Cambridge, MA: Blackwell, 1992), 75–84; Herbst, *From Crisis to Crisis*, 1.

5. William D. Carrell, "American College Professors: 1750–1800," *History of Education Quarterly* 8 (1968): 289–305.

6. Herbst, *From Crisis to Crisis*, 82–137; Howard Miller, *The Revolutionary College: American Presbyterian Higher Education, 1707–1837* (New York: New York University Press, 1976), 65–75.

7. Beverly McAnear, "College Founding in the American Colonies: 1745–1775," *Mississippi Valley Historical Review* 42 (1952): 24–44.

8. David C. Humphrey, *From King's College to Columbia, 1746–1800* (New York: Columbia University Press, 1976), 199; Robert McCaughey, *Stand Columbia: A History of Columbia University* (New York: Columbia University Press, 2003); Morison, *Three Centuries*, 102–3; James McLachlan, introduction to *The Princetonians, 1748–1768: A Biographical Dictionary* (Princeton, NJ: Princeton University Press, 1977).

9. Edmund S. Morgan, *The Gentle Puritan: A Life of Ezra Styles, 1727–1795* (Chapel Hill: University of North Carolina Press, 1962), 47–57; Henry F. May, *The Enlightenment in America* (New York: Oxford University Press, 1976); Hoeveler, *Creating the American Mind*.

10. Mark A. Noll, *Princeton and the Republic, 1768–1822: The Search for a Christian Enlightenment in the Era of Samuel Stanhope Smith* (Princeton, NJ: Princeton University Press, 1989), 16–98; Miller, *Revolutionary College*, 82–94.

11. Noll, *Princeton and the Republic*, 185–213, 297–99; David W. Robson, *Educating Republicans: The Colleges in the Era of the American Revolution, 1750–1800* (Westport, CT: Greenwood, 1985), 143–77.

12. Robson, *Educating Republicans*, 247.

13. Hofstadter, *Academic Freedom*, 209–53. However, see Roger L. Geiger, "The Reformation of the Colleges in the Early Republic," *History of Universities* 16, no. 2 (2000): 129–81.

14. *A History of Columbia University, 1754–1904* (New York: Columbia University Press, 1904), 100. See also McCaughey, *Stand Columbia*.

15. Steven J. Novak, *The Rights of Youth: American Colleges and Student Revolt, 1798–1815* (Cambridge, MA: Harvard University Press, 1977); Leon Jackson, "The Rights of Man and the Rites of Youth: Fraternity and Riot at Eighteenth-Century Harvard," in Geiger, *American College*, 46–79.

16. Novak, *Rights of Youth*, 166. However, see also Caroline Winterer, *The Culture of Classicism: Ancient Greece and Rome in American Intellectual Life, 1780–1910* (Baltimore: Johns Hopkins University Press, 2002).

17. Alfred Z. Reed, *Training for the Public Profession of the Law* (New York: Scribner, 1921), 116–60; William F. Norwood, *Medical Education in the United States before the Civil War* (Philadelphia: University of Pennsylvania Press, 1944).

18. Natalie A. Naylor, "The Theological Seminary in the Configuration of American Higher Education: The Ante-Bellum Years," *History of Education Quarterly* 17 (1977): 17–30; Glenn T. Miller, *Piety and Intellect: The Aims and Purposes of Ante-Bellum Theological Education* (Atlanta: Scholar's Press, 1990).

19. Herbst, *From Crisis to Crisis*, 232–43; Leon Burr Richardson, *History of Dartmouth College* (Hanover, NH: Dartmouth College Publications, 1932), 287–346; John

S. Whitehead and Jurgen Herbst, "How to Think about the Dartmouth College Case," *History of Education Quarterly* 26 (1986): 333–50.

20. Roger L. Geiger, "Introduction: New Themes in the History of Nineteenth-Century Colleges," in Geiger, *American College*, 1–36, esp. 16–24.

21. Stanley M. Guralnik, *Science and the Ante-Bellum American College* (Philadelphia: American Philosophical Society, 1975), 18–46.

22. David B. Potts, *Liberal Learning for a Land of Colleges* (New York: Palgrave Macmillan, 2010); *Reports on the Course of Instruction in Yale College; By a Committee of the Corporation and the Academical Faculty* (New Haven, CT: H. Howe, 1828).

23. Frederick Rudolph, *Mark Hopkins and the Log: Williams College, 1836–1872* (New Haven, CT: Yale University Press, 1956); Roger L. Geiger, with Julie Ann Bubolz, "College as It Was in the Mid-Nineteenth Century," in Geiger, *American College*, 80–90.

24. Charles H. Glatfelter, *A Salutary Influence: Gettysburg College, 1832–1985*, 2 vols. (Gettysburg, PA: Gettysburg College, 1987), vol. 1, 175; David B. Potts, " 'College Enthusiasm' as Public Response: 1800–1860," *Harvard Education Review* 47 (1977): 28–42.

25. Colin Burke, *American Collegiate Populations: A Test of the Traditional View* (New York: New York University Press, 1982).

26. Francis Wayland, *Report to the Corporation of Brown University on Changes in the System of Collegiate Education* (Providence, RI: G. H. Whitney, 1850).

27. Daniel Coit Gilman, "Our National Schools of Science," *North American Review* (Oct. 1867): 495–520; Richard J. Storr, *The Beginnings of Graduate Education in America* (Chicago: University of Chicago Press, 1953), 60–65, 112–17.

28. Thomas Woody, *A History of Women's Education in the United States*, 2 vols. (New York: Science Press, 1929), vol. 1, 145–47; Christie Anne Farnham, *The Education of the Southern Belle: Higher Education and Student Socialization in the Antebellum South* (New York: New York University Press, 1994); Sidney Sherwood, *The University of the State of New York* (Washington, DC: U.S. Government Printing Office, 1900), quotation on 447.

29. Roger L. Geiger, "The Era of Multipurpose Colleges in American Higher Education, 1850–1890" in Geiger, *American College*, 127–52; Doris Malkmus, "Small Towns, Small Sects, and Coeducation in Midwestern Colleges," *History of Higher Education Annual* 22 (2002): 33–66.

30. Roger L. Geiger, "The Rise and Fall of Useful Knowledge," in Geiger, *American College*, 153–68; Roger L. Williams, *The Origins of Federal Support for Higher Education: George W. Atherton and the Land-Grant College Movement* (University Park: Pennsylvania State University Press, 1991).

31. "The Morrill Act, 1862," in *Higher Education: A Documentary History*, 2 vols., ed. Richard Hofstadter and Wilson Smith (Chicago: University of Chicago Press, 1961), vol. 2, 568–69 [emphasis added].

32. Helen Lefkowitz Horowitz, *Alma Mater: Design and Experience in the Women's Colleges from Their Nineteenth Century Origins to the 1930s* (Boston: Beacon, 1984).

33. Hugh Hawkins, *Between Harvard and America: The Educational Leadership of Charles W. Eliot* (New York: Oxford University Press, 1972); Morison, *Three Centuries,*

323–99, quotation on 361; Laurence Veysey, *The Emergence of the American University* (Chicago: University of Chicago Press, 1965).

34. Roger L. Geiger, *To Advance Knowledge: The Growth of American Research Universities, 1900–1940* (New York: Oxford University Press, 1986), 270–71.

35. Roger L. Geiger, "The 'Superior Instruction of Women,' 1836–1890," in Geiger, *American College*, 183–95; Barbara Miller Solomon, *In the Company of Educated Women: A History of Women and Higher Education in America* (New Haven, CT: Yale University Press, 1985); Lynn D. Gordon, *Gender and Higher Education in the Progressive Era* (New Haven, CT: Yale University Press, 1990).

36. Veysey, *Emergence*; Geiger, *To Advance Knowledge*, 14–19; enrollments by professional school or department are given in Edwin E. Slosson, *Great American Universities* (New York: Macmillan, 1910).

37. Geiger, *To Advance Knowledge*, 30–39; Walter P. Metzger, "Origins of the Association," *AAUP Bulletin* 51 (1965): 229–37.

38. W. Bruce Leslie, *Gentlemen and Scholars: College and Community in the "Age of the University," 1865–1917* (University Park: Pennsylvania State University Press, 1992); Ronald A. Smith, *Sports and Freedom: The Rise of Big-Time College Athletics* (New York: Oxford University Press, 1988); David P. Setran, *The College "Y": Student Religion in an Age of Secularization* (New York: Palgrave Macmillan, 2007).

39. Geiger, *To Advance Knowledge*, 45–47; Ellen Condliffe Lagemann, *Private Power for the Public Good: A History of the Carnegie Foundation for the Advancement of Teaching* (Middletown, CT: Wesleyan University Press, 1983), 3–53.

40. Hugh Hawkins, *Banding Together: The Rise of the National Associations in American Higher Education, 1887–1950* (Baltimore: Johns Hopkins University Press, 1992), 107–10.

41. Martin Trow, *The Transition from Elite to Mass Higher Education* (Paris: Organisation for Economic Co-operation and Development, 1974).

42. David O. Levine, *The American College and the Culture of Aspiration, 1915–1940* (Ithaca, NY: Cornell University Press, 1986).

43. Geiger, *To Advance Knowledge*; Abraham Flexner, *Universities: American, English, German* (New Brunswick, NJ: Transaction, 1994 [1930]).

44. Harold Wechsler, *The Qualified Student: A History of Selective Admissions in America* (New York: Wiley, 1977); Marcia G. Synnott, *The Half-Opened Door: Discrimination in Admissions to Harvard, Yale, and Princeton, 1900–1970* (Westport, CT: Greenwood, 1977); Geiger, *To Advance Knowledge*, 129–39.

45. Geiger, *To Advance Knowledge*, 206, and also see appendices for institutional finances.

46. Burton R. Clark, *The Distinctive College* (New Brunswick, NJ: Transaction, 1992 [1970]), 184–232.

47. Enrollment data are from the National Center for Education Statistics, *Digest of Education Statistics*, http://nces.ed.gov/programs/digest/. For postwar academic development, see Richard M. Freeland, *Academia's Golden Age: Universities in Massachusetts, 1945–1970* (New York: Oxford University Press, 1992); Roger L. Geiger, *Research*

and *Relevant Knowledge: American Research Universities since World War II* (New York: Oxford University Press, 1993).

48. Harvard University, *General Education in a Free Society* (Cambridge, MA: Harvard University Press, 1945).

49. Roger L. Geiger, "Demography and Curriculum: The Humanities in American Higher Education, 1945–1985," in *The Humanities and the Dynamics of Inclusion since World War II*, ed. David A. Hollinger (Baltimore: Johns Hopkins University Press, 2006), 50–72.

50. The following draws on Geiger, *Research and Relevant Knowledge*.

51. Christopher Jencks and David Riesman, *The Academic Revolution* (Chicago: University of Chicago Press, 1968); Geiger, *Research and Relevant Knowledge*, 198–203.

52. Claudia Goldin and Lawrence F. Katz, *The Race between Education and Technology* (Cambridge, MA: Harvard University Press, 2008), 276.

53. Roger L. Geiger, *Knowledge and Money: Research Universities and the Paradox of the Marketplace* (Stanford, CA: Stanford University Press, 2004).

54. Roger L. Geiger and Creso M. Sá, *Tapping the Riches of Science: Universities and the Promise of Economic Growth* (Cambridge, MA: Harvard University Press, 2009).

CHAPTER THREE

Autonomy and Accountability

Who Controls Academe?

Frank A. Schmidtlein and Robert O. Berdahl

If a college or university is effectively to define its purposes and select or invent the means of attaining them, it must have a high degree of autonomy. Bowen has observed that the "production process" in higher education is far more intricate and complicated than that in any industrial enterprise.[1] Turning resources into human values defies standardization. Students vary enormously in academic aptitude, interests, intellectual dispositions, social and cultural characteristics, educational and vocational objectives, and many other ways. Furthermore, the disciplines and professions with which institutions of higher learning are concerned require diverse methods of investigation, intellectual structures, means of relating methods of inquiry and ideas to personal and social values, and processes of relating knowledge to human experience. Learning, consequently, is a subtle process, the nature of which may vary from student to student, institution to institution, discipline to discipline, one scholar or teacher to another, and one level of student development to another. The intricacy and unpredictability of both learning and investigation require a high degree of freedom from intellectually limiting external intervention and control if an institution of higher education is to perform effectively.

These characteristics of colleges and universities have led Etzioni to make a distinction between *administrative* and *professional* authority.[2] This distinction has important implications for understanding the tensions between the concepts of autonomy and accountability in higher education. The primary expertise in higher education is possessed by the faculty, the base of the organizational pyramid. A physics professor does not presume to tell a history or business professor what to teach and research. In a business firm, however, those in the central leadership typically possess the primary knowledge needed to instruct those making the product, or providing the service, about how it should be done. Unfortunately, this distinction commonly is not understood nor, perhaps, appreciated by public officials who are more familiar with the administrative concept of organizational coordination and control and who believe that direct bureaucratic intervention can, or should be able to, effectively alter academic practices in institutions. These distinctions have been best expressed by Etzioni, who contrasts decision-making authority in organizations where the workforce is primarily composed of professionals with those where the primary workforces possess less complex skills: "Administration assumes a power hierarchy. Without a clear ordering of higher and lower in rank, in which the higher in rank have more power than the lower ones and hence can control and coordinate the latter's activities, the basic principle of administration is violated; the organization ceases to be a coordinated tool. However, knowledge is largely an individual property; unlike other organization means, it cannot be transferred from one person to another by decree. Creativity is basically individual and can only to a very limited degree be ordered and coordinated by the superior in rank." He then concludes that, in organizations made up of professionals, "the surgeon has to decide whether or not to operate. Students of the professions have pointed out that the autonomy granted to professionals who are basically responsible to their consciences (though they may be censured by their peers and in extreme cases by the courts) is necessary for effective professional work. It is this highly individualized principle which is diametrically opposed to the very essence of the organizational principle of control and coordination by superiors—i.e., the principle of administrative authority."

Autonomy and Academic Freedom

On first thought, one might identify academic freedom with autonomy. Certainly a high degree of intellectual independence is necessary for faculty and students in choosing their subjects of study and investigation, searching for the truth without unreasonable or arbitrary restrictions, and expressing scholarly conclusions without censorship. Some forms of external control—or even subtle efforts to influence teaching, learning, or research—may endanger intellectual freedom. However, academic freedom and university autonomy, though related, are not synonymous. Academic freedom as a concept is universal and absolute, whereas autonomy is, of necessity, parochial and relative.

Presumably, state boards of higher education designating the missions of sectors or particular institutions after appropriate studies and consultation would not be an unwarranted invasion of autonomy. But specifying the content of academic programs, academic organization, the curriculum, and methods of teaching in order to attain designated missions is likely to be considered unjustified intervention. A coordinating or governing board might phase out a doctoral program at a particular campus (after appropriate study and consultation) without an unwarranted invasion of institutional autonomy or a violation of academic freedom. The federal government might impose antidiscrimination procedures in admitting students or appointing and promoting faculty members without interfering unjustifiably in academic affairs, provided the means do not make unreasonable demands on the institutions or violate the necessary confidentiality of records. If appropriate safeguards are followed, no invasion of academic freedom need be suffered.

Requirements for accountability may impose onerous procedures on an institution, but even these restraints may not endanger academic freedom. Whether restrictions on DNA research put an undesirable limit on the choice of problems for investigation remains a controversial issue. In this case, cultural norms and public protection are asserted to justify some interventions that seem to infringe on academic freedom. Less controversial are restrictions placed on researchers to protect human and animal subjects. The absence of external controls does not guarantee academic freedom, and certain elements of external control do not endanger intellectual independence, but an institution's right to mobilize its intellectual resources and, within reasonable limits, even its financial resources toward the attainment of its agreed-upon purposes is at least strongly fortified by a relatively high degree of autonomy.[3]

The Nature of Accountability

Zumeta, in an excellent review of accountability in higher education, notes that institutions historically were viewed "as necessarily freewheeling and unconstrained."[4] He quotes Martin Trow, saying they "were treated with unusual deference by their state sponsors, who were often content to 'leave the money on the stump' with few questions asked." Today, however, Zumeta observes that colleges and universities face unprecedented external demands, and that "this shift in states' expectations and relations with colleges and universities is significant not only for academe's own interests but . . . for important societal values."

Growing external demands on institutions have produced conflicting concepts of how to maintain institutional accountability. Some states have reduced some substantive and procedural controls on institutions, usually to encourage market forces that are expected to promote consumer interests and innovation, while others have strengthened administrative controls. In some cases, states have reduced financial, personnel, procurement, and other direct procedural controls while imposing less-direct substantive and procedural controls by mandating accountability, quality assessment, and performance budgeting processes. There is a vigorous debate over what mix of market incentives and administrative controls are appropriate and effective to assure that institutions meet their public responsibilities. Both administrative controls and marketplace pressures can restrict institutions' autonomy, but they generally prefer accommodating the more diverse pressures of the marketplace over the centralized imposition of administrative controls. A delicate balance is required between an unregulated marketplace and expensive and stultifying government-imposed administrative controls.

Shulock observes that "the meaning of accountability has evolved as new models of public management have emerged in the last fifteen years. The older view emphasizes accountability for sound fiscal management and following rules. The newer view emphasizes outcomes and argues that public managers should be given flexibility to produce the desired outcomes with minimal oversight of how funds were allocated or what methods were used—a kind of oversight viewed as micromanagement."[5] She also points out that accountability and assessment of student learning are not the same: "State-level accountability is about the effectiveness of our institutions and public policies, *collectively*, in meeting the educational needs of the citizens of the state; it is not about assessing the effectiveness of each institution or providing consumer information to support the private choices of citizens" (emphasis in original).

Financial austerity causes legislatures, state coordinating boards, and even consolidated governing boards to look more critically at institutional roles, the availability and distribution of functions and programs, effectiveness, and educational and operational costs. As the federal government extends support for higher education, it prohibits discrimination in the admission of students and the appointment and promotion of faculty members. The public at large has become more conscious of its institutions of higher education. States and localities are more demanding in terms of education and service, more critical of what they perceive institutions to be doing, and more vocal in expressing their criticisms and desires. Public institutions, always answerable to the general interest, can no longer avoid defending what they do or do not do. They increasingly have to explain themselves, defend their essential character, and demonstrate that their service is worth the cost. They will become increasingly answerable (i.e., accountable) to numerous constituencies for the range of their services and the effectiveness of their performance.

Institutions are accountable to a variety of clients, in addition to government agencies. They serve the business community, students and their parents, and not-for-profit organizations. Nor is accountability confined to an institution's external relationships. Internally, a college or university is a complex of mutual responsibilities and reciprocal pressures for accountability, with a wide variety of ongoing and periodic performance assessments. As Etzioni points out, professionals have a primary accountability to their peers for the quality and integrity of their efforts.[6] These include not only the peers at their institutions, but also those in their disciplines and professional fields nationally and, increasingly, internationally. External accountability to peers is accomplished largely through processes such as accreditation, peer review of manuscripts for publication, and peer review of research proposals. Important as these bases of accountability are, this chapter is nonetheless devoted to a discussion of accountability to external agencies.

In this environment of increasing demands for accountability, intellectual freedom in colleges and universities generally has maintained widespread public and governmental support, although occasionally governmental officials attempt to sanction academics who express unpopular views or criticize government policies. Also, some institutions have abolished tenure, thus potentially inhibiting faculty expression of unpopular views.

Accountability to the Public

Ultimately, public institutions of higher education are broadly answerable to the people who support them. After California voters previously failed to approve a state bond issue providing large sums for the construction of medical school facilities and gave other evidences of disaffection, the then president of the University of California recognized the ultimate public accountability of the university. "Make no mistake," he said to the Assembly of the Academic Senate, "the university is a public institution, supported by the people through the actions of their elected representatives and executives. They will not allow it to be operated in ways which are excessively at variance with the general public will. By various pressures and devices, the university will be forced to yield and to conform if it gets too far away from what the public expects and wants."[7]

At one time, people were relatively remote from their public institutions, but citizens now find their future economic, social, and cultural lives increasingly influenced, and in some cases virtually determined, by their colleges and universities. Consequently, public institutions have had to become responsive to a wider range of economic interests and a more diverse pattern of ethnic and cultural backgrounds and aspirations. Minority groups are pressing for financial assistance, remedial programs when necessary for admission or the attainment of academic standards, and academic programs that will meet their interests and perceived needs. Just as interest groups have pressed the university to provide the services they believe they need, students have organized to promote their interests. Over the years, many colleges and universities have responded to that student market by establishing new vocational and professional programs of study, and most institutions are struggling to redistribute faculty, equipment, and resources as students shift from liberal arts courses to vocational and professional curricula.

Serving the public interest is a complicated process; institutions have diverse missions and serve a variety of student and public interests. Accountability is further complicated by a question of which interests should be served and which ones should be put aside by institutions with differing missions. The interests to be served by an institution are determined through both external and internal political processes, resulting in complex compromises and the accommodation of many, often conflicting, objectives. As a consequence, accountability, which implies agreed-upon purposes and objectives, has significant political as well as technical dimensions. Many attempts to institute accountability processes have failed, because they were based on an inaccurate assumption that substantial agreement was possible on a stable set of measurable institutional goals and objectives. The directions institutions take result from a constantly evolving, complex set of compromises among a variety of contending internal and external interests and from the accommodation of resource and time constraints.

Conflicts over the appropriate locations for making various kinds of decisions have occurred since tribal times. They typically involve balancing collective and private interests. Schmidtlein describes a number of factors that influence where decisions are located.[8] He notes that persons at various locations in governance structures have ready access to differing kinds of information. Those in state government are in a better position to observe the relationships among colleges and universities and typically have a more holistic sense of public sentiment. Consequently, they are likely to be more sensitive than institutions to the appropriateness of the entire pattern of institutions and their missions, the relationships among institutions, and priorities across the entire state system of higher education.

In contrast, those located in colleges and universities possess more information about local circumstances and the tradeoffs involved in making decisions affecting local issues. When decisions involve internal institutional issues, central officials are likely to have oversimplified views of the factors involved and make inappropriate decisions. Many highly relevant kinds of information are hard to quantify and communicate effectively to those in government and difficult for them to evaluate. Consequently, they are likely to delay decisions by requesting increasing numbers of costly reports and data to assure themselves that their decisions are correct, because often they are aware of their relative ignorance of local complexities. Lacking an intimate knowledge of these complexities, they also are more susceptible to simplistic solutions to issues, more likely to embrace management fads, and tend to focus more on information collection and decision-making processes than on the substance of the decisions. However, governments can appropriately seek to assure that institutions maintain effective internal accountability systems.

In practice, higher education systems need to achieve a balance between the benefits and costs of central and local decision making. Government oversight and steering are needed to assure, for example, that a set of institutions exist whose missions serve the diverse needs of the public, and to counter occasional attempts of two-year colleges to become four-year institutions and four-year teaching institutions to become graduate/research universities. Changes in institutional missions should serve the public interest and not be based primarily on institutional ambitions to move up the prestige ladder. Government oversight also is needed to assure that a diverse set of academic programs exists that meets the legitimate needs of the public while avoiding unnecessary duplication. Institutions, however, should have the freedom to design the content of their academic programs and courses and their research initiatives. They also should have the procedural freedom needed to pursue their programs in an efficient manner. As Berdahl notes, governments need to retain authority over substantive issues related to the character of higher education systems, while institutions should be given a very large measure of freedom over procedural aspects of their programs.[9] Unstructured competition reduces diversity and increases costs through program duplication, while excessive regulation restricts the ability of competent institutional leaders to take expeditious advantage of new opportunities and adjust to new circumstances. Government controls seldom remedy the errors of those lacking competence. Thus accountability is both general (responding to definitions of the broad public interest) and particular (responding to institutional constituencies).

Later chapters in this book will elaborate on the tensions between autonomy and accountability in higher education with respect to state governments, the federal government, and the courts. Here, we merely provide brief overviews.

Governmental Oversight

State Government

Accountability to the public is mediated by the operation of several governance layers between it and the institutions in question. Colleges and universities are answerable most immediately to their governing boards. Most public boards have statutory status: they were created by legislatures and are, in nearly all respects, under legislative control. Twelve states have given some of their public universities some form of constitutional autonomy; however, that autonomy is severely limited in at least two of these states.[10] Giving institutions constitutional status sought to remove questions of management, control, and supervision of the universities from politicians in state legislatures and governors' offices.[11] However, several state courts have rejected the interpretation that autonomy creates boards as a separate branch of state government. Consequently, this legal status may only make them "a distinctive part of state government."[12]

The purpose for creating universities' constitutional status was to give them a much greater degree of autonomy and self-direction than statutory status would provide. Their autonomy, however, has been materially eroded over the years. A study of statutory and constitutional boards in 1973 showed that the supposedly constitutionally autonomous university "is losing a good deal of its ability to exercise final judgment on the use not only of its state funds but also of those derived from other sources. It now undergoes intensive reviews of budgets and programs by several different state agencies, by special commissions, and by legislative committees, all of which look for ways to control [it]."[13]

The evidence is mixed regarding further increases in government intrusions. Whether an institution has statutory or constitutional status, or even whether it is public or private, it is moving into the governmental orbit.

Most students of university governance believe that government officials should not serve on governing boards, since this identifies the institution too closely with political and governmental agencies. However, in California the governor, the lieutenant governor, the superintendent of public instruction, the president of the state board of agriculture, and the speaker of the legislative assembly are among the ex officio voting members of the board of regents of the University of California. Governors may also use their appointive power to attempt to influence governing boards, although most boards have staggered terms that prevent governors from appointing a majority of members until they have served several years in office.

However, sometimes governors can accomplish through other means what they lack the power to do through the direct appointment of trustees or regents. For example, when Ronald Reagan was governor of California, he heartily disapproved of the way President Clark Kerr was handling the mid-1960s student uprisings. A minority of university regents agreed with Governor Reagan; to them he added a few appointments to seats that had fallen vacant. He still lacked a majority who agreed with him, however, until he emphatically noted that the university's budget did not have constitutional autonomy and that he would not look kindly at continued resistance to his point of view. Consequently, Clark Kerr, as he later commented, left the university as he had come to it, "fired with enthusiasm!" Enough additional regents had been intimidated by the governor's statements to swing opinions over to his side.

Although governors may thus influence institutions via their governing boards, they make their greatest impact through the executive budget process.[14] The state finance or budget officer, who is ordinarily responsible to the governor, may also exercise an important element of authority by controlling shifts or changes in line-item budgets. Some state finance departments conduct preaudits of expenditures that not only pass on the legality of the use of itemized funds, but also give the state officer the opportunity to rule on the substance or purpose of the expenditures.

As important as the executive officers of state government may be to public colleges and universities, state legislatures are even more so. These institutions are dependent on the legislature's understanding of their broad missions and programs, its financial support, and its judgment of the institutions' educational effectiveness. Even a constitutionally autonomous public university is ultimately accountable to the legislature for the ways in which it uses its state-appropriated funds and for the effectiveness of its educational services. Legislators often become restless in the face of what some regard as the continuing neglect of undergraduate teaching and an overemphasis on research at graduate/research universities. Studies of faculty workloads are common, with some legislatures considering mandated faculty teaching loads. At times the long arms of state finance officers have reached into academic affairs by conducting program audits or even program evaluations.

Issues raised in program evaluation include the consistency of the program with the assigned institutional role and function; the adequacy of planning with regard to the objectives, program structure, processes, implementation, and evaluation of outcomes; either the adherence of the program's operation to the objectives, structural features, processes, sequence, and outcome appraisal originally specified or the presentation of a sound rationale for any deviations from the original prescription; an evaluation of planning and operations and the use of feedback for alterations and improvements; and provision for cost-benefit analyses.

State governments determine eligibility for state aid to both public and private postsecondary institutions. Most states charter and license degree-granting institutions, but some observers believe that in most instances the standards specified are insufficient to ensure quality. The Education Commission of the States has urged that the states establish minimum quality standards for all postsecondary institutions.

As reported in chapter 6, states are seeking to hold institutions answerable for the attainment of their professed goals in the form of demonstrable changes in students. Historically, there appeared to be an implicit assumption that responsibility for learning outcomes should be placed primarily on students. However, over the past three or four decades, institutions increasingly have been viewed as having a major portion of this responsibility. Today, institutional demonstrations of student learning outcomes are commonly viewed as part of their responsibility for public accountability, and states are seeking evidence that they are meeting this challenge. However, as noted earlier, Shulock asserts that a demonstration of learning outcomes is *assessment* and thus is an internal institutional responsibility. Complex learning outcomes are extremely difficult to identify, to agree on and then assign priorities, and to communicate to government officials and the public. This view may be simple in conception, but it is extremely difficult in implementation. First, it is essential to translate goals into relevant and agreed-upon outcomes. An even more complicated task is to devise means of determining the extent to which students have attained these outcomes. The first question to be asked is, how has the student changed at a given point in relation to this characteristic at entrance? This requires information on how students vary at the starting point, not only in previous academic achievement but also in general and special academic aptitude; information on students' intellectual dispositions, such as a theoretical or pragmatic orientation; and information on students' interests, attitudes, values, and motivations, to mention only some of the dimensions relevant to the educational process. These attributes establish baselines for estimating the amount of change over stated periods, and some are indicative of students' educability.

Studies of the influence of institutions on student development also require means of measuring or describing college characteristics, "the prevailing atmosphere, the social and intellectual climate, the style of a campus," as well as "educational treatments."[15] One of the complications involved in describing college environments is that student characteristics and institutional qualities are by no means unrelated. Furthermore, most institutions are not all of a piece, and the total environment may have less influence on particular students than the suborganizations or subcultures of which they are members.

It is even more difficult to determine the impact of the institution's environment on students. First, environmental variables probably do not act singly, but in combination. Second, changes that occur in students may not be attributable to the effect of the college environment itself. Developmental processes established early in an individual's experience may continue through his or her college years; some of these processes take place normally within a wide range of environmental conditions, and in order to alter the course and extent of develop-ment, it would be necessary to introduce fairly great changes in environmental stimulation. Third, changes that occur during the college years may be less the effect of the college experience as such than of the general social environment in which the college exists and the students live.[16]

For these and many other reasons, it is extremely difficult to relate changes in behavior to specific characteristics of the college or to particular patterns of educa-tional activity. Studies of change in students' characteristics reveal wide differences from person to person and detectable differences from institution to institution. Bowen summarizes the evidence on change in students in both cognitive and non-cognitive outcomes, and also the differences in the effects of various institu-tions: "On the whole, the evidence supports the hypothesis that the differences in impact are relatively small—when impact is defined as value added in the form of change in students during the college years."[17] Given these complexities, the assessment of student learning outcomes and their implications for academic pro-grams appear best accomplished within institutions, by faculty, who are the ones with detailed knowledge of the students and their academic progress and accom-plishments. The appropriate role of state government and accrediting agencies should be to ensure that institutions have appropriate policies and procedures for assessing student learning outcomes and to review the effectiveness of their aca-demic programs.

Notwithstanding the complexity of the processes described above, a number of states have established policies seeking to assess student learning. But in most states, policy makers were persuaded to place the responsibility for developing the assessment program on the individual public institutions, allowing each one to develop a program appropriate to its particular role and mission. Only by al-lowing for such diversity is it likely that any institution will gain a sense of own-ership of the process and be encouraged to use the results for self-improvement.

The Federal Government

Autonomy and accountability issues of American higher education vis-à-vis the federal government primarily involve three major relevant federal policy areas: federal support for research, federal support for student aid, and federal inter-ventions to support social justice. While later chapters in this volume will dis-cuss both the federal policies and the role of the courts in much greater detail, here we present a brief overview of our perspectives on those key issues relating to autonomy and accountability. Issues in the research domain include the following:

—Are internal research priorities among major research universities unnaturally distorted by federal priorities?
—Does the peer review process for awarding federal research grants allow enough recognition to women and minority scientists at so-called second-level research institutions?
—Has the right balance been struck between the need for federal accounting requirements and the setting of indirect research costs, and the need for research institutions to have both flexibility and sufficient research funds to cover their internal related costs?
—Are the costs and limitations of federal requirements for the protection of human subjects and the avoidance of fraud excessive?

Federal policies have obviously tilted research universities' priorities in ways that they might not have chosen, absent the federal funds, but the bottom line has been to aid a small but very important set of public and private research institutions to become world class, as noted by their international achievements. Thus, on balance, the results of this federal role appear to be somewhat mixed but, overall, to have had a very positive influence.

Similarly, regarding the criticisms of peer review as being too elite oriented, the broadening of most peer review panels to reflect a greater diversity of institutions has benefits, but the basic principle of concentrating most of the federal research funds at a limited number of institutions and on a limited number of scientists widely recognized as constituting "the best" appears to have served the nation well. Obviously, the persons judging "the best" must be drawn from a fair cross-section of qualified scientists.

The federal government's accounting requirements whereby institutions justify their overhead costs are expensive, but they are designed to ensure that cost calculations are accurate and comparable across institutions. The federal government needs to work closely with institutions to minimize this burden and avoid the impression of being driven by overzealous attempts primarily aimed at reducing federal costs, and to recognize and support the infrastructure costs associated with the research projects or programs.

The federal government has instituted extensive requirements to help ensure that researchers at colleges and universities do not engage in practices that harm research subjects, and to reduce incidences of academic fraud. The principal issue is whether these requirements have become overly restrictive and so rigidly applied that they hamper legitimate research and add to its costs. There appears to be a tendency for the federal government to react strongly to individual cases of misconduct by imposing burdensome requirements on all those receiving federal support. Reaching an appropriate balance between reducing misconduct through regulation, on the one hand, and hampering legitimate research practices and increasing the costs of research, on the other, is a difficult task that merits further attention.

Issues in the area of student aid policies relate to federal efforts to tighten up on student loan defaults. More recent proposals from a few individuals in Congress and in the U.S. Department of Education consider linking eligibility for federal funds to student attrition and graduation rates and even, possibly, to student grades and quality dimensions. Here we recognize that loan default rates have declined markedly in the face of reform efforts, although recessions may compromise this progress. Proposed federal moves to link student aid to assessments of student quality outcomes may be no more successful than the outcomes suggested by our earlier analysis of the shortcomings of state efforts along the same dimensions.

Issues concerning the federal government's role in promoting social justice pertain to the effects of executive orders and court rulings on such institutional policies as student admissions, faculty hiring and promotion, and the composition of governing boards. Federal activities in these areas have obviously lessened the former autonomy of most public and private institutions, but are justified in the name of broader social values. Some aspects of this set of issues are still controversial, and people of good will can disagree. A later chapter will examine the role of the courts in this area in greater detail.

Financing student access through tax policies has a somewhat indirect effect on institutions' autonomy and accountability. Scholars concerned with higher education finance point out that tax deductions for enrolling in a postsecondary institution benefit only those who have sufficient income to qualify for that reduction in their taxes. Thus it does not contribute to equalizing access for students regardless of their financial status. In addition, financing programs through tax policy, rather than through appropriations included in annual budgets, tends to obscure the full costs of federal programs.

Judicial Intervention

The increasingly intimate relationship between government and higher education means that colleges and universities are in and of the world, not removed and
protected from it. Toward the end of the earlier period of student disruption on
college campuses, it was observed that "judicial decisions and the presence on
campus of the community police, the highway patrol, and the National Guard
symbolize the fact that colleges and universities have increasingly lost the privilege of self-regulation to the external authority of the police and the courts . . . It
is apparent that colleges and universities have become increasingly accountable to
the judicial system of the community, the state, and the national government."[18]

Kaplin's book on higher education and the law summarizes legal conditions
bearing on higher education institutions and gives numerous examples of court
decisions involving trustees, administrators, faculty members, and students, as
well as cases involving relationships between institutions and both state and federal governments.[19] Recourse to the courts to settle disputes has increased greatly
during the past four decades. Faculty members may sue over dismissal, appointment, tenure, and accessibility to personnel records. Students may sue to secure
access to their records, over discrimination in admissions, and over failure by an
institution to deliver what it promised from classroom and other academic resources. Institutions may take governments to court in protection of their constitutional status and, as illustrated above, in contention over the enforcement of
federal regulations.

The historic aloofness of the campus has been shattered. Kaplin points out that
"higher education was often viewed as a unique enterprise, which could regulate
itself through reliance on tradition and consensual agreement. It operated best
by operating autonomously, and it thrived on the privacy which autonomy afforded."[20] The idea of a college or university as a sanctuary was once considered
necessary to protect the institution and its constituencies from repressive external control and invasions on their intellectual freedom. Now, other means must
be devised to safeguard an institution's essential spirit while it bows to the world
of law and the tribunal.

Accrediting Agencies

Accreditation is a process for holding postsecondary institutions accountable to
voluntary nongovernmental agencies for meeting certain minimum educational

standards. Institutional reviews are conducted by representatives from institutions, according to standards derived by member institutions.

Institutional and program accreditation are the two types usually noted. Six regional agencies are responsible for accrediting entire institutions' schools, departments, academic programs, and related activities. Program accreditation, by professional societies or other groups of specialists or vocational associations, is extended to a specific school, department, or academic program in such fields as medicine, law, social work, chemistry, engineering, and business administration. A variation is an agency for accrediting single-purpose institutions, such as trade and technical schools.

If the institution or program being accredited fails to meet minimum standards, the obvious sanction is withdrawal of approval (or rejection for a first-time candidate). Since accreditation is, in theory, voluntary and nongovernmental, an institution or program judged inadequate will suffer a loss of prestige but could presumably survive without it. However, in practice, since the federal government requires accreditation by some federally recognized accrediting association for the institution to be eligible for federal research and student aid funds, the process has in effect become much less "voluntary."

The issue then shifts to the federal government's decision to approve a given accrediting association for inclusion on the Department of Education's list. For these decisions, the department is presumably influenced by the recognition status accorded to the association in question by the Council for Higher Education Accreditation (CHEA), formed in 1996. CHEA functions as an umbrella national group for accreditation activities and works actively with the federal government on matters of quality assurance, student outcomes, and internationalizing higher education. Accreditation issues and the particular role of CHEA are discussed at greater length in chapter 8.

Conclusion

Although autonomy cannot be absolute, only a high degree of independence will permit colleges and universities to devise and choose effective academic means for realizing their professed goals. First of all, institutions must ensure academic freedom for faculty and students. Autonomy does not guarantee intellectual independence, but some forms of external intervention, whether overt or covert, may undermine such freedom.

While intellectual fetters must be opposed, institutions may legitimately be expected to be held accountable to their constituencies for the integrity of their operations and, as far as possible, for the efficiency of these operations. Colleges and universities are answerable to the general public, which supports them and needs their services. In response to this public interest, federal and state governments intervene in institutional affairs. At times government pressure may induce an institution to offer appropriate services; at other times, government agencies may attempt to turn an institution, or even a system, in inappropriate directions. Only constructive consultation and requirements for accountability that recognize the fundamental characteristics of academe will effectively serve the public interest and give vitality to the educational enterprise.

Most institutions, including those supported by legislatures, are not immediately controlled by the general public. Rather, public accountability is mediated by several layers of representation. Institutions are directly answerable to their governing boards. Here they may be responsible to a consolidated governing board, or they may first be responsible to institutional or systemwide governing boards, and these in turn may be under the surveillance of statewide coordinating boards. They also must respond to the requirements of accrediting agencies. Institutions thus may be controlled by a hierarchy of agencies, an arrangement that may complicate their procedures for accountability, but that may also provide a measure of protection from unwise or unnecessary external intervention.

Colleges and universities are now in a period when they are being asked to provide not only data on the attainment of defined outcomes—including changes in students during undergraduate, graduate, and professional education—but also evidence that results have been gained at a "reasonable" cost. They are confronted with the difficult challenge of resisting inappropriate government accountability processes, with their added costs and damages to the academic enterprise, while recognizing legitimate state interests and avoiding the appearance of both self-interest and a resistance to sincere efforts to improve their performance. Institutions need to communicate clearly the accountability and assessment practices they currently employ, as well as take the lead in designing processes that are compatible not only with the character of colleges and universities, but also with the complex political and professional judgments faculty and institutional administrators must make to maintain and achieve a quality academic program.

NOTES

This chapter is a revision of a previously published chapter by T. R. McConnell, now deceased. It is dedicated to his memory.

1. Howard R. Bowen, *Investment in Learning* (San Francisco: Jossey-Bass, 1977), 12.

2. Amitai Etzioni, *Modern Organizations* (Englewood Cliffs, NJ: Prentice-Hall, 1964), 75–84.

3. Eric Ashby discusses the relationship between academic freedom and autonomy in *Universities: British, Indian, African* (Cambridge, MA: Harvard University Press, 1976), ch. 10.

4. William Zumeta, "Public Policy and Accountability in Higher Education: Lessons from the Past and Present for the New Millennium," in *States and Public Higher Education Policy: Affordability, Access, and Accountability*, ed. Donald E. Heller (Baltimore: Johns Hopkins University Press, 2001), 155–97.

5. Nancy Shulock, *An Accountability Framework for California Higher Education: Informing Public Policy and Improving Outcomes* (Sacramento: California State University, Institute for Higher Education Leadership and Policy, Nov. 2002).

6. Etzioni, *Modern Organizations.*

7. Charles J. Hitch, "Remarks of the President," address delivered to the Assembly of the California Academic Senate, June 15, 1970.

8. Frank Schmidtlein, "Assumptions Commonly Underlying Governmental Quality Assessment Practices," paper presented at the 25th EAIR Forum, Limerick, Ireland, Aug. 25, 2003.

9. Robert O. Berdahl, "Universities and Governments in the 21st Century: Possible Relevance of U.S. Experience to Other Parts of the World," in *Toward a New Model of Governance for Universities?* ed. Dietmar Braun and Francois-Xavier Merrien (London: Jessica Kingsley, 1999).

10. Neal Hutchens, "Preserving the Independence of Public Higher Education: An Examination of State Constitutional Autonomy Provisions for Public Colleges and Universities," *Journal of College and University Law* 35 (2009): 271–322.

11. Lyman A. Glenny and Thomas K. Dalglish, *Public Universities, State Agencies, and the Law: Constitutional Autonomy in Decline* (Berkeley: University of California, Center for Research and Development in Higher Education, 1973), 42.

12. Hutchens, "Preserving the Independence."

13. Glenny and Dalglish, *Public Universities*, 43.

14. John W. Lederle, "Governors and Higher Education," in *State Politics and Higher Education*, ed. Leonard E. Goodall (Dearborn: University of Michigan Press, 1976), 43–50.

15. C. Robert Pace, "When Students Judge Their College," *College Board Review* 58 (Spring 1960): 26–28.

16. T. R. McConnell, "Accountability and Autonomy," *Journal of Higher Education* 42 (1971): 446–63.

17. Bowen, *Investment in Learning*, 257. Other evidence on changes in students over the college years is presented in Alexander W. Astin, *Four Critical Years* (San Francisco: Jossey-Bass, 1977); see also Patrick Terenzini and Ernest Pascarella, *How College Affects Students* (San Francisco: Jossey-Bass, 1991).

18. McConnell, "Accountability and Autonomy."

19. William A. Kaplin, *The Law of Higher Education* (San Francisco: Jossey-Bass, 1983).

20. Ibid., 4.

CHAPTER FOUR

Academic Freedom

Past, Present, and Future

Robert M. O'Neil

The subject of academic freedom has been a central theme throughout the recent history of American higher education. Within the collegiate community, there have been widely differing perspectives on certain key issues—for example, whether academic freedom applies as fully to students as to professors, how far beyond the classroom and laboratory such protection extends, and what circumstances might warrant the curtailment of academic freedom to serve broader societal interests. This chapter explores the meaning and scope of academic freedom in four phases: its origins and early historical development, its current status in the courts and in institutional policy, challenges that are certain to arise as teaching and learning occur increasingly in an electronic environment, and the fate of academic freedom in the years since the terrorist attacks of September 11, 2001.

Academic Freedom's Roots and Legacy

The origins of the concept of academic freedom lie deep in the history of teaching and scholarly inquiry.[1] German universities long recognized the concept of *Lehr-*

freiheit, or freedom of professors to teach, with a corollary *Lernfreiheit*, or free-dom of students to learn. Other countries recognized the distinctive status of uni-versity teachers and students in different ways and in widely varying degrees. What is most striking about the importation of these concepts to the United States is the recency of any systematic protection for academic freedom in a currently recognizable form. As late as the second decade of the twentieth century, some of our most eminent universities could discharge—or refuse even to hire—professors solely because their views on economic or social issues were deemed radical or subversive. While many within the academic community found such actions ab-horrent, and many governing boards took a more tolerant view of outspoken schol-ars, the establishment of clear principles protecting the expression of unpopular views within or outside the classroom occurred surprisingly late in our history.

The formal origins of academic freedom in this country almost certainly lie in the issuance in 1915 of a "declaration of principles" by a committee of senior scholars who had been convened by the fledgling American Association of Uni-versity Professors (AAUP). That declaration, some twenty pages in length, can-vassed a wide range of issues. Professor Walter Metzger, the preeminent historian of academic freedom, describes the declaration in this way: "Utilitarian in tem-per and conviction, the theorists of 1915 did not view the expressional freedoms of academics as a bundle of abstract rights. They regarded them as corollaries of the contemporary public need for universities that would increase the sum of hu-man knowledge and furnish experts for public service—new functions that had been added to the time-honored one of qualifying students for degrees."[2] The drafters of the declaration thus characterized the emerging university of their time as an "intellectual experiment station, where new ideas may germinate and where the fruit, though still distasteful to the community as a whole, may be al-lowed to ripen until finally, perchance, it may become part of the accepted intel-lectual food of the nation and the world."[3]

Such an institution must, the declaration went on to insist, be prepared to tolerate a range of views on controversial issues. It must also tolerate those mem-bers of its faculty who expressed such aberrant views. Academic institutions that sought to repress or silence such views simply did not deserve the respect of the higher education community. Thus, concluded the declaration, any university that places restrictions on the intellectual and expressive freedom of its profes-sors effectively proclaims itself a proprietary institution and should be so de-scribed in making any appeal for funds, and the general public should be advised that the institution has no claim to general support or esteem.

The reception of these views was not entirely harmonious, even in intellectual circles. The *New York Times*, in an editorial fairly representative of the more conservative media of the time, scoffed at the newly declared principles: " 'Academic freedom,' that is, the inalienable right of every college instructor to make a fool of himself and his college by . . . intemperate, sensational prattle about every subject under heaven . . . and still keep on the payroll or be reft therefrom only by an elaborate process, is cried to the winds by the organized dons."[4] The reference to "an elaborate process" was not entirely unfair, since a major element of the declaration was a cornerstone of what would become the concept of academic tenure—the precept that academic freedom entailed procedural due process for the dismissal of faculty as much as a limitation on the reasons for which such dismissal might occur.[5]

Thus by the time the United States entered World War I (an event that would create new tensions between professors and society), three vital elements were already in place. There was a rather elaborate and forceful declaration of the basic principles of academic freedom. There was the nucleus of a guarantee of tenure, in the form of procedures that should be followed in the event an institution wished to remove or terminate a professor. And there was an organization, created by and for the benefit of university faculty, committed not only to promulgating and publicizing the new principles, but also to enforcing those principles by investigating egregious departures from them and disseminating the results of such inquiries in a form that would eventually become known as *censure*.

The next major milestone along the route to broader recognition of academic freedom was a statement adopted in 1940 as a joint effort between the AAUP and the Association of American Colleges (now the Association of American Colleges and Universities), a longtime partner in this enterprise. The 1940 "Statement of Principles of Academic Freedom and Tenure" soon drew the support and adherence of many learned societies and academic organizations. By the time of its sixtieth anniversary at the turn of a new century, the Statement had the formal endorsement of more than 150 such groups, representing virtually every facet of academic life and every scholarly discipline, as well as the endorsement of the great majority of research universities and liberal arts colleges.[6]

The 1940 Statement remains nearly as inviolate as the U.S. Constitution. There have been a few "interpretive comments" added over the years (and codified in 1970), and the gender-based language of the original document was modified to achieve neutrality in 1990. The core of the Statement is a declaration, remarkably brief, that university professors are entitled to academic freedom in three vital dimensions—freedom in research and in the publication of the results of research, freedom in the classroom in discussing the subject matter of the course and when speaking or writing as citizens, and freedom from institutional censorship or unwarranted sanction. Each of these freedoms entails corollary responsibilities and limitations; with regard to research, for example, the Statement cautions that "research for pecuniary return should be based upon an understanding with the authorities of the institution." In the classroom, college professors "should be careful not to introduce . . . controversial matter which has no relation to their subject." Teachers, when speaking or writing as citizens, "should at all times be accurate, should exercise appropriate restraint, should show respect for the opinions of others, and should make every effort to indicate that they are not speaking for the institution."

The balance of the 1940 Statement defines the basic elements of faculty tenure, including the need for every institution to adopt a clear statement of the terms and conditions of appointment; a finite probationary period (recommended, but not mandated, to last for seven years), during which a nontenured teacher on the tenure track fully enjoys academic freedom; and rigorous procedures for the handling of charges that might lead to dismissal for cause. The Statement also envisions that tenured and continuing appointments might be terminated for demonstrated "financial exigency," or when a program or department is eliminated for sound academic reasons, or on the basis of a proven medical disability.

Over the years since 1940, the AAUP has adopted many statements and policies, most of which appear today both in the *Redbook* (most recently revised in 2000) and on the Association's Web site, www.aaup.org. Especially cogent to the evolution of professorial interests is a 1994 "Statement on the Relationship of Faculty Governance to Academic Freedom." This statement notes the crucial link between meaningful faculty participation in the governance of a university and the probable condition of academic freedom on that campus. Central to such freedom is the right of a faculty member, without fear of reprisal or loss of influence, to criticize the administration and the governing board on matters of faculty concern. Thus the nexus between governance and academic freedom is vital, as this recent statement serves to remind those on both sides of this relationship.

It is not only the endorsement of virtually all learned societies and very many universities that has given the 1940 Statement such stature as a source of academic common law. The U.S. Supreme Court in one major case, and the lower federal and state courts on numerous occasions, have cited the Statement as an exemplar, guide, and template of the principles of academic freedom.[7] "Probably because it was formulated by both administrators and professors," observed a federal appeals court in a 1978 case, "all of the secondary authorities seem to agree [that the 1940 Statement] is the 'most widely accepted academic definition of tenure.'" Another federal court of appeals approvingly cited the AAUP policy on nonrenewal of continuing appointments, noting that its language "strikes an appropriate balance between academic freedom and educational excellence on the one hand and individual rights to fair consideration on the other." Judges have also recurrently invoked AAUP standards for determining financial exigency as a prelude to the dismissal of tenured faculty. On most issues of that sort, there simply are few, if any, other credible and widely accepted sources to guide lawyers and judges. Moreover, AAUP standards tend to emerge from practical experience at the campus level and have often been revised in light of further and constantly changing experience in the field. Thus it is not surprising to discover the degree of judicial reliance and respect they have received.

The actions and practices to which these standards are addressed have changed substantially over time as well. In the early years, those faculty members at greatest risk were economists and others in the social sciences who had spoken and written unpopular views about the nation's foreign policy or its domestic economic system, making the business and government leaders who comprised typical boards of trustees and alumni officers acutely uncomfortable. The pressures that such leaders brought to bear on the administration led even so illustrious an institution as the University of Pennsylvania to discharge the nonrevolutionary Marxist Scott Nearing from the faculty of its Wharton School; for the next several years, Nearing was an unemployable pariah in higher education, until finally the University of Toledo offered him a teaching position.[8] There were other egregious cases of outspoken critics of capitalism who were either not hired at all or, if their controversial views became known after they began teaching, were summarily dismissed, even by the most prestigious universities.

Of course there were also striking cases to the contrary. Some universities fought to keep, and to protect, "radical" or "subversive" professors, even without the application of the full force of academic freedom and tenure—much less, at this early stage, without contemplating the prospect of an AAUP investigation that might result in censure. Harvard's example was notable in this regard. President A. Lawrence Lowell refused in 1916 to discipline a prominent professor for his avowedly pro-German statements and outspoken opposition to U.S. entry into World War I. Lowell wisely observed that a university that officially condemns faculty views it dislikes would quickly find attributed to it—simply by the absence of such condemnation—a host of professorial utterances from which it had not formally distanced itself.

Though there were a few serious breaches during the 1920s and 1930s, the gravest challenges to academic freedom and tenure occurred during the McCarthy era of the late 1940s and early 1950s. Many professors (as well as screenwriters, actors, and others) were summoned before federal and state antisubversive legislative hearings. Often there was no evidence that the target of such inquiry had personally done anything remotely "subversive" or "anti-American," much less actually joined the Communist Party. Rather, the witness had often befriended, collaborated, or simply casually met one or more suspected Communists or front-group members. Many professors summoned under such conditions either declined to appear at all, fearing that their mere presence would place them at risk, or appeared and (while sometimes candidly describing their own activities and associations) refused to identify suspected colleagues, describe political gatherings they had attended, or in other ways jeopardize long-standing relationships of trust within the academic community.

In many such cases recalcitrance led to demands for reprisal. Few administrations and governing boards, especially at public institutions, were able to resist such pressures completely. The stakes were too high, the publicity too intense, and the forces too powerful to avoid taking some action against faculty members who invoked constitutional claims to avoid compelled testimony, even when many had nothing of their own to hide. Professor Ellen Schrecker, the preeminent chronicler of faculty fates in those unhappy times, has reported that nearly 170 tenured or tenure-track professors were dismissed during the McCarthy era, mostly for suspected disloyalty that was never convincingly documented.[9] The most reputable (and normally most protective) institutions were among the most culpable—Harvard, Michigan, Rutgers, the University of Washington, and other top research institutions.

Much of the damage to faculty freedoms came not through outright dismissals, but in subtler (if no less insidious) forms, such as the exaction of disclaimer-type loyalty oaths. When all University of California professors were required to sign such oaths in the early 1950s, some principled nonsigners simply left the faculty as a matter of conscience, though they had nothing to hide or conceal. Others brought a lawsuit in state court, which yielded a classically Pyrrhic victory. The California Supreme Court agreed with the professors that, given the constitutional autonomy of the university and its regents, they could not be made to take an oath prescribed by the legislature for all state employees. Instead, in a bitter irony, they were left subject to the even more intrusive and distrustful loyalty oath devised by the regents exclusively for University of California faculty and staff. It was not until 1967, long after the political climate had changed, that the California courts finally invalidated all loyalty oaths, following the lead the U.S. Supreme Court had set several years earlier.

Since the McCarthy era happened just a decade after the issuance of the AAUP's 1940 Statement, and after most of the academic community had signed on, it is fair to ask whether academic freedom and tenure failed their first critical test. This is a difficult and complex question, to which at least two contrasting views are responsive. One view is that the academic community, which is especially vulnerable at all times and was unusually suspect during this perilous time, would have fared even worse had not such safeguards existed—that many careers were in fact saved because protective administrators and trustees could tell livid legislators and angry alumni that "our hands are tied since he/she has tenure." Some evidence supports that hypothesis; for example, the fact that no faculty were fired at institutions like Indiana University (despite pressure from an extremely conservative congressional delegation) because the insiders gave the outsiders an unwelcome but irrefutable account of the legal protections that professors enjoyed. The contrary view takes to task not only those eminent universities that caved in under anti-Communist pressure, but also notes that the AAUP, as well as organizations such as the American Civil Liberties Union (ACLU), were slow to respond. During the later stages of the McCarthy period, these groups did become active both on campus and in court in ways that undoubtedly afforded some protection, even if, arguably, it was too little and too late. Thus the jury remains out on the question of whether the 1940 Statement failed its inaugural test; surely a less auspicious time for a debut could hardly be imagined.

The end of the McCarthy era brought a period of relative calm to the academic world. The 1960s launched a massive expansion of higher education, during which the demand for young scholars grew geometrically and strongly diminished the likelihood of reprisals against those with unconventional views. Besides, this was a time when young people were expected to have and express unconventional views, with college professors likely to be leading the pack. The later years of the Vietnam War did bring some institutional pressures to bear on outspoken faculty, both for publicly expressed attacks on U.S. policy in Southeast Asia, and for such collateral actions as "reconstituting" courses to focus on the rising disenchantment with Vietnam policy, as well as on poverty, racism, and the environment. But the sanctions were few and relatively mild and dismissals (at least by major institutions) almost unknown. The AAUP's investigative caseload, which certainly did not diminish during these years, consisted disproportionately of mishandled personnel actions at smaller and less-sophisticated institutions, relating more to strained finances or lack of experience than to aberrant faculty voices.

The recent history of academic freedom contains one other promising feature. While those who teach in private colleges and universities cannot claim the protection of the First Amendment against their institutions—it applies only to government action—state university professors enjoy not only the speech rights of citizens, but also a special sensitivity that courts have shown for the academic setting. Starting with a 1950s case that barred a governmental demand for a teacher's lecture notes, through several key rulings in the next decade that struck down loyalty oaths, to later judgments invalidating laws of other sorts that repressed campus speech, the courts consistently recognized a special role for academic freedom. Perhaps the clearest statement is that of Justice William J. Brennan, Jr., in sounding the death knell for New York State's loyalty oath in 1967:

> Academic freedom . . . is of transcendent value to all of us and not merely to the teachers concerned. That freedom is therefore a special concern of the First Amendment, which does not tolerate laws that cast a pall of orthodoxy over the classroom . . . The classroom is peculiarly a marketplace of ideas. The Nation's future depends upon leaders trained through wide exposure to its robust exchange of ideas which discovers truth out of a multitude of tongues, [rather] than through any kind of authoritative selection.[10]

Although the Supreme Court has never retreated from that view of academic freedom—indeed, the Court has amplified it in such varied contexts as race-sensitive admission policies of state universities—there has been some recent erosion in lower federal courts. In cases during the late 1990s and the first years of the new century, several appeals courts effectively created a new tension between individual and institutional academic freedom. When a faculty member challenges on First Amendment grounds a government policy by which the institution is bound, several recent cases seem to favor the institutional interest, to the detriment of the individual professor's interest. Most dramatically, when the Fourth Circuit Court of Appeals sustained a 1996 Virginia law that bars the use of state-owned or state-leased computers by state employees to access sexually explicit material, save with official approval for "bona fide research projects," the majority expressly rejected a professorial academic freedom claim, recognizing only an institutional interest.[11] Scholars and chroniclers of academic freedom have written critically of that and several other recent rulings that similarly disparage individual academic freedom claims.

Despite occasional setbacks, and despite important differences between court-declared and institutionally shaped academic freedom precepts, these two sources have interacted and blended throughout the twentieth century in ways that, as Professor William Van Alstyne notes, constantly reinforce one another. Although the First Amendment does not bind them, most major private universities pride themselves on voluntary adherence to standards (typically those crafted by the AAUP) that are at least as rigorous as the standards legally imposed on their state-supported counterparts. The historic development of academic freedom, covering as it does most of the twentieth century, reflects gradual and, at times, checkered progress toward enhanced security for professorial speech and political activity. Along the way there have been (and continue even now, as we shall see in the review of post-9/11 developments) some truly chilling casualties. Yet that history suggests, in the main, how much less well the American professoriate would have fared had there not emerged, early in the last century, a set of widely accepted principles and a nearly universal commitment to fair procedures for the termination of faculty appointments.

Academic Freedom Faces New Tests and Challenges

University professors have not, for many years, been forced to sign loyalty oaths or demonstrate their loyalty in other ways. Rarely in the twenty-first century are lecture notes or laboratory files subpoenaed by legislative committees or law enforcement officials seeking to prove that college campuses are enclaves for radical or subversive activity. Save for an occasional professor who may still become embroiled in a political controversy, as indeed several have been since September 11, most of today's academic freedom issues are subtler, if no less urgent, for those whose careers may be at risk.

The emergence of sexual harassment as a campus concern illustrates this change. Disparaging and insensitive remarks by male professors to and about female colleagues and students were surely prevalent a half century ago—indeed, probably far more so than they are today. Yet such transgressions went largely unredressed in the absence of specific policies and procedures designed to target and prevent such harassment. Only within the past two decades has the academic community given adequate attention to such abuses and their corrosive effect on the collegial and learning environments. The implications both for gender equity and for academic freedom are profound.

A major court case illustrates how different the current challenges are. Faculty member Dean Cohen had for some years been an English teacher at a California community college. He used a teaching style that he conceded to be at times "abrasive" and "confrontational." He also read occasional excerpts to his classes from sources such as *Penthouse* and *Hustler*, and used vulgarity, profanity, and sexual themes to "enliven" class discussion. Many students and colleagues lauded Cohen's ability to reach and excite slower learners and students whose spontaneous interest was minimal. But in 1993, one female student formally charged Cohen with sexual harassment. A campus committee agreed with the charges and ordered Cohen to "become sensitive to the needs of his students" and "modify his teaching strategy when it becomes apparent that his techniques create a climate which impedes the students' ability to learn."

Cohen went to federal court and filed suit against the college, claiming that his freedom of speech and his academic freedom had been abridged. The trial judge disagreed, though recognizing that the college's harassment policy was hardly a model of clarity, and that the policy might give a veto over course content and class discussion to "the most sensitive and easily affected students." The appeals court, finding greater merit in Cohen's claims, reversed the trial judge.[12] To the higher court, the sexual harassment policy created a "legal ambush" because the terms were too vague to afford adequate guidance, especially to a teacher whose classroom style had for many years "been considered pedagogically sound and within the bounds of teaching methodology permitted at the College." Thus Cohen prevailed on all counts, and the college suffered a humiliating setback in the pursuit of its laudable concern to spare its students from sexually hostile learning experiences.

The Cohen case was the first judgment directly addressing the growing tension between academic freedom and sexual harassment. The Cohen court did not say that the use of vulgarity or sexual themes are categorically within the scope of a professor's free speech; indeed, some years later a federal appeals court in Michigan would take a much less tolerant view of similar classroom speech in a strikingly similar case that involved a Detroit-area community college teacher.[13] That very same federal appeals court had earlier reviewed the case of a basketball coach who had been fired for using racial slurs to motivate a mostly minority group of athletes; the court split the difference there, striking down on First Amendment grounds the university's speech code but upholding the coach's dismissal on the basis of singularly poor judgment in guiding a racially mixed team.[14] Several other harassment cases since Cohen have reached conflicting results, though more often than not faulting vague standards or summary procedures while stopping short of any ringing declarations about academic freedom.

The AAUP felt called on to enter the fray as dissonance between its policies on harassment and on academic freedom became increasingly apparent and troubling. Thus at its annual meeting in 1995, the Association approved a policy that defines as forbidden harassment such relatively readily identifiable (and intolerable) verbal abuses as offering a student a higher grade in exchange for sexual favors or targeting an individual student with persistent gender-demeaning epithets and insults. The policy also addresses the much harder and subtler issues of nontargeted but offensive speech posed by cases like Cohen's. Before it may be punished as harassment, "speech . . . of a sexual nature . . . directed against another" must be shown to be "abusive" or "severely humiliating" or to "persist . . . despite objection," or, alternatively, that it be "reasonably regarded as offensive and substantially impair the academic work opportunity of students." That last option carries an essential corollary: "If [speech] takes place in the teaching context, it must also be persistent, pervasive, and not germane to the subject matter."

Would such a policy help in cases like Professor Cohen's? It almost certainly would help in two very distinct ways. First, such a policy would provide precision that should cure the vagueness and lack of fair warning that so troubled the Cohen court. Second, it would enable institutions to distinguish between the merely salty teaching style, on the one hand—even if it is occasionally offensive to a few students—and the unacceptable classroom infliction of persistent and pervasive sexism, on the other. A single example should make the point: if a professor begins every other class with a round of sexist jokes, the conditions of the AAUP policy would seem to be met (unless they were made in the rare course on "Modern American Humor"). Assuming the jokes offended some students enough to provoke a formal harassment complaint, such material could be found to be "persistent, pervasive, and not germane to the subject matter."

The AAUP policy also addresses the cognate and equally critical element of procedure, insisting on due process as well as ideological neutrality. Many institutions, including most of those that have been faulted through formal investigations or taken to court over such issues, relied on informal or ad hoc procedures to handle harassment claims. Where any other serious charge of faculty misconduct that could lead to dismissal—plagiarism, for example—would involve a committee of faculty peers, strict secrecy, and full due process, the separate harassment procedures often dispense with such safeguards and entrust the fate of a senior professor to a panel that may include nonfaculty members and may follow casual or informal rules on evidence, confidentiality, and the like. Such processes would be unacceptable for any other charge that might place a professor's status at risk. In one example, the federal court that ruled in Professor J. Donald Silva's favor, ordering his reinstatement at the University of New Hampshire, faulted on many grounds the informal, ad hoc procedure for handling harassment claims.[15] However appealing the case for informality and flexibility may seem in the investigative stages, dispensing with or bypassing the guarantees of due process in the trial of such charges seems unacceptable (as several courts have made clear). The concern of academic freedom is as much a concern for process as it is for substantive standards and policies.

If sexual harassment has been the most visible and contentious area of academic freedom in recent years, several other catalysts have evoked major concern from the professorial community. Faculty expression and political activity have been notably less free in certain types of institutions, mainly those with weak or even nonexistent traditions of shared academic governance and certain church-related institutions where curbs on faculty speech not only serve theological needs, but may go well beyond theology in ways that have no secular counterpart. Yet there is no monopoly on academic freedom violations at small and untutored campuses; in recent years the AAUP's list of censured administrations has included such eminent institutions as New York University and the University of Southern California (both now having taken corrective action that brought about their removal from the censure list).

The censure list increasingly involves procedural violations rather than direct reprisals for expressions of professorial views or activities (as was more common in earlier times). Moreover, termination of continuing academic appointments for reasons of financial exigency continues to draw AAUP scrutiny and, on occasion, litigation. Association policies and court decisions define a clear and acceptable path by which to declare financial exigency and, if necessary, to reduce the faculty size in a way that does not reflect strict seniority. Often it is done by the book, as when seventy tenured faculty at several University of Wisconsin campuses were laid off in the 1970s. However, investigations at Bennington College and St. Bonaventure University showed the darker side of the process—not because the latter institutions clearly lacked adequate financial reasons for cutting back the number of teaching personnel, but because the determination of such "exigency" and the way in which that judgment was applied fell far short of pre-scribed standards and procedures. Here, as with terminations "for cause" or be-cause of the "bona fide elimination of a program or department," the way in which it is done may provide far greater reason for concern and scrutiny—including the potential for censure—than that action itself.

These discussions raise an issue that deserves closer attention: does academic freedom require, or does it depend on, the existence of tenure? The pros and cons of academic freedom have been vigorously debated for at least the past three or four decades, since the founding of several institutions (notably Hampshire College) that did not offer tenure but promised their faculties academic freedom. Of the small number of such institutions that began without a tenure track, several (for example, Evergreen State College in Oregon and the University of Texas–Permian Basin) have since adopted at least de facto, if not de jure, tenure.

Even so, nothing in AAUP policy requires a tenure system. Hampshire College, for example, would never risk censure by declining to offer tenure to a new teacher or by refusing to renew the contract of a person who had served well beyond seven years—so long as the scrupulous procedures that Hampshire has adopted were faithfully followed and the nonrenewal was not based on an invalid premise, such as reprisal for an unpopular statement or activity or affiliation. Rather, the AAUP position is that tenure best serves the interests of both individuals and institutions. It is not only the likeliest guarantor of academic freedom, but it offers other benefits. Tenure provides continuity and stability of employment in a profession whose members often engage in long-term research and where institutions need the capacity to project curricular needs and staffing well into the future. A tenure system also forces (toward the close of the probationary period) a critical review and assessment of the potential of every junior faculty member. In the absence of tenure, there is no such imperative.

Despite these virtues, even the strongest champions of tenure would concede some reservations. First, the current system is far from perfect. More rigorous review of the performance of those seeking tenure would benefit them and their careers, as well as their students and the institution. Those who have achieved tenure are not, and should not be, immune from continuing scrutiny despite the greater security they enjoy. Nothing in the principles of academic freedom converts senior faculty status to a sinecure. Second, alternative safeguards for academic freedom may exist and should be carefully considered. The fact that almost all universities and baccalaureate colleges do confer tenure does not settle the matter, as Hampshire's experience and that of a few other non-tenure-track institutions suggests. Finally, among the flaws, there is no doubt that tenure creates the risk of an exaggerated hierarchy within the academic profession. There have surely been abuses by senior faculty of junior colleagues who should be their protégés. It is hardly surprising that some younger faculty, with or without tenure, view the current system with ambivalence or even resentment. For some, the tradeoff between greater protection for those who survive the system and the hardships for those who do not may appear an excessive cost. The quest for alternatives should thus continue, and even the most securely tenured professors should bear some responsibility to improve the current system.

Academic Freedom in the Digital Age

As new technologies convey an ever-growing share of intellectual exchanges, academic freedom issues are certain to arise in new and sometimes very different media, even though the substance of those issues may change only slightly as the means of communication evolve. There are several obvious differences between print and electronic messages: digital messages may reach thousands (if not millions) of recipients within a matter of seconds. The source of an electronic message may be far harder to discern or trace. The absence from the Internet of any affect or other indicia of print communications may cause fear or anxiety at the other end to a degree unknown in the print era. Yet academic freedom must adapt to cyberspace, however uncomfortably.[16] An initial question is whether expressive freedoms even apply to digital or electronic communications. When it comes to constitutional safeguards, the framers clearly never envisioned digital or electronic material as "speech" or "press"—though there seems no logical reason why a message entitled to protection in print form should not be equally protected when it travels by wires or wireless electronic means. After all, the First Amendment has adapted over time to encompass motion pictures, broadcasting and cable, fax machines, and other new media. Thus it was no surprise when, in the spring of 1997, the Supreme Court unanimously declared that communication on the Internet was as fully protected as was communication through more traditional and familiar means. That view remains central, even though later cases have brought some qualifications; in the summer of 2003, for example, the high court upheld Congress's requirement that public libraries filter Internet access as a condition of continued eligibility for federal funding. However, in 2002 the justices struck down a federal law that would have criminalized "virtual child pornography," wherein the majority found that such a ban would severely constrain artistic expression for a purpose that could not be directly linked to the clearly valid interest in protecting real children from abuse and exploitation.

Academic freedom issues in cyberspace are bound to be somewhat different from those that arise from spoken or printed words and images. The sanctity of the university classroom, and of the expression or communication that occurs in that space, are at the core of academic freedom. Yet when an instructor creates a course home page, and when a growing portion of exchanges between teacher and student occurs through e-mail, we need at least to ask whether such media are an extension of the physical classroom or whether they should invite a completely different analysis. Distinctions that have existed since time immemorial between "on-campus" and "off-campus" activity obviously break down in an electronic environment. Other familiar tests blur on the Internet. For example, professors are constrained by the 1940 Statement to avoid any implication that they speak for their institutions when they are not authorized to do so. The force of that rule is clear when letters are written on either institutional or personal stationery. But when many communications are exchanged via e-mail, with an address or heading that may or may not appear to implicate the server, the lines become far less distinct. Surprisingly, both legal guidelines and institutional policies have been remarkably slow to recognize these differences and adapt to the inescapable reality of the virtual classroom.

During the 1990s, several early skirmishes over access to electronic material underscored the need for cyber-sensitive approaches. When a University of Oklahoma journalism professor challenged his institution's refusal to make a full array of alt.sex newsgroups available to the faculty, he sued in federal court. The judge found the case an easy one to dismiss when the plaintiff conceded that he could obtain the same material through a commercial Internet service provider. The university, meanwhile, adopted a two-tiered Internet access system, with a broader menu for faculty and advanced graduate students than for undergraduates.

On the other hand, when a student at California State University, Northridge, posted on his Web site, through the university server, a hideous image of a state senator morphing into a skull, the administration felt it had no choice but to remove the offending image when the senator's staff complained. The student went to court, claiming his free speech had been abridged, and a state trial judge agreed, noting that political expression enjoyed the highest level of protection. The judge ordered the university to restore the Web page, which posed an impossible dilemma for the administration until another judge upheld new university policies adopted during the litigation that regulated political expression on the university's media. When four male freshmen at Cornell University sent rampantly sexist e-mails to a group of female classmates, and when a homophobic student at Virginia Tech invaded and upended a chat room for gay and lesbian students, both institutions discovered, as had Oklahoma and Northridge, the limitations of print-era law in the age of cyberspace and the difficulty of anticipating a host of new challenges with a still largely unfamiliar technology.

The Oklahoma case also posed a different and novel issue—what restrictions, if any, should universities impose on Internet access through the campus server? Ironically, the issue first surfaced in the mid-1990s at Carnegie Mellon University, the nation's first fully wired campus. The administration announced severe restrictions on such access, after revelations (which turned out to be highly exaggerated) of the range of salacious material that students could easily download. The administration's initial concern was that providing unrestricted access could make the university complicit in violating state obscenity and child pornography laws. After an outcry that went well beyond Pittsburgh, the policy was substantially modified and seems to have invited no followers elsewhere. Meanwhile, the futility of such efforts became increasingly obvious, because students at Carnegie Mellon, or elsewhere, who wished to access material they could not obtain through the campus server had many alternative channels.

A host of other issues await resolution, sometimes including litigation. When Northwestern University professor Arthur Butz published a book in which he effectively denied the existence of the Holocaust, the institution could and did distance itself from such abhorrent views, as long as he never imposed them on his students or used campus facilities to disseminate his thesis. But when the very same message appeared on Butz's home page, accessible through the university server, the process of distancing Northwestern from Holocaust denial became vastly more difficult.[17] Nonetheless, Northwestern continued to treat such deeply abhorrent messages in electronic form as beyond reprisal or sanction, just as they had been immune in print; at least two other major institutions (Washington University–St. Louis and Indiana University–Bloomington) adopted a similarly tolerant view of homophobic statements posted by professors on Web pages accessible through (and maintained on) the university's server. On the other hand, colleges and universities have been unable or disinclined to intervene to protect members of their faculties from sometimes scurrilous and unfair attacks posted on anonymous Web sites such as Campuswatch.org or Noindoctrination.org. Targeted teachers may typically post responsive statements on their own sites or through the accusatory medium, but little else is possible, even in the most hei-nous or extreme cases.

Finally, myriad complications have arisen with regard to the privacy or sanc-tity of e-mail messages in the university setting. Clearly, a sealed envelope arriv-ing in a professor's physical mailbox, either through an internal mail system or from the U.S. Postal Service, has always been considered inviolate. Arguably, electronic messages should enjoy no lesser degree of protection. There are, how-ever, major practical differences. For one, every university's information technol-ogy system routinely backs up some portion of each day's e-mail, and thus inad-vertently invades the sender's and recipient's privacy, save for the most securely encrypted messages. Moreover, emergency situations may occasionally warrant using the technical power that every institution holds to redirect certain mes-sages. Thus the AAUP and other groups have urged adoption of policies designed to protect electronic privacy by sharply limiting the exigencies that would warrant such intrusion and, even then, requiring notification of the person whose account is at risk in time to seek legal redress. The University of California System seems to have led the way in this regard by promulgating unusually sensitive and protec-tive e-mail policies, recognizing the need to define clearly the conditions under which privacy might be invaded, and to ensure timely notice of such actions.

Academic Freedom and National Security in a Time of Crisis

For most American professors, even those who taught during the Vietnam era, relative peace and stability have been a major premise of academic life. The events of September 11, 2001, dramatically altered such placid assumptions. The attacks on the World Trade Center heralded virtually inevitable changes in the relationship between government and the academy. At first those events even seemed to threaten challenges to academic freedom comparable to those of the Mc-Carthy era. Yet by the end of the twenty-first century's first decade, such fears simply have not materialized. The first few highly controversial and outspoken university professors were (with remarkably few exceptions) suspended pending inquiry, not dismissed outright, as happened so often in the 1950s. In place of the summary sanc-tions of the cold war era that abruptly (and unjustifiably) ended the careers of nearly a hundred university scholars, post-9/11 brought a degree of deliberation and a re-spect for due process that, sadly, was usually lacking in the McCarthy days.[18]

The very first such case is illustrative, one which occurred in a University of New Mexico freshman history class on the very afternoon of the World Trade

Center and Pentagon attacks. Professor Richard Berthold, on hearing the news from lower Manhattan and northern Virginia, quipped to his students, "anyone who can blow up the Pentagon gets my vote." Outraged state officials demanded Berthold's immediate ouster, but the administration placed him on leave while launching a careful inquiry. Berthold, meanwhile, conceded he had been "a jerk" and that his classroom conduct had been "stupid." After several months of painstaking review, Berthold was reinstated, although barred from teaching freshman classes—a condition that many academics would view with relief rather than regret. Eventually, after a sexual harassment charge, Berthold took early retirement.[19] Comparable to the Berthold case, and in contrast to the 1950s, was the somewhat later case of University of Colorado ethnic studies professor Ward Churchill, who had written an essay soon after the terrorist attacks in which he lauded the hijackers for having "the courage of their convictions" and disparaged many of the World Trade Center victims as "little Eichmanns." Colorado officials demanded his summary dismissal, but the university's regents launched an inquiry which soon reaffirmed his tenured faculty post, finding that his shocking statements fell within the scope of free speech and academic freedom. (Churchill was eventually dismissed by the governing board, but over the wholly different charge of research misconduct.) In these and a dozen or more early, post-9/11 cases set a pattern that seemed dramatically different from what academics with long memories recalled from the dark days of the cold war.

A wholly positive view of academic freedom in the early twenty-first century would, however, be naive or myopic. To look first at the undeniably darker side of the ledger, freedom regarding university research has suffered in important respects. Reliance on the heretofore unused concept of "sensitive but unclassified" research has undoubtedly slowed the release and publication of some important studies, and it may have discouraged some investigators from even seeking federal support because of growing uncertainty about the degree to which the sharing of data might be inhibited. The handling of certain research materials has been restricted; the availability of important data on governmental (and even nongovernmental) Web sites, and in libraries, has also been affected by post-9/11 policies. Scientists from certain parts of the world have been barred from some research activity within the United States, and those who seek entry from "sensitive" countries—by no means all of them in the Middle East—have found the journey tortuous and, at times, impossible.

The effect on access and entry of foreign graduate students has been especially severe. A monitoring system that was supposed to be in full operation by the middle of the decade languished for many months, with growing doubt that it would ever be fully operational and effective. Monitoring of graduate students already in the United States has included bizarre incidents, such as a group of Saudi Arabians in Colorado who were summarily arrested for having (quite innocently, as it turned out) underregistered by one credit hour for the coming semester and were thus deemed to have forfeited their visa status. There is at least reliably anecdotal evidence that an appreciable number of foreign students who would ordinarily have studied here have gone instead to England, Germany, or Japan, simply because the burdens and risks of coming to the United States seemed, for the first time in history, to outweigh the obvious benefits.

Access to information seems to have suffered in ways other than the removal or classification of research data. Prominent in the U.S.A. PATRIOT Act is a "business records" provision that empowers federal law enforcement officials to obtain, through subpoenas issued by a secret court, sensitive materials chosen by library borrowers or bookstore purchasers. The problem is compounded by a clause that prevents a librarian or bookseller served with such an order from disclosing that fact to anyone, including the person whose records have been sought and obtained. Thus it had been impossible to estimate the probable volume of such activity until, in late September 2003, Attorney General John Ashcroft revealed the Justice Department had made no use of the business records provision. Such news brought small comfort to the academic community, because the prospect of future use remained likely without any public knowledge of its extent and focus. Indeed, a major concern for scholars and the institutions in which they teach has been the growing difficulty of determining the extent to which special governmental powers have been invoked. Moreover, the anticipated major relaxation of legislation such as the U.S.A. PATRIOT Act failed to materialize—at one dramatic moment in 2007, for example, because action by the U.S. House of Representatives followed by one day a terrorist attack in the London subway, after which much of the congressional support for mitigation simply evaporated overnight.

Meanwhile, the cautious optimism engendered by the early and relatively benign treatment of outspoken professors has largely persisted through the post-9/11 decade. The academic year 2006–7, for example, provided three examples of a generally calmer climate than those with long memories recalled of the McCarthy era. A University of Wisconsin–Madison political scientist, Kevin Barrett, became increasingly vocal and public in his attacks on the George W. Bush administration for alleged complicity in the terrorist attacks on the World Trade

Center. Despite demands by legislators and other state officials that he be silenced or banished, accompanied by threatened reprisals to the university's budget if such action were not taken, the university's provost defended his maverick colleague, stressing—after a careful review of his performance—that he had fulfilled his assigned duties and that "his personal views are not imposed on his students." A few months later a strikingly similar controversy plagued the University of New Hampshire, where William Woodward, a senior psychology professor, quite vocally insisted that 9/11 had resulted from a conspiracy at the highest levels of U.S. government. Like his Wisconsin counterpart, New Hampshire's provost reviewed the record of his defiant colleague and, on that basis, affirmed his right to remain in the classroom, stressing the university's commitment to academic freedom and noting that while "we may not agree with Professor Woodward . . . he is entitled to his opinion." A slightly less happy outcome awaited Brigham Young University physicist Steven Jones, long a Bush supporter who had recently espoused the same revisionist views that Barrett and Woodward proclaimed. Though BYU officials resisted pressure for Jones's dismissal or suspension, they did launch—apparently in response to his public statements and support of Scholars for 9/11 Truth—a review of his published research, which led to an early retirement. The first two of these revisionists were completely vindicated under conditions where their McCarthy-era predecessors would have fared poorly indeed, and even the third would probably have survived had he chosen to fight.

With nearly a decade of experience, it may be worth speculating briefly on why academic freedom has seemingly fared so much better in the 2000s than it did a half century earlier. There are several contextual differences that offer partial insight. The target of attack and repression has changed markedly; what got professors into trouble with McCarthy and his cold war partners was typically membership in or support of (even sympathy for) politically or ideologically suspect organizations; targets of post-9/11 hostility have been outbursts or intemperate remarks, although in a few cases (the Scholars for 9/11 Truth, for example) the parallels are somewhat closer. The twenty-first-century ideological divide has been more complex than it was a half century ago, when subversive academics were always on the left end of the spectrum, while today unwelcome professorial views cross the aisles. Perhaps even more significant are the far greater capacity and determination of the academic community and their supporters to step up and resist pressure to conform; when Army intelligence officers launched an inquiry into a suspected conference of Islamic women, University of Texas officials vigorously protested, and the Pentagon not only dropped the inquiry but formally apologized—a response that has been replicated elsewhere in the first post-9/11 decade. When, for example, federal prosecutors demanded detailed information and files from a legal conference held at Drake University, campus officials strenuously objected, with support from national civil liberties and lawyers groups; the U.S. attorney eventually apologized for unwarranted intrusion and withdrew the subpoenas. Meanwhile, Congress has also been listening; proposals that would have severely compromised the role of foreign scholars in sensitive sponsored-research projects—treating those scholars as "deemed experts" and thus forced to be specially licensed—were eventually scrapped after vigorous protests by the major research universities and their leaders. Quite simply, the academic community has felt far freer and bolder in stepping up to protect its interests, and its voice has often (though clearly not always) been heeded.

Not only have new protective forces entered the stage in the last half century, but those that existed in the McCarthy days (like the ACLU and the AAUP) have been far readier to come forward and even to take recalcitrant government officials to court. In several cases, visas that were initially denied to foreign scholars for U.S. visits became the subject of litigation, with mixed but occasionally favorable results. Largely as a result of such courageous efforts in recent times, the climate seems to have improved markedly. When a Senate subcommittee recently unsealed files containing information about potential (but never actually summoned) McCarthy-era witnesses, Senator Carl Levin reflected on the difference: "I think there's a greater awareness of McCarthyism and what tactics can be used by people who are trying to quiet dissenters. And there's greater resistance against those who would try to still voices that they disagree with."

As though to confirm such a healthier and more receptive climate in the post-9/11 era, no less unlikely a voice than that of Fox News' Bill O'Reilly has spoken out several times in support of academic freedom. When discussing the Columbia University anthropologist who urged "a million Mogadishus," O'Reilly rejected viewers' demands for the young professor's head and his job: "If I were [Columbia's president] I wouldn't fire this guy . . . because you've got to tolerate this kind of speech." A couple of years later, O'Reilly came to the defense of University of Colorado's Ward Churchill after the "little Eichmanns" essay led to demands for instant dismissal. "I don't think," the conservative commentator cautioned his Fox audience, "he should be fired. That would send the wrong message to the rest of the world. America's a strong enough country to put up with the likes of Professor Churchill. Punishing him further would just make him a martyr."

When a guest on the Fox program suggested that Holocaust denier Arthur Butz should be removed from teaching Northwestern University classes, O'Reilly again raised the flag, noting that his skeptical guest was herself a professor who should know that "the university . . . is a place where all views, even abhorrent views, are tolerated for the sake of freedom of expression." Then he added, lest his view be misperceived, "you don't want to inhibit anybody." Although academic freedom these days has other champions more familiar and more congenial than Fox News' prime-time pundit, the contrast between O'Reilly's views today and the anti-intellectual diatribes of cold war predecessors like Walter Winchell, Dorothy Kilgallen, and Gabriel Heatter is striking. That contrast also suggests that while academic freedom still needs all the help it can get in the public forum, and may still be widely misunderstood, it is no longer despised or undervalued, as was the case a half century ago.

It may still be too early to draw conclusions with confidence about the effect on academic freedom of the September 11 trauma and the nation's response. Nearly a decade later, the returns are still mixed—a more benign treatment of outspoken professors or members of suspect groups, on the one hand, but worrisome incursions on research support, governmental demands for sensitive documents and files, and other policies that would not have emerged (nor would they be tolerated) in more tranquil times, on the other. Clearly those groups and individuals who are committed to defend and protect academic freedom and free expression are far bolder and more confident in stepping up and speaking out in the twenty-first century than was true during the cold war. Even later threats to national security as dramatic as the near disaster on a U.S.-bound aircraft on Christmas Day 2009 have not brought demands for repression or reprisal comparable to those launched by Senator McCarthy and his allies in much earlier times. As the new millennium evolves, and basic principles of academic freedom mature, the academic community remains alert, vigilant, and anxious—but cautiously optimistic.

NOTES

1. See Walter Metzger, "The 1940 Statement of Principles on Academic Freedom and Tenure," in *Freedom and Tenure in the Academy*, ed. William W. Van Alstyne (Durham, NC: Duke University Press, 1993).

2. Ibid., 13.

3. "General Report of the Committee on Academic Freedom and Academic Tenure," *AAUP Bulletin* 17 (1915): 1.

4. Quoted in "The Professors Union," *School and Society* 175 (1916): 3.

5. See Metzger, "1940 Statement," 9.

6. See American Association of University Professors, *Policy Documents and Reports* (Washington, DC: American Association of University Professors, 2000), 3–10.

7. See *Tilton v. Richardson*, 403 U.S. 672, 681–2 (1971); *Jiminez v. Almodovar*, 650 F.2d 363, 369 (1st Cir. 1981); *Krotkoff v. Goucher College*, 585 F.2d 675, 679 (4th Cir. 1978); *Gray v. Board of Higher Education*, 692 F.2d 901, 907 (2d Cir. 1982); *Levitt v. Board of Trustees*, 376 F. Supp. 945, 950 (D. Neb. 1974). See also Matthew W. Finkin, ed., *The Case for Tenure* (Ithaca, NY: Cornell University Press, 1966); Ralph S. Brown, Jr., and Matthew W. Finkin, "The Usefulness of AAUP Statements," *Educational Record* 59 (1978): 30–44.

8. See "Report of the Committee of Inquiry on the Case of Professor Scott Nearing of the University of Pennsylvania," *AAUP Bulletin* 127 (1916): 2.

9. Ellen Schrecker, *No Ivory Tower: McCarthyism and the Universities* (New York: Oxford University Press, 1986).

10. *Keyishian v. Board of Regents*, 385 U.S. 589, 603 (1967).

11. *Urofsky v. Gilmore*, 216 F.3d 401 (4th Cir. 2001).

12. *Cohen v. San Bernardino Valley College*, 92 F.3d 968 (9th Cir. 1996).

13. *Bonnell v. Lorenzo*, 241 F.3d 800 (6th Cir. 2001).

14. *Dambrodt v. Central Michigan University*, 55 F.3d 1177 (6th Cir. 1995).

15. *Silva v. University of New Hampshire*, 888 F. Supp. 293 (D.N.H. 1994).

16. See generally, for a discussion of such issues of academic freedom in cyberspace, Robert M. O'Neil, *Free Speech in the College Community* (Bloomington: Indiana University Press, 1997), 52–76.

17. Ibid., 74.

18. See generally Special Committee of the American Association of University Professors, "Academic Freedom and National Security in a Time of Crisis," *Academe* 89, no.6 (Nov.–Dec. 2003): 34–59.

19. For discussion of both the Berthold and Ken Hearlson cases, see Robin Wilson and Scott Smallwood, "One Professor Cleared, Another Disciplined over September 11 Remarks," *Chronicle of Higher Education*, Jan. 11, 2002, A12.

PART II / External Forces

CHAPTER FIVE

The Federal Government and Higher Education

Michael Mumper, Lawrence E. Gladieux, Jacqueline E. King, and Melanie E. Corrigan

The federal government, notwithstanding the primary role of the states in our federal system, has played an essential role in shaping the size, scope, and character of American higher education. Today it provides nearly $100 billion annually to assist students in covering college costs, help institutions expand their capacity to serve disadvantaged students, and engage faculty in the types of scientific and medical research that advance the national interest.

Despite this huge investment, the federal government's role has always been secondary or supplementary. It is the states and the institutions that are the primary policy makers for higher education. In this chapter, we summarize the evolving role that the federal government has played in higher education, including a review of the major interventions that have influenced and shaped the course of America's colleges and universities. Then we describe, in some detail, several of the areas where the federal role has been most crucial. These include the provision of direct aid to college students, the allocation of tax deductions and credits to students and colleges, federal funding of research and development, and the impact of federal regulations on colleges and universities. These are the areas both of the greatest federal expansion over the years and where the greatest tensions remain. Finally, we reflect briefly on some of the major issues facing the federal government in higher education today and the prospects for federal relations with higher education over the coming decades.

The Evolving Federal Role in Higher Education

In the U.S. Constitutional system, the states have primary responsibility for all levels of education. The Tenth Amendment reserves all powers not delegated to the central government to the states. Since education is not explicitly mentioned in the Constitution, the states have taken the lead in this area, with the federal government playing a secondary role. While most·of the framers supported this division of responsibilities, a few, including George Washington, favored the creation of a national university. However, all proposals to establish such a university have failed. As a result, the federal government does not directly sponsor specific institutions of higher education, apart from the military academies and a few institutions serving special populations.

While the role of the federal government has been secondary, it has certainly not been unimportant. It has played a critical part in promoting the development and expansion of the nation's system of higher education. This growth in the influence of the federal government, however, did not unfold in a steady or linear pattern. Instead, it has proceeded in a series of sequential expansions over many decades, with each new expansion advancing the federal role in new and often fundamental ways. At critical times in the nation's history, these federal interventions proved to be the driving force in the growth and expansion of the American higher education system. For the most part, these new federal programs were offered as "grants" under the Constitutional power to "promote the general welfare." While states could turn down such grants, the political reality is that they were never rejected, and the federal role has accordingly increased.

The first of these significant federal interventions occurred in the 1860s, as part of a federal effort to encourage Americans to migrate west and develop the nation's public lands along the way. While the Morrill Land Grant Act of 1862 was aimed at encouraging this western expansion, the approach it used has had a profound impact on the nation's colleges and universities.[1] Rather than embracing the classical liberal arts curriculum, the Morrill Act encouraged the creation of new institutions focused on the study of disciplines critical to westward expansion, including agriculture, engineering, mechanics, and mining. Within a few years, thirty-seven institutions were designated as land-grant colleges. In some states, the legislature opted to graft a new program onto at existing college. Other states created wholly new institutions. The result of this federal expansion was the creation and development of what are now some of the nation's great universities, including the University of Wisconsin, the University of California, the Pennsylvania State University, Texas A&M University, and parts of Cornell University.

The next significant expansion in American higher education driven by the federal government was the post–World War II enrollment boom resulting from the GI Bill. While the Servicemen's Readjustment Act of 1944, popularly known as the GI Bill of Rights, was not intended to be higher education policy in a narrow sense, its impact on American colleges and universities is difficult to overstate. The GI Bill provided returning veterans with a wide range of benefits, but to the general public it became synonymous with tuition assistance in attending college.

The most obvious impact of the GI Bill was on college enrollment. In 1945, as the war was coming to an end, there were about 1.6 million students enrolled in higher education. Only about 88,000 of those were veterans. Just two years later, college enrollments had increased 45 percent, to 2.3 million, and more than 1 million of those students were veterans.[2] With the assistance of the GI Bill, hundreds of thousands of Americans who otherwise would not have attended college returned to earn degrees. One important feature of the GI Bill was that it provided its benefits equally to all veterans, regardless of gender, racial, or ethnic background. Although the armed forces remained segregated at the end of World War II, the benefits of the GI Bill were available to anyone who had been on active duty for at least ninety days and had not been dishonorably discharged. The benefits of the GI Bill allowed many black and Hispanic veterans to use their education to boost themselves and their families into the middle class.

The massive influx of veterans onto the nation's campuses resulted in substantial changes in their facilities and physical plants, admissions procedures, and even their curricula and pedagogies. New housing and classroom space needed to be built, methods needed to be developed to assess the college readiness of veterans, and adjustments needed to be made for veterans who were anxious to become wage-earners as quickly as possible. All of this expansion, much of which remained after the initial wave of veterans had completed their education, was funded by the tuition dollars provided through the GI Bill.

Glen Altschuler and Stuart Blumin argue that the most import contribution of the GI Bill was that the academic achievements of the veterans "enhanced the prestige, practical value, and visibility of a college diploma."[3] It also helped to "forge a consensus that the number of college caliber candidates drawn from all socioeconomic and ethnic groups was far larger than previously thought. Americans began to perceive undergraduate and graduate degrees as gateways to the professions, the new route to the American dream."[4] It is difficult to imagine how this could have happened without the GI Bill.

Federal involvement and investment in higher education accelerated through the cold war years of the 1950s, 1960s, and 1970s. This occurred primarily through a larger federal role in university-based research and in the development of financial aid to college students. In direct and immediate response to the launch of the Sputnik satellite by the Soviet Union in 1957, Congress sought to ensure the nation's economic and military hegemony by encouraging more students to pursue higher education and making substantial investments in programs to boost scientific research.

During the cold war, Congress sought to encourage more students to attend college and study in areas of national interest, such as science, engineering, and foreign languages. The cold war also produced a strengthening of the research partnership between the federal government and the nation's universities that had developed so strongly during World War II. This partnership aimed at creating the technology to explore space and supporting the science necessary to maintain dominance over the Soviet Union.

The next real breakthrough in the expansion of the federal role in higher education came in 1965, as a part of President Lyndon Johnson's Great Society program.[5] This was an aggressive effort to achieve equal opportunity for all Americans, and a central part of that effort was insuring that everyone had an equal opportunity to attend college. The logic behind the first equal opportunity programs was that by bringing college within the financial reach of all Americans, lower-income students would enroll in greater numbers. This would result in their finding better jobs, earning higher wages, and moving out of poverty. Based largely on this economic rationale, the federal government developed an elaborate new plan to provide financial aid to needy college students. As we will describe later, these federal programs have grown until today they offer billions of dollars in aid to 8.5 million students attending almost every accredited institution of higher education in the nation.[6]

In 2009, the federal government made a new and largely unexpected intervention that is likely to have long-term implications for American higher education. As Barack Obama entered office in January 2009, the national and international economy was in an almost unprecedented decline. Credit markets were frozen, the unemployment rate was soaring, and federal and state tax revenues had slowed dramatically. In the face of this crisis, President Obama persuaded Congress to adopt the American Reinvestment and Recovery Act (ARRA), widely known as the Economic Stimulus Bill. A major part of this multifaceted legislation was a massive infusion of federal funds to state governments, intended to prop up their budgets, which were staggering under the combination of declining tax revenues and increasing state and local demands for health care and social services.[7]

Since most states have constitutional requirements to maintain balanced budgets, their declining revenues would have left governors and state legislatures with no choice but to make devastating reductions in higher education funding. Public colleges and universities, in turn, would have been left to cope with those reductions by reducing staff, cutting operating budgets, and sharply increasing tuition and fees. While the states and public colleges were certainly hurt by the 2009 budget crises, the full potential of that impact was substantially reduced by the federal support provided by ARRA. Federal dollars flowed directly and quickly to the states to "backfill" for their lost tax revenues. This reduced the amount states were forced to cut from all areas. More importantly for higher education, ARRA included a critical "Maintenance of Effort" provision that required states to continue to use the ARRA dollars to fund higher education at the same level as each state had in the previous year. This provision protected many public institutions from enormous reductions in state support and lessened the impact those reductions would have had on students attending those institutions.[8]

The Scope of the Federal Role

In the nineteenth century, the states served as intermediaries in federal support for higher education, as this federal support flowed to institutions through state governments. Toward the beginning of the twentieth century, however, federal support increasingly bypassed the states and went directly to institutions. Today, nearly all federal support has been channeled to institutions (departments, research centers, schools, or individual faculty members within institutions) or to individual students. For this reason, there is not really a federal-state partnership in either the direction or financing of higher education. In fact, there is very little conscious coordination of funding purposes and patterns between the two levels of government. Federal activity proceeds independently of state activity. Chester Finn observes that "with a few modest exceptions, federal postsecondary spending arrangements make no attempt to stimulate state spending or compensate for differences in state wealth or effort, or to give state governments money to allot as they see fit."[9]

Today, the federal government's activities affecting higher education are so decentralized and so intermixed with other policy objectives that trying to enumerate the programs and tally the total investment is problematic. The creation of the U.S. Department of Education in 1979 consolidated only about one-fourth of the more than 400 programs that existed at the time, and less than one-third of the total federal expenditures for higher education. The remaining programs and funds are still scattered across a number of federal agencies, including the departments of Defense, Labor, Agriculture, Homeland Security, Transportation, Health and Human Services, the Veterans Administration, the Agency for International Development, the National Aeronautics and Space Administration, and the Smithsonian Institution.

Table 5.1 provides an overview of federal support for higher education. In 2008, the federal spending total on higher education, including tax expenditures, was $99.6 billion. Of that total, 45 percent went to university-based research, 32 percent to programs providing direct aid to college students (including student loans), 11 percent to tax programs providing benefits for students and their families, and 6 percent to tax benefits affecting nonprofit institutions of higher education. The more than $32 billion spent on student aid programs is considerably less than the $95 billion in federal aid actually made available to students through the federal programs.[10] This is because the federal government guarantees and subsidizes private loans, requires nonfederal matching in certain programs, and recoups some of the cost of student aid expenditures through interest payments on federal educational loans.

Direct Federal Aid to College Students

Since the mid-1960s, the area where the federal government has had the greatest impact on the nation's colleges and universities is in the provision of direct aid to college students. The federal legislation that provided the rationale for this involvement and laid out its programmatic structure was the Higher Education Act of 1965 (HEA). Passed in the flurry of Great Society legislation—including the Voting Rights Act, the Civil Rights Act, and the Elementary and Secondary Education Act, as well as expansions in the availability of health care coverage (in-

Table 5.1   Estimated federal assistance to higher education by type, 2008

Type of federal aid	Billions of dollars	Percentage of federal total
Student assistance	32.3	32.4
Student financial assistance	17.5	
Federal Direct Student Loans	5.6	
Federal Family Education Loans	3.9	
Tuition assistance for military personnel	1.1	
Veterans' tuition benefits	3.1	
Health professions scholarships/fellowships	1.2	
Research and development	45.0	45.2
Basic research	22.5	
Applied research and development	22.5	
Other federal expenditures	4.8	4.8
Service academies	0.4	
All other on-budget expenditures for higher education	4.4	
Tax expenditures for students and families	11.2	11.3
Tax credits for tuition for postsecondary education	4.4	
Deductions for student loan interest	0.9	
Exclusion of scholarship and fellowship income	1.7	
Other tax expenditures for families	4.2	
Tax expenditures for institutions	6.2	6.2
Deduction for charitable contributions	6.2	
Total federal assistance	99.6	99.8

Sources: U.S. Congress, Joint Committee on Taxation, *Estimates of Federal Tax Expenditures for Fiscal Years 2008-2012*, JCS-2-08 (Washington, DC: U.S. Government Printing Office, Oct. 31, 2008); National Science Foundation, *Federal Government Is Largest Source of University R&D Funding in S&E; Share Drops in FY 2008* (Washington, DC: National Science Foundation, 2009); National Center for Education Statistics, *Digest of Education Statistics 2008* (Washington, DC: U.S. Department of Education, 2009), table 375.
    Note: Student financial assistance includes all Title IV programs, in addition to various scholarship programs where monies are directly awarded to the student (except National Health Service Corps scholarships). Tuition assistance for military personnel also includes the Senior Reserve Officer Training Corps. Veterans' tuition benefits also includes the Department of Veterans Affairs' postsecondary education–related expenses. Health professions scholarships/fellowships also include Department of Health and Human Services postsecondary education–related expenses and Indian Health Manpower. Research and development includes all federal obligations for research and development. Service academies also include the Merchant Marine Academy. Other federal expenditures include historically black colleges and universities (HBCUs), Hurricane Katrina aid, the Agricultural Extension Service, mineral leasing, federal aid to Washington, D.C., and educational exchanges.

cluding the creation of Medicare and Medicaid)—the HEA established a new federal role and purpose in higher education: promoting equal opportunity. For the first time, the federal government was going to set the goal of removing the barriers, especially price barriers, which keep low-income students out of higher education.

Title IV of the HEA created three types of federal student aid programs, and their basic structures more or less remain today. The centerpiece of the student aid system was a large, need-based grant program. Originally called the Educational Opportunity Grant, then the Basic Educational Opportunity Grant, the federal grant program was first designed to be administered by each campus. In 1972, the HEA was amended to centralize the administration and awarding of the program under a new name, the Pell Grant. Pell grants were intended to form the foundation of the federal student aid effort. Using a calculation based on a student's estimated family resources and the cost of the college to be attended, the student would receive a grant directly from the federal government to reduce his or her cost of attendance.[11] Pell grants were designed to make awards to students with the greatest financial need.

Second, for those students who had greater family resources but still needed additional federal support in attending college, the HEA created the Guaranteed Student Loan Program, now called the Stafford Student Loan Program. Under this program, students would be able to borrow from a private bank for their education. The federal government would make those loans more widely available and at a lower cost by providing the banks with limited subsidies and a guarantee of repayment. This federal loan program was designed to provide secondary support for those students who did not qualify for the grant program, and it was expected to remain much smaller than the federal grant program.

Third, the federal government developed or redesigned a number of other programs that were intended to give campus financial aid offices resources that they could use to address the needs of individual students on a case-by-case basis. These campus-based programs included the Federal Work-Study Program, the Perkins Loan Program, and the Supplemental Educational Opportunity Grant Program.

Rapid Expansion and Policy Drift

By the end of the 1970s, the federal student aid programs had all expanded rapidly and seemed to be well on their way to achieving their original purpose.[12] By 1980, as a result of the Title IV programs, lower-income families could make use of a wide range of federal resources in their efforts to pay for college. These included Pell grants and work-study aid. Students could also borrow directly from their school through the Perkins loan program or from a private lender through the federally guaranteed loan program. These resources combined to significantly reduce the net price of higher education facing low-income students. Similarly, the expansion of federal student aid also improved the situation of most middle-income families during the 1970s. The changes to the HEA made in 1978 expanded eligibility for federally guaranteed and subsidized loans to all students, regardless of their family income. The expansion of student loans allowed many middle-income families to shift the responsibilities of paying for college to their children.

By the early 1980s, the nation's economic and political circumstances changed in ways that made it difficult for policy makers to continue to pursue the original objectives of the Title IV programs. As these programs became more popular in the 1970s and 1980s, federal policy makers found themselves under tremendous pressure to spread their benefits out to a wider range of students. As college prices began to spiral upward and family incomes remained flat, parents demanded increased eligibility for Pell grants and continued access to ever-larger federally subsidized loans. Similarly, policy makers were under pressure from for-profit and technical schools to broaden eligibility for the Title IV programs from traditional colleges to the full universe of postsecondary education programs.

The eligibility of more students and more schools, in an environment of rising college prices, required the federal government to pump an ever-larger amount of funding into the Title IV programs in order to maintain their purchasing power for lower-income students.[13] Unlike his predecessors, President Reagan was not interested in increasing federal expenditures. He set out to reduce them, except in the realm of military defense. Reagan's efforts to cut the federal student aid programs were generally thwarted by a congress that sought to continue their expansion. The result was a political stalemate, where policy makers continued to expand eligibility for the Title IV programs even when they did not appropriate the dollars to support the growth of those programs. This meant that during the 1980s, the purchasing power of Pell grants began to decline sharply relative to college prices. More students were receiving grants each year, but those grants were covering smaller and smaller portions of their educational expenses. Caught between rising prices and stable Pell grants, more lower- and middle-income students were forced to turn to the federal student loan programs.

As college prices began to rise and federal policy makers struggled with limited resources, they changed the orientation of the federal programs in two fundamental ways. First, they allowed the erosion of need-based allocation standards in order to provide at least some federal aid to a larger number of students. Second, by allowing the federal loan programs to grow much more rapidly than the grant programs, what had been a grant-centered system was transformed into

Table 5.2   Changes in size and purchasing power of Pell grants, 1977–78 to 2007–8, in constant 2008 dollars

	Total annual charges at public four-year institutions	Maximum Pell grant	Pell grant as a percentage of total charges	Number of Pell grant recipients (in thousands)	Total federal expenditures on Pell grants (in millions)
1977–78	6,923	5,393	78	1,944	5,685
1982–83	6,801	4,738	70	2,523	5,461
1987–88	7,631	4,446	58	2,660	7,257
1992–93	8,608	4,853	56	4,002	9,669
1997–98	9,657	6,167	64	3,733	8,677
2002–3	11,128	6,595	59	5,140	14,218
2007–8	13,589	6,125	45	5,542	15,498

Sources: College Board, *Trends in Student Aid 2009* and *Trends in College Prices 2009*, both at www.collegeboard.com/html/trends/.

a loan-centered system. Both of these changes resulted in shifting limited federal resources away from the neediest students and toward less-needy students.

The impact of this federal policy drift can be most clearly seen in table 5.2. In 1978, the full cost of attendance for one year at an average-priced public institution was $6,923 (in constant 2008 dollars). The maximum Pell grant would cover 78 percent of that cost. But a decade later, the cost of attendance had increased rapidly and Pell grants now only covered 58 percent of that cost. This decline was not the direct result of reductions in aggregate federal support. The number of students receiving Pell grants had actually increased by one-third over the decade, and total federal expenditures on the Pell grant program had increased to more than $7 billion dollars. More students were eligible for grants, but the value of those grants was falling rapidly.

During the 1990s, the declining purchasing power of the Pell grant was reversed for a few years, but by the early 2000s, that decline had returned. Since that time, the decline has accelerated. By 2007–8, federal spending on Pell grants had spiked to an all-time high of $15.4 billion, with 5.5 million students receiving awards. The value of the maximum grant now covered only 45 percent of the cost of attendance, leaving many students with no choice but to borrow the difference from the federal loan programs.

As the number of students borrowing through the federal loan programs has grown, Congress had become increasingly concerned about the level of student debt.[14] Federal policy makers continue to argue that they want a better balance between grants and loans, but their policy choices have accelerated the drift in the opposite direction. In 1992, under great public pressure, Congress established a new unsubsidized version of the Stafford loan program that was not restricted by need. This made federal loans available to middle- and upper-income students who had previously been squeezed out of eligibility for regular student loans. This new program dramatically expanded the borrowing capacity of students and parents at all income levels, spurring a huge increase in borrowing through federal loan programs in the years after the law took effect.

Not only has the number of federal borrowers grown more rapidly that the number of Pell grant recipients, the number of unsubsidized borrows had expanded more rapidly than the number of subsidized borrowers. Table 5.3 shows that since 1998–99, the number of borrowers in the subsidized loan program has increased by about 75 percent. During that same time, the number of unsubsidized borrowers increased by 180 percent. Today, nearly as many students are borrowing through the unsubsidized program as they are through the subsidized program. It is also important to note that many students are borrowing through both programs.

Access to What?

Since the passage of the HEA, federal student aid policies have been directed primarily toward the goal of increasing access to higher education, especially

Table 5.3   Number of borrowers and average loan amounts borrowed through the federal Stafford loan program (subsidized and unsubsidized), in constant 2008 dollars

	1998–99	2003–4	2008–9
Total borrowers (subsidized and unsubsidized)			
Number of borrowers (in thousands)	4,843	6,492	8,667
Average loan per borrower	$7,579	$7,671	$8,175
Borrowers (subsidized)			
Number of borrowers (in thousands)	4,232	5,531	7,403
Average loan per borrower	$4,514	$4,114	$3,692
Borrowers (unsubsidized)			
Number of borrowers (in thousands)	2,496	3,989	7,009
Average loan per borrower	$4,990	$4,941	$4,303

Source: College Board, "Types of Loans," in *Trends in Student Aid 2009.*
Note: The number of total borrowers counts each borrower only once, but many students are borrowing through both programs.

among those students from the neediest families. Since the 1990s, a number of policy makers have also sought to ensure that these programs are supporting access to academic and vocational programs. They question whether federal dollars are being directed effectively to those who really need the help and have a reasonable chance of benefiting from the education and training that is being subsidized. Are the programs attended by federal aid recipients of a reasonable quality? Do federal aid recipients complete their programs? Do they secure jobs in the fields for which they have been prepared? In short, are students and taxpayers getting their money's worth from their substantial investment in student aid?

Proprietary trade schools have been a primary concern regarding quality and standards.[15] In the 1970s, Congress substituted the term "postsecondary" for "higher" in the student aid statutes and broadened their eligibility to include short-term vocational training provided by for-profit schools, as well the traditional programs of public and private nonprofit institutions. In doing so, Congress embraced the view that students would "vote with their feet" and take their federal aid to those institutions that best served their educational and training needs. Unfortunately, the deregulation that followed did not address the critical questions of institutional quality and effectiveness. The result of this broadened eligibility was a burgeoning of the trade-school industry. Many for-profits emerged that were subsidized almost entirely by tax dollars. Some of these institutions even set their prices based on the federal aid packages available to their students. Over the next decade, students attending many of these institutions reported high levels of dissatisfaction with their programs and, in large numbers, defaulted on the loans they had taken out to cover their costs.

For quality control, the federal government has traditionally relied on a so-called triad of institutional accreditation, state reviews, and federal oversight. Federal responsibility, as carried out by the Department of Education, has included certifying accreditation agencies as well as ultimately approving institutions to participate in the federal programs. Over time, however, a growing number of observers have come to conclude that the triad arrangement is simply inadequate for the task.

Over the years, federal policy makers have tried to crack down on institutions with excessively high student-loan default rates. That effort has helped to reduce the overall level of defaults and eliminate schools that were clearly abusing the system. Some of the worst problems have been remedied. For example, the national default rate has dropped from a high of 22 percent in 1990 to less than 7 percent in 2008,[16] but the default rate for borrowers attending for-profit institutions remains above 20 percent.[17]

The George W. Bush administration, in particular, was concerned about whether institutions were serving as good stewards of federal student aid funds.[18] In particular, it believed that many colleges and universities were not paying sufficient attention to their low retention and graduation rates. To try to pressure institutions to focus on improving these rates, the Bush administration pursued several unsuccessful proposals that would reward or punish institutions based on the success rates of their students. The potential intrusiveness and complexity of implementing these proposals, and strong opposition from colleges and their representatives in Washington, undermined their enactment. As college prices continue to increase, and the costs of the student aid programs follow, there are likely to be continuing concerns over whether students and taxpayers are getting their money's worth.[19]

Reforming the Delivery of Student Loans

In 1993, President Clinton proposed changing the way that student loans were originated, financed, serviced, and repaid. This would have been an entirely new system that would make loans directly to students rather than making use of traditional bank-based government guaranteed loans, now called the federal Family Education Loan program (FELP). The promise of direct loans was that they would streamline the lending process, better serve student borrowers, promote improvements in the bank-based system through competition, and saves tax dollars by reducing subsidies to private lenders and guarantee agencies.[20] After a heated debate, Congress agreed to create the Direct Loan Program, but rather than eliminating the bank-based system as Clinton had proposed, they decided to allow the two systems to operate as rival programs. Institutions would be free to choose the program they decided would serve their students more effectively. Despite a general agreement that direct lending has improved services to schools and students, Republicans remain skeptical that an entirely state-run system is necessary.[21]

The Obama administration has renewed the debate over the best method for the federal government to use in making student loans. Seeking ways to increase the dollars available for Pell grants and other need-based aid, Obama has sought to require all institutions to participate in the Direct Loan program. This would eliminate the subsidies to lenders and save billions of dollars that could then be redirected to expand the grant programs. However, the effort to eliminate the traditional bank-based lending system has meet with intense opposition.[22] Banks, loan processors, and secondary markets such as Sallie Mae mobilized to save the traditional loan program. A part of this opposition was driven by the view that these programs serve students better.[23] Nevertheless, there is also no doubt that these programs are enormously profitable for lenders, and that their elimination would lead to a significant restructuring of many corporations that rely on federal student loan subsidies to remain solvent. Today, the stalemate continues with both loan programs operating simultaneously. In late 2009, the Department of Education sent a letter to all institutions participating in the FELP program, urging them to change over to direct lending in anticipation of a mandated shift. In response, many institutions have chosen to switch programs, but the outcome of the competition between the two loan programs remains in doubt.

Federal Tax Policies

In addition to direct funding of students and institutions, the federal government assists college students and their families, as well as colleges and universities, through a variety of tax policies. A number of exclusions, exemptions, credits, and deductions have been added to the federal tax code over the years to benefit education at all levels. Some of these provisions—for example, the personal exemption parents may claim for dependent students aged nineteen to twenty-four, tax-advantaged savings plans, and tuition tax credits—affect the ability of individuals and families to save for and pay college costs. Other provisions affect the revenue and financing arrangements of colleges and universities—for example, their charitable 501(c)(3) status allows them to receive tax-deductable contributions. The monetary benefits of these tax expenditures to institutions and students are measured by the estimated amount of federal revenue that would be collected in the absence of such provisions. In 2008, the estimated annual federal tax expenditures for higher education (including for both students and institutions) totaled $17.4 billion.[24]

In 1997, the Clinton administration persuaded Congress to enact the Taxpayer Relief Act, which included a number of higher-education-related new tax breaks for students and families.[25] Since that time, individual tax-based relief has become an important and expanding tool of federal policy to address rising college costs. The challenge to policy makers was to find a way to promote affordability to middle-income families—the primary beneficiaries of these tax policies—without detracting from efforts to improve access for the neediest students through direct student aid. The scope of the Taxpayer Relief Act was dramatic. Indeed, it proved to be a watershed in the use of federal tax policy to address the burden of rising college prices on middle- and upper-income college students. The Hope and Lifelong Learning tax credits were the largest of the tuition tax benefits incorporated into the law. The nonrefundable Hope tax credit provides a $1,500 credit per student per year for tuition expenses during the first two years of postsecondary education. Since it can only be claimed up to the amount of the taxpayer's liability, it effectively eliminates the eligibility of a large number of lower-income families. The Lifetime Learning tax credit provides up to one credit per household for up to $2,000, or 20 percent of tuition and related expenses. These credits represent a major shift away from targeted aid to low-income families and toward cost relief primarily benefiting middle- and upper-income families.[26]

The Taxpayer Relief Act also created several new vehicles for tax-advantaged savings for higher education expenses: Roth Individual Retirement Accounts (IRAs), Education IRAs (now called Coverdale Education Savings accounts), State Prepaid Tuition Plans, and College Savings Plans (now generally called 529 Plans after the provision in the tax code). These new instruments expanded and complicated the landscape for families saving for future college expenses.

The new tuition tax credits received broad and immediate public approval, and in 2001 President Bush expanded their scope. The Economic Growth and Tax Reconciliation Act of 2002 raised the applicable income limits for Hope and Lifelong Learning credits, increased annual limits on contributions to educational IRAs, and eliminated interest earned under prepaid tuition programs and college savings plans. This new law further exacerbated the shifting of benefits from the more needy to middle- and upper-income families.[27] This is because lower-income families pay little or no federal tax and thus are not eligible to use these tax breaks. Along with educational IRAs and other tax-sheltered federal savings vehicles, which also primarily benefit upper- and middle-income families, these benefits were estimated to cost the federal treasury $11.2 billion in lost revenue in 2008.

Institutional tax-exempt status and the deduction of contributions from the taxable income of donors are the crucial tax policies benefiting institutions of higher education. The tax exemption predates most of the nation's colleges and universities and the federal tax code, so its long-standing precedent, and the political implications of change, have preserved the tax-exempt status of colleges and universities. However, institutions are required to pay a federal tax on unrelated business income for all activities that are not a part of their charitable purpose.

As shown in table 5.1, the total cost in lost revenues of institutional tax expenditures is estimated to be $6.2 billion.

Federal Support for Research

Federal spending to support research and related activities goes back to 1883, when Congress voted to support agricultural experiment stations. The federal investment in academic science remained fairly small until the demands of World War II caused spending for campus-based research to skyrocket. Guided by the newly created National Science Foundation (NSF), the boom in federally sponsored research continued through the 1950s and early 1960s. Today, the federal government remains the largest source of financing for campus-based research, supplying $45 billion in 2008.

Unlike student aid, federal research funding is highly concentrated on a relatively small number of institutions, most of them large research universities. According to the NSF, one hundred doctoral-degree-granting institutions receive more than 50 percent of all federal science and engineering obligations to academia.[28] This support flows from multiple federal agencies and is directed toward multiple policy objectives. While the NSF was originally conceived as a single agency having broad purview over federal research funding, this vision never came to be. Instead, there are diffuse priority-setting and allocation systems. Today more than a dozen mission-oriented agencies fund significant portions of academic

Table 5.4   Federal obligations for research, by agency, 1990–2008, in constant 2000 dollars (in millions)

	1990	1995	2000	2005	2008
Health & Human Services	9,190	10,931	17,913	25,392	24,138
Defense	4,344	4,555	4,920	5,263	5,594
Energy	3,164	3,753	4,101	5,061	5,026
National Science Foundation	2,079	2,332	2,726	3,321	3,289
Agriculture	1,316	1,409	1,612	1,777	1,784
NASA	3,767	4,389	3,964	3,309	1,735
Other	2,752	3,478	3,235	3,559	3,389
Total for all federal agencies	26,612	30,847	38,471	47,682	44,955

Source: National Science Foundation, Division of Science Resources Statistics, Survey of Federal Funds for Research and Development: FY 2007–08, www.nsf.gov/statistics/srvyfedfunds/.

science. These agencies serve multiple purposes and operate hundreds of competitive and noncompetitive sponsored-research programs.

The large federal investment in scientific research has allowed a relatively small cadre of American research universities to achieve global preeminence in many fields. Further, the diffusion of funds into various agencies has prevented any single set of federal bureaucrats from setting the nation's entire research agenda. However, the growth of federally funded research has clearly influenced the priorities of research universities and, in the view of many observers, created an incentive structure that has lead many universities to emphasize research over teaching, graduate over undergraduate education, and the sciences over the social sciences and humanities.[29]

During the 1970s, 1980s, and 1990s, total research expenditures, from all sources, increased steadily. Federal research support grew, but research contributions from industry, institutional funds, and other sources also increased during this period. In retrospect, this was an extraordinary time for investment in university-based research. The growth curve continued despite the end of the cold war and the collapse of the Soviet Union. While these events diminished public interest in military research and the "big science" projects that characterized this competition between the superpowers, in large part this growth curve represented a shift toward medical research within federal funding priorities.

That long period of growth came to an end in the early 2000s.[30] Federal research funding flattened out and has remained largely stable, as measured in constant dollars, for nearly a decade. The operating costs of the wars in Iraq and Afghanistan, as well as the reductions in federal revenue resulting from the George W. Bush administration's tax cuts, left the federal government with very little budget flexibility. This pattern of flat funding seems unlikely to change soon. In the absence of a common research goal, such as that provided first by Sputnik and later by the space race and the cold war, it will be difficult to assemble the public and legislative support necessary to significantly increase federal spending on research and development. There are simply too many other priorities competing for limited discretionary federal dollars.

In addition to differences among policy makers on what goals federal research dollars should be directed toward, they are also divided over how those dollars should be awarded. Traditionally, federal campus-based research funds have been awarded via competitions involving a peer review process, where experts evaluated grant proposals in their field. Supporters of this peer review system argue that it ensures that the best research is funded. Opponents see it as an "old boy's network" that precludes many worthwhile projects because the researchers are not tied into the network, and that discriminates against younger faculty members, women, and minorities.[31]

In the past two decades there has been rapid growth in the portion of federal research funding that is allocated through congressional earmarking. In this process, which bypasses formal competition and peer review, Congress specifies the particular projects that will be funded. Such earmarking has ballooned to almost $20 billion, sparking criticism that it is nothing more than "pork-barrel science" where elected officials are able to award research grants and contracts to campuses in their home districts.[32] In part congressional earmarking is a reaction to the heavy concentration of research funding to relatively few institutions. Institutions outside of this select group can now go to their elected representatives directly to plead their case—often with the help of lobbyists and government-relations consultants. Earmarking is also a response to a long-term problem affecting virtually all research universities—the deterioration and obsolescence of scientific equipment and facilities. Only a small portion of federal research funds support renovation, new construction, and the purchase of equipment. In the 1950s and 1960s, separate federal appropriations were made for these categories. More recently, the federal government has persisted in a policy of funding research activities at universities, but requiring those institutions to provide and maintain the research infrastructure. In reaction, some institutions have gone directly to the congressional appropriations committees to find funding for construction and renovation of particular facilities.

Whether funded by traditional competitions or by earmarks, the nation's investment in science and technology must now compete directly with funding requests for interstate highways, national parks, environmental protection, housing, and a host of other domestic needs. These are all vying for a smaller portion of the federal pie. Not only will budgets be tight through the next decade, but questions surrounding the management and conduct of university research may have weakened the support for academic science. Since the end of World War I, the nation's substantial investment in science has been repaid many times over in both pathbreaking discoveries and practical applications. The computer, radar, the polio vaccine, and America's world leadership in agriculture can all be traced back to academic science. Yet controversy and skepticism have beset the university research community in recent years. Publicized cases of research fraud and other ethical breaches by federally sponsored researchers have triggered investigations and doubts about the integrity of scientific research.

All of these issues take on particular significance in light of the dependence of many universities on federal research dollars. While federal grants and contracts represent less than 10 percent of total revenues to higher education, at some major research institutions federal dollars constitute 25 percent or more of their revenues. The decline in federal funding, coupled with budgetary problems faced by state governments and many private contributors, have placed many research universities in difficult financial situations. If the diminution of federal support continues, these institutions will be unable to afford to acquire the newest technologies, others will be unable to maintain and replace their existing research equipment, and most institutions will have difficulty in funding existing staff and operations.

Federal Regulation

Federal regulation of higher education derives from two principal sources: (1) the requirements of accountability that accompany the receipt of federal funds, and (2) the dictates of social legislation, as well as the regulations, executive orders, and judicial decisions that stem from that legislation. In addition, the Civil War amendments to the Constitution have strengthened the role of the federal government to protect civil rights. To the degree that government officials insist on accountability and congressional mandates addressing a range of social problems remain in place, there will be complexity and strain in the relationship between the federal government and higher education. Tensions are inevitable, given the traditions of institutional autonomy in higher education, the mandates of Congress, the missions of federal agencies, and the responsibilities of those agencies for the stewardship of taxpayer dollars.

One area where federal regulation has had an enormous impact on higher education is in the area of desegregation. From the 1890s until the 1960s, many states operated dual systems of higher education—one for black students and another for white students. Although desegregation of these systems was implied by the 1954 *Brown v. Board of Education* decision by the Supreme Court, meaningful steps toward that end did not take place until after the enactment of the Civil Rights Act of 1965. Since that time, through legislation and court decisions, the federal government has been involved with decisions about who colleges can (or must) admit, how they hire faculty and staff, and how they award scholarships. While these interventions represent a fundamental aspect of the federal government's role in higher education, the details of that role are discussed in chapter 7, on the legal environment in higher education.

Federal regulation has rarely been welcomed by the nation's colleges. Indeed, the academic community has always been wary of entanglement with government. Still, despite their concerns, only a few, mainly independent, religiously affiliated institutions have been willing to refuse funds from Washington. The great majority of colleges have accepted federal patronage, even though it carries a high price in terms of compliance and external control. The federal government influences higher education through scores of statutes and regulations. Some mandates, such as the Americans with Disabilities Act or the regulations of the Environmental Protection Agency or the Occupational Safety and Health Administration, affect all types of organizations. Others, such as the Federal Educational Records Privacy Act and Title IX of the Education Amendments of 1972, which bars gender bias, are specific to higher education. Colleges have long argued that such regulations represent a burden that contributes to the rapidly rising price of higher education. They are seen as a series of "unfunded mandates" from Washington that impose regulatory requirements that leave institutions no choice but to pass those costs onto students in the form of higher prices.

While many in higher education support the broad goals of environmental and consumer protection, open records and meetings, and campus safety, they are concerned that the costs of compliance with the blizzard of federal regulations in these areas outweigh the benefits. One college president is recently quoted as saying:

We have a gazillion people working on compliance. The government requires us to do it. Is it reasonable? Do we do too much? At least from where I sit, it looks as though we have an excessive number of people working on this. But if we don't have them we would be in violation of the law.[33]

An often-cited example of such a federal mandate is the Jeanne Cleary Disclosure of Campus Security and Policy and Campus Crime Statistics Act. This law, signed by President George H. W. Bush in 1990, requires all colleges and universities to disclose specific information about crime on their campuses and in the surrounding communities. The act, which is enforced by the U.S. Department of Education, can result in severe penalties to institutions that do not comply. On the one hand, campus leaders can argue that it is precisely such federal mandates that drive up college costs, as gathering and reporting such data requires substantial staff time. The Department of Education has a constantly changing manual of more than 200 pages on its Web site describing the actions campuses must take to comply with the law.[34] On the other hand, while such reporting requirements

certainly have costs for institutions, there is no evidence that such regu
have much of an impact on college tuition inflation.

Federal Policy and College Costs

Concern over the rising price of a college education has been one of the primary
animating forces in federal policy at least since the late 1970s. The rapid tuition
inflation after 2009 has only heightened federal concern over college costs. As
tuitions spiral upward, so does the demand for increases in federal student aid. It
was tuition inflation that finally brought enough public pressure to enact tuition
tax credits, as well as the various educational savings programs and the 529 state
savings plans. Similarly, the pressures for accountability and the resulting federal
regulations sprang directly from concerns over rising prices.

In 1997 Congress established the National Commission on the Cost of Higher
Education to determine what was driving tuition upward and what could be done
about it. When the commission issued its report, however, it concluded that there
is no single explanation for the tuition spiral.[35] The commission examined factors
that may be driving up institutional costs—everything from faculty salaries, facilities, curriculum, technology, government regulation, and expectations of students (and their parents) about quality and amenities on campus. It concluded
that "the available data on higher education expenditures and revenues make it
difficult to ascertain direct relationships among the cost drivers and increases in
the price of higher education. Institutions of higher education, even to most people in the academy, are financially opaque."[36]

In the end, the commission also decided that there was little that the federal
government could, or should, do about tuition inflation. The commission admonished colleges to intensify their efforts to increase institutional productivity and
inform the public about the actual price of postsecondary education, the returns
on investment, and preparation for college. As for the federal role, the commission urged policy makers to do a better job of collecting and reporting standardized data on costs, prices, and subsidies in higher education and of analyzing the
relationship between tuition and institutional expenditures—but not to impose
any cost or price controls.

Today, more than decade after the commission had completed its work, the
question of whether the federal government should take action to contain college
costs continues to be controversial. It should not be surprising, however, that all

Gladieux, J. E. King, and M. E. Corrigan

to any federal interventions in college pricing policies. It
[fede]ral government has sufficient authority, or political will,
[p]ricing. While the federal government does provide the
[stu]dent aid, it still supplies only 15 percent of college and
[at l]east for now, federal policy makers have concluded that
[not to tak]e action and ought to leave cost containment and price
setting to states, campuses, and market forces.

Prospects for the Federal Role in Higher Education

In summary, here are some of the issues that will influence the federal role in higher
education as we move into the second decade of the twenty-first century:

—The massive budgetary shortfalls faced by nearly all of the states, and the
high unemployment and slow economic growth rates that underlie those
shortfalls, are forcing state governments to reduce their support for
higher education. This is likely to accelerate tuition inflation at public
colleges and universities at precisely the time when families have fewer
resources to pay that tuition. These trends are overwhelming the federal
student aid system, as more and more students are borrowing ever-larger
amounts to cover their rising costs.

—Congress remains divided on the best way to deliver the enormous volume
of federal student loans. The efforts of the Obama administration to
replace the bank-based loan system with direct loans seem to have
stalled for now. But the administration's more popular effort to increase
the size of the Pell grant program requires it to use the savings that
would result from a shift to Direct Loans. Sorting out these issues will
be at the top of the federal higher education agenda until they are
resolved one way or the other.

—Policy makers continue to worry about the consequences of growing
student indebtedness for individuals and for society. There will be
efforts to restore the purchasing power of federal grant aid, but the
policy drift toward a loan-based system seems likely to continue. Issues
of quality control, the costs of education, and consumer protection will
also continue to concern federal policy makers.

—Clouding the generally positive outlook for federal patronage of university-
based research are persistent concerns about research practices in

academia and pressures to reduce federal spending. Some federal policy
makers are calling for science and technology investments to be more
sharply focused on areas of national need. Universities will be challenged to articulate more clearly how their research contributes to
societal goals. Debates will also focus on the balance of funding between research and commercial applications, the need to upgrade the
physical infrastructure of scientific research, and the adequacy of
government support to train the country's next generation of top-flight
scientists and engineers.

—Higher education will continue to press the federal government for
regulatory relief. Yet as long as government officials insist on accountability for taxpayer dollars and legislative mandates addressing a range
of educational and social problems remain in force, the burden of rules
and regulations will continue to be the price that universities must pay
for federal support.

From the Morrill Act, to the GI Bill, to the Higher Education Act, to the American Recovery and Reinvestment Act, the federal government has played a pivotal
role in extending opportunities for higher education to a wider segment of American society. As the nation enters the second decade of the twenty-first century,
the number of students entering college each year continues to grow, and these
new students are more diverse than ever. Given this reality, coupled with rising
college prices and ballooning budget deficits, it is not clear whether the federal
government will be able to sustain its historic commitment to assuring a fair
chance of a college education for all citizens.

The federal government will undoubtedly continue to make important contributions to enhancing the academic enterprise and equalizing educational opportunities in America. As in the past, federal support will supplement the basic
funding provided by states and private sources, and it will spring from objectives
such as economic competitiveness, health, and the quality of life rather than on
an interest in education for its own sake. Funds, along with regulatory controls,
will continue to flow from a variety of agencies in Washington. Such support is
untidy, piecemeal, and not without its headaches for institutions, students, and
states, But the pattern serves a variety of national purposes and, in fact, ultimately may better serve to protect institutional diversity, a student's freedom of
choice, and independent thought in American higher education than would an
overarching federal policy.

NOTES

The chapter was originally prepared by Lawrence Gladieux, Jacqueline King, and Melanie E. Corrigan for the first edition of American Higher Education in the Twenty-First Century. *For this edition, Michael Mumper revised and updated the chapter. Any errors or mistakes in this version are his and not those of the previous authors.*

1. For two thoughtful discussions of the development of the federal role in higher education, see George N. Rainford, *Congress and Higher Education in the Nineteenth Century* (Knoxville: University of Tennessee Press, 1972); and John Thelin, "Higher Education and the Public Trough: A Historical Perspective," in *Public Funding of Higher Education: Changing Contexts and New Rationales*, ed. Edward St. Johns and Michael Parsons (Baltimore: Johns Hopkins University Press, 2004), 21–40.

2. Glenn C. Altschuler and Stuart Blumin, *The G.I. Bill: A New Deal for Veterans* (Oxford: Oxford University Press, 2009), 85.

3. Ibid., 87.

4. Ibid.

5. Francis Keppler, "The Higher Education Acts Contrasted, 1965 and 1986: Has Federal Policy Come of Age? *Harvard Education Review* 57 (Spring 1987): 49–67.

6. College Board, *Trends in Student Aid 2009*, www.trends-collegeboard.com/student_aid/.

7. For an analysis of the impact of this act on state governments, see a report by the National Governors Association, *Education and Workforce* (Mar. 2, 2009), www.nga.org/Files/pdf/ARRAANALYSIS.PDF. For a review of the impact of the act on state colleges and universities, see Daniel Hurley, *Considerations for State Colleges and Universities in a Post-Recession America*, www.congressweb.com/aascu/docfiles/Considerations-AASCU11-09.pdf.

8. Daniel Hurley, "The Second Fiscal Crisis: Preparing for the Funding Cliff," *Public Purpose* (Sept./Oct. 2009): 2–3.

9. Chester Finn, Jr., "A Federal Policy for Higher Education?" *Alternative* (May 1975): 18–19.

10. College Board, *Trends in Student Aid 2009*.

11. For a detailed analysis of the creation of the Pell Grant program, see Lawrence E. Gladieux and Thomas R. Wolanin, *Congress and the Colleges: The National Politics of Higher Education* (Lexington, MA: Lexington Books, 1976).

12. Michael Mumper, "The Affordability of Public Higher Education: 1970–1990," *Review of Higher Education* 16, no. 2 (Winter 1993): 157–80.

13. James Hearn and Janet Holdsworth, "Federal Student Aid: The Shift from Grants to Loans," in St. Johns and Parsons, *Public Funding of Higher Education*, 21–40.

14. David Cho, "As College Costs Rise, Loans Become Harder to Get," *Washington Post*, Dec. 28, 2009, www.washingtonpost.com/wp-dyn/content/article/2009/12/27/AR2009122702116.html.

15. A more complete discussion of the impact of the growth of the proprietary sector on federal student-aid policy can be found in Richard Apling, "Proprietary Schools and Their Students," *Journal of Higher Education* 64 (July/Aug. 1993): 379–415.

16. U.S. Department of Education, *National Student Loan Default Rates*, www2.ed .gov/offices/OSFAP/defaultmanagement/defaultrates.html.

17. Government Accountability Office, *Proprietary Schools: Stronger Department of Education Oversight Needed to Help Ensure Only Eligible Students Receive Federal Student Aid* (Aug. 2009), www.gao.gov/highlights/d09600high.pdf.

18. Stephen Burd, "Bush's Next Target?" *Chronicle of Higher Education*, July 11, 2003, http://chronicle.com/article/Bushs-Next-Target-/24767/.

19. Eric Kelderman, "Accountability Issues Persist under New Administration," *Chronicle of Higher Education*, Nov. 17, 2009, http://chronicle.com/article/Account ability-Issues-Persist/49190/.

20. General Accounting Office, *Direct Loans Could Save Billions in 5 Years with Proper Implementation* (Washington, DC: U.S. Government Printing Office, Nov. 1993).

21. Gilbert Cruz, "Obama's Student Loan Plan: A Good Takeover?" *Time*, Sept. 16, 2009, www.time.com/time/politics/article/0,8599,1924128,00.html.

22. Eliza Adelson, "Lenders Search for Alternatives to Loan Proposal," *Hill*, July 30, 2009, http://thehill.com/homenews/administration/52893–lenders-search-for -alternatives-to-loan-proposal/.

23. Libby Nelson, "Sallie Mae Fights for Student-Loan Role in a Campaign That's All About Jobs," *Chronicle of Higher Education*, Nov. 22, 2009, http://chronicle.com/ article/Sallie-Mae-Fights-for-Stude/49224/.

24. Joint Congressional Committee on Taxation, *Estimates of Federal Tax Expenditures for Fiscal Years 2008–2012* (Oct. 31, 2008), www.jct.gov/s-2-08.pdf.

25. Thomas Wolanin, *Rhetoric and Reality* (Washington, DC: Institute for Higher Education Policy, 2001).

26. Ibid.

27. KPMG, *The Economic Growth and Tax Relief Reconciliation Act of 2001*, http:// us.kpmg.com/microsite/taxnewsflash/2001/TaxBook/2001TaxBill.pdf.

28. Ronda Britt, "Federal Government Is Largest Source of University R&D Funding in S&E: Share Drops in FY 2008," *InfoBrief*, NSF 09-318 (Washington, DC: National Science Foundation, Sept. 2009).

29. Clark Kerr, *The Uses of the University* (Cambridge MA: Harvard University Press, 1995).

30. Britt, "Federal Government."

31. General Accounting Office, Peer Review, *Reforms Needed to Ensure Fairness in Federal Agency Grant Selection*, GAO/PEMD-94-1 (Washington, DC: General Accounting Office, 1994).

32. Gail Russell Chaddock, " 'Pig Book': Congressional 'Pork' Hits $19.6 Billion in 2009," *Christian Science Monitor*, Apr. 14, 2009, www.csmonitor.com/USA/Politics/ 2009/0414/pig-book-congressional-pork-hits-196-billion-in-2009/.

33. John Immerwahr, Jean Johnson, and Paul Gasbarra, *The Iron Triangle: College Presidents Talk about Costs, Access, and Quality* (Washington, DC: National Center for Public Policy and Higher Education, Oct. 2008), 13.

34. Diana Ward and Janice Lee, *The Handbook for Campus Crime Reporting* (Washington, DC: U.S. Department of Education, 2005), www.ed.gov/admins/lead/safety/handbook.pdf.

35. National Commission on the Cost of Higher Education, *Straight Talk about College Costs and Prices* (Phoenix: Oryx Press, 1998).

36. Ibid., 12.

CHAPTER SIX

The States and Higher Education

Aims C. McGuinness, Jr.

The period of the early years of the twenty-first century is likely to be one of the most challenging in the history of the nation's higher education enterprise. Relations between state government and higher education are likely to be especially strained because of four broad trends:

1. Escalating demands: These are driven not only by numbers, but also by higher expectations for what an increasingly diverse student population should know and be able to do as the result of a college education. The demands extend to virtually every dimension of higher education, including research and service. President Obama's call for the United States to regain global competitiveness and have the highest proportion of students graduating from college in the world by 2020 intensifies the challenge.

2. Severe economic constraints: Even with gradual economic recovery, it is unlikely that higher education will see significant improvements in funding, at least on a per student basis, within the next decade. The federal deficit, competing priorities for public funds, public anger about

rising student costs, and severe competition for limited corporate and philanthropic funds will all contribute to the continuing financial constraints.

3. The academy's inherent resistance to change: As demands increase and resources dwindle, institutions are slowly recognizing that, if they continue to do business as usual, their ability to educate students and continue their research and service missions will be seriously compromised. But translating this slow awareness into changes at the institutional core—in the curriculum, in modes of teaching and learning, and in faculty governance—will be a long-term, incremental process. The resulting public frustration with the academy's inability to respond to major societal needs only intensifies the danger of blunt governmental intervention.

4. Instability of state political leadership: The trend toward term limitations and the demands of political office are contributing to major changes in state leadership. This is especially pronounced in state legislatures. As each legislative session begins, the proportion of new members increases. The relative stability provided by the memory of long-term legislative leaders about state higher education policies is being lost. Other issues are dominating the agendas. The twenty-year trend toward larger and more dominant legislative staffs is accelerating.

These conditions are certain to exacerbate already frayed state relationships with higher education. Constructive resolution of these conflicts is essential both to the continued strength of American higher education and to its capacity to respond to major societal priorities. The purpose of this chapter is to present a framework and basic information about the state role as a beginning point for further reading and study.

Role of the State: Historical Perspective

The state role in higher education has evolved significantly over the nation's history. Higher education in the nineteenth century was primarily private. With only a few exceptions—such as the establishment of the University of Georgia in 1785, Ohio University in 1804, and the University of Virginia in 1819—states played a limited role in higher education until the establishment of land-grant universities in the 1860s and 1870s. Another important development was the establishment of state normal schools to prepare teachers, schools that evolved into state colleges and universities by the mid-twentieth century. Historically, states have always provided the legal framework within which both public and private institutions operated. Following the principles established by the U.S. Supreme Court's ruling in the Dartmouth College case (*Dartmouth College v. Woodward*) in 1819, states accorded both public and private institutions significant autonomy, especially on "substantive" decisions on whom to admit, what should be taught, and who should teach.[1] It was not until the massive expansion of higher education in the 1950s and 1960s that the states began to undertake more deliberate efforts to promote the coordinated development of public higher education to establish more systematic approaches to the allocation of state funding.

From the 1950s to the end of the 1980s, the share of total enrollments in public institutions (including many community colleges partially funded from local revenue) increased from about 60 to 76 percent.[2] The private sector continued to grow, but this was outstripped by enrollment increases of one and a half times in public four-year institutions and five times in public two-year ones. The proportion of institutions in the private sector dropped from 65 to 59 percent.[3]

State and local governments now provide approximately 35 percent of the current revenue for higher education, both public and private, excluding sales and services (for example, hospitals, dormitories, and restaurants). This compares with 16 percent from the federal government, 38 percent from student tuition and fees, and 11 percent from other sources (including endowments, private gifts, and grants).

Changing Relationship between State Government and Higher Education

For some within higher education, even the mention of state government conjures up negative images. There continues to be a widespread sense within the academy that virtually any state involvement, other than providing funding with no strings attached, is an infringement on legitimate institutional autonomy. The relationships are viewed along a continuum: at one end, complete institutional autonomy is good; at the other end, state involvement is seen as bad. Frank Newman suggests a different, more constructive view. His point is that both institutional autonomy and state involvement are important. Governments have a legitimate interest in the responsiveness of the academy to major societal needs. At the same time, it is important for both society and the academy that higher education be able to pursue values and purposes that are different from and, in some cases, may conflict with the prevailing values and priorities of the state. "What becomes clear," Newman states, "is that the real need is not simply for more autonomy but for a relationship between the university and the state that is constructive for both, built up over a long period of time by careful attention on the part of all parties."[4]

Robert Berdahl makes a similar distinction between the concept of academic freedom, which is universal and absolute, and autonomy, which is "of necessity parochial and relative." He continues by emphasizing that "the real issue with respect to autonomy . . . is not whether there will be interference by the state but whether the inevitable interference will be confined to the proper topics and expressed through a suitably sensitive mechanism."[5] The key is for the higher education community to recognize that it has a stake, and even a responsibility, to engage actively with state political leaders in defining the nature of the relationship. This includes defining the major societal ends toward which the academy should direct its energies, and shaping the policies and other "suitably sensitive" mechanisms that will govern the relationships.

Evolving State and Federal Roles

The state role differs distinctly from that of the federal government. Since the historic decision in the Education Amendments of 1972 to reject direct general purpose aid to institutions, the federal government has emphasized aid to students, not to institutions. Federal funding to institutions is either through students, in the form of student financial assistance, or restricted funding for research and other purposes. The federal government is generally impartial about a particular provider's ownership and control (public, private, or proprietary), assuming other conditions for receiving a subsidy are met. The federal government thus tends to emphasize a strict separation between the government's role as "overseer of the public interest" and the institutional role of providing services.

In contrast to the federal government, states primarily finance higher education through the direct subsidy of public institutions. In this respect, states play a dual role of overseer of the public interest and provider of higher education services. States also provide aid to students, ranging from large programs in states such as New York to small programs in states such as Alabama.[6] However, only a few states (for example, Illinois, Maryland, Michigan, New Jersey, New York, and Pennsylvania) provide grants to private not-for-profit institutions for the purposes of general institutional subsidy;[7] in the recent state fiscal crisis, several of these states discontinued or severely limited funding for these programs.

The balance between federal and state roles has changed over time. Clark Kerr predicted in 1985 that the decade of the mid-1980s to mid-1990s (and perhaps beyond) would be one of state and private leadership in higher education. He pointed out that this has been the dominant pattern in U.S. history. Periods of federal leadership have been relatively brief: 1860–90 and 1955–85. He further observed that as the effect of higher education on states' economies has become more politically important, state governors have emerged as the most important political figures.[8]

Fulfilling Kerr's prediction, the states were the focus of higher education reform in the period from 1985 through the 1990s. Spurred by reports of national task forces and commissions sponsored by state-based organizations such as the Education Commission of the States and the National Governors Association, governors and state legislators led a fundamental change in the definition of accountability, and these changes continue to underlie many of the state policy initiatives. Up to the 1980s, states had primarily focused on issues of resource allocation and utilization and rarely became involved in basic questions about the outcomes of a college or university education. By the end of the 1980s, questions about outcomes—especially student outcomes—dominated states' agendas. More than any other force, it was state policies requiring institutions to assess student learning and provide information to the states and the public that stimulated higher education's attention to these issues. Many colleges and universities now report that they have active efforts to assess student learning. Although state mandates initially spurred this attention, voluntary accreditation, national pressures such as the report of the Spellings Commission, and the Voluntary System of Accountability initiative sustain that attention.

During the 1980s, the states also led in developing new funding systems, such as competitive, incentive, and performance funding. The use of funding "on the margin" to support centers of excellence in research and technology and stimulate improvement in undergraduate education was widespread.[9] Relating this to the earlier discussion of autonomy, since the early 1980s states have been much more willing to enter into the area Berdahl defines as "substantive autonomy."

In the early twenty-first century, a more mixed pattern is evolving, one of greater connection and interdependence between the federal and state roles in higher education. A long-standing link remains in the eligibility requirements for federal aid. In order to receive federal aid, an institution must be "authorized" or licensed by the state in which it is going to operate or deliver services. The more significant interrelationships relate to finance. Beyond the specific domain of higher education, federal budget and tax policies establish the fiscal framework for state finance. The basic rules governing not-for-profit institutions are generally based on federal, not state policy. The declining percentage of state funding for public institutions is the result, to a large extent, of the escalating costs of the federal Medicaid program. Specifically within higher education, federal regulations related to the financing of research drive state and institutional decision making. State student financial aid programs commonly are tied to federal student aid policies, especially the methodology for determining eligibility for federal aid (the Federal Application Form for Student Aid). The Secretary of Education's Commission on the Future of Higher Education (the Spellings Commission) touched on a number of issues related to accreditation, data systems, and accountability that concerned both federal and state policy.[10] The Obama administration has signaled a far more aggressive leadership stance on higher education with the president's stated goal of regaining the United States' status as a global leader in educational attainment. The new federal initiatives, including those within the American Recovery and Reinvestment Act of 2009, provide for extensive involvement of the states. The state fiscal crisis is also prompting calls for a stronger federal role in funding public research universities.[11] These changes in the state role and its increasing interdependence with federal policy are requiring fundamental changes in state-level capacity for policy leadership, as well as in the mechanisms for coordinating federal and state policy.

Differences in State Structures

The basic patterns of state-level organization across the nation today were in place in the early 1970s. The year 1972 marked the culmination of more than a decade of development of state higher education agencies formed to coordinate the massive expansion in the late 1950s and 1960s. By that year, forty-seven states had established either consolidated governing boards responsible for all senior institutions (and, in some cases, community colleges also) or coordinating boards responsible for statewide planning and coordination of two or more governing boards. Three small states with a limited number of institutions did not form a special statutory agency, but instead continued to handle statewide higher education issues through existing governing boards, informal coordination, and direct involvement of the governor and state legislature.

The general pattern, as well as tradition, in the United States is that state governments (meaning the governor, the executive branch, administrative and fiscal agencies, and the state legislature) treat public higher education differently from other state agencies, such as state transportation departments.

Each state has a unique state structure and relationship between government and higher education.[12] The differences among states reflect, amid other points, variations in their general governmental structure (for example, different legal responsibilities of the executive and legislative branches), political culture, and history. Most states have established an entity (for example, a state board of higher education, state board of regents, or higher education commission) explicitly charged with statewide policy for higher education.

Despite the complexity of the differences, the approaches taken by states can be understood in terms of the variations in the authority and responsibility of state higher education entities for key policy tools and processes—such as budget review and approval, review and approval of academic programs, and public accountability—and the extent to which these entities are directly involved in institutional operations (governance). The following is an overview of these variations.

The distinction between *governance* and *coordination* is fundamental for understanding state higher education structures and the assignment of responsibility for budgetary and financial decision making and for institutional financial management. Some structures are established to *govern institutions*, while others are established to *coordinate the state postsecondary education system or sectors* (for example, a system of locally governed community colleges).

The term governance has a particular meaning when applied to the authority and responsibility of governing boards of public colleges and universities. American postsecondary education has a strong historical and legal tradition of institutional autonomy—a high degree of freedom from external intervention and control. A basic responsibility of governing boards is to oversee the delicate balance between institutional autonomy and public accountability.

All states assign responsibility for governing public colleges and universities to one or more boards, which are most often composed of a majority of lay citizens representing the public interest. The names of these boards vary, but "board of trustees" and "board of regents" are the most common. The responsibilities of these boards are similar to those of boards of directors for nonprofit corporations. Public institution governing boards were modeled after the lay boards of private colleges and universities. Private college boards usually govern a single institution. In contrast, public institution boards most often govern several public institutions. In fact, 65 percent of the students in American public postsecondary education attend institutions whose governing boards cover multiple campuses.[13]

Common responsibilities of public governing boards include governing a single corporate entity, including all the rights and responsibilities of that corporation as defined by state law and, if it is a system board, encompassing all institutions within a system. Individual institutions within the board's jurisdiction usually do not have separate corporate status, although governing boards may have subsidiary corporations for hospitals, foundations, or other purposes. Other responsibilities include appointing, setting the compensation for, and evaluating both system and institutional chief executives; planning strategically, budgeting (operating and capital), and allocating resources between and among the institutions within the board's jurisdiction; ensuring public accountability for the effective and efficient use of resources to achieve institutional missions; maintaining the institution's assets (human, programmatic, and physical), and ensuring alignment of these assets with the institutional mission; developing and implementing policy on a wide range of institutional concerns (for example, academic and student affairs policies) that do not need the approval of external agencies or authorities; awarding academic degrees; advocating for the needs of the institutions under the board's jurisdiction to the legislature and governor; and establishing faculty and other personnel policies, including approving the awarding of tenure and serving as the final point of appeal on personnel grievances.

There are a number of ways to categorize public governing boards, but the approach suggested by Clark Kerr and Marian Gade in *The Guardians: Boards of Trustees of American Colleges and Universities* is particularly useful.[14] They categorize public governing boards in three ways. First, there are consolidated governance systems in which one board governs all public two- and four-year institutions, or one board covers all four-year campuses (with separate arrangements for two-year institutions). Second, there are segmental systems in which separate boards govern distinct types of campuses (for example, research universities, comprehensive colleges and universities, and community colleges; this may include separate boards for postsecondary technical institutes or colleges and for adult education, as well). Third, there are campus-level governing boards that have full, "autonomous" authority over a single campus that is not part of a consolidated governing board or multicampus system. Several states combine consolidated governance and campus-level boards. For example, in North Carolina and Utah, campus-level boards have authority delegated by the central board and can make some decisions on their own. The State University of New York System, the University of Maine System, and the University System of Maryland also have campus boards, though they are largely advisory.

A number of states have established coordinating boards responsible for key aspects of the state's role in postsecondary education. Some coordinating boards have the responsibility for statewide coordination of many policy tools or functions (for example, planning and policy leadership, institutional missions, program review and approval, and budget development and resource allocation). Other coordinating boards are responsible for only a single sector, such as community colleges.

The important point is that coordinating boards do *not* govern institutions, in the sense defined above (for example, appointing institutional chief executives or setting faculty personnel policies). Specifically, coordinating boards appoint, set compensation for, and evaluate only the agency executive officer and staff, but not the institutional chief executives. In several states, the governor is the final appointing authority for the agency executive, although usually with recommendations from the coordinating board. Coordinating boards do not generally have corporate status independent of state government; they focus more on state and system needs and priorities than on advocating the interests of a particular institution or system of institutions, and they plan primarily for the state postsecondary education system as a whole. In most coordinating board states, this planning includes both public and private institutions and, in some states, for-profit institutions. Coordinating boards may or may not review and make recommendations on budgets for the state system as a whole, rather than only for one part of that system. A few coordinating agencies recommend consolidated budgets for the whole public system. Others simply make recommendations to the governor or legislature on individual institutional or segmental budgets. Most coordinating boards have a responsibility to implement budget policy only for funds appropriated specifically to the agency for operations and special initiatives, or for reallocations to the institutions for performance, incentives, or other purposes; they may or may not review or approve proposals for new academic programs and may or may not have authority to require institutions to review existing programs. They are not directly involved in setting or carrying out human resource or personnel policies, except to carry out legislative mandates for studies of issues such as faculty workload and productivity or tenure policy.

Twenty-three states plus the District of Columbia and Puerto Rico are consolidated governing board states. These states organize all public higher education under one or two statewide governing boards. None of these states has established a statewide coordinating agency with significant academic policy or budgetary authority between the governing board and state government. Nine of these states organize all public higher education under a single governing board. The other fourteen states have two boards: most often a board for universities and a board for community colleges and/or technical colleges. In several of these states, the second board is a coordinating board for community and technical colleges. Twenty-four states are coordinating board states. Twenty-two of these states have regulatory coordinating boards with approval authority for academic programs. Fifteen of these boards have significant budgetary authority, six have limited budget authority, and one has no role in the budgetary process. Two states have advisory boards with no program approval authority and only authority to review and recommend budgets. One consolidated governing board state (Alaska) also has an advisory board with limited authority to review and make recommendations on budgets. The remaining three states (Delaware, Michigan, and Pennsylvania) have planning or service agencies, but no other boards between the governing boards for public institutions and state government. In addition, three other states (Minnesota, New Hampshire, and Oregon) plus the District of Columbia and Puerto Rico have planning or service agencies between their consolidated governing boards and state government. These agencies perform functions such as the administration of student aid and institutional licensure and authorization. In Vermont, the Higher Education Council is a nonstatutory voluntary planning entity. Five states (Florida, Idaho, Michigan, New York, and Pennsylvania) have state boards with formal legal authority for all levels of education (early childhood education through higher education). Nevertheless, the formal authority these boards have over higher education varies significantly. Among these five states, only the state boards in Idaho and New York have significant authority related to all higher education. A constitutional amendment approved by Florida voters in November 2002 removed the responsibility for universities from the previous P–20 (early childhood through graduate education) State Board of Education and created a new Board of Governors with governing responsibility for the state universities. The state universities continue to have local boards, and the State Board of Education continues to have responsibility for coordinating the locally governed community colleges.

Differences in Budgeting and Financing Relationships between States and Institutions

Within the broad categories of states with coordinating or governing boards, states differ fundamentally in the legal status accorded to public colleges and

Table 6.1   Levels of state control and institutional legal status

Level	Type	Legal status
High regulatory control	A. Institution as state agency	Higher education institutions are treated in a manner similar to other state agencies, such as the transportation/highway department.
	B. State-controlled institution	The distinctiveness of higher education institutions from other state agencies is recognized, but most of the budget and financing policies applied to other state agencies are also applied to higher education.
	C. State-aided institution	Higher education institutions have a legal status according them substantial autonomy from state government. The state provides base, categorical, and capital funding, but with an expectation of substantial nonstate funding (tuition, private giving, etc.).
Low regulatory control	D. Corporate model for institutional governance	As in model C, institutions have a legal status (e.g., a public corporation) according them substantial autonomy. The expectation of state funding is less certain and may be allocated not in grants to the institution, but in the form of vouchers or grants to students to offset tuition charges.

universities and, as a consequence, in the nature of their budgeting and financing relationships. The four levels of state control of institutions can be represented on a continuum from high to low (table 6.1).

The four categories of institutional legal status represent theoretical types. In practice, no state currently treats all of its public institutions as if they were in either of the two extremes: institution as a state agency or institution as an independent corporation.[15] There are three common patterns:

—Pattern 1: Different sectors are accorded different levels of independence from state procedural controls. For example, both the University of California and the California State University systems are treated as "state-aided" institutions, although each is subject to specific regulations that treat the institutions as "state controlled." The University of California System is established in the state constitution and has a higher level of independence from state procedural controls than the California State University System, which is established in state statutes and, until the early 1990s, was closely linked to state budget, personnel, and purchasing requirements. In contrast to the two university systems, the California Community Colleges are governed by extensive state statutory and regulatory policies and, in many respects, are treated as state-controlled institutions.

—Pattern 2: All public universities are established as public corporations (state aided) but are subject to detailed state oversight in specific areas, such as capital construction or personnel. North Dakota and Kentucky are examples of this pattern—the North Dakota University System as a single university system and Kentucky's system, where each university is a separate public corporation. In both cases, the institutions are subject to specific state procedural controls related to capital construction and other areas. As another example, the University of Wisconsin System is organized as a public corporation but is subject to detailed oversight by the Wisconsin State Department of Administration on all capital projects, and all classified (nonprofessional) personnel are included in the state civil service system.

—Pattern 3: Most public institutions are established as public corporations (state aided), but specific institutions are accorded greater independence from state procedural controls as a result of deliberate state actions to decentralize governance and diversify revenue sources. The University System of Maryland, for example, is accorded a degree of independence as a public corporation (state aided), but St. Mary's College of Maryland was granted increased autonomy in return for meeting specific accountability requirements.[16] The State of Colorado has implemented a similar policy through which institutions may enter into "compacts" with the state in return for increased autonomy.[17]

Since the early 1980s, several states have adopted measures to deregulate public higher education institutions. Understandably, the states where these changes occurred were those that had high levels of procedural controls of their public institutions. New Jersey was one of the leading states in making changes. The state colleges, which had been under tight state control compared with the relatively high degree of autonomy of Rutgers University, were granted a measure of autonomy. In the same period, several other states (e.g., Kentucky and Maryland) granted their universities increased management flexibility.[18] This trend accelerated in the 1990s with the interest in "reinventing government," the growing impact of market forces on higher education, and interest in "new public management."[19] One of the most publicized changes was the New Jersey Higher Education Restructuring Act, enacted to implement Governor Christie Whitman's reform proposals. The legislation extended earlier efforts to grant the state colleges increased autonomy and altered the state structure to create both a presidents' council as a coordinating mechanism and a newly constituted coordinating board, the Commission on Higher Education.[20]

The pressures for increased institutional autonomy and management flexibility tend to intensify in periods of severe fiscal stress. As the fiscal crisis of the early 2000s hit the states and the percentage of public institutions' funding from states decreased precipitously, university leaders argued that increased flexibility was essential for their institutions to sustain access and quality and to compete in the global knowledge economy.[21] These calls for change coincided with other calls, especially from political conservatives, for fundamental shifts in the financing of higher education: from institutional subsidy to student subsidy or student vouchers. Two state reforms in the early 2000s illustrate these changes. Virginia enacted the 2005 Restructured Higher Education Financial and Administrative Operations Act to grant the public higher education system increased autonomy in return for explicit requirements for state accountability.[22] Colorado enacted far-reaching reforms in 2004 to establish a College Opportunity Fund to provide voucherlike payments to students in lieu of direct payments to institutions, with other provisions to change this from an institutional subsidy to a "purchase of services" consistent with state priorities. A major force behind the Colorado reforms was the desire of state and university leaders to circumvent restrictions in the state's constitutional Tax Payer's Bill of Rights, which imposes severe tax and expenditure limitations.[23] Both these reforms addressed conditions that were unique to these two states. Nevertheless, they attracted widespread attention in other states, raising the perennial concern that solutions to one state's problems would be inappropriately applied in other states that did not have the same problems.[24]

Other Differences among States

In addition to the obvious variations in size, population, and enrollments, the fifty states differ significantly in history, culture, and political and economic dynamics. These differences are further reflected in the overall performance of their higher education systems, as well as in their financing policies, governance, and state regulatory culture related to higher education. A particularly informative, yet controversial, way of thinking about state variations is presented by political science literature on state political "cultures." Daniel Elazar, for example, sets forth a theory of political subcultures and classifies states according to whether they are moralistic, individualistic, or traditionalistic; their culture and ethnicity; and whether their "ethos" is "public-regarding" or "private-regarding."[25] Two other differences are especially important: financing policy and overall system outcomes.

Financing Policy

States differ significantly in their capacity and effort to finance higher education. States also fluctuate widely in the shares of funding for public institutions borne by state and local governments, students, and other sources. States range from those that provide more than 65 percent of the core funding for public institutions from state and local appropriations (for example, Alaska, Florida, North Carolina, and Mississippi) to those that provide less than 40 percent of the funding from these sources (for example, Montana, Colorado, Pennsylvania, Delaware, New Hampshire, and Vermont). The extent to which states supplement state appropriations with revenue from tuition and other sources also varies greatly. North Carolina, for example, has historically maintained comparatively low public tuition, while Vermont has deliberately relied on high tuition offset by state student financial aid.[26]

States differ in the extent to which they fund need-based financial aid for low-income students.[27] A measure of the level of this funding is calculating state funding as a percentage of federal Pell grant aid to low-income families in the state. Four states (Illinois, Pennsylvania, Minnesota, and New Jersey) provide state need-based aid at a level of more than 100 percent of Pell grant aid; sixteen states, however, provide less than 10 percent of Pell grants.[28] States with limited need-based student financial aid may provide access through low tuition, and they may also have other non-need-based (merit-based) student financial aid programs.[29]

State financing of higher education has followed a rollercoaster pattern over the decades, with periods of significant increases in state appropriations when economic times are good followed by dramatic decreases in periods of economic downturns or recessions. Because governors and state legislatures recognize that higher education has a revenue source (tuition and fees), in contrast to most other governmental services, higher education tends to be the "budget balancer." Consequently, in each period of economic downturn, tuition and fees have increased dramatically.[30] The long-term direction of state policy is away from institutional subsidies and low tuition and toward higher tuition and greater institutional reliance on tuition and other nonstate revenue sources. As shown in figure 6.1, total funding in constant dollars for public higher education per full-time-equivalent (FTE) student increased in the late 1980s and then again in the late 1990s, with periods of significant decline in the early 1990s and early 2000s. Before the

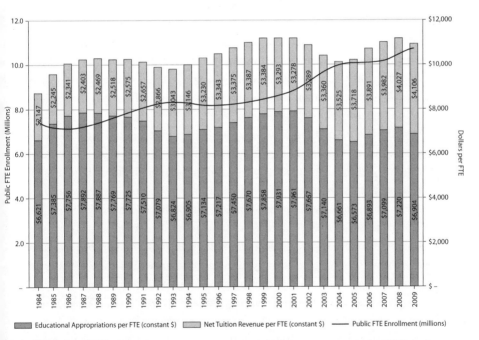

Figure 6.1 Public FTE enrollment and educational appropriations per FTE, United States, fiscal 1984–2009

Net tuition revenue used for capital debt service is included in the figure. Constant 2009 dollars are adjusted by the State Higher Education Executive Officers' (SHEEO) Higher Education Cost Adjustment (HECA). Reprinted by permission of SHEEO from their *State Higher Education Finance Survey* (Boulder, CO: State Higher Education Executive Officers, 2010).

financial crisis in 2008, total funding had regained earlier highs. Nevertheless, the percentage of funding from tuition and fees increased from about 23 percent in 1982 to 36 percent in 2007.[31]

State funding for student aid (student subsidies) to offset tuition increases is growing, but the trend is for this aid to be awarded largely on the basis of merit (academic performance and qualifications) rather than need.[32] The shift from institutional subsidy to a greater reliance on tuition is taking place on a largely ad hoc basis, primarily without coordination with student aid policy and attention to the long-term implications for student access and opportunity.[33]

The dramatic cuts in state funding for higher education in the fiscal crises of the early 2000s and then again beginning in 2008 were raising fundamental questions about the states' commitment to higher education as a public good and their future role in the oversight and funding of public higher education.[34] The crises reflected a long-term trend toward a decreasing share of revenue for higher education from public sources. Even when the economy recovers, higher education is likely to feel a continued squeeze in state funding. The reasons for the long-term decline in state support are more structural than the result of deliberate decisions about higher education per se. In many states, the demand for higher education is far outstripping the states' fiscal capacity—a consequence of conditions such as the faltering economy, mandated increases in funding for health care and K–12 education, and deliberate tax reductions.[35]

Since the late 1980s, there has been a recurring interest in linking state funding to performance. Joseph C. Burke and associates at the Rockefeller Institute of Government began tracking state policies linking accountability with funding in 1997 and continued these annual surveys until 2003. The initial surveys tracked two kinds of policies: performance funding and performance budgeting.[36] The *Seventh Annual Survey* added an additional but closely related policy—performance reporting.[37] The surveys used several definitions. *Performance funding* ties specified state funding *directly* and *tightly* to the performance of public campuses on individual indicators. Performance funding focuses on the distribution phase of the budget process. *Performance budgeting* allows governors, legislators, and coordinating or system boards to *consider* campus achievement on performance indicators as *one factor* in determining allocations for public campuses. Performance budgeting concentrates on budget preparation and presentation and often neglects or even ignores the distribution phase of budgeting. In performance funding, the relationship between funding and performance is tight, automatic, and formulaic. If a public college or university achieves a prescribed target or an improvement level on defined indicators, it receives a designated amount or percentage of state funding. In performance budgeting, the possibility of additional funding due to good or improved performance depends solely on the judgment and discretion of state, coordinating, or system officials. Finally, *performance reporting* recounts statewide results (and often the institutional results)—mostly of public higher education—on priority indicators, similar to those found in performance funding and budgeting. However, since they have no formal link to allocations, performance reports can have a much longer list of indicators than performance budgeting and especially performance funding. The reports are usually sent to governors, legislators, and campus leaders and increasingly appear on the Web sites of coordinating or system boards and individual institutions.

The number of states using performance funding and performance budgeting increased significantly during the late 1990s. The number peaked in 2000, at a time when state budgets were still robust. In 2000, eighteen states had performance funding and twenty-eight states had performance budgeting. The number of states with these policies dropped as the state fiscal crisis developed. In the 2003 survey, fifteen states indicated that they were using performance funding and twenty-one indicated that they were using performance budgeting. At the same time, the number of states indicating that they had policies of performance reporting increased significantly. Burke and associates attribute the upswing in performance reporting to the reality that this form of accountability is both less costly and less controversial than the other two forms, and to the effect of the national state-by-state report card on higher education, *Measuring Up*. The number of states with performance reporting increased from thirty-nine in 2001 to forty-six in 2003.

The findings of the 2003 Burke survey were that performance reporting—which now covers all but four states—was by far the preferred approach to accountability for higher education. However, bad budgets for both states and higher education continued to erode support for performance funding and performance budgeting. More policy makers in state government and higher education agencies seemed to see performance reporting as a "no cost" alternative to performance funding and budgeting, although some policy makers still viewed performance reporting as an informal form of performance budgeting. *Measuring Up* continued to spur interest in statewide performance reporting, but only a limited number of states were revising their reports to link them with those reports cards. State governments were making only modest—and coordinating and system boards only moderate—use of performance reports in planning and policy making. None of the three programs demonstrated the desired effect of improving performance, but performance funding showed more of an effect than budgeting or reporting.[38]

With the growing focus on increasing educational attainment following President Obama's challenge, the emphasis of public policy is shifting from encouraging access to completion—increasing the states' degree production to achieve globally competitive levels of the American population with an associate's degree and above. Even as states are facing fiscal crises, they are enacting changes in financing policy to provide incentives for increasing productivity, with *productivity* being defined in terms of graduating more students at a lower cost to the students and the public but without diminishing (and, if possible, increasing) quality.[39]

Overall Performance of State Higher Education Systems

Measuring Up, the state-by-state report card on state performance in higher education published every other year by the National Center for Public Policy and Higher Education, assigns grades to states based on their performance compared with the best-performing states.[40] The report card grades each state on the performance of its higher education system as a whole in terms of its effect on the state's population and economy. The report card does not grade institutions, but the grades indirectly reflect each state's combined institutional capacity and the alignment of that capacity with state priorities. The important point is that differences in state performance are related to differences in *state policies* (financing, regulation, accountability, and structure/governance). States are graded on five measures. *Preparation*: How well are students in each state prepared to take advantage of college? *Participation*: Do state residents have sufficient opportunities to enroll in college-level programs? *Affordability*: How affordable is higher education for students and families in each state? *Completion*: Do those who enroll make progress toward and complete their certificates and degrees in a timely manner? *Benefits*: What economic and civic benefits does each state receive from the education of its residents? In future report cards, states will be graded on a sixth measure, *Learning*: What do we know about student learning as a result of education and training beyond high school?

Comparatively little research has been conducted on the relationship between state policy and performance in terms of student outcomes. Richardson and Martinez analyzed the performance of California, New Jersey, New Mexico, New York, and South Dakota on *Measuring Up* in relationship to several policy variables.[41] Their analysis led to a call for new thinking about state policy and performance and the policy levers most likely to have a long-term impact. The National Center for Higher Education Management Systems (NCHEMS) has developed a Web-based resource, the NCHEMS Information Center for Policymaking and Analysis (www.higheredinfo.org), that provides access to nationally available information resources for analyzing state performance. Many states, with the support of private foundations, especially the Lumina Foundation and the Bill and Melinda Gates Foundation, are now embarking on multiyear initiatives to support state reforms to increase student success in postsecondary education and degree completion, toward the long-term goal of reaching globally competitive educational attainment levels. Lessons are likely to emerge from these reform efforts regarding the policy tools—financing incentives, regulatory mandates, governance changes, and the like—that have had the greatest impact on improved institutional and system performances.[42]

Changes in State Structures

Despite the apparent continuity in state structures over time, significant changes have taken place and continue to take place in the form and substance of state coordination and governance.[43] Changes in political leadership (for example, newly elected governors or changes in party control of the state legislature) are often the occasions for restructuring. The forces behind the changes can be grouped in two broad categories: first, "perennial" issues that throughout the past have consistently spurred governors and legislators to make higher education reorganization proposals and, second, broader changes in state expectations and roles.

Perennial issues tend to be long-standing problems that may fester for years but then, especially at points of changes in political leadership or severe economic downturns, trigger debates, lead to special study commissions, and often eventually result in full-scale reorganization. The following are examples of several of the most common issues:

—Access to high-cost graduate and professional programs: In most states, regional economic, political, and cultural differences present serious challenges to state policy makers. These regional stresses are amplified and played out in conflicts within the states' postsecondary education systems. A common scenario begins with pressure from a growing urban area to have accessible graduate and professional programs. Subsequent local campaigns and state lobbying efforts seek to expand

these initiatives from a few courses to full-scale programs, and then the
new campuses lead to opposition from existing universities and other
regions. The same scenario often plays out when isolated rural areas
struggle to gain access to programs for place-bound adults. Local and
regional end runs to the governor or legislature to get special attention
either to advance or block such initiatives usually spark political struggles
that inevitably lead to major restructuring proposals.

—Conflict between the aspirations of two institutions (often under separate
governing boards) in the same geographic area: Again, conflicts tend to
be over which institution should offer high-cost graduate and professional programs. Major reorganization proposals, usually mergers or
consolidations, frequently occur after years of other efforts to achieve
improved cooperation and coordination.

—Political reaction to institutional lobbying: As governors and legislators
face politically difficult and unattractive choices to curtail rather than
expand programs, intense lobbying by narrow, competing institutional
interests can spark demands for restructuring. Political leaders seek to
push such battles away from the immediate political process by increasing
the authority of a state board, with the hope that the board will be able
to resolve the conflicts before they get to the legislature. The reverse
situation also occurs frequently, when a state board will act to curtail an
institutional end run and then face a legislative proposal, frequently
stimulated by the offending institution, to abolish the board. Short-term
victories gained through end running the established coordinating
structures usually lead to greater centralization.

—Frustrations with barriers to student transfer and articulation: Cumulative
evidence that student transfers between institutions are difficult, or
that the number of transfer credits is limited, often leads to proposals
to create a "seamless" system. Before the mid-1990s, most of the
reorganization proposals were limited to postsecondary education (for
example, consolidating institutions under a single governing board),
but an increasing number of states are debating proposals to create
P–16 (primary through postsecondary education) structures.

—Concerns about too many institutions with ill-defined or overlapping
missions: At issue may be small, isolated rural institutions or institutions
with similar missions in close proximity to one another. The governance
debates often emerge from proposals to merge, consolidate, or close

institutions or to make radical changes in institutional missions. The intense lobbying and publicity by persons who oppose the changes often lead to proposals for governance changes. In some cases, the proposals are to abolish the board that proposed the changes. In other cases, just the opposite is proposed—to increase the board's authority out of frustration with its inability to carry out a recommended closure or merger.

—Lack of regional coordination among institutions (for example, community colleges, technical colleges, and branch campuses) offering one- and two-year vocational, technical, occupational, and transfer programs: Many states have regions or communities where two or more public institutions, each responsible to a different state board or agency, are competing to offer similar one- and two-year programs. In the worst situations, this may involve a postsecondary technical institute, a community college, and two-year lower-division university branches competing for an overlapping market in the same region.

—Concerns about the current state board's effectiveness or continuing relevance to state priorities: Reorganizations often result from efforts to change leaders or leadership styles. As illustrated by the brief summary of changes over the past twenty-five years, state leaders tend to see the importance of statewide coordination in times of severe fiscal constraints, but when the economy is strong and these leaders face fewer difficult choices among competing priorities, the relevance of state agencies is less evident. Common triggers for change include a sense that a board, or its staff, is ineffective or lacks the political influence or judgment to address critical issues facing the state, which are often one or more of the other perennial issues. The board or staff may be perceived as unable to resolve problems before they become major political controversies, or they may have handled difficult issues poorly in the past. Another trigger is often a desire to change the leadership style or the underlying philosophy of the state role. This may be a reaction to aggressive, centralized leadership and an effort to shift to a more passive, consultative leadership approach—or the reverse. The change may be to move from a focus on administrative, regulatory, or management issues internal to postsecondary education to a focus on policy leadership relative to a broader public agenda. Finally, state leaders also may propose reorganization not because the structure has problems, but simply to change the leadership or personalities involved in the process.

Other governance changes result from changing state expectations and roles. Even in a period of constrained resources, many state leaders—as well as governmental leaders throughout the world—increasingly recognize that higher education is the key to the future of the quality of life for the state's population and the ability of the state to compete in the global knowledge economy. The disjuncture between higher education and state leaders is not that states don't care, it is that they care about agendas different from those that drive institutional behaviors.[44]

Developing a Public Agenda

The 1990s marked a basic change in the emphasis of state policy: from building and sustaining the capacity of public institutions to linking public institutions to a state strategy to improve the educational attainment of the state's population and the state's economy. The new emphasis was on developing a "public agenda" for higher education. Prominent examples include the Kentucky Postsecondary Reform Act of 1997, linking higher education reforms to a long-term goal of increasing the state's per capita income to the national average or above by 2020,[45] and the Texas Higher Education Coordinating Board's *Closing the Gaps* campaign to improve the state's higher education performance by 2015.[46] An increasing number of governors and state legislatures undertook initiatives to tie higher education reform to efforts to improve elementary and secondary education (P–20: preschool through higher education and lifelong learning), linking research and development to economic development and other efforts to strengthen states' global competitiveness. In the early 2000s, the publication of the national report card on state performance, *Measuring Up*; the creation of a collaborative state higher education project supported by the Pew Charitable Trusts, among others;[47] and national reports from the State Higher Education Executive Officers, the National Conference of State Legislatures, the National Governors Association, and the Education Commission of the States all gave greater impetus to state public agenda reforms.[48]

Rather than emphasizing state support for higher education per se, the new leaders are increasingly advocating a broader public agenda. A *public agenda* defines long-term goals to address a state's major social, economic, and educational challenges and sets forth strategies to link higher education to the achievement of these goals. An example of a long-term goal would be to raise a state's per capita income to the national average or above. Strategies would link higher education to that goal through raising the state's educational attainment, contributing to economic development through research and technology transfer, and creating other educational initiatives. In contrast to the traditional state master plan for higher education, a public agenda focuses not on higher education issues per se, but on issues concerning the status and performance of the state's population and educational system as a whole. These issues are distinctly different from issues that concern institutional leaders: issues about institutional mission and the basic capacity to accomplish that mission (faculty resources, programs, and facilities and other assets). A public agenda also sets forth strategies that cut across higher education sectors, all educational levels, and other public policy domains (such as economic development and health).[49]

The issues raised by the national report card, *Measuring Up*, illustrate the kinds of concerns addressed by a public agenda. The scores on Preparation raise questions about the effectiveness of preschool or kindergarten through high school (P/K–12) reform: standards, assessment, curriculum, and course-taking patterns; secondary school retention and completion; and the alignment of K–12 standards with requirements for college-level work or employment in a twenty-first-century workforce. The scores on Participation raise questions about differences in college-going rates among different groups (for example, race, ethnicity, gender, and income) and the state's regions; about relationships between the adequacy of preparation and affordability; and about the nature of provision (for example, the regional availability of community college services). The scores on Affordability raise questions about the overall relationship of student financing policy (tuition and student aid) to incomes of the state's families and students; and about the interrelationship between tuition policy, student aid policy, and state appropriations for higher education. The scores on Completion raise questions related to the adequacy of preparation and affordability, as well as to incentives and accountability requirements for institutional performance. Initiatives to improve retention and completion and the proportion of a state's population completing a degree require articulation and coordination between education levels and an environment that focuses on student success rather than institutional status. The scores on Benefits raise questions related to state strategies to raise educational attainment, improve the quality of the state's workforce, and improve the civic participation of and quality of life for the state's population. The new emphasis on a public agenda suggests that the case for future state support for higher education will be made in fundamentally different terms than in the past.

Accompanying the changes in state expectations is a subtle yet fundamental shift in the basic assumptions about the role of government in higher education. These changes are summarized as shifts in policy assumptions (table 6.2).

As described by Dennis Jones, the focus of state financing policy is shifting from a traditional emphasis on institutional viability—on *building and maintaining institutional capacity*—to a focus on targeted funding policies to *utilize institutional capacity* to achieve state purposes. Institutional viability remains an important

Table 6.2   Changing assumptions about the role of government in tertiary education

A shift from:	To:
Rational planning for static institutional models	Strategic planning for dynamic market models
A focus on providers, primarily public institutions	A focus on clients: students/learners, employers, and governments
Service areas defined by geographic boundaries of the state and monopolistic markets	Service areas defined by the needs of clients without regard to geographic boundaries
Clients served by single providers (e.g., a public university)	Clients served by multiple providers (e.g., students enrolling simultaneously with two or more institutions)
A tendency toward centralized control and regulation through tightly defined institutional missions, financial accountability, and retrospective reporting	More decentralized governance and management using policy tools to stimulate a desired response (e.g., incentives, performance funding, consumer information)
Policies and regulation to limit competition and unnecessary duplication	Policies to "enter the market on behalf of the public" and to channel competitive forces toward public purposes
Quality defined primarily in terms of resources (inputs such as faculty credentials or library resources) as established within tertiary education	Quality defined in terms of outcomes, performance, and competence, which are defined by multiple clients (students/learners, employers, governments)
Policies and services developed and carried out primarily through public agencies and public institutions	Increased use of nongovernmental organizations and mixed public/private providers to meet public/client needs (e.g., developing curricula and learning modules, providing student services, assessing competencies, providing quality assurance)

Source: Aims C. McGuinness, Jr., *A Conceptual and Analytic Framework for Review of National Regulatory Policies and Practices in Higher Education*, prepared for the Education Committee, OECD, Feb., EDU/EC (2006) 3 (Paris: Organisation for Economic Co-operation and Development, 2006).

state funding priority—not as an end in itself, but as a means for maintaining the capacity to address state priorities.[50] State financing policies have traditionally emphasized primarily creating and maintaining institutional capacity. The principal approaches to budgeting and resource allocation have been either "base-plus" funding (taking the previous year's funding and adjusting it for increased costs and other variables) or formulas based on a combination of costs and a measure of workload, such as enrollment or credit hours. Policies regarding student financing have traditionally focused on establishing tuition and student aid policies designed to maximize institutional revenues. The changes in expectations and state roles have far-reaching implications for state leadership or governance structures. Structures and policies established when states were primarily "owner-operators" and were the principal revenue sources for public institutions are no longer appropriate. The alternatives are likely to be found not in the traditional modes of governance, but in new structures for policy leadership and the alignment of finance and other policies with a clearly defined public agenda.[51]

Reality of Change in the States

Despite the need for new approaches to state policy leadership, the reality of change varies dramatically across the states.[52] In the 1990s, several states led the nation in implementing new approaches not only to state leadership, but also to related policies of finance and accountability. These included changes within their existing structures as well as major restructuring initiated by the governor or state legislature. In most states, however, the trends were far less certain. State decision-making structures were seemingly unable to make the transition to new missions and modes of operation. Governors focused on short-term agendas or immediate budget crises. Legislatures increasingly were unable to sustain attention to long-term-change agendas because of legislative turnover, short-term agendas, intensified pressures from interest groups, and a lack of core staff capability focused on the "public interest" perspective of higher education. There is no venue within most legislative processes to link a strategic agenda with strategic financing policy.[53]

State-level governing boards (consolidated systems as well as multicampus universities) continued to focus primarily on *internal* institutional concerns. They often functioned as vertically organized, closed systems that were designed to protect the institutions from competition for students and for resources from other providers, and that continued to emphasize one-size-fits-all policies that ran counter to strategies to address the unique needs of each state's regions. Their effectiveness was increasingly challenged by weaknesses in the quality of board and system leadership.

State coordinating boards remained mired in regulatory practices shaped by the statutory mandates of the 1970s and 1980s. They continued to focus primarily on *coordinating public institutions* and not on leading a public agenda. They were increasingly politicized through appointments of both board members and staff, and they were experiencing an accelerating turnover of senior staff leadership. These agencies had significant deficits in terms of core information and analytic capabilities (especially those necessary for leading a public agenda as summarized above).

State structures and politics continued to create barriers to collaboration between and among sectors to address common, crosscutting issues (for example, "picket-fence" relationships among the three California segments that resulted in competing, uncoordinated services within each of the state's regions). Many higher education and other state policies were *not* aligned with a public agenda—in fact, they were not aligned with any long-term agenda. The structures resulted in splintered decision making organized around specific programs or sectors. Financing policy was characterized by short-term agendas and was driven by the most immediate fiscal crisis. States continued to make decisions separately on the interrelated areas of state appropriations, student aid, and tuition policy. Financing policies provided few incentives for performance and collaboration. State regulatory policies in areas such as human resources, purchasing, and capital financing were often mired in state bureaucratic processes; did little to achieve efficiencies; and often hindered the capacity of the higher education system to respond to public priorities.

In summary, despite growing concerns about the public or societal purposes of higher education and the need for new approaches to policy leadership and related policies, the reality is that few states have the capacity to pursue a long-term agenda focused on public purposes.[54] In blunt terms, there is "no one at home" when it comes to the responsibility to articulate and defend basic public purposes. State leaders are preoccupied with fiscal crises and short-term political agendas. Higher education leaders appear far more concerned about the future of their own institutions in turbulent fiscal and competitive times than about the need for policy leadership structures and policies essential to ensure that higher education responds to public priorities.[55]

Conclusion

Sustaining attention toward the public and societal purposes of higher educ.
in the turbulent times of the next decade and beyond will require fundament.
improvements in state-level capacity to lead change in the public interest. As
summarized above, few states now can meet the fundamental prerequisites for
that leadership. Many of the state structures formed for other purposes in an earlier time cannot be expected to make the transition to new missions and modes of
leadership. New thinking is needed about the ways states can shape decision-
making structures and policies designed explicitly for new missions and functions. Crafting new alternatives must be a shared responsibility of both higher education and state leaders.

NOTES

1. Robert Berdahl makes an important distinction between "substantive" autonomy, meaning autonomy on matters of standards, curriculum, faculty appointments,
and similar matters, and "procedural" autonomy, meaning autonomy from state procedural controls. See Robert O. Berdahl, *Statewide Coordination of Higher Education*
(Washington, DC: American Council on Education, 1971).
2. National Center for Education Statistics [NCES], *Digest of Education Statistics*,
http://nces.ed.gov/programs/digest/.
3. Ibid.
4. Frank Newman, *Choosing Quality* (Denver: Education Commission of the
States, 1987), xiii.
5. Berdahl, *Statewide Coordination*, 9.
6. National Association of State Scholarship and Grant Programs [NASSGAP], *39th
Annual Survey Report for the 2007–2008 Academic Year*, 2009, www.nassgap.org.
7. Education Commission of the States, *Preservation of Excellence in American
Higher Education* (Denver: Education Commission of the States, 1990).
8. Clark Kerr, "The States and Higher Education: Changes Ahead," *State Government* 58, no. 2 (1985): 45–50.
9. Newman, *Choosing Quality*; Robert O. Berdahl and Barbara A. Holland, eds.,
*Developing State Fiscal Incentives to Improve Higher Education: Proceedings from a Na-
tional Invitational Conference, Denver, Colorado, Nov. 9–11, 1989* (College Park, MD:
National Center for Postsecondary Governance and Finance, 1990); Peter T. Ewell
and Dennis P. Jones, *Assessing and Reporting Student Progress: A Response to the "New
Accountability"* (Denver: State Higher Education Executive Officers, 1991); James R.
Mingle, *State Policy and Productivity in Higher Education* (Denver: State Higher Education Executive Officers, 1992).

10. U.S. Department of Education, *A Test of Leadership: Charting the Future of U.S. Higher Education* (a.k.a. the Spellings Commission) (Washington, DC: U.S. Department of Education, 2006).

11. Paul N. Courant, James J. Duderstadt, and Edie N. Goldenberg, "Needed: A National Strategy to Preserve Public Research Universities," *Chronicle of Higher Education*, Jan. 3, 2010.

12. For more detail on state structures, see Education Commission of the States, *State Postsecondary Education Governance Database*, www.ecs.org/html/educationIssues/Governance/GovPSDB_intro.asp.

13. Eugene C. Lee and Frank M. Bowen, *The Multicampus University* (New York: McGraw-Hill, 1971); Aims C. McGuinness, Jr., *Perspectives on the Current Status and Emerging Policy Issues for Public Multi-Campus Higher Education Systems*, AGB Occasional Paper No. 3 (Washington, DC: Association of Governing Boards of Universities and Colleges, 1991); Marian L. Gade, *Four Multicampus Systems: Some Policies and Practices that Work* (Washington, DC: Association of Governing Boards of Universities and Colleges, 1993); Gerald H. Gaither, ed., *The Multicampus System: Perspectives and Prospects* (Sterling, VA: Stylus, 1999); E. K. Fretwell, Jr., *More than Management: Guidelines for System Governing Boards and Their Chief Executives* (Washington, DC: Association of Governing Boards of Universities and Colleges, 2000).

14. Clark Kerr and Marian L. Gade, *The Guardians: Boards of Trustees of American Colleges and Universities: What They Do and How Well They Do It* (Washington, DC: Association of Governing Boards of Universities and Colleges, 1989).

15. Aims C. McGuinness, Jr., *A Conceptual and Analytic Framework for Review of National Regulatory Policies and Practices in Higher Education*, prepared for the Education Committee, OECD, Feb., EDU/EC (2006) 3 (Paris: Organisation for Economic Co-operation and Development, 2006).

16. Robert O. Berdahl, "Balancing Self-Interest and Accountability: St. Mary's College of Maryland," in *Seeking Excellence through Independence*, ed. Terrence J. MacTaggart (San Francisco: Jossey-Bass, 1998), 59–84.

17. Western Interstate Commission for Higher Education [WICHE], *An Evaluation of Colorado's College Opportunity Fund and Related Policies: A Report for the Colorado Department of Higher Education* (Boulder, CO: Western Interstate Commission for Higher Education, 2009).

18. James R. Mingle, ed., *Management Flexibility and State Regulation in Higher Education* (Atlanta: Southern Regional Education Board, 1983).

19. James R. Mingle and Rhonda Martin Epper, "State Coordination and Planning in an Age of Entrepreneurship," in *Planning and Management for a Changing Environment*, ed. Marvin W. Peterson, David D. Dill, and Lisa A. Mets (San Francisco: Jossey-Bass, 1997), 45–65; MacTaggart, *Seeking Excellence through Independence*.

20. Aims C. McGuinness, Jr., *Restructuring State Roles in Higher Education: A Case Study of the 1994 New Jersey Higher Education Restructuring Act* (Denver: Education Commission of the States, 1995).

21. Katherine C. Lyle and Kathleen R. Sell, *The True Genius of America at Risk: Are We Losing Our Public Universities by De Facto Privatization?* (Westport, CT: American Council on Education / Praeger Series on Higher Education, 2006); Michael K. McLendon, "Setting the Governmental Agenda for State Decentralization of Higher Education," *Journal of Higher Education* 74, no. 5 (2003): 479–516.

22. Lara K. Couturier, *Checks and Balances at Work: The Restructuring of Virginia's Public Higher Education System*, June (San Jose, CA: National Center for Public Policy and Higher Education, 2006), www.highereducation.org/reports/checks_balances/.

23. WICHE, *Evaluation of Colorado's College Opportunity Fund.*

24. Michael K. McLendon, Donald E. Heller, and Steven P. Young. "State Postsecondary Education Policy Innovation: Politics, Competition, and the Interstate Migration of Policy Ideas," *Journal of Higher Education* 76, no. 4 (July/Aug. 2005): 343–400.

25. Daniel J. Elazar, *American Federalism: A View from the States* (New York: Thomas Y. Crowell, 1966).

26. For the latest information on state financing differences and trends, see State Higher Education Executive Officers [SHEEO], *State Higher Education Finance FY 2009* (Boulder, CO: State Higher Education Executive Officers, 2010).

27. NASSGAP, *39th Annual Survey Report.*

28. National Center for Public Policy and Higher Education [NCPPHE], *Measuring Up 2008* (San Jose, CA: National Center for Public Policy and Higher Education, 2008), http://measuringup2008.highereducation.org.

29. NASSGAP, *39th Annual Survey Report.*

30. Dennis P. Jones, *Financing in Sync* (Boulder, CO: Western Interstate Commission for Higher Education, 2003).

31. SHEEO, *Higher Education Finance FY 2009.*

32. William R. Doyle, "Adoption of Merit-Based Student Grant Programs: An Event History Analysis," *Educational Evaluation and Policy Analysis* 28, no. 3 (2006): 259–85.

33. Jones, *Financing in Sync*; Patrick M. Callan and Joni E. Finney, eds., *Public Policy and Private Financing of Higher Education: Shaping Public Policy in the Future* (Phoenix: Oryx Press, 1997); NCPPHE, *The Challenge to States: Preserving College Access and Affordability in a Time of Change* (San Jose, CA: National Center for Public Policy and Higher Education, Mar. 2009, www.highereducation.org.

34. Lyle and Sell, *True Genius of America.*

35. Dennis P. Jones, "State Shortfalls Projected to Continue Despite Economic Gains: Long-Term Prospects for Higher Education No Better," *Policy Alert*, Feb. (San Jose, CA: National Center for Public Policy and Higher Education, 2006), www.higher education.org; Donald J. Boyd, "What Will Happen to State Budgets when the Money Runs Out?" *Fiscal Features*, Feb. 19 (Albany, NY: Nelson A. Rockefeller Institute of Government, 2009), www.rockinst.org.

36. These initial surveys ranged from Joseph C Burke and Andreea M Serban, *Performance Funding of Public Higher Education: Results Should Count* (Albany, NY:

Nelson A. Rockefeller Institute of Government, 1997) through Joseph C. Burke and Associates, *Funding Public Colleges and Universities for Performance: Popularity, Problems, and Prospects* (Albany, NY: Rockefeller Institute Press, 2002).

37. Joseph C. Burke and Henrik P. Minassians, *Performance Reporting: "Real" Accountability or Accountability "Lite"; Seventh Annual Survey* (Albany, NY: Nelson A. Rockefeller Institute of Government, 2003).

38. Ibid.

39. Patrick M. Callan, Peter T. Ewell, and Dennis P. Jones, *Good Policy, Good Practice: Improving Productivity in Higher Education; A Guide for Policymakers* (Boulder, CO: National Center for Higher Education Management Systems, 2007).

40. NCPPHE, *Measuring Up 2008.*

41. Richard C. Richardson, Jr., and Mario Martinez, *Policy and Performance in American Higher Education* (Baltimore: Johns Hopkins University Press, 2009).

42. Callan, Ewell, and Jones, *Good Policy, Good Practice.*

43. Malcolm C. Moos and Francis E. Rourke, *The Campus and the State* (Baltimore: Johns Hopkins University Press, 1959); Lyman A. Glenny, *Autonomy of Public Colleges* (New York: McGraw-Hill, 1959); Carnegie Commission on Higher Education, *The Capitol and the Campus: State Responsibility for Postsecondary Education* (New York: McGraw-Hill, 1971); Lyman A. Glenny, Robert O. Berdahl, Ernest G. Palola, and James G. Paltridge, *Coordinating Higher Education for the '70s* (Berkeley: University of California, Center for Research and Development in Higher Education, 1971); Education Commission of the States, *Challenge: Coordination and Governance in the 1980s* (Denver: Education Commission of the States, 1980); John D. Millet, *Conflict in Higher Education: State Government versus Institutional Independence* (San Francisco: Jossey-Bass, 1982); Mingle and Epper, "State Coordination and Planning"; Richard C. Richardson, Jr., Kathy Reeves Bracco, Patrick M. Callan, and Joni E. Finney, *Designing State Higher Education Systems for a New Century* (Phoenix: Oryx Press, 1999); Paul E. Lingenfelter, *State Policy for Higher Education: The 21st Century Challenge* (Boulder, CO: State Higher Education Executive Officers, 2003); Aims C. McGuinness, Jr., "State Policy Leadership in the Public Interest: Is Anyone at Home?" in *Trends in Strengthening State Policy Leadership for Higher Education in the Nation and Western States*, WICHE Reports on Higher Education in the West (Boulder, CO: Western Interstate Commission on Higher Education, forthcoming).

44. MacTaggart, *Restructuring Higher Education*; Michael K. McLendon, "State Governance Reform of Higher Education: Patterns, Trends, and Theories of the Public Policy Process," in *Higher Education: Handbook of Theory and Research*, vols. 1–, ed. John C. Smart (London: Kluwer, 2003), vol. 18, 57–143; David W. Leslie and Richard J. Novak, "Substance vs. Politics: Through the Dark Mirror of Governance Reform," *Educational Policy* 17, no. 1 (2003): 98–120; McGuinness, "State Policy Leadership."

45. Kentucky Council on Postsecondary Education, *Five Questions—One Mission: Better Lives for Kentucky's People; A Public Agenda for Postsecondary and Adult Education, 2005–2010* (Frankfort, KY: Kentucky Council on Postsecondary Education, 2005), http://cpe.ky.gov/planning/strategic/; Aims C. McGuinness, Jr., "Globally Competitive,

Locally Engaged: The Case Study of Kentucky," *Higher Education Management and Policy* 20, no. 2 (2008): 74–89.

46. Texas Higher Education Coordinating Board, *Closing the Gaps: The Texas Higher Education Plan* (Austin: Texas Higher Education Coordinating Board, 1999).

47. Gordon K. Davies, *Setting A Public Agenda for Higher Education in the States: Lessons Learned from the National Collaborative for Higher Education*, Dec. (San Jose, CA: National Center for Public Policy and Higher Education, 2006), http://higher education.org/reports/public_agenda/.

48. State Higher Education Executive Officers, *Accountability for Better Results: A National Imperative for Higher Education*, Report of the National Commission on Accountability in Higher Education (Boulder, CO: State Higher Education Executive Officers, 2005); National Conference of State Legislatures, *Transforming Higher Education: National Imperative—State Responsibility* (Denver: National Conference of State Legislatures, 2006); National Governors Association, *A Compact for Postsecondary Education* (Washington, DC: National Governors Association, 2006).

49. Davies, *Setting A Public Agenda*.

50. Jones, *Financing in Sync*.

51. NCPPHE, "State Capacity for Higher Education Policy," *National Crosstalk* 13, no. 3 (Special Supplement, July 2005): 1A–4A.

52. McGuinness, "State Policy Leadership."

53. Leslie and Novak, "Substance vs. Politics"; McLendon, "State Governance Reform"; Michael K. McLendon, Russ Deaton, and James C. Hearn, "The Enactment of Reforms in State Governance of Higher Education: Testing the Political Instability Hypothesis," *Journal of Higher Education* 78, no. 6 (Nov./Dec. 2007): 645–75.

54. NCPPHE, "State Capacity."

55. McGuinness, "State Policy Leadership."

CHAPTER SEVEN

The Legal Environment

The Implementation of Legal Change on Campus

Michael A. Olivas and Benjamin Baez

In modern higher education, few major decisions are made without considering the legal consequences, and though the core functions of higher education—instruction and scholarship—are remarkably free from external legal influences, no one would plausibly deny the increase of legalization on campus. We know surprisingly little about the law's effect on higher education, but virtually no one in the enterprise is untouched by statutes, regulations, case law, or institutional rules promulgated to implement legal regimes.

Lewis Thomas, perhaps our most thoughtful commentator on medicine and science in society, ascribes organic qualities to the university, and his view of a college as a "community of scholars" is grounded in an appreciation of the history of education. Paul Goodman and John Millett also exemplify this perspective. Like a prism refracting light differently depending on how you hold it up for viewing, higher education can appear differently. For Herbert Stroup and many other sociologists, colleges are essentially bureaucracies, and no student confronting course registration today is likely to be dissuaded from this view. To Victor Baldridge, universities are indisputably political organizations, as they also appear to Clark Kerr and Burton Clark. To critics, higher education is stratified by class

(Randall Collins), resistant to legal change (Harry Edwards), and in need of fundamental restructuring (Paolo Freire).[1] As many observers would insist, all are equally close to the truth or truths, depending on which truth is being refracted. The cases in this chapter reveal many truths and, often frustratingly, few answers. As the following cases demonstrate, legal considerations can pare governance issues down to the essential question, what is a college?

Legal Governance

Despite the seeming obviousness of the question posed above, a variety of cases probe the fundamental definitional issue. In *Coffee v. Rice University*, the issues were whether the 1891 trust charter founding Rice University (then Rice Institute), which restricted admissions to "white inhabitants" and required that no tuition be charged, could be maintained in 1966.[2] The court held that an "institute" was a postsecondary institution by any other name, and its postcompulsory, collegiate nature rendered it a college. On the issue of whether the trust could be maintained with its racial restrictions and tuition prohibition, the court applied the doctrine of *cy pres*, which allowed the trustees to reformulate the provisions and admit minorities and charge tuition, for to continue the practices would have been impracticable; if the trust provisions can no longer be realistically carried out, a court can reconstitute the trust to make it conform to the changed circumstances.

A court is not always so disposed as the *Coffee* court was. In *Shapiro v. Columbia Union National Bank and Trust Co.*, the court allowed a trust reserved only for male students to remain male only, refusing to apply *cy pres*.[3] An interesting case is *U.S. on Behalf of U.S. Coast Guard v. Cerio*, in which a judge allowed the Coast Guard Academy to reformulate a major student prize when the endowment's interest had grown to more than $100,000.[4] The judge began, "This is essentially a case of looking a gift horse in the mouth and finding it too good to accept as is," and allowed the academy to use some of the prize interest for other support services.

Sometimes a zoning ordinance raises the issue of what constitutes a college. In *Fountain Gate Ministries v. City of Plano*, a city wished to keep colleges from locating in residentially zoned housing areas.[5] The church argued that its activities were those of a church rather than those of a college. However, the court took notice of the educational instruction, faculty, degree activities, and other collegelike activities and determined that these constituted a college, protestations to the contrary notwithstanding. In the opposite direction, a court held that a consultant firm's use of the term "Quality College" to describe its activities did not make it a college or subject it to state regulation. In wry fashion, the court noted that to make use of the word *college* in an organization's title would make a college bookstore or the Catholic College of Cardinals into institutions!

Sometimes the definition drives a divorce decree. In *Hacker v. Hacker*, a father who had agreed to pay for his daughter's college tuition did so while she was a theater major at the University of California but refused to do so when she moved to Manhattan and enrolled in The Neighborhood Playhouse (TNP), a renowned acting school; that it was not degree granting persuaded the judge that TNP failed to meet the definition of a college.[6] Occasionally, the definition turns on accreditation language (*Beth Rochel Seminary v. Bennett*), while at other times it turns on taxation issues (*City of Morgantown v. West Virginia Board of Regents*).[7]

Due to the different constitutional considerations between public and private colleges, such as free speech and due process not applying to private colleges, it is important to distinguish between the two forms in order to understand the full panoply of rights and duties owed to institutional community members. Consider the public-private distinction as a continuum, with *Trustees of Dartmouth College v. Woodward* at the purely private end and *Krynicky v. University of Pittsburgh* at the other end, that of purely public colleges.[8] In *Dartmouth*, the first higher education case considered by the U.S. Supreme Court, the State of New Hampshire had attempted to rescind the private charter of Dartmouth College, which was incorporated in the state nearly fifty years earlier, and make it a public college with legislatively appointed trustees to replace the college's private trustees. The Supreme Court held that the college, once chartered, was private and not subject to the legislature's actions, unless the trustees wished to reconstitute themselves as a public institution. At the other end of the spectrum, *Krynicky* held that Temple University and the University of Pittsburgh were public colleges, due to the amount of money given to them by the state, the reconstitution of the board to include publicly appointed trustees (including ex officio elected officials), state reporting requirements, and other characteristics that injected state actions into the act of reconstituting these universities into the state system of higher education.

Complex issues arise in public institutions, such as the reach of sovereign immunity. A state's sovereign immunity is often referred to as its "Eleventh Amendment immunity," although this nomenclature is somewhat of a misnomer. The Eleventh Amendment provides that "the Judicial power of the United States shall not be construed to extend to any suit in law or equity, commenced or prosecuted against one of the United States by Citizens of another State, or by Citizens or

Subjects of any Foreign State." While the Eleventh Amendment grants a state immunity from suit in federal court by its citizens and citizens of other states, sovereign immunity is much more.

When the United States was formed, the Constitution created a system of government consisting of two sovereigns—one national and one state. Although the states did concede some of their sovereign powers to the national government, they did retain substantial sovereign powers under the constitutional scheme. On this relationship, the U.S. Supreme Court has observed: "The sovereign immunity of the States neither derives from, nor is limited by, the terms of the Eleventh Amendment. Rather, as the Constitution's structure, its history, and the authoritative interpretations by this Court make clear, the States' immunity from suit is a fundamental aspect of the sovereignty which the States enjoyed before the ratification of the Constitution, and which they retain today . . . except as altered by the plan of the Convention or certain constitutional Amendments." Although a state's sovereign immunity is significant, it is not absolute.[9]

Of course, if there are pure archetypes such as Dartmouth and the University of Pittsburgh, there must be intermediate forms, such as Alfred University, where several students were arrested, the court holding in *Powe v. Miles* that regular students were entitled to no elaborate due process, as the institution was private.[10] However, the ceramics engineering students were entitled to hearings before dismissal, as the Ceramics College in which they were enrolled was a state-supported entity; the State of New York contracted with the private college to provide this program rather than establish such a program in a state school. Other hybrid examples of a state-contracted unit within a private school include Cornell University's agricultural sciences program and Baylor's College of Medicine, both of which operate as if they were state institutions.

Other important foundational issues have also resulted in litigation, which has created a complex definitional process. For example, in *Cahn and Cahn v. Antioch University*, trustees of the institution were sued by codeans of the law school to determine who had authority for governance decisions; the court ruled that trustees have the ultimate authority and fiduciary duty.[11] In contrast to *Dartmouth*, where there was a "hostile takeover" of the institution by the state, private trustees can close a college or surrender its assets, such as its accreditation (*Fenn College v. Nance* and *Nasson College v. New England Association of Schools and Colleges*).[12] Another important issue involving the definition and legal governance of colleges turns on the consortial or collective behavior of institutions: does their mutual recognition in athletics accreditation and information sharing subject them to state action? In *NCAA v. University of Oklahoma*, the U.S. Supreme Court held that the NCAA was a "classic cartel" engaged in restraint of trade by its negotiated television contract; another court held that the activities of the Overlap Group—a group of elite institutions that share information on financial aid offers with other colleges admitting the same students, so as to "coordinate" the awards— similarly violated antitrust law (*U.S. v. Brown University*).[13] However, in accreditation activities, mutual-recognition agreements have been allowed by courts as not constituting a restraint of trade, as in *Marjorie Webster Junior College v. Middle States Association* and *Beth Rochel Seminary v. Bennett*, in which an institution that was not yet accredited failed to negotiate the complex exceptions to the accreditation requirement for financial aid eligibility.[14]

In sum, despite the seeming simplicity of legally defining a college, it is not always easy. Cases were cited on which entities not labeled colleges were found to be colleges, while some that resembled colleges were held not to be, including a commercial program ("Quality College") that was held not to be an institution of higher education. For some technical, eligibility-driven issues—such as child support or taxation—the definition was extremely important. The bottom line appears, from these cases, to be that a college is an entity with instructional programs and degree-granting authority. In addition, the definitional issue is raised in the context of who is responsible for governance of the institution. The answer is ultimately the trustees, although the *Yeshiva* case, discussed in the following section, appears to hold the opposite.[15] With this foundational layer in place, we turn to the two major campus actors: faculty and students.

Faculty and the Law

Although there have not been many studies of patterns in postsecondary law, the few that have been undertaken show that faculty bring many of the suits in higher education. A 1987 study of Iowa case law shows that litigation against colleges brought by students totaled 11 percent, while faculty brought 31 percent; a 1988 study of Texas litigation shows that faculty brought 35 percent of all college cases in that state.[16] These numbers are surprising for two reasons. First, higher education has traditionally been a "gentlemen's club," to use William Kaplin's apt term.[17] This meant that if faculty members did not receive tenure, or were forced to move for another reason, they would simply find another position or fall upon their sword. To do otherwise would brand them as troublemakers or contentious colleagues. Second, there were no civil rights laws or widespread collective bargaining until the 1960s and 1970s, so faculty had fewer opportunities to bring suit or engage in collective protection, such as that afforded by security provisions in collective bargaining agreements.

Tenure

The two leading U.S. Supreme Court tenure cases were decided on the same day in 1972, and both *Perry v. Sinderman* and *Board of Regents v. Roth* turn on what process is due to faculty, should institutions wish to remove them.[18] In *Perry*, a community college instructor who had been a thorn in the side of college administrators was fired for "insubordination," without a hearing or official reasons. The college had no tenure policy, except one that said, "the Administration of the College wishes the faculty member to feel that he has permanent tenure as long as his teaching services are satisfactory and as long as he displays a cooperative attitude toward his coworkers and his supervisors, and as long as he is happy in his work." The court held that the instructor thus had a property interest in his continued employment and ordered the lower court to determine whether he had been fired for his protected speech or for cause. In short, the administrators were required to give him notice of the reasons for his firing and an opportunity to explain his side of the matter. This is what tenure grants: a presumption of continued employment, absent certain circumstances (financial exigency, etc.). In *Roth*, the Court held that an untenured professor had no constitutional right to continued employment beyond the contractual period for which he was hired.

These two cases, together with several others fleshing out the terms of faculty employment, delineate the contours of tenure. For example, in *Wellner v. Minnesota State Junior College Board*, an untenured teacher was removed from his position for allegedly making racist remarks; he was sanctioned without a hearing or an opportunity to explain his behavior.[19] The appeals court ordered that he be accorded a hearing, as his liberty interest had been infringed. That is, his record was stigmatized and his reputation was at stake, so the court ordered a hearing to allow him to clear his name.

In addition to contract and liberty interests, faculty may also have property interests, as in *State ex rel. McLendon v. Morton*, in which the court held that Professor McLendon had a property interest in being considered for tenure, since she ostensibly qualified by being in rank the requisite period of time.[20] Although many cases, including *Roth*, have held that no reasons need be given for denying tenure, McLendon had, on the surface, appeared to earn tenure by default, and a hearing was required to show why she was not entitled to tenure. These cases are very grounded in fact and case specific, due to individual institutional policies and each state's contract or employment law.

A surprising number of cases deal with the ambiguities of tenure rights, as in whether or not the guidelines of the American Association of University Professors (AAUP) apply (*Hill v. Talladega College*); exactly when the tenure clock applies (*Honore v. Douglas*); if financial reasons apply once a candidate has been evaluated in the tenure review process (*Spuler v. Pickar*); whether institutional error can be sufficient grounds for overturning a tenure denial (*Lewis v. Loyola University of Chicago*); and whether tenure is really only just a fixed-term contract (*Otero-Burgos v. Inter-American University*).[21]

As for discrimination in the tenure process, hundreds of cases have been reported, most of which defer to institutional judgments about the candidates. Most find that the plaintiff, whether a person of color or an Anglo woman, did not prove that the institution acted in an unfair or discriminatory fashion. In *Scott v. University of Delaware*, the court held that "while some of this evidence is indicative of racial prejudice on the University campus, it does not suggest to me that Scott was a victim of racial discrimination by the University in its renewal process, or that he was treated differently than non-black faculty by the University."[22] That this is so is particularly due to the extraordinary deference accorded academic judgments, as in *Faro v. NYU*: "Of all fields, which the federal courts should hesitate to invade and take over, education and faculty appointments at a University level are probably the least suited for federal court supervision."[23]

Even so, occasionally an institution goes too far, as the Claremont Graduate School (CGS) did in the 1992 case of *Clark v. Claremont Graduate School*.[24] In this case, a black professor chanced upon the meeting in which his tenure consideration was being reviewed. From the room, whose door was apparently left ajar, he overheard the committee making racist remarks, such as "us white folks have rights, too" and "I couldn't work on a permanent basis with a black man." When the court and jury reviewed his entire record, compared it with others who had recently been considered for (and received) tenure, and noted that no other minority professor had ever received tenure at CGS, it was determined that Professor Clark had been discriminated against due to his race, and he was awarded $1 million in compensatory damages as well as punitive damages and lawyers' fees.

Women have won several cases in which it was held that they were treated discriminatorily, as in *Sweeney v. Board of Trustees of Keene State College*, *Kunda v. Muhlenberg College*, *Mecklenberg v. Montana State Board of Regents*, and *Kemp v. Ervin*, among others, in which courts or juries found for women faculty plaintiffs.[25] Professor Jan Kemp particularly prevailed, winning six years on the tenure clock and more than $2.5 million in compensatory and punitive damages from the University of Georgia. She left the university without being awarded tenure.

Recent developments in employment law have made it more difficult for faculty to prevail in state and federal courts, particularly by extending cases outside higher education to the college enterprise. Thus *Hazelwood School District v. Kuhlmeier*, a U.S. Supreme Court decision about the right of school boards to control editorial content in a public K–12 school setting, has been cited in college faculty cases such as *Bishop v. Aranov* and *Scallet v. Rosenblum*, while *Waters v. Churchill*, a public hospital case that held that public employees whose speech was "disruptive" could be removed for cause, was cited in *Jeffries v. Harleston*.[26] Professor Leonard Jeffries, removed from his departmental chair position for his offensive and anti-Semitic speech, had won at trial and upon appeal, but the Supreme Court remanded and ordered the appeals court to review his case in light of *Waters*. After this review, the appeals court overturned and vacated its earlier opinion.

Collective Bargaining

Since the first college faculties were unionized in the 1960s and 1970s, collective bargaining has become widespread in higher education. Union data indicate that 830 of the 3,284 institutions in the United States (25%) were covered by faculty collective bargaining agreements; figures for nonfaculty college employees were even higher.[27] By 1984, nearly 200,000 faculty (27% of all faculty) were unionized, 83 percent of them in public colleges and 17 percent in private institutions. Unionized public senior colleges totaled 220, private four-year colleges 69, public two-year colleges 524, and private two-year colleges 13. In the last two decades, there were 138 full-time college faculty strikes (or work stoppages), averaging almost 15 days; the longest, 150 days, was at St. John's University in 1966.

Collective bargaining is governed by federal and state laws, although several states also authorize local boards of junior colleges (hence, local laws) to govern labor. Twenty-six states and the District of Columbia have such authorizing legislation. While state or local laws, if they exist, govern the respective state or local institutions, the National Labor Relations Act (NLRA) governs faculty collective bargaining in private institutions. In 1951, the National Labor Relations Board (NLRB) decided that colleges would not fall under NLRB jurisdiction if their mission was "noncommercial in nature and intimately connected with charitable purposes and education activities."[28] This refusal to assert jurisdiction remained in force until 1970, when the NLRB reversed itself.[29] After reviewing labor law trends in the twenty years that had passed, the NLRB noted, "We are convinced that assertion of jurisdiction is required over those private colleges and universities whose operations have a substantial effect on commerce to insure the orderly, effective, and uniform application of the national labor policy." The board set a $1 million gross revenue test for its standard, a figure that would today cover even the very smallest colleges.

The NLRB decision to extend collective bargaining privileges to Yeshiva University faculty, however, was overruled by the U.S. Supreme Court, which held that faculty were, in effect, supervisory personnel and therefore not covered by the NLRA. This important decision, of course, reversed a decade of organizing activity and struck a heavy blow to faculty unionizing efforts. Since the decision not to entitle Yeshiva faculty to organize collectively, nearly a hundred private colleges have sought to decertify existing faculty unions or have refused to bargain with faculty on *Yeshiva* grounds. Dozens of faculty unions have been decertified, and an untold number of organizing efforts have been thwarted because of the decision or because of the absence of state enabling legislation.

The decision, which affected only private colleges, has recently been applied to public institutions, such as the University of Pittsburgh. The State of Pennsylvania has a labor law (Public Employment Relations Act, or PERA) that was construed by a Pennsylvania Labor Relations Board hearing examiner to exclude faculty: "As the faculty of the University of Pittsburgh participate with regularity in the essential process which results in a policy proposal and the decision to [hold a union election] and have a responsible role in giving practical effect to insuring the actual fulfillment of policy by concrete measures, the faculty of the university are management level employees within the meaning of PERA and thereby are excluded from PERA's coverage."[30]

In some instances, a court has found that *Yeshiva* criteria were not met and that the faculty did not govern the institution, as in *NLRB v. Cooper Union* and *NLRB v. Florida Memorial College.*[31] Scholars and courts will continue to sort out the consequences of *Yeshiva* and its successors, and unless legislation is enacted at the federal level (to amend the NLRA, for instance) or in the states (to repeal "right to work" legislation), this issue will remain a major bone of contention between faculty and their institutions, both public and private. In addition, in the late 1990s, graduate student employees, adjunct faculty, and academic staff have successfully negotiated labor contracts, although these remain a small part of the landscape.

Students and the Law

There are many ways to approach the topic of students and the law, but the most interesting and historically based approach is to track the changes in the common law definition of the legal relationship between colleges and college students. This history, which resembles that of faculty and the colleges, began with few rights but now includes many protections. Private institutions afford students fewer rights than public institutions do, and constitutional rights extend only to students in public institutions. Moreover, there is no evidence of statutory development comparable to Title VII or the Equal Pay Act. Although since *Bakke v. Regents of University of California*,[32] students have used Title VI to gain legal standing and student athletes, especially women, have utilized Title IX to litigate for parity in intercollegiate athletic programs, the status of students is largely the province of constitutional protections.

The traditional status of students relative to their colleges was that of child to parent or ward to trustee: *in loco parentis*, literally, "in the place of the parent." This plenary power gave colleges virtually unfettered authority over students' lives and affairs. Thus the hapless Miss Anthony of *Anthony v. Syracuse University* could be expelled from school for the simple offense of "not being a typical Syracuse girl," which, the record reveals, meant that she could be expelled from school for smoking a cigarette and sitting on a man's lap. An earlier case, *Gott v. Berea College*, held that colleges could regulate off-campus behavior, while more recent cases up until the 1970s still held that students were substantially under institutional control. The weakening of this doctrine began with *Dixon v. Alabama State Board of Education*, a case involving black students dismissed from a public college for engaging in civil disobedience at a lunch counter. When the court held that they were entitled to a due process hearing before expulsion, it was the first time such rights had been recognized.[33]

The age of majority changed from twenty-one to eighteen years old in 1971, and since that time student rights have either been grounded in tort law (*Tarasoff v. Regents of University of California, Mullins v. Pine Manor College*) or contract theories (*Johnson v. Lincoln Christian College, Ross v. Creighton University*).[34] An area that has developed recently accords protection to students under legislation addressing consumer fraud and deceptive trade practices. While these arguments have been used primarily for tuition refund or for proprietary school (for-profit) cases, they have picked up momentum and in some states can provide for damage awards. For example, courts used the theory of fraudulent misrepresentations against a college in *Gonzalez v. North American College of Louisiana* (1988), and consumer statutes in *American Commercial Colleges, Inc. v. Davis* (1991).[35]

The case studies that follow are excellent proxies for the many cases in admissions, affirmative action, and other student issues that might be appropriate for this review. Two case studies involve subjects that are litigated often and represent important societal developments outside the academy. We situate the case studies in their legal and societal context to suggest alternative ways in which they could have been decided. In law, as in life, it is not always the end result that is important, but the reasoning itself.

Admissions and Race

Before two Supreme Court cases in 2003 involving the University of Michigan (UM), the most important court decision on affirmative action was that in *Bakke*. The *Bakke* case struck down racial quotas in higher education but allowed race as a discretionary factor in admissions. Between *Bakke* and the UM cases there were a number of inconsistent lower court decisions on affirmative action in higher education, perhaps the most notorious being *Hopwood v. State of Texas*, which—in striking down the affirmative action policies for institutions of higher education in Louisiana, Mississippi, and Texas—was both more and less than *Bakke*.[36] Justice Lewis Powell's carefully crafted and nuanced plurality opinion in *Bakke* attempted to balance the rights and the values at stake in this issue. While some absolutists have since lampooned Powell's balancing act, it served a great purpose in reassuring universities that they still had discretion and latitude in choosing from among their many applicants.

Before *Hopwood*, a number of Supreme Court decisions had rejected affirmative action policies in the employment context.[37] These prior decisions, exhibiting what can only be called willful blindness to the social realities of our time as well as to any historical context, had rejected the idea that racial preferences might be justifiable to remedy current inequities or to address past wrongs, and they established exacting tests for enacting preference programs. The Fifth Circuit Court in *Hopwood* similarly justified its decision and distinguished the only decision on point, *Bakke*, by characterizing Justice Powell's decision as a "lonely" opinion. The court argued that "any consideration of race or ethnicity by the law school for the purpose of achieving a diverse student body is not a compelling interest under the Fourteenth Amendment."[38] This opinion was unequivocally wrong, as the UM cases established.[39]

There exists an incredible disparity in income and educational achievements for most racial and ethnic minorities in the United States. Thus racial equity has yet to be achieved. Moreover, white beneficiaries of racial practices often assume that they have reached their station in life on their merits and that minority communities have advanced only through bending the rules. Critics of affirmative action and some federal judges believe that higher scores translate into more meritorious applications and that "objective" measures are race neutral. The evidence for this proposition is more intuitive than verifiable; indeed, a substantial body of research literature and academic practice refutes it. Heavy reliance on test scores and the near-magical properties accorded them inflate the narrow use to which these scores should be put. Accepted psychometric principles, testing-industry norms of good practice, and research on the efficacy of testing all suggest more modest claims for test scores, whether standing alone or combined with other proxy measures. Test scores are at best imperfect measures to predict first-year grades, and first-year grades are only a small part of the aptitude for law study. More importantly, the same score means different things for different populations. For example, studies consistently show that scores on standardized tests are less predictive of minority students' first-year grade point averages (both underpredicting and overpredicting) than Anglo students' averages. This finding substantially weakens the claim by affirmative action critics that standardized tests should be given more weight in the admissions process.

In a sense, institutions could always underplay their use of standardized tests, but the problem was how to be able to maintain a privileging of standardized tests while also attempting to diversify student bodies. *Bakke* implied that institutions could have their cake and eat it too; *Hopwood* suggested otherwise; and now *Bakke*'s logic prevails. In June 2003, the U.S. Supreme Court decided two admissions cases involving the University of Michigan: the undergraduate program (*Gratz v. Bollinger*), and the law school (*Grutter v. Bollinger*).[40] The moral arguments about redistributive justice that shaped the context in which previous affirmative action cases were couched were discarded by the University of Michigan, which amassed a cadre of researchers and educational and corporate supporters to argue that its affirmative action policies promoted the educational benefits of diversity. Acknowledging the serious underrepresentation of most racial and ethnic minorities in higher education, and particularly at elite institutions, and seeing this underrepresentation as problematic in a racially diverse global world, the Supreme Court upheld, at least in principle, the use of racial preferences in college admissions.

In *Gratz*, the Court struck down UM's use of a racial point system in undergraduate admissions by a 6 to 3 majority. The Court found the use of a points system was not sufficiently "narrowly tailored" to survive strict scrutiny. The University of Michigan had awarded twenty points (on a one-hundred-point scale) to minority applicants, and the Court ended this particular practice. However, by a 5 to 4 decision, the Court upheld the full-file review practice of the UM Law School, which took racial criteria into account for reasons of diversity (upholding the original rationale of *Bakke*) and to obtain a "critical mass" of minority students. In both decisions, however, the Supreme Court established that promoting the educational benefits of a diverse student body is a compelling state interest, and where the opinions differed was in the determination of whether the polices at issue were "narrowly tailored" to further that interest.

The Court determined that in the *Gratz* case, the point system used to admit students was invalid. The Court approved the individualized review process used by the law school in *Grutter*. (Of course, one can argue that reviewing a few thousand applications individually for admission to law school is altogether different from having to review individually 25,000 applications to undergraduate studies, but, nevertheless, one can also argue that affirmative action is mostly an issue for elite institutions, which can well afford do something less crass than giving someone 20 points for being, say, black.) The essential point here is that the *Grutter* opinion has become the key decision, as many schools follow the full-file review of the *Grutter* case and now have the imprimatur of the Supreme Court to use race as allowed in the *Bakke* decision more than twenty-five years ago. The sheer crush of applicants—Georgetown University receives over 10,000 applications per year—means that admissions officers can choose among many exceptionally qualified persons. This is a key point. When they can choose from thousands of applicants, most of whom have the credentials to do the work, admissions committees are doing exactly what they are charged to do: assembling a qualified, diverse student body. And, given the current demographics and globalization of much of our economic and political lives, assembling such a diverse student body becomes much more important than simply making students more racially tolerant but allowing them to go on and continue to lead segregated lives, as they have in the past. Our future depends on our ability to interact with others who are surely going to differ from ourselves, and this was the argument that made sense to the Supreme Court in *Grutter* and *Gratz*. *Bakke* and *Grutter* sanction this approach, common sense dictates it, and no anecdotal horror stories or isolated allegations can change this central fact.

Race is a fugue that plays throughout U.S. society, including higher education. In the 1990s, there has been a societal backlash against affirmative action,
as evidenced by a major political party's platform plank against the principles,
California voters' ballot initiative to outlaw affirmative action in state services
and employment, the University of California regents' action to overturn admissions affirmative action (later rescinded), and congressional action to dismantle
a number of federal education programs. In addition, there is a new and resurgent
nativism evident, as in California Ballot Initiative 197 to deny undocumented
alien children public education (struck down by the California courts) and in
federal initiatives to deny benefits to legal permanent residents. As society has
become more conservative on affirmative action, so too have the courts and
legislatures. The *Grutter* decision will likely lead to other state ballot initiatives,
as well as legal challenges that will seek to undermine it (see *Fisher v. University
of Texas*).[41]

Faculty Rights versus Student Rights

In several important legal cases, faculty and student rights have come into direct
conflict.[42] One involved prayer in the public college classroom, in which the court
precluded the practice, finding that the Establishment Clause mandated that the
college discontinue the practice. Another religion case, *Bishop v. Aranov*, pitted a
public university against an exercise physiology professor who invited students in
his class to judge him by Christian standards and to admonish him if he deviated
from these tenets.[43] The appeals court held that colleges exercised broad authority over pedagogical issues and that "a teacher's speech can be taken as directly
and deliberately representative of the school." This troubling logic reached the
correct decision to admonish the professor, but it did so for the wrong reasons
and rested on the erroneous ground that faculty views are those of the institution.
The court could have more parsimoniously and persuasively decided the same
result by analyzing the peculiar role of religion injected into secular fields of
study, especially when the teacher invites a particular religious scrutiny.

In another course, a studio art teacher was dismissed for his habit of not supervising his students; he argued that this technique taught students to act more
independently. The court disagreed with his contention that his behavior was a
protected form of professorial speech, as did a court that considered a professor's
extensive use of profanity in the classroom. In a similar view, a basketball coach,
dismissed for angrily calling his players "niggers" on the court to inspire them,
found an unsympathetic court, which held that the remarks were not a matter of

public concern and, therefore, not protected speech. A white professor also lost his position at a black college for making a remark that was interpreted by students as racist and for refusing to go back to teaching until the college administrators removed a student he considered disruptive.[44]

These and other cases have made it clear that students have some rights in a classroom, while well-known cases such as *Levin v. Harleston* and *Silva v. University of New Hampshire* have made it clear that courts still protect professors' ideas, however controversial (*Levin*), and their teaching styles, however offensive (*Silva*).[45] A proper configuration of professorial academic freedom is resilient enough to resist extremes from without or within, fending off the New Hampshire legislative inquiry of *Sweezy* and the proselytizing of *Bishop*.[46] In this view, professors have wide-ranging discretion to undertake their research and formulate teaching methods in their classrooms and laboratories. However, this autonomy is, within broad limits, contingent on traditional norms of peer review, codes of ethical behavior, and institutional standards. In the most favorable circumstances, these norms will be subject to administrative guidelines for ensuring requisite due process and fairness. Even the highly optimistic and altruistic 1915 AAUP Declaration of Principles holds that "individual teachers should [not] be exempt from all restraints as to the matter or manner of their utterances, either within or without the university."[47] In short, academic freedom does not give carte blanche to professors but, rather, vests faculty with the establishment and enforcement of standards of behavior, which are to be reasonably and appropriately applied in evaluations. Although we attempt to persuade here that the academic common law is highly normative, contextual, and faculty driven, we do not lose sight of the range of acceptable practices and extraordinary heterogeneity found in classroom styles.

Additionally, persuasive research has emerged to show that persons trained in different academic disciplines view pedagogy differently. John Braxton and his colleagues summarize how these norms operate across disciplines:

> Personal controls that induce individual conformity to teaching norms are internalized to varying degrees through the graduate school socialization process. Graduate school attendance in general and doctoral study in particular are regarded as a powerful socialization experience. The potency of this process lies not only in the development of knowledge, skills, and competencies but also in the inculcation of norms, attitudes, and values. This socialization

process entails the total learning situation . . . Through these interpersonal relationships with faculty, values, knowledge, and skills are inculcated.[48]

Moreover, they are all inculcated differently. To grab a student and put one's hands on his chest would be extraordinarily wrong in an immigration law class, but it could happen regularly and appropriately in a voice class, physical education course, or acting workshop. Discussing one's religious views in an exercise physiology class may be inappropriate, but certainly it is appropriate in a comparative religion course. Discussions of sexuality, which would be salacious in a legal ethics course, would be appropriately central to a seminar in human sexuality. Each academic field has evolved its own norms and conventions.

However, courts are not in the business of contextualizing pedagogical disputes, as is evident from *Mincone v. Nassau County Community College*, a case that wended its awkward way through the judicial system.[49] Although *Mincone* has forbears in other decisions, it is sufficient to make our points: if colleges do not police themselves, others will; disputes between teachers and pupils are on the rise; and poor fact patterns and sloppy practices will lead to substantial external control over the classroom. One other thread is that *Mincone* arose in a two-year community college, making it likely that the results will be taken by subsequent judges as directly pertinent for higher education in a way that K–12 cases (notwithstanding *Hazelwood*'s leaching into postsecondary cases) have not been held to be controlling. Given their overlap with the mission of senior institutions and their usual transfer function, two-year colleges will not be easily distinguished. If a K–12 case is not in one's favor, one can always try to convince a judge to limit it to the elementary-secondary sector; one will not be able to muster such a finely graded distinction in a postcompulsory world, even though two-year colleges are, on the average, more authoritarian and administrator driven than are four-year colleges. The widespread use of part-time and non-tenure-track faculty makes academic freedom more problematic at community colleges, where faculty do not always have the security or autonomy to develop traditional protections of tenure and academic freedom.

Mincone is the second round of a case that began as a request for public records, in this instance, course materials for Physical Education 251 (PER 251), "Family Life and Human Sexuality." The course is taught in several sections to nearly 3,000 students each year, and in *Mincone*, a senior citizen auditor (enrolled under terms of a free, noncredit program for adults over sixty-five years of age), who reviewed the course materials before he took the class (which was to be offered in summer 1995), sued to enjoin the course from using the materials or from using federal funds to "counsel abortion in the PER 251 course materials." Mincone, the representative of a coplaintiff party, the Organization of Senior Citizens and Retailers, in May 1995 filed a lawsuit with nine causes of action: PER 251, under these theories, (1) violates the strict religious neutrality required of public institutions by the New York State constitution; (2) burdens and violates state law concerning the free exercise clause of the New York State constitution by "disparagement" of Judeo-Christian faiths and by promoting the religious teaching of Eastern religions with regard to sexuality; (3) violates the federal First Amendment; (4) violates the plaintiffs' civil rights guaranteed under Section 1983; (5) teaches behavior that violates Section 130.00 of the New York State Penal Law (sodomy statutes); (6) violates federal law concerning religious neutrality by singling out one "correct view of human sexuality"; (7) disregards the duty to warn students of course content so they can decide whether or not to enroll in the course; (8) endangers minors who may be enrolled in the course; and (9) violates federal law enjoining abortion counseling.

This broad frontal attack on the course is virtually without precedent, as the plaintiff was not even enrolled in the course for credit and enjoined the course even before the term began and before he took the course as an auditor. But the wide-ranging claims, particularly those that allege religious bias, are so vague and poorly formulated that it is difficult to believe they will survive.

If we begin with the premise that faculty members have the absolute right, within the limits of germaneness and institutional practice, to assign whatever text they wish, subject only to the text being appropriate for the course and to academic custom, then professors can pick whichever texts seem best for their courses (though some states, such as Florida, have passed laws seeking to restrict the ability of professors to assign expensive texts). Sometimes this means a compromise, as in using a central text supplemented by the extra materials they might wish were in the basic text (not everyone can or is inclined to write their own book). Therefore, materials could be assigned that are a compromise, or materials may be not assigned because they are inappropriate. Surely, for a course known to be a lightning rod (by the earlier suit), sex education and physiology faculty carefully chose the filmstrips and materials; this is the contextual and professional judgment that our theory requires. There should be no qualms in defending the course materials: they were picked by professionals with considerable expertise in this field; the course is widely accepted and regularly fully enrolled; it does what it sets out to do—expose students to wide-ranging issues of sexuality; and the materials clearly put students on notice about what the course covers. Except for the personal and moral objections of the plaintiffs concerning the materials, this course is generically like any course. Context is all, as is professional authority to determine how it will be taught.

Cases like this are fraught with implications for higher education practice, especially for teacher behavior. In *Cohen v. San Bernardino Community College*, the District Court could have gone in the opposite direction, as it had for Professors Silva and Levin, by stressing their academic freedom rather than by balancing the competing interests.[50] However, by characterizing the issues as ones of classroom control and the students' learning environment, Professor Cohen's interests are trumped, at least with the admonishment he received. (His orders were to do essentially what Professor Silva was ordered to do by the University of New Hampshire: take counseling, alter his class style, etc.) He had been admonished to stop teaching from *Hustler* and other "pornographic" materials in his remedial English class. And the court did suggest that the admonishment was mild: "A case in which a professor is terminated or directly censored presents a far different balancing question." But does it? Can there be any doubt that Cohen considers himself "directly censored" by the formal complaint of one student? Was Levin censored by the City University of New York's "shadow section"? Is reading *Hustler* letters a good idea for a remedial English class?

Additionally, there is the issue of a solution to the conundrum of faculty autonomy and sexual harassment jurisprudence. The difficulty is acknowledging that a classroom can be a hostile environment in some instances. The AAUP has hammered out a compromise attempt to preserve faculty autonomy and yet acknowledge and deal with an environment so hostile that it can stifle learning opportunities. The AAUP Proposed Statement of Policy for Sexual Harassment reads as follows:

It is the policy of this institution that no member of the academic community may sexually harass another. Sexual advances, requests for sexual favors, and other speech or conduct of a sexual nature constitute sexual harassment when

1. such advances or requests are made under circumstances implying that one's response might affect academic or personnel decisions that are subject to the influence of the person making the proposal; or

2. such speech or conduct is directed against another and is either abusive or severely humiliating, or persists despite the objection of the person targeted by the speech or conduct; or

3. such speech or conduct is reasonably regarded as offensive and substantially impairs the academic or work opportunity of students, colleagues, or coworkers. If it takes place in the teaching context, it must also be persistent, pervasive, and not germane to the subject matter.[51]

The academic setting is distinct from the workplace in that wide latitude is required for professional judgment in determining the appropriate content and presentation of academic material. In our search for the perfect, clarifying epiphany, this proposed policy falls short: What is "severely humiliating"? Is it more than "humiliating"? How much more? How long does harassment have to persist in order to be found "persistent"? Isn't the classroom a "workplace" for faculty?

To us, in interpreting academic standards, it is not surprising that things work so badly but, rather, that they work so well. Our own experiences as students and as professors lead us to believe that any comprehensive theory of professorial authority to determine "how it shall be taught" must incorporate a feedback mechanism for students to take issue, voice complaints, and point out remarks or attitudes that may be insensitive or disparaging. At a minimum, faculty should encourage students to speak privately with them to identify uncomfortable situations. Professor Bishop asked his students to point out inconsistencies between his Christian perspectives and his lifestyle. This is excessive and could itself provoke anxiety on the part of both Christian and non-Christian students. But a modest attempt to avoid stigmatizing words and examples is certainly in order for teachers, and schools should have in place some mechanism to address these issues. We cringe when exams consign "José," "Maria," or "Rufus" to criminal questions or when in-class hypotheticals use "illegal aliens" or sexist examples and stereotypes to illustrate legal points. Such misuse may be especially prevalent in fact patterns involving criminal activities, such as rape and consent. Students have a right to expect more thoughtful pedagogical practices.

Finally, there is the issue of grading, a hotly contested arena. One would assume that a professor's ability to assign grades is sacrosanct, but that was before *Sylvester v. Texas Southern University*.[52] *Sylvester* is, arguably, the first federal case where a grade is overturned. Yet the circumstances are so bizarre that no one can really insist that the grade was "properly awarded." Therein lies a very odd tale, one that

demonstrates just how obstinate a faculty member can be and how badly
take can be compounded without proper faculty or administrative leadership.

Karen Sylvester, a 2L at Thurgood Marshall Law School at Texas Southern
University (TSU) in Houston, was at the top of her class, having received almost
all As. In the spring of 1994, she completed Professor James Bullock's Wills and
Trusts class and was awarded a D. This had the effect of dropping her from first
in her class, whereas a C or a "pass" would have kept her in first place.

First, she protested orally to the associate dean, who did not respond. The next
semester, she protested in writing and did so several times without receiving any
response from the professor or the law school administration. Bullock was later
asked to produce Sylvester's exam book, and he said it had been lost. After a more
thorough search, it was discovered. She had appealed to the law school's oversight
committee, a standing committee (which included faculty and student members)
that reviewed such disputes. Nearly a year later, when she was scheduled to graduate, Sylvester sought to enjoin the graduation ceremony until her grade and its
effect on her rank-in-class could be resolved. TSU promised the judge that if she
allowed the ceremony to go forward, it would review the case and adjust her
standing accordingly.

What follows is not pretty. The judge found that "Bullock was defiant." The
court ordered him to meet with the student to review the grade. She returned to
Houston from Dallas, where she learned that Bullock either had no answer key
or had not used one, so he could not review the exam properly. Angered, the judge
ordered him to pay her travel expenses and to attend all subsequent meetings
scheduled on this issue. The record tersely records that "he did neither." At the
next court session, the judge sent marshals to fetch the missing professor, who
admitted that he had received proper notice.

The issue was punted back to the law school committee, which decided—
contrary to its published regulations—that students could not serve on the committee because of privacy issues. The committee, without its student members,
decided that the review had been adequate and that "no inconsistencies were
found." Yet one member told the court that the committee had been informed by
Bullock that the correct answer to the essay question had been "yes." The judge,
incredulous that this defiance had been ratified by the committee, threw the
book at them.

He wrote, in a remarkable and sweeping voice, "Governmental actions cannot
be arbitrary. Having no basis for comparison is arbitrary. Changing the committee on the chairman's malicious whim is arbitrary. Once the committee had been

university-constituted form it was nothing but a mob."
ester be given a "pass" for the course and that she be listed
aordinary actions needed to provide an "equitable adjust-
the contours of bad faith in awarding a grade and the inex-
t leads critics to complain about tenured (and, ironically, in
essors such as Bullock.

Policy Implications and Conclusion

Higher education has undoubtedly become legalized, by the traditional means of legislation, regulation, and litigation as well as by the growing areas of informal lawmaking, such as ballot initiatives, insurance carrier policies, and commercial or contract law in research. This cascade will shower down upon institutions, each leaving its residue in the form of administrative responsibility for acknowledging and implementing these obligations.

Understanding how legal initiatives become policy, particularly complex regulatory or legislative initiatives, should contribute greatly to improving administrative implementation of legal change on campus. Even with this modest review, it is clear that some legal policies will be more readily adopted than others. It is also clear that academic policy makers have substantial opportunities and resources to shape legal policy and smooth the way for legal changes on campus. Of course, no one can be expected to endorse all legal initiatives with equal enthusiasm or to administer them as if they were all high institutional priorities. Not will all of them be so. Some will be implemented only grudgingly. However, understanding what is involved in the implementation of legal change will influence the amount of policy output produced, the distribution of policy outputs, and the overall extent of compliance achieved.

The considerable autonomy and deference accorded higher education often translate into institutions designing their own compliance regimes for legislative and litigative change, and greater understanding of this complex legal phenomenon should increase this independence. As no small matter, higher education officials could begin to convince legislators that mandated legal change has a better chance of achieving the desired effects if institutions are allowed to design their own compliance and implementation strategies. This role could ease the sting so many campuses feel when another regulatory program is thrust upon them, or when they lose an important case in court, as happened at the University of Texas in *Hopwood v. State of Texas*. It could also lead higher education officials to seek reasonable compliance rather than exemption, which occurs often in practice. As higher education becomes more reliant on government support, and as colleges offer themselves for hire as participants in commercial ventures and as social change agents, legal restrictions are sure to follow. Understanding the consequences of legalization is a first step toward controlling our fate.[53]

This and the other chapters in this book show how interdependent the higher education system is and reveal why we need to adapt to the times. Our timeless values, such as academic freedom, tenure, institutional autonomy, and due process are in danger of being legislated or litigated away if we do not remain vigilant and alert, and if we do not self-police. There are many police outside the academy all too willing to do so if we do not.

NOTES

1. Lewis Thomas, *The Youngest Science: Notes of a Medicine Watcher* (New York: Viking, 1983); Paul Goodman, *The Community of Scholars* (New York: Free Press, 1962); John Millett, *The Academic Community* (New York: McGraw-Hill, 1962); Herbert Stroup, *Bureaucracy in Higher Education* (New York: Free Press, 1966); Victor Baldridge, *Power and Conflict in the University* (New York: Wiley, 1971); Clark Kerr, *The Uses of the University* (Cambridge, MA: Harvard University Press, 1982); Burton R. Clark, *The Higher Education System* (Berkeley: University of California Press, 1983); Randall Collins, *The Credential Society* (New York: Academic, 1979); Harry T. Edwards, *Higher Education and the Unholy Crusade against Governmental Regulation* (Cambridge, MA: Institute for Educational Management, 1980); Paolo Freire, *Education for Critical Consciousness* (New York: Seabury, 1973).

2. *Coffee v. Rice University*, 408 S.W.2d 269 (1966).

3. *Shapiro v. Columbia Union*, 576 S.W.2d 310 (1979).

4. *U.S. on behalf of U.S. Coast Guard v. Cerio*, 831 F. Supp. 530 (E.D. Va. 1993).

5. *Fountain Gate Ministries, Inc. v. City of Plano*, 654 S.W.2d 841 (Tex. App. 5 Dist. 1983).

6. *Hacker v. Hacker*, 522 N.Y.S. 768 (Supp. 1987).

7. *Beth Rochel Seminary v. Bennett*, 825 F.2d 478 (D.C. Cir. 1987); *City of Morgantown v. West Virginia Board of Regents*, 354 S.E.2d 616 (W. Va. 1987).

8. *Trustees of Dartmouth v. Woodward*, 4 Wheaton (U.S.) 518 (1819); *Krynicky v. University of Pittsburgh*, 742 F.2d 94 (1984).

9. Three exceptions have been created by the Supreme Court to limit a state's sovereign immunity: waiver, abrogation, and the *ex parte Young* exceptions. The first exception to the doctrine of sovereign immunity occurs when a state waives its immunity. A state's waiver of sovereign immunity may subject it to suit in state court, but it is not enough, absent some other indicator of intent, to subject the state to suit

in federal court. A state can also waive its Eleventh Amendment immunity against suits in federal court by other clearly stated means, such as successfully moving a federal case to state court. Congress can abrogate a state's sovereign immunity by exercising its powers under section 5 of the Fourteenth Amendment. Since the 1996 decision in *Seminole Tribe of Florida v. Florida*, the Court has begun to limit Congress's rights to abrogate a state's sovereign immunity. Thus Congress has the power to abrogate a state's sovereign immunity when it is acting pursuant to its Fourteenth Amendment powers under section 5. However, the Court requires Congress to act unambiguously when doing so. For an excellent summary of these issues, see Brian Snow and William Thro, "The Significance of Blackstone's Understanding of Sovereign Immunity for America's Public Institutions of Higher Education," *Journal of College and University Law* 28 (2002): 97–128. Snow and Thro have summarized the *ex parte Young* exemption: "This doctrine holds that sovereign immunity does not bar federal court actions against individual state officers . . . seeking (1) declaratory judgment that the state officer is currently violating federal law and (2) an injunction forcing the state officer to conform his current conduct to federal law." This exception does not apply to violations that occurred in the past; rather, it "applies only where there is an on-going violation of federal law, which can be cured by declaratory or injunctive relief."

10. *Powe v. Miles*, 407 F.2d 73 (1968).

11. *Cahn and Cahn v. Antioch University*, 482 A.2d 120 (1984).

12. *Fenn College v. Nance*, 210 N.E.2d 418 (1965); *Nasson College v. New England Association of Schools and Colleges*, 16 B.C.D. 1299 (1988).

13. *NCAA v. University of Oklahoma*, 488 U.S. 85 (1984); *U.S. v. Brown University*, 5 F.3d 658 (3d Cir. 1993).

14. *Marjorie Webster Junior College v. Middle States Association*, 139 U.S. App. D.C. 217, 432 F.2d 650 (1970); *Beth Rochel Seminary v. Bennett*.

15. *NLRB v. Yeshiva University*, 444 U.S. 672 (1980).

16. Lelia Helms, "Patterns of Litigation in Postsecondary Education: A Caselaw Study," *Journal of College and University Law* 14 (1987): 99–110; Margaret Lam, *Patterns of Litigation at Institutions of Higher Education in Texas, 1878–1978* (Houston: Institute for Higher Education Law and Governance, 1988).

17. William Kaplin and Barbara Lee, *The Law of Higher Education*, 4th ed. (San Francisco: Jossey-Bass, 2006). Also see George LaNoue and Barbara Lee, *Academics in Court* (Ann Arbor: University of Michigan Press, 1985); Steven G. Poskanzer, *Higher Education Law: The Faculty* (Baltimore: Johns Hopkins University Press, 2002); Patricia Spacks, ed., *Advocacy in the Classroom* (New York: St. Martin's Press, 1996).

18. *Perry v. Sindermann*, 408 U.S. 593 (1972); *Board of Regents v. Roth*, 408 U.S. 564 (1972).

19. *Wellner v. Minnesota State Junior College Board*, 487 F.2d 153 (1973).

20. *State ex rel. McLendon v. Morton*, 162 W.Va. 431, 249 S.E.2d 919 (1978).

21. *Hill v. Talladega College*, 502 So.2d 735 (Ala. 1987); *Honore v. Douglas*, 833 F.2d 565 (5th Cir. 1987); *Spuler v. Pickar*, 958 F.2d 103 (5th Cir. 1992); *Lewis v. Loyola Uni-

versity of Chicago, 500 N.E.2d 47 (Ill. App. 1 Dist. 1996); *Otero-Burgos v. Inter-American University,* 558 F.3d 1 (1st Cir. 2009).

22. *Scott v. University of Delaware,* 455 F. Supp. 1102 (1978).

23. *Faro v. NYU,* 502 F.2d 1229 (1974).

24. *Clark v. Claremont Graduate School,* 8 Cal. Rptr. 2d 151 (Cal. App. 2 Dist. 1992).

25. *Sweeney v. Board of Trustees of Keene State College,* 569 F.2d 169 (1978); *Kunda v. Muhlenberg College,* 463 F. Supp. 294 (E.D. Pa. 1978); *Mecklenberg v. Montana State Board of Regents,* 13 EPD 11, 438 (1976); *Kemp v. Ervin,* 651 F.Supp. 495 (N.D. Ga. 1986).

26. *Hazelwood School District v. Kuhlmeier,* 108 S. Ct. 562 (1988); *Bishop v. Aranov,* 926 F.2d 1066 (11th Cir. 1991); *Scallet v. Rosenblum,* unpublished opinion, U.S. Court of Appeals, 4th Cir., Jan. 29, 1997 (C.A. 94-16-c); *Waters v. Churchill,* 114 S. Ct. 1878 (1994); *Jeffries v. Harleston,* 828 F.Supp. 1066 (S.D.N.Y. 1993), 21 F.3d 1238 (2d Cir. 1994), vac. and rem. 115 S. Ct. 502 (1995), vac. and rev'd. 52 F.3d 9 (2d Cir. 1995), cert den. 116 S. Ct.173 (1995).

27. Data from Joel Douglas, "Professors on Strike: An Analysis of Two Decades of Faculty Work Stoppages, 1960–1985," *Labor Lawyer* 4 (1988): 87–101.

28. *Trustees of Columbia University,* 29 LRRM 1098 (1951).

29. *Cornell University,* 183 NLRB 329 (1970).

30. *United Faculty v. University of Pittsburgh,* PLRB No. PERAR-84-53W (Mar. 11, 1987).

31. *NLRB v. Cooper Union,* 783 F.2d 29 (2d Cir. 1985); *NLRB v. Florida Memorial College,* 820 F.2d 1182 (11th Cir. 1987).

32. *Bakke v. Regents of University of California,* 438 U.S. 265 (1978).

33. *Anthony v. Syracuse University,* 231 N.Y.S. 435 (1928); *Gott v. Berea,* 156 Ky. 376, 161 S.W. 204 (1913); *Dixon v. Alabama State Board of Education,* 294 F.2d 150 (1961).

34. *Tarasoff v. Regents of University of California,* 551 F.2d 334 (1976); *Mullins v. Pine Manor College,* 449 N.E.2d 331 (Mass. 1983); *Johnson v. Lincoln Christian College,* 501 N.E.2d 1380 (Ill. App. 4 Dist. 1986); *Ross v. Creighton University,* 957 F.2d 410 (7th Cir. 1992).

35. *Gonzalez v. North American College of Louisiana,* 700 F. Supp. 362 (S.D. Tex. 1988); *American Commercial Colleges, Inc. v. Davis,* 821 S.W.2d 450 (Tex. App.–Eastland 1991).

36. *Hopwood v. State of Texas,* 78 F.3d 945 (5th Cir. 1996) (reviewing constitutional standards). For a review of this and other higher education cases, see Michael A. Olivas, *The Law and Higher Education,* 3rd ed. (Durham, NC: Carolina Academic Press, 2006).

37. *Wygant v. Jackson Board of Education,* 476 U.S. 267 (1986); *City of Richmond v. Croson,* 488 U.S. 469 (1989); *Adarand v. Pena,* 115 S. Ct. 2097 (1995).

38. *Hopwood v. Texas,* 948.

39. As this panel misread *Bakke,* so it misread the admissions process. The panel also did not understand that Cheryl Hopwood wanted affirmative action to apply in her case: she was a mother with a child born with cerebral palsy, and the panel found the case one of "unique background," in which Hopwood's "circumstances would bring a different perspective to the law school." But when she applied, the University

of Texas law school committee did not have this information. Incredibly, Hopwood provided no letters of recommendation and no personal statement outlining her unique background (*Hopwood v. Texas*, 946). Yet she was certain she was displaced from her rightful place by lesser-qualified minorities. Another of the plaintiffs had a letter of recommendation from a professor describing the plaintiff's academic performance at his undergraduate institution as "uneven, disappointing, and mediocre" (*Hopwood v. State of Texas*, 861 F. Supp. 551, 566–67 (W.D. Tex. 1994)). That such students could score high on an index utilizing only grade point averages and LSAT (Law School Admission Test) scores indicates why law schools look to features other than mere scores. Any law school would be wary of incomplete applications or ones in which letters of recommendation singled out a student for "mediocre" academic achievement.

40. *Gratz v. Bollinger*, 123 S. Ct. 2411 (2003); *Grutter v. Bollinger*, 123 S. Ct. 2325 (2003).

41. *Fisher v. University of Texas*, 645 F. Supp. 2d 587 (W.D. Tex. 2009).

42. Michael A. Olivas, "Professorial Academic Freedom: Second Thoughts on the 'Third Essential Freedom,'" *Stanford Law Review* 45 (1993): 1835–58.

43. *Bishop v. Aranov*.

44. *McConnell v. Howard University*, 818 F.2d 58 (D.C. Cir. 1987).

45. *Levin v. Harleston*, 770 F. Supp. 895 (S.D.N.Y. 1991), aff'd in relevant part, vac. on other grounds, 996 F.2d 85 (2d Cir. 1992); *Silva v. University of New Hampshire*, 888 F. Supp. 293 (D.N.H. 1994).

46. *Sweezy v. New Hampshire*, 354 U.S. 234 (1957); *Bishop v. Aranov*.

47. "General Report of the Committee on Academic Freedom and Academic Tenure," *AAUP Bulletin* 17 (1915): 1, reprinted in *Law and Contemporary Problems* 393 (1990): 53.

48. John M. Braxton, Alan Bayer, and Martin Finkelstein, "Teaching Performance Norms in Academia," *Research in Higher Education* 33 (1992): 533–70, quotation on 535–36.

49. *Mincone v. Nassau County Community College*, 923 F. Supp. 398 (E.D.N.Y. 1996). See also *Gheta v. NCCC*, 33 F. Supp. 2nd 179 (E.D.N.Y. 1999).

50. *Cohen v. San Bernadino Valley Community College*, 883 F. Supp. 1407 (C.D. Cal. 1995), rev'd in part, 92 F.3d 968 (9th Cir. 1996).

51. American Association of University Professors, "AAUP Proposed Statement of Policy for Sexual Harassment," in *Policy Documents and Reports* (Washington, DC: American Association of University Professors, 1995), 171.

52. *Sylvester v. Texas Southern University*, 957 F. Supp. 944 (S.D. Tex. 1997).

53. There is a growing narrative literature concerning college law cases, with particular attention to race and faculty issues; examples include Benjamin Baez, *Affirmative Action, Hate Speech, and Tenure: Narratives about Race and Law in the Academy* (New York: Routledge Falmer, 2002), and Amy Gajda, *The Trials of Academe: The New Era of Campus Litigation* (Cambridge, MA: Harvard University Press, 2009).

CHAPTER EIGHT

The Hidden Hand

External Constituencies and Their Impact

Fred F. Harcleroad and Judith S. Eaton

Postsecondary institutions have endured in the United States for over three and one-half centuries. All except those established recently have been modified over the years and have changed greatly in response to pressures from external forces. Particularly in the last century and a half, literally thousands of diverse institutions have opened their doors, only to close when they were no longer needed by a sufficient number of students or by the public and private constituencies that had founded and supported them. Those in existence today are the survivors, the institutions that adapted to the needs of their constituencies.

The varied external forces affecting postsecondary education in the United States have grown out of our unique three-sector system of providing goods and services for both collective consumption and private use. First, the *voluntary enterprise sector*, composed of millions of independent nonprofit organizations, often has initiated efforts to provide such things as schools, hospitals, bridges, libraries, environmental controls, and public parks. Such organizations are protected by constitutional rights to peaceful assembly, free speech, and petition for redress of grievances. These formidable protections, plus the nonprofits' record of useful service, led to their being nontaxable, with contributions to them being tax free.

Second, the *public enterprise group*, comprising all local, state, and federal governments, administers the laws that hold our society together. Third, the *private enterprise sector*, composed of profit-seeking businesses and commerce, provides much of the excess wealth needed to support the other two sectors. This pluralistic and diverse set of organizations implements the basic ideas behind our federated republic.

Our constitution provides for a detailed separation of powers at the federal level among the presidency, the Congress, and the judiciary. The Tenth Amendment establishes the states as governments with "general" powers, delegating "limited" powers to the federal government. Education is not a delegated power and therefore is reserved to the states, whose constitutions often treat it almost as a fourth branch of government. In addition, the Tenth Amendment reserves "general" powers to citizens, who operate through their own voluntary organizations, their state governments, or state-authorized private enterprise. Consequently, only a few higher education institutions are creations of the federal government (mostly military institutions, to provide for the common defense); more than 99 percent of postsecondary institutions are authorized or chartered by individual states and created and managed by the states, voluntary organizations, or profit-seeking businesses.

Both of the oldest institutions in the country, Harvard University (established in 1636) and the College of William and Mary (established in 1693), have closed for different reasons but opened up again when changes were made. Harvard (then a college) closed for what would have been its second year (in 1639–40), after Nathaniel Eaton, its first head, was dismissed for cruelty to students and the theft of college funds. After being closed for the year, government officials determined that the Massachusetts Bay Colony still needed a college to train ministers and advance learning. A new president, Henry Dunster, reopened the college in 1640, and by changing regularly, and sometimes dramatically, Harvard has remained in operation ever since. Two small examples illustrate this process. As Massachusetts grew and secularized, ministerial training at Harvard became only one function of this institution, so it was placed in a separate divinity school. Also, by the late 1700s, required instruction in Hebrew was replaced by student choice, a beginning of our current elective system.

William and Mary was the richest of the colonial colleges, supported by the Commonwealth of Virginia, with income from taxes on tobacco, skins, and hides. Nevertheless, the college had to make many adaptations in order to remain politically supported. For example, after the Revolution, in 1779, it dropped its chair of divinity and established the nation's first professorship of law and police. The college closed during the Civil War (1861–65), reopened briefly, but closed again in 1881. It eventually reopened in 1888, when the state agreed to make it a state-supported institution if it would become Virginia's main teacher education college. Thus it changed from being essentially a private college operated by the Episcopal Church to a public one, an excellent example of a government taking over a private institution to meet the developing needs of society as a whole. Interaction of this type between government and private constituencies is a characteristic of the democratic republic established in the United States, and it is important to consider this in studying the relationships of colleges and universities to their external environment.

External groups, associations, and agencies from all three sectors can have an impact on the autonomy of the postsecondary educational institutions. This diverse group of external organizations includes everything from athletic conferences and alumni associations to employer associations and unions (or organized faculty groups that function as unions). The corporate boards that administer all of the private colleges, universities, and institutes authorized to operate in the respective states obviously belong in this group. Their power to determine institutional policies is clear and well known. However, many other voluntary associations can and do have significant effects on specific institutions or on units of the institutions. This is particularly true in the funding of colleges and universities, since the American system is based on income from varied sources. As states have decreased the proportion coming from their budgets for both public and private institutions, other sources of income and ways to economize have become increasingly crucial in the twenty-first century. External associations can play an important role in providing badly needed alternative funding and more effective operational use of existing funds. Five of these groups—private foundations, institutionally based membership associations, voluntary accrediting organizations, voluntary consortia, and regional compacts—are described below in some detail, indicating their backgrounds, their development, and their possible impact on institutional autonomy and academic freedom.

Private Foundations

The beginnings of private foundations in the United States took place over two centuries ago.[1] Benjamin Franklin led in the establishment, in Philadelphia, of a number of voluntary-sector organizations, including the American Philosophical

Society in 1743, an association with many foundation characteristics. In 1800 the Magdalen Society of Philadelphia, possibly the first private foundation in the United States, was established as a perpetual trust to assist "unhappy females who had been seduced from the paths of virtue." In the 1890s and early 1900s, long before the federal income tax became legal, due to the Sixteenth Amend- ment to the U.S. Constitution, the Carnegie foundations, followed shortly by the Rockefeller foundations, set a pattern that continues to this day.

Andrew Carnegie established 1,681 free public libraries; contributed signifi-cantly to the University of Chicago; and founded the Carnegie Institute, which later became Carnegie-Mellon University. In addition, he established the Carne-gie Foundation for the Advancement of Teaching, the Carnegie Corporation of New York, the Carnegie Endowment for International Peace, the Carnegie Insti-tution Of Washington, and Carnegie Hall. John D. Rockefeller established the University of Chicago, Spelman College, the Rockefeller Institute for Medical Research (now Rockefeller University) and, in 1955, he provided 630 liberal arts colleges with faculty salary improvement funds equal to each institution's total for the previous year. These examples illustrate how Carnegie and Rockefeller established a high standard of operations and service. Few academics realize that their current TIAA pensions were developed and are currently administered by a foundation resulting from Andrew Carnegie's feeling of public service responsi-bility. Decades before such "contributions" became tax deductible, he gave sev-eral million dollars to set up the first pension fund for college teachers.

Today, private foundations vary greatly in form, purpose, size, function, and constituency. Some are corporate in nature, many are trusts, and others are only associations. Many of them can affect postsecondary institutions through their choice of areas to support. They can be classified into five types: (1) community foundations, often citywide or regional, which make a variety of bequests or gifts (local postsecondary institutions often can count on some support from such foundations for locally related projects); (2) family or personal foundations, often with limited purposes; (3) special purpose foundations (including such varied examples as the Harvard Glee Club and a fund set up to provide every girl at Bryn Mawr with one baked potato at each meal); (4) company foundations established to channel corporate giving through one main source; and (5) national indepen-dent foundations (including many of the large, well-known foundations, such as Carnegie, Rockefeller, Ford, Lilly, Kellogg, Mellon, and Johnson, plus more re-cent ones such as Murdock, Hewlett, Packard, Lumina, and the Pew Trusts). The number of grant-making foundations, estimated at 60,000 in 2004–5, grows constantly. Their total assets are variously estimated at $420 billion to $600 billion, and their awards range from $32 to $35 billion yearly. A significant portion of these funds regularly go to higher education. A recent special report from the Foundation Center stressed the wide range of their fields of interest and their increasing attraction as a valuable resource for institutions with budget problems.[2]

By their choice of areas to finance, foundations, especially those in the national independent category, entice supposedly autonomous colleges to do things they might not do otherwise. Institutional change continues to be a prime goal of foundations, as it has been for most of the past century. Thus, although their grants still provide a relatively small proportion of the total financing for institutions, they have had significant effects on program development and even operations. Grants from foundations have been instrumental in the establishment of new academic fields such as microbiology and anthropology, and in the redirection of the fields of business and teacher education.

An excellent, somewhat different example of a valuable foundation-supported activity during the first decade of the twenty-first century is the National Center for Public Policy and Higher Education (NCPPHE), which was supported initially by the Pew Trusts and the Ford Foundation and currently by the Lumina Foundation and the Bill and Melinda Gates Foundation. It provides numerous useful studies for decision making. The NCPPHE recognizes the importance of state responsibility for chartering, regulating, and supporting higher education in most colleges and universities, and it publishes a "report card" on each of the states in six areas: (1) student preparation, (2) participation (opportunities to enroll), (3) affordability, (4) student completion of programs, (5) benefits to the states from an educated population, and (6) student learning. Titled *Measuring Up*, these reports for 2000, 2002, 2004, 2006, and 2008 have produced vital information on which to base state efforts to improve opportunity in, and operations of, their colleges and universities. Other key publications include *Losing Ground* (in-depth data on affordability) and *State Policy and Community College–Baccalaureate Transfer*. These data, and many others from this foundation-supported center (available at www.highereducation.org), provide useful beginnings of benchmarks, or social indicators, for improving higher education in the United States.

It is important to stress, however, that private foundations affect institutional freedom only if the institutions voluntarily accept the funds for the purposes prescribed by the foundation. The redirection of programs, and even of private institutional goals, is possible and has occurred on occasion. Nevertheless, the private foundation model has been so successful that government has adopted it in forming and funding such agencies as the National Science Foundation, the Fund for the Improvement of Postsecondary Education, and the National Endowments for the Arts and for the Humanities. Clearly, private foundations have been and undoubtedly will continue to be important external forces affecting postsecondary education.

Institutionally Based Membership Organizations

Voluntary membership organizations of this type are almost infinite in their possible number.[3] The *Higher Education Directory*, a compendium of higher education associations, institutions, and government agencies, lists 298 of these organizations. Although formed by institution officials for their own purposes, the associations often end up having indirect or direct effects on the institutions themselves. The American Council on Education (ACE), probably the major policy advocate for postsecondary education at the national level, plays a critical coordinative role as an umbrella organization, composed of a wide spectrum of institutions. Other major national institutional organizations include the Association of American Colleges and Universities, the American Association of Community Colleges, the American Association of State Colleges and Universities, the Association of American Universities, the Council for Higher Education Accreditation, the Council of Independent Colleges, the National Association of Independent Colleges and Universities, and the National Association of State Universities and Land-Grant Colleges. ACE also coordinates a larger group of fifty higher education associations, known as the Washington Higher Education Secretariat; the Secretariat convenes eight times per year to exchange information and discuss current or projected activities, many of them national policy issues, often regarding federal financing or control. These organizations represent most of the public and private nonprofit and some for-profit postsecondary institutions in the United States, with some institutions belonging to two or three of them. Based for the most part in Washington, D.C., they represent the differing interests of the varied institutions. Also, especially when these organizations work together as a united front, they can influence congressional committees and government agencies on key issues affecting higher education.

The strength of these national associations will continue to grow, along with taxes, the federal budget, and federal purchase of selected services from their member institutions. Even though most postsecondary institutions are state chartered and many are basically state funded, the increasing power of the federal tax system will make such national associations even more necessary.

Many specialized voluntary membership associations contribute in diverse ways to the development and operations of functional areas within institutions. For example, the American College Testing Program (now ACT) and the College Entrance Examination Board (its service bureau, the Educational Testing Service, is not a membership organization) provide extensive information resources for their members: institutions and program areas within institutions. These data are vital for counseling and guidance purposes, student admissions, student financial aid programs, and related activities. In addition, different administrative functions (such as graduate schools, registrars, institutional research units, and business offices) have their own, extremely useful representative associations. Likewise, most academic fields and their constantly increasing subdivisions or spinoffs have set up specialized groups. Prime examples are engineering and the allied health professions, both with dozens of separate associations. Many of these academic organizations affect institutions and their program planning in direct ways. In particular, the associations that set up detailed criteria for membership in the association often directly influence the allocation of resources. Of the several thousand member organizations in this category, almost one hundred of them, from architecture to veterinary medicine, probably exert the greatest influence, since those programs or academic units admitted to membership are considered to be accredited. (The following section provides more detail on this group.) A sampling of these organizations illustrates their services, emphasizes their significance, and shows, in a limited way, their potential impact.

The American Council on Education includes separate institutions and other associations, with approximately 1,800 institutional members representing more than 70 percent of all college and university enrollments in the United States. (There are an additional 200 or so noninstitutional members.) Since the council's establishment in 1918, its work has changed from an emphasis on "consensus building," its primary charge for the first fifty years, to initiating action to improve higher education. Some of its special offices and centers indicate its thrusts: Center for the Advancement of Racial and Ethnic Equity, Adult Learner Programs, Center for Effective Leadership, Center for International Initiatives, Center for Policy Analysis, Office of Women in Higher Education, Center for Lifelong Learning, ACE Credit and Transcript services, ACE Fellows Program, Executive Search Roundtable, and numerous other specialized programs.

The publication program of ACE provides major documents on the field of higher education and a constant flow of documents and papers on current federal legislative activities and on major studies completed or underway. Many of these documents are available through the ACE Online Store (http://store.acenet.edu/). The ACE magazine, *The Presidency*, is available there and is very useful for current or aspiring institutional presidents. A regular series of publications on all aspects of higher education cover such topics as changing economics and funding, overseas branch campuses, the *Directory of Accredited Institutions of Postsecondary Education*, and especially their constant reports from the policy analysis service.

The Association of Governing Boards of Universities and Colleges (AGB) is a nonprofit association serving more than 34,000 trustees and officials of 1,200 colleges and universities or their foundations, representing all types of boards— private, public, two-year, four-year, governing, coordinating, and advisory. Its mission is "to strengthen the practice of voluntary trusteeship as the best alternative to direct government and political control of higher education." In addition to membership fees, its support comes from several dozen national, personal, private, and corporate foundations. Its extensive program of publications, videotapes, conferences, and seminars is designed to provide trustees and institutional leaders with timely and useful resources in this specialized area. One package of materials, *Fundamentals of Trusteeship*, is designed for the orientation of new trustees. Another specialized service is its Presidential Search Consultation Service, which often serves several dozen institutions a year. Other projects include the AGB "Survival Kits," providing publications covering eight board basics, including such items as fundraising, leadership of a board, financial matters, foundation relations, and effective committees. Other of their publications cover public policy and governance, presidential compensation, and understanding financial statements.

The American Association of State Colleges and Universities (AASCU) represents 430 public colleges and universities, constituting 56 percent of the enrollments in public four-year institutions. Since its beginnings in 1961, the AASCU has been a leading stimulator of all facets of international education. Its many presidential missions to such countries as Egypt, Israel, Greece, Poland, the People's Republic of China, Cuba, Argentina, Taiwan, Malaysia, and Mexico have fostered continuing educational exchange and on-campus programs. It has taken national leadership in developing cooperative interassociation and interinstitutional programs and networks, such as the Service Members Opportunity Colleges (with many AASCU institutions involved) and the Urban College and University Network. Its Office of Federal Programs monitors current funding programs and priorities and has been instrumental in increasing the participation of AASCU institutions in this ever-increasing source of funds. Its Office of Governmental Relations and Policy Analysis analyzes pending legislation, prepares testimony on major national issues, monitors state issues affecting public higher education, conducts surveys, studies trends, and keeps institutional officials informed. The Academic Affairs Resource Center and Academic Leadership Academy serve the chief academic officers of higher education institutions, emphasizing planning, faculty development, opportunities for minorities and women to attain senior administrative positions, leadership training, financial management, legal matters, and innovative educational ideas for new clientele.

An extensive seminar, conference, and publication program supports this alignment of institutional services. Some examples are the annual Summer Council of Presidents, which emphasizes current issues and presidential leadership; regular meetings of the chief academic affairs officials; the annual President's Academy for new campus chief executive officers; and the Voluntary System of Accountability (VSA), developed in partnership with the National Association of State Universities and Land-Grant Colleges. The VSA project is a long-term, critically important project to provide detailed information on education outcomes and demonstrate accountability and stewardship by these public institutions to the public. Overall, the AASCU has had a profound effect on the institutions that founded it in 1961, and their graduates represent more than one-fourth of all those earning baccalaureate degrees and one-third of those earning master's degrees in the United States.

The Association of American Universities (AAU) is a distinctive higher education association, because it is open only to those institutions that are invited to join. Invitations are sparingly issued after they are approved by 75 percent of existing members. The AAU was first organized in 1900 by fourteen universities offering doctoral degrees. The original purpose was to strengthen and set standards for these degrees. A century later, the AAU focuses primarily on the PhD degree, although the multiple present-day doctoral degrees—which started at Harvard in 1872—have increased in number to almost 100. The sixty-two current invited members "focus on issues of importance to research intensive universities," such as research policy issues, research funding from all sources, and research education. From 1913 to 1948, the AAU was the "gold standard" for accrediting institutions. Its lists of three levels of institutional quality were based on student success in the graduate schools of its member institutions. The AAU's membership numbers varied from twenty to thirty of the thousands of other institutions during this period.

Currently, the AAU concentrates on research leading to "innovation, scholarship, and solutions that contribute to our nation's economy, security, and wellbeing." Since 1932, the AAU has had a policy encouraging degrees other than the PhD to emphasize preparation for college teaching. In the 1960s, the AAU supported the new, developing DA degree as a college teaching degree.

AAU member institutions lead the world in discovery research, with faculties that include 43 percent of all Nobel Prize winners since 1999. Their faculty discoveries have been patented and licensed, providing thousands of "discoveries and technologies that have led to breakthroughs in medicine, information technology, communications, and energy, to name just a few areas." AAU members award over 50 percent of all doctoral degrees earned in the United States and receive almost 60 percent of federal research funding going to the nation's universities.

These summaries illustrate the significance and impact of this type of voluntary association. Each contributes in varied ways to the diverse needs of their member institutions or the program units within them. Fundamentally, the organizations are the creatures of their founding and continuing members, and they serve important functions for these institutions. When institutions need assistance in preserving such important features as autonomy of operation or academic freedom for students and faculty, these professional associations are buffers and important sources of support.

Voluntary Accrediting Organizations

The membership organizations in this important group barely existed a century ago.[4] However, the end of the nineteenth century was a confused and uneasy time in higher education, and major changes were under way. Five key factors contributed to the turbulent state of affairs in the period from 1870 to 1910: (1) the final breakdown of the fixed, classical curriculum and the broad expansion of the elective system; (2) the development and legitimation of new academic fields (psychology, education, sociology, American literature); (3) the organization of new, diverse types of institutions to meet developing social needs (teachers colleges, junior colleges, land-grant colleges, research universities, specialized professional schools); (4) the expansion of both secondary and postsecondary education and their resultant overlapping, leading to the question, What is a college?; and (5) a lack of commonly accepted standards for admission to college and for completing a college degree.

To work on some of these problems, as early as 1871 the University of Michigan sent out faculty members to inspect high schools and admitted graduates of the acceptable and approved high schools on the basis of their diplomas. Shortly thereafter, pressures developed for regional approaches to these problems, in order to facilitate uniform college entrance requirements.

In keeping with accepted American practice and custom, groups of educators banded together in various regions to organize private, voluntary membership groups for this purpose. In New England, for example, a group of secondary schoolmasters took the initiative. In the southern states, it was Chancellor Kirkland and the faculty of Vanderbilt University. Six regional associations have developed throughout the United States, starting with the New England Association of Schools and Colleges in 1885. It was followed in 1887 by the Middle States Association of Colleges and Schools, in 1895 by the Southern Association of Colleges and Schools and the North Central Association of Colleges and Schools, in 1917 by the Northwest Association of Schools and Colleges, and in 1923 by the Western Association of Schools and Colleges. Criteria and requirements for institutional membership (which now serve as the basis for institutions being considered as accredited) were formally established by these six associations at different times: in 1910 by North Central, with the first list of accredited colleges in 1913; in 1919 by Southern; in 1921 by Northwest and Middle States; in 1949 by Western; and in 1954 by New England. Thus, at the same time that the federal government instituted regulatory commissions to control similar problems (the Interstate Commerce Commission in 1887, the Federal Trade Commission in 1914, and the Federal Power Commission in 1920), these nongovernmental voluntary membership groups sprang up to provide yardsticks for student achievement, quality assurance, and institutional operations.

Regional groups dealt in the main with colleges, rather than with specialized professional schools or programs. The North Central Association finally decided to admit normal schools and teachers colleges, but on a separate list of acceptable institutions. Practitioners and faculty in professional associations gradually set up their own membership associations. These groups established criteria for approving schools and, based on these criteria, made lists of accredited schools and program units. In some cases, only individuals with degrees from an approved school could join the professional association. Later, some membership groups made the approved program unit or school a basis for association membership. In any case, the specialized academic program and its operational unit had to meet exacting criteria, externally imposed, to acquire and retain standing in the field.

The first of the specialized or programmatic discipline-oriented associations was the American Medical Association (AMA) in 1847. However, approving processes for medical schools did not start until the early 1900s. From 1905 to 1907, the Council on Medical Education of the AMA led a movement to rate medical schools. The first ratings, in 1905, were a list based on the percentages of failures on licensing examinations by students from each school. This was followed in 1906–7 by a more sophisticated system, based on ten specific areas to be examined and inspections of each school. Of the 160 schools inspected, classified, and listed, 32 were in Class C, "unapproved"; 46 were in Class B, "probation"; and 82 were in Class A, "approved." The Council on Medical Education was attacked vigorously for this listing and approving activity. The then recently established Carnegie Foundation for the Advancement of Teaching (1905) provided funds for Abraham Flexner and N. P. Colwell to make their famous study (1908–10) of the 155 medical schools still in existence (5 already had closed). By 1915, only 95 medical schools remained, a 40 percent reduction, and they were again classified by the AMA Council on Medical Education, with 66 approved, 17 on probation, and 12 still unapproved. This voluntary effort led to the ultimate in accountability: the merger and closing of 65 medical schools. In the process, medical education was changed drastically, and the remaining schools completely revised and changed their curricula, a process still continuing to this day. This case provides an excellent example of the work of an external voluntary professional association that, with financial support from a private foundation, took the initiative to protect the public interest. Thus, in some cases, intrusions into autonomy can have beneficial results.

The success of the AMA did not go unnoticed. The National Home Study Council (now the Distance Education and Training Council) started in 1926 to do for correspondence education what the AMA had done for medical education. Between 1914 and 1935, many other professional disciplinary and service associations were started in the fields of business, dentistry, law, library science, music, engineering, forestry, and dietetics, plus the medically related fields of podiatry, pharmacy, veterinary medicine, optometry, and nurse anesthesia. From 1935 to 1948, new associations that were starting up included architecture, art, Bible schools, chemistry, journalism, and theology, plus four more medically related fields (medical technology, medical records, occupational therapy, and physical

therapy). Between 1948 and 1975, the number of specialized associations continued to expand rapidly, for programs from social service to graduate psychology
and from construction education to funeral direction. Medical care subspecial-
ties also proliferated, particularly in the allied health field, which included more
than twenty-five separate groups. After 1975 the expansion slowed greatly, and
only a few new specialized associations were created during the following two
decades, these few being formed in developing allied health areas (for nontraditional types of institutions that could not obtain "listing" by recognized national
associations) or to expand accreditation opportunities in fields in which existing
associations were unduly restrictive. One such example is the Association of Collegiate Business Schools and Programs (ACBSP), established in 1988.

   In the meantime, new needs led to additional accrediting bodies developing in
special areas. Recent examples are the American Academy for Liberal Education
(AALE, 1993) and the Teacher Education Accreditation Council (TEAC, 1997), as
well as the ACBSP. All have complete programs of accreditation and have been
listed by the U.S. Department of Education or the Council for Higher Education
Accreditation as recognized accrediting bodies in their fields. The ACBSP emphasizes teaching quality in the business field, in both community colleges and
baccalaureate or graduate institutions. AALE is recognized as the first accrediting body for liberal arts institutions and programs, based on its emphasis on
teaching, a commitment to undergraduate education, and a core of studies in the
arts, sciences, and humanities. TEAC is devoted to the improvement of academic
degree programs for professional educators. To achieve this goal, TEAC's accreditation process places primary emphasis on an audit of evidence of student achievement. These three new, quite different voluntary accrediting bodies graphically
illustrate both the importance of the voluntary sector in our society and its constant renewal.

   All of these external professional associations directly affect institutional operations, including curricular patterns, faculty, degrees offered, teaching methods, support staff patterns, and capital outlay decisions. In many cases, priorities
in internal judgments result from their outside pressures. Local resource allocations often are heavily influenced by accreditation reports. For example, a law
library, a chemistry or engineering laboratory, and teaching loads in business or
social work may have been judged substandard by these external private constituents. Yet if teaching loads in English or history also are heavy, or physics laboratories are inadequate, will they get the same attention and treatment as specialized program areas with outside pressures? In cases such as these, association

memberships are not really voluntary if the institution is placed on probation, is no longer an accredited member, and has sanctions actually applied. Frequently, students will withdraw from or not consider attending a professional school or college that is not accredited. States often limit the professional licenses for individuals to practice in a field to graduates of accredited schools. Federal agencies may not allow students from unaccredited institutions to obtain scholarships, loans, or work-study funds. The leverage of a voluntary association in such cases becomes tremendous, and the pressure for accredited status can be extremely powerful.

Starting in 1924, presidents of some of the larger institutions have attempted to limit the effects of accrediting associations. Through some of the institutionally based associations described in the previous section, they established limited sanctions and attempted to restrict the number of accrediting associations to which they would pay dues and that would be allowed on campus for site visits. These efforts to limit association membership and accreditation repeatedly failed to stem the tide. In 1949, a group of university presidents organized the National Commission on Accrediting (NCA), a separate voluntary membership association of their own, designed to cut down on the demands and influence of existing external associations and to delay or stop the development of new ones. The number of new accrediting associations dropped for a few years, but the pressures of new, developing disciplines on campus led, since the 1950s, to many new organizations of this type.

In 1949, the regional associations also felt the need for a new cooperative association and set up what became the Federation of Regional Accrediting Commissions of Higher Education (FRACHE). In 1975 the two organizations, FRACHE and NCA, agreed to merge, and they became major factors in the founding of the new Council on Postsecondary Accreditation (COPA). COPA also included four national groups accrediting specialized institutions, plus seven major, institutionally based associations. They, in turn, endorsed COPA as the central, leading voluntary association for the establishment of policies and procedures in postsecondary accreditation. After a few years, its large representative board became unwieldy and was made much smaller. Also, the institutional presidents, through their various associations, pushed vigorously for more representation. As a result, COPA reorganized further, into three assemblies: the Assembly of Institutional Accrediting Bodies (six national and eight regional), the Assembly of Specialized Accrediting Bodies (forty-two associations), and the Presidents Policy Assembly on Accreditation (seven national associations of presidents from differing types of institutions).

The system for funding COPA required the member associations, particularly the large regional associations, to collect COPA dues along with their own dues, which were tied to institutional accreditation. When, in 1993, several regional associations decided not to collect the dues for COPA, it found itself without financial support and disbanded on December 31, 1993. One of COPA's major functions was the "recognition" and "listing" of approved voluntary accrediting bodies, and on January 1, 1994, the less-expensive, streamlined Commission on Recognition of Postsecondary Accreditation (CORPA) was set up by a voluntary founding commission to maintain this phase of the work. Nine organizations paid sustaining fees to keep this critical accrediting function alive. They included the American Association of Community Colleges, the American Association of Dental Schools, the American Association of State Colleges and Universities, the American Council on Education, the Association of American Universities, the Association of Collegiate Business Schools and Programs, the Association of Governing Boards of Universities and Colleges, the National Association of Independent Colleges and Universities, and the National Association of State Universities and Land-Grant Colleges. A tenth was later added, the Western Association of Bible Colleges and Christian Schools.

From 1994 through 1996, various alternatives were debated throughout higher education, alternatives designed to continue a more extensive national accrediting presence beyond the efforts of CORPA. Finally, a presidents' work group on accreditation, consisting of twenty-five leaders from all types of institutions, developed a prospective new association to be called the Council for Higher Education Accreditation (CHEA). After a number of associations voted to approve its plan for operation, in 1995–96 a ballot was sent to 2,990 colleges and universities. Replies were received from 1,574 (52.5%) of these, and 1,476 (94%) voted to support the new organization.

CHEA differs from COPA and CORPA in three critical respects. First, it is an institutional membership organization led by college and university presidents. Second, this membership is available only to degree-granting (associate's degree and above) institutions. Third, CHEA controls its own financial destiny by directly billing institutions for dues. CHEA is the largest higher education institutional membership organization in the United States; it includes approximately 3,000 degree-granting colleges and universities.

CHEA is the only national higher education association exclusively devoted to advocacy for quality assurance and improvement through accreditation. The organization sustains three major functions: government affairs, recognition of accrediting organizations, and membership services.

Government affairs involves work with the U.S. Department of Education and Congress on federal policy matters that relate to accreditation. Many of the federal policy issues with which CHEA deals stem from the 1965 Higher Education Act (HEA), as amended, Title IV (Student Assistance), Part H (Program Integrity Triad). This section of the law provides for federal scrutiny of accrediting organizations (also known as *recognition*). Since 1952, the federal government has relied on accrediting organizations for affirmation of the quality of institutions and programs for which federal funds (e.g., for student grants and loans and for research) are made available. However, these organizations must be federally recognized. Only institutions and programs that are accredited by these federally recognized accreditors are eligible for federal funds. As of 2008, fifty-eight accreditors were recognized by the Department of Education. Government affairs issues before CHEA include, for example, how well accreditation addresses quality in distance learning; accreditation and student learning outcomes; accountability; and the effect on U.S. accreditation of efforts by the World Trade Organization to address quality in higher education through the General Agreement on Trade in Services.

CHEA's recognition function began in 1999. By the end of 2008, sixty institutional and programmatic accrediting organizations have been recognized by CHEA. Many of these organizations are also recognized by the Department of Education. CHEA's membership services include conferences and meetings, and an extensive publications program. CHEA conducts research and undertakes policy analyses of accreditation; it makes this work available in print and electronic form.

With the 2002–8 reauthorization of the HEA, CHEA became a leading advocate to sustain and enhance the traditional institutional leadership role of colleges and universities in academic decision making. Both the HEA's reauthorization in the legislative branch and the work of the executive branch—through the Secretary of Education's Commission on the Future of Higher Education, established in 2005—reflected a significant effort to shift at least some of this decision making to the federal government, using federal authority over accrediting organizations as a key vehicle to achieve this goal. CHEA, in concert with other higher education associations, worked to assure that academic decisions related to curriculum, faculty, and academic standards remained at the institutional level and did not move to federal agencies.

CHEA, after eleven years, has emerged as a major policy forum for U.S. accreditation through the framing of key complex topics such as accreditation and public accountability. CHEA's research and policy analyses are focused on emerging issues and on enhancing accreditation's capacity to deal with the extensive changes and challenges facing quality assurance in higher education, such as the internationalization of higher education. CHEA also plays a significant role in international quality assurance and accreditation, regularly convening experts from countries around the world and routinely participating in the ongoing international dialogue on quality-related issues. CHEA has been formally identified as the official, national, competent authority on accreditation and quality assurance in the United States.

The relationship of voluntary accrediting associations to state and federal governments also is a major factor in current considerations of academic freedom, institutional autonomy, and institutional accountability. The states charter most of the postsecondary institutions and, thus, establish their missions, general purposes, and the level of degrees offered. However, the states also license individuals to practice most vocations and professions. In many fields, the licensing of individuals is based on graduation from accredited programs. Thus a form of sanction has developed, and membership in the involved, specialized professional associations, supposedly voluntary, becomes almost obligatory.

In the federal arena, the listing of institutions by federal government agencies had little or no effect before World War II. However, the entrance of the federal government into the funding of higher education on a massive basis since World War II has drastically changed the overall uses of accreditation. Reported abuses of the Servicemen's Readjustment Act of 1944 (the GI Bill) led to a series of congressional hearings, which led in turn to major additions related to accreditation in Public Law 550, the Veterans Readjustment Act of 1952. Section 253 of that law empowered the Commissioner of Education to publish a list of accrediting agencies and associations that could be relied on to assess the quality of training offered by educational institutions. State-based approving agencies then used the resulting actions of such accrediting associations or agencies as a basis for approval of the courses specifically accredited. The enormous increase in federal assistance to students attending postsecondary educational institutions since 1972 made this federal listing process extremely important. Federal efforts to exert control over institutional processes have been constant for the past thirty years, with institutional membership in a listed accrediting association becoming almost obligatory. Default rates on student loans have been blamed on the post-secondary institutions and accrediting associations, and laws have been passed making the institutions enforce the police power of the government. Since voluntary associations cannot be either forced or allowed to enforce state police powers, in 1992 Congress established a new state enforcement system, called state postsecondary review entities (SPREs). The public outcry against this law led Congress to rescind it in 1994–95 by not funding it. And in 1995 the president's budget contained no request for funds to continue SPREs, effectively eliminating them. SPREs were formally eliminated from the law in 1998.

Extensive legal arguments about the resulting powers of the Department of Education still continue. However, greater institutional dependence on eligibility for funding is now based on membership in much-less-voluntary accrediting associations. A delicate relationship exists between the federal government (and eligibility for federal funding), state government (and its responsibilities for establishing or chartering institutions and credentialing individuals through certification or licensure), and voluntary membership associations (which require accreditation for membership).

Thus these voluntary associations have come to represent a major form of private constituency, with a direct impact on an institution's internal activities. Possible sanctions that would prevent state licensing of graduates, the loss of eligibility for funds from federal agencies, and problems caused by peer approval or disapproval enhance the importance of these sometimes overlooked educational organizations.

Voluntary Consortia

Formal arrangements for voluntary consortia, based on interinstitutional cooperation among and between postsecondary institutions, have been in operation for many decades. Probably the oldest continuous consortium is the Ohio College Association, founded in 1867 and finally incorporated in 1967, after its first century of operation. Its *Administrative Directory* is called "the telephone book" of Ohio higher education. Its rating programs for workers' compensation have saved more than forty of its almost one hundred current institutions more than a million dollars yearly. Decades later, Claremont Colleges (in California) started in 1925 with Pomona College and the Claremont University Center, and they were joined by Scripps College in 1926. The Atlanta University Center (in Georgia), sometimes called the Affiliation, started shortly thereafter, in 1929, and included Morehouse College, Spelman College, and Atlanta University. Over the decades, both of these latter groups have added additional institutions to their cooperative arrangements and proven that voluntary consortia can be valuable for long periods of time. Some early examples from the 1927–29 period illustrate the reality of the cooperation between Morehouse and Spelman. In those years, several faculty were jointly appointed to both faculties. Upper-division students could take courses offered by the other college. Also, they operated a joint summer school with Atlanta University. In 1932, a new library was built, and the three libraries were consolidated into a joint library serving all three institutions. Thus, although they remained separate institutions, they sacrificed some autonomy to extend their academic offerings and services.

In the years since these early beginnings, hundreds of institutions have developed informal and increasingly formal arrangements for interinstitutional cooperation. By 1966, a national study by the U.S. Office of Education found 1,107 consortia operating in the United States, with some evidence that a number of them had not responded. The Council for Interinstitutional Leadership, a voluntary national organization formed in 1968, was composed of many of the consortia. It published an updated directory regularly for more than two decades, until 1991; shortly thereafter, it was replaced by the newly established, national Association for Consortium Leadership (ACL). The most recent edition of ACL's *Consortium Directory*, published in 2004, listed data from more than one hundred consortia of many diverse types, representing about 1,800 institutional members. A planned new directory, in 2010, undoubtedly will be considerably larger. A significant number of the consortia also include business, commercial, public service nonprofit, and public school district associate members. A careful reading of the directory and its listing of consortium activities clearly demonstrates the importance of consortia in cutting-edge innovations in higher education, as well as in overall operational efficiency in providing educational services.

The importance of voluntary consortia to concerns regarding institutional autonomy also becomes evident with the enumeration of their activities. The 2004 directory listed several dozen widely differing programs and services being carried on cooperatively, in seven major areas: administrative and business services; enrollment and admissions; academic programs, including continuing education; libraries, information services, and computer services; student services; faculty; and community services, including economic development. Cross-registration between nearby institutions is quite common, as are joint library services, professional development activities, seminars, joint purchasing through group-negotiated contracts, high school and college career-advising services, and joint development projects for new technology. Many of the consortia have World Wide Web pages, e-mail, and fax capability, and some have teleconferencing capability.

A few brief examples illustrate the diversity of services expedited by the consortium method of organizing. The Massachusetts Higher Education Consortium provides an exceptional and extensive group-purchasing service for almost one hundred institutions, including members of seven smaller consortia (with varied projects). It saves each college from having to develop individual contracts (the consortium has more than eighty contracts for its institutions to use), and its joint buying power saves many millions of dollars on purchases totaling more than $150 million a year. The Council of Christian Colleges and Universities (founded in 1976 and incorporated in 1982) has ninety member institutions and provides internship, travel, and service-learning opportunities to their students in such regions as Russia, the Middle East (particularly Egypt), and Latin America (especially Costa Rica).

A relatively recent consortium is the Center for Academic Integrity, with over 360 member institutions. Funded by the Hewlett and Templeton foundations, its official location is at Clemson University. It provides research, information, and assistance to campuses in assessing the integrity climate. It publishes the *Fundamental Values of Academic Integrity* and an *Academic Integrity Assessment Guide*, and it conducts related conferences and training programs. With the increasing use of technology and the Internet for distance-learning courses, there have been dozens of consortia formed to develop and deliver courses and degree programs in this way. The Internet2 project, for example, has become such a consortium for over a hundred institutions. A U.S. Department of Education study of public universities recently found that almost 90 percent of these institutions offered electronic distance-learning opportunities, and 60 percent were in a consortium to do so. Of those, 75 percent were part of a state- or system-level group.

The diversity of academic consortia is further illustrated by the following examples. The U.S. Office of the Director of National Intelligence awarded $3 million to fund a consortium of seven campuses of the California State University (CSU) System to develop an intelligence-community center of academic excellence. The lead institution is CSU–San Bernardino, along with six other campuses in the southern part of the state. In Chicago, the Project Align Consortium involves the public schools, the city colleges, and five local public and private universities. They cooperate with the ACT organizational data system so that students are able to move "seamlessly" through the high schools, the two-year city college, and on to universities. The goal is to use the ACT system and excellent guidance to ensure that students are ready for college and that the articulation from a two- to a four-year institution is effective. Another example of a diverse consortium function is in the field of teacher education. In Texas, the CREATE Center and a select group of seven universities are working to identify data and incorporate its use in creating continuing improvement in their teacher education programs. The Texas group organized as a consortium in order to expand their data, when it has been fully developed as credible evidence of quality, so that it could be widely used.

One other, more extensive example illustrates the nature of the many comprehensive consortia and their program possibilities. The Virginia Tidewater Consortium for Higher Education (VTC) is one of six regional consortia covering all of Virginia. They were established in 1973 by state law to coordinate off-campus continuing education courses. The VTC is an example of what can happen when institutional leadership works cooperatively. It now offers a variety of services, including the cross-registration of students, faculty exchanges, interlibrary courier services, cooperative degree programs, and faculty and administrative development programs. In addition, it operates the consortium's higher education digital cable channel, off-campus centers and their continuing education programs, and the Educational Opportunity Center.

In the years since its founding in the Hampton Roads area, the VTC has grown from eight original institutions to fifteen, and includes the following: four community colleges; four public colleges and universities; four private institutions; two nonresident public universities; a national defense university (the Joint Forces Staff College); two associate members, Skyline College (formerly ECPI Technical College) and Troy University; and two affiliate members, Cox Communications and WHRO-TV. This is similar to many of the comprehensive consortia that have varied memberships, such as businesses, community organizations, and multiple school districts.

The VTC's early cooperative projects have expanded and new ones have been developed. Cross-registration has been enlarged to include the new college and university members, on both a credit and an audit basis. Articulation programs between the community colleges and the four-year, baccalaureate degree institutions have been created so students earning two-year associate of arts and associate of science degrees have them fully recognized when transferred. The Educational Opportunity Center provides free educational, career, and financial aid counseling at eleven locations. The digital cable channel operates full time and serves almost 500,000 homes, offering college courses. Study abroad programs are coordinated and offered by seven of the institutions, and an International Education Committee was designed to broaden global understanding and cooperative academic efforts. For over a quarter century, a Summer Institute on College Teaching has been attended by hundreds of college teachers. More recently, specialized programs on substance abuse prevention and institutional security have been developed. In addition, the consortium works closely with the military community, maintaining offices at differing military bases.

Another important service of the Virginia Tidewater Consortium is in hosting the national office for the Association for Consortium Leadership. After its beginning in 1968, the national office was housed at the Kansas Regional Council for Higher Education until 1991. After 1991, the VTC assumed this key responsibility, with great success. Nearly seventy groups of all types—ranging from ones with three members to ones with 1,500 members—comprise the ACL. The ACL's expanded *Consortium Directory* now includes extensive data on more than one hundred consortia.[5] The "Topic Index" lists the major activities of consortia (twenty-eight categories of service) and each individual consortium provides one in its directory entry. The "Geographic Index" lists consortia by state location. Data for each individually listed consortium contains its name and location, governance and staffing, funding, membership, and programs and services. The ACL also provides mentoring services for new groups of institutions interested in consortial-type collaboration, and it publishes a quarterly magazine of consortia activity. A detailed book, *Leveraging Resources through Partnerships*, was prepared by the leaders of the VTC and published for the ACL.[6] A yearly conference/workshop on consortia activity and future-oriented programs rounds out the extensive and valuable efforts that the ACL has undertaken through the VTC's leadership, and the ACL is open to other groups that can profit by such cooperative ventures.

The examples above illustrate the move by consortia from being primarily private institutions to representing developments in all three sectors. Although started essentially by the voluntary enterprise sector, the public enterprise sector has moved in, and several consortia now include the profit-seeking sector. The federal government passed the National Cooperative Research Act in 1984, which awards special status to research and development consortia regarding antitrust statues and gives them a monopoly exception, and a number of states passed laws to facilitate their start-up. The Illinois Higher Education Cooperative Act of 1972 provided some state support for voluntary combinations of private and public institutions. California, Connecticut, Massachusetts, Minnesota, Ohio, Pennsylvania, Texas, and Virginia have used the consortium approach for specific purposes. This trend toward public financing of consortia thus becomes a factor in institutional planning, and even in regional intrastate planning.

In the past, consortia have been developed to provide for interinstitutional needs both in times of growth and in times of decline. They are uniquely capable of handling the mutual problems of public and private institutions, and thus they provide a powerful deterrent to further governmental incursions into private and sometimes public institutional operations. At various levels of formality, consortia currently are being used by significant numbers of institutions of all types to adjust to changing curricular and funding necessities. As governmental controls continue to increase, and thus to affect institutional autonomy and academic freedom, voluntary consortia provide another way to plan independently for future operations and program development.

Regional Compacts

Regional compacts, although they are nonprofit, private organizations, are quasi governmental. Groups of states create them, provide their basic funding, and contract for services through them. They operate much like private organizations and receive considerable funding from other sources, including private foundations. Some of their studies (including policy ones), seminars, and workshops directly affect the institutions in their regions.

Soon after World War II, three regional interstate compacts developed to meet postsecondary education needs that crossed state lines. Originally, they concentrated on student exchange programs in the field of medical education; however, in the past half-century their areas of service and influence have expanded considerably. Although established, funded, and supported basically by state governors and legislatures, their indirect effects on institutional programs and operations can be significant. Listed in order of their establishment, these regional compacts are the Southern Regional Education Board (SREB, 1948), the Western Interstate Commission for Higher Education (WICHE, 1953), the New England Board of Higher Education (NEBHE, 1955), and the Midwestern Higher Education Compact (MHEC, 1991). By 2004, forty-seven of the fifty states were actively involved in one of the four state compacts. Only New York, New Jersey, and Pennsylvania were not members.

The valuable and varied programs of the compacts have often expanded far beyond the four state groups. Some interesting examples are what is now the National Center For Higher Education Management Systems, which developed out of WICHE. SREB developed a "High Schools that Work" network that has greatly expanded into thirty-one states. Several other joint projects between compacts include SREB's Educational Cooperative and WICHE's Technology Costing Methodology. WICHE has joined the MHEC's Master Property Program to improve risk management and lower insurance costs for their member institutions, saving over one hundred campuses between $3 and $4 million a year. WICHE also administered a national State Scholars Initiative, funded by the U.S. Department of Education, to arrange state-level business and education partnerships to encourage student readiness for college. These assorted projects illustrate the current and potential value of the compacts beyond their regional borders, but each one still meets regional needs in varied ways.

The Southern Regional Education Board includes governors, legislators, and other figures (some from higher education) from sixteen states (Alabama, Arkansas, Delaware, Florida, Georgia, Kentucky, Louisiana, Maryland, Mississippi, North Carolina, Oklahoma, South Carolina, Tennessee, Texas, Virginia, and West Virginia). SREB was formed by the political leaders of its member states, and they retain leadership in the organization. SREB has played a major part in the development of such important areas as equal opportunity for all students in higher education and expanded graduate and professional education. Its research and information program has been vital in state and institutional planning. Its regular legislative work conferences, planned by its Legislative Advisory Council, have been influential in setting policy and funding directions in the region.

Regionally, SREB has provided extensive "state services," including the State Data Exchange and its outstanding *Fact Book on Higher Education*. Its Academic Common Market and Doctoral Scholars programs assist students in attending out-of-state colleges and provide states with cost-effective programs that do not duplicate expensive majors unnecessarily. The Electronic Campus uses modern technology to deliver educational opportunity throughout the region (and beyond). It offers more than 8,000 courses and 325 major programs at more than 300 institutions for online, anytime, anyplace education. The Distance Learning Policy Laboratory provides key studies on all phases of distance and e-learning, regionally and nationally. SREB's special institute designed to help minority scholars is an essential part of the effort that has resulted in a 90 percent graduation rate of doctoral scholars from the program who are preparing to be college professors. The Council on Collegiate Education for Nursing keeps nurse educators informed about regional developments in their field. Current initiatives include a leadership program for staff from state agencies in higher education and a college readiness project to better prepare prospective students for study in higher education institutions. These varied areas illustrate the breadth and positive effects of this first regional compact and its influence on collegiate institutions.

The Western Interstate Commission for Higher Education has members from fifteen states: Alaska, Arizona, California, Colorado, Hawaii, Idaho, Montana, Nevada, New Mexico, North Dakota, Oregon, South Dakota, Utah, Washington, and Wyoming. WICHE was formed originally to pool educational resources; to help the states plan jointly for the preparation of specialized skilled manpower; and to avoid, where feasible, the duplication of expensive facilities. The student exchange program has been a major effort. Originally set up in the fields of medicine, dentistry, and veterinary medicine, it expanded greatly to include physical therapy, occupational therapy, optometry, podiatry, osteopathic medicine, dental hygiene, nursing, mental health, physician's assistants, pharmacy, public health, architecture, and graduate library studies. Later, the Western Regional Graduate Program (for all member states except California) included specialized interdisciplinary fields not commonly available in the WICHE states, allowing nonresident students to pay in-state rates. Thousands of professionals, mostly in health care areas, have received this assistance while enrolled in one of the contract programs in another WICHE state. Another special program supports efforts to recruit minority students into graduate degree programs and assist them in becoming college and university faculty members. All told, WICHE programs of this type assist close to 20,000 students a year, making maximum use of regional institutional facilities and saving costs for both the states involved and the students who participate. A more recent development, the Internet Course Exchange and its operations manual, provides member institutions with specialized course options and information about transferability and cost. WICHE's professional student exchange program, plus its state inventory of rural-health-practice incentives, helps students in twelve of its states to enroll in programs not yet available in their homes states.

WICHE contributes by sponsoring annual legislative workshops and timely special projects. Currently, it makes policy analyses and data available, through the Internet, on higher education in North America. A comparative research series was published on major policy issues and differences in higher education in Mexico and the United States. WICHE has developed a Western Cooperative for

Educational Telecommunications, which serves at least forty states and four continents in promoting the effective use of technology in higher education. Also, WICHE has produced quality standards for distance learning (Principles of Good Practice), developed a purchasing service for electronic equipment and services, and conducted research on actual returns in learning from these investments, as well as attempted to meet the needs of students in rural or under-served areas.

Another unique WICHE program with national and international impact is the Consortium for North American Higher Education Collaboration (CONA-HEC). As a founding partner, WICHE has been active in establishing a regional bank of institutions and programs available to students from participating colleges and universities in Canada, Mexico, and the United States. CONAHEC sponsors the North American Student Exchange Program and fosters higher education's role in building economic ties and development in the North American trade area.

The enormous diversity of the WICHE programs and their ability to change to meet new needs is again indicative of the value of regional compacts. Their diverse services provide flexibility in the states they serve, often with positive influences far beyond their immediate region.

The New England Board of Higher Education serves six states—Connecticut, Maine, Massachusetts, New Hampshire, Rhode Island, and Vermont—and is authorized by the U.S. Congress. It administers such projects as the regional student exchange program and conducts studies regarding current needs in higher education that cross state lines. Data on higher education in the New England states are collected, analyzed, and published widely for use by all interested groups in the region. Its Excellence through Diversity project gathers data from all six states and analyzes and publishes this information for regional planning purposes in each of the states. Also, timely special projects are coordinated through NEBHE, such as Project Photon, a funded endeavor stressing photonics as an important educational subject in all phases of education, from elementary schools through higher education. The program has been funded four times by the National Science Foundation, and the most recent grant employs problem-based learning where technology students solve real-world challenges from industry and research partners. Another topic, the STEM project, emphasizes work in science, technology, engineering, and mathematics through the NEBHE Science Network; it is another example of meeting a critical need in the six states. However, NEBHE's major program continues to be the student exchange, with its savings for students and optimum use of facilities. In one year, 8,000 New England students saved more than $37 million in tuition and fees.

One interesting NEBHE project was its studies of the need for veterinary medicine in the region. Political disputes about the potential location for such a program were so great that it did not develop until Tufts University started one in 1978. In this way, an important project of a regional compact (to bring a needed academic program to its area) led to the service being established by a private university. Currently, about six hundred students from many locations apply for admission, and sixty-five to seventy are accepted in each class, for a four-year program leading to a doctoral degree in veterinary medicine. This is an excellent example of the law of unintended consequences in higher education and of the importance of voluntary enterprise in American higher education.

The Midwestern Higher Education Compact serves twelve states: Illinois, Indiana, Iowa, Kansas, Michigan, Minnesota, Missouri, Nebraska, North Dakota, Ohio, South Dakota, and Wisconsin. Its three current core functions are cost savings, student access, and policy research. Its service area involves 1,000 public and private nonprofit institutions and over 4 million students. MHEC was the last of the four regional compacts to be formed. Originally, it was established to provide for interstate student exchanges at in-state tuition rates, similar to the other compacts. In addition, it included cooperative programs in vocational and higher education, and an areawide approach to gathering and reporting information that facilitates state educational planning. MHEC is recognized by legislation in each of its member states and governed by a fifty-member commission made up of legislators, governors' appointed representatives, and leaders in higher education appointed by the governors and legislatures.

In its first decade, MHEC's productivity and cost-saving projects resulted in savings of $146 million. Key initiatives came from such items as a natural gas contract system, risk management (property insurance), purchasing contracts for computer hardware and operational software, and operational maintenance. MHEC set up the original American TelEd Communications Alliance with a nonprofit Michigan group (MiCTA). This was so successful that SREB, WICHE, and NEBHE joined it. It provides nationwide contracts for local area networks, wide area networks, and national wireless technology systems, including local voice services.

MHEC's original student exchange program has involved thousands of students attending more than one hundred of the member institutions' colleges. The

gram for Minority Scholars combined three smaller proj-
d both scholarship aid and completion by future faculty
project, funded by the Lumina Foundation, expanded the
k to provide further analyses of distance learning in the Mid-
wth factors and other policy priorities regarding student action, and adult education in the region.

MHEC	he last of the regional compacts to develop, but it has clearly shown that such an organization of states can have significant effects for colleges and universities. With the member states' governors and key legislators being an active part of the system, MHEC can influence the operation and services of the region's colleges and universities.

The current four interstate compacts cover all but a few of the states in the entire country. Their diversified programs alter as the needs of their regions change. The basic costs of their operations are funded by state legislatures from tax revenues, but foundation grants plus federal projects pay for several of the new thrusts of the regional commissions. This provides another excellent example of the flexible way that the mixed society of the United States operates to adapt to changing needs and emphases.

Conclusion

During the first two centuries of American higher education's existence, religious tenets and basic social agreements resulted in a relatively fixed, classically oriented program of studies. However, as society began to open up, industrialize, and expand, it demanded change in its colleges. When this was slow to occur, new institutions met these needs, and many existing ones closed. Between 1830 and 1900, normal schools, engineering schools, military academies, and universities were copied from institutions in Europe and adapted to American norms. However, even these were not sufficient to meet democracy's needs. New types of institutions were developed, unique or almost unique to America. The land-grant colleges of 1862 and 1890, the junior colleges of the early 1900s, the comprehensive state colleges of the 1960s to 1980s, and the post–World War II community colleges all represent essentially new types of institutions. Private constituency groups often pressured state or local governments to establish them, and in some cases these private groups pressured Congress into funding some of them, including the 1862 land-grant colleges and, particularly, the 1890 land-grant colleges. The critical point, again, is that in the United States, new institutions replace existing ones that do not change.

Private constituencies, such as the five types detailed in this chapter, have a significant impact on institutional autonomy and academic freedom. Much of this impact is positive, supportive, and welcome. However, those that provide funds can affect institutional trends and directions by determining what types of academic programs or research efforts are supported. As federal and state monies tighten up even more in the years ahead, funds from alternate sources will become even more attractive. Acceptance of grants moves institutions in the directions dictated by the funding sources, and faculties are well advised to consider this possibility as the "crunch" of the twenty-first century becomes greater.

Finally, the real benefits accorded to institutions by private organizations must be mentioned again. Many membership organizations have been created to provide such advantages. In some cases, these benefits have been greater than anyone could have foreseen. Probably the most dramatic examples have come from private accrediting associations in relation to state political efforts to limit the autonomy and academic freedom of their public institutions. In 1938 the North Central Association of Colleges and Schools dropped North Dakota Agricultural College from membership because of undue political interference. The U.S. Court of Appeals upheld the action of North Central, and the state government backed away from its prior method of political interference in internal institutional affairs. In the post–World War II period, sanctions of the Southern Association of Colleges and Schools stopped legislation banning on-campus speakers in North Carolina and, after 1954, contributed strongly to the development of open campuses in other states in its region. As the nation has worked to expand higher education opportunities for minorities, almost every type of association has participated. And as society has demanded that higher education become more cost-effective, many of these associations and commissions have adopted systems that have saved large amounts of money, so that academic programs may still be offered to the students they were established to serve.

Private organizations related in some way to postsecondary education clearly continue the great tradition of direct action by voluntary citizen associations. Increasingly, they stand in the middle, between control-oriented federal and state agencies and the private and public institutions. Governments have abandoned the self-denying ordinance that in recent decades kept a state at a distance from the essence of many of its institutions. The nurturance of supportive and helpful private constituencies, therefore, becomes even more crucial as higher education enters the twenty-first century.

NOTES

1. For detailed information about foundations, the best overall source is the Foundation Center. Twelve regular publications constitute its core collection. They also have offices and reference collections in Atlanta, San Francisco, Washington, D.C., and Cleveland and cooperating collection centers in numerous libraries in each state. Its two main references are its own annual *Foundation Directory*, and the *Annual Register of Grant Support*, published by Information Today, Inc.

2. Two very useful foundation references are Joel L. Fleishman, *The Foundation: A Great American Secret: How Private Wealth is Changing the World* (New York: Public Affairs / Perseus Books Group, 2007); and the Chronicle of Philanthropy's *The Non-Profit Handbook*.

3. Three major references with extensive information about institutionally based associations are the *Encyclopedia of Associations*, published annually by Gale / Cengage Learning; the regular editions of *American Universities and Colleges*, available from the American Council on Education; and the *Higher Education Directory*, published annually by Higher Education Publications, Inc.

4. Two key sources of historical background information regarding voluntary institutional accreditation are Kenneth E. Young, Charles Chambers, and H. R. Kells and Associates, *Understanding Accreditation* (San Francisco: Jossey-Bass, 1983); and Fred F. Harcleroad, *Accreditation: History, Process, and Problems* (Washington, DC: ERIC Clearinghouse on Higher Education, 1980). Since 1997, the Council for Higher Education Accreditation (CHEA) has published an electronic *Directory of CHEA Participating and Recognized Organizations* (updated as changes become known) and a biannual print *Almanac of External Quality Review*. A somewhat different list of accrediting associations, by the U.S. Department of Education, has been available since it was required in the Veterans Readjustment Assistance Act of 1952. Inclusion on this list is one of several ways in which institutions can participate in a number of federal funding programs.

5. The best source of current information on consortia is this *Consortium Directory*, published by the Association for Consortium Leadership, c/o The Virginia Tidewater Consortium for Higher Education. Two major references about the work of consortia are Lawrence G. Dotolo and John B. Noftsinger, eds., *Leveraging Resources through Partnerships* (San Francisco: Jossey-Bass, 2002); and Lawrence G. Dotolo, *Access to Higher Education through Consortia* (San Francisco: Jossey-Bass, 2007.

6. Dotolo and Noftsinger, *Leveraging Resources*.

PART III / The Academic Community

CHAPTER NINE

Harsh Realities

The Professoriate in the Twenty-First Century

Philip G. Altbach

A merican higher education finds itself in a period of significant strain. Financial cutbacks, enrollment uncertainties, pressures for accountability, and
confusion about academic goals are among the challenges facing American colleges and universities at the end of the twentieth century and into the early part
of the twenty-first. The situation is in many ways paradoxical. The American academic model is the most successful in the world, admired internationally for
providing access to higher education to a mass clientele as well as for possessing
some of the best universities in the world. Yet higher education has come under
widespread criticism. Some argue that the academic system is wasteful and inefficient, and they place the professoriate at the heart of the problem.[1] Others
urge that higher education reconsider its priorities and place more emphasis on
teaching, reasoning that the core function of the university has been underem-
phasized as the professoriate has focused on research.[2] Again, the professoriate
is central to this criticism.

America's economic problems, related to the 2008–10 recession, structural
adjustments, and a change in thinking about the role of higher education, all
create serious long-term difficulties for the professoriate. Many policy makers

increasingly see higher education as a private good that does not deserve as much state support as it has had—and that the "users" (i.e., students) should pay more of the cost. Increasing resistance to tuition increases in private colleges and universities have created financial problems as well. Many observers believe that higher education will not fully recover financially in the foreseeable future. It has been argued that higher education's golden age—the period of strong enrollment growth, increasing research budgets, and general public support—is over.[3] This means that the academic profession, as well as higher education in general, must adjust to new circumstances. This adjustment, which has already begun, would be difficult under any circumstances, but it is all the more troubling to the professoriate, coming directly after the greatest period of growth and prosperity in the history of American higher education.

The American professoriate has been shaped by the social, political, and economic context of higher education. While academe enjoys relatively strong internal autonomy and considerable academic freedom, societal trends and public policy have affected both institutions of higher education and national and state policies concerning academe. There are many examples. In the 1860s, the Land Grant acts contributed to the expansion of public higher education and an emphasis on both service and research, while after World War II the GI Bill led to the greatest and most sustained period of growth in American higher education. Court decisions on government's role in private higher education, race relations, affirmative action, the scope of unions on campus, and other issues have affected higher education policy and the professoriate. Education is a basic responsibility of the states, and the actions of the various state governments have ranged from support for the "Wisconsin idea" in the nineteenth century to the promulgation of the California "master plan" in the 1960s. In New York and Massachusetts, as elsewhere, state policies in the postwar period had a formative influence on postsecondary education and the professoriate.[4] A recurring theme in this chapter is the tension between the autonomy and internal life of the academic profession and the many external forces for accountability.

Precisely because the university is one of the central institutions of postindustrial society, the professoriate finds itself under pressure from many directions. Increasingly complicated accounting procedures attempt to measure professorial productivity as part of the effort to increase accountability. The measurement of educational outcomes has become a major national concern, and efforts are being made to measure the effectiveness of teaching and the productivity of professors. Calls for the professoriate to provide social relevance in the 1960s were replaced in the 1980s by student demands for vocationally oriented courses. A deteriorating academic job market raised the standards for the award of tenure and increased the emphasis on research and publication. At the same time, there were demands for faculty to devote more time and attention to teaching.

A constant tension exists between the traditional autonomy of the academic profession and external pressures. The processes of academic hiring and promotion remain in professorial hands, but with significant changes: affirmative action requirements, tenure quotas in some institutions, the occasional intrusion of the courts into promotion and tenure decisions. The curriculum is still largely a responsibility of the faculty, but the debates over multicultural courses or over the number of vocational courses, for example, affect curricular decisions. Governmental agencies influence the curriculum through grants and awards. The states engage in program reviews and approvals and, through these procedures, have gained some power in areas traditionally in the hands of the faculty.

The academic profession has largely failed to explain its centrality to society and to make the case for traditional academic values. Entrenched power, a complicated governance structure, and the weight of tradition have helped protect academic perquisites in a difficult period. But the professoriate itself has not articulated its own ethos.[5] The rise of academic unions helped to increase salaries during the 1970s, but it also contributed to an increasingly adversarial relationship between the faculty and administrators in some universities.[6]

The unions, with the partial exception of the American Association of University Professors (AAUP), have not defended or articulated the traditional professorial role. Few have effectively argued that the traditional autonomy of the faculty and faculty control over many aspects of academic governance should be maintained. We are in a period of profound change in American higher education, and it is likely that these changes will result in further weakening of the power and autonomy of the professoriate. This chapter considers the interplay of forces that have influenced the changing role of the American academic profession.

A Diverse Profession

The American professoriate is large and highly differentiated, making generalizations difficult. There are more than 1.3 million full- and part-time faculty members in America's 4,300 institutions of postsecondary education. Almost 1,400 of these institutions grant baccalaureate or higher degrees, and 213 give doctoral degrees. More than a quarter of the total number of institutions are community colleges. A growing number of faculty are part-time academic staff, numbering more than half of the professoriate nationwide—and having grown by 376 percent between 1970 and 2001. They enjoy little or no job security and only tenuous ties with their employing institutions. The proportion of part-time staff has risen in recent years, reflecting fiscal constraints. Full-time but non-tenure-track appointees are a new and growing category of faculty. They usually hold limited-term jobs and often have a major responsibility for teaching. Faculty are further divided by discipline and department. While one may speak broadly of the American professoriate, the working life and culture of most academics is encapsulated in a disciplinary and institutional framework. Variations among the different sectors within the academic system—research universities, community colleges, liberal arts institutions, and others—also shape the academic profession.[7] Vast differences exist in working styles, outlooks, remuneration, and responsibilities between a senior professor at Harvard University and a beginning assistant professor at a community college. Further distinctions reflect field and discipline; the outlook of medical school professors, for example, and that of scholars of medieval philosophy are quite dissimilar. Indeed, given the changing nature of the academic workforce, it is becoming more and more irrelevant to speak of a unified academic profession. One must focus on the increasingly differentiated segments of the professoriate.

A half century ago, the academic profession was largely white, male, and Protestant. It has grown increasingly diverse. In recent years, the proportion of women in academe has grown steadily; it is now 36 percent of the total and about half of the new entrants to the profession, although women are concentrated at the lower academic ranks and suffer some salary discrimination.[8] While salary inequalities based on gender persist, women are now a majority in many humanities fields and can increasingly be found at all academic ranks. Racial and ethnic minority participation has also increased, and while Asian Americans are well represented in the academic profession, African Americans and Latinos remain proportionately few. African Americans constitute around 15 percent of the total professoriate.[9] Racial and ethnic minorities make up more than a quarter of the total academic profession. The substantial discrimination that once existed against Catholics and Jews has been largely overcome, and there has been a modest decline in the middle- and upper-middle-class domination of the professoriate.[10] Despite these demographic changes and expansion in higher education, the academic profession has retained considerable continuity in terms of its overall composition.

Any consideration of the role of the professoriate must take into account demographic, cultural, disciplinary, and other variations in the academic profession. If there ever was a sense of community among professors in the United States, it has long since disappeared. At the same time, the large majority of the professoriate retain a basic commitment to the essential values of the profession—teaching, research, and service—and they maintain considerable optimism about the profession.

The Historical Context

The academic profession is conditioned by a complex historical development. Universities have a long tradition, dating to medieval Europe, and the professoriate is the most visible repository of this tradition.[11] While national academic systems differ, all stem from common roots in Europe. The model of professorial authority that characterized the medieval University of Paris, the power of the dons at Oxford and Cambridge universities, and the centrality of the "chairs" in nineteenth-century German universities all contributed to the ideal of the American academic profession. Its medieval origins established the self-governing nature of the professorial community and the idea that universities are communities of scholars. The reforms in German higher education in the nineteenth century augmented the authority and prestige of the professoriate, while at the same time linking both the universities and the academic profession to the state.[12] Professors were civil servants, and the universities were expected to contribute to the development of Germany as a modern industrial nation.[13] Research, for the first time, became a key responsibility of universities. The role and status of the academic profession at Oxford and Cambridge in England also had an impact on the American professoriate, since the early American colleges were patterned on the British model, and the United States, for many years, was greatly influenced by intellectual trends from Britain.[14]

These models, plus academic realities in the United States, helped to shape the American academic profession. To understand this profession in it contemporary form requires a look at its most crucial period of development, beginning with the rise of land-grant colleges following the Civil War and the establishment of innovative, research-oriented private universities in the last decade of the nineteenth century.[15] The commitment of the university to public service and to "relevance" meant that many academics became involved with societal issues, applied aspects of scholarship, and training for the emerging professions and for skilled occupations involving technology. The contribution of land-grant colleges to American agriculture was the first and best-known example. Following the German lead, the new innovative private universities (Johns Hopkins, Chicago, Stanford, and Cornell), followed a little later by such public universities as Michigan, Wisconsin, and California, emphasized research and graduate training. A doctorate soon became a requirement for entry into at least the upper reaches of the academic profession; earlier, in the mid-nineteenth century, top American professors had obtained their doctorates in Germany. The prestige of elite universities gradually came to dominate the academic system, and the ethos of research, graduate training, and professionalism spread throughout much of American academe. As these norms and values gradually permeated the American academic enterprise, they have come to form the base of professorial values.

The hallmark of the post–World War II period has been massive growth in all sectors of American higher education. The profession tripled, and student numbers expanded just as rapidly. The number of institutions also grew, and many universities added graduate programs. Expansion characterized every sector, from community colleges to research universities. Growth was especially rapid in the decade of the 1960s. Expansion became the norm, and departments, academic institutions, and individuals based their plans on expectations of continued growth.

This expansion ended in the early 1970s, however, as a result of a combination of circumstances, including population shifts, inflation, and government fiscal deficits. Part of the problem in adjusting to conditions of diminished resources is the very fact that the previous period of unusual growth was a temporary phase.[16] From the 1980s to the present time, there has been increasing enrollment and an expansion of the professoriate—but the bulk of this growth has been among part-timers and non-tenure-track faculty.

Expansion shaped the vision of the academic profession for several decades, just as structural change now affects perceptions. Postwar growth introduced other changes, which came to be seen as permanent when, in fact, they were not. The academic job market became a seller's market, in which individual professors were able to sell their services at a premium. Almost every field had a shortage of teachers and researchers.[17] Average academic salaries improved significantly, and the American professor moved from a state of semipenury into the increasingly affluent middle class.[18] The image of Mr. Chips was replaced by the jet-set professor. University budgets increased, and research-oriented institutions at the top of the academic hierarchy enjoyed unprecedented access to research funds. The space program, the cold war, rapid advances in technology, and a fear in 1958

(after Sputnik) that the United States was "falling behind" educationally contributed to greater spending by the federal government for higher education. Expanding enrollments meant that the states also invested more in higher education and that private institutions prospered.

The academic profession benefited substantially. Those obtaining their doctorates found ready employment. Rapid career advancement could be expected,
and interinstitutional mobility was fairly easy. This contributed to diminished
institutional loyalty and commitment. To retain faculty, colleges and universities
lessened teaching loads, and the average time spent in the classroom declined.
Salaries and fringe benefits increased. Access to research funds from external
sources expanded greatly, not only in the sciences but also, to a lesser extent, in
the social sciences and humanities. The availability of external research funds
made academics with such access less dependent on their institutions. Those professors able to obtain significant funds were able to build institutes or centers and,
in general, to develop "empires" within their institutions.

The turmoil of the 1960s had an impact on contemporary higher education
and the consciousness of the professoriate. A number of factors in the turbulent
sixties contributed to emerging problems for higher education. The very success
of the universities in moving to the center of society meant that they were taken
more seriously. In the heady days of expansion, many in the academic community
thought that higher education could solve the nation's social problems, from providing mobility to minorities to suggesting solutions to urban blight and deteriorating standards in the public schools. In this context, it is not surprising that
colleges and universities became involved in the most traumatic social crises of
the period, the civil rights struggle and the antiwar movement triggered by the
Vietnam War. The antiwar movement emerged from the campuses, where it was
most powerful.[19] Student activism came to be seen by many, including government officials, as a social problem for which the universities were to be blamed.
Many saw professors as contributing to student militancy.

The campus crisis of the 1960s went deeper than the antiwar movement. Its
new and much larger generation of students, from more diverse backgrounds,
seemed less committed to traditional academic values. The faculty turned its attention away from undergraduate education, abandoned *in loco parentis*, and allowed the undergraduate curriculum to fall into disarray. Overcrowded facilities
were common. The overwhelming malaise caused by the Vietnam War, racial unrest, and related social problems produced a powerful sense of discontent. Many
faculty members, unable to deal constructively with the crisis and feeling under

attack from students, the public, and governmental authority, became demoralized. Faculty governance structures proved unable to bring the diverse interests of the academic community together. This period was one of considerable debate and intellectual liveliness on campus, with faculty taking part in teach-ins and a small number of professors becoming involved in the antiwar movement. However, the lasting legacy of the 1960s for the professoriate was largely one of divisiveness and the politicization of the campus. The past several decades have been largely free of activism, either from professors or students, although the "culture wars" of an earlier period have some resonance.

The Sociological and Organizational Context

Academics are, at the same time, both professionals and employees of large bureaucratic organizations. Their self-image as independent scholars dominating their working environment is increasingly at odds with the realities of the modern American university.[20] Indeed, the conflict between the traditional autonomy of the scholar and demands for accountability to a variety of internal and external constituencies is one of the central issues of contemporary American higher education. The rules of academic institutions, from stipulations concerning teaching loads to policies on the granting of tenure, govern the working lives of the professoriate. Despite the existence in most institutions of an infrastructure of collegial self-government, academics feel increasingly alienated from their institutions. In a 1990 survey, two-thirds described faculty morale as fair or poor, and 60 percent had negative feelings about the "sense of community" at their institutions.[21] Things have not improved since then.

Academics continue to exercise considerable autonomy over their basic working conditions, although even here pressures are evident. The classroom remains largely sacrosanct and beyond bureaucratic controls, although recent debates about "political correctness" have had some impact on teaching in a few disciplines, and emerging technologies may stimulate some changes in teaching styles. Professors retain a significant degree of autonomy over the use of their time outside of the classroom. They choose their own research topics and largely determine what and how much they publish, although research in some fields and on some topics requires substantial funding and therefore depends on external support. There are significant variations based on institutional type, with faculty at community colleges and at nonselective, teaching-oriented institutions subject to more constraints their on autonomy than professors at prestigious research universities.[22] Non-tenure-track and part-time faculty also have much less autonomy than their tenured colleagues and, as noted earlier, these groups are an increasingly large part of the profession—half of all new appointments fall into these categories.

As colleges and universities have become more and more bureaucratized and demands for accountability have extended to professors, this autonomy has come under attack. The trend toward decreased teaching loads for academics during the 1960s has been reversed, and now more emphasis is placed on teaching and, to some extent, on the quality of teaching. The movement to measure learning outcomes will bring further pressures on professors to demonstrate their teaching effectiveness. Without question, there is now tension between the norm (some would say the myth) of professional autonomy and demands for accountability. There is little doubt that the academic profession will be subjected to increased controls as academic institutions seek to survive in an environment of financial difficulties. Professorial myths—of collegial decision making, individual autonomy, and the disinterested pursuit of knowledge—have come into conflict with the realities of complex organizational structures and bureaucracies. Important academic decisions are reviewed by a bewildering assortment of committees and administrators. These levels of authority have become more powerful as arbiters of academic decision making.

The American academic system is enmeshed in a series of complex hierarchies. These hierarchies, framed by discipline, institution, rank, and specialty, help to determine working conditions, prestige, and, in many ways, orientation to the profession. As David Riesman pointed out a half century ago, American higher education is a "meandering procession," dominated by the prestigious graduate schools and ebbing downward through other universities, four-year colleges, and, finally, to the community college system.[23] Most of the profession attempts to follow the norms, and the fads, of the prestigious research-oriented universities. Notable exceptions are the community colleges, which employ one-fourth of the academics in the United States, and some of the less-selective four-year schools. Generally, prestige is defined by how close an institution, or an individual professor's working life, comes to the norm of publication and research—a cosmopolitan orientation to the discipline and the national profession—rather than to local teaching and institutionally focused norms.[24] Even in periods of fiscal constraint, the hold of the traditional academic models remains strong indeed.

Within institutions, academics are also part of a hierarchical system, with the distinctions between tenured and untenured staff a key to this hierarchy. The dramatic growth of part-time instructors has added another layer at the bottom of the institutional hierarchy.[25] Disciplines and departments are also ranked into hierarchies, with the traditional academic specialties in the arts and sciences, along with medicine and, to some extent, law at the top. The hard sciences tend to have more prestige than the social sciences or humanities. Other applied fields, such as education and agriculture, are considerably lower on the scale. These hierarchies are very much part of the realities and perceptions of the academic profession.

Just as the realities of the expansion of the second half of the twentieth century shaped academic organizations, affecting salaries, prestige, and working conditions and giving more power to the professoriate over the governance of colleges and universities, current diminished circumstances also bring change. In an unheralded academic revolution, there has been an increase in the authority of administrators and unprecedented bureaucratic control over working conditions on campus. In general, professors have lost a significant part of their bargaining power, which was rooted in moral authority as well as traditional shared governance. As academic institutions adjust to a period of declining resources, there will be additional organizational shifts that will inevitably work to diminish the perquisites—and the authority—of the academic profession. Universities, as organizations, adjust to changing realities, and these adjustments will work against the professoriate.

Legislation, Regulations, Guidelines, and the Courts

The academic profession has been directly affected in a number of areas by the decisions of external authorities. American higher education has always been subject to external decisions, from the Dartmouth College case in the period immediately following the American Revolution to the Land Grant Act in the mid-nineteenth century and the GI Bill in the mid-twentieth century. Actions by the courts and legislative authority have profoundly affected higher education and the professoriate. In the contemporary period, governmental decisions continue to have an impact on American higher education and the academic profession. The financial problems of higher education have already been discussed. However, academe's difficulties stem not only from new economic priorities, but also from quite deliberate policies by government at both the federal and state levels to change funding patterns for higher education and research. Other pressing social needs, combined with public reluctance to pay higher taxes, have worked to restrict higher education budget allocations. Cuts in research funding have been felt by both public and private institutions and their faculties.

Specific governmental policies have also had an impact on the profession. One area of considerable controversy has been affirmative action, the effort to ensure that college and university faculties include women and members of underrepresented minorities, so as to reflect the national population.[26] A variety of specific regulations have been mandated by federal and state governments relating to hiring, promotion, and other aspects of faculty life to ensure that women and minorities have greater opportunities in the academic profession. Some professors have opposed these regulations, viewing them as an unwarranted intrusion on academic autonomy. These policies have, nonetheless, had an impact on academic life. Special admissions and remedial programs for underrepresented students have also caused considerable controversy on campus and have been opposed by many faculty. These, too, are programs that have been implemented by governmental intervention.

The legal system has had a significant influence on the academic profession in the past several decades. The courts have ruled on university hiring and promotion policies, as well as on specific personnel cases. While the courts are generally reluctant to interfere in the internal workings of academic institutions, they have reviewed cases of gender or other discrimination, sometimes reversing academic decisions.[27] The U.S. Supreme Court decision that compulsory retirement regulations are unconstitutional has had a major impact on the academic profession and has meant that many faculty are retiring later; as a result, fewer new positions open up.

These examples illustrate the significance and pervasiveness of governmental policies on the academic profession. In a few states, there is now legislation concerning faculty workloads. Other accountability measures have also been considered. Such laws, as well as those dealing with affirmative action, directly affect the professoriate. Shifts in public opinion are often reflected in governmental policies on higher education and the professoriate. The courts, through the cases they are called on to decide, also play a role. The cumulative impact of governmental policies, laws, and decisions of all kinds has profoundly influenced the professoriate.[28] In the post–World War II era, as higher education has become more central to society, government has involved itself to a greater extent with higher education, and this trend is likely to continue.

The Realities of the Twenty-First Century

The past several decades have been problematic for the academic profession. During the 1990s, when university budgets were reasonably good, the academic profession did not expand much. With the recent economic crisis, budgets deteriorated significantly, with hiring and salary freezes. The immediate future does not offer the promise of any great improvement. The demographic changes that have resulted in more retirements have also resulted in a larger number of part-time and non-tenure-track, full-time faculty, rather than more regular appointments. The following issues are likely to be central in the debates of the coming period.

Teaching, Research, and Service

One of the main debates, the appropriate balance between teaching and research in academe, goes to the heart of the university as an institution and is crucial for the academic profession. Many outside academe, and quite a few within it, have argued that there should be more emphasis on teaching in the American higher education system. It is generally agreed that research is overvalued and that, especially considering fiscal constraints and demands for accountability, professors should be more productive.[29] The reward system in academe has produced this imbalance. Critics charge that, outside of the hundred or so major research universities, the quality and relevance of much academic research is questionable. Some have gone further, saying that much of academic research is a scam.[30]

The issue of faculty productivity has produced action in several states and on a few campuses. Massachusetts, Nevada, New York, Arizona, and Wisconsin are among the states that have been involved in workload studies. The California State University System has compared the teaching loads of its faculty members with professors in other institutions. A few states require annual reports on workloads, and some have mandated minimum teaching loads: Hawaii and Florida, for example, require twelve hours of classroom instruction or the equivalent for faculty in four-year institutions.[31] Academic institutions are also studying workloads.

American professors seem to be working longer, not shorter, hours, and classroom hours have not declined in recent years. In 1992, according to a study by the Carnegie Foundation for the Advancement of Teaching, full-time American professors spent a median 18.7 hours a week in activities relating to teaching (including preparation and student advisement).[32] On average, professors spend 13.1 hours per week in direct instructional activity: those in research universities teach 11.4 hours per week, and those in other four-year institutions, 13.8 hours.[33] Not surprisingly, professors in research universities produce more publications than do their colleagues in other institutions. For example, 61 percent of faculty in research universities reported publishing six or more journal articles in the past three years, compared with 31 percent of faculty working elsewhere.[34] If anything, workloads and the pressure for publication and research have intensified at the beginning of the twenty-first century.

With pressure for the professoriate to focus more on teaching and, probably, to spend more time in the classroom, there is likely to be more differentiation among sectors within the academic system, so that academics at the top research universities will teach significantly less than their colleagues in comprehensive colleges and universities. Greater stratification between the academic sectors, and perhaps less mobility among them, are probable outcomes. A shift in thinking has taken place about research and its role. External funding for research has declined in most fields, and competition for resources is intense. There is also an orientation toward more applied research, closer links between industry and universities, and more service to the private sector. These changes will affect the kind of research that is conducted. There may well be less basic research and more small-scale research linked to products.

Thus far, the professoriate has not fully responded to these externally initiated debates and changes, although the profession has sought to adapt to changing patterns in funding and to the more competitive research climate. In the long run, however, these structural changes will transform research culture and the organization of research. In some ways, academics have moved closer to their clientele through the emphasis on service to external constituencies. The debate about total quality management, or TQM, in higher education is, in part, an effort to convince academic institutions and the professoriate to think more directly about student needs, using a model designed to focus attention on the customer.[35]

Demographic Changes and the Decline of Community

As discussed earlier, the "age bulge" has meant that the large cohort of academics who entered the profession in the 1960s and 1970s takes up a disproportionate share of jobs, especially when openings are restricted. Part-time faculty make up an increasing segment of the profession, further altering its nature and orientation.[36] It is much harder for a midcareer academic to find another position if he or she becomes dissatisfied or desires a change in location. The safety valve of job mobility no longer functions as well. While the number of retirements is rising rapidly, and many institutions have used early-retirement incentives to meet mandated budget cuts, this has not produced significant numbers of full-time academic jobs. The current period remains a time of diminished expectations.

The academic job market for new entrants has dramatically deteriorated as well, although there are major variations by field and discipline. Smaller numbers of recent PhDs are being hired, and as it has become clear that the academic job market has contracted, enrollments in many fields at the graduate level have declined or leveled off, especially in the traditional arts and sciences disciplines. Bright undergraduates have gravitated to law school or management studies. Perhaps the greatest long-term implication is a missing generation of younger scholars, although there is also a generation of gypsy scholars who are relegated to part-time teaching with little chance of a full-time, tenure-track position. Further, a generation of fresh ideas has been lost. While there is currently a need for new PhDs to handle growing enrollments and take the place of retirees, there has been only a modest growth in full-time faculty positions, because part-timers and non-tenure-track appointees are being hired in large numbers.[37]

The size and increased diversity of the academic profession have made achieving a sense of community more difficult.[38] As institutions have grown to include well over a thousand academic staff, with elected senates and other, more bureaucratic governance arrangements taking the place of the traditional general faculty meeting, a sense of shared academic purpose has become elusive. Academic departments in larger American universities can number up to fifty. Committees have become ubiquitous, and the sense of participation in a common academic enterprise has declined. Increasing specialization in the disciplines contributed to this trend. Two-thirds of the American professoriate in the Carnegie study judged morale to be fair or poor on campus, and 60 percent felt similarly about the sense of community at their institution.[39]

Tenure, Retrenchment, and Unions

The profession has seen its economic status eroded after a decade of significant gains in real income during the 1960s. Academic salaries began to decline in terms of purchasing power in the 1970s, although there was a leveling off in the 1980s and a modest improvement in the 1990s. During the recession of the late 1970s and early 1980s, faculty members in Massachusetts and California saw actual salary cuts, while many states, including New York and Maryland, froze salaries, sometimes for more than a year. The 2008 recession brought unprecedented salary freezes, mandatory furloughs, and other cost-cutting measures that have affected the professoriate. Professional prerogatives seemed less secure, and autonomy was threatened.

Perhaps most significantly, the tenure system came under attack in the 1970s and again in the 1990s. Some argued that the permanent appointments offered to professors once they had been evaluated and promoted from assistant to associate professor bred sloth among those with tenure, although there was little evidence to back up this claim.[40] Tenure was also criticized because it interfered with the institution's ability to respond to fiscal problems or changes in program needs. Professors could not easily be replaced or fired. Originally intended to protect academic freedom, the tenure system expanded into a means of evaluating assistant professors, as well as a way to offer lifetime appointments. As fiscal problems grew and the job market deteriorated, it became more difficult for young assistant professors to be promoted. Tenure quotas were imposed at some institutions, and many raised their standards for awarding tenure. These measures added to the pressures felt by junior staff.

The tenure debates of the 1970s ended without any significant changes and with tenure intact. The renewed discussion in the 1990s, stimulated by many of the same concerns as in the earlier period, also resulted in little direct change.[41] To some extent, post-tenure review and other reforms have been implemented. There are also a growing number of academics who are not part of the tenure system, and these full-time, non-tenure-track staff are likely to increase in number as institutions try to maximize their flexibility.

Retrenchment—the firing of academic staff without regard to tenure—has always been one of the major fears of the professoriate.[42] During the first wave of fiscal crises in the 1970s, a number of universities attempted to solve their financial problems by firing professors, including some with tenure, following programmatic reviews and analyses of enrollment trends. The AAUP, several academic unions, and a number of individual professors sued the universities in the courts, claiming that such retrenchment was against the implied lifetime employment arrangement offered through the tenure system. The courts consistently ruled against the professors, arguing that tenure protects academic freedom but does not prevent firings due to fiscal crisis. Universities that were especially hard hit, such as the City University of New York and the State University of New York System, declared fiscal emergencies, firing a small number of academic staff, including tenured professors, and closing several departments and programs. Many institutions found that the financial savings were not worth the legal challenges, decline in morale, and bad national publicity, and in later crises fewer tenured faculty were terminated. The fact is that tenure in American higher education does not fully protect lifetime employment, although, in general, commitments are honored by colleges and universities.[43] The retrenchments, and discussions and debates about retrenchment, left an imprint on the thinking of the academic profession, contributing to low morale and feelings of alienation.

The growth of academic unions in the 1970s was a direct reaction to the difficulties faced by the professoriate. Most professors turned to unions with some reluctance, and despite accelerating difficulties in the universities, the union movement has not become dominant. Indeed, the growth of unions slowed and even stopped in the late 1980s. In 1980, 682 campuses were represented by academic unions. Of this number, 254 were four-year institutions, and the numbers have only modestly increased since then. Very few research universities are unionized; only one of the members of the prestigious Association of American Universities is unionized, for example. Unions are concentrated in the community college sector and in the public lower and middle tiers of the system.[44] Relatively few private colleges and universities are unionized, in part because the U.S. Supreme Court, in the *Yeshiva* case, made unionization in private institutions quite difficult. The Court ruled that faculty members in private institutions were, by definition, part of "management" and could not be seen as "workers" in the traditional sense. However, further court rulings have made it easier for private college faculty to organize unions.

The growth of academic unions has slowed in the 1990s and beyond. Legal challenges such as the *Yeshiva* decision and a realization that academic unions were not able to solve the basic problems of higher education have been contributing factors. In addition, while unions brought significant increases in salaries in the first years of contractual arrangements, this advantage lessened in later contract periods. In normal times, many faculty see unions as opposed to the traditional values of academe, such as meritocratic evaluation. Often, unions are voted in following severe campus conflict between faculty and administration. Further, unions have been unable to save faculty from retrenchment or a deterioration in working conditions. Both public university systems in New York State are unionized, but both have been hard hit by fiscal problems, and their faculty unions have not shielded staff from retrenchment, salary freezes, and the like. Unions, however, were part of an effort in the 1970s to stop the erosion of faculty advantages. Unions were also an expression of the attempt by professors in institutions with only limited autonomy and weak faculty governance structures to assert faculty power. In both of these areas, unions had only limited success.

Accountability and Autonomy

The academic profession has traditionally enjoyed a high degree of autonomy, particularly in the classroom and in research. While most academics are only dimly aware of it, the move toward accountability affects their professional lives. This trend will intensify, not only due to fiscal constraints, but also because all public institutions have come under greater scrutiny. Institutions, often impelled (in the case of public universities) by state budget offices, require an increasing amount of data concerning faculty work, research productivity, the expenditure of funds for ancillary support, and other aspects of academic life. What is more, criteria have been established for student-faculty ratios, levels of financial support for postsecondary education, and the productivity of academic staff. New sources of data permit fiscal authorities to monitor how institutions meet established criteria, so that adjustments in budgets can be quickly implemented. While most of these measures of accountability are only indirectly felt by most academics, they nonetheless have a considerable impact on the operation of universities and colleges, since resources are allocated on the basis of closely measured formulas. The basic outputs of academic institutions—quality of teaching and quality and impact of research—cannot be calculated through these efforts at accountability. Indeed, even the definitions of teaching quality and research productivity remain elusive.

If autonomy is the opposite side of the accountability coin, then one would expect academic autonomy to have significantly declined. But, at least on the surface, this has not occurred. Basic decisions concerning the curriculum, course and degree requirements, the process of teaching and learning, and indeed most of the matters traditionally the domain of the faculty have largely remained in the hands of departments and other parts of the faculty governance structure. Most academics retain the sense of autonomy that has characterized higher education for a century—although confidence is slipping. Autonomy, however, remains relatively strong at the top-tier institutions. There have been few efforts to dismantle the basic structure of academic work in ways that would destroy the traditional arrangements.

Change is nonetheless taking place, which will continue to shift the balance increasingly from autonomy to accountability and erode the base of faculty power. Decisions concerning class size, the future of low-enrollment fields, the overall academic direction of the institution, and other issues have been shifted from the faculty to the administration, or even to systemwide agencies. Academic planning, traditionally far removed from the individual professor and seldom impinging on academic careers, has become more of a reality as institutions seek to streamline their operations and worry more about external measures of productivity.

Academic Freedom

American professors at present enjoy a fairly high degree of academic freedom, although just half of the professoriate agrees that there are "no political or ideological restrictions on what a scholar may publish."[45] There are few demands for ensuring the political or intellectual conformity of professors, and the concept of academic freedom seems well entrenched. The AAUP has noted very few cases in which institutions have sought to violate the academic freedom of their staff, and there has been virtually no governmental pressure to limit academic freedom. The tensions of the McCarthy era seem far removed from the current period.[46] The fact that the past decade or more has not experienced the major ideological and political unrest and activism that characterized some earlier periods, such as the Vietnam War era, certainly has contributed to the calm on campus; however, even during the Vietnam War, academic freedom remained relatively secure. This record was, however, not entirely spotless. A number of junior faculty were denied tenure during this period because of their political views.[47] In the aftermath of September 11, 2001, there have been a few incidents relating to the academic freedom of Muslim scholars.

Academic freedom nevertheless remains a contentious issue. One of the most visible academic debates of the 1980s and 1990s relates to "political correctness," an unfortunate shorthand term for a variety of disputes concerning the nature and organization of the undergraduate curriculum, interpretations of American culture, the perspectives of some disciplines in the humanities and social sciences, and what some conservatives claim is the infusion of ideology into academe. Dinesh D'Souza, a conservative writer, argued in his 1991 book, *Illiberal Education*, that American higher education is being taken over by left-wing ideologists seeking to transform the curriculum through the infusion of multicultural approaches and the destruction of academe's traditional focus on Western values and civilization.[48] Conservative critics, including then secretary of education William Bennett, took up the call, and a major national debate ensued.[49] Some conservatives claim that the academic freedom of some conservative faculty is being violated, although there is no evidence that this is the case. The debate, however, has affected thinking about the curriculum and the role of multiculturalism on campus. While it has not touched on academic freedom directly, the politics of race, gender, and ethnicity has left a mark on academic life.[50] These social issues have entered into discussions of the curriculum, and some faculty have claimed that these issues have inappropriately influenced decision making. There have also been incidents of racial or gender-based intolerance on some campuses.

Some analysts see threats to academic freedom from more indirect but, in some ways, just as dangerous sources. The increasing links between universities and industry in terms of research and other relationships have, in the view of some critics, created a certain amount of tension on campus regarding academic freedom. In some cases, corporations have made agreements with universities that restrict the publication of research results, and corporate influence, in general, is seen to constrain faculty members who may be in departments or schools with such corporate links. However, academic freedom is largely free of basic structural constraints. During the past few decades, while there have been occasional external pressures, and issues such as political correctness on campuses have become controversial, academic freedom has been reasonably secure.

Students

The two central parts of any college or university are students and faculty. These two groups are not often linked in analyses of higher education, although students have profoundly affected the academic profession throughout the history of American higher education. Before the rise of the research university at the end of the nineteenth century, American higher education was student oriented and interaction between faculty and students was substantial. Even in the postwar period, most colleges remained oriented to teaching, although, with the decline of *in loco parentis* in the 1960s, faculty became less centrally involved in the lives of students.[51] Students affect faculty in many ways. Increases in student numbers have had the result of expanding the professoriate, and changes in patterns of enrollments also affect the academic profession. Student demands for relevance in the 1960s had implications for the faculty, as did the later vocationalism of student interests. American higher education has traditionally responded to changing student curricular interests by expanding fields and departments or by cutting offerings in unpopular areas. Student consumerism is a central part of the ethos of American higher education.[52]

Student interests have also had some impact on academic policy and governance. In the 1960s, students demanded participation in academic governance, and many colleges and universities opened committees and other structures to them. These changes were short lived, but the student demands aroused considerable debate and tension on campus.[53] Recently, students have shown little interest in participating in governance and have been only minimally involved in political activism, on campus or off, although there has been a recent increase in student volunteerism for social causes. Student interests and attitudes affect the classroom and enrollments in different fields of study. Students are themselves influenced by societal trends, government policies concerning the financial aspects of higher education, perceptions of the employment market, and many other factors. These student perceptions are brought to the campus and are translated into attitudes, choices, and orientations to higher education. Student opinions about the faculty and the academic enterprise have a significant influence on institutional culture and morale.[54]

Technology and the For-Profits

Society, and of course higher education, is undergoing an unprecedented technological revolution, and technology is having a significant impact on academic life. Traditional academic publishing is affected by online journals and electronic publishing. The peer review system for evaluating scholarly work is threatened. Blogs and other informal knowledge-communication networks have salience. For example, universities have not yet discovered how to adjust evaluation arrangements for faculty to the technological revolution. How do electronic publications "count" for promotion and tenure? How does evaluation take place in this new environment? An increasing number of professors are teaching online courses. This has required acquiring new skills and new styles of teaching and evaluating students. The rise of for-profit academic institutions, such as the University of Phoenix, has created an entirely new academic environment for a growing number of faculty. The University of Phoenix is now the largest private academic institution in the United States in terms of enrollments—and it employs a growing number of faculty. None have tenure or permanent appointments; none are expected to do research; and most are part-timers. While the for-profit sector constitutes only a tiny part of the academic system at present, it is growing and will employ more faculty in the future.

Conclusion

The analysis presented in this chapter is not optimistic. The academic profession has been under considerable pressure, and the basic conditions of academic work in America have deteriorated. Some of the gains made during the period of postwar expansion have been lost. The golden age of the American university is probably over. The basic fact, however, is that the essential structure of American higher education remains unaltered, and it is unlikely to change fundamentally. Despite the probably overall stability of the American academic system, considerable change is taking place, and much of this will adversely affect the academic profession. The professoriate stands at the center of any academic institution and is, in a way, buffered from direct interaction with many of higher education's external constituencies. Academics do not generally deal with trustees, legislators, or parents. Their concerns are with their own teaching and research and with their immediate academic surroundings, such as their departments. Yet external constituencies and realities increasingly affect academic life.

Some of the basic trends that have been discussed in this analysis, factors that are likely to continue to affect the academic profession in the coming period, can be summarized as follows:

—Increased competition for federal research funds made such funds more difficult to obtain in most fields.[55] Governmental commitment to basic research declined as well, and funding for the social sciences and humanities fell. With the end of the cold war, the emphasis on military research has diminished somewhat.

—Financial difficulties for scholarly publishers and cutbacks in budgets for academic libraries reduced opportunities for publishing scholarly work, thereby placing added stress on younger scholars, in particular, and on the entire knowledge system in academe. Reductions in library funds also place restrictions on access to knowledge. The impact of electronic publishing and online journals is beginning to be felt and will have a significant impact, although its scope and nature are not yet clear.

—Changes in student curricular choices have been significant: from the social sciences in the 1960s to business, engineering, and law in the 1980s, all with a strong vocational focus. Declines in enrollments in the traditional arts and sciences at the graduate level have also been notable.

—Demands from government for budgetary and programmatic accountability have affected higher education at every level.

—In this climate of increased accountability, academic administrators have gained power over their institutions and, inevitably, over the professoriate.

—Economic problems in society have caused major financial difficulties for higher education, affecting the faculty directly in terms of salaries, perquisites, and teaching loads. The financial future of higher education, regardless of broader economic trends, is not favorable in the medium term.

—A modest decline in public esteem and support for higher education, triggered first by the unrest of the 1960s and enhanced by some questioning of the academic benefits of a college degree, has caused additional stress for the professoriate. There is a tendency to see an academic degree as a private instead of a public good, so individuals and families—rather than the state—should pay for higher education.

—The academic profession will become further differentiated. The full-time, tenure-track professoriate is already shrinking, and the numbers of part-timers and non-tenure-track teachers are growing. In addition, terms and conditions of academic work in the different segments of the academic system will be more diverse and unequal.

—The shrinking academic employment market has meant that fewer younger scholars have been able to enter the profession, and it has limited the mobility of those currently in the profession. The increased use of part-time faculty has further restricted growth.

Given these factors, it is perhaps surprising that the basic working conditions of the American professoriate have remained relatively stable. The structure of postsecondary education remains essentially unchanged, but there have been important qualitative changes that, from the perspective of the professoriate, are generally in a negative direction. Academic freedom and the tenure system remain largely intact, but there have been increased demands for accountability. Academics retain basic control over the curriculum, and most institutions continue to be based on the department, which remains strongly influenced by the professoriate. Institutional governance, although increasingly impacted by administrators, remains unchanged.

The period of expansion and professorial power during the middle years of the twentieth century will not return. How, then, can academics face the challenges of the coming period? At one level, the academic profession needs to represent itself effectively to external constituencies. If academic unions could more effectively assimilate traditional academic norms, they might have the potential of representing the professoriate. Traditional academic governance structures are the most logical agencies to take responsibility for presenting the case for the academic profession to a wider audience, both to the public and to political leaders, probably in cooperation with university administrators.

The professoriate reacted to the challenges of the postwar period. It was glad to accept more responsibilities, move into research, and seek funding from external agencies. It relinquished much of its responsibility to students. The curriculum lost its coherence in the rush toward specialization. Now it is necessary to reestablish a sense of academic mission that emphasizes teaching and the curriculum. To a certain extent, this has occurred on many campuses, with the rebuilding of the undergraduate general education curriculum and the reestablishment of liberal education as a key curricular goal. The current emphasis on teaching is another important trend that may restore the credibility of the profession.

NOTES

I am indebted to Lionel S. Lewis, Patricia Gumport, Robert Berdahl, and Edith S. Hoshino for comments on this chapter.

1. See Allan Bloom, *The Closing of the American Mind: How Higher Education Has Failed Democracy and Impoverished the Souls of Today's Students* (New York: Simon and Schuster, 1987); Charles J. Sykes, *Profscam: Professors and the Demise of Higher Education* (Washington, DC: Regnery Gateway, 1988); Martin Anderson, *Imposters in the Temple* (New York: Simon and Schuster, 1992). For a more optimistic perspective, see Philip G. Altbach, Patricia J. Gumport, and D. Bruce Johnstone, eds., *In Defense of American Higher Education* (Baltimore: Johns Hopkins University Press, 2001).

2. Ernest L. Boyer, *Scholarship Reconsidered: Priorities of the Professoriate* (Princeton, NJ: Carnegie Foundation for the Advancement of Teaching, 1990).

3. Harold T. Shapiro, "The Functions and Resources of the American University of the Twenty-First Century," *Minerva* 30 (1992): 163–74.

4. Richard M. Freeland, *Academia's Golden Age: Universities in Massachusetts, 1945–1970* (New York: Oxford University Press, 1992).

5. Edward Shils, "The Academic Ethos under Strain," *Minerva* 13 (1975): 1–37. See also Henry Rosovsky, *The University: An Owner's Manual* (New York: Norton, 1990).

6. Robert Birnbaum, "Unionization and Faculty Compensation, Part II," *Educational Record* 57 (1976): 116–18.

7. Kenneth P. Ruscio, "Many Sectors, Many Professions," in *The Academic Profession: National, Disciplinary, and Institutional Settings*, ed. Burton R. Clark (Berkeley: University of California Press, 1987).

8. Mary M. Dwyer, Arlene A. Flynn, and Patricia S. Inman, "Differential Progress of Women Faculty: Status 1980–1990," in *Higher Education: Handbook of Theory and Research*, vols. 1–, ed. John C. Smart (New York: Agathon, 1991), vol. 7.

9. The most through analysis of the American academic profession is in Jack H. Schuster and Martin J. Finkelstein, *The American Faculty: The Restructuring of Academic Work and Careers* (Baltimore: Johns Hopkins University Press, 2006).

10. Jake Ryan and Charles Sackrey, *Strangers in Paradise: Academics from the Working Class* (Boston: South End, 1984).

11. Charles Homer Haskins, *The Rise of Universities* (Ithaca, NY: Cornell University Press, 1965).

12. Joseph Ben-David and Awraham Zloczower, "Universities and Academic Systems in Modern Societies," *European Journal of Sociology* 3 (1962): 45–84.

13. Fritz K. Ringer, *The Decline of the German Mandarins: The German Academic Community, 1890–1933* (Cambridge, MA: Harvard University Press, 1969).

14. Frederick Rudolph, *The American College and University: A History* (New York: Vintage, 1965 [1962]).

15. Laurence Veysey, *The Emergence of the American University* (Chicago: University of Chicago Press, 1965).

16. This theme is developed at greater length in David Henry, *Challenges Past, Challenges Present* (San Francisco: Jossey-Bass, 1975).

17. The academic job market of this period is captured in Theodore Caplow and Reece J. McGee, *The Academic Marketplace* (New York: Basic Books, 1958). Current realities are reflected in Dolores L. Burke, *A New Academic Marketplace* (Westport, CT: Greenwood, 1988), a replication of the earlier Caplow and McGee study.

18. See Logan Wilson, *American Academics: Then and Now* (New York: Oxford University Press, 1979).

19. Seymour Martin Lipset, *Rebellion in the University* (New Brunswick, NJ: Transaction, 1993).

20. Burton R. Clark, *The Academic Life* (Princeton, NJ: Carnegie Foundation for the Advancement of Teaching, 1987). For a structural discussion of American higher education, see Talcott Parsons and Gerald Platt, *The American University* (Cambridge, MA: Harvard University Press, 1973).

21. These figures come from a survey of the views of the American academic profession undertaken by the Carnegie Foundation for the Advancement of Teaching in 1992. See J. Eugene Haas, "The American Academic Profession," in *The Interna-*

tional Academic Profession: Portraits of Fourteen Countries, ed. Philip G. Altbach (Princeton, NJ: Carnegie Foundation for the Advancement of Teaching, 1997).

22. See James S. Fairweather, *Faculty Work and Public Trust: Restoring the Value of Teaching and Public Service in American Academic Life* (Boston: Allyn and Bacon, 1996); Robert T. Blackburn and Janet H. Lawrence, *Faculty at Work: Motivation, Expectation, Satisfaction* (Baltimore: Johns Hopkins University Press, 1995).

23. David Riesman, *Constraint and Variety in American Education* (Garden City, NY: Doubleday, 1958), 25–65.

24. Alvin Gouldner, "Cosmopolitans and Locals: Toward an Analysis of Latent Social Roles, 1," *Administrative Science Quarterly* 2, no. 3 (Dec. 1957): 281–303; Alvin Gouldner, "Cosmopolitans and Locals: Toward an Analysis of Latent Social Roles, 2," *Administrative Science Quarterly* 2, no. 4 (Mar. 1958): 445–67.

25. Judith M. Gappa and David W. Leslie, *The Invisible Faculty: Improving the Status of Part-Timers in Higher Education* (San Francisco: Jossey-Bass, 1993).

26. See, for example, Valora Washington and William Harvey, *Affirmative Rhetoric, Negative Action: African-American and Hispanic Faculty at Predominantly White Institutions* (Washington, DC: George Washington University, School of Education, 1989).

27. William A. Kaplin and Barbara A. Lee, *The Law of Higher Education: A Comprehensive Guide to Legal Implications of Administrative Decision Making* (San Francisco: Jossey-Bass, 1995).

28. Edward R. Hines and Leif S. Hartmark, *The Politics of Higher Education* (Washington, DC: American Association for Higher Education, 1980).

29. The most influential consideration of this topic is in Boyer, *Scholarship Reconsidered*. See also William F. Massy and Robert Zemsky, *Faculty Discretionary Time: Departments and the Academic Ratchet* (Philadelphia: Pew Higher Education Research Program, 1992).

30. Sykes, *Profscam*. See also Page Smith, *Killing the Spirit: Higher Education in America* (New York: Viking, 1990). Both of these volumes received widespread attention in the popular media and sold well.

31. Arthur Levine and Jana Nidiffer, "Faculty Productivity: A Re-Examination of Current Attitudes and Actions," unpublished manuscript, Institute of Educational Management, Harvard Graduate School of Education, 1993.

32. See Ernest L. Boyer, Philip G. Altbach, and Mary Jean Whitelaw, *The Academic Profession: An International Perspective* (Princeton, NJ: Carnegie Foundation for the Advancement of Teaching, 1994). Academics in other countries report that they teach similar amounts: Germany, 16.4 hours per week; Japan, 19.4; Sweden, 15.9; England, 21.3.

33. Haas, "American Academic Profession," 351.

34. Ibid.

35. Daniel Seymour, "TQM: Focus on Performance, Not Resources," *Educational Record* 74 (1993): 6–14. See also Robert Birnbaum, *Management Fads in Higher Education* (San Francisco: Jossey-Bass, 2000).

36. Elaine El-Khawas, *Campus Trends, 1991* (Washington, DC: American Council on Education, 1991), 7.

37. William G. Bowen and Julie Ann Sosa, *Prospects for Faculty in the Arts and Sciences* (Princeton, NJ: Princeton University Press, 1989). Demographic projections, however, must be carefully evaluated, because they have frequently been wrong. See also Martin J. Finkelstein, Robert K. Seal, and Jack H. Schuster, *A New Academic Generation* (Baltimore: Johns Hopkins University Press, 1998).

38. Carnegie Foundation for the Advancement of Teaching, *Campus Life: In Search of Community* (Princeton, NJ: Carnegie Foundation for the Advancement of Teaching, 1990). See also Irving J. Spitzberg, Jr., and Virginia V. Thorndike, *Creating Community on College Campuses* (Albany: State University of New York Press, 1992).

39. Haas, "American Academic Profession."

40. Bardwell Smith, ed., *The Tenure Debate* (San Francisco: Jossey-Bass, 1973). For a more recent attack on tenure, see Anderson, *Imposters in the Temple.*

41. Matthew W. Finken, ed., *The Case for Tenure* (Ithaca, NY: Cornell University Press, 1996). See also Cathy A. Trower, *Tenure Snapshot* (Washington, DC: American Association for Higher Education, 1996); Richard P. Chait, ed., *The Questions of Tenure* (Cambridge, MA: Harvard University Press, 2002).

42. See Marjorie C. Mix, *Tenure and Termination in Financial Exigency* (Washington, DC: American Association for Higher Education, 1978).

43. Sheila A. Slaughter, "Retrenchment in the 1980s: The Politics of Prestige and Gender," *Journal of Higher Education* 64 (1993): 250–82. See also Patricia J. Gumport, "The Contested Terrain of Academic Program Reduction," *Journal of Higher Education* 64 (1993): 283–311.

44. For example, in the sixty-four-campus State University of New York System, which is unionized, there is a bifurcation between the four research-oriented university centers, which have been reluctant to unionize, and the fourteen four-year colleges, which favor unionization. Since the four-year college faculty are in the majority, the union has prevailed.

45. Boyer, Altbach, and Whitelaw, *International Academic Profession,* 101. The United States falls at the lower end on this spectrum, with scholars in Russia, Sweden, Mexico, Germany, Japan, and other countries feeling more positive about their freedom to publish.

46. See Noam Chomsky, ed., *The Cold War and the University* (New York: New Press, 1997), for a general discussion of the impact of the cold war period on American higher education.

47. Joseph Fashing and Stephen F. Deutsch, *Academics in Retreat* (Albuquerque: University of New Mexico Press, 1971).

48. Dinesh D'Souza, *Illiberal Education: The Politics of Race and Sex on Campus* (New York: Free Press, 1991).

49. Among the numerous books on the topic, see Paul Berman, ed., *Debating P.C.: The Controversy over Political Correctness on College Campuses* (New York: Dell, 1992); Patricia Aufderheide, ed., *Beyond PC: Toward a Politics of Understanding* (Saint Paul,

MN: Graywolf, 1992); Francis J. Beckwith and Michael E. Bauman, eds., *Are You Politically Correct? Debating America's Cultural Standards* (Buffalo, NY: Prometheus, 1993).

50. William A. Smith, Philip G. Altbach, and Kofi Lomotey, eds., *The Racial Crisis in American Higher Education* (Albany: State University of New York Press, 2002).

51. Helen Lefkowitz Horowitz, *Campus Life: Undergraduate Cultures from the End of the Eighteenth Century to the Present* (Chicago: University of Chicago Press, 1987).

52. Arthur Levine, *When Dreams and Heroes Died: A Portrait of Today's College Student* (San Francisco: Jossey-Bass, 1980).

53. Alexander W. Astin, Helen Astin, Alan Bayer, and Ann Bisconti, *The Power of Protest* (San Francisco: Jossey-Bass, 1975).

54. Alexander W. Astin, *What Matters in College: Four Critical Years Revisited* (San Francisco: Jossey-Bass, 1993).

55. See Roger L. Geiger, *Research and Relevant Knowledge: American Research Universities since World War II* (New York: Oxford University Press, 1993).

CHAPTER TEN

College Students in Changing Contexts

Sara Goldrick-Rab and Marjorie A. E. Cook

One of the most fundamental shifts in American higher education over the last half-century occurred among its students. Corresponding with dramatic changes in public policy, cultural norms about education, and demographics, the undergraduate population came to much more closely reflect the broader populace. While in the past college-goers constituted a highly elite group, today's undergraduates often resemble the "average" American.[1] As a result, the challenges and opportunities affecting our society also shape how and under what conditions students experience college. For example, contemporary students frequently struggle with financial needs and academic limitations; tensions between friends, family, and school; and health issues.

While popular and scholarly literatures have long recognized that college students are central to understanding higher education, typically little attention is paid to the role of undergraduates as actors within the social aspects of colleges and universities. In particular, the way in which mutually interactive changes in institutions and students over time shifted the meaning and experience of college going is often neglected. Thus our goal in this chapter is to review key trends affecting the composition of both the undergraduate population and the colleges that serve them, and to consider how, together, those changes contribute to current college experiences.

As the empirical data we present in this chapter explains, the move toward universal enrollment in American postsecondary education means that participation is much less exclusive than it used to be, resulting in (and from) greater heterogeneity in the college-going population. While heterogeneity comes with benefits (e.g., more racial and ethnic diversity), it also brings consequences (e.g., an increased need for remedial education).[2] In addition, college experiences are intertwined with other experiences, such as work and family life.

We also consider the implications of these changing contexts for academic theory and research, as well as for policy and practice. Explaining the decisions, behaviors, and outcomes of an incredibly diverse set of students is much more challenging than accounting for those of a homogenous population. An interdisciplinary approach to the study of higher education, one incorporating economic, sociological, psychological, and even psycho-biological approaches, is needed and ought to be developed. In particular, there are social, cognitive, and developmental processes—ones that have largely gone unexamined but affect the expression of college students' decisions—that could prompt us to rethink how we explain college choices in America. Also, such an approach would undoubtedly lead to different means of serving and supporting students.

Demography and Stratification in Higher Education

Over time, higher education in the United States changed substantially to include more citizens, and that move was accompanied by shifts in the composition of both students and schools. In this section we describe those trends, emphasizing that as the student body grew more diverse, so did the kinds of colleges and universities serving them. At the same time, opportunities both expanded in number and became more distinct and disparate, reflecting and preserving key aspects of the inequality of opportunity and outcomes.

Widening Participation

College is a progressively more common part of American life, and this means that the characteristics of undergraduates are far different than they once were. Fully 95 percent of all high school seniors expect to have at least some form of a college education (up from 79% in 1981). There is relatively little variation in those expectations based on race or gender, and expectations are quite high

(90%) even among children of low-income families.[3] At the same time, routes to and through college vary greatly.

Many people are realizing their expectations through at least some form of college attendance. In 1970, there were 6.3 million undergraduates in the United States, and the number of participants increased by more than one-third over the next ten years, to over 9 million. Between 1980 and 2000, undergraduate enrollment continued to enlarge at a more modest 26 percent. From 2000 to 2008, it grew further, swelling an additional 17 percent to bring the total to nearly 15 million undergraduates in higher education. That number is projected to increase to nearly 17.5 million by 2018.[4]

The increase in overall enrollment rates is partly attributable to population growth. For example, even though the percentage of eighteen- to twenty-four-year-olds enrolling in college remained flat between 1997 and 2007, the representation of that age group in the U.S. population increased from 25.5 million to 29.5 million, resulting in a 16 percent increase in college attendance.[5] In addition, high school graduation rates expanded, affecting the percentage of young adults receiving at least basic preparation for college entrance. In 1970, only 52 percent of adults aged 25 or over completed a high school education. By 2007, that number reached 84 percent.[6]

Changes in the American labor market also prompted many people to pursue a college education as the country transitioned from manufacturing to a knowledge-based economy. Between 1986 and 2006, the share of high-skill jobs (those requiring a bachelor's degree or more) grew, while the share of low-skill jobs (requiring a high school diploma or less) saw a decline.[7] The Bureau of Labor Statistics estimates that by 2014, fully 45 percent of all job openings will be middle-skill positions (requiring more than a high school education but less than a bachelor's degree), with another 33 percent consisting of high-skill occupations. Only 22 percent of the jobs will be low-skill service positions requiring no college education.[8]

In general, when jobs offering decent wages are in short supply, college becomes an attractive option, since individuals strive to become more competitive for existing and future positions. College enrollment hit an all-time high in 2009, when the national unemployment rate was the highest in more than a quarter of a century. Unemployment had the greatest impact on the age group most closely associated with college attendance. Only 46 percent of Americans aged sixteen to twenty-four were employed during the beginning of fall 2009, the lowest rate of employment for this group since the Department of Labor began collecting these data in 1948.[9]

The value of a college education is reflected in the stability of wages for bachelor's degree holders compared with individuals with less education. In 1980, the average wage for full-time workers, aged twenty-five to thirty-four, with a bachelor's degree or more was $45,000. By 2007, that average wage had increase by just 6.7 percent, to $48,000. In contrast, earnings for those with a high school diploma declined 17 percent, and for those with less than a high school diploma, 23 percent. Such numbers suggest a lifetime penalty for individuals who forego higher education and may compel many Americans to enroll in college.[10]

Compositional Change: Students

While absolute growth in the college-going population helped shape today's college milieu, compositional changes also impacted the college experience, turning it into a set of highly diverse experiences that lead to very different outcomes. Today's students are heterogeneous in many dimensions, including race and ethnicity, academic ability, precollege achievement, effort level, study skills, ambitions, and religious background.[11]

The undergraduate population in the United States has altered in numerous respects since 1970. For example, it has become increasingly diverse in terms of race, gender, and social class. The proportion of white students steadily declined between 1976 and 2006 (from 84% to 67%), while the proportion of Hispanic students tripled (from 3.6% to 11.4%), the proportion of Asian students nearly quadrupled (from 1.8% to 6.8%), and the proportion of black students grew by over 40 percent (from 9.6% to 13.3%). As barriers to college entry for women diminished, they became a dominant presence in higher education. Now, more than half of all undergraduates are female, and, while the presence of men attending college full time has declined (from 48.5% in 1970 to 35% in 2008), the representation of women attending part time has increased (from nearly 8% in 1970 to nearly 14% in 2008). By 2018, women are expected to account for nearly three out of every five undergraduates.[12]

While many policies and practices have attempted to diminish the extent to which family background predicts college access, over time the linkages between parental education, family income, and college going have increased.[13] For example, among college-goers in the National Longitudinal Study of 1972 (NLS-72), 28 percent had a father holding a bachelor's degree and 16 percent had a mother with that degree. In contrast, among college-goers in the National Educational Longitudinal Study of 1988 (NELS:88), fully 35 percent of college-goers had that paternal educational advantage, and 30 percent had a mother with a bachelor's degree. There have also been shifts in the income distribution of college students, although these are more difficult to document, since colleges and universities rarely collect family income information on all students. According to estimates comparing the NLS and NELS studies, the proportions of undergraduates from the lowest and highest family-income brackets have increased over time, while the proportion from middle-income families has declined somewhat. The number of Pell grant recipients has nearly tripled, and their representation among all undergraduates has grown (increasing from 14% to 23% from 1976 to 2008).[14]

There have also been notable changes in the age distribution of students. While the average age of undergraduates has increased, that change was primarily driven by shifts in the proportion of students aged nineteen and under (which declined from 46% in 1970 to 29% in 2008) and the proportion aged twenty-five and older (which increased from 12% in 1970 to nearly 28% in 2008).[15]

One of the most-often-derided changes to American higher education is the declining academic preparation of its students. That shift is at least partly a function of widening participation. In other words, as more students from a variety of backgrounds entered college, the average levels of academic preparation had to decline (similarly, as SAT test taking has become more common, the average score has declined). Comparisons over time are hard to document, as they are complicated by factors such as grade inflation. According to one measure—tested math ability—the proportion of college-goers in the bottom quartile of the distribution has increased (from 11% to 16% between 1970 and 1990) while the representation of students with scores in the top quartile has decreased (from 41% to 33%).[16] Taking these changes into account, it should come as no surprise that 40 percent of college students require at least one remedial course. More than one-fifth of college freshmen, for example, are enrolled in remedial math.[17] Rates of remediation are the highest among the groups that have most dramatically increased their representation in higher education over time—for example, fully 63 percent of students who come from families in the bottom socioeconomic quintile need remediation, typically in reading.[18] Their growing presence in postsecondary education therefore represents great strides in the nation's goals for an inclusionary tertiary system, and brings with it the need to rethink the particular goals of "higher" education.

While there have been notable alterations in the kinds of postsecondary institutions available to students (see the next section), the distributions of undergraduate enrollment have not shifted dramatically over the last forty years, with one exception. While approximately 80 percent of undergraduates are, and have been, enrolled in the public sector, the proportion enrolled in community colleges has increased, from 39 percent in 1970 to 52 percent in 2007.[19]

Compositional Change: Institutions

As the composition of students in higher education has altered, the institutions that serve them have also evolved, giving rise to new institutions and prompting changes in existing colleges. Like students, colleges are more varied than ever.

In 1870 there were 563 institutions of higher education in the United States. By the turn of the twentieth century there were 977, and 4,182 by the turn of the twenty-first century. Between 1976 and 2006, the number of public institutions grew: by 17 percent for four-year universities and nearly 16 percent for two-year colleges. Private not-for-profit institutions experienced very different changes. While, over the same thirty-year period, the number of four-year institutions in that sector rose by almost 14 percent, private two-year not-for-profits experienced a dramatic decline of 43 percent (in 1976 there were 188 institutions of this type, but in 2006 just 107 remained).[20]

At the same time, the representation of private for-profit institutions increased dramatically. In 1976, there were only fifty-five for-profit institutions in the United States. Forty of these colleges served students seeking associate degrees and short-term certificates, and only fifteen offered bachelor's degrees. By 2006, the number of two-year for-profits had increased to 533. Four-year for-profit institutions experienced the greatest thirty-year increase, to 453 institutions. In 1976 these institutions accounted for just 2 percent of all postsecondary institutions; today nearly one in four colleges and universities are part of that sector.[21]

Community colleges and for-profit institutions represent very different educational options for college students. They vary in their missions, admissions standards, approaches to student services such as job placement, and in how they set tuition and leverage financial aid dollars. Much of the focus of proprietary schools and community colleges is on providing students with a career-focused education, but there are more differences between the two types of institutions than similarities, including mission, governance, size, cost, and market orientation. Compared with students at public two-year colleges, students at for-profit institutions are disproportionately women, African American or Latino, and single parents.[22] Students may be attracted to these institutions because they benefit from a higher level of support and guidance, and from admissions through career placement, compared with students enrolled at community colleges. These institutions also have far fewer options in terms of programs and electives, compared with community colleges. The curricula tend to be more standardized at proprietary schools, presumably to allow faculty with varying experience levels to provide a consistent degree of instruction to students.

These institutions also differ in the financial aid participation rates of their students. For example, among students earning associate's degrees from public two-year colleges in 2007–8, 38 percent graduate with some level of student loan debt. In comparison, 98 percent of students receiving associate's degrees from private for-profit institutions incur that debt.[23] For students earning an associate's degree from a public two-year college, 8 percent have student loan debt between $20,000 and $30,000 and 5 percent owe $30,000 or more. Among students earning their associate's degree from a for-profit institution, one-quarter owe between $20,000 and $30,000, and nearly one-fifth (19%) carry student loan debt in excess of $30,000.[24]

Not only do students who attend proprietary schools take on more student loan debt, they are also more likely to default on those loans. The default rate for students who attend private nonprofit two-year institutions is 16.2 percent four years after borrowers enter repayment, compared with 16.6 percent for students who attend public two-year institutions, and 27.2 percent for students who attend for-profit two-year institutions.[25]

During the 1990s, proprietary schools were forced to become more similar to community colleges, due to tighter accreditation standards and federal financial aid policies. While still maintaining their focus on preparing students for careers, these colleges now are requiring general education courses as part of their degree requirements, as well as offering developmental education courses and classes for English-language learners.[26] Their rapid growth and market orientation indicate alterations in the climate of higher education that may have lasting implications.

Other changes shape undergraduate education as well. For example, over time the proportion of female faculty has increased substantially—in 1870 barely one in ten faculty were women, but by 1950 that percentage had grown to one in four, and today nearly one in two faculty members are female.[27] However, the representation of women faculty varies by rank and institutional type: just 48 percent of them are tenured (compared with 72% of male faculty), and nearly one in five are employed as lecturers, instructors, or in other no-rank positions (compared with just 9% of male faculty). Women represent 38 percent of the faculty at lower status colleges, compared with 27 percent at more prestigious universities.[28]

The student-faculty ratio has also increased by nearly ten (to 39 to 1), and expenditures per student have declined—changes that most likely stem from the swells in undergraduate enrollment and persistent efforts to contain costs. According to one estimate, today's productivity in the nation's public colleges and universities (as measured by the ratio of degrees to expenditures) is less than half of what it was forty years ago.[29]

Degree Completion

Despite a greater awareness of the need for postsecondary education in terms of wages, job security, and job satisfaction, according to some estimates the percentage of entering students who achieve their goal of earning a bachelor's degree is lower today than it was in the 1970s.[30] A comparison of the eight-year college completion rates for members of the 1972 and 1992 cohorts of graduating seniors reveals that the overall college graduation rate declined slightly, from 50.5 percent to 46 percent.[31]

Degree completion rates vary dramatically between and within the types of institutions students first attend. In 1972, graduation rates were comparable (64%) for students attending four-year public and four-year private institutions, even though bachelor's degree completion varied greatly, based on the selectivity of the institutions within each category. The graduation rate at flagship public schools was 73.5 percent, compared with 62 percent at nonflagship public colleges.[32] The gap was even wider in the private four-year sector, with 80 percent of students at highly selective colleges earning a bachelor's degree, compared with 58 percent at less-selective private colleges. Only one-fifth of community college students in that cohort completed a bachelor's degree within eight years of high school graduation.

For the high school class of 1992, graduation rates rose among private and selective public four-year institutions, with increases of between 9 and 12 percentage points in the proportion of students who earned bachelor's degrees. Less-selective public four-year colleges saw a 5 percentage point decline in graduation rates among this same group of students, and community colleges experienced only a slight decline of 2 percentage points.[33]

One reason for the decline—or at least stagnation—in college completion rates is the increased enrollment of less-prepared students. For example, as noted earlier, rates of remediation have grown, and the incidence of degree completion among remedial students is quite low.[34] While that relationship is not clearly causal, and some studies even indicate positive effects of remediation on academic progress, it does suggest that inadequate preparation for college contributes to declines in completion rates—at least at the descriptive level.[35]

Rigorous research nonetheless indicates that declines in average academic preparation do not account for all of the stagnation in completion rates.[36] In fact, at nonselective four-year universities (where 28% of the nation's undergraduates are enrolled), declining resources play a much more important role.[37]

Changing completion rates could also be linked to the increasing role of the community college. The nation has relied on community colleges to absorb much of the growth in undergraduate enrollment. But median per-student expenditures during the 1990s were just $2,610 at community colleges, having declined 14 percent since the 1970s (in comparison, spending at public four-year nonflagship colleges was 52% higher).[38] A growing number of students are enrolled in this underresourced sector, and some studies suggest that inadequate spending compromises students' chances for degree completion by contributing to overcrowding, outdated technology, and a shortage of permanent, full-time faculty.[39] Some analysts also suggest that while community colleges offer a wide range of educational options and services, they could do more to help students make appropriate choices that lead to degree completion, including securing financial aid.[40] Others would argue that those services would be difficult to provide without greater resources.[41] In either case, with nearly 40 percent of community college students hailing from homes where neither parent attended college, this lack of knowledge and guidance is particularly deleterious. While these students are less likely to apply for financial aid, they are more likely to enroll in classes they do not need, thereby increasing the time and expense of attending college, resulting in a greater likelihood of dropouts.[42]

Shifting Inequality

Even though many policies endeavor to promote equality of educational opportunity, college continuation rates for high school graduates remain highly stratified by family background. Consider, for example, trends by family income. In 1972, just under one-fourth (23%) of high school seniors from the poorest families entered college the fall after high school graduation. Over the next 35 years the proportion of low-income students entering college immediately after high school rose dramatically, reaching 45 percent in 1990 and 55 percent in 2007. Increases among middle- and upper-income students were less pronounced. Therefore, despite policy efforts to diminish inequality, the income gap in college going narrowed over time but remained sizable (for example, the gap between upper- and lower-income groups decreased from 41% to 23%).[43]

Disparities based on parental educational attainment are even larger. Rates of college going among the children of parents lacking a bachelor's degree have not increased since 1992, while growing 5 percentage points among those with at least one parent holding a BA. As a result, the gap between those from the best educated families and those from the least educated homes is 35 percentage points. Furthermore, the difference in college-going rates between the children of BA-educated parents and those of parents with "some college" widened from 14 to 21 percentage points.[44]

While higher education has become more diverse in terms of race and ethnicity, racial inequality in college-going rates has not diminished much since 1972. Even though the black college-going rate swelled to nearly 56 percent (from 38%) since that time, the white college-going rate also grew substantially—leaving the gap nearly stagnant (from 11% to 14%). Because college-going rates of Hispanics have not changed much since the 1970s, a Hispanic-white gap was created and grew substantially (from 0% in 1972 to nearly 9% in 2007).[45]

Thus, as the first decade of the new millennium comes to a close, much of the enrollment in postsecondary institutions in America is composed of low-income, first-generation, and/or racial and ethnic minority college students. But access is not always translated into success, for these students are much more likely than their peers to leave college without a degree. For example, low socioeconomic status students are five times less likely to earn a bachelor's degree within six years, compared with their more advantaged peers (11% versus 55%). For students attending public four-year institutions, one-third of the most disadvantaged students earned degrees within six years, compared with two-thirds of the students from more privileged homes. The attainment gap in the private not-for-profit four-year sector was even greater, with a difference of 43 percent compared with 80 percent.[46]

The Changing College Experience

The characteristics of both students and colleges have clearly changed over time. Evidence of a corresponding alteration in how and under what conditions students attend college abounds.

How Students Attend College

In the past, the dominant pattern of college enrollment involved high school students transitioning directly into college the fall after graduation. Now, delaying entrance into college after high school is becoming more common. Among students who enrolled in postsecondary education for the first time in 1995–96, nearly one-third waited a year or more after graduating from high school before attending college.[47] Using data from NELS:88, researchers found that, among 1992 high school seniors, 16 percent of the students delayed their entry into college following high school. Students taking time off are six times more likely to come from families in the bottom socioeconomic quintile, compared with high school graduates from well-off families.[48] This is true even among academically able students—for example, one study found that only 52 percent of low-income students who were well prepared to enroll in college actually did so within two years after high school, while 83 percent of high-income, well-prepared students enrolled immediately after graduation.[49] Students who did not delay entrance into college were more likely to have taken advanced courses in high school, and less likely to have married or had children. Students from low socioeconomic backgrounds were far less likely to engage in advanced courses while in high school, and far more likely to start a family prior to entering college. These factors may contribute to the observed gap of 26 percentage points in the time of college entry between students in the highest and lowest socioeconomic quintiles.[50]

Today's students also change colleges frequently (sometimes called *swirling*).[51] For example, according to one study, within eight years of high school graduation, one-third of the students who began their college education at a four-year school transferred at least once: nearly one-fifth transferred to another four-year institution, and 15 percent transferred to a two-year college. Among the group that transferred from a four-year to a two-year college (referred to as *reverse transfer*), 41 percent eventually transferred back into a four-year college or university.[52] In addition to transfer, college *stop out* is prevalent, with at least one-fourth of the students taking time off before returning to school.[53]

These shifts in enrollment behavior are at least partly attributable to the increase in educational options available to students. Not only are there a greater number and variety of institutions from which to choose, but the types of programs and their delivery methods create additional options.[54] At the same time, evidence indicates that students are not entirely free to choose their college pathways. There is a correlation between students' social class and their attendance patterns, and that relationship holds after taking high school preparation into account. For example, students from families in the lowest socioeconomic quintile are over four times more likely than students from advantaged socioeconomic backgrounds to either stop out of college or stop out before transferring to another institution. Students in the bottom socioeconomic quintile are half as likely as those in the top quintile to transfer between four-year colleges, yet they are three times more likely than their more privileged peers to reverse transfer. Reverse transfer is significantly less common among students whose parents are well educated, and this appears to be related to their greater tendency to achieve higher college grade point averages.[55]

Given those inequalities, it is especially troubling that the rates of bachelor's degree attainment are lower among students who change colleges—at least in some directions. In one study, the average BA attainment rate among four-year starters who did not transfer was 78 percent, compared with 69 percent among students who transferred to another four-year school, and only 22 percent among reverse transfers.[56]

Emerging College Contexts

The above statistics depict attendance patterns, but understanding those patterns requires recognizing that meaningful college experiences are constructed in social contexts. *Contexts* are typically thought of as the environments in which individuals experience life, where developmental processes take place. To describe college students in their contexts requires first addressing a crucial question: what constitutes a context in contemporary postsecondary education? While, in the past, college attendance was for a select group only—those who could afford to live at school and enroll in classes with little time devoted to outside work—the statistics presented in this chapter clearly indicate that this is no longer the case. This begs an important but difficult question: is college today anything more than a time period partly characterized by some (intermittent) periods of schooling beyond high school?

According to dominant theoretical models in higher education, the college experience constitutes an interaction between students and schools, with fit between the two being of paramount importance.[57] The setting is simply the college environment, measured in terms of racial composition, student-faculty ratio, resources, and (occasionally) measures of "engagement" based on in-classroom surveys of students.[58] While the most rigorous studies of institutional or school effects have not found them to be particularly strong predictors of student outcomes, interventions to enhance college life continue to proliferate (see, for example, the widespread use of learning communities).[59] Given the changing nature of student and institutional bodies, we may need to (re)consider the extent to which these on-campus efforts can be effective for students who experience college in "momentary and marginal ways" because of factors that lie beyond the characteristics or practices of the college itself.[60]

For example, in contrast to high school, when most students are in the classroom for a substantial portion of their waking hours, most of college life occurs outside the classroom. The time, energy, and resources required to pursue an education create further limitations on how, where, and when students work, live, and care for themselves.

Consider the issue of affordability. The price of attending any public college or university has nearly doubled in the last thirty years when comparing the price of tuition, room, and board in constant 2006–7 dollars. Between 1997 and 2007, prices for undergraduate tuition, room, and board at public institutions rose by 30 percent, and prices at private institutions by 23 percent, when adjusted for inflation. For the 2007–8 academic year, undergraduate tuition, room, and board at public institutions averaged $11,600, with a price of $30,000 at private colleges.[61] Correspondingly, the number of hours students needed to work in order to finance college swelled—in 1976 it was possible to pay the full costs of attending a public university by working just twenty-three hours per week at minimum wage, but by 2006 financing those costs required seventy-two hours per week of minimum-wage work.[62]

The economic downturn that ushered in the second decade of the twenty-first century has exacerbated the financial struggles of students and their families. The proportion of freshman who stated that cost impacted their choice of where to attend college reached an all-time high in 2009. Over 40 percent of respondents stated that cost was a "very important" factor in determining where they enrolled. Nearly 45 percent stated that an offer of financial aid was a "very important" factor in their decision making, up from 43 percent in 2008 and 39 percent in 2007. According to the 2009 Cooperative Institutional Research Program Freshman Survey, administered to first-year students at four-year colleges and universities across the nation, more freshman are concerned about paying for college than any time since 1971. In 2009, 55 percent of respondents expressed "some" concern about paying for college, with 11 percent stating that this was a "major" concern. More students were also relying on student loans to cover those costs—53 percent, up nearly 4 percentage points from the year before and the highest proportion over the last nine years.[63]

The percentage of traditional-age college students who attend classes full time and also work has increased from 34 percent in 1970 to 46 percent in 2007. The number of hours full-time students are working has surged. In 1970, 10 percent of full-time students worked twenty to thirty-four hours per week, and 10 percent worked full time (thirty-five-plus hours per week), in addition to full-time college attendance. At the start of this century, 21 percent of full-time students worked twenty to thirty-four hours, and 8 percent worked at least forty hours per week.[64]

Students' living conditions have changed as well. At a time when most college freshman moved directly from their parents' home into a college dormitory, the greatest concern was being distracted from one's homework by an inconsiderate roommate. Today's college students cannot simply flee to an ivy-adorned library to escape the stressors of their living conditions. Over half of high school seniors and their parents feel it is important for a student to live at home during college, and this is particularly true in Hispanic families. Students who live at home are much more likely to care for siblings or other relatives, and to help pay rent.[65]

Students who have children also face the increased financial burden of housing and feeding their children, and sometimes a partner. They must simultaneously care for their children while finding the time and space to do homework. Individuals from impoverished backgrounds tend to find themselves sharing this limited space and money with other family members. Dierdre, a participant in the Wisconsin Scholars Longitudinal Study (codirected by the first author), provides an illustrative case. As a student attending a selective four-year university, she shares an apartment with her two-year-old daughter, her sister and her sister's two children, and her mother.[66] Her family members moved in with her to escape dangerous living situations, and Dierdre felt she had no choice but to accept them. She is now supporting the entire family, since she is the only one with a job, and at the same time she is attending college full time. How does she respond to her living situation? She says, "I just try to stay away from home."

Dierdre is not alone. Full-time students are spending more hours on the job than they did forty years ago, and correspondingly they are spending less time on academic work. As a result, contexts such as work and family may be even more determinative for students than classroom settings, yet they are also more difficult to document and evaluate. One study examining how much time full-time college students devote to attending classes, study, work, and leisure pursuits found that in 1961, full-time students enrolled in four-year institutions spent forty hours per week on attending classes and studying. More than forty years later, students are spending just twenty-three to twenty-six hours on these activities. The decline in time spent on academics cannot be accounted for based just on student demographics of race, gender, ability, family background, and hours worked. There was also a decline in all groups based on the type, size, and level of selectivity of the four-year college attended, as well as within majors.[67] Those trends are echoed by the work of an ethnographer studying college students at a midwestern university, who observed that students appeared much more focused on their nonacademic life. At the same time, her explanations for the trends may insufficiently recognize the constraints on students' lives, as she attributed those trends to a preference for "settings where they [students] experience themselves having higher levels of choice, control, and the ability to be authentic."[68]

The stress of the circumstances in which students live and learn may have a negative impact on their functioning and their educational outcomes. In a study of why students fail to complete college, researchers found that the number one reason given for leaving college early was the stress associated with working while attending classes. More than 60 percent of noncompleters cited the stress of work while taking classes as their reason for not continuing their education. Students' concerns surrounded day-to-day living expenses, not simply paying tuition. Thirty-six percent of the students who left college said that, even if they could secure a grant (not a loan) to pay for tuition, fees, and books, it would still be difficult to return to school.[69]

Ninety percent of the directors of college counseling centers report that over the last ten years, there has been an increase in the number of students with severe mental health issues. Psychiatric medication use by students seeking counseling on campus has also risen dramatically, from 9 percent in 1994 to 23 percent in 2006, with 7.5 percent of the students experiencing mental health issues that made it impossible for them to continue their education, or to do so without a high degree of psychiatric or psychological support.[70] A survey by the National Institute on Alcohol Abuse and Alcoholism indicates that nearly one-third of college students meet the criteria for alcohol abuse, and 6 percent have been diagnosed with alcohol dependence.[71] More than 18 percent of college students report symptoms of depression, and nearly 15 percent have received a diagnosis of depression.[72] In one study fully 43 percent of the students reported feeling so depressed at some time in the previous academic year that they found it hard to function. Suicide had been seriously considered by 1 in 10 students, with just under 2 percent reporting having made a suicide attempt. It is estimated that there are about 1,100 suicides on college campuses each year.[73]

Stress has important health implications, and it can create a dangerous cycle that exacerbates educational troubles. For example, stress can compromise sleep. There is a "preponderance of scientific evidence [showing] that human perception, cognition, and decision making suffer when people are sleep deprived."[74] Periods of sleep longer or shorter than seven to eight hours per night have been shown to be associated with learning and memory problems, depression, obesity, and accidents.[75] Experts state that in order to be optimally alert, adolescents need 9.25 hours of sleep per night through their early twenties.[76] While studies of sleep among college students are uncommon, a nationally representative study of adults found that 28 percent sleep less than seven hours per night, while 9 percent sleep nine hours or more.[77] An ongoing study of low-income Wisconsin college students attending two- and four-year colleges found that first-year students reported 7.8 hours of sleep per night on average, with 29 percent sleeping less than seven hours and 10 percent sleeping more than nine hours.[78] This suggests that these low-income students are not getting the sleep needed for high-quality cognitive functioning—and this is probably not uncommon among low-income college students, particularly since they are also known to keep erratic schedules.[79]

Constraints and Opportunities

The emphasis in American higher education throughout much of the twentieth century and well into the twenty-first is on expanding opportunity. For example, in his 1998 State of the Union address, then president Bill Clinton assured all Americans that they could attend college. In 2009, President Barack Obama encouraged the nation to embrace a thirteenth year of education. These statements reflect a college-for-all philosophy aimed at expanding opportunities and raising hopes and ambitions. That approach promotes ambition, and at the same time it may introduce constraints. For example, some argue that its ascendance has contributed to a culture in which many high school students rely on community colleges and other open-admissions institutions to fulfill the promise of a college education.[80] As a result, some claim that high school students expect to attend college, even while expending little effort to make that happen.[81] A phenomenon of mismatched students and colleges may be the result.[82]

Some students have made strides in entering through college doors while never completing degrees, further illustrating the challenges of dealing with the new opportunities and constraints of today's college culture. Changes in the representation of unmarried parents in higher education provide one example. Over the last twenty years, the proportion of undergraduate students who are single parents has doubled, from 7 percent to just over 13 percent. But the rates of degree completion in that group is very low—for example, just 5 percent complete a BA within six years of starting college (compared with 29% on average)—at least in part because of inadequate academic and financial supports. For example, only 5 percent have taken at least one Advanced Placement course before college (compared with 20% of other students), and nearly half (45%) score less than 700 on the ACT or SAT (compared with 18% of other students). Three-fourths of all unmarried parents enrolled in college full time work at least fifteen hours per week; and 30 percent work forty or more hours per week. This represents a dramatic change—in 1989–90, less than half (48%) of unmarried parents enrolled in college full time worked at all.[83]

These substantial constraints could be alleviated, but currently the rhetoric of opportunity is not matched with sufficient provisions. For example, even as mothers with young children are encouraged to attend college, resources for on-campus childcare have diminished. Only half of all postsecondary education institutions provide any form of childcare on campus, and most are overenrolled. In fact, national data indicate a severe shortage of campus childcare centers, with existing resources meetings only one-tenth of the demand. This is particularly true when it comes to infant care, as only about one-third of campus childcare centers accept infants. At the same time, federal support for the Child Care Access Means Parents in School Program (the sole federal funder of such centers) declined by 40 percent (to just $15 million) between 2002 and 2009. According to calculations by the Institute for Women's Policy Research, this means an allocation of just $8 per family headed by a parenting student.[84]

Implications and Conclusions

The trends described in this chapter clearly illustrate that American higher education in the twenty-first century serves a much more heterogeneous undergraduate population than ever before. Students vary not only in their family backgrounds and demographic characteristics, but also their approaches to college enrollment (e.g., where, how, and under what conditions they attend) and their pathways through college (e.g., their attendance patterns and choices about degree completion). For growing numbers of students, aspects of life outside of the classroom are overlapping with college life. It is therefore increasingly difficult to think in terms of an average college student or an average college experience.

The need to document and reflect a multiplicity of experiences has important implications for how researchers depict college choices, and for how policymakers and practitioners think about the ways in which undergraduates make decisions. In the absence of stronger theoretical models paying greater attention to variation, the behavior of some students may be inaccurately interpreted as irrational. For example, an ethnographer in a state university called undergraduates "confusing" and "bizarre." In comparing them with the ideal learner, that researcher asked:

> Why don't undergraduates ever drop by for my office hours unless they are in dire trouble? . . . Why don't they respond to my (generous) invitations to do out-of-class research? . . . What about those students who . . . eat and drink during class . . . or [take] a nap?[85]

The problem is that this researcher is comparing the students she is observing to an outdated "norm." While cataloging available student activities, she found that more than one-quarter of dorm-based activities centered on psychological and physical health; she also noticed that some students slept hardly at all, and that some reported not having time to eat. In addition, she discovered that students did not join the Greek system because it required time and resources. But in drawing her final conclusions, she made a common mistake, failing to connect those observations to the new realities of some college students' lives. Instead, she lamented the loss of "community" in college life and, in particular, articulated a sense that colleges are faced with a student body much less interested in academics than ever before.

This is not an uncommon problem. Despite enormous changes in the composition of both undergraduates and their colleges, the "road through college" remains commonly painted as individualized and middle class in its orientation.[86] Representations of college as a time for "meandering" and "identity exploration," a period of "finding out what you want to do," often do not jibe with today's undergraduates.[87] In many ways, that view of college as a period of exploration is similar to the characterization of it as a time of experimentation.[88] But for students faced with high costs and external pressures, there appears to be little room to safely experiment. It is difficult to explore when one is juggling long hours of work, family responsibilities, and classes.

Thinking more deeply about the multiple contexts affecting the lives of college students also raises significant questions about the utility of studying the college classroom in order to understand the settings of college life. For example, a researcher who initially aimed to use public spaces (such as classrooms and gathering areas in dorms) to learn about students quickly came to realize that "student life . . . occur[s] behind closed doors and [is] not amenable to participation or observation."[89] Studying the first-year college experience by hanging out on campus may not lead much of anywhere, since "there is little in the way of shared first-year experiences." Instead, researchers should consider ways to capture the more relevant experiences of today's undergraduates, including those who commute.

Of course, these changes also raise the stakes for policy makers and practitioners hoping to enhance overall attainment. As a broader swath of high school graduates from across the socioeconomic spectrum enters college, we need to consider how best to educate *all* students, while at the same time utilizing the most effective and efficient approaches. The heterogeneity of college contexts and experiences increases the likelihood of heterogeneous effects of specific policies and programs. This should lead more policy makers to consider targeting and tailoring those efforts—and lead evaluators to consider emphasizing the effectiveness of those efforts for specific subgroups. For example, students coming from the most supportive home environments may derive the most benefit from policies such as mandatory student advising. On the other hand, the biggest impacts of financial aid could occur for students in the most challenging living conditions (e.g., multiple roommates, significant obligations and demands from family members, no space to study, limited sleep, challenging emotions), if they are supported by strong, healthy relationships and other positive assets.[90] It is therefore imperative that the vast diversity of students and their experiences are considered in all endeavors to serve them.

Undergraduate education in the twenty-first century means different things, depending on how students encounter it. Since heterogeneity is so often associated with stratification in the United States, that is troubling in one sense. Some encounters with postsecondary education lead to positive outcomes, while others do not—and this contributes to wide disparities in whether and how a college education promotes social mobility. At the same time, the ability of American higher education to become ever more varied, and to accommodate individuals and institutions from all walks of life, is perhaps its attribute most worth emulating.

NOTES

1. Sarah Igo, *The Averaged American* (Cambridge, MA: Harvard University Press, 2007).

2. Jeffrey A. Smith, "Heterogeneity and Higher Education," in *Succeeding in College: What It Means and How to Make It Happen*, ed. Michael S. McPherson and Morton Owen Schapiro (New York: College Board, 2008), 131–44.

3. National Center for Education Statistics [NCES], *The Condition of Education 2006* (Washington, DC: National Center for Education Statistics, 2006), table 23–1.

4. U.S. Census Bureau, "Table A-7: College Enrollment of Students 14 Years Old and Over, by Type of College, Attendance Status, Age, and Gender; October 1970 to 2008," *Current Population Survey*, www.census.gov/population/www/socdemo/school.html.

5. NCES, *Digest of Education Statistics 2008* (Washington, DC: National Center for Education Statistics, 2009), chapter 3.

6. Sarah R. Crissey, *Educational Attainment in the United States: 2007; Population Characteristics* (Washington, DC: U.S. Census Bureau, Jan. 2009).

7. Harry J. Holzer and Robert I. Lerman, *The Future of Middle-Skill Jobs*, Brief #41 (Washington, DC: Brookings Center on Children and Families, Feb. 2009).

8. U.S. Department of Labor, *Occupational Projections and Training Data: 2006–07 Edition* (Washington, DC: U.S. Government Printing Office, 2006).

9. Richard Frye, *College Enrollment Hits All-Time High, Fueled by Community College Surge*, Pew Research Center Report, Oct. 2009, http://pewsocialtrends.org/pubs/747/college-enrollment-hits-all-time-high-fueled-by-community-college-surge [accessed Jan. 10, 2010].

10. NCES, *The Condition of Education 2009* (Washington, DC: National Center for Education Statistics, 2009), table A-17-1.

11. Smith, "Heterogeneity and Higher Education."

12. NCES, *Digest of Education Statistics 2008*, table 226.

13. Robert Haveman and Timothy Smeeding, "The Role of Higher Education in Social Mobility," *Opportunity in America* issue, *Future of Children* 16, no. 2 (2006): 1225–150.

14. Postsecondary Education Opportunity, *Pell Grant Recipient Data by State, 1976–77 to 2007–08* (Aug. 2009), www.postsecondary.org.

15. U.S. Census Bureau, "Table A-7: College Enrollment."

16. The NCES Math Test figures are for NLS-72 and NELS:88 college-goers; in John Bound, Michael Lovenheim, and Sarah Turner, "Why Have College Completion Rates Declined? An Analysis of Changing Student Preparation and Collegiate Resources," NBER Working Paper No. 15566, National Bureau of Economic Research (Dec. 2009), www.nber.org/papers/w15566 [accessed Feb. 5, 2010].

17. Postsecondary Education Opportunity, *Academic Preparation for College, 1983 to 2002* (Feb. 2003), www.postsecondary.org.

18. NCES, *The Condition of Education 2004* (Washington, DC: National Center for Education Statistics, 2004), table 18-1.

19. NCES, *Condition of Education 2009*, table A-10-2.

20. NCES, *Digest of Education Statistics 2008*, table 265.

21. Ibid.

22. Thomas Bailey, Norena Badway, and Patricia J. Gumport, *For-Profit Higher Education and Community Colleges*, ERIC Document No. ED463824 (2001), www.eric.ed.gov.

23. College Board, *Community Colleges*, Trends in Higher Education Series 2010, http://professionals.collegeboard.com/profdownload/trends-community-colleges.pdf.

24. National Postsecondary Student Aid Study [NPSAS] 2007–8 data; in Patricia Steele and Sandy Baum, *How Much Are College Student Borrowing?* College Board Policy Brief (Aug. 2009), http://professionals.collegeboard.com/profdownload/cb-policy-brief-college-stu-borrowing-aug-2009.pdf.

25. U.S. Government Accountability Office analysis of 2004 cohort data from the National Student Loan Data System (NSLDS), provided by the Department of Education, for two-year, three-year, and four-year default rates by sector, using December 2007 student loan data; in U.S. Government Accountability Office, *Proprietary Schools: Stronger Department of Education Oversight Needed to Help Ensure Only Eligible Students Receive Federal Student Aid*, GAO-09-600 (Washington, DC: U.S. Government Accountability Office, 2009).

26. Bailey, Badway, and Gumport, *For-Profit Higher Education.*

27. NCES, *Digest of Education Statistics 2008*, table 187.

28. Virginia Valian, *Why So Slow? The Advancement of Women* (Cambridge, MA: MIT Press, 1998).

29. Douglas Harris and Sara Goldrick-Rab, *The (Un)Productivity of American Colleges: From "Cost Disease" to Cost-Effectiveness* (Indianapolis: Lumina Foundation, 2009).

30. Others dispute this claim, which is based on the full universe of college-goers. A more restrictive definition of college going, such as one that requires on-time participation and BA aspirations, yields a slight increase in completion rates over time (Clifford Adelman, pers. comm., Dec. 8, 2009).

31. Bound, Lovenheim, and Turner, "College Completion Rates."

32. Ibid. These are based on *U.S. News and World Report* rankings. In the original text, "top 50" and "non-top 50" designations were used instead of "flagship" and "nonflagship,"

33. Bound, Lovenheim, and Turner, "College Completion Rates."

34. Sara Goldrick-Rab, "Challenges and Opportunities for Improving Community College Success," *Review of Educational Research* (forthcoming, Sept. 2010).

35. Paul A. Attewell, David E. Lavin, Thurston Domina, and Tania Levey, "New Evidence on College Remediation," *Journal of Higher Education* 77 (2006): 886–924; Eric P. Bettinger and Bridget Terry Long, "Remediation at the Community College: Student Participation and Outcomes," in *Responding to the Challenges of Developmen-*

tal Education, ed. Carol A. Kozeracki, New Directions for Community Colleges No. 129 (San Francisco: Jossey-Bass, 2005), 17–26; Juan Carlos Calcagno and Bridget Terry Long, "The Impact of Postsecondary Remediation Using a Regression Discontinuity Approach: Addressing Endogenous Sorting and Noncompliance," working paper, Harvard University (2008); Christopher Jepsen, "Remedial Education in California's Community Colleges," paper presented at the American Education Research Association conference, Apr. 2006; Ebenezer F. Kolajo, "From Developmental Education to Graduation: A Community College Experience," *Community College Journal of Research and Practice* 28 (2004): 365–71; Brian G. Moss and William H. Yeaton, "Shaping Policies Related to Developmental Education: An Evaluation Using the Regression-Discontinuity Design," *Educational Evaluation and Policy Analysis* 28 (2006): 215–30.

36. Bound, Lovenheim, and Turner, "College Completion Rates."

37. Ibid. See also Clifford Adelman, *The Toolbox Revisited: Paths to Degree Completion from High School through College* (Washington DC: U.S. Department of Education, 2006).

38. Bound, Lovenheim, and Turner, "College Completion Rates."

39. Of course, this link is not necessarily causal. Students who select into each type of institution may have unobservable characteristics, related to motivation or intent, that may affect their outcomes. See Sara Goldrick-Rab, Douglas Harris, Christopher Mazzeo, and Gregory Kienzl, *Transforming Community Colleges* (Washington DC: Brookings Institution, 2009).

40. Regina Deil-Amen, "To Teach or Not to Teach 'Social' Skills: Comparing Community Colleges and Private Occupational Colleges," *Teachers College Record* 108 (2006): 397–421; Ann E. Person and James E. Rosenbaum, "'Chain Enrollment' and College 'Enclaves': Benefits and Drawbacks of Latino College Students' Enrollment Decisions," in *Latino Educational Opportunity*, ed. Catherine L. Horn, Stella Flores, and Gary Orfield, New Directions for Community Colleges No. 133 (San Francisco: Jossey-Bass, 2006), 51–60; James E. Rosenbaum, Julie Redline, and Jennifer L. Stephan, "Community College: The Unfinished Revolution," *Issues in Science and Technology* 23 (2007): 49–56.

41. Goldrick-Rab, Harris, Mazzeo, and Kienzl, *Transforming Community Colleges*.

42. Goldrick-Rab, "Challenges and Opportunities."

43. NCES, *Condition of Education 2009*, table A-21-1.

44. Ibid., table A-21-2.

45. Ibid., table A-21-3.

46. Jennifer Engle and Vincent Tinto, *Moving beyond Access: College Success for Low-Income, First-Generation Students*, Pell Institute for the Study of Opportunity in Higher Education (2008), www.pellinstitute.org/files/COE_MovingBeyondReport_Final.pdf [accessed Jan. 31, 2010].

47. Laura Horn, Emily Forrest Cataldi, and Anna Sikora, *Waiting to Attend College: Undergraduates Who Delay Their Postsecondary Enrollment* (Washington, DC: National Center for Education Statistics, 2005).

48. Sara Goldrick-Rab and Seong Won Han, "The Class Gap in 'The Gap Year': Academic Coursetaking, Family Formation, and Socioeconomic Differences in Delaying the Transition to College," *Review of Higher Education* (forthcoming).

49. Edward P. St. John, *Refinancing the College Dream* (Baltimore: Johns Hopkins University Press, 2003).

50. Goldrick-Rab and Han, "The Class Gap."

51. Sara Goldrick-Rab and Fabian T. Pfeffer, "Beyond Access: Explaining Socioeconomic Differences in College Transfer," *Sociology of Education* 82 (2009): 101–25.

52. Ibid.

53. Lutz Berkner, *Descriptive Summary of 1995–1996 Beginning Postsecondary Students: Six Years Later* (Washington DC: National Center for Education Statistics, 2002).

54. Sara Goldrick-Rab, "Following Their Every Move: An Investigation of Social-Class Differences in College Pathways," *Sociology of Education* 79 (2006): 61–79.

55. Goldrick-Rab and Pfeffer, "Beyond Access."

56. Ibid.

57. For example, see Vincent Tinto, *Leaving College: Rethinking the Causes and Cures of Student Attrition*, 2nd ed. (Chicago: University of Chicago Press, 1993); John M. Braxton, *Reworking the Student Departure Puzzle* (Nashville, TN: Vanderbilt University Press, 2000); Alan Seidman, *College Student Retention: Formula for Student Success* (Santa Barbara, CA: Praeger, 2005).

58. George D. Kuh, Jillian Kinzie, Jennifer A. Buckley, Brian K. Bridges, and John C. Hayek, *What Matters to Student Success: A Review of the Literature* (Washington, DC: National Postsecondary Education Cooperative, 2006).

59. Marc Scott, Thomas Bailey, and Greg Kienzl, "Relative Success? Determinants of College Graduation Rates in Public and Private Colleges in the U.S.," *Research in Higher Education* 47 (2006): 249–79.

60. Rebekah Nathan, *My Freshman Year: What a Professor Learned by Becoming a Student* (Ithaca, NY: Cornell University Press, 2005), 44.

61. NCES, *Digest of Education Statistics 2008*, table 331.

62. Postsecondary Education Opportunity, *"I Worked My Way through College. You Should Too"* (July 2009), www.postsecondary.org.

63. John H. Pryor, Sylvia Hurtado, Linda DeAngelo, Laura Palucki Blake, and Serge Tran, *The American Freshman: National Norms, Fall 2009* (Los Angeles: Higher Education Research Institute, University of California, Los Angeles, 2009).

64. NCES, *Condition of Education 2009*, table A-44-3.

65. Ruth Turley, "When Parents Want Children to Stay Home for College," *Research in Higher Education* 47 (2006): 823– 46.

66. For more on the Wisconsin Scholars Longitudinal Study, see www.finaidstudy.org. Results reported here are unpublished at this time.

67. Philip Babcock and Mindy Marks, "The Falling Time Cost of College: Evidence from Half a Century of Time Use Data," unpublished paper, Department of Economics, University of California, Santa Barbara, and Department of Economics, University of California, Riverside (2009).

68. Mary Grigsby, *College Life through the Eyes of Students* (Albany: State University of New York Press, 2009), 2.

69. John Johnson, Jon Rochkind, Amber N. Ott, and Samantha DuPont, *With Their Whole Lives Ahead of Them: Myths and Realities about Why So Many Students Fail to Finish College* (San Francisco: Public Agenda, 2009), www.publicagenda.org/their WholelivesAheadofthem.

70. Victor Schwartz and Jerald Kay, "The Crisis in College and University Mental Health," *Psychiatric Times* 26, no. 10 (2009), www.psychiatrictimes.com/display/ar ticle/10168/1472474 [accessed Mar. 11, 2010].

71. National Institute on Alcohol Abuse and Alcoholism, *College Drinking—Changing the Culture* (2010), www.collegedrinkingprevention.gov [accessed Mar. 12, 2010].

72. American College Health Association, *National College Health Assessment* (Spring 2008), www.acha-ncha.org/pubs_rpts.html [accessed Mar. 12, 2010].

73. Jed Foundation, *Preventing Suicide and Reducing Emotional Distress* (2010), www.jedfoundation.org [accessed Mar. 12, 2010].

74. Nita Lewis Miller and Lawrence G. Shattuck, "Sleep Patterns of Young Men and Women Enrolled at the United States Military Academy: Results from Year 1 of a 4-Year Longitudinal Study," *Sleep* 28 (2005): 837.

75. Patrick M. Krueger and Elliot M. Friedman, "Sleep Duration in the United States: A Cross-Sectional Population-Based Study," *American Journal of Epidemiology* 169 (2009): 1052–63.

76. Interview with Mary A. Carskadon, "Inside the Teenage Brain," *Frontline* (n.d.), www.pbs.org/wgbh/pages/frontline/shows/teenbrain/interviews/carskadon.html [accessed June 30, 2009]; Siri Carpenter, "Sleep Deprivation May Be Undermining Teen Health," *Monitor on Psychology* 32, no. 9 (Oct. 2001), www.apa.org/monitor/oct01/sleepteen.html [accessed June 30, 2009]; Francie Grace, "Help for Sleep-Deprived Students," Associated Press, Apr. 19, 2004, www.cbsnews.com/stories/2004/04/19/health/main612476.shtml [accessed June 30, 2009].

77. Krueger and Friedman, "Sleep Duration," 1059.

78. Wisconsin Scholars Longitudinal Study, www.finaidstudy.org.

79. Mary A. Carskadon, *Adolescent Sleep Patterns: Biological, Social, and Psychological Influences* (Cambridge: Cambridge University Press, 2002).

80. Alberto F. Cabrera and Steven M. La Nasa, "Understanding the College Choice of Disadvantaged Students," *New Directions for Institutional Research* (San Francisco: Jossey-Bass, 2000).

81. James E. Rosenbaum, *Beyond College for All* (New York: Russell Sage, 2001).

82. William Bowen, Michael McPherson, and Matthew Chingos, *Crossing the Finish Line* (Princeton, NJ: Princeton University Press, 2009).

83. Sara Goldrick-Rab and Kia Sorensen, "Unmarried Parents in College: How Postsecondary Education Affects Family Stability," *Future of Children* (forthcoming).

84. Ibid.

85. Nathan, *My Freshman Year*, 2.

86. Jeffrey Jenson Arnett, *Emerging Adulthood: The Winding Road from Late Teens through the Twenties* (New York: Oxford University Press, 2004); Grigsby, *College Life.*

87. Arnett, *Emerging Adulthood*; Grigsby, *College Life.*

88. Charles F. Manski and David A. Wise, *College Choice in America* (Cambridge, MA: Harvard University Press, 1983).

89. Nathan, *My Freshman Year.*

90. Ann A. Masten, "Ordinary Magic: Resilience Processes in Development," *American Psychologist* 36 (2001): 227–38.

CHAPTER ELEVEN

Presidents Leading

The Dynamics and Complexities of Campus Leadership

Peter D. Eckel and Adrianna Kezar

While the work of academics—teaching, research, and service—is the core of an institution, they need someone who can attend to the following:

1. Manage their finances and budgets and provide key services, such as payroll, and health and retirement benefits
2. Serve as a go-between to the scholars from different disciplines and coordinate individual course offerings to create a coherent curriculum
3. Act as a conduit to outside councils, government agencies, alumni, donors, and communities when representing, as well as defending, the academics
4. Steward, but more importantly increase, the available financial resources
5. Oversee facilities and ensure their maintenance
6. Serve periodically as a target for academic ardor and aggression

The nature of this position requires a single individual to be a leader, academic, planner, mediator, politician, advocate, investment banker, conductor, showman, church elder, supporter, cheerleader, and, of course, manager. These roles, and many more functions—including providing leadership; setting institutional

strategy; planning; financing; and ensuring compliance with multiple regulations, laws, and policies (and politics)—are the domain of a campus head, a position labeled president or chancellor, vice-chancellor or rector, depending on the
continent and the system.

Today's colleges and universities rely on presidents for many things and have
high expectations for their campus chief executive officer.[1] As the Association of
Governing Boards of Colleges and Universities noted in its statement by the Task
Force on the State of the Presidency in American Higher Education: "No leader
comes to personify an institution in the way a president does. A president must
provide leadership in maintaining the institution's academic integrity and reputation. He or she must assimilate and tell the institution's story to build pride
internally and support externally. The president has the primary responsibility
for increasing pubic understanding and support for the institution . . . and must
lead the institution as it confronts new external challenges."[2]

Thus the organization of colleges and universities, the influence of the external environment, the multiple roles that presidents must play, and the constituencies they must please make it challenging for presidents to fulfill expectations.
This chapter explores contemporary dimensions of the position, including the
roles and functions of presidents, the organizational and environmental factors
that shape the position, notions of presidential leadership, and what the future of
the presidency might look like. While the nation's 4,000-plus colleges and universities each have a president, the job, context, and leadership most likely vary. This
chapter strives to be representative of the position, as it cannot be inclusive, given
the tremendous diversity of institutions.

The Presidential Profile

Presidents do not come from a single mold; however, some patterns exist in key
characteristics. The typical president is approximately sixty years old; holds a
doctorate, most commonly in education or higher education, social sciences, or
humanities; and has served in his or her current position for 8.5 years, according
to the American Council on Education (ACE), which has been tracking presidential profiles for twenty years.[3] In 2006, approximately 70 percent of presidents
had served as a faculty member, a decrease from 75 percent in 1986. Women hold
23 percent of all presidencies, an approximate doubling in twenty years. Minorities hold 14 percent of presidencies, with African Americans holding 6 percent,
Hispanics holding 5 percent, Asian Americans and Native Americans holding 1

percent each, and 2 percent who note themselves as *other*. This is an increase from the 8 percent of presidencies held by minorities in 1986. The most typical path into the presidency is from that of chief academic officer (CAO), such as provost or vice president for academic affairs (31%); followed by other presidential positions (21%); posts outside of higher education (13%); and other academic affairs positions, such as dean or vice president for research (12%). Most presidents are newcomers to their institutions, with 72 percent of their prior positions being outside of the campuses they now lead (i.e., external hires).

The Job of the President

While presidents may not deliver the key functions of a campus, they create the context that supports (or in the case of poor leadership, impedes) that important work. They are arguably the single most influential person on a campus, having their authority delegated from legally recognized boards.[4] Presidents are charged with leading their institutions. They are responsible for the wise use of scarce resources and are accountable for their institution's effectiveness. They coordinate institutional strategic direction, develop and put into action both master and strategic plans, and are accountable for the institution's future well-being. They support faculty work by making choices—for instance, regarding space and facilities, enrollments, and budgets. They liaise with critical external stakeholders, such as policy makers, alumni, and donors, and hire and manage other key campus leaders. Their leadership matters, as does the attention they choose to give to certain activities, functions, and issues. Further evidence of their importance is the sizable financial investment made by trustees in identifying and retaining talented presidents, with the highest salaries and benefits headed toward $1 million (but still lagging behind football and basketball coaches).[5] Successful presidents are essential to dynamic, relevant, and robust colleges and universities. Seen from the other direction, failed presidencies are costly in all-too-numerous ways. Regrettably, higher education is often reminded of these unfortunate costs.

Presidents face a series of complexities—organizationally, politically, and systemically—that shape their ability to lead and influence how they approach their responsibilities. They are the administrative heads of the institutions, serving as chief executive officers (CEO). They spend their time on fund raising, budget and financial management, community relations, strategic planning, and governing-board relations.[6] They manage an administrative cabinet typically composed of vice presidents responsible for key divisions, such as academic affairs,

administration, student affairs, and external relations. The majority of presidents
report to a board of trustees, although in some public campuses presidents report
to a system head, and some for-profit, health- and church-related presidents may
report to corporate or church executives.[7] Most presidents have written contracts
for their appointments, varying between one and five years; however, close to 30
percent serve "at the pleasure of the board," meaning that their tenure is dependent on meeting board-specified performance objectives.[8]

Much of the president's time is spent outside of the campus, with off-campus
constituencies, and the external demands on the position are growing. In an ACE
study of college presidents, 57 percent of long-serving presidents (those who have
been in their positions for ten years or more) report that as new presidents, the
constituents with whom they spent the most time were internal campus stakeholders. In contrast, only 14 percent report that as experienced presidents, internal constituents still occupy the majority of their time. Instead, 39 percent spend
the most time with external constituents, and 47 percent spend time equally with
external and internal constituents.[9] While new presidents are likely to invest
time on campus establishing themselves as the new leader, the sizable difference
experienced presidents have reported in the amount of time previously and currently spent on campus suggests that the nature and demands of the job today are
also different. Much of the on-campus leadership is now delegated to the CAO,
who tends to be the campus number-two leader (behind the president) and reports spending little to moderate time on off-campus activities.[10]

The external work of campus leaders is tied to the growing importance of the
need to secure more resources as expenses grow and public dollars do not keep
pace, and institutions cannot raise tuition high enough to support their expenses.[11] Presidents find themselves as the lead entrepreneur.[12] Of the ten areas
identified most frequently by long-serving presidents as taking more time today
than these areas initially did during their tenure, half are directly related to securing or spending dollars (fund raising, capital improvement, budget and financial management, entrepreneurship, and operating costs) and three others are
indirectly related to this (technology planning, strategic planning, and enrollment management). Furthermore, fund raising is the task all presidents, regardless of their time in office, most often identified as being the one they were underprepared to address when they began their position.[13] Presidents meet with
potential donors to the institution, such as alumni, and they are the key lobbyists
interacting with public officials in the statehouse as well as in Washington, D.C.
They build relationships with corporate leaders and sign off on technology trans-

fer and licensing agreements; sponsor new business incubators; seek to capitalize on patents and intellectual property rights; and are ultimately responsible for traditional and innovative auxiliary services (such as hospitals, residence halls, and athletics), investments, and endowment returns.

The nature of the presidency is only partially explained by the tasks on which presidents spend their time. Presidents also play important symbolic roles as campus heads.[14] They are expected to articulate the values and image of the institution. In his study on presidential leadership, Robert Birnbaum notes that "presidents, by virtue of their hierarchical positions and legitimacy, are believed by others to have a coherent sense of the institution and are therefore permitted, if not expected, to articulate institutional purposes."[15] They express these institutional objectives both externally and internally. Because of these external responsibilities, a president often is the primary spokesperson for the institution and thus become the "face" of the institution, or, as the president of Muhlenberg College calls the role, that of "the living logo."[16] The images presidents convey—based on how they act, what they say, and what they emphasize (and on what they do not say, act, or stress)—become viewed by internal constituents and external stakeholders as being those of the institution, not of the individual leading the institution. On campus, presidents play important symbolic roles not only at highly ceremonial events and academic rituals, such as convocation and commencement, but also at what may seem like more common events, such as football games, state of the university addresses, or annual alumni-recognition galas. Academic organizations are rife with events that are highly meaningful, and presidents help to build common understandings among disparate constituents who may have their own interpretations of campus events.[17]

The symbolic work of leading can be one of the most time-consuming and tiresome activities of presidents. Such a role is not limited to a particular audience, arena, or activity. It is ongoing and can be exhausting. For former University of Michigan president James Duderstadt, the symbolic role of the president defending academic values conjured images of the Wild West:

The president is expected to be the defender of the faith, both of the institution itself and the academic values so important to the university. I sometimes thought of this latter role as roughly akin to that of a tired, old sheriff in a frontier western town. Every day I would have to drag my bruised, wounded carcass out of bed, strap on my guns, and go out into the main street to face whatever gunslingers had ridden in to shoot up the town that day. Sometimes these were politicians; other times the media; still other times various special interest groups on campus; even occasionally other university leaders such as deans or regents.[18]

The Evolution of the Presidency

The tasks and nature of the presidency have evolved as higher education has matured as an industry. The presidency has not always been as just described. Early American colleges were tightly connected to various religious denominations, and religious appointees (often reverends) served as their heads. In the very early colonial colleges, the president was first among equals in a faculty of resident masters; the position had no previous training or career ladder, as individuals came immediately from a faculty position to become president. From these beginnings, early tensions emerged regarding the amount of influence presidents versus boards had on the institution and its direction.[19]

By the 1800s, the presidency had evolved from the first-among-equals tradition to one in which presidents were sole authority figures, a position of power over college matters that Christopher Lucas described as "nearly absolute."[20] During this period, the college president's job became increasingly complex and burdensome as presidents oversaw activities ranging from raising funds to disciplining students, collecting tuition and dispersing funds, recordkeeping, and also teaching.[21] Administrative specialization and decentralization had not yet taken hold. By the mid-1800s, a philosophical belief and practical reality emerged: colleges needed to separate faculty and administration. Faculty were better suited for engaging in instruction, and administrators were needed for running the college. From this understanding, a distinct administrative class emerged and the authority of the president grew.[22]

In the late 1880s, a new type of postsecondary institution emerged, one much more complex in its activities, mission, and oversight—universities—and, with them, secular college presidents. Although they often assumed the same authoritative power that old-time college presidents maintained, their jobs were different. The old-time president "lived at the college, was not absent for long periods of time, probably taught every member of the senior class, and knew most of the students by name," noted Frederick Rudolph.[23] New-time university presidents, in contrast, were more removed from students and teaching and became more involved in the management of their increasingly complex institutions, even in the early days of universities. Academic disciplines emerged in the late 1800s and created departmental structures within institutions, particularly in the universities. Faculty further asserted their responsibility over the curriculum and the importance of their involvement in academic decision making, challenging the reach of the president.

At the turn of the twentieth century, university presidents' positions became increasingly complex as the missions of the institutions grew. Administrative oversight expanded to include research laboratories and observatories, libraries, athletics, facilities, and performing arts centers. With this functional diversification, the size of the administration expanded, as did the scope of presidential responsibility. As a result, a bureaucratic model emerged in order to manage the multifaceted organizations; the old-time collegiate model no longer worked. Universities were looking for presidents who would be akin to captains of industry and finance, and thus less intimately steeped in students and student discipline, the curriculum, and other educational affairs. The increased bureaucratization of higher education institutions created tension regarding faculty participation in academic decision making, and presidents grew more and more distant from such key decisions. External fund raising also became vastly important. Said Rudolph, "The financing of the American college and university was one of the problems that would keep many of the presidents overworked . . . It was also the age of the alumnus and the philanthropic foundation."[24] Even small colleges began to break with the tradition of religious presidents and started to hire secular presidents with broader financial and managerial experience.[25]

After World War II, the roles and responsibilities of college and university presidents became broader and more external. Important trends during this time included a tremendous enrollment explosion and the expansion of large-scale research funded by the federal government, which was mostly the domain of public and private research universities. Research universities also developed comprehensive medical centers and athletic programs. Many began to establish an international footprint, often through development work abroad, as well as joint research projects and the intentional recruitment of international students and scholars. Presidents found themselves more and more involved with external affairs as these external demands grew, and they began to delegate much of the internal academic affairs of their institutions to provosts and deans, and the finances to chief business officers. The increased external demands on public institutions corresponded with the rise of state coordinating boards, which sought to more directly shape institutional priorities and missions, and thus added another layer of governance oversight. Clark Kerr, the chancellor of the University of California System, keenly described the difficulty of presidents having to serve so many different stakeholders: from traditional ones such as faculty, students, and alumni to newer stakeholders such as business and industry, federal and state governments, local communities, and, over time, international communities. Institutions faced more pressure to be accountable for institutional performance, often to stakeholders—such as governors, trustees, alumni, and legislators—with competing goals and agendas.[26]

While some generalizations can be made about the changing historical role of and challenges for presidents, there are incredible differences in the evolution of the presidency by institutional type. As the nation's postsecondary institutions became more diverse, so did the job of the president. For example, because many community colleges emerged out of primary and secondary school systems, the presidency of early community colleges often was akin to a school superintendent and was a more hierarchical position than that of contemporaries at four-year institutions. Historically black colleges, women's colleges, and tribal colleges also developed their own unique cultures and traditions that shaped their presidencies. For instance, tribal colleges often followed tribal tradition, and the president operated as a community elder, often working directly with the tribal community in developing policies and decisions. Large comprehensive institutions and urban universities tended to follow the traditions of research universities in terms of the breadth and expectations of the college presidential role. Liberal arts colleges and religiously affiliated colleges often continued some of the historic traditions of the old-time college president from the 1800s, with high presidential involvement on campus, both directly with students and faculty and, frequently, in the classroom.

The roles and responsibilities of college and university presidents varied across different types of institutions, based on the culture and traditions that had been part of these institutions. The sections below focus on the current demands on presidents and the nature of today's presidency. While this chapter cannot do justice to the breadth of presidential experiences, given the diversity of institutions that make up American higher education, it does paint a general portrait of the contemporary presidency.

The Presidency Shaped by Contexts

With the important functions and symbolic role of a president, this position should wield great influence. However, the realities of the organization and the environments in which the individual is trying to be effective makes what presidential leadership scholars have called an "impossible job" and, at an extreme, "an illusion."[27] Michael Cohen and James March wrote, "Important aspects of the role seem to disappear on close examination . . . Compared to the heroic expectations he [*sic*] and others might have, the president has modest control over the events of college life. The contributions he makes can easily be swamped by outside events or diffuse the quality of university decision making."[28] As Birnbaum notes, "presidential leadership is influenced by interacting webs of administrative routines, environmental pressures, and political processes that take place in the context of institutional history and culture."[29]

Organizational Contexts

Colleges and universities, while having characteristics similar to other types of organizations, have a set of atypical dynamics that shape the presidency. This section explores three of them: dual sources of authority, loose coupling, and garbage-can decision making.

First, unlike more traditional hierarchical organizations, where authority is correlated with one's administrative position, colleges and universities are defined by their dual sources of authority—bureaucratic (or administrative) and professional (or academic).[30] As discussed above, colleges and universities evolved in ways that gave faculty priority over the curriculum and administrators responsibility over administrative elements. The result of this evolution is two sources of authority within a single organization. Bureaucratic authority is grounded in the organization's structure and arises from the legal rights of senior administrators, such as the president, to set direction, control and monitor budgets, develop institution strategy, hire and terminate employees, develop and implement policies, and assess progress toward objectives and priorities. On the other hand, the second source of authority—professional authority—stems from the high degree of knowledge, expertise, and specialization required to perform the core functions of the institution (i.e., teaching and research). This authority provides the faculty with a different and often competing source of influence. The effect is that authority is not consolidated in the hands of the organization's positional leaders. Instead, it is dispersed; some might suggest that authority is shared. But rather than two sets of hands dipping into the same stream of authority, two different streams exist. Depending on the topic and the context (such as budgeting and planning), administrative authority can be the stronger source. However, professional authority is dominant in decisions about faculty hiring, curricular offerings, and the research that is pursued. Nothing defines the core functions of a college or university more than its teaching and research activities, key elements that are shaped by professional and not administrative authority.

This dynamic is codified in the 1966 *Statement on Government of Colleges and Universities*, jointly formulated by the American Association of University Professors, the American Council on Education, and the Association of Governing Boards of Universities and Colleges.[31] The statement attempts to outline areas of responsibility for faculty, administrators, and trustees, as well as areas of shared authority. However, decisions are not easy to categorize, and a topic can easily overlap traditional areas of responsibility, leading to conflict between sources of authority. When the University of Illinois attempted to create its (now aborted) World Campus to offer online programs and degrees, administrators invoked administrative authority regarding planning, budgeting, and setting the strategic priority of the institution. Faculty, however, invoked professional authority focusing on the curriculum. The result was a long-standing stalemate that needed continued negotiation between influence wielders.[32]

Second, the relationships between various units and the central administration and between the units and departments themselves can be described as loosely coupled, which makes central coordination and oversight, and, by extension, the role of the president, difficult.[33] Loose coupling describes weak connections among organizational units. Both the relationship between units, and that between units and the center, are weak. Information travels slowly and indirectly between these areas, and coordination among them is difficult and minimal. Long-time University of Chicago president Robert Hutchins's definition of a university serves as a pointed reminder of the nature of loose coupling in higher education: "The university is a collection of departments tied together by a common steam plant."[34] While it can be expected that loose coupling is most descriptive of large institutions, even smaller colleges are defined by it. While loosely coupled organizations create problems for central administrators seeking to coordinate organizational activities, these weak relationships also give some advantages.[35] First, loosely coupled systems are able to respond more sensitively to environmental changes. However, the likelihood is just as great that the unit will pay attention to external stimuli rather than requests from a president. The benefit here, for example, is that new professional standards in accounting may affect one department, but they do not require a curricular overhaul throughout the institution. Second, loosely coupled organizations promote and encourage localized innovations and, at the same time, prevent poor adaptations from spreading to other parts of the organization. The curricular change described above does not require the consent of a busy president or consensus by other departments; instead, the individual department concerned can respond more quickly. Furthermore, poor ideas are not spread easily throughout the institution. Keeping bad decisions quarantined means that although presidents may not know about the adaptations occurring throughout the organization or may not be able to coordinate those adaptations, they will probably not have to fix widespread damage caused by bad ideas. Third, loosely coupled organizations benefit from localized expertise. For instance, the president does not need to be an expert in all disciplines. Local decisions can be made by the people who know best. Lastly, loosely coupled organizations have few coordination and centralization costs. A large central bureaucracy is not required, allowing institutions to invest more resources locally rather than centrally.

Regardless of the organizational pluses of loose coupling, one drawback is that presidents cannot easily create organizational efficiency because of weak central coordination. Instead, they struggle to disseminate helpful innovations widely, because communication between units occurs indirectly, sporadically, and unevenly.[36] Presidents may learn that units are working at odds with one another, and with the central administration, as they each scan their own environments and pursue local adaptations. One unit may be advancing its service-learning activities, while another is focusing on graduate education, and a third internationalizing its curricula. Aligning activities and priorities is a continual challenge for university leaders, what the Kellogg Commission on the Future of State and Land-Grant Universities called "institutional coherence."[37]

A final dynamic is garbage-can decision making. Decision making in colleges and universities is complex, and, to the frustration of most presidents, the decisions that are rendered often seem only peripherally related to the problems that leaders thought they were attempting to solve. Three additional organizational dynamics beyond the control even of presidents create these conditions. First, colleges and universities pursue a set of inconsistent, ambiguous, and uncertain goals, and these goals may conflict. For instance, institutions are concerned both with serving local students *and* with having a global effect; they seek the unfettered pursuit of knowledge *and* the leveraging of scientific breakthroughs for economic gain. Second, the ways in which they conduct their core functions— particularly teaching and learning—are complex. Most faculty do not really agree on how students learn best, nor do they understand the essential processes involved in creating civic-minded students or globally competent citizens. The result is that multiple informal theories of what should happen and how it should happen exist within the institution. Third, because time and attention are limited, participation in decisions is fluid as faculty and administrators choose among competing opportunities, based on their own preferences as to what is important. Although they are busy people, key decision makers cannot be in all places at all times. "Every entrance is an exit somewhere else . . . Participation stems from other demands on the participants' time."[38] Taken together, these three elements create situations Cohen and March label "organized anarchies."[39]

The effect of these organizational realities is that decision outcomes depend on the combined flow of (1) decision makers, (2) institutional problems, and (3) potential solutions that are present in the institution. In places where they are in contact, these three streams of people, problems, and solutions come together in a range of metaphoric garbage cans throughout the institution. Solutions are in search of problems as much as problems are in search of solutions, and decisions depend on the mix of people, problems, and solutions in the garbage can at any particular time.[40] Organizations are often thought to render decisions after leaders have defined the problem, explored potential outcomes, and selected a course of action to maximize the effect of the decision.[41] However, the dynamics of colleges and universities create a situation within organized anarchies—described as garbage-can decision making—in which the prototypical, rational approach to rendering decisions is only one way to actually reach a decision.[42]

In the garbage-can model, decision making takes place in one of three ways. Decisions can be made by *resolution*, in which participants make a concerted effort to apply solutions to recognized problems. Decisions can also be made by *flight*, when problems become attached to other unintended solutions or participants. For example, a suggested science or foreign language requirement can easily turn into conversations about faculty hiring, classroom space utilization, or the undue influence of accrediting agencies, different and potentially seemingly unrelated sets of problems and solutions. Finally, decisions can be made by *oversight*. Key participants are too busy to participate in all decisions, so problems and solutions in another garbage can become coupled together with little attention and involvement from key campus leaders.

It is the mix of problems, solutions, and people in a decision opportunity that shape the outcome, not just the preferences of administrative leaders. To render their desired outcomes, presidents can (1) spend time on the problem, since people willing to invest time on any particular decision are likely to have a disproportionate effect on its outcomes; (2) persist in the decision process and see the decisions through to fruition, as intended outcomes may be undone as the mix in the garbage can changes; (3) exchange status for substance, since individuals may be more concerned about being involved than in achieving a particular outcome, and facilitating their involvement in decision processes may be more important to them than the actual outcomes; (4) put a large number of decisions on the table to hedge one's bets, so that eventually a decision on one of these presidential issues will be rendered unobtrusively; (5) provide multiple garbage cans to attract undesired solutions to other problems; and (6) focus on a series of small-scale changes that have a cumulative effect and avoid the attractiveness of a high-stakes decision.[43]

Environmental Contexts

Presidents not only operate within an organizational context, but also in a larger environmental one.[44] Public college and university presidents lead institutions that are either a part of a state system for higher education or under the auspices of a statewide coordinating board. Although the reach and degree of influence of coordinating boards varies among states (and even within states) on an almost yearly cycle, they do shape presidential influence.[45] For instance, presidents are frequently frustrated when they seek to offer a new major or degree, only to be stopped because of perceived program duplication among public institutions in the system. Additionally, state boards set hiring policies and operating procedures, such as procurement, lease agreements, and capital projects.

Part of the political environment also includes state legislatures. They determine the amount of general state support for public institutions through block grants. Furthermore, in many states legislatures set tuition levels (although this is sometimes done by state boards), thus determining the amount of resources from the institution's primary source of revenue. Legislatures also develop accountability goals and metrics for public institutions that shape institutional priorities. For instance, Virginia has outlined a set of eleven goals, referred to as the "state ask," which institutions must negotiate individually and then address.[46] Such accountability schemes often press priorities on institutions that the institutions may not think are important strategically.[47] Birnbaum notes that "as the locus of influence moves from the campus to the state, public sector presidents may find themselves becoming like middle managers in public agencies rather than campus leaders."[48]

Such oversight is not limited to state governments and coordinating boards; federal regulation and the courts also shape the context in which presidents operate. Decisions regarding admissions and financial aid—as they relate to diversity and affirmative action goals—are common, if not frustrating, examples of federal and legal influence. As Charles Bantz, the president of Indiana University–Purdue University at Indianapolis, said, "Every one of us has read the Michigan cases. Everyone's trying to follow as carefully as possible what Justice O'Connor approved, but I sense an enormous nervousness. There's a fear that if you push to the edge, you'll see anti-affirmative-action activists swoop into town. It's a worry. At [our university] we got around that by doing things like giving scholarships to students from the inner city. But I wonder if there is a [national] backing off?"[49] Other topics—such as electronic file sharing, international student visas and admissions, patent policy, college costs, and even toxic waste produced in university labs—are additional issues shaped by federal and legal interventions.

Voluntary accreditation, both regional for institutions and specialized for particular fields and disciplines, also shapes presidential discretion. Accreditation, although not federally regulated, is tied to federal oversight. In order to be eligible for federal funding, including student financial aid, accreditation is essential for most institutions; it allows campus graduates to work in some fields; and it can seem, as one president said, to be "a straightjacket of many colors."[50] For instance, accreditors can threaten to withhold accreditation unless the institution hires more full-time faculty in a particular department, alters curricula, develops new assessment methods, or provides more resources. Even the head of the Council for Higher Education Accreditation, the oversight organization for higher education accreditation, notes that "while presidents and provosts want to sustain a voluntary system of quality review and self-regulation, they are quick to complain that accreditation is intrusive, costly, and ineffective.[51]

Presidents lead their institutions not only in a political environment, but also in one that is strongly shaped by competitive market forces. The rise of market-based state policies, the creation of quasi markets for public services, and a decline in public support have resulted in a heightened competitive environment for colleges and universities.[52] One insightful description of the dynamics of the competitive environment is what Robert Frank and Philip Cook call a "winner-take-all market."[53] They argue that the result is a competitive system in which those at the top get a disproportionate share of the rewards. This encourages more institutions to want to move up the pecking order. This strategy has fundamental flaws; no more than ten institutions can be "top-ten" institutions at any given time, and those at the top are uninterested in moving down. Ellen Hazelkorn's global study of rankings found that 70 percent of the university leaders surveyed said they wished to be in the top 10 percent nationally, and 71 percent said they wanted to be in the top 25 percent internationally.[54]

To move up, institutions look to mimic the current winners, regardless of their own institutional strengths and resources and without solid evidence that what they seek to mimic will improve their standing. They seek the best researchers, try to field the best athletic teams, recruit the brightest students, and build the most elaborate student and research facilities. All of these strategies are pursued not for absolute gains, but in terms of what other competitors are accomplishing. This behavior creates an overreliance on prestige, which is not an outright performance indicator, but rather the *appearance* of doing what highly regarded institutions do. According to Brewer, Gates, and Goldman, "certain characteristics of a college or university become associated with good providers, even though these characteristics are not directly related to the quality of the output."[55] Finally, newcomers overestimate their chances of winning; thus too many competitors become easily attracted to a situation that will only pay off for a small number of people. Most institutions will invest to keep up and not significantly improve their lot. They are trying to complete against already successful leaders, and they do so by mimicking them from inferior positions.

The result is that institutions end up outspending one another and, by doing so, cancel one another's investments. Such behavior creates an arms race among contestants, with few winners and many negated investments. Roger Geiger notes that "universities must continually seek improvement even to remain in the same relative position."[56] In the end, all players run harder to stay in place, and those that choose not to play the game quickly slip behind. The implication for presidents is that they have little choice but to do what others are doing. An extreme but illustrative example focuses on recreational climbing walls, as described in the *Chronicle of Higher Education*:

> The competition for students and recognition is fierce in Texas . . . The new distinction [of the biggest climbing wall] will help separate [the University of Texas, San Antonio] from the rest of the pack. The wall . . . beats out [the University of] Houston's wall by one measly foot. That should sound familiar to Houston officials. Two years ago they built their climbing wall to be exactly one foot taller than the one at Baylor University . . . Texas State at San Marcos plans to build in 2008 "the tallest Texas collegiate climbing wall."[57]

The organizational and environmental contexts in which presidents must operate create a complex set of rules of the game. However, effective presidents understand these dynamics and act accordingly.

Effective Presidential Leadership

There is no lack of interest in or attempts to explore effective presidential leadership. They approach the common question from a range of perspectives, driven by different assumptions.

Perhaps the most insightful school of thought has focused on the *contingency of leadership*. Effective presidents understand the importance of the context in which they are operating, and they know that being a good president varies by the institutional context, environmental conditions, campus culture, and leadership dilemma being addressed (technology versus diversity, for example).[58] Essentially, effective presidential leadership varies by context and situation. As John Levin notes, "in all cases, institutional context is equally or more important than the perception of presidential influence in contributing to organizational actions and outcomes . . . Presidents who were perceived as the most influential are those who fit into the socially constructed story of the institution."[59] In other words, the organizational and environmental contexts vary so much that effective presidents modify their actions to make sense of and be effective within their specific campus context.

One very important contextual element that effective presidents pay attention to is the set of unique characteristics individual institutions possess.[60] As discussed above and throughout this volume, colleges and universities are characterized by certain features that distinguish them from other organizations and, in turn, affect their leadership. Some examples of these features are shared governance; academic freedom and autonomy; tenure; multiple and complex authority structures, with boards of trustees and faculty senates; and unique reward structures that are distributed between the disciplines and the institutions. Birnbaum noted that presidents in his studies were more successful when they worked within and acknowledged these various aspects of the academic culture.[61] After reviewing the findings from studies of presidential effectiveness discussed below, this insight will become apparent across a variety of research efforts. At the institutional level, for instance, Anna Neumann noted that presidents who develop communication skills, style, and a strategy that is culturally appropriate are perceived as more effective by key constituencies.[62]

It is not the specific behaviors, styles, traits, or actions of leaders that make them effective, but the extent to which those elements are accepted and viewed as legitimate by key stakeholders. Underlying contingency theories of leadership is the notion that presidents need the support of different groups of individuals in an institution, groups that often have very different priorities, passions, and perspectives.[63] Effective presidents are able to meet all of these different and often competing expectations.[64] As Birnbaum notes, "good leadership is what its constituents believe it to be—and they don't always agree."[65] For faculty members, presidential effectiveness may mean giving them significant autonomy and including them in key decision-making processes, while for trustees, it may mean defining an aggressive campus growth agenda or raising money to advance the institution's mission.

A third element in the contingency approach to effective leadership is temporal. Over the last forty years, the characterization of effective presidents has altered quite markedly, and these shifting notions of presidential effectiveness reflect changing views in society about what is effective leadership.[66] Forty years bounds the timeframe, because it is the period during which the college presidency has been more formally studied. Forty years ago, more hierarchical and authoritative images of college presidents were seen as being effective.[67] The characteristics noted for effective presidents were also often considered typical masculine traits, such as risk taking, task orientation, confidence, and the ability to work alone. Contemporary views of effective presidents focus more on relationship building, collaboration, and a quest for input, characteristics often associated with women and reflective of more contemporary social customs.[68] It is only more recently that women have moved into college presidencies in substantive proportions, and therefore these changing qualities may reflect alterations in expectations of what is deemed appropriate. In 1986, women held approximately 10 percent of all presidencies, while in 2006 their share more than doubled, to 23 percent.[69] For instance, James Fisher and James Koch, drawing largely on studies done in the 1980s, suggest that presidents should use more unilateral forms of power, and judiciously punish and reward; demonstrate expertise; maintain appropriate distance; and develop charisma and public presence.[70] Later studies, in contrast, focus on power and influence as a two-way process and show that effective leaders are negotiators, coalition builders, and facilitators.[71] The fact that presidents use power effectively has remained important throughout the decades, but the understanding of the concept of power and its dynamics is different. This understanding is evolutionary, reflecting changes in management and business literature and in contemporary society, as Western views were challenged and expanded by the success of Japanese firms. While time itself is important, the key point is that time is a proxy for the ways in which environments continue to change and evolve, ways that might suggest that different behaviors and skills are needed to be effective.

Although the most complex and nuanced approach to understanding presidential effectiveness is through contingency theories, there is a long tradition in higher education and in the broader leadership literature that focuses on the *traits and behaviors* of effective leaders. Bensimon, Neumann, and Birnbaum summarized much of this tradition that tried to identify certain traits that would make a leader effective.[72] Rather than actually testing whether certain traits were associated with more effectiveness, they argue that most of the studies seek characteristics of people who had been identified as effective presidents. The problem with this approach is that such studies strongly mirror expected characteristics, corresponding to the period of time in which each study was conducted.[73]

Studies that concentrate on behaviors, such as whether presidents should focus on goals, vision, planning, or motivating people to action, fall into similar traps. These studies reflect people's expectations or perceptions, rather than testing effective behavior by looking at how behavior affects certain outcomes. If expectations of traits and behaviors differ by campus climate and culture as well as time (as they often do), then the identified traits and behaviors of effective presidents will vary with individual expectations within the setting, but they may not be correlated with change or effectiveness. These studies, for example, do not look at specific presidential outcomes and measure traits or behaviors against others to see which traits achieved certain outcomes or goals. Many studies of presidential behavior have examined the importance of being task oriented or relationally oriented. While findings vary by campus context, most studies suggest that presidents need to balance an emphasis on completing tasks and demonstrating outcomes with a need to build relationships and effectively manage a variety of stakeholders; in the end such studies reveal little about effective behaviors.[74]

Research has generated some consensus regarding certain qualities that tend to be identified as important across any institutional setting, such as trustworthiness; fairness; honesty; respect, or treating people with dignity; caring; and credibility or integrity.[75] The importance of qualities such as credibility and integrity suggests that presidents must be clear about their values and act authentically; they will jeopardize their effectiveness if they are perceived as lacking these qualities.

Overall, the search for universal traits and qualities has not proven to be particularly helpful. Instead, such studies tend to offer time- and contextual-specific insights. Yet, as a set, certain themes do appear vital to understanding presidential effectiveness: honesty, integrity, and respect, for example, seem to transcend context, stakeholder, and institutional type.

An ongoing debate in presidential leadership literature is whether presidents should play a *transformational* or *transactional* leadership role.[76] Transactional leadership focuses on leader-follower exchange, such as allocating resources, rewards, or status; controlling budgetary processes; creating priorities; and establishing accountability and assessment structures. Transformational leadership, alternatively, involves leaders who interact with followers in ways that appeal to their higher needs and aspirations. They motivate others by connecting through higher moral purposes. Bensimon, Neumann, and Birnbaum argue that transactional leadership might be the more effective approach in higher education, given the relationships between presidents and faculty and the organizational contexts in which they must work (such as loose coupling), as a more directive influence by a president may not be effective.[77] They believe that presidents should rely on exchange, rather than a higher calling, and be influential through ongoing organizational activities such as the yearly budgetary process, the allocation of rewards, and accountability structures. Other studies, however, suggest that effective presidents can be transformational by creating an overarching vision for the campus, playing a role in its overall guidance and direction by motivating and inspiring, and demonstrating commitment for moving forward in a new direction.[78] A middle ground exists, and recent studies demonstrate that effective presidents use both transactional and transformational approaches. For example, we examined college presidents who are successful in advancing campuswide diversity agendas and found that such presidents articulate a preference for strategies that could be described as transformational, but that they were much more effective when they used both transactional and transformational approaches.[79] These presidents recognize that different stakeholders respond to different approaches, and that both are needed. They found that the appropriateness of certain approaches is often tied to the stage of the change efforts. For instance, when a campus is initially starting a concerted effort to advance campus diversity, strategies that inspire (transformational leadership) are necessary. As the campus advances in its efforts, more transactional leadership is necessary, using rewards and accountability structures. Our study also reinforces the importance of thinking about effectiveness as varying by stake-holder, phase of change, and cultural context—again reinforcing contingency approaches to leadership.

While theories of transaction and transformation suggest that leadership is more than behavior or traits, *cognitive theories* of leadership focus specifically on the ways presidents make sense of and shape understanding within a campus. Cognitive theories examine the socially constructed world of organizations.[80] The premise of such approaches is that organizations consist of events and actions that are open to interpretation: What does it mean when the president is away from campus for a month while fund raising? Does it mean he or she is a disengaged or absent leader, or that he or she is cultivating important donors for needed and desired support? Is opening a state-of-the-art student recreation center a good thing? It probably depends on whether the institution serves traditional-age, residential students or whether students are only on campus for classes. Action and behavior thus proceed from cognition. Shaping and understanding the meaning and cognition associated with ambiguous and uncertain elements of campus life is the centerpiece of this approach.

One of the largest studies of college presidents examined how presidents approach and view their organizations, and people's actions within them, through archetypes: bureaucratic, collegial, political, and symbolic.[81] Leaders using a bureaucratic frame observe their campuses through a lens of structure and organization, pay attention to goals and priorities, and invoke authority and control. Leaders using a collegial frame focus on people, relationships, team building, consensus, and loyalty. Leaders using a political frame see the inherent politics of organizations, build agendas, mobilize coalitions, and focus on negotiation and conflict. Lastly, presidents using a symbolic frame focus on mission, vision, values, symbols, stories, and the history of the institution. Birnbaum's research suggests that most college and university presidents see the world through one or two sets of assumptions or frames.[82] In particular, presidents tend to focus on viewing the organization and its people through the bureaucratic framework and on approaching their work in a linear and mostly rational fashion. However, his research also demonstrated that leaders were considered more effective by stakeholders when they used three or more lenses, invoking greater cognitive complexity.

Presidents' cognitive approaches shape how they go about particular activities, such as budgeting, planning, or leading change. Pamela Eddy, for example, identified how leaders who have a symbolic framework tend to approach change as a visionary activity, whereas bureaucratic leaders tend to rely on planning processes and documents.[83] Kezar, Eckel, and Contreras-McGavin demonstrated how college presidents were more successful in advancing diversity agendas when they applied all four frames.[84] Because such change typically involves the use of multiple strategies from all frameworks, presidents who do not adopt complex approaches have limited effectiveness in advancing their agendas.

Since so many studies have identified the importance of cognitive complexity in relation to presidential success, and since few presidents appear to develop ease in using multiple frames, researchers have shifted the unit of analysis from an individual leader to a team of leaders. A single individual may rarely possess all of the skills and knowledge required to be an effective leader. Leadership teams provide an avenue for creating greater presidential effectiveness by capitalizing on different people's strengths—some people might be good working with others and developing relationships, different individuals can influence institutional politics, others can effectively examine data, while still others can communicate and translate information in effective ways to the campus community. Bensimon and Neumann propose that presidents can be much more effective if they work in "real" leadership teams (as opposed to illusionary teams), using examples such as working with the presidential cabinet and capitalizing on greater expertise throughout the institution.[85] They encourage college and university presidents to move beyond the image of leadership as being invested in a single individual and to conceptualize leadership as a group process. Their research on presidential leadership teams demonstrates that teams can develop and leverage greater cognitive complexity and be more effective, but only if the teams act in what the authors call "authentic ways." Their study outlines many of the characteristics needed to develop real leadership teams, such as ensuring that criticism is embraced, building relationships among the team members so that people feel free to share information, guaranteeing that the president is truly open to sharing power and being challenged, and recognizing the importance of the collective sense leadership team members make together. They also note that real leadership teams fit into the unique culture and context of higher education that has traditionally been based on consensus, collaboration, and an intellectual environment.

A variety of studies from business and industry also demonstrate the value and importance of team-based or shared models of leadership.[86] This research confirms that successful leaders not only create leadership teams (such as presidential cabinets), but also demonstrate how people throughout the organization should be seen as part of a shared leadership process. In the case of higher education, this would include rank-and-file faculty as well as staff. Leadership, through this framework, is a collective activity (rather than a position) that is distributed among members of an organization. Within these approaches to leadership, faculty and staff are delegated more authority when they show promise of creating an important change for the campus and playing a leadership role. In addition, effective presidents identify individuals throughout the institution who can be effective leaders; the president's role is to foster this leadership. Business and industry are increasingly breaking down hierarchical structures and creating cross-functional teams with more delegated authority for decisions, in order to more effectively meet the mission of the institution. In many ways, traditional hierarchical companies are adopting practices that look very much like the ways in which academic organizations work. Presidents become highly dependent on and interdependent with the expertise of their team members and the distributed leadership groups they create within the organization. Peter Senge's work on organizational learning and effective organizations further suggests that the traditional role of the authority figure (as embodied within executive positions) needs to change so that the leadership capacities of others in the organization can grow.[87] While little research has been conducted to date regarding these trends within higher education, literature from other sectors suggests that effectiveness can be increased when presidents see themselves as one leader among many throughout the campus.

As a set, these theories of leadership provide insight into presidential effectiveness and, used in combination, can help us better understand the complexities of what makes presidents successful. Presidents must analyze and be fully aware of the multiple contexts and environments in which they operate. In a word, they must be anthropologists. They must also balance tasks and relationship building. They need to examine and understand organizations, problems, and people in complex ways that lead to complex actions. And they need to build effective leadership teams, as well as distribute leadership by helping to identify and develop leaders throughout the campus. Given today's complex and contradictory environment, contingency approaches are particularly important, suggesting that what it takes to be an effective leader depends on stakeholder expectations, time period, and institutional context.

The Pipeline for Tomorrow's Presidents

As this chapter has shown, the presidency is important. It can be a challenging position, and theories on what constitutes effective leadership are evolving. However, the greatest challenge of the presidency in the future may simply be having talented leaders in this position; higher education may quickly find itself without the necessary talent pool at the top. Forty-nine percent of all presidents are aged sixty-one or older and quickly approaching traditional retirement age.[88] In contrast, twenty years ago only 14 percent of presidents fell within this age group. In the last five years, the average length of presidential tenure has jumped from a fifteen-year running average of 6.8 years to 8.5 years, indicating that a larger share of presidents are likely to leave the presidency in the near future, and those who traditionally might have stepped down have remained in the positions longer. Combined, these two factors suggest that higher education may well be facing a large-scale turnover in the presidency.

To look for the next generation of presidents, one has to look at today's chief administrative officers. Forty percent of first-time presidents come from CAO positions, compared with 23 percent from nonacademic offices (such as student affairs, development, or administration), 17 percent from outside of higher education, 16 percent from other academic affairs positions, and 5 percent from chair or faculty positions.[89] Given that the CAO position is the most likely prior position for new presidents, two key questions emerge: What are the presidential aspirations of this group? And how well suited are their positions as a training ground for the presidency?

A problem exists in that less than one-third of CAOs in a recent national study indicated that they intend to seek a presidency; 45 percent have no such intention, and the remaining 25 percent are undecided.[90] Furthermore, only 25 percent of female CAOs report presidential aspirations, and another 28 percent report being undecided about seeking a presidency. One-third of male CAOs have presidential ambitions, and 23 percent are undecided. Forty-eight percent of African American CAOs report presidential aspirations, as do 35 percent of Asian American CAOs and 34 percent of Hispanic CAOs. While these percentages are higher than the aspirations of white CAOs (28%), minorities hold only 15 percent of all CAO positions, meaning that only a few CAOs are members of minority groups and have presidential ambitions.[91] The lack of interest in pursuing a presidency suggests that the traditional pipeline to the presidency may not be adequate to meet the expected demand for new presidents.

The top reasons CAOs give for not being interested in a presidency are that they view the nature of presidential work as unappealing, are ready to retire, are concerned about the time demands of the position, don't want to live in a fishbowl, and want to return to teaching or research. Minority CAOs are more likely to report wanting to return to academic work than white CAOs (29% versus 20%), and to have more concerns about the search process than their white counterparts (13% as compared with 3%). Female and male CAOs give similar answers, except that men are more likely to think of themselves as too old to be considered.[92] CAOs who are ambivalent about seeking a presidency give similar reasons to those not seeking a presidency—uncertainty about the nature of the work, concerns about balancing family and job demands, and the draw of the classroom.[93]

The second question asks, to what extent are possible future presidents prepared to assume this complex leadership position? Recent data about CAOs implies that their current position only partially prepares them for the presidency.[94] On the positive side, they have an institutional perspective (as compared with a dean), and their portfolio, while directly focused on academic affairs (including research at institutions with that activity in their mission), often touches on physical infrastructure via classrooms and laboratories; a large portion of an institution's budget is linked to academic activities and personnel. However, while the presidency is externally focused, CAOs spend little time on external activities. For example, 72 percent of CAOs report little or no time on fund raising (the presidents' top use of time); 75 percent spend little or no time on alumni relations; 58 percent spend little or no time on corporate relations or economic development; and 64 percent spend little or no time on government relations, all important presidential activities. These findings do not suggest that CAOs have never had these responsibilities, as many probably have (one-third previously served as dean, a position that often has sizable external activities), but their skills may be a bit rusty by the time they ascend to a presidency. Furthermore, differences do exist across types of institutions. For example, CAOs at doctorate-granting institutions are much more likely to spend a moderate to significant amount of time fund raising (62%), on corporate relations and economic development (51%), on government relations (50%), and on alumni relations (45%) than their counterparts at other types of institutions. Only CAOs from associate's-degree colleges spend more time on corporate relations and economic development (61%). Nevertheless, most CAOs do not gain important experiences and tested skills on these typical presidential activities.

External activities are only part of the presidential portfolio. The most important institutional activities for presidents are budgeting and financial management, strategic planning, board relations, and personnel.[95] Although many CAOs have experience with personnel issues, only CAOs from doctorate-granting institutions noted strategic planning and budgeting as one of the top three presidential-type activities on which they spend their time.[96] Instead, CAOs report spending the most time on curriculum and academic programs; accountability, accreditation, and assessment (master's, baccalaureate, associate's, and special focus CAOs); and hiring, promoting, and retiring faculty (baccalaureate CAOs)—all topics that presidents do not report as their concerns.

The data suggest that if the next generation of presidents are to come from CAO positions, there is much work to be done to both ensure that they want to become presidents and that they are well prepared for the challenges of the position. As discussed earlier, the stakes are high and new leaders must hit the ground running, because even minor mistakes can have potentially large consequences. First, the nature of the presidency is unappealing to most in line for such positions. The dynamics of the job, the press of the external environment, and the activities of presidents are mostly nonnegotiable. The work of the presidency is difficult to change, if not impossible, given the demands and dynamics highlighted throughout this chapter. However, more attention given to the joys and benefits of the presidency may be helpful in convincing CAOs to seek presidencies. Second, the most common prior position of presidents is not a comprehensive training ground for the presidency; however, as leadership is more widely shared, others will have more meaningful experiences to better prepare them for presidential responsibilities. CAOs with presidential ambitions must look beyond their responsibilities to gain additional experiences that will serve them well as presidents. Concerned presidents can craft the CAO position to include more presidential-like activities, or give their provosts enough time and encouragement to develop skills and gain experiences outside of their job. Third, the traditional pipeline to the presidency seems to be insufficient to meet emerging needs. More intentional efforts to develop a deeper, more robust pipeline are necessary, particularly for people of color, and more attention is required to convince those already at the top of the pipeline to seek presidencies, particularly women. Fourth, alternative pathways to the presidency could be developed. Trajectories from other positions both inside and outside of academia, while insufficient training grounds on their own, may open other potentially viable avenues into the top position. Boards and search committees must be convinced to look

tes and focus on skills, accomplishments, and experiences
n positions held.[97] However, thinking broadly about the path-
ency does not disregard academic experience and a deep aware-
culture.

Conclusion: Toward a Future of Shared Leadership

As this chapter has demonstrated, the presidency is an important and influential position that must lead, manage, communicate, inspire, and shape, as well as achieve all of the other elements described above. The effectiveness of individuals in the presidency depends very much on their ability to meet the expectations of diverse stakeholders in a fluid context, rather than, for instance, to act or behave in a particular way. However, the presidency will continue to evolve, and one can expect the job to become more complex, with higher stakes and more pressure to succeed.

Effective presidential leadership in the future may depend on an individual's ability to leverage an integrated, shared leadership approach that encourages coordinated and synergistic leadership among many actors. As former University of Michigan president James Duderstadt notes, "leadership is dispersed throughout academic institutions, through department chairs and program directors, deans and executive officers, and influential leaders of the faculty and student body. However, in most institutions, both the responsibility and authority of leadership flow from the top of the organizational pyramid."[98] Future presidents may approach leadership as integrated, synergistic, cooperative, and collaborative, effectively moving them from the top of the pyramid to the key node on a network.[99] Given the organizational nature of the institutions they are trying to lead, with their loose coupling, dual sources of authority, and decentralized decision making, leadership throughout the campus may be the key to future institutional success. What can be different and difficult is creating synergies among what may be, by default, isolated pockets of leaders.

Furthermore, while shared governance is common, shared leadership is not, and traditional forms of governance are not substitutes for shared leadership. Shared governance typically involves faculty in leadership roles, but it often limits their roles and rarely capitalizes on staff and students as potential leaders; however, on campuses with university assemblies rather than faculty senates, there may be a structure closer to shared leadership. Structure may also limit impact. Second, shared leadership involves the delegation of authority, and very little authority is delegated in shared governance; instead, it is often divided or limited to particular topics. Leadership often occurs in parallel play, rather than in an integrated manner. In shared leadership, administrators and faculty are asked to approach leadership challenges much more collaboratively, rather than sequentially. While there are other distinctions (such as shared leadership involving a great number of individuals and shared governance involving only officially voted or nominated individuals), the above elements provide a sense of the differences between the two models.

A shared leadership team has many advantages, and it also overcomes many of the constraints noted above for college presidents, but it is challenging. Shared leadership is particularly well adapted to address the organizational characteristics noted earlier, such as dual sources of authority, loose coupling, and garbage-can decision making. Moreover, in shared leadership environments, alternative structures for delegating authority and accountability are established, which can take advantage of loose coupling, but also provide levers to make these systems more effectively integrated. For example, within a shared leadership approach, presidents vest more power in leaders across campus, and they put accountability systems in place to monitor decision making and its effect. These new accountability structures might yield more decisions through resolution and less through oversight.

Shared leadership also can help better address challenges that leaders face in the external environment. The rate and pace of decision making has increased; a single individual is no longer capable of understanding the vast array of issues that face higher education, and leaders need to increasingly rely on a broad group of people with varying expertise to address all of these challenges. An overwhelming number of tasks vie for presidential attention. As leadership is shared with more individuals, presidents can delegate responsibility to others and ensure that they spend their own time only on the most critical issues. Second, a shared leadership model allows the institution to address a larger and more diverse agenda more effectively. Colleges and universities will have more priorities, rather than fewer. Shared leadership helps to ensure that an issue is being worked on by the campus, even though the president is not directly addressing this issue. Third, a shared leadership model expands the number of people who embody the values of the institution. Presidents cannot be all things to all people, and a singular focus on the president as the sole embodiment of what is important is guaranteed to disappoint many. Diversity, access and affordability, and quality are often values that are in conflict, and a shared leadership approach may be better able to cope with such disparate priorities. Finally, a leadership team is a natural evolution of the history of higher education, which has gone from relatively small institutions with a narrow mission to complex corporate structures with multiple missions and a vast array of stakeholders and external influences.

In conclusion, the job of the president is in flux. Presidents of early colleges could be and were successful as *the* leader, but as times changed, so did the nature of the position. Today and into tomorrow, the effectiveness of a president may well depend on how strong a complex web of leadership—involving cabinet, external stakeholders, faculty, staff, and students—is created for what Birnbaum argued, in the original version of this chapter, may still be an impossible job.[100]

NOTES

The authors would like to thank Bob Birnbaum, who wrote the original chapter on presidential leadership for this book. His ideas, thoughts, and reactions are reflected in this chapter.

1. To simplify the discussion, we will use the term *president* to refer to the campus chief executive.

2. Association of Governing Boards of Colleges and Universities, *The Leadership Imperative: The Report of the AGB Task Force on the State of the Presidency in American Higher Education* (Washington, DC: Association of Governing Boards of Colleges and Universities, 2006), vi.

3. American Council on Education [ACE], *The American College President: 2007 Edition* (Washington, DC: American Council on Education, 2007).

4. Robert Birnbaum, *How Academic Leadership Works* (San Francisco: Jossey-Bass, 1992); Michael D. Cohen and James G. March, *Leadership and Ambiguity*, 2nd ed. (Boston: Harvard Business School Press, 1986).

5. "As Economy Sours, Presidential Pay Draws Increased Scrutiny," *Chronicle of Higher Education*, Nov. 21, 2008, http://chronicle.com/weekly/v55/i13/13b00301.htm [accessed May 15, 2009].

6. ACE, *American College President*.

7. Ibid.

8. Ibid.

9. Ibid.

10. Peter D. Eckel, Brian J. Cook, and Jacqueline E. King, *The CAO Census: A National Profile of Chief Academic Officers* (Washington, DC: American Council on Education, 2009).

11. See, for example, Michael K. McLendon and Christine G. Mohker, "The Origins and Growth of State Policies that Privatize Public Higher Education," in *Privatizing the Public University: Perspectives from Across the Academy*, ed. Christopher C. Morphew and Peter D. Eckel (Baltimore: Johns Hopkins University Press, 2009), 7–32.; Robert Toutkoushian, "An Economist's Perspective on the Privatization of Public Higher Education," in Morphew and Eckel, *Privatizing the Public University*, 60–86.

12. James L. Fisher and James V. Koch, *The Entrepreneurial College President* (Westport, CT: Praeger, 2004).

13. ACE, *American College President*.

14. Robert Birnbaum and Peter D. Eckel, "The Dilemma of Presidential Leadership," in *American Higher Education in the Twenty-First Century: Social, Political, and Economic Challenges*, 2nd ed., ed. Philip G. Altbach, Robert O. Berdahl, and Patricia J. Gumport (Baltimore: Johns Hopkins University Press, 2002), 340–65.

15. Birnbaum, *How Academic Leadership Works*, 154.

16. Peyton R. Helm, "The President, Alumni, and Fund Raising," in *Out in Front: The College President as the Face of the Institution*, ed. Lawrence V. Weill (Lanham, MD: Rowman and Littlefield, 2008), 49.

17. Robert Birnbaum, *How College Works* (San Francisco: Jossey-Bass, 1988); Dennis A. Gioia and James B. Thomas, "Identity, Image, and Issue Interpretation: Sensemaking During Strategic Change in Academia," *Administrative Science Quarterly* 41 (1996): 370–403.

18. James J. Duderstadt, *A University for the 21st Century* (Ann Arbor: University of Michigan Press, 2000), xi.

19. Frederick Rudolph, *The American College and University: A History* (Athens: University of Georgia Press, 1990 [1962]).

20. Christopher J. Lucas, *American Higher Education: A History* (New York: St. Martin's Press, 1994), 124.

21. Lucas, *American Higher Education*.

22. Ibid.

23. Rudolph, *American College and University*, 167.

24. Ibid., 424.

25. Ibid.

26. Clark Kerr, *The Uses of the University*, 4th ed. (Cambridge, MA: Harvard University Press, 1995).

27. Robert Birnbaum, "The Dilemma of Presidential Leadership," in *American Higher Education in the Twenty-First Century: Social, Political, and Economic Challenges*, 1st ed., ed. Philip G. Altbach, Robert O. Berdahl, and Patricia J. Gumport (Baltimore: Johns Hopkins University Press, 1999), 328; Cohen and March, *Leadership and Ambiguity*, 2.

28. Birnbaum, "Dilemma of Presidential Leadership"; Cohen and March, *Leadership and Ambiguity*.

29. Birnbaum, *How Academic Leadership Works*, 146.

30. Birnbaum, *How College Works*; Henry Mintzberg, *Structures in Fives: Designing Effective Organizations* (Englewood Cliffs, NJ: Prentice Hall, 1983).

31. American Association of University Professors, *Policy Documents and Reports*, 8th ed. (Washington, DC: American Association of University Professors, 1995).

32. Andrea L. Foster, "Illinois Plans to Draw 70,000 Students to Distance Education by 2018," *Chronicle of Higher Education*, Apr. 27, 2007, http://chronicle.com/weekly/v53/i34/34a05001.htm [accessed May 15, 2009].

33. Karl E. Weick, "Educational Organizations as Loosely Coupled Systems," *Administrative Science Quarterly* 21, no. 1 (1976): 1–19.

34. As cited in Robert Birnbaum, *Speaking of Higher Education* (Westport, CT: Praeger, 2004), 185.

35. Weick, "Educational Organizations."

36. Ibid.

37. Kellogg Commission on the Future of State and Land-Grant Universities, *Returning to Our Roots: Toward a Coherent Campus Culture* (Washington, DC: National Association of State Universities and Land-Grant Colleges, 2000), 41.

38. Cohen and March, *Leadership and Ambiguity*, 82.

39. Cohen and March, *Leadership and Ambiguity*.

40. Ibid.

41. James G. March, *A Primer on Decision Making: How Decisions Happen* (New York: Free Press, 1994).

42. Cohen and March, *Leadership and Ambiguity*.

43. Birnbaum, *How College Works*; Cohen and March, *Leadership and Ambiguity*.

44. Birnbaum, "Dilemma of Presidential Leadership."

45. Michael K. McLendon, "State Governance Reform of Higher Education: Patterns, Trends, and Theories of the Public Policy Process," in *Higher Education: Handbook of Theory and Research*, vols. 1–, ed. John C. Smart (Norwell, MA: Kluwer Academic, 2003), vol. 18, 57–143.

46. Lara K. Couturier, *Checks and Balances at Work: The Restructuring of Virginia's Public Higher Education System* (San Jose, CA: National Center for Public Policy and Higher Education, June 2006).

47. Michael W. Redding, *Autonomy Policy in U.S. Public Higher Education: A Comparative Case Study of Oregon and Virginia*, PhD diss., University of Pennsylvania, 2009.

48. Birnbaum, "Dilemma of Presidential Leadership," 330.

49. Matthew Hartley, Peter D. Eckel, and Jacqueline E. King, *Looking Beyond the Numbers: The Leadership Implications of the Shifting Demographics of Students, Faculty, and Administrators*, Discussing Higher Education's Future No. 3 (Washington, DC: American Council on Education, 2009).

50. William R. Dill, "Specialized Accreditation: An Idea Whose Time Has Come? Or Gone?" *Change* 30, no. 4 (July/Aug. 1998): 18–25.

51. Judith S. Eaton, "Regional Accreditation Reform: Who Is Served?" *Change* 33, no. 2 (Mar./Apr. 2001): 40.

52. Roger L. Geiger, *Knowledge and Money* (Stanford, CA: Stanford University Press, 2004); David L. Kirp, *Shakespeare, Einstein, and the Bottom Line* (Cambridge, MA: Harvard University Press, 2003); Morphew and Eckel, *Privatizing the Public University.*

53. Robert H. Frank and Philip J. Cook, *The Winner-Take-All Society* (New York: Penguin Books, 1995).

54. Ellen Hazelkorn, "Rankings and the Battle for World Class Excellence: Institutional Strategies and Policy Choices," paper presented at the Organisation for Economic Co-operation and Development, Institute for Higher Education Management General Conference, Paris, France, Sept. 2008.

55. Dominic J. Brewer, Susan M. Gates, and Charles A. Goldman, *In Pursuit of Prestige: Strategy and Competition in U.S. Higher Education* (New Brunswick, NJ: Transaction, 2002), 28.

56. Geiger, *Knowledge and Money,* 15.

57. Eugene McCormick, "A Battle of Inches," *Chronicle of Higher Education,* Apr. 22, 2005, A6.

58. Birnbaum, *How Academic Leadership Works.*

59. John S. Levin, "Presidential Influence, Leadership Succession, and Multiple Interpretations of Organizational Change," *Review of Higher Education* 21, no.4 (1998): 420.

60. Birnbaum, *How Academic Leadership Works;* Anna Neumann, "Context, Cognition, and Culture: A Case Analysis of Collegiate Leadership and Cultural Change," *American Educational Research Journal* 32, no. 2 (1995): 251–79.

61. Birnbaum, *How Academic Leadership Works.*

62. Neumann, "Context, Cognition, and Culture."

63. Birnbaum, *How Academic Leadership Works.*

64. Jeffrey Pfeffer and Gerald R. Salancik, *The External Control of Organizations: A Resource Dependence Perspective* (New York: HarperCollins, 1978).

65. Birnbaum, *How Academic Leadership Works,* 55.

66. Adrianna J. Kezar, Rozana Carducci, and Melissa Contreras-McGavin, *Rethinking the "L" Word in Higher Education: The Revolution on Research in Leadership,* ASHE Higher Education Report, Vol. 31, No 6 (San Francisco: Jossey-Bass, 2006).

67. Estela M. Bensimon, Anna Neumann, and Robert Birnbaum, *Making Sense of Administrative Leadership: The "L" Word in Higher Education,* ASHE-ERIC Higher Education Report 1989, No. 1 (Washington, DC: George Washington University, School of Education and Human Development, 1989).

68. Kezar, Carducci, and Contreras-McGavin, *Rethinking the "L" Word.*

69. ACE, *American College President.*

70. James L. Fisher and James V. Koch, *Presidential Leadership: Making a Difference* (Phoenix: Oryx Press, 1996).

71. Vicki J. Rosser, Linda K. Johnsrud, and Ronald H. Heck, "Mapping the Domains of Effective Leadership," paper presented at the annual meeting of the Association for the Study of Higher Education, Sacramento, California, Nov. 2000.

72. Bensimon, Neumann, and Birnbaum, *Making Sense of Administrative Leadership.*

73. Kezar, Carducci, and Contreras-McGavin, *Rethinking the "L" Word.*

74. Ibid.

75. Ibid.

76. Ibid.

77. Bensimon, Neumann, and Birnbaum, *Making Sense of Administrative Leadership.*

78. See, for example, William G. Tierney, "Advancing Democracy: A Critical Interpretation of Leadership," *Peabody Journal of Higher Education* 66, no. 3 (1991): 157–75.

79. Adrianna J. Kezar and Peter D. Eckel, "Advancing Diversity Agendas on Campus: Examining Transactional and Transformational Presidential Leadership Styles," *International Journal of Leadership in Education* 11, no. 4 (2008): 379–405.

80. Bensimon, Neumann, and Birnbaum, *Making Sense of Administrative Leadership*; Karl L. Weick, *Sensemaking in Organizations* (Thousand Oaks, CA: Sage, 1995).

81. Birnbaum, *How Academic Leadership Works.*

82. Ibid.

83. Pamela L. Eddy, "The Influence of Presidential Cognition and Power on Framing Change at Community Colleges," paper presented at the annual American Educational Research Conference, Chicago, Illinois, Apr. 2003.

84. Kezar, Eckel, and Contreras-McGavin, , *Rethinking the "L" Word.*

85. Estela M. Bensimon and Anna Neumann, *Redesigning Collegiate Leadership* (Baltimore: Johns Hopkins University Press, 1993).

86. Craig L Pearce and Jay Alden Conger, eds., *Shared Leadership: Reframing the Hows and Whys of Leadership* (Thousand Oaks, CA: Sage, 2003).

87. Peter M. Senge, *The Fifth Discipline: The Art and Practice of the Learning Organization* (New York: Doubleday, 1990).

88. ACE, *American College President.*

89. Jacqueline E. King and Gigi G. Gomez, *On the Pathway to the Presidency: Characteristics of Higher Education's Senior Leadership* (Washington, DC: American Council on Education and College and University Professional Association for Human Resources, 2008).

90. Eckel, Cook, and King, *CAO Census.*

91. Ibid.

92. Ibid.

93. Ibid.

94. Ibid.

95. ACE, *American College President.*

96. Eckel, Cook, and King, *CAO Census.*

97. Brian K. Bridges, Peter D. Eckel, Diana I. Córdova, and Byron P. White, *Broadening the Leadership Spectrum: Advancing Diversity in the American College Presidency* (Washington DC: American Council on Education, 2008).

98. Duderstadt, *University for the 21st Century*, 249.

99. Henry Mintzberg, *Managing* (San Francisco: Berrett-Koehler, 2009).

100. Birnbaum, "Dilemma of Presidential Leadership."

PART IV / Central Issues for the Twenty-First Century

CHAPTER TWELVE

Financing Higher Education

Who Should Pay?

D. Bruce Johnstone

The funding of higher education is a large and complex topic. It is complex in part because of its multiple sources of revenue and its multiple outputs, or products, which are only loosely connected to those different revenue sources. Furthermore, these revenue and expenditure patterns vary significantly by the type of institution (university, four-year college, two-year college), mode of governance (public or private), and state. Within the private sector, expenditure levels as well as patterns of pricing and price discounting differ greatly, according to institutional wealth and the depth, demographics, and family affluence of the applicant pool. In the public sector, these patterns also vary according to state funding levels, tuition policies, and enrollment limits that are set by state governments or public multicampus governing boards.

The topic is large because finance underlies much of the three overarching themes of contemporary higher education policy: *quality*, and the relationship between funding and quality in any of its several dimensions; *access*, or the search for social equity in who benefits from, and who pays for, higher education; and *efficiency*, or the search for a cost-effective relationship between revenues (particularly those that come from students, parents, and taxpayers) and outputs (whether measured in enrollments, graduates, student learning, or the scholarly activity of the faculty).

Within these broad themes lie public and institutional policy questions that are informed, if not always answered, by economic and financial perspectives. How, if at all, can costs—especially to the taxpayer and the student—be lowered without damage to academic quality or to principles of access and participation? What are appropriate ratios of students to faculty and to professional and administrative staff at various kinds of institutions? What are reasonable conceptions and expectations of higher educational productivity? How can institutional aid, or price discounting, be used either to attract students with qualities or characteristics sought by the institution or to maximize net tuition revenue? Are taxpayer dollars in the public sector best used to hold down tuition, or should they go toward expanding need-based aid, with public tuitions raised closer to the full average costs of undergraduate instruction? Are public aid dollars best used for grants or for loan subsidies? Should public aid be based on academic promise and performance as well as on family financial need? And what is the appropriate response by institutions and governments to the pervasive condition of austerity in higher education, whether brought on by declining enrollments, reduced state tax assistance, allegations of runaway costs, or (especially vivid at the time of this chapter updating) the severe economic downturn of 2008–10 that has ravaged endowments, state budgets, current giving, and the ability of many families to cover the high and still rising costs of a college education?[1]

Although this chapter concentrates on American higher education, the financial principles and problems are much the same worldwide.[2] Our understanding of the particular financial conditions and problems of American higher education can be sharpened by noting what is peculiar to the financing of the American university: the sheer size and consequent accessibility, or what the Europeans call "massification"; the large private sector, which includes the most and the least prestigious institutions; and the great reliance on nongovernmental revenue—mainly tuition, but also private gifts and the return on endowments.

Who pays, and who should pay? Students and parents? Taxpayers? Philanthropists? How much higher education? At what cost or level of efficiency? Does the seemingly profound economic downturn at the end of the first decade of the century portend fundamental and lasting changes in the way most of our colleges and universities operate? Or are the financial troubles at the time of this writing to be overcome with time and additional revenue—and, if so, from where? These questions can be adequately addressed only within the broader context of American society in the early twenty-first century.

The Economic, Social, and Political Context

Higher education is recognized both as an engine of economic growth and as a gatekeeper to individual positions of high remuneration and status. Advanced education—particularly in high technology, information processing, and sophisticated management and analysis—is thought to be essential to maintaining America's economic position in the increasingly competitive global economy. It follows that most high salary, high status jobs will require an advanced degree, probably beyond the baccalaureate, and it further follows that a lack of postsecondary education creates a likelihood of marginal income and status. These propositions, however, do not mean that advanced education necessarily makes individuals more productive or that all recipients of an advanced education will find remunerative, high-status employment. Higher education can increase productivity; but it can also simply screen, or select, for the kinds of intellectual, social, and personal characteristics required for the high-remuneration, high-status jobs that may be available. In short, higher education is essential for most good jobs, and the absence of an education beyond high school will be an increasingly formidable barrier to obtaining them; but the mere possession of an advanced degree will not guarantee either good, or lasting, employment.

American society continues to be polarized by class, race, and ethnicity. More and more children grow up in poverty, both rural and urban. The dilemma presented by higher education's gatekeeper function is that access to, and especially success in, college and university remains highly correlated with socioeconomic class. This correlation has not significantly diminished in recent years, even though American higher education is more accessible than the higher education systems of other countries. Thus, with the widening disparities of income in the decades ending the twentieth and beginning the twenty-first centuries, and with the increasing relationship of economic success in life to success in college, there is reason to be alarmed at the degree to which our colleges and universities perpetuate, and even accelerate, the intergenerational transmission of wealth and status.

As to the political context, American society, or at least the voting electorate, has become increasingly polarized and conservative. Notwithstanding the elections of 2008, key elements of this conservatism continue, including resistance to the notion of a benign government, to the expansion of social welfare programs, and to transfer payments from the rich to the poor. Insofar as there is to be a public agenda for education, conservatives would have it advanced through private, or at least market-oriented, mechanisms such as charter schools, vouchers, tuition tax credits, and portable need-based aid to increase accessibility to higher education. A third element of this resurgent conservatism, continuing at least into the second decade of the century, is increasing concern over crime and moral laxity, coupled with a diminishing inclination to view either poverty or racism as an acceptable excuse for "deviant" (i.e., non-middle-class) behavior.

Finally, college and university finance at the start of the second decade of the twenty-first century has a special salience, due to the worldwide economic downturn that began in the United States in 2008 and has caused the deepest recession since the Great Depression of the 1930s. At the time of this writing (late in 2009), the United States and most other countries seem to be recovering, albeit slowly. However, revenues in most states remain severely strained, without recourse to the deficit financing that cushions expenditures at the federal level. Since current operating budgets of public colleges and universities are dependent on state budgets for 60 to 70 percent of instructional costs, and as the continued shift of costs from states to parents and students is meeting economic as well as political resistance, public institutions of higher education are experiencing financial strains that are unprecedented since before the Second World War. While the financial fortunes of private colleges and universities vary enormously, depending on such factors as the depth of applicant pools (and thus the ability to maintain tuition revenues in the face of falling applications and yields) and the resilience of endowments and current giving, many endowments lost up to 40 percent of their value in the market crash of 2008, and most private colleges and universities, even selective ones, continue through 2009–10 to experience losses of students to public institutions of similar selectivity and much lower tuitions.

The resulting financial strains, manifesting in academic years 2009 and 2010, in both public and private institutions of higher education are forcing deep budget cuts, including the deferral of planned capital projects and maintenance, positions being left vacant, and the nonrenewal of junior and adjunct faculty; and even extending, in many institutions, to layoffs, mandatory furloughs, salary reductions, and cuts of entire programs. It is difficult to predict the longer-range consequences of this austerity, especially the degree to which it is a temporary downturn from which most institutions will recover in a few years, or whether many or even most colleges and universities will have to fundamentally alter their instructional production functions to effect major and permanent increases in productivity. In either event, the future course of higher education's quality, accessibility, and efficiency, from the vantage point of the second decade of the century, seems increasingly dependent on matters of finance.

These themes are intertwined, of course. For example, the political inclination to seek private solutions to what used to be viewed as public problems is given impetus by the decline in public revenues that (quite aside from the deep economic turndown of 2008–10) is a function, at least in part, of the globalization of the economy and the increasing propensity of wealthy individuals to flee to low-tax havens and move their enterprises to low-wage economies. There are also internal inconsistencies among these themes: for example, increasing dissatisfaction with governmental intrusion contradicts not only the demand for more costly and intrusive accountability, but also direct political intervention into matters of curriculum and programs. Nonetheless, these economic, social, and political themes, for all their complexity, provide a context for consideration of the three broad issues in higher education finance:

—The size of America's publicly funded higher education enterprise (including the publicly funded portion of the private sector): How much publicly supported higher education do we need or will we choose to afford, measured either in total expenditures or as a percentage of our gross domestic product?

—The efficiency and productivity of this enterprise: What should higher education, particularly public higher education, cost per unit (whether the *unit* is students enrolled, degrees granted, scholarship produced, service rendered, or combinations thereof)?

—The sources of revenue to support this enterprise: Who pays (or who should pay) for the costs of higher education? Students and parents? Government and taxpayers? Philanthropists?

Size of the Enterprise

The American higher education enterprise is enormous, even when controlling for our great wealth and population. For example:

—Total current-fund expenditures for all public and private nonprofit institutions of higher education in 2005–6 were $334 billion, of which operating expenditures on instruction alone (that is, excluding research, public service, academic and institutional support, student services, institutionally

provided room and board and other auxiliary enterprises, university
hospitals, scholarships and fellowships from all sources, and depreciation)
were more than $100 billion.[3]

—Total public and private per-student expenditures on higher education in
2005 were the highest of any of the thirty major industrialized countries, and almost double the expenditures of either France or Germany.[4]

—A total of 18,240,000 undergraduate, graduate, and first-professional
students were enrolled in the fall of 2007. Of these, more than 57
percent were undergraduates; 56 percent female; 38 percent part time;
and 32 percent minority (12% black, 11% Hispanic, and 7% Asian or
Pacific Islander). In fall 2007, just under 20 percent were enrolled in
private nonprofit institutions.[5]

—Among twenty-five- to twenty-nine-year-olds, in 2008 59 percent had
completed some college, and 30.8 percent had completed a bachelor's
degree. Those with some college included 80.2 percent Asian and Pacific
Inlanders, 67.1 percent whites, 51 percent blacks, and 35.9 percent Hispanics; those completing a bachelor's degree, aggregated by race or ethnicity,
included 57.9 percent Asian and Pacific Inlanders, 37.1 percent whites, 20.4
percent blacks, and 12.4 percent Hispanics.[6]

—These students were enrolled in 4,352 colleges and universities (counting
branch campuses and institutions outside of the fifty states) in 2007–8,
including 2,667 public and 1,624 private institutions, as well as some
550 degree-granting proprietary institutions (in addition to more than
5,000 non-degree-granting, mainly very short-term, proprietary
vocational institutions).[7]

By these and other measures, it is clear that America has chosen to support a
large, accessible—both in cost and in admission standards—and highly diverse
system (some would say a "nonsystem") of higher education. These "choices" are
made in the form of literally millions of decisions by parents and students to pay
the costs of college—thereby giving expression to the value they place on higher
education for themselves or for their children—and by even more citizens and
elected officials, mainly at the state level, who spend tax funds to maintain public
colleges and universities; provide assistance, mostly via student aid, to private
colleges and universities; and, finally, support an academic research enterprise
that is far and away the largest and most productive in the world.

In the twenty-first century, four forces will expand this already large enterprise. The first is an enlargement of the eighteen- to twenty-four-year-old age cohort. The National Center for Education Statistics projects an enrollment growth for the decade 2008 to 2018 ranging from a low estimate of 9 percent to a high estimate of 17 percent, with the middle estimate pushing enrollment projections to 20,620,000 full- and part-time students.[8] This expansion will occur unevenly, concentrated mainly in the high-growth states of the West, Southwest, and South. (California, for example, continues to experience what policy experts in the 1990s were forecasting as a "tidal wave" of enrollment growth—on top of what in 2009–10 is considered to be one of the most serious economic downturns of any state.)[9]

A second force for more growth in higher education is an expansion of participation and completion, due to a perception of higher private rates of return and the need for at least some higher education so as to acquire positions of remuneration and status, compounded by political pressures for increasing accessibility and decreasing rates of attrition. If the current (as of 2010) efforts to increase participation and reduce dropouts are successful, enrollments will be accelerated by the three-fold drivers of demographics, enhanced participation, and reduced attrition.

A third force, related to the above, is the accretion of degree levels sought by many students. This phenomenon is probably a function of the increasing amount and complexity of knowledge, the rising educational demands of the nation's productive economy (whether for actual skills or simply for higher education's screening function), and the tendency of most professions to enhance their status by requiring ever more education prior to entry and, perhaps, more continuing education to maintain licensure.

A fourth force—working more to increase costs than to enlarge enrollments, and identified more through conjecture than hard evidence—is the incentive for enhancements that seems to be built into the traditions of the academy. William Massy and Robert Zemsky identify this force as "the ratchet."[10] It manifests itself in a perpetual dissatisfaction with the status quo on the part of professors, staff, and administrators and in a determination to do more and better: to teach new materials, to advise students more effectively, to perform more sophisticated (and usually more costly) research, and generally to advance in the highly competitive pecking order of individual and institutional scholarly prestige—all of these without regard to whether *more and better* is either cost-effective or is demanded by those who must pay the bills.

The Efficiency and Productivity of the Enterprise

Another issue within the financing of higher education is the efficiency, or expected productivity, with which all of these resources are employed in the higher education enterprise. Productivity and efficiency look at both costs, or expenditures, and at benefits, or outputs. These concepts deal with costs *per*: whether per student (which, of course, is not really an output but which has the advantage of being easily and unambiguously measured), or per unit of research, or per unit of learning (however measured), or per learning added by the institution. Because the real outputs of the university (the discovery, transmission, and promulgation of knowledge) are both multiple and difficult to measure, and because revenue, at least for the support of instructional expenditures, generally tracks student enrollment in both the public and private sectors, the cost per student inevitably and overwhelmingly dominates approaches to questions of productivity and efficiency. But we ought never to forget that enrollment, however measured—and however sensitive to fields of study, levels of education, or methods of instruction—is still merely a proxy for the hard-to-measure real output, which is student learning.

Variation in Unit Costs

In the production of goods, there are usually multiple ways of combining productive inputs—mainly different combinations of labor, capital, materials, and managerial effectiveness—to produce a unit of output. The most efficient combination of inputs is determined by alternative manufacturing technologies and the relative costs of the inputs. Given a set of input costs and a set of technologies for combining inputs into desired outputs, there generally is an unambiguously *most efficient way*: that is, a lowest cost per unit. The efficiency, then, of any alternative producer or production process can be measured by how that producer or that process compares with the most efficient way.

Higher education is not as fortunate as these goods-producing enterprises. The technology of university production (i.e., of learning and scholarship) is unclear and highly idiosyncratic to the institution, the department, and the individual professor. We know that per-student costs vary greatly. For example, higher education is generally assumed to be more costly at research universities than at undergraduate colleges, due to the higher salaries, lower teaching loads, and more extensive academic support (e.g., libraries and computer facilities) accorded to the faculty of a research university. However, the direct instructional costs (especially at the margin), at least of freshmen and sophomores at a typical public research university, can be rather low, due to the prevalence of low-cost teaching assistants and very large lecture courses—in contrast to the typical public four-year college, where more instruction may be carried out by regular faculty in moderate-sized classes, albeit with heavier average teaching loads. In the end, it is probably appropriate to claim that per-student costs even for undergraduates are higher at most research universities than at four-year colleges; but it must not be forgotten that this is so at least partly because of certain assumptions and cost allocations that, while reasonable, are nonetheless judgmental and sometimes questionable.

Among like institutions, most interinstitutional variation in per-student costs can be attributed to differences either in the amenities provided to the students (recreational and cultural facilities, for example, or academic and student-services support staff) or in the costs of faculty. Differential faculty costs, in turn, reflect differences not only in salaries—which are low for part-time faculty, who provide much of the teaching at low-cost colleges, and high for the full-time senior professoriate at prestigious private colleges—but also in that other major faculty expense, time, which translates into light teaching loads at wealthy colleges and heavy teaching loads at low-cost "access" colleges.

Howard Bowen, in his classic 1980 study of higher education costs, found great variation in costs among seemingly similar institutions with seemingly similar outcomes. In a sample of research and doctoral-granting universities arranged from lowest to highest in per-student expenditures, the average university in the third quartile spent twice as much per student as the average one in the second quartile, and the highest-spending university in the sample spent almost seven and one-half times as much as the first quartile average. The variation among colleges was less, but the colleges in the third quartile of per-student costs still spent about 50 percent more than the colleges in the second quartile.[11] While Bowen's data are old, these cost disparities have continued: fiscal year 2000 data on current-fund expenditures on instruction show per-student spending as high as $20,815 at elite private research universities, but only $8,417 at all public universities, $4,617 at public master's colleges, and $3,912 at public two-year colleges.[12]

This great spread in unit costs is seen by some as profligacy on the part of the highest-cost institutions. Bowen accounts for such variation with his revenue theory of costs, which states that institutions raise all the money they can (which, in the case of highly endowed institutions with wealthy alumni that continue to attract children of affluent families, is a very large amount indeed), and spend all that they raise, purposefully and honorably, even though the amounts spent do not emerge from any discernible production function per se, such as they do in the industrial manufacture of goods.[13]

Even if the "cost" we use to calculate the cost per student at Harvard were to mean the same thing as the "cost" in per-student costs at, say, neighboring Whee-lock College or at the University of Massachusetts, Boston, we still cannot say unambiguously that Wheelock and UMass, Boston, are more efficient or more productive than Harvard. They may be cheaper per student, to be sure, but whether they are more efficient requires a measure of output that we do not have and that we probably could not agree on. Moreover, if Harvard were to contest its possible characterization as "inefficient" or "unproductive," it would point to the extraordinary knowledge and competence of its graduates, or to the lifetime of added benefits that Harvard presumably helped to produce, or to the value to society (not captured by private lifetime income streams) that Harvard "created."

In short, without better agreement on the proper outputs of higher education, not to mention on how to weight and measure them, we are left with the cost per full-time-equivalent student, as best as we can measure it, as the dominant metric of higher educational productivity—and as something that should presumably get lower (or cheaper) in response to the demands of students, parents, and taxpayers that higher education become less costly.

Inflation in Unit Costs

Actually, the problem of unit costs and efficiency (or inefficiency) in higher education is less a function of unit costs per se, and more a function of the seemingly inexorable increase of such costs and the resulting tuition increases at rates that are considerably in excess of the rate of inflation. This is the "cost disease" described by William Baumol as characteristic of the so-called productivity-immune sectors of the economy, which are generally labor-intensive, with few opportunities for substituting capital or new production technologies for labor (including, for example, live theater, symphony orchestras, social welfare agencies, and education).[14] Unit costs in such enterprises track their increases in terms of compensation. Because workers in such enterprises (e.g., faculty) typically get the same wage and salary increases as those in the productivity-sensitive, goods-producing sectors of the economy, in which constant infusions of capital and technology produce real productivity gains and allow unit-cost increases to be less than compensation increases, the unit costs in productivity-immune sectors will inevitably exceed those in goods-producing sectors. Thus unit-cost increases in higher education will be "above average." In addition, since the rate of inflation is nothing more than a weighted average of many price increases, it is inevitable that unit costs—and thus tuitions—in higher education in normal years will rise faster than the rate of inflation.

This, then, is the normal, or default, condition in higher education: unit costs that increase slightly in excess of the prevailing rate of inflation. Tuitions, however, tend to increase at even higher rates, substantially exceeding the prevailing rates of inflation. This results from the following practices:

—state governments that continue year after year to shift the cost burden from taxpayers to students and families, through very-high-percentage tuition increases in the public sector

—private colleges that year after year have to put more of their marginal tuition dollars back into student aid, thus requiring even larger tuition increases to keep up with rising costs

—increases in faculty compensation that, for many institutions, exceed the compensation increases prevailing in the economy generally

—higher education that becomes more and more "input rich" in the form, say, of more technology per student, higher ratios of faculty and staff to students, or a more costly physical plant per student

All of these factors have been at work for most of the past several decades (at least up to the severe recession of 2008), resulting in very substantial tuition increases in both the private and public sectors. From 1997–98 to 2007–8, the average cost of attendance (tuition and required fees plus room and board) at private universities rose from $13,075 to $40,640, or 211 percent. The percentage increase at public universities over the same two decades was from $4,619 to $14,915, an increase of 230 percent. The very high rates of tuition increases alone in private universities—from $8,771 in 1987–88 to $30,260 in 2007–8, or an increase of 245 percent—was largely the result of enriching their amenities, lowering faculty-student and staff-student ratios, and increasing institutionally provided financial aid (i.e., lowering the net revenue yield from a dollar's tuition increase). Rising tuitions in public universities—from $1,726 in 1987–88 to $7,171 in 2007–8, or an increase of some 315 percent—are caused mainly (in addition to inflation) by the withdrawal of state tax revenue and a shift in the relative cost burden from the taxpayer to students and parents.[15]

Diverging Trajectories of Costs and Revenues

As described above, the natural trajectory of unit costs in higher education is steeply upward, at rates in excess of the prevailing rates of inflation. The corresponding rate of increase of anticipated revenues is substantially flatter, being dampened by the following:

—price resistance from upper-middle-class parents, manifested both in a shift in demand to selective public universities and in "bargain hunting" for increased financial aid (lowering *net* tuition revenues), with both of these phenomena increasing during the economic downturn that began in 2008

—price resistance from older students and from graduate and advanced professional students facing mounting debt loads

—the sharp decline in the stock market beginning in 2008 and the resulting collapse of college and university endowments, which especially affects private institutions

—decreasing support from governors and state legislatures faced with other compelling public needs as well as restive state taxpayers—a decline also severely exacerbated by the collapse of state revenues in the recession of 2008–10

—increasing costs of "big science" without concomitant increases in federal research support

—decreasing support for academic health centers, caught between cost-cutting insurers and low-cost alternative providers

The resulting financial scenario is worrisome and, for some institutions, even frightening: particularly for high-priced private institutions, feeling price resistance and declining applications and yields, as well as for public colleges and universities, facing declining state tax revenues and politicians and taxpayers unconvinced of their productivity and accountability. Some institutions have turned their fortunes around through vigorous cost cutting, restructuring, and moving into a narrow market niche, but the future will continue to hold great uncertainty and continuing financial stress for most colleges and universities.

Sources of Revenue for the Enterprise

The financing of higher education poses the question of how its costs should be apportioned among four parties: parents, students, taxpayers, and philanthropists.[16] Parents would finance their children's education from current income, savings, or future income via increased indebtedness (such as a home equity loan). Students would finance their own education from savings, summer earnings, term-time earnings, and future earnings via loans. Taxpayers at the federal, state, and local levels would finance students' education through taxes on income; through sales, property, assets, and business or manufacturing taxes (via the higher prices of the goods or services so taxed); or through the indirect "tax" of inflation brought about by public deficit spending. Philanthropists would finance students' education either through endowments or current giving.

The sharing and shifting of the costs of higher education among these parties can be a zero-sum game, in which a lessening of the burden upon, or revenue from, one party must be compensated for in other ways, either by a reduction of underlying costs or by a shift of the burden to another party. Thus if the state taxpayers' share of higher education costs is to be lessened, that reduced share must either lead to reduced institutional costs or be shifted, probably to students and parents via higher tuition. However, if parents cannot pay or do not have enough political power to limit, by statute or regulation, a higher parental contribution (as happened when voter pressure forced Congress to eliminate home equity from the assets to be considered in determining "need" for awarding federal Pell grants), the burden would shift to students, principally through higher debt loads. This scenario—lower taxpayer contributions, reduced institutional budgets, higher tuitions, level parental contributions, and much higher debt burdens—is exactly what has happened in the last decades of the twentieth and the first decade of the twenty-first centuries.

A number of policy questions regarding tuitions and financial assistance are sharpened by the cost-sharing perspective. For example, what is the appropriate amount that should be expected from parents to cover the higher education costs of their children? Is this share to be a function only of current income, to be met by family belt tightening? Or are parents also expected to have saved from the past or to borrow against the future? Are assets to be figured in the calculation of need? How long should parental financial responsibility continue: through undergraduate years only, or until the age of, say, twenty-four or twenty-five? And what is the expected contribution from a noncustodial parent?

With regard to the students' share, are there any limits to the hours of term-time work that are compatible with full-time study? Are there any limits to the amount of indebtedness that students should be allowed to incur in pursuit of their education? Should this limit be a function of the probability of completing their studies, or of the anticipated earning power of their intended occupation or profession? Would this deferred payment obligation be best handled via a conventional mortgage-type loan, an income-contingent obligation, or a tax obligation after graduation (assuming that the present value of the repayment stream under all options would yield the same repayments, at least over a cohort of borrowers)?

With regard to tuition policies, particularly for public colleges and universities, and whether paid by parents or students or both, should tuitions reflect differences in instructional costs: that is, should they be higher in research universities than in four-year or community colleges? Should they reflect differences in individual program costs, as between, say, engineering and sociology? Or should tuitions reflect market demand, as between a more selective and a less selective public college, or between a major in history versus, say, economics or management? And should the combination of tuition and student assistance—that is, the net price of attendance—be used to favor certain institutions, programs, or students that the government wants to favor?

There has been a considerable increase in education costs borne by students and parents, mainly through higher tuitions, in both the private and the public sector in the first decade of the twenty-first century (and for many preceding years). These increases, in both current and constant dollars, are shown in table 12.1. Table 12.2 indicates the total cost of attendance and the percentage taken from family incomes at selected income quintiles. While adjustments for inflation (that is, converting from current to constant price increases) bring the increased costs of attendance between 1997–98 and 2007–8 down considerably, the increases as percentages of mean family incomes by income quintiles reveal that the increased costs of attendance are taking a greater proportion of family incomes in almost all circumstances. More significantly, the stagnation of family incomes, beginning in the latter decades of the twentieth century and continuing through the first decade of the twenty-first, particularly at the lowest income quintile, has raised the total cost of attendance for low-income families at a public university from 85 to 129 percent of income, and at a private university from 211 to a staggering 351 percent of family income. Clearly, these costs (or, more accurately, prices) are substantially moderated by financial assistance, such that low-income students can access most colleges and universities—but only with very generous (and partially merit-based) institutional aid at private institutions, and with high levels of term-time work and very high levels of student debt at almost all institutions.[17]

Tables 12.3 and 12.4 show how the expenses of private and public institutions, both high cost and low cost, are met through combinations of family contributions, federal and state aid, loans, and institutional (philanthropic) grants for high-, middle-, and low-income families. The numbers shown in the tables are illustrative only, as actual numbers will vary greatly, depending on both the institution and the family. These numbers, however, suggest several policy-relevant observations.

First, the annual costs of attendance at private colleges and universities (table 12.3) are very high for high-income parents, and they are also high for low- and middle-income students. At high-cost private institutions, the costs borne by the institutions (which are assumed to be from endowments, but in some cases might also be from institutional discounts) are also very high, but colleges would be inaccessible to low- and middle-class students without such institutional aid.

Second, the costs borne by students are very high—even for many students from relatively high-income families—and are composed of varying amounts of loans and earnings. In fact, the key to financial accessibility, particularly for private colleges and universities, lies less in the level of tuition, or even in the expected parental contribution, than in the students' willingness to incur substantial indebtedness.

Table 12.1 Annual tuition and required fees, private and public colleges, 1987–88 to 2007–8, in current dollars

	Private institutions		Public institutions	
Year	University	Four-year college	University	Two-year college
1987–88	8,771	6,574	1,726	706
1992–93	13,055	9,533	2,604	1,025
1997–98	17,229	12,338	3,486	1,314
2002–3	22,176	15,416	4,686	1,483
2007–8	30,260	19,798	7,171	2,063
Percent increase 2002–7	36	28	53	39
Percent increase 1997–2007	76	60	106	57

Source: National Center for Education Statistics, *Digest of Education Statistics 2008*, (Washington, DC: National Center for Education Statistics, 2009), table 331.

Note: Data has not been adjusted for changes in the purchasing power of the dollar over time.

Table 12.2   Increase in average total costs (tuition, room, and board), 1997–98 to 2007–8, by sector, in current and constant (2006–7) dollars, and as a percentage of mean family income by quintile in 2007 CPI-U-RS adjusted dollars

	Average total cost			
	Private university	Private other four-year	Public university	Public two-year
Total cost 2007–8, current dollars	40,640	28,142	14,915	6,966
Total cost 1997–98, current dollars	24,116	17,717	8,210	4,509
Total cost 1997–98, constant (2006–7) dollars	24,069*	16,308	9,685*	5,691
Percent increase, current (unadjusted) dollars	66	59	82	54
Percent increase, constant (2006–7) dollars	22*	NA	34*	18
Total cost 2007–8, current dollars, as a percentage of mean family income by quintile, 2007				
High quintile	24	17	8	4
Third quintile	81	56	30	14
Low quintile	351	243	129	60
Total cost 1997–98, constant dollars, as a percentage of mean family income by quintile, 1997				
High quintile	15	10	6	4
Third quintile	50	34	20	12
Low quintile	211	143	85	50

Sources: Total costs from National Center for Education Statistics, Digest of Education Statistics 2008 (Washington, DC: National Center for Education Statistics, 2009), table 331; mean family income by quintiles from U.S. Census Bureau, Income, Poverty, and Health Insurance Coverage in the United States: 2007 (Washington, DC: U.S. Government Printing Office, 2008), table A-3.
*All four-year institutions.

Table 12.3 Student budgets at private institutions, sources of support by family income (in dollars)

Sources of support	High-cost institution ($40,000)			Low-cost institution ($28,000)		
	Low-income family	Middle-income family	High-income family	Low-income family	Middle-income family	High-income family
Parental contribution*	0	3,508	27,362	0	3,508	27,362
Federal grants†	9,350	2,760	0	9,350	2,760	0
State grants‡	2,000	1,500	0	2,000	1,500	0
Institutional grants	12,650	18,732	5,638	2,430	7,732	0
Summer savings	3,000	3,000	3,000	2,500	2,500	638
Student term-time earnings	2,000	2,000	2,000	1,500	1,500	0
Stafford student loans (max. subsidized and unsubsidized)	5,500	5,500	2,000	4,720	5,500	0
Perkins student loans (max.)	5,500	3,000	0	5,500	3,000	0
Total from taxpayer§	14,630	6,583	0	14,630	6,583	0
Total from parents**	0	3,508	27,362	0	3,508	27,362
Total from student††	12,720	11,177	7,000	10,940	10,177	638
Total from philanthropists‡‡	12,650	18,732	5,638	2,430	7,732	0
Total	40,000	40,000	40,000	28,000	28,000	28,000

Note: Low family income is the point below which a family qualifies for maximum grants and has no expected financial contribution. Middle income is household earnings of $50,000, and high income is household earnings of $150,000.

*Expected family contribution calculated using the FinAid calculator, www.finaid.org/calculators/scripts/estimate.cgi.

†Assume maximum Pell plus Federal Supplemental Educational Opportunity grants.

‡Assume maximum need-based grants.

§Sum of federal and state grants, plus the present value of the loan subsidy for subsidized Stafford loans (interest paid by the government while the student is in school and for six months following completion, plus a subsidized interest rate of 5.6 percent during the repayment period) and Perkins loans (interest paid by the government while the student is in school and for nine months following completion, plus a subsidized interest rate of 5 percent during the repayment period).

**Expected family contribution minus summer savings from the student.

††Sum of expected term-time earnings, plus summer savings, plus present value of the loan repayments.

‡‡Total from philanthropists includes all institutional grants.

Total student debt for four or more years of undergraduate education alone can reach from $30,000 to $50,000, and three or more years of graduate or advanced professional school can increase that aggregate student debt to more than $100,000, presenting low- and middle-income students with repayment obligations that can either discourage advanced higher education altogether or distort career and other life choices.

Third, access to private higher education by low- and middle-income students also depends heavily on taxpayer support through federal and state grants, as well as through estimates of the taxpayer-borne costs of student loan subsidies.

Table 12.4, showing the division of the cost burden at public institutions, reveals that high-cost public institutions (high tuition plus residency) also require substantial indebtedness, particularly from middle-income students, considerably diminishing their price advantage over high-cost private institutions to students, although not to parents.

The costs borne by families and students at low-cost public institutions—essentially the costs of commuting to a public community college—remain modest and require little from the student, at least in terms of a low cost of living. With the addition of loans and earnings, low-cost public higher education is clearly still accessible, at least to traditional-age youth who are appropriately accommodated by their local community colleges.

High Tuition–High Aid

From time to time, a proposal is made that direct public funding of state colleges and universities, at least with regard to support for instruction, either be drastically reduced or eliminated altogether, and that tuitions be raised to full or near-full cost, thus eliminating or greatly reducing what the proponents of this view call the "subsidy" to the students and the families of students attending public colleges and universities. In place of direct state revenue, which currently supports from 60 percent to 90 percent of public four-year undergraduate instructional costs, proponents of the high tuition–high aid model would substitute a much-expanded program of need-based grants that would diminish as parental or student incomes rose. The grants would phase out entirely for families and students whose income was deemed to be sufficient to pay the full cost of tuition in addition to other expenses.[18]

The high tuition–high aid model is based on claims of efficiency and equity. The efficiency claim begins with a tenet of public finance theory: any public subsidy of a good or a service that consumers are likely to purchase anyway, in

Table 12.4 Student budgets at public institutions, sources of support by family income (in dollars)

Sources of support	High-cost institution ($15,000)			Low-cost institution ($7,200)		
	Low-income family	Middle-income family	High-income family	Low-income family	Middle-income family	High-income family
Parental contribution*	0	3,508	15,000	0	3,508	7,200
Federal grants†	9,350	1,333	0	7,200	1,333	0
State grants‡	2,000	1,000	0	0	1,000	0
Institutional grants	650	720	0	0	0	0
Summer savings	1,500	2,000	0	0	598	0
Student term-time earnings	1,500	1,000	0	0	761	0
Stafford student loans (max. subsidized and unsubsidized)	0	5,439	0	0	0	0
Perkins student loans (max.)	0	0	0	0	0	0
Total from taxpayer§	11,350	2,333	0	7,200	2,333	0
Total from parents**	0	3,508	15,000	0	3,508	7,200
Total from student††	3,000	8,439	0	0	1,359	0
Total from philanthropists‡‡	650	720	0	0	0	0
Total	15,000	15,000	15,000	7,200	7,200	7,200

Note: Low family income is the point below which a family qualifies for maximum grants and has no expected financial contribution. Middle income is household earnings of $50,000, and high income is household earnings of $150,000.

*Expected family contribution calculated using the FinAid calculator, www.finaid.org/calculators/scripts/estimate.cgi.

†Assume maximum Pell plus Federal Supplemental Educational Opportunity grants.

‡Assume maximum need-based grants.

§Sum of federal and state grants, plus the present value of the loan subsidy for subsidized Stafford Loans (interest paid by the government while the student is in school and for six months following completion, plus a subsidized interest rate of 5.6 percent during the repayment period) and Perkins Loans (interest paid by the government while the student is in school and for nine months following completion, plus a subsidized interest rate of 5 percent during the repayment period).

**Expected family contribution minus assumed summer savings from the student.

††Sum of expected term-time earnings, plus summer savings, plus present value of the loan repayments.

‡‡Total from philanthropists includes all institutional grants.

the absence or diminution of the subsidy, is an inefficient use of public tax dollars. The tax dollars released, if public-sector tuitions were allowed to rise (or forced to be raised) would supposedly go toward public needs of greater priority: more need-based student aid, health care, public infrastructure, tax cuts, or public deficit reduction. Moreover, if the demand for public higher education should decline as a result of lower subsidies and higher prices, this, too, might be a move in the direction of a more efficient use of the nation's resources. Subsidies can generate overproduction of a good or service, and a higher-priced public higher education might discourage ambivalent, ill-prepared students, whom advocates of high tuition–high aid assume are taking up space in and wasting precious resources of our public colleges and universities.

A corollary of the efficiency claim is that there exists, at least in some states, underutilized capacity in the private higher education sector that could be filled at relatively low marginal cost. A shift of tax dollars from the direct support of public colleges and universities to need-based student aid, portable to the private sector, would presumably shift enrollments there and enable a socially optimal level of enrollments to be supported more in the private sector, but at a lower additional net cost to the taxpayer.

The equity argument in favor of high tuition–high aid is based on two assumptions: first, that public higher education is actually partaken of disproportionately by students from upper-middle-income and affluent families; and second, that the state taxes used to support public higher education tend to be proportionate, or even regressive, and thus are paid by many lower-middle-income and poor families who are unlikely to benefit from it. Thus the high tuition–high aid model of public higher education finance is claimed to be more equitable than across-the-board low tuition, because it targets all of the public subsidy only on the needy and imposes full costs on students or families affluent enough to pay those costs.

The case against the high tuition–high aid model rests partly on the oversimplification and political naïveté of the case made on its behalf, summarized above, and partly on the case to be made below for the very existence of a public higher education sector. The case against high tuition–high aid may be summarized by four points.

First, a full cost-recovery "sticker price" of $20,000 to $30,000 or more for a full-time year at a public college or university would almost certainly discourage many from aspiring to a higher education, even with the prospect of financial aid or lower tuition for those in need. The total costs to students and parents of a year of full-time study at a public four-year college or university, as shown in table 12.4, make even public higher education a relatively heavy financial burden today for most families and for nearly all independent students. This fact alone does not fully negate the more theoretical arguments of efficiency and equity presented on behalf of full-cost or near-full-cost pricing for public higher education, as summarized above. But even with financial aid, costs at a public college might seem daunting to many students and their parents, especially to students from disadvantaged and nonwhite families.

Second, a high tuition–high aid policy would lessen the quality of public colleges and universities. The purpose of high tuition–high aid plans is to reduce the state tax revenues currently going to public colleges and universities, even though some proponents claim that this revenue loss would be made up for by increased revenue from the much higher tuitions paid by the more well-to-do. Private-sector proponents of high tuition–high aid, however, make no secret of their aim to shift enrollments and the tuition dollars of middle- and upper-middle-income students (or at least the most attractive and able ones) from the public sector to the private sector. With little or no price advantage left in the public sector; with the resource advantages of large endowments, wealthy alumni, and a tradition of philanthropic support in the private sector; with the patina of elitism and selectivity associated with private colleges and universities (especially in the Northeast); and with greater constraints and burdens remaining on the public sector, many of the nation's 1,600 public colleges and universities would become places for students whom the private colleges, if priced the same as public colleges, would not accept. Such an erosion in the relative status and quality of public colleges and universities does not seem to be in the nation's public interest.

A third element in the case against high tuition–high aid is that high tuition in and of itself does not guarantee high aid. Governors, legislators, and voters, continually pressed by public needs exceeding available resources, are likely to support that part of the public sector in which they perceive that they or their children have a stake. They are much less likely to maintain the financial aid, or "tuition discount," portion of the public higher education budget when it is devoted almost exclusively to the poor. Rather than creating purported enhancements of efficiency and equity, the not-unlikely consequences of a policy of high tuition–high aid are higher tuition, lower taxes, inadequate aid, diminished access, and deteriorating public colleges and universities.

Fourth and fundamentally, the high tuition–high aid model is a denial of the appropriateness of higher education as a public good. The nation's public colleges and universities have not been built and supported over the last century and a half merely to provide a subsidized education to those who might not otherwise have an opportunity for higher education. Rather, voters and elected officials wanted public colleges and universities that would attract and hold the best and brightest students and scholars, serve society, aid the economy, and be a signal of the state's culture. The high tuition–high aid model essentially denies most of these public purposes to public higher education and substitutes only a public subsidy for those who are too poor to afford what would become an otherwise unsubsidized, expensive, and essentially privatized product. States need to consider whether these public purposes continue to be important reasons for supporting public higher education, or whether they mainly want to get needy students into some college, in which case high tuition–high aid is almost certainly, as public finance theory correctly states, less expensive to the taxpayer.

Summary and Conclusions

The financial fortunes of American colleges and universities vary greatly by institution. Those relatively few private institutions with large endowments, traditions of generous alumni giving, and deep and affluent student applicant pools will experience continuing cost pressures, as well as what many observers in 2010 believe will be only a temporary setback, due to losses in endowment income and current giving from the 2008–10 recession. Some public institutions—similarly situated with deep and affluent applicant pools, established traditions of philanthropic support, and research strengths in areas of continuing public investment (e.g., biomedical and applied sciences)—may suffer temporary state revenue cutbacks, but they will continue to prosper and may even gain some market share from the troubles of the less-selective private institutions. Some less-selective and less-endowed private institutions may be able to seize a specialized market niche, either vocational (e.g., health-related professions) or cultural-ideological (e.g., conservative Christian), and, with good management and low faculty costs, also prosper. Most private colleges and universities, however, will experience a fierce revenue squeeze, primarily driven by a lack of growth both in the number of upper-middle-class parents able or willing to pay their high tuitions and in the number of students willing to take on increasing levels of indebtedness. Finally, most public colleges and universities will continue to experience flat or declining state tax support, forcing them to have even higher tuitions, more program closures, and an increasing reliance on part-time and adjunct faculty.

As more and more colleges and universities exhaust the available cost-side measures for increasing productivity, some interest is being turned towards measures to increase productivity by enhancing higher education's output: that is, learning.[19] Expressed another way, the major remaining productivity problem in higher education may lie less in excessive costs and more in insufficient learning—a function of such features as redundant learning; aimless academic exploration; the unavailability of courses at the right time; excessive nonlearning time in the academic day, week, and year; insufficient use of self-paced learning; and insufficient realization of the potential of collegiate-level learning during the high school years. Enhancing the productivity of learning, then, would reduce vacation time and other time spent in other-than-learning activities; provide better advising and other incentives to lessen aimless curricular exploration; enhance opportunities for self-paced learning, perhaps with the aid of instructional technology; minimize curricular redundancy; and maximize the potential of college-level learning during the high school years.

Technology—in the form of personal computers, new instructional software, the Internet, and instructional videocassettes—will profoundly affect the way faculty and advanced students conduct research, and it will enrich some teaching. However—aside from some pockets of distance learning and from the users of a virtual university, who are generally limited to nontraditional and technologically inclined students—technology will mainly enable more and better, but not cheaper, learning.

The current shift in the cost burden from parents and taxpayers onto students, paid for with more part-time (and even more full-time) work and much more debt, will continue, but there is reason to believe that the long-expected price resistance is happening. Marketing will become even more frenzied, as will various governmental efforts to "solve the problem" without spending any taxpayer revenue: tuition prepayment, tax-exempt savings plans, non-need-based price discounting, income-contingent repayment plans, and the like.

State higher education budgets will be smaller, but in most states this reduction will be accompanied by greater flexibility, together with performance criteria and incentives, such as premiums to institutions that improve retention and completion rates. Most institutions have been shaping their missions for years to adjust to more low-income, minority, older, part-time, and place-bound students; greater applied and vocational interest among most students; and less revenue and the need to trim or eliminate that which is neither excellent nor popular nor central to the institution. In short, much of the vaunted restructuring that management consultants and many observers and analysts of higher education have been calling for as a solution to the financial dilemma of U.S. colleges and universities is probably not a solution at all, for the simple reason that it has been going on for years. Most of the smaller and comprehensive colleges have reallocated resources and altered their programs and faculty profiles dramatically; many have changed their missions altogether. It is impossible to forecast whether more small, nonselective, nonendowed colleges will close their doors in the wake of the recession that is still current at the time of this writing, but some almost assuredly will.

Some institutions may be in financial jeopardy: those universities, both public and private, that are largely regional, have minimal or uneven scholarly reputations, and continue to pursue the research university model yet are unlikely to penetrate the top ranks, measured by either the scholarly prestige of their faculty or their graduate programs. Here, pressures to control costs are likely to focus on an increasing separation of funding for instruction and for research, much as has occurred in the United Kingdom. If these measures are successful, the result could be less indirect public subsidization of faculty scholarship, a widening difference in faculty workloads, and reduced administrative overhead on competitive research grants.

Although American higher education does more than the systems of any other nation to provide postsecondary opportunities to those from low socioeconomic backgrounds, the larger American society is becoming not only more unequal, but also more predictable in the intergenerational transmission of higher educational attainment. In other words, the children of well-educated, well-off parents generally achieve and persist in college, and those of the extremely poor, unless they are very bright and very lucky, generally do not. The likely continuation of sharply rising public tuitions, political attacks against remedial courses, the elimination of affirmative action considerations in admissions and financial aid, and the conservative assault against curricula acknowledging multicultural values may accentuate this pattern.

NOTES

1. The prevailing condition of austerity in higher education is described in such works as David W. Breneman, *Liberal Arts Colleges: Thriving, Surviving, or Endangered?* (Washington, DC: Brookings Institution, 1994); and D. Bruce Johnstone, "Higher Education and Those 'Out-of-Control Costs'" in *In Defense of American Higher Educa-*

tion, ed. Philip G. Altbach, Patricia J. Gumport, and D. Bruce Johnstone (Baltimore: Johns Hopkins University Press, 2001), 144–80.

2. For a perspective on the overwhelming condition of austerity in higher education in developing countries, and its similarity—in both the analyses and policy solutions—with the United States and Europe, see World Bank, *Higher Education: The Lessons of Experience* (Washington, DC: World Bank, 1994); Adrian Ziderman and Douglas Albrecht, *Financing Universities in Developing Countries* (Washington, DC: Falmer Press, 1995); Task Force on Higher Education and Society, *Higher Education in Developing Countries: Peril and Promise* (Washington, DC: World Bank and UNESCO); World Bank, *Constructing Knowledge Societies: New Challenges for Tertiary Education* (Washington, DC: World Bank, 2002); Maureen Woodhall, guest editor, *Paying for Learning: The Debate on Student Fees, Grants, and Loans in International Perspective,* a special international issue of the *Welsh Journal of Education* 11, no. 1 (2002).

3. National Center for Education Statistics [NCES], *Digest of Education Statistics 2008* (Washington, DC: National Center for Education Statistics, 2009), tables 362, 365.

4. Ibid., table 418.

5. Ibid., table 188.

6. NCES, *Condition of Education 2009* (Washington, DC: National Center for Education Statistics, 2009), table A-23-1.

7. NCES, *Digest of Education Statistics 2008,* table 265.

8. NCES, *Condition of Education 2009,* table 14; NCES, *Digest of Education Statistics 2002* (Washington, DC: National Center for Education Statistics, 2002), table 174.

9. California Postsecondary Education Commission, *The Challenge of the Century* (Sacramento: California Postsecondary Education Commission, Apr. 1995). The privately financed California Policy Center sets the number at 488,000; see California Higher Education Policy Center, *Shared Responsibility: Strategies to Enhance Quality and Opportunity in California Higher Education* (San Jose: California Higher Education Policy Center, 1996).

10. William F. Massy and Robert Zemsky, "The Lattice and the Ratchet," *Policy Perspectives* 2, no. 4 (1990): 1–8. Also see Robert Zemsky and William F. Massy, "Toward an Understanding of Our Current Predicaments," *Change* (Nov./Dec. 1995): 41–49.

11. Howard R. Bowen, *The Costs of Higher Education* (San Francisco: Jossey-Bass, 1980), 116–19.

12. NCES, *Digest of Education Statistics 2002,* tables 343, 345, 386.

13. Bowen, *Costs of Higher Education,* 19–26.

14. William J. Baumol and William G. Bowen, *Performing Arts: The Economic Dilemma* (New York: Twentieth Century Fund, 1966); see also William G. Bowen, *The Economics of the Major Private Universities* (Berkeley, CA: Carnegie Commission on the Future of Higher Education, 1968).

15. Figures taken from NCES, *Digest of Education Statistics 2008*, table 331. For more on rising tuition fees, see Charles T. Clotfelter, *Buying the Best: Cost Escalation in Elite Higher Education* (Princeton, NJ: Princeton University Press, 1996); Ronald G. Ehrenberg, *Tuition Rising: Why College Costs So Much* (Cambridge, MA: Harvard University Press, 2000); D. Bruce Johnstone, "'Out-of-Control Costs.'" For time series, see College Board, *Trends in College Pricing*, available annually at www.collegeboard .com.

16. Some consider "business" a possible fifth party to bear a share of higher education costs. However, grants from business to higher education can be viewed in one of three ways: (1) as the purchase of a service, whether research or specialized training, in which case the grant should cover the costs of the added service but is not expected to bear a share of the core instructional costs of the college or university; (2) as voluntary contributions coming out of owner profits, in which case they would fall under "philanthropy"; or (3) as contributions considered as part of the cost of doing business, included in the price of the products and paid for by the general consumer, like a sales or consumption tax, in which case the incidence, or burden, is indistinguishable from that of other taxes and may be considered to be included, at least conceptually, in the "taxpayer" party. See D. Bruce Johnstone, *Sharing the Costs of Education* (New York: College Board, 1986).

17. NCES, *Digest of Education Statistics 2008*, table 331. See also College Board, *Trends in College Pricing* [yearly].

18. The case for high tuition–high aid was popularized in W. Lee Hansen and Burton A. Weisbrod, *Benefits, Costs, and Finance of Public Higher Education* (Chicago: Markham, 1969). See also Carnegie Commission on Higher Education, *Higher Education: Who Pays? Who Benefits? Who Should Pay?* (New York: McGraw-Hill, 1973); Frederick J. Fischer, "State Financing of Higher Education: A New Look at an Old Problem," *Change* 22, no. 1 (Jan./Feb. 1990): 42–56; McPherson, Shapiro, and Winston, *Paying the Piper*. The case against it draws heavily on D. Bruce Johnstone, *The High Tuition–High Aid Model of Public Higher Education Finance: The Case Against* (Albany: State University of New York, for National Association of System Heads, 1993).

19. D. Bruce Johnstone, "The Productivity of Learning," *Journal for Higher Education Management* (Summer/Fall 1995): 11–17.

CHAPTER THIRTEEN

The Digital Technologies of Learning and Research

John Willinsky, Gustavo Fischman, and
Amy Scott Metcalfe

This chapter addresses how twenty-first-century digital technologies are transforming, or have the potential to transform, teaching and research in higher education. Having crossed the threshold into this digital era, leaders in higher education face critical decisions and promising opportunities around questions of how best to utilize these technologies to advance higher education. This chapter sets out the principal issues and challenges that, as we see it, will need to be considered in making wise and sound choices for advancing the work of higher education. While universities continue to develop advanced technical systems, from astronomical observatories to particle accelerators, this chapter restricts itself to the impact of digital information and communication technologies. Digital systems are, of course, crucial for operating observatories and accelerators, but, more importantly, they have everything to do with the teaching and learning, as well as research and scholarship, taking place across the disciplines and throughout the university. Our focus, then, is on the educational and epistemological principles that should, in our estimation, inform the deployment of digital technologies. We are approaching this sense of *what is to be done* with an eye on the rearview mirror, that is, with some regard for how earlier and current technologies have furthered the mission and reach of higher education.

Digital Openings

The digital era is marked by a reordering of world markets and knowledge-based services in which the intense capitalization of knowledge provides both opportunities and challenges to universities. In times of restrained public funding, higher education is feeling the temptation to become increasingly responsive to market forces, whether in pursuing new high-tech ventures, such as online degree programs, or getting behind knowledge-based spinoffs. Yet at the same time, this digital era has also given rise to a contrary set of forces, aimed at increasing the openness of research and scholarship, as well the degree of cooperation among institutions, projects, and researchers. It is still too early into this digital era to see anything more certain ahead than multiple and varied possibilities, with no one direction necessarily excluding the other.

What is clear, however, is that through their constant quest for new ways of learning more about the world, researchers and scholars are shaping digital information and communication systems. Those technologies, in turn, are shaping academic life, facilitating an increased international flow of correspondence and collaborations, as well as of data and publications, in ways that resonate with themes running throughout this collection. Digital systems are supporting a parallel growth in the number of journals, even as faculty, for their part, are consulting an increasing number of articles from a greater number of sources, including older works, through electronic means.[1]

These digital technologies are contributing, in a word, to a further *opening* of learning and knowledge. That is, these systems are being used to open higher education to more people, to more active forms of learning, to more globally distributed research, and to more widely available research. This extended openness is not without its natural limits, its immediate financial hurdles, and its share of trial and error, fumbles and successes, in remaining true to the public mission and purpose of higher education. That mission has long involved contributing to the public good through the highest forms of learning, which may well seem to work against this new spirit of openness, making it all the more interesting in how higher education takes advantage of this new medium amid questions of knowledge access and distribution.

We see the current and potential degrees of a greater openness in higher education not as a particular artifact or gift of the digital era, nor as unqualified good, but as furthering a relatively constant theme within the proud heritage of higher education. The opening of learning has long been part of the challenge and achievement of these institutions, with today's new forms being very much a part of that history, whether one considers online distance education (think of the twelfth-century correspondence between Abelard and Heloise) or the new openness of digital scholarship (much as the early universities sought to open up Greek and Arabic learning to Europe). Higher education's engagement with present-day technologies retains the marks of its historic and imperfect pursuit of learning, while facing critical and pressing issues in the years ahead. We have thus organized what follows around themes of the digital age's impact on teaching and learning; the development of research cyberinfrastructure; the new digital economies; and the opening access to research and scholarship.

Digital Impact on Teaching and Learning

It may seem obvious that the ability to move information across vast distances, delivering it to individual users in virtually no time at all and at very little cost, would prove a boon for what is now known as "online education" and "e-learning" models. Yet the process of developing the models and appropriate systems has been uneven and complex, marked by numerous challenges affecting efficiency, access, cost, and equity.[2] What is beyond doubt is that digital systems are ubiquitous in American higher education, and universities are now almost "unthinkable" without them.[3] According to a survey by the Sloan Group (a consortium of providers of online education) during the fall of 2007, over 3.9 million students in the United States took at least one online course, representing a 12 percent annual increase from 2006, compared with a 1.2 percent growth in the overall higher education student population.[4]

From around the turn of the twenty-first century, a number of institutions have experimented with offering not only courses, but also complete degree programs online. On one level, this was a natural outgrowth or extension of "open university" services to nontraditional students, such as minorities, rural populations, or working adults. Yet often enough, these online distance education ventures were positioned as for-profit, high-tech startups, intent on selling the university "brand" to a global audience. The most promising collective instances, among them Fathom and Universitas 21, have stumbled and failed for want of enrollment, despite the distinguished institutions participating in them, with resulting losses in the millions of dollars.[5]

Still, some institutions have found a way to make the online model of program delivery work on a for-profit basis, as well as being educationally attractive to students. The University of Phoenix was, at the beginning of this century, enrolling a quarter of its more than 100,000 students in its online campus, and this continues to be a part of its program.[6] Cornell University's eCornell, which began in 2001, has had some 25,000 students, drawn from over 180 countries, pass through its business and management programs.[7] Such programs represent a threat to the traditional values of higher education for some, while others point to them as demonstrating the capacity of universities to utilize new technologies to serve a wider audience on a self-sustaining basis.[8]

This sort of either/or thinking—with technology either *spelling the end* or *serving the ends* of learning—is all too common to discussions in this field.[9] There are those, for example, who consider the digital transformation of higher education as absolutely crucial to preparing the young for the high-tech demands of the "new economy."[10] At the same time, Philip Brown and Hugh Lauder are among those who have cast serious doubts on the widespread demand for tech-savvy knowledge workers and symbolic analysts: "This problem is not only numerical—there are not enough high-skilled jobs—but the quality of work experience is also in question . . . [as] there are not enough good quality jobs available and [there is] the failure of employers to exploit the potential for higher productivity and growth that mass education now offers."[11]

In addition, efforts to portray e-learning as the redeemer of outdated teaching practices have been challenged by others, such Robert Bernard and a number of colleagues, over the validity of trying to compare learning in different settings: "We have learned that the very nature of the question [How does distance education compare with classroom instruction?] impedes our ability to discover what makes distance education effective or ineffective, because the question is cast as a contrast between such starkly different forms for achieving the same end."[12] Framing digital technologies as simply an improved delivery mechanism fails to take into account how the medium massages the message, as well as, in this case, the pedagogy.

Despite the challenges posed by assessing the digital age's impact on learning, instances of technologies leading to better teaching and learning have emerged. Having students use "clickers" or student personal response systems (to indicate their understanding of the materials being presented during class) offers a good example, with several studies showing that these devices effectively address two long-standing challenges for teachers facing larger classes, namely, assessing students' learning during instruction and motivating student engagement.[13] A broader source of pedagogical innovation is found in the emergence of Open Educational Resources, with the OpenCourseWare Consortium (OCW) being a prime instance. OCW makes available instructional content from approximately 200 universities across the world, with the Massachusetts Institute of Technology's (MIT's) site, now involving virtually every course taught at that institution, receiving more than a million visitors monthly.

It is important to continue experimenting with digital means of increasing engagement in and sharing of learning, even while knowing that much sorting out and refinement will be needed with the introduction of new approaches and devices in a largely untried teaching medium.[14] No one can predict the future impact of technologies on teaching and learning in higher education, but it remains relatively certain that the American universities of tomorrow will continue to seek out and assess the pedagogical advantages to be wrought from innovative and imaginative uses of these new technologies.[15] Whether you consider simulations in surgical training, access to primary documents from historical archives, the management of peer review in undergraduate research programs, or the provision of service-learning opportunities around the globe, the potential pedagogical contribution of networked technologies is just getting underway and, as such, awaits much experimentation, testing, and assessment of benefits.[16]

At this point, when we are still in the first wave of the wireless campus, concerns aplenty are being expressed by instructors facing a sea of open screens and otherwise-connected students who are updating their Facebook pages and text messaging. Comparative studies provide evidence for the value of closed-laptop policies and wireless-free classrooms, at least if the use of laptops is not playing a vital role in the learning taking place.[17] Yet rather than seeking to isolate the classroom from the Web, others are exploring a new category of electronic tools, known as Wireless Internet Learning Devices, that enable classroom activities to be both individualized and networked.[18] Internet conferencing services are being used not just in distance education settings, where much of this work has been pioneered in order to improve the educational experience of students; given the portability of wireless networking, they are also now being taken advantage of to have experts informally drop into a class to address specific points, or to have a class drop in on a site or project under discussion.[19] Some instructors, in our experience, are calling on connected students to provide Web-based intellectual backup by supplementing classroom discussions, to the educational benefit of both the instructor and the students, whether in the moment or through a follow-up after class. The digital opening of the classroom and the extension of learning has a number of credits and missteps to its name, while much—in terms of digitally enhanced ways of teaching and improving the quality of learning—awaits exploring and assessing.

Development of Research Cyberinfrastructure

The term *computer* goes back to the seventeenth century, when it was first used to refer to those who computed and calculated (Newton had one, or rather hired one, while at Cambridge). The complex calculations that distinguish research from other forms of knowledge continue to be a focus of twenty-first-century digital technologies. What distinguishes these technologies, as this century begins to unfold, is not only their tremendous computing power, but also how that power is being realized and augmented through distributed networks among scientists, which in turn are affecting the way research is conducted at every stage. The key term for these online systems supporting research activities (including collaborative project sites, shared research tools, and data and workflow management platforms) is *cyberinfrastructure* (or *e-research*, as it is referred to in Europe). Cyberinfrastructure promises not only to enhance the quality of scientific work and resources, but also to further integrate American research activities within a global grid of investigation and inquiry, with benefits for both the scale and pace of research and the advantages that it might bring to learning and practice.[20]

The growing use and development of cyberinfrastructure not only changes the scale and speed of connections that are forming among hundreds, if not thousands, of researchers, but also alters the very process of planning and building research grants; establishing virtual research organizations; and marshalling computing power for data collection, analysis, visualization, and publication—all from within this digital sphere.[21] Daniel Atkins and the other authors of the National Science Foundation's 2003 study on cyberinfrastructure are convinced that this new manner of working has economic implications that go well beyond academic life; they hold, in historical terms, that "if *infrastructure* is required for an *industrial* economy, then we could say that *cyberinfrastructure* is required for a *knowledge* economy."[22]

While the term originated with "big science," cyberinfrastructure is no longer exclusively the purview of the sciences on university campuses. In 2006, the Commission on Cyberinfrastructure for the Humanities and Social Sciences, formed by the American Council of Learned Societies with support from the Andrew W. Mellon Foundation, issued *Our Cultural Commonwealth*. The commission stakes its own digital claim in this extensive rewiring of higher education, asserting that "digital cultural heritage resources are a fundamental dataset for the humanities."[23] Here, then, is the interdisciplinary influence of these shared technologies for research and scholarship, even if it will be some time before the language of *digital datasets* will come easily for the majority of humanities scholars. What distinguishes *Our Cultural Commonwealth* from the sciences' approach to cyberinfrastructure, however, is its emphasis on working toward a *shared* or common wealth of knowledge. As the commission puts it, cyberinfrastructure is to be, first of all, "accessible as a public good," while the need to "support experimentation" comes in fifth among its stated goals.[24] This group of scholars in the humanities and social sciences are committed to *opening* to the public both the "digital cultural heritage resources" (read *digitized* cultural artifacts) and their closely linked accompanying scholarship.[25] And, like their colleagues in the sciences, these scholars are doing so using online platforms and tools that offer "open standards" intended to enable other projects to readily take up and augment these resources on a worldwide basis.[26]

Across the disciplines, the introduction of these new structures poses something of a challenge to America's traditional role as a clearly demarcated global academic *center* that serves a distant, loosely connected *periphery* of higher education institutes spread across the developing world.[27] The emerging cybergrid—in which the full array of data-collection and data-analysis tools are equally accessible to all participating researchers—represents a distributed model for scholarly participation. Cyberinfrastructure holds at least the promise of what could well be far more of a global knowledge exchange. Now, make no mistake, collaboration on a global scale faces considerable infrastructural challenges.[28] Yet studies of international research teams, as reflected in measures of coauthorship, show that there is a growth in the international distribution of these collaborations, along with an increase in the number of participating countries.[29]

The accumulation of massive data sets, as a result in part of innovative cyberinfrastructure, has led to new techniques of data visualization in pursuit of more effective and dynamic means of analysis.[30] There is far more than a pretty picture at stake. An early pioneer in data visualization, Ben Schneiderman, has stressed how data visualization allows researchers, whether as "authors" or "readers," to first gain an overview and then zoom in on specific aspects, as well as to filter and call up details on demand.[31] Through this cyberinfrastructure, the data sets are openly available to the larger community for continuing analysis and interpretation, for testing alternative hypotheses, or for identifying different patterns.[32] The data can also be augmented by harvesting the results of smaller and earlier studies, thereby reducing research isolation and the fragmentation that can undermine the accumulation of knowledge. Still, it should be noted that harvesting various studies addressing the same question has proven to be no simple matter.

The U.S. federal government's Genetic Association Identification Network (GAIN), in attempting to coordinate data from twenty years of extensive bipolar disorder studies, found that considerable differences in data collection methods, as well the basis on which the data could be shared, created formidable obstacles.[33] The challenge in going forward, given the obvious value of better-coordinated research studies, has been summed up by Eric Meyer: "The question, of course, is to what extent data management demands should dictate scientific decisions, and conversely to what extent should individual scientists be allowed to ignore issues of compatibility and data availability."[34]

As one step forward in seeking greater coordination, the U.S. government now regulates the sharing of human genome data within the research it sponsors, with its goal being "to make the sequence data generated by the Human Genome Project rapidly and freely accessible to scientific communities worldwide."[35] In support of this initiative, leading genetics journals now require the deposit of the relevant genome sequence data, in effect extending the old saw about publishing to "share data or perish." But sharing data on this scale requires an element of "data curation" through sophisticated database systems, which the National Institutes of Health is providing through its GenBank.[36] This new curatorial responsibility includes maintaining the data in a complete, well-structured, and clearly indexed format, and it may make available user annotations and links to relevant research literature.

The prospects of improving the quality of science through systems that support far more open data (open to reanalysis, replication, and hypothesis-testing on a much greater global scale), while reducing the expense (or impossibility, in some cases) of otherwise gathering available data, are substantial. The challenge remains one of motivating researchers to share their data—given a tradition of treating data as a proprietary aspect of one's competitive advantage—as well as providing funding for preparing data for sharing.[37] While concerns are being expressed about empty data archives, a number of promising approaches for crediting authors for the use and citation of their data are under development, so that this technically enabled process can play its part in the university's recognition economy.[38]

New Digital Economies

A further development in cyberinfrastructure and the use of digital technologies in higher education has been the emergence of open-source software models for developing systems for courseware, institutional repositories, financial systems, and student services, among others. Open-source software is a movement among software developers to create programs such as the Linux operating system and the Firefox browser that can be freely used and adapted, while being supported by communities of users. It is an approach that has begun to offer higher education a nonproprietary means of meeting its software needs. The distributed development of open-source software has its academic parallel in the values of peer review and the scientific method. The larger spirit of digital openness, within the academic climate of American higher education, has had a direct effect on the ability of individual institutions to create and sustain open-source software to meet campus computing needs (that is, systems and software utilized in the day-to-day functions of colleges and universities).

Indeed, a symbiotic relationship has emerged on many campuses between research in the academic field of computer science (and related fields of electrical engineering, management information systems, and educational technology) and the production cycles of campus computing. Robust cyberinfrastructure, which contributes to the development of computer hardware and software—entailing a global innovation network that stretches far beyond the higher education sector and the United States—contributes to the very structures and functions of academic computing. Campus computing staff are often trained on college and university computing systems, influenced by the marketing efforts of particular software and hardware vendors through campuswide contracts with academic bookstores, and certified by technology companies that began life as spinoff ventures of university projects, which is to say that academic computing in the twenty-first century is increasingly recursive and recombinant in productive ways.

If the open-source movement, as a nonproprietary and nonmarket model of software production, represents a significant shift in the academic computing environment, it remains only part of the picture.[39] Much of the software used in higher education is commercial in nature and purchased from vendors, while a good deal of the software created on campuses is commercialized on a proprietary basis. The universities are necessarily embedded within a global economy and, as such, are subject to various intellectual property regimes, industrial research and development support, and public-sector investments to promote regional and national competitiveness. The open-source software model in American higher education thus requires careful examination, and it must be understood within the context of a market-driven and status-oriented system that prevails within higher education, as well as within other sectors.

First, it is important to note that open-source software is *not* free. There are many levels to this statement. At the base of it, the "free" exchange of ideas between open-source software developers and users is supported by a vast public-private telecommunications network that has become the veritable "backbone" of the new economy. Without the historical and ongoing governmental and industrial investments in the Internet, telecom networks, and other communications technologies, open-source software would scarcely exist. At the next level, the technical expertise that provides the foundation of many open-source systems was obtained at great personal and public expense, through the tuition dollars of the individuals who became programmers and users, governmental allocations of public dollars to their education (ever since primary school), and the "opportunity costs" of the many hours they spent toiling away at a keyboard. Even software created at private American universities or by the alumni of private institutions was most likely influenced by heavy public subsidies from the U.S. government through federal research grants and the like. Finally, at the most overt level of the software itself, open-source software, while not always requiring a licensing fee, still requires dedicated maintenance support and technical infrastructure, none of which is free.[40]

Yet open-source software initiatives can provide real economic incentives that make them an attractive choice for campus information technology (IT) managers and technology users. In this sense, open source affords savings relative to other options, although it is not expense neutral. To the extent that open source leads to licensing revenues for a developer or an institution, the resources (both human and technical) dedicated to it can be considered as investments. Possibly the strongest economic argument for pursuing open-source software in an academic setting, and one that resonates with the themes of this book on a broader basis, is the ability to retain or regain organizational autonomy in an environment of increasing marketization (at the levels of both systems and institutions). In terms of systems, the academic computing market has burgeoned as higher education has "gone digital" in the last two decades. Whereas academic computing was originally a grow-your-own affair, the emergence of the World Wide Web in the late twentieth century provided an opportunity structure for consultants, commercial systems, and off-the-shelf products for personal computers that enabled campuses to "go online." A sign of the growing academic computing sector was creation of Educause, the result of a 1998 merger between two organizations, CAUSE and Educom.[41] Today, Educause is the primary professional association for campus IT specialists in North America, publishing several leading periodicals and maintaining strong alliances with both the open-source community and the technology industry. The attempts to balance the interests of public and private stakeholders of Educause itself can be seen as a sign of the tightrope that campus IT professionals walk between the commercial and "homegrown" worlds of software development.

At the level of institutions, campus computing is both a service function and a potential source of revenue. From the institutional perspective, it is important to note that *academic computing is not optional.* So-called world-class institutions require world-class computing infrastructures to attract high-fee-paying international students, the "best and brightest" domestic students, and top-notch faculty. Bandwidth has become synonymous with research capacity and teaching quality. Savings in one arena of academic computing (such as teaching) may pay dividends in the long run by helping to support another arena (for example, research). In the aftermath of the global economic downturn of at the close of this century's first decade and the reality of additional constraints on institutional budgets, IT costs are scrutinized and resource optimization is paramount.[42] The era of big computing expenditures in the 1990s, made amid the promise of "economies of scale" and the high-tech boom, is over. The true costs of "refresh" have finally been understood.[43]

Enter open source, and the new opportunities it presents in the twenty-first century.[44] The scope of these initiatives can be classified by their institutional function: as "enterprise" systems that serve administrative purposes, teaching systems that support courseware and learning objects, and research systems that support digital repositories, intra- and extra-nets, or collaboration at a distance. By choosing open-source instead of proprietary software, institutions enter into a community of peer-to-peer cooperation that is unlike that found in any economic sector, due to the co-location of research, development, and use that is unique to higher education. That said, institutional alliances within the open-software arena are also marked by competition, as institutions leverage their open-source initiatives to attract high-quality students and faculty, thereby maximizing resources in the pursuit or maintenance of status and prestige.

Among the more recent examples of open-source enterprise software within higher education is the Kuali Foundation, which represents, in its own words, a "growing community of universities, colleges, businesses, and other organizations that have partnered to build an open-source administrative software for higher education, by higher education."[45] With its start as a Community Source Software initiative, Kuali began in the early 2000s as an alternative to a proprietary software system for financial services. With support from organizations such as the Mellon Foundation and the National Association of College and University Business Officers, and with a consortium of public and private universities, the Kuali Financial System was born. Today the Kuali development community includes a variety of financial and student-information-systems projects, and it has over thirty-five member institutions.

A similar story lies behind the development of Sakai ("designed by educators for educators"), an open-source courseware management system.[46] Finding homegrown systems too costly for a single institution to support, a consortium of public and private universities—including Stanford University, the University of Michigan, Indiana University, MIT, and the University of California, Berkeley—jointly developed Sakai at the beginning of the twenty-first century. Like the Kuali project, Sakai had substantial seed money from the Andrew W. Mellon Foundation, which continues to play a key start-up role in advanced digital initiatives in higher education, even as the consortium moves toward sustainable membership funding through the Sakai Partnership Program, as well as a Commercial Affiliate program. Although membership is optional for institutional users, the Partnership Program offers members a say in the software and its management.

Broadly speaking, Sakai offers what is commonly called a Course Management System (CMS), although the group prefers to describe the platform as a Collaboration and Learning Environment (CLE).[47] As with commercially available Web-based course systems, Sakai enables instructors to use wikis, chat functions, notification boards, e-mail, and blogs, as well as lessons, assignments, and tests. Sakai also allows users to create e-portfolios, with enhanced social networking features targeted for later versions. While some of these features could be utilized to support collaborative research, it appears that the open-source community continues to maintain the long-standing distinction between teaching and research applications, with the potential crossover benefits between these two core strengths of higher education still to be explored and tested within the open-source development community.

Another example of a higher education open-source development is the Shibboleth Project, which supports utilization of the Internet2, a public-private partnership established in 1996 to enhance the digital backbone of America's new cyberinfrastructure. Internet2 membership includes the leading U.S. research universities, federal funding agencies, national research institutes, and high-tech corporations. Early projects for Internet2 include healthcare applications, international science and engineering partnerships, and the creation of networked research centers. Unlike Kuali and Sakai, the Shibboleth System is a middleware endeavor that facilitates the authentication of users within the Internet2 domain.

The future of open-source projects in American colleges and universities may have everything to do with its economic and social role in the "global imaginary" of higher education.[48] Open-source and other community-based software developments demonstrate the extent to which the exchange of knowledge is both a production function and a product of higher education.[49] Furthermore, it may be that the process of open-source development and its postcapitalist sensibilities can provide a modicum of resistance to the lures of the external environment and academic capitalism.[50] Perhaps this alignment of open-source software development and the "public good" justification for nonprofit higher education is not only coincidental, but also inevitably interdependent.

Opening Access to Research and Scholarship

A celebrated educational aspect of the digital age, on which we wish to conclude this chapter, is how online systems are increasing access to knowledge. The question of who is able to attend a college, university, or other postsecondary institution receives greater prominence in higher education, but who has access to research and scholarship also matters, whether to researchers around the world, professionals, policy makers, or the interested public. The Internet has certainly altered who is able to tap into university-based research and scholarship. An aspect of this arises from cyberinfrastructure initiatives that lead to freely shared publications and the creation of scholarly resources, such as archives. But there are also initiatives underway specifically directed toward increasing access to scholarly publications, which are changing both the economic basis and the proprietary basis on which this knowledge circulates.

Beginning in the fifteenth century, the development of the printing press formed a critical technology in the opening of science and other learning, greatly extending and strengthening an international network of book and journal publishers who significantly advanced the circulation of knowledge and, in the seventeenth century, played a vital part in what is known as the Scientific Revolution.[51] Print not only established a record of discovery, but was, in itself, a great incentive for research, as it enabled others, who were distributed far and wide, to incrementally extend existing information, as well as to test, replicate, and critique this ongoing stream of scientific and scholarly work.

The twenty-first-century scholarly journal has taken this opening of scholarly communication a step further, with online publication considerably increasing the reach of this work compared with what could be achieved by print.[52] In addition to simply posting journals and, in some cases, books online for sale by subscription or purchase, a new breed of journals is taking advantage of the transformative possibilities of this new technology to make their contents freely available online at the moment of publication. This free online access to research has become known as *open access* (with the name drawing its own parallel with open-source software, even if complicating the use of "open" terms). Most traditional subscription journals now have policies that permit authors to post their articles on their Web sites and open-access library archives, even if the articles are posted in their final draft version rather than their published form.[53] In addition, there are now thousands of peer-reviewed journals across the disciplines that no longer charge subscription fees, but instead make their contents open access on publication.[54]

Also contributing to this body of freely available work are yet other journals that make their contents freely available after a certain period of time. *The New England Journal of Medicine*, for example, asks nonsubscribing readers to wait six months for free access to its content. To have research and scholarship forming part of the public sphere, with so many going online to look for information (particularly in areas of health, for example) speaks to changes in the university's contribution as a source of knowledge, often in the immediate and direct service of the larger community.[55] These open-access journals use a variety of economic models—from charging article-processing fees (similar to the page charges levied by science journals for many years) to relying on faculty and students, as well as subsidies, to see the journals out. As a result, at this point close a quarter of the research literature, from up and down the ranks of journals, as well as across the disciplines, is publicly available in open-access formats.[56]

Further support for this increased openness is coming from research-funding agencies, such as the U.S. government's National Institutes of Health (NIH), which now requires funded researchers to post a copy of resulting publications in NIH's open-access repository, known as PubMed Central, within a year of publication. In addition, faculty members at a number of universities—at this point Harvard University, Stanford, MIT, and the University of Kansas—have adopted open-access policies that commit them, whether as a school or an entire university, to archiving copies of their published work.

This movement towards open access represents a further opening of academe's program of research and scholarship on a global and public basis. Given the emergence of these alternatives to the traditional economic models for scholarly publishing, universities, scholarly societies, research funding agencies, university presses, commercial publishers, and individual faculty members are realizing that this new publishing medium may well afford yet another expansion in access to this knowledge. In terms of new publishing models, this is clearly a transitional period. Many commercial publishers feel that the growing interest in open access from government funding agencies such as NIH represents an unwarranted source of government interference in their investment in scholarly publishing.[57] Others are pointing out the degree to which there exists an excessive range of pricing for digital scholarly resources, from free to dear, without regard to quality or even quantity, which argues for a transformation of the basis on which scholarly publishing operates.[58] Clearly, the economics of scholarly publishing is still finding its feet in cyberspace, with some signs pointing to it all leading, by whatever means, to increased global and public circulation of this knowledge.

At the same time, archival scholarly resources are being digitized on a number of fronts. For example, a historic (and still current) journal such as *Philosophical Transactions*, dating back to its first issue in March 1665, is now digitally available on JSTOR, along with complete online editions of hundreds of other long-standing journals, by both subscription to university libraries and (on a fee-per-article basis) the public. The Early English Books Online database provides another instance, offering to subscribing institutions nothing less than, as its front page declares, "digital facsimile page images of virtually every work printed in England, Ireland, Scotland, Wales, and British North America and works in English printed elsewhere from 1473–1700." Over the course of the last two decades, a mix of commercial, philanthropic, and public interests have been underwriting what amounts to an emerging universal digital library, which, if not affordable in its entirety by all institutions in America, let alone elsewhere in the world, is still radically transforming the scholarly reach of faculty and students.[59] The first decade of this century has demonstrated the potential scope of this new level of openness, which would seem to hold much promise for advancing the sciences and deepening the work of the humanities, as well as enhancing the role and contribution of this scholarly work as a source of public good.

In considering the impact of new technologies on twenty-first-century higher education, it seems fair to conclude that these digital systems are playing a critical role in advancing the mission and contributions of these institutions. The transition to digital information and communication systems cannot help but seem, at this point at least, to represent a historic moment, on a scale comparable to the introduction of the printing press. If such judgments still seem premature, then, at a minimum, these digital technologies can be said to pose opportunities, challenges, and distractions, not least of all in working out new economies of learning, or, as one might say, affording the affordances. Many trials and not a few false starts still lie ahead in aligning the potential transformations that might be wrought from these systems by that mission.

It is above all the *quality* of learning and knowledge that is at stake, even as we may be easily distracted, if not misled, by how readily these digital systems serve up measures of the quantity and speed involved in scholarly communication today. The quality of learning is the most valued part of that historically continuous tradition, often fraught, as it has been before, with struggles over the meaning, value, and purposes of education. What matters most, in this epistemological sense, is a further opening—to critique and review, as well as to sharing and utilization—of what is to be learned through instruction, research, and scholarship.

It may seem to go without saying that the technologies in question are but tools and a digital means to a greater educational end, but it also bears repeating that the choice and particular use of such tools will surely affect the opening of this learning to more people around the world. Higher education stands as a leading force in digital-era developments. It provides the incubation for the principal corporate developments of the era, led by the likes of Google and Facebook, and it is breaking new ground in the sharing and opening of knowledge resources: from open access, to research, to data sharing on the level of the Genome Project. At the same time, higher education has only begun to make gains in the quality of learning that appears possible through an emerging panoply of digitally networked resources. Challenges lie ahead, as well, particularly in continuing to find innovative financing and resourcing models at a time of reduced public support for higher education. Open-source cooperative ventures appear to be but one way forward in supplying the technologies needed to provide advanced forms of education to a growing population that is increasingly global in scope. There's reason enough, then, to call for the most careful consideration in technologies of learning that are deployed in higher education over the years ahead.

NOTES

1. Brian D. Edgar and John Willinsky, "A Survey of Journals Using Open Journals Systems," *Scholarly and Research Communication* 1 (2010); Carol Tenopir, Donald W. King, Sheri Edwards, and Lei Wu, "Electronic Journals and Changes in Scholarly Article Seeking and Reading Patterns," *Aslib Proceedings: New Information Perspectives* 61, no. 1 (2009): 5–32.

2. See Richard Andrews and Caroline Haythornthwaite, eds., *The SAGE Handbook of E-Learning Research* (London: Sage, 2007); Ray J. Amirault and Yusra L. Visser, "The University in Periods of Technological Change: A Historically Grounded Perspective," *Journal of Computing in Higher Education* 21 (2009): 62–79; Shirley Bach, Philip Haynes, and Jennifer Lewis-Smith, *Online Learning and Teaching in Higher Education* (Berkshire, UK: Open University Press / McGraw-Hill Education, 2007).

3. Since the Second World War, the American university has been in constant expansion, but it is important to distinguish between two stages. Between 1945 and 1975, in the first period (also known as the Golden Age) the "identity" or composition of the system maintained its previous characteristics while increasing its size quite dramatically. During the second period, from 1975 to the present, the expansion has continued, but its most salient characteristic is the diversification of the system, ranging from new providers of higher education services, to new models of faculty employment, to new groups accessing faculty positions, to new populations accessing universities, to new forms of completing degrees. This diversification cannot be reduced to the massive use of computer technologies in universities, but it also cannot be understood without them.

4. Isabel Elaine Allen and Jeff Seaman, *Staying the Course: Online Education in the United States* (Needham, MA: Sloan Group, 2008).

5. Among the failed ventures, Fathom is perhaps the most notable, led by Columbia University in a partnership with the University of Chicago, the London School of Economics, and other leading institutions, but then there is also New York University's NYUonline, UMUC (University of Maryland University College) Online, and Temple University's Virtual Temple; see Scott Carlson, "After Losing Millions, Columbia U. Will Close Online-Learning Venture," *Chronicle of Higher Education*, Jan. 17, 2003, A30. The University of Illinois Global Campus and Universitas 21 have

closed as well; see Steve Kolowich, "Another One Bites the Dust," *Inside Higher Education*, Dec. 9, 2009, www.insidehighered.com/news/2009/12/09/u21.

6. Anthony Trippe, *Student Satisfaction at the University of Phoenix Online Campus*, unpublished paper, University of Phoenix, 2001.

7. See eCornell, www.ecornell.com.

8. "The university, as an institution, is in 'crisis' . . . Information and communication technologies (ICTs) play a significant role in this situation, either as 'angels of deliverance' or 'devils of damnation,'" according to James Cornford and Neil Pollock, *Putting the University Online: Information, Technology and Organizational Change* (Buckingham, UK: Society for Research into Higher Education and Open University, 2003), 1. See also Bill Readings, *The University in Ruins* (Cambridge, MA: Harvard University Press, 1997).

9. Similar divides have been found to exist between faculty perceptions of how they taking advantage of new technologies to improve their teaching and born-digital students who beg to differ; see Scott Jaschik, "Technology Gap," *Inside Higher Education*, Nov. 5, 2009, www.insidehighered.com/news/2009/11/05/survey.

10. Gerard Delanty, "The University in the Knowledge Society," *Organization* 8 (2001): 149–53; Michael Gibbons, Camille Limoges, Helga Nowotny, Simon Schwartzman, Peter Scott, and Martin Trow, *The New Production of Knowledge* (London: Sage, 1984).

11. Philip Brown and Hugh Lauder, *Globalization and the Knowledge Economy: Some Observations on Recent Trends in Employment, Education, and the Labour Market*, Working Paper No. 43, School of Social Sciences, University of Cardiff (2003). See also Manuel Castells, *The Power of Identity*, vol. 2 of *The Information Age: Economy, Society, and Culture*, 2nd ed. (Oxford: Wiley-Blackwell, 2009); Joseph E. Stiglitz, *Globalization and Its Discontents* (New York: Norton, 2002). On the limited high-tech dominance of the new economy, Steve Shapin writes that of "the world's top thirty companies (by revenue), only three are mainly in the business of high tech—General Electric (No. 11), Siemens (No. 22), and I.B.M. (No. 29)—and all three go back more than a century. The heights of the early-twenty-first-century corporate world are still occupied—as they have long been—by petroleum companies (Exxon Mobil, Royal Dutch Shell, and B.P., Nos. 1, 3, and 4), retailing (Wal-Mart, No. 2), automobiles (General Motors, No. 5), and finance (I.N.G. and Citigroup, Nos. 13 and 14). No Hewlett-Packard (No. 33); no Microsoft (No. 140); no Merck (No. 289)" ("What Else is New: How Uses, Not Innovation, Drive Human Technology," *New Yorker*, May 14, 2007, 147).

12. Robert M. Bernard, Philip C. Abrami, Eugene Borokhovski, C. Anne Wade, Rana M. Tamim, Michael A. Surkes, and Edward Clement Bethel, "A Meta-Analysis of Three Types of Interaction Treatments in Distance Education," *Review of Educational Research* 79, no. 3 (2009): 1243–89.

13. Maryfran Barber and David Njus, "Clicker Evolution: Seeking Intelligent Design," *CBE Life Science Education* 6, no. 1 (Spring 2007): 1–8; Douglas K. Duncan, *Clickers in the Astronomy Classroom* (New York: Pearson / Addison-Wesley, 2006). "An example of where computer-based tools have been shown to be effective is when ap-

plications provide support for cognition and scaffold meta-cognitive skills and other self-regulated learning strategies such as planning and goal setting" (Richard F. Schmid, Robert M. Bernard, Eugene Borokhovski, Rana Tamim, Philip C. Abrami, C. Anne Wade, Michael A. Surkes, and Gretchen Lowerison, "Technology's Effect on Achievement in Higher Education: A Stage I Meta-Analysis of Classroom Applications," *Journal of Computing in Higher Education* 21 [2009]: 95–109).

14. David Edgerton, *The Shock of the Old: Technology and Global History since the 1900s* (London, Profile Books, 2006).

15. "Sometimes, in accounts of the university it seems as if the university has developed from a singular and continuous 'idea,' arising full-fledged from Cardinal Newman's *Idea of the University* (1852) or Kant's *Conflict of Faculties* (1798). But, in the actual history of the American university, if there is a principle, it is adaptability" (Jeffrey Williams, "The Post–Welfare State University," *American Literary History* 18, no. 1 [2006]: 190).

16. Kathleen R. Rosen, Jennifer M. McBride, and Richard L. Drake, "The Use of Simulation in Medical Education to Enhance Students' Understanding of Basic Sciences," *Medical Teacher* 31, no. 9 (2009): 842–46; Nancy Dennis, "Using Inquiry Methods to Foster Information Literacy Partnerships," *Reference Services Review* 29, no. 2 (2001): 122–32.

17. Carrie B. Fried, "In-Class Laptop Use and Its Effects on Student Learning," *Computers & Education* 50, no. 3 (2008): 906–14; Helene Hembrooke and Geri Gay, "The Laptop and the Lecture: The Effects of Multitasking in Learning Environments," *Journal of Computing in Higher Education* 15, no. 1 (2003): 46–54.

18. To date, these devices have been largely used in the schools and in teacher education programs; see Jeremy Roschelle and Roy Pea, "A Walk on the WILD Side: How Wireless Handhelds May Change Computer-Supported Collaborative Learning," *International Journal of Cognition and Technology* 1, no. 1 (2002): 145–68.

19. Aliye Karabulut and Ana Correia, "Skype, Elluminate, Adobe Connect, Ivisit: A Comparison of Web-Based Video Conferencing Systems for Learning and Teaching," in *Proceedings of the Society for Information Technology & Teacher Education International Conference, Mar. 3–7, 2008, Las Vegas, Nevada*, ed. Karen McFerrin (Chesapeake, VA: Association for the Advancement of Computing in Education), 481–84.

20. The portmanteau concoction *cyberinfrastructure* suggests just how extensive the role of digital technologies is, as it is taken from the science fiction notion of *cyberspace*, another plane of reality in which one can exist and operate (as a researcher, in this case). In an instance of life imitating art, novelist William Gibson is credited with coining "cyberspace" in *Neuromancer* (New York: Ace, 1987).

21. The aim of this cybergrid (as one of the metaphors for the Internet/science) is to turn "the global network of computers into one vast computational resource," which Anne Beaulieu and Paul Woters cite from an anonymous Grid Café posting in "e-Research as Intervention," in *e-Research: Transformation in Scholarly Practice*, ed. Nicholas W. Jankowski (London: Routledge, 2009), 55. For the ways in which researchers working in large networks handle collective authorship in such projects (sometimes

running to hundreds of names on a single article), see Peter Galison, "The Collective Author," in *Scientific Authorship: Credit and Intellectual Property in Science,* ed. Mario Biagioli and Peter Galison (New York: Routledge, 2003); Mario Biagioli, "Rights and Rewards? Changing Frameworks of Scientific Authorship," also in Biagioli and Galison, *Scientific Authorship.*

22. Daniel Atkins, Kelvin K. Droegemeier, Stuart I. Feldman, Hector Garcia-Molina, Michael L. Klein, David G. Messerschmitt, Paul Messina, Jeremiah P. Ostriker, and Margaret H. Wright, *Revolutionizing Science and Engineering through Cyberinfrastructure: Report of the National Science Foundation Blue-Ribbon Advisory Panel on Cyberinfrastructure* (Washington DC: National Science Foundation, 2003), 5.

23. John Unsworth, with commission members and ed. Marlo Welshons, *Our Cultural Commonwealth: Report of the American Council of Learned Socieites' Commission on Cyberinfrastructure for the Humanities and Social Sciences* (Washington, DC: American Council of Learned Societies, 2006), 1. The report's sense of "the infrastructure of scholarship" as including archives and "diverse collections of primary sources" may seem to confuse the objects of study with the apparatus or device that enables them to be studied.

24. Ibid., 2–3.

25. See, for example, *Nines: Nineteenth Century Scholarship Online* (www.nines.org), with its coordination of peer-reviewed digital objects from fifty-nine federated sites. The *Stanford Encyclopedia of Philosophy* (http://plato.stanford.edu/) represents another form of openly accessible, peer-reviewed digital assemblies, run by independent groups of scholars. Beaulieu and Woters hold that what is at issue is not only a *modernization,* but a *rationalization* of work in these areas, as if the *e* in *e-research* stood for *enhanced* ("e-Research as Intervention," 63).

26. Unsworth, *Our Cultural Commonwealth,* 36.

27. Traditionally, the centers of learning (first of all in Europe, and now led by America) would draw on the rest of the world as a source of artifacts and wonders, data and specimens, only to offer back a true knowledge of that world. It is a pattern that continues amid the global distribution of higher education, but not without explicit critiques from postcolonial scholarship and the ameliorating movement of scholars from the periphery to the center and back. Postcolonialism's landmark work is by Edward Said, *Orientalism* (New York: Knopf, 1978); but see also A. Suresh Canagarajah, *The Geopolitics of Academic Writing* (Pittsburgh: University of Pittsburgh Press, 2002); John Willinsky, *Learning to Divide the World: Education at Empire's End* (Minneapolis: University of Minnesota Press, 1998).

28. Consider sub-Saharan Africa, for example, where power outages and excessively priced and unreliable Internet services remain all too common; see Calestous Juma and Elisabeth Moyer, "Broadband Internet for Africa," *Science* 320, no. 5881 (2008): 1261.

29. Caroline S. Wagner and Loet Leydesdorff, "Mapping the Network of Global Science: Comparing International Co-Authorships from 1990 to 2000," *International Journal of Technology and Globalisation* 1, no. 2 (2005). Kathryn H. Jacobson's study of

epidemiology articles demonstrates that collaborations within the global North are strong, and studies conducted in the South primarily have North-to-South coauthorships, with only rare instances of South-to-North or South-South partnerships ("Patterns of Co-Authorship in International Epidemiology," *Journal of Epidemiological Community Health* 63 [2009]: 665–69).

30. Rather than referencing today's most interesting instances, in the spirit of real-time data representation we invite readers to simply do an online search for images on "data visualization."

31. Benjamin Schneiderman, "The Eyes Have It: A Task by Data Type Taxonomy for Information Visualizations," *Proceedings of the IEEE Symposium on Visual Languages, Sept. 3–6, Boulder, Colorado* (Los Alamitos, CA: Institute of Electrical Electronic Engineering, 1996), 337. Or, as Howard T. Wesler, Tomas M. Lento, Marc Smith, Eric Gleave, and Itai Himelbom put it, these systems enable researchers "to cut the data along multiple facets to reveal commonalities and key differences" as part of "increasingly rich self-documenting social systems" ("A Picture Is Worth a Thousand Questions: Visualization Techniques for Social Science Discovery in Computational Spaces," in Jankowski, *e-Research*, 196).

32. Wesler et al., "Picture," 182. Hans Rosling has done much to also demonstrate the public value of historically animated visualization of data related to health, through his Trendanalyzer software (which Google now makes freely available as Motion Chart). He has used this public attention to make the case for a greater openness among the principal sources of data, particularly from major sources such as the World Bank, the Organisation for Economic Co-operation and Development, and various governments ("Visual Technology Unveils the Beauty of Statistics and Swaps Policy from Dissemination to Access," *Journal of the International Association for Official Statistics* 24, no. 1–2 [2007]: 103–4).

33. Eric T. Meyer, "Moving from the Small Science to Big Science," in Jankowski, *e-Research*, 152–55.

34. Ibid., 157.

35. National Center for Biotechnology Information [NCBI], *An Introduction to NCBI's Genome Resource* (2009), www.ncbi.nlm.nih.gov/About/Doc/hs_genomeintro .html.

36. Helena Karasti, Karen Baker, and Eija Halkola use the related phrases "information management preparedness" and "data stewardship awareness" in relation to the U.S. Long Term Ecological Research Network in their "Enriching the Notion of Data Curation in e-Science: Data Managing and Information Infrastructuring in the Long Term Ecological Research (LTER) Network," *Computer Supported Cooperative Work* 15, no. 2–3 (2006): 351. In the case of WormBase (covering *Caenorhabditis elegans*) and FlyBase (for *Drosophila*), in which data deposit is not yet required of researchers, NIH has data curators scour the literature, seeking out the relevant data sets to assemble in publicly accessible form. The aim is to "relieve researchers from the responsibilities and effort to make the data available for sharing" (Ann Zimmerman, Nathan Bos, Judith S. Olson, and Gary M. Olson, "The Promise of Data in

e-Research: Many Challenges, Multiple Solutions, Diverse Outcomes," in Jankowski, *e-Research*, 228).

37. See Carole Goble and David De Roure, "myExperiment: Social Networking for Workflow-Using e-Scientists," *Proceedings of the 2nd Workshop on Workflows in Support of Large-Scale Science, June 25–27, Monterey, California*, ed. Ewa Deelman and Ian J. Taylor (New York: ACM Press, 2007): 2. A *Nature* editorial entitled "Data's Shameful Neglect" refers to "a scandalous shortfall in the sharing of data by researchers," while pointing out that the "United States, by contrast [to the UK], is playing catch-up" (*Nature* 461 [2009]: 145). The Public Library of Science journals require authors to make the data "freely available without restriction, provided that appropriate attribution is given and that suitable mechanisms exist for sharing the data used in a manuscript" ("Editorial and Publishing Policies," *PLoS Biology*, www.plosbiology.org/static/policies.action#sharing). In ecology, a number of journals have had some success in actively inviting authors to share their data (Jane L. Bain, "An Introduction to Ecological Archives," *Bulletin of the Ecological Society of America* 86, no. 2 [Apr. 2005]: 86–91). On the question of prepublication data, see also Nathan Blos, "Motivation to Contribute to Collaboratories: A Public Goods Approach," in *Scientific Collaboration on the Internet*, ed. Gary M. Olson, Ann Zimmerman, and Nathan Blos (Cambridge, MA: MIT Press, 2008), 260.

38. Bryn Nelson, "Data Sharing: Empty Archives," *Nature* 461 (2009): 160–63. Zimmerman et al. ("Promise of Data," 230–31) review data-crediting initiatives such as *Nature*'s Molecule Pages, as well as the Ecological Society of America's Data Papers, which both represent peer-reviewed data publishing; for the social sciences, see Gary King, "An Introduction to the Dataverse Network as an Infrastructure for Data Sharing," *Sociological Methods & Research* 36, no. 2 (2007): 173–99.

39. See Yochai Benkler, *Wealth of Networks* (New Haven, CT: Yale University Press, 2006); Shahron Williams van Rooij, "Adopting Open-Source Software Applications in U.S. Higher Education: A Cross-Disciplinary Review of the Literature," *Review of Educational Research* 79, no. 2 (2009): 682–701.

40. For a review open source licensing models, see Thomas J. Trappler, "Is There Such a Thing as Free Software? The Pros and Cons of Open-Source Software," *Educause Quarterly* 32, no. 2 (2009).

41. CAUSE, whose name was an acronym for the College and University Systems Exchange, was founded in 1962 by a group of college and university data administrators who were interested in new developments in computers and information processing in academic settings. Educom, formally known as the Interuniversity Communications Council, Inc., was founded in 1964 by a group of medical school deans and vice presidents for the purpose of exploring ways in which universities could share digital data.

42. For a discussion of the key items on the minds of Chief Information Officers (CIOs) during this period of fiscal crisis, see Bruce Maas, Fredrick Miller, Pattie Orr, Julie Ouska, and Shelton M. Waggener, "CIOs Talk about Budgets: Emerging Stronger and Leaner," *Educause Review* 44, no. 4 (2009): 20–35.

43. The Campus Computing Project, begun in 1990, was formed to track the expenditures made by U.S. institutions in the area of information technology. With an annual survey of institutions, the project has reported the growth and expenditures of campus computing projects for over a decade. The 2008 survey included a new item that asked if institutions were likely to migrate to open source within five years. The survey revealed that 24.4 percent of the institutions were planning or likely to move to an open-source learning-management system in the near future (www.cam puscomputing.net).

44. See Patrick Carmichael and Leslie Honour, "Open Source as Appropriate Technology for Global Education," *International Journal of Educational Development* 22 (2002): 47–53.

45. Kuali Foundation Web site, www.kuali.org/about/ [accessed Jan. 25, 2009].

46. Sakai Foundation Web site, http://sakaiproject.org/ [accessed Jan. 25, 2009].

47. Sakai Foundation Web site, http://sakaiproject.org/product-overview/ [accessed Jan. 25, 2009].

48. Simon Marginson, "Open Source Knowledge and University Rankings," *Thesis Eleven* 96 (2009): 9–39.

49. For a discussion of open-source and private-sector software development, see Josh Lerner and Jean Tirole, "The Economics of Technology Sharing: Open Source and Beyond," *Journal of Economic Perspectives* 19, no. 2 (2005): 99–120.

50. Sheila A. Slaughter and Gary Rhoades, *Academic Capitalism and the New Economy: Markets, State, and Higher Education* (Baltimore: Johns Hopkins University Press, 2004).

51. This process, in itself, represented an opening of science. See William Eamon, *Science and the Secrets of Nature: Books of Secrets in Medieval and Early Modern Culture* (Princeton, NJ: Princeton University Press, 1994); Pamela O. Long, *Openness, Secrecy, Authorship: Technical Arts and the Culture of Knowledge from Antiquity to the Renaissance* (Baltimore: Johns Hopkins University Press, 2001); and, on a broader historical scale, Paul A. David, "Common Agency Contracting and the Emergence of 'Open Science' Institutions," *American Economic Review* 188, no. 2 (1998): 15–21.

52. Perhaps the most dramatic instances of this increased circulation of knowledge are the programs (e.g., HINARI, AGORA, OARE), well supported by journal publishers, that enable academics in developing countries to access online editions of thousands of journals.

53. See the SHERPA RoMEO database of publisher copyright and archiving policies, www.sherpa.ac.uk/romeo/. On the oldest of these open-access archives (dating back to 1993), which has transformed the field of high-energy physics, see Paul Ginsparg, "As We May Read," *Journal of Neuroscience* 26, no. 38 (2006): 9606–8.

54. See the Directory of Open Access Journals, www.doaj.org.

55. Susannah Fox and Sydney Jones, *The Social Life of Health Information* (Washington, DC: Pew Internet and American Life Project, 2009), www.pewinternet.org/ Presentations/2009/30—The-Patient-is-In.aspx. For other examples of the university's increased public impact through its open access to knowledge, see Timothy Ferris,

Seeing in the Dark: How Backyard Stargazers Are Probing Deep Space and Guarding Earth from Interplanetary Peril (New York: Simon & Schuster, 2002); John Willinsky, "Socrates Back on the Street: Wikipedia's Citing of the *Stanford Encyclopedia of Philosophy*," *International Journal of Communication* 2 (2008): 1269–88.

56. Bo-Christian Björk, Annikki Roos, and Mari Lauri, "Scientific Journal Publishing: Yearly Volume and Open Access Availability," *Information Research* 14, no. 1 (2009), paper 391. The publication figures in this paper (which only went through 2006) were updated in 2008 for a presentation at the Open Access Scholarly Publishers Association Conference, Lund, Sweden, Sept. 15, 2009.

57. The International Association for Scientific, Technical, and Medical Publishers (www.stm-assoc.org/about.php) has identified a number of concerns with a variety of proposals to increase open access to the literature, while pointing to the contributions of its member publishers to open access and other initiatives intended to increase access to this body of work.

58. See Theodore C. Bergstrom, "Free Labor for Costly Journals?" *Journal of Economic Perspectives* 15 (2000): 183–98, www.econ.ucsb.edu/~tedb/Journals/jeprevised .pdf; John Willinsky, *The Access Principle: The Case for Open Access to Research and Scholarship* (Cambridge, MA: MIT Press, 2006).

59. Google's efforts to digitize the research libraries (including those at the University of Michigan, Stanford, and Harvard), which began in 2004, did lead to a major copyright infringement suit, brought against Google by the Authors Guild and the Association of American Publishers, for which, as we write, a settlement agreement is still under discussion, intended to make the resulting collection available to research libraries for a fee.

CHAPTER FOURTEEN

Graduate Education and Research

Interdependence and Strain

Patricia J. Gumport

This chapter examines over a century of forces that have reshaped the content and conduct of graduate education in American research universities. I focus on the graduate education–research nexus, to show the interdependence and strain between doctoral education, academic research, and the federal government. Despite the long-standing and pervasive view that American graduate education is the best in the world, signs of strain are evident on campuses and at the national level. Most of the tensions arise from perennial challenges, albeit with some ebb and flow in the particulars, given changing economic conditions and differences across fields of study.

In admissions, faculty lament the need to reduce the size of incoming doctoral cohorts due to funding constraints; while labor market projections suggest an oversupply reminiscent of the early 1970s, especially of PhD recipients for academic jobs. Talented doctoral students consider abandoning their academic career ambitions. Although their predecessors also anticipated years of long hours at low pay, this generation is all the more concerned about disappearing tenure-line faculty jobs. Graduate student loan debt has climbed to record highs. National data from selected disciplines show longer times to doctoral degree completion for women and underrepresented U.S. minorities than for men, white students, and international students. On the world stage, moreover, the United States may be losing its significant market share of international students—a longtime source of pride and affirmation. In the research-training arena, increased competition for funding has sped up the clock in labs, pressuring researchers to produce faster yet still novel findings. Intellectual property interests are cast as diminishing the free exchange of ideas and collegiality. As teaching assistants, graduate students are estimated to provide one-quarter of all undergraduate instruction nationally. Collective bargaining activities at forty universities involve over 40,000 graduate student "employees" working in assistantships while pursuing their degrees. While graduate school has long been characterized as an exercise in deferred gratification, reports reveal students' perceptions of unrelenting competition, unrealistic expectations, and powerlessness—all of which exacerbate mental health issues.[1]

Although some readers may be inclined to minimize these trends as selective or exaggerated representations, I make the case that several axes of persistent tension have redefined the graduate education–research nexus: volatile sources of funding for graduate education; increased competition, especially for federal research funding; uncertain labor market projections; and, writ large, unprecedented shifts in the global economy. Viewed historically, the above tensions exemplify the larger challenges for universities as they strive to preserve standards of excellence in teaching and research while meeting the rising costs of maintaining a complex research infrastructure to attract talented faculty and students. Public universities in particular have additional constraints, especially in those states where bleak economies have triggered sizable and successive budget cuts. These signs of strain—and the contextual influences that exacerbate them—frame the contemporary image of how the character of the university is incrementally reshaped with each passing decade.

Against that backdrop, this chapter examines graduate education and research; specifically, the intersection between doctoral education, academic research, and the federal government. The interdependence of these three activities has strong historical roots in the expansion of research universities and the specialization of faculty across the disciplines. While the core structural foundations of graduate programs reflect some continuity, the conduct of graduate programs in many fields has undeniably been altered—directly, in research training practices; and indirectly, through changes in academic research. Historians have varying accounts of this interdependence between graduate education and research, set within the broader story of how well universities have adapted to external sponsors or have maintained their academic autonomy.[2] Nonetheless, some basic changes are undisputed.

As universities have transformed into modern research complexes, the organizational character and rhythm of academic work changed to accommodate the increased centrality of externally sponsored research.[3] Research training of graduate students became oriented to the stark realities of ongoing quests for research funding, especially from federal sources: uncertain funding levels, changing agendas of federal agencies, and increased competition.[4] The imperatives of seeking external funding for university research have, at times, directly strained ideals for graduate education: when knowledge transfer, patents, and financial gain are primary aims, instead of the disinterested pursuit of inquiry; when students must focus on topics and skills for funded projects, rather than exploring what interests them; when faculty hire postdoctoral researchers, instead of funding novice doctoral students. Each of these exemplifies the pull away from prioritizing the educational and advising needs of students.

In the context of these tensions, university officials, faculty, and even graduate students have sought greater control in the conduct of academic affairs in order to protect their interests. Yet each is also well aware of interdependence with the others: university reputations are bolstered by successfully competing for high-profile faculty and talented graduate students; universities rely on their faculty's success in obtaining grants and producing valuable research results to balance budgets and maintain prestige; faculty rely on grants to support their research and doctoral students; faculty with stable grant funds are able to recruit talented graduate students to work on their research grants; graduate students need faculty mentoring and research training in their chosen professional specializations; students, after completing their PhDs, need jobs from universities as postdoctoral researchers or new faculty members; and so on. Although more visible in the sciences and engineering, some of these complex interdependencies also apply to the social sciences and humanities. As a prominent common denominator across academic fields, the expansion of undergraduate education came to depend on graduate students to serve as teaching assistants. Talented graduate teaching assistants (TAs) can be excellent instructors and inspiring role models for undergraduates. This also benefits the universities, insofar as they are inclined to replace faculty time for the lower cost of TAs. Yet the TA role can be detrimental to graduate students if it becomes a primary focus and lengthens their time to degree completion. Inevitably, with these inextricable links, changes in one area affect the entire complex—a set of dynamics reviewed in this chapter.[5]

Historical Overview

The major transformations in American higher education over the past century have had their effects in graduate education, as they have in other areas. Among the many external forces, funding from the federal government has reshaped the enterprise. Changes in the forms and amounts of federal funding signal society's changing expectations for graduate education—substantively and symbolically. In the evolving relationship between universities and the federal government, graduate education became intertwined in complex organizational symbioses with academic research, research funding, and undergraduate education. This historical overview traces a paradox of continuity alongside change: expansion in higher education's structural foundations on the one hand, with key qualitative changes in the academic work of faculty and graduate students on the other.

Although graduate education in the United States has been neither unified nor standardized, its expansion during the twentieth century retained a fundamental structural consistency, especially at the doctoral level. By cross-national standards, this country has the largest, most decentralized, and most highly differentiated arrangements for advanced education—spanning more than 1,200 campuses; enrolling about 2 million students in graduate degree programs; and granting more than 650,000 master's degrees, over 90,000 first-professional degrees, and 48,000 doctorates annually.[6] This tremendous breadth of activity notwithstanding, decentralized organization, with faculty authority established at the department level, has remained, as has the basic model for doctoral education: a few years of prescribed courses, followed by examinations for advancement to degree candidacy, culminating in a dissertation that reflects original research conducted by the student under the guidance of a faculty committee. The ideal, dating back to Wilhelm von Humboldt in the early nineteenth century, has been for students to engage in advanced study and research.[7] Research training has reflected distinct disciplinary patterns: in the sciences, where research is laboratory intensive, students work under faculty supervision, with the dissertation as a piece of a faculty member's research project; while in the humanities, where research is library intensive, students work independently, with little or no faculty contact, unless they initiated it, often for months at a time. These differing patterns of social relations are, in part, intrinsic to the disciplines and tied to professional norms, the nature of disciplinary inquiry, and the research technologies,[8] although I will argue they have been sharpened in recent decades by external demands for academic research in the sciences and engineering.

In contrast to these structural continuities, the historical arc simultaneously reveals profound changes in the nature of graduate study's social and intellectual relations, especially among students and faculty. Nevitt Sanford assessed this with critical concern back in 1976:

> The structure of graduate education seems to have changed hardly at all since the 1930s . . . What has changed are the purposes for which the structure is used and the spirit with which it is managed. The motives of professors and graduate students are less purely intellectual and more professional . . . The general climate of today is one of competitiveness among universities, between departments in a given university, and between subgroups and individuals within the same department. Students are regarded less as potential intellectual leaders and more as resources to be used in the struggle for a place in the sun.[9]

To the extent that this characterization is apt today, the research foundations of graduate education are clearly central to an analysis of how this shift came about and what the consequences have been. Specifically, changes in the funding patterns for graduate education and university research can be pinpointed as a critical mediating force in this transformation.

Historically, graduate education has been financed primarily through university research sponsorship and secondarily through a variety of loan programs, as well as by state-funded and institutionally funded teaching assistantships. Federal support for academic research has been concentrated in the top one hundred research universities, and this remains; the top one hundred account for 80 percent of federal research and development (R&D) expenditures in 2007. In 2000, the top one hundred produced nearly 50 percent of doctoral degrees and nearly 25 percent of all master's degrees that year.[10] Sponsored university research thus has had the greatest effect in these universities and on the heavily funded sciences within them. Still, it does have salience for others throughout the system—if only by denying them funds.

Federal involvement in graduate education and research can be traced back to the late nineteenth century, when the organizational structure of the modern research university emerged to accommodate graduate programs and scientific research. As these activities expanded in scale, and as faculty and campus administrators sought more external sponsors, the funding base for both activities became a source and a condition for further organizational changes on campuses and throughout the higher education system. Since the federal government has been a principal source of funds, it has played a pivotal role in these and other, more subtle alterations in graduate education. Three changes have been most apparent: increasing specialization in faculty and administrative work; greater stratification, together with heightened within-sector competition for fiscal and human resources; and a proliferation of organizational subunits for academic research to reflect the instrumental and increasingly economic agenda of external sponsors. How these changes came about is the next piece of the story.

Nineteenth-Century Beginnings

Graduate education achieved a stable American presence during the last two decades of the nineteenth century, when awarding the PhD degree became a laudable academic goal. The founding of Johns Hopkins University in 1876 is often thought of as marking the establishment of graduate education in the United States. Johns Hopkins became known as the "prototype and propagator" of research as a major university function.[11] Coupled with its commitment to scientific research, Johns Hopkins offered merit-based graduate fellowships for full-time study that included state-of-the-art research training.

Both within and immediately surrounding higher education, interest in scientific research had burgeoned since the mid-nineteenth century. With great frequency, scientists and those seeking advanced study traveled to Germany for the requisite exposure. Work in chemistry, even into the 1870s, required a trip to Germany. On the American front, after initial resistance to the German idea of studying science for its own sake—and after conflicts between self-identified pure and applied scientists—scientific research gradually gained more acceptance. It took on a distinctive meaning in the American context: science would be "a collective enterprise like those in business. Modern science needed labor, capital, and management."[12] Proclamations at Johns Hopkins reflected this change in scientific research from "a rare and peculiar opportunity for study and research, eagerly seized by men who had been hungering and thirsting for such a possibility" to an increasingly more prestigious endeavor, proclaimed by G. Stanley Hall, Clark University's first president, as "the very highest vocation of man—research."[13] Science became an increasingly specialized activity that professors could pursue autonomously—yet with the security of support, personal advancement, and even prominence within an academic institution.

Following Johns Hopkins' ideal of linking scientific research and graduate education, other graduate schools emerged in the 1890s, usually within larger universities whose undergraduate missions and size offered a broad and stable base of support in endowment funds and tuition. Some were established at the founding of a new university, so as to offer both undergraduate and graduate instruction from their inception, as at Stanford University (1891) and the University of Chicago (1892). Others added a graduate school onto an older, established, private college, as in the case of Harvard University and Columbia University. Some existing state universities—Wisconsin, Michigan, and Illinois—evolved out of origins as land-grant institutions, or land-grants, established with government funds for agriculture and mechanical arts (through the Morrill acts of 1862 and 1890), and for experimental agricultural stations (fueled through the Hatch Act of 1887). By 1900, the number of PhD-granting institutions had grown to fourteen, awarding a total of three hundred doctorates in an expanding array of fields.[14]

In addition to taking on scientific research commitments, PhD programs came to be viewed as attractive for expanding and advancing an institution's competitive position in the growing higher education system. Desiring to confer prestige on their institutions, universities sought out both faculty with research interests and sponsored research funds to build laboratories that would attract eminent scientists. Since faculty increasingly wanted to pursue basic research and train selectively chosen graduate students, universities were compelled to provide such opportunities for research and advanced training and, hence, graduate programs across disciplines.

Organizing Principles: Departmentalization and Disciplinary Specialization

The widespread adoption of graduate programs within higher education institutions was enhanced by the departmental organization that developed in the last quarter of the nineteenth century. Departments provided a flexible organizational structure for decentralizing and compartmentalizing graduate instruction. While PhD programs were organizationally integrated as a separate level from the liberal education of undergraduate colleges, they were also made part of departments responsible for undergraduate instruction in a discipline—a linking arrangement that has been remarkably stable and uniform over time and across universities. The drive to conform to this structure was so strong that Johns Hopkins expanded its organizational structure to offer undergraduate as well as graduate programs.

This organizational arrangement allowed for the same faculty to exercise authority over both undergraduate and graduate programs.[15] Courses and research training appropriate to each discipline could be designed and coordinated by each department's faculty. One functional byproduct of this arrangement was that graduate programs maintained both faculty and institutional continuity and cohesion: faculty propagated themselves and their field of study by training their professional successors; and responsibility for their graduate students kept faculty attentive to their departments. Graduate programs kept research and teaching activities interlocked and the institution functionally integrated, at least at the department level, in spite of increased disciplinary specialization.

This interdependence was crucial to the success of graduate study, perhaps most specifically in facilitating the doctoral student's transition from course work to dissertation—which, among the many hurdles encountered by PhD students across the disciplines, emerged as paramount and has persisted to this day. Research-training experience is central to a student's shift from consumer to producer of research, and thus is also integral to successful degree completion. In correspondence with established areas of knowledge, departments could design different kinds of research apprenticeships appropriate to specialized training in each discipline.

Specialization in the disciplines—which the departments mirrored—represented professors' vocational interests and aspirations. This was particularly apparent in newly established natural and social science departments, whose very existence was justified on the basis of specialized research. Beyond the campus level, as disciplines crystallized into national professional associations, they came to serve as visible external referent groups that would provide a semblance of standardization across graduate programs: "disciplines and departments had powerful reciprocal effects upon one another" in reinforcing the authority of departments on campus and the professional judgments of faculty nationally.[16]

Especially during the 1890s, the size and complexity of the graduate-education-and-research enterprise encouraged coordination and control, which were reflected in the emergent university administrative structures. Although the departments served faculty interests in terms of autonomy in research and instruction, hierarchies of academic rank within the departments and competition for resources across departments resulted in more incentives—and therefore more "productive work"—generated from more research activity. As one observer has noted, "clearly it had become a necessity, from the administrator's point of view, to foster the prestigeful evidences of original inquiry."[17] The dual tasks of graduate education and research were institutionalized most easily in organizations that had greater resources, both financial and reputational. Those that succeeded in the competitive drive became a peer group of leading institutions. The prominence of this tier was reflected in its founding the Association of American Universities (AAU) in 1900. The AAU was ostensibly established to ensure uniformity of standards, yet it simultaneously functioned as an exclusive club.[18] The AAU signified an implicit systemwide division of labor in the United States, where the highest-prestige institutions differentiated themselves at the top of the hierarchy, which was legitimately engaged in graduate education and research. Although many universities have competed for faculty, graduate students, and philanthropic support, the persistent concentration of fiscal and status resources at the top of this sector became a distinctive feature of the U.S. system, wherein success begets future success, an institutional version of Robert Merton's Matthew Effect.[19]

Termed "a new epoch of institutional empire-building," this period of American higher education was characterized by universities' explicit aims for status in an increasingly stratified system. It was seen in academic rivalry, such as bidding for faculty, and in emulating each other's highly regarded academic departments. While the American system is not unique in its inclination toward stratification, the institutional drive for competitive advancement within the research university sector has been characterized by one American scholar as "almost an obsession."[20]

Thus the end of the nineteenth century saw the research university emerge as a new kind of social institution, devoted to scientific research as well as to graduate education. Pursuing this institutional ambition became pervasive. Across the country, homogeneity in proliferating graduate programs and faculty positions suggests that universities thereby sought to acquire not only intellectual legitimacy, but also a new kind of economic and political legitimacy. These priorities have stayed at the forefront for a growing number of universities throughout the twentieth century and to the present day.

Twentieth-Century Rise of Sponsored Academic Research

The expansion of graduate education in the modern university subsequently developed hand-in-hand with the expanding national system of sponsored research. Initially, external resources for academic science were amassed principally from philanthropic foundations, while industry played a minimal role. After World War II, foundations and industry were eclipsed by a surge in federal sponsorship; the government became the major funder of academic research into the twenty-first century.

The earliest sources of research sponsorship were wealthy benefactors and their philanthropic foundations. In the 1870s, philanthropic contributions to higher education averaged $6 million per year—mainly to individual scientists. By 1890, philanthropic support showed a more widespread and instrumental orientation, directing funds to emerging universities for their potential contributions to industrial growth, employment, and commercial endeavors. The funds supported a wide array of institutional activities, especially in the applied sciences—including equipment, overall plant expansion, and new professional schools. In some cases philanthropists provided large sums of money, such as John D. Rockefeller's $35 million endowment to the University of Chicago. On a national scale, Rockefeller and Andrew Carnegie established the two largest foundations supporting research: the Rockefeller Foundation, started in 1913 with an endowment of $182 million; and the Carnegie Corporation, created in 1911 with $125 million. However, in the early 1920s these foundations favored donations to separate research institutes, such as the Rockefeller Institute of Medicine and the Carnegie Institute of Washington.[21]

By the 1930s, universities could no longer depend on philanthropic foundations as a stable sponsor for academic science. While still essential, the foundations reoriented their allocations to take the form of project grants and postdoctoral fellowships, especially in medical research, the natural sciences, and, to a lesser extent, the social sciences. In 1934, the Rockefeller Foundation's funding constituted 35 percent of overall foundation giving, comprising 64 percent of what went to the social sciences and 72 percent of gifts to the natural sciences.[22] Such voluntary contributions provided universities with resources essential to institutionalizing graduate education and scientific research as two interdependent functions.

The course was set. Universities and their faculties built their own rationales and adapted organizational structures to expand the scope of their research activities, while training the next generation of knowledge producers. Upholding university autonomy and academic freedom became important not only for the institution, but equally for individual faculty. The professionalization efforts of faculty during this era were, in part, an effort to buffer themselves from an array of powerful external interests, and not merely an outgrowth of the knowledge explosion, as is commonly cited.[23] In claiming expert authority, faculty established some distance for themselves from the agendas of prominent philanthropists.

Private industry entered the academic scene as an unexpected and unpredictable supplement.[24] As industry R&D expenditures rose in the 1920s, corporations conducted both applied and basic research in their own industrial laboratories, both in communications and chemical technologies. Two prestigious research universities—the Massachusetts Institute of Technology and the California Institute of Technology—exemplified successful industry sponsorship of university research during this era. Overall, however, corporate R&D funds stayed in their industrial laboratories through the 1930s.

By the late 1930s, university research was genuinely flourishing, primarily in the nation's most visible universities. American universities also became a haven for preeminent scientists from Europe, which helped elevate the universities' scientific capability and reputation. This concentration of research activity was paralleled by a similar concentration of research training activity: in 1937, sixteen universities accounted for half of the total expenditures on university research and granted 58 percent of all doctorates.[25] The consolidation of research resources with doctoral-granting activity was a pattern that would persist even after the era of privately financed university research. This basic imprint for university research acquired a taken-for-granted status, along with its promise for self-reproduction: a concentration of external research resources, conferred on talented faculty providing research training for the next generation while also yielding first-class academic research—all of which was recognized as valuable by external sponsors.

Surge of Federal Investment

The government's sponsorship of research and research training evolved incrementally, rather than through a coordinated policy on science or on graduate education, as was the case in some countries. Beginning with the federal and state governments' role in land-grants through agricultural research, universities were increasingly regarded as a national resource for basic research and training that could assist economic growth, national security, and health care. Over time, including during the two world wars, the government became the major sponsor of scientific research and higher education.

Federal involvement in academic science began with organizational efforts to designate advisory boards for scientific research. Acknowledging both the value of modern science and a perceived need to oversee the country's research intentions, the first national organization, the National Academy of Sciences (NAS), was founded in 1863.[26] In 1919, the National Research Council (NRC) was established by NAS essentially to carry out the earlier congressional mandate. As the principal operating agency of both NAS and—after 1964—the National Academy of Engineering, the NRC was intended to bridge the interests of its constituents: the federal government, the public, and the community of scientists and engineers. Over time, the NRC became a principal organizational vehicle for overseeing national research efforts and for monitoring how federal funds are channeled into university research.

The NRC, along with the American Council of Learned Societies (also founded in 1919) and the Social Sciences Research Council (founded in 1923), relied on the resources of philanthropic foundations to assume a prominent role in facilitating and promoting university research. As channels for foundation funds, these organizations provided interested sponsors with access to scientists and scholars, as well as with administrative assistance in selecting recipients for small research grants and postdoctoral fellowships in the areas of mathematics, physics, and chemistry. By the 1920s, American science was mobilized under "the guidance of the private elites," who "came together for the purpose of furthering science." The memberships of the NRC and NAS were constituted by "the same group of individuals [who] encountered one another, in slightly different combinations."[27]

The federal government's large-scale, multiagency funding system to support academic science expanded incrementally during and after each world war. In the late 1930s, annual federal expenditures for American science were estimated at $100 million; most of these funds went to applied research within federal bureaus, especially agriculture, meteorology, geology, and conservation. The shift to university-based research occurred when the expertise of academic researchers became valuable for national defense efforts.[28] In World War I, for example, the government financed psychologists to construct intelligence tests and encouraged scientists to follow up on diagnostic physical examinations for nearly 4 million draftees. For such work, universities granted leaves to full-time life scientists and physical scientists, as well as to social scientists and historians. The government also allocated funds for researchers working from their own campuses. By World War II, this type of funding had become more extensive. During the 1940s, the Office of Naval Research contracted with more than two hundred universities to conduct about 1,200 research projects involving some 3,000 scientists and 2,500 graduate students. Between 1941 and 1945, the United States spent a total of $3 billion on R&D—one-third of which went to university-based research aimed at winning the war and devising "new instruments of destruction and defense."[29]

This expansion of sponsored research within universities was coupled with doctoral training. Between World War I and World War II, the number of institutions awarding doctoral degrees rose from fifty in 1920 to one hundred in 1940; and the number of doctorates awarded increased fivefold, from 620 in 1920 to 3,300 in 1940.[30] In addition to such growth, one priority became enhancing the caliber of doctoral students; in the 1920s, the majority of graduate students had been "undistinguished," reflecting "uneven preparation, uncertain motivation, and unproven ability."[31]

By the end of World War II, the federal government viewed research universities as a precious public resource for research and research training, worthy of the government's investment and partnership—even during peacetime. The establishment of the National Science Foundation (NSF) in 1950 reflected an explicit federal agenda that science would indeed offer "an endless frontier," and that universities could be ideal settings for such research, as Vannevar Bush stated in his 1945 report to President Franklin Roosevelt: funding would go to scientists working in their home universities, rather than bringing them to the few existing government labs. In the 1950s, the federal research budget grew steadily, and the academic research enterprise expanded in the top tier of institutions. In 1953–54, the top twenty spent 66 percent of all federal research funds and awarded 52 percent of all doctorates—most in the life sciences, physical sciences, and engineering, the same fields receiving the most research funds.[32]

Postwar Expansion of Funds for University Research and Doctoral Education

Spurred by the Soviet launch of Sputnik in 1957, the U.S. government provided even more funds for basic research. Federal sponsorship of research increased every year from 1958 to 1968. In that decade alone, there was a fivefold expansion in annual federal contributions to academic research. As this investment increased, so did the universities' share of total basic research in the United States, from one-third to one-half during that decade.[33] Thus the post–World War II period clearly established research as a separate operation, largely paid for by the government, wherein universities performed a large share of the nation's research effort. As higher education was increasingly viewed as legitimate in this research role, overall enrollments rose from 3 million to 7 million students, and enrollments doubled within doctorate-granting universities—up from 1.24 million to 2.5 million for undergraduate and graduate levels combined. Annual PhD production in science and engineering grew from 5,800 in 1958 to 14,300 in 1968.[34]

The allocation of federal research funds followed two basic imperatives: multiagency support, and competition among proposals for specified projects of limited terms. Federal sponsorship had a clear presidential directive—Executive Order 10521, in 1954—for multiagency support, such that no single agency within the government was to be given sole responsibility for distributing research funds. Rather, each agency was to sponsor research related to its mission, such as health, defense, and energy. In 1959, 96 percent of funding came from five agencies: the Department of Defense; the Department of Health, Education, and Welfare, largely through the National Institutes of Health (NIH); the Atomic Energy Commission; NSF; and the Department of Agriculture. In the same year, nearly all of the $1.4 billion allocated for research was channeled into the life sciences, physical sciences, and engineering, leaving the social sciences, and particularly the humanities, virtually neglected.[35]

Funding allocations were determined through merit-based peer review by researchers in the scientific community. This competitive system was presumed to ensure that the best research would be performed, and further excellence cultivated. The result was to reinforce the strength of the science fields in the leading tier of research universities—with the life sciences and physical sciences accounting for over half of their the basic research budgets. For the most part, the federal agencies focused on merit, although, over time, some effort was made to disperse resources across geographic locations and to smaller institutions.

Federal support for doctoral education expanded as well, with the government's rationale being to train science and engineering personnel. Aside from short-term interests to advance science and technology, improving research capacity ("manpower training," as it was called) required a longer-term investment to develop "the pipeline" of trained scientists and engineers to meet the country's needs. A variety of mechanisms attracted talented students into the pipeline: direct student aid, such as fellowships; student aid channeled through institutions, as traineeships; and project grants to individual faculty that included salaries for graduate student research assistants. The precedent for this explicit twofold agenda—to ensure the strength of the research and the workforce—was established in the National Cancer Act of 1937, which set up grant-in-aid funds to nongovernmental scientists and direct aid to students (in the form of fellowships). By the 1950s, NSF offered more than five hundred prestigious portable fellowships to students.

Similarly, the National Defense Education Act of 1958 conveyed a commitment to rebuild the nation's research capability through "manpower training"; specifically, to support science education through a host of fellowship and traineeship programs from a variety of federal agencies—NIH, NSF, and NASA (National Aeronautics and Space Administration). The National Research Service awards, which were administered through three federal agencies in the 1960s, had the same aim. These training programs were intended to attract talented students, offering them stipends for predoctoral and postdoctoral support, as well as to improve training on campuses through institutional allowances. Between 1961 and 1972, these programs assisted more than 30,000 graduate students and 27,000 postdoctoral scholars.[36]

While direct support of doctoral education—fellowships and traineeships— was allocated to students on a competitive basis, it ended up funding students at the leading research universities, which were conducting the bulk of federally funded academic research. This concentration of resources for both research and doctoral education gave these institutions a doubly competitive edge in attracting high-quality students and faculty.

Post–World War II federal initiatives were even more instrumental in cementing the legitimacy of this interdependence: funding university research had short-term R&D value, and graduate education promoted "manpower training." Between the end of World War II and 1972, the government spent $200 billion cumulatively on R&D; the academic institutions' share of total R&D expenditures rose from 5 to 10 percent. More notably, their share of basic research expenditures went from one-quarter of all funds in 1953 to one-half in the early 1970s. By the end of this era, the surge of federal sponsorship resulted in a pattern that would persist over subsequent decades: about half of the country's basic research was done in universities; about two-thirds of university research expenditures came from the federal government; and about half the federal funds for basic academic research went to the top twenty-five research universities.

Postwar Expansion of Graduate Education

The end of World War II marked a turning point. Within this context of funded research opportunities, the graduate education system grew at a constant rate during each decade.[37] More doctorates were granted in the 1950s than in all the preceding years; the number of doctorates granted increased from 6,000 in 1950 to 10,000 in 1960. The 1960s experienced an even more pronounced expansion: a threefold increase in one decade alone—from 10,000 to nearly 30,000. The number of master's degrees also increased dramatically, rising from about 25,000 in 1940 to a genuine flourishing in the decades following World War II—about 60,000 in 1950, 75,000 in 1960, and nearly 300,000 two decades later.

This proliferation of doctorates and master's degrees reflects both overall growth in degree production and expansion into more fields of study, especially in the sciences and professional fields. The physical sciences, life sciences, and engineering accounted for close to half of the doctorates awarded in 1965; two decades later they still predominated, although PhDs in the life sciences edged out the other two fields. Social science and psychology remained fairly constant, at about 20 percent; humanities dropped from 20 to 10 percent; and education increased from about 15 to 25 percent, reflecting an increasingly professional orientation in graduate study. The overall diversification of doctoral fields was marked—there were more than 550 fields in 1960. Beyond additional areas of concentration, several dozen types of doctoral degrees developed besides the PhD, which remained the most common research doctorate: for example, degrees in education (EdD), social work (DSW), and business administration (DBA).

A similar orientation to the demands of the marketplace is evident in the growth of master's degrees since 1965, especially in practitioner-oriented fields. By 1982–83, only 16 percent of master's degrees were conferred in research-oriented MA programs. Business master's degrees increased from 7 to 23 percent; engineering accounted for 10 percent; and the health professions for about 6 percent. Education held the largest share of master's degrees, although that dropped from 40 to 30 percent.[38]

On the whole, in the decades following World War II, graduate education at the master's and doctoral levels developed into a vast enterprise in which the leading tier of research universities became the model for aspiring institutions to emulate, both in the United States and around the world. Less-elite institutions have had a smaller resource base in terms of the scale of their facilities, the amount of departmental funds, and a critical mass of sought-after faculty and students. Their approach was to invest in selected fields, although it was not until the 1970s that asserting a distinctive institutional mission become a clear strategy for gaining a competitive edge in specialized areas. At the leading institutions, the dynamic was different: able to cover many fields with depth, their strategy was to undertake even more sponsored research and to expand PhD enrollment and production. This is the modern research imperative—the vehicle whereby universities protect, if not advance, their institutional mobility. It became taken for granted that "the institution which is not steadily advancing is certainly falling behind."[39]

Thus, up to the contemporary period, graduate education and research in the leading universities were guided by opportunities funded by the government: scientific research for national priorities in defense and the economy; the government's rising research budget for R&D, specifically in basic research; and a peer review system aiming to distribute resources to the best science. The fact that multiple funding agencies were supporting academic research reduced the universities' dependence on a single agency. However, during the last quarter of the twentieth century, shifts in organization and sponsorship brought greater uncertainty in the amounts and mechanisms of funding, posing new challenges for the research foundations of graduate education, and for research universities to further diversify their funding base.

The Contemporary Era: Signs of Strain

While the patterns that crystallized in the post–World War II period remained prominent, as wider economic, social, and political conditions changed, university-government relations showed signs of strain. The early 1970s witnessed an economic crisis that threatened even the strong research-training link within the sciences, as well as the solid resource base of the most prominent research universities. An era of retrenchment—roughly between 1969 and 1975—began with a tightening academic labor market and inflation in the wider economy. The events of this era signaled an unanticipated fact: that the federal government was an unstable base of economic support for university research and graduate education. Political support was also unpredictable, with Democratic and Republican administrations modifying these funds to reflect their own distinctive priorities.

The dramatic expansion fueled by the post–World War II surge of federal support for university research and graduate education had appeared limitless. By the 1970s, research universities had greatly extended their capital-intensive research infrastructure, thereby securing their position as international centers of excellence for research and research training. Still a desirable destination for researchers from other countries, U.S universities also had a steady stream of foreign students earning doctorates, which had increased to almost 10 percent of the doctorates awarded across all fields by the late 1960s.

More doctoral students worked as research assistants for faculty who were engaged in sponsored research projects. This need, and the scale of funding, became a major determinant of the size and types of graduate programs. In addition, on the teaching side, surging enrollments meant that more graduate students could serve as teaching assistants for undergraduate classes. So, even while most applicants to graduate school sought to engage in advanced study and obtain advanced degrees, their contributions as research and teaching assistants shaped their learning experiences, while concurrently enabling universities to expand their institutional capacities for research and undergraduate education. Moreover, government-funded traineeships and portable fellowships supported those fortunate graduate students, covering their educational and living expenses. Such direct federal aid was limited to U.S. citizens and permanent residents, leading to challenges in funding foreign students, most of whom held temporary visas.

The early 1970s brought changes in the funding climate, signaling sharp declines in direct federal support for fellowships and the reorientation of basic research funds to more applied projects that prioritized economic competitiveness. These shifts, in turn, catalyzed hopes that industry would become more involved in funding academic research. Joseph Ben-David characterized this new reality: a reduction of the massive federal support was "inevitable, but . . . the system was entirely unprepared for it when it came."[40] Graduate enrollment and degrees awarded reached unprecedented highs and then leveled off during this period, another indicator that expansion was not limitless. There was concern that supply had exceeded demand, as exemplified by "taxi-driving ABDs" (students who completed all but the dissertation). How universities would manage to achieve stability, let alone thrive, in the context of uncertain job prospects and volatile federal funding became an ongoing question, along with how to sustain an infrastructure to continue to attract and nurture excellence in both research and research training. Indeed, the ongoing viability of graduate programs at several hundred campuses across the United States has been remarkable, given these broad concerns and a future of uncertain external support.

As for the changes in funding, between 1968 and 1971 the national basic research budget fell more than 10 percent in real terms.[41] Annual academic research expenditures contributed by the federal government declined from $5 billion in 1968 to $4.7 billion in 1974. The government's priority was for research that made scientific knowledge technologically relevant. As a result, physical resources—such as equipment and campus buildings—were neglected. In addition to declining funds for academic science, support for graduate students declined. Thus both research and research training became "victims of federal benign neglect."[42] The government abruptly withdrew the bulk of its direct fellowship support for graduate students, especially some of the larger programs funded by NIH. By one count, the 57,000 federal fellowships and traineeships funded in 1968 shrank to 41,000 in 1970; another estimate is that federal fellowships fell from 51,000 in 1968 to 6,000 by 1981.[43] As graduate fellowships were "cut back too fast and too far," a series of national reports looked at graduate education financing.[44] They cited the destabilizing effects of "stop-and-go" federal funds and the disadvantages of smaller-scale fellowships. The decline left the bulk of doctoral students seeking direct support from loans, which increased substantially during one decade alone: from 15 percent of the total graduate student enrollment in 1974 to 44 percent in 1984. It is estimated that by 1984, more than 600,000 students working toward graduate degrees had borrowed $2 billion from the federal government in Guaranteed Student Loans (later known as Stafford Loans).

The federal government's funding for doctoral education became more of an indirect support, through research assistantships. In the 1980s, funds for graduate student research assistantships were embedded in $13 billion of federal academic R&D. However, besides cuts in fellowships and traineeships in the early 1970s, the stipends for research assistantships were, in effect, reduced when the Tax Reform Act of 1986 reconfigured them as taxable pay for work (hence salaries) rather than tax-exempt educational subsidies. In addition, this initiative taxed state-funded teaching assistantships, which also were previously excluded from income taxes. Universities and their national representatives, along with outspoken graduate students, moved to have this legislation amended.[45] The tax reform, which required technical changes in the administration of graduate student financial assistance, marked a shift in attitude towards graduate students: seeing students as instrumentally valuable for their work, rather than as inherently worthy of direct support. Angered and saddened by the change, many saw it as "a big bite" out of "survival wages" and still consider it an unreasonable burden today.

Nonetheless, doctoral degree production resumed its growth, and by the late 1980s universities had regained the numerical losses that had occurred in the mid-1970s; the number of doctoral degrees awarded annually stabilized at above 35,000, surpassing the 1973 peak. When examined cumulatively over the last three decades of the twentieth century, the overall growth is impressive: doctoral degrees awarded from 1969 to 1999 increased by 60 percent, with only brief periods of decline. The first decade of the new century shows more growth, despite fluctuations between 1998 and 2002; growth from 2003 to 2008 led to a record number of doctorates—over 48,000 in 2008.[46]

Foreign students account for some of this increase in doctorates. In the last four decades of the twentieth century, the proportion of U.S. doctorates awarded to foreign students rose from about 10 percent in the 1960s to 23 percent in the late 1990s. Even more impressive, the proportion of foreign students earning doctorates in science and engineering tripled over this period, increasing from 13 to 39 percent. Engineering stands out, increasing from 16 to 44 percent of the doctorates in that field.[47]

Growth in the number of doctoral degrees has also been attributed to an increase in women earning doctorates. Marking progress over the past 40 years in the proportion of doctoral degrees awarded to women in the fields of science, technology, engineering, and mathematics (STEM), the number of doctorates earned by women from 1966 to 2006 are as follows: in the biological sciences, from one-eighth to one-half of the doctorates; in computer science, engineering, and physics, from less than 3 percent to about one-fifth of the doctorates. Despite this progress, women still comprise less than 50 percent of graduates in all STEM fields except the largest, the biological sciences.[48] Less progress has been made for underrepresented U.S. minorities, although their proportion of STEM doctorates increased from 4 percent in 1995 to 7 percent in 2007.[49] Aside from social justice motives, improving the participation of underrepresented U.S. minorities has been cast as a national necessity in order to maintain global competitiveness. Observers fear that if degree attainment rates of underrepresented minorities do not improve, the increased diversity of the American population will lead to a less highly trained workforce. Obviously this is a longer-term pipeline challenge than increasing success in graduate education, as the former extends from each lower level of education up through faculty ranks. The federal government has intervened in this arena, creating and funding a number of "pipeline" programs, including those aimed at graduate education (e.g., Ronald E. McNair Post-Baccalaureate

Achievement Program, Louis Stokes Alliances for Minority Participation Program, Alliances for Graduate Education and the Professoriate).

The relatively narrow concentration of doctoral degree production in the same universities has persisted in recent decades, with only a very slight decline in share. In 1992, the top fifty universities granted 54 percent of all doctorates; and the top ten, 17 percent of the total. By 2007, the fifty biggest doctoral-producing universities granted over half the doctorates, while the top 10 universities granted 15 percent. Looking at the particular universities, of the top fifty producers in 1992, all but six remained in the top fifty fifteen years later. Their concurrent research activity has also continued. Of those top fifty doctorate-granting universities in 2007, thirty-four are also in the top fifty for federally funded R&D expenditures; of the top twenty-five doctoral producers, all but one are also in the top fifty for federal R&D support, again showing the concentration of those activities in the same locales. The converse is also the case: of the top ten universities receiving federal R&D funds, seven are in the top twenty-five for doctorates awarded.[50]

Disaggregated by field of study, however, doctoral degree trends suggest more complex shifts: an increase in the life sciences and engineering, a marked decline in the humanities, and slightly less of a decline in the social sciences. The life sciences, the largest single field since 1990, continued to grant the most doctorates (over 11,000 of the 48,000 awarded) in 2008. Looking broadly at these disciplines, doctoral degree production figures between 1978 and 2008 reveal large increases in the share of doctorates earned in the life sciences, physical sciences, and engineering, while the relative share of doctorates in the humanities, social sciences, and education has decreased. Increases in federal research funds in science and engineering fields have continued to facilitate their doctoral degree production, while universities have relied on their own funding, as well as graduate students' self-support, to help finance doctoral education in other disciplines.

Postdoctoral researchers (postdocs) have become indispensable to the graduate education–research nexus for their contributions in research, supervision, grant writing, and publications. In some science and engineering fields (e.g., life sciences), postdoctoral experience is regarded as a necessary career step for new PhDs, and it has become more common in the social sciences. Educators are concerned that this extended time discourages PhDs from academic careers by prolonging their work in relatively low-status positions for low pay (about one-third that of faculty) and delaying the start of independent projects that are foundational to advancing in the faculty ranks. While skeptics point to this mass of about

50,000 postdocs as an "academic reserve army of unemployed PhDs," it is ideally a transitional phase of professional development, providing additional training and mentoring. Up to three-quarters of these postdocs are estimated to be funded by federal grants, revealing their centrality to the enterprise.[51]

In the first decade of the twenty-first century, universities have continued to perform over half of the country's basic research (56% in 2006)—a significant proportion of the overall national R&D effort. Most R&D funds go to development ($206 billion in 2006, compared with $75 billion to applied research and $62 billion to basic research). Nationwide R&D activities doubled, from $171 billion in 1995 to $340 billion in 2006. Of that 2006 total, 28 percent was provided by the federal government and 66 percent by industry. Even though industry became a big performer in R&D, its support for academic research has remained small, close to the level in the mid-1980s. In 2008, colleges and universities were relying on external—still primarily governmental—sources for R&D support, with 60 percent of academic R&D funded by the federal government (roughly the same as forty years previously), and 6.5 percent by state and local governments, compared with 5.5 percent by industry. The most dramatic proportional growth was from the universities themselves, covering 20 percent of academic R&D with their own funds.[52]

The distribution of basic research funds among academic institutions reflects the persistent concentration of research activity and sponsored research resources noted above. In dollars, by 2007 the top 100 institutions accounted for almost $40 billion—80 percent of all academic R&D expenditures; the top fifty, $27 billion (55%); the top ten, just under $9 billion (17%). Again, research funds have remained concentrated in a top tier of colleges and universities that has been relatively stable. Only five of the top one hundred institutions in 2008 were not on the list twenty years earlier.

The distribution of academic R&D across fields also remained stable in the past decade. The life sciences continued to receive the bulk of R&D funding (60% in 2006), followed by engineering (15% in 2006), while the social sciences suffered losses. Between 1996 and 2006, the life sciences and psychology earned an increased share of R&D funding; the physical sciences had modest increases; engineering decreased slightly, after increases between 1975 and 1996; while the social sciences had the largest decrease over the previous three decades (from 7.5% to 3.6% between 1975 and 2006).[53]

The patterns of federal support for doctoral students established at the end of the last century remain largely unchanged today. Since 1971, the share of federal science and engineering funding used for fellowships, research traineeships, and training grants has declined, from a high point of 20 percent of all federal science and engineering funding in 1971 to less than 4 percent in the 2000s.[54] These changes in sources of support have been experienced by successive cohorts of doctoral students since the mid-1970s: their graduate education became more labor-intensive (working in assistantships) and more reliant on self-support (loans rather than fellowships). Nearly half of the doctoral recipients in 2008 reported their primary source of financial support as teaching and research assistants; one-quarter relied on fellowships; and one-fifth used their own resources.[55]

The leading research universities, well aware of the uneven and unstable financial base in external sources, keep close tabs on what peer universities offer in financial aid (without violating federal antitrust requirements) to compete for the best students. To buffer themselves from changes in external funding sources, not only in financing graduate education but also in research, universities have launched their own fundraising initiatives. Establishing endowed funds for research and for graduate fellowships in specific fields provides income for research initiatives and fellowships. The scale of fundraising has become breathtaking, with graduate fellowships embedded in larger university campaigns. For example, in 2006 Stanford University announced the launch of a $4.3 billion campaign, the largest to date in higher education. Their theme, "Seeking Solutions, Educating Leaders," succinctly depicts the interdependence of research and graduate education and, more significantly, the stark reality that even this top research university had to turn to alumni and friends to support its capacity to pursue these core missions. Nonetheless, it is a success story, as that fundraising goal was reached—with pledges—in 2009. In fact, even in the sharp economic downturn of 2009, when charitable giving to colleges and universities nationwide dropped 12 percent, Stanford brought in $640 million, earning its ranking as the leading fundraising university in the United States for the fifth consecutive year.[56] This case is especially noteworthy, because of Stanford's previous 1997 success at raising $200 million in endowed fellowships for graduate students in the sciences and engineering; by 2010, more than 1,500 students had been supported on these multiyear fellowships.

Organized Research Units

In their efforts to broaden their funding base, universities have created extradepartmental research units that reflect specialized areas of interdisciplinary and applied research. In the historical organization of departmental structures, faculty in the departments work both as investigators and as mentors to their advanced graduate students in the department's degree programs. The post–World War II period has given rise to the major exception to this mode of organization, the organized research unit (ORU). Before the twentieth century, ORUs were primarily observatories and museums, but the post–World War II expansion of academic research fueled the proliferation of ORUs on campuses to meet new societal demands for research that did not correspond with instructional areas outlined by departments, such as for research projects that were disproportionate to departments in their magnitude and expense. Funded by the national government, state governments, industry, and foundations, over the past several decades ORUs have extended university research into interdisciplinary, applied, and capital-intensive endeavors. They have become common in the fields of biotechnology, artificial intelligence, microelectronics, and material sciences, as well as more recent fields explicitly oriented to solving complex problems in bioengineering, nanotechnology, neuroscience and imaging, photon science, and global climate and energy issues.[57] ORUs have proven successful because they are visible and highly adaptive. Flexibility is achieved by employing specialists who are highly qualified researchers and technicians, often on term appointments, in addition to drawing on time, as needed, from tenure-line faculty and graduate students. Some of the country's most competitive research universities have ORUs with external funding, as well as their own research institutes and centers funded by gifts or endowment revenue. By the end of the 1980s, estimates of the number of ORUs ranged from a total of 2,000 to more than 10,000 across U.S. universities. By 2000, estimates ranged from a few dozen to several hundred ORUs *at any given research university*, and they existed either within or across schools.

Many universities have also used their own funds to support some of these cost-intensive research activities—including facilities and equipment improvement—in addition to accelerating efforts to collaborate with industry.[58] Industrial sponsorship—whether arranged in these kinds of ORUs as formal research agreements, or as informal collaborations—carries some potential constraints in terms of the research process (for example, secrecy), the product (for example, negotiation over intellectual property), and exclusivity clauses against the formation of other alliances. These affect research activities, generating concern about a potential blurring of boundaries—if not purposes—between academic researchers and external sponsors. When profit is likely and students are involved, other issues emerge: while the quasi exploitation of students for a faculty member's academic advancement is historically grounded in the university research system, it is another matter for a professor to profit financially from a student's work on a commercial venture.[59] That said, these collaborations can provide unique research opportunities and facilitate the transfer of research results to users, and they are more commonly seen as a win-win situation, so long as these issues are well managed.

As sites of research training for doctoral students, ORUs can mediate between the world of disciplinary training and "real world needs and problems."[60] Practically, they may provide dissertation research support and stipends for graduate students. Often they make better research equipment available. Finally, as an indirect benefit, they employ specialists—postdoctoral or nonfaculty researchers—in a temporary home akin to a departmental home. This evokes a set of challenges, however, if it works at cross-purposes with departmental organization. In general, students and younger faculty want the opportunity to work with researchers and up-to-date equipment in such a setting. The fear is that ORUs may draw intellectual, organizational, and economic vitality away from department-based graduate programs as faculty and graduate students join these research groups. Research personnel may supervise graduate research assistants, but they do not have faculty status.[61] Graduate students in ORUs may become more distant from their "home" departments, which can also raise competing expectations from faculty in different locations. ORU budgets are overseen by different managers than those anchored in departments. The result is a complex set of administrative arrangements for research and research training that fall outside of the department. Even if these concerns can be satisfactorily addressed, ORUs may meet resistance from faculty who advocate for students to have strong disciplinary training before they engage in any other work. Thus far in the twenty-first century, enthusiasm for such extradepartmental research activities has been steadily rising, attracting faculty and students who want to pursue ideas beyond disciplinary boundaries, acquiring whatever skills are called for as the research unfolds, forming collaborations with peers as they see fit, and potentially gaining recognition for pathbreaking research that will help solve vexing problems—from developing advanced energy technologies to finding cures for pervasive illnesses.

Despite uncertainties and attendant tensions, ORUs are unarguably a very effective organizational mechanism to quickly assemble a critical mass of researchers to undertake new projects, and to compete for funding that will support cutting-edge investigations beneficial to the researchers' careers and to graduate

students' research training. The downside for universities is that, once established, ORUs that use cost-intensive equipment and facilities demand to be fed by
a stable flow of funds. By the same token, they are difficult to close. Thus assessing the risks of establishing an ORU against the potential benefits is an ongoing
challenge for universities, especially in fields with unclear trajectories. For example, should a university invest in neuroscience and, if so, in what form, when
the infrastructure needs and research expertise are so costly? If this looks daunting for a university and, by their criteria, they cannot afford to do so, they may
nonetheless conclude that they cannot afford not to—especially if they want to
remain competitive in attracting top faculty and students. Given state economic
contexts, there is growing concern about public universities' ability to keep pace
with privates in this regard. These decisions—just what business a university
should be in—have implications for research, research training, degree specializations, and the capacity to pull in future research funding.

Indirect Costs

Universities recover some of the enormous costs incurred in campus research by
charging overhead on research grants. Infrastructure expenses (such as lighting,
heat, and libraries) are indirect costs for research projects that are charged to
sponsors. Each university negotiates its indirect cost rate with the government to
gain an additional percentage for every dollar of government funds; as a result,
the rates vary from one campus to the next.[62] For decades, university administrators, campus-based researchers, and federal agencies have struggled to reconcile
conflicting interests in this arena, fueling internal tensions on campus between
faculty who want as much funding as possible going to the research project and
administrators' wanting a higher indirect cost rate to recoup more for the
infrastructure.

Underlying some discussions over insufficient indirect cost recovery is a widespread perception on the part of research university advocates that the instrumentation in university laboratories fares poorly when compared with government or commercial laboratories, along with the belief that a decline in quality
may cause a decline in the research productivity of academic scientists, as well as
in first-rate training opportunities for graduate students. In 2010, advocates for
research universities assert that they still bear enormous unreimbursed indirect
costs for federally sponsored research, with national estimates totaling between
$2.5 and $4 billion. In addition to the financial burden of cost-sharing expecta-

tions associated with grants, another concern is over faculty time spent on the administration of research grants, estimated to have increased from 18 to 42 percent over the past twenty years.[63] Public universities that are already stretched financially are clearly not well positioned to afford such unreimbursed costs, especially after budget cuts that included administrative staff layoffs. This jeopardizes the quality of research, research training, and financial support for graduate education. It suggests that even in the near term, universities may become even more stratified in the quality and reputation of both their academic research and their doctoral education.

A related concern is that universities may lose cutting-edge research if they are unable to provide sufficient resources for innovative interdisciplinary research and research training. The fear is that if universities do not have the support to make "some realistic accommodation . . . an increasingly large portion of basic research and academic activity which is necessary to the quality of [graduate] education . . . will move outside the university structure." [64] The long-range concern is that faculty will not have the resources to continue on the frontiers of research, and that the best researchers may move away from graduate students, thereby jeopardizing a premise of the system—that "the best and the brightest" produce the best science and scientists at centers of excellence.

Consequences for Graduate Students

Over the past four decades, graduate education has become more expensive, yet its funding base continues in an ad hoc way. This has been most evident for PhD students in the sciences, where funding uncertainties have deeply affected their research training experiences, and it continues to affect PhD students in the humanities, where there has been no real federal support. As noted above, recent decades have seen assistantships as a major source of financial aid for graduate students, along with grants and loans. The number of graduate assistants has increased dramatically. It grew from 160,000 in 1975 to 216,000 in 1995. By 1999–2000, of those pursuing master's degrees, 16 percent had assistantships, up from 9 percent in 1990; and of those pursuing doctoral degrees, 47 percent had assistantships, up from 29 percent in 1990. The numbers in 2004 revealed a slight decline in the share of students holding assistantships, as 13 percent of students pursuing master's degrees held assistantships, while 41 percent of doctoral students held such positions.[65] In other words, many more graduate students have been working at their institutions concurrently with their graduate study. Uncertainty about funding is one among many factors thought to impact attrition from PhD programs, estimated to be as high as 50 percent nationally.[66]

The financing of graduate education also has implications for time to degree. In 1983, doctoral graduates in all fields spent a median time of 8.2 years between starting and completing their graduate study. By 1993, it was 8.7 years. Yet in recent years the trend has moved in the opposite direction: 8.5 by 2003 and 7.7 in 2008. This could be explained by the increase in students in fields with shorter times to degree, or by fields with more international students, who have strong incentives to finish more quickly (i.e., those on temporary visas are ineligible for direct federal aid and their spouses cannot work). It must be noted that the overall median time to degree of 7.7 years obscures substantial differences across fields of study. In 2008, the field of education took the longest (a median of 12.7 years of enrollment between starting graduate school and earning a doctorate), and physical sciences and engineering had the least time (6.7 years).[67] Beyond factors intrinsic to differences in disciplinary research, an unstable and unequal funding base seems to be a major factor. In disciplines without research funds, such as the humanities, or with declining research support (education, social sciences), doctoral students tend to rely on teaching assistantships and self-support. For these students, the quest for funding is a distraction from completing their dissertation, rather than being intimately tied to their dissertation projects.

High loan debt for graduate students has become an ongoing concern. Students acquire more loan debt the longer they defer employment, and they become discouraged from the loss of momentum. In an effort to speed up the process, some programs have reduced requirements for course work, so that students begin working on their dissertations earlier. The University of Chicago instituted a reduced-course-work policy in 1982 to encourage students "to engage in their doctoral research as quickly, as clearly, and as self-consciously as possible," which would lead to "a healthier emphasis on the research stage of graduate student work."[68] The need for such a change is especially apt in the humanities, where the tendency has been to handle knowledge changes cumulatively—with more and more material to incorporate into graduate course work—while in the sciences, for example in physics and the biological sciences, the faculty revamp the curricula more often. Along similar lines, expectations for the dissertation may be revised, as seen thus far in the sciences and in economics, where a compilation of published or publishable research articles (usually with a framing introduction and conclusion) has become common.[69] Such changes help students make a smoother transition to a faculty position, with material ready for submission to a top journal, or a dissertation ready for a book deal in fields where that is the currency. Competitive pressures have ratcheted up expectations, to the point that students even at the leading universities ask themselves, how can I compete with that? The tendency may be to stay in school longer to do ever more.

At the same time, recent studies documenting an overproduction of doctorates in science and engineering supplement the already bleak picture for new PhDs in the humanities and social sciences, who are disheartened by an unfavorable academic labor market.[70] Many universities are widely replacing tenure-line positions with "off-track" full-time and part-time positions, commonly referred to as "contingent" faculty. Borrowed from the discourse on labor, this term reflects concerns about job security for contingent workers, and about exploitation of these highly skilled individuals. Yet the trend is advantageous for the hiring organizations, giving them flexibility to adapt to changing resources and to compete by hiring experts in academic areas where student interest is on the rise. From roughly 1975 to 2007, the percentage of tenure-line faculty declined from 57 to 31 percent, according to the American Association of University Professors. Current estimates are that 60 percent of new hires are off-track, which is decidedly less desirable than tenure track. This trend is likely to swell, given the impact of the economic crisis that hit in 2009, which left universities eliminating jobs or freezing faculty hiring. In the absence of projections for an academic hiring boom, faculty across disciplines have begun working with doctoral students early in their programs to prepare them for alternatives to an academic career. In addition, admissions committees have been considering whether they should limit the number of new doctoral students or, alternatively, provide prospective students with precise placement information concerning graduates in each department.

Changes in federal sponsorship of research and graduate education have produced an even less visible, and yet potentially more profound transformation in the nature of student-faculty relationships during research training, especially for students in the sciences. While the historical ideal entailed a student working "at the bench" with a mentor, sponsored research is now the central medium for supervision and potential collaboration. Concerns have been raised that faculty have become more like project managers and administrators than mentor-professors, and that students are being supervised in a more directive manner—treated like employees and technicians rather than as apprentices. As one observer suggests, "the roles of faculty member (mentor) and principal investigator (employer) are becoming inconsistent, straining the incumbents. Principles and practices that the mentor would prefer are inconsistent with the needs of the scientist as employer."[71]

While the flow of federal research funds to the sciences and engineering may appear preferable to conditions in the humanities and social sciences, increased competition for research grants has squeezed professors into developing leaner budgets with tighter time constraints. This has dramatic consequences for graduate students, as they, too, face the exigencies of an increasingly competitive arena of research support. The time schedules of short-term grants mean less leeway for mistakes; less available grant money means more competition and pressure to produce better results; sharing capital-intensive instrumentation means longer hours of work, often in other geographic locations; the increased size of research teams entails perfecting a technique on one part of a project, rather than completing an entire project from beginning to end; and time spent in research is valued over time spent teaching younger students—or time for family responsibilities, since nowadays more doctoral students have gotten older and have families. The contemporary arrangements call for an unprecedented intensity for students and faculty alike.

One manifestation of this can be found in the organizing efforts of graduate students to gain bargaining status as employees.[72] Changes in the academic workplace, along with momentum from faculty collective-bargaining activities, have strengthened the willingness and ability of graduate students to unionize. In the 1970s, dismal labor market prospects for emerging PhDs exacerbated graduate students' concerns about a longer time to degree. These concerns were amplified into the 1980s and 1990s, due to students' higher levels of financial debt, their perceptions of inadequate faculty advising, and the stark realization that benefits accrued to universities as a result of the institutions leveraging faculty time through the "cheap labor" of graduate assistants. In 1989, graduate students founded the National Association of Graduate-Professional Students to advocate for improved living and working conditions. By the end of the 1990s, these factors contributed to a growing awareness of discrepancies between ideals and realities, and, at the national level, fostered widespread discussions about the quality of doctoral education.[73]

In 2001, a key ruling by the National Labor Relations Board (NLRB) reversed precedent on the collective bargaining rights of graduate students. That decision found that graduate students who hold positions as teaching or research assistants, or similar titles, were eligible to unionize; other graduate students were not suited to making the case that they were employees. In 2002, more than 40,000 graduate students at more than forty universities were either involved in organizing drives or already had formal collective bargaining representation, more than 16,000 of whom were members of the United Auto Workers (UAW).[74] However, graduate student unionization efforts were dealt a serious blow by a 2004 NLRB ruling that reversed the 2001 regional decision, stating that graduate students at private universities were not employees and thus lacked the right to collective bargaining.[75] While recognizing that state law permits collective bargaining at public universities, the NLRB chose to impose a single federal standard on the private universities under its jurisdiction. Graduate students continue to organize themselves to gain collective bargaining leverage, but private universities are under no legal obligation to negotiate with them. Despite the legal hurdles for graduate students at private universities, estimates are that by 2006, graduate unions—some without collectively negotiated contracts—were active on some forty U.S. campuses.[76] To underscore the high stakes, the graduate dean of arts and sciences at New York University voiced a view widely held among academic leaders, expressing her skepticism about the UAW's promises of what a graduate union could do there: "At heart, what matters in the university are academic values, and I am wary of any force that might corrode them."[77]

Approaching the end of the first decade of the twenty-first century, the worst financial crisis since the Great Depression has had widespread impacts on every part of higher education, and it is expected to have long-term repercussions. This is so despite a very short-term gain from some of the federal government's $787 billion in stimulus funding.[78] Universities are adapting to losses in anticipated revenues (from endowment payouts, from external sources such as foundations, and—if public—from declines in state funding) by utilizing such cost-saving measures as budget cuts to core academic programs, enrollment reductions, hiring freezes, and layoffs and furloughs for full-time employees, including tenure-line faculty. Morale on campuses has been low, especially at public universities. The job outlook is bleak for students soon to complete their degrees, especially those seeking to launch academic careers. Finding a decent job—let alone a dream job—seems unattainable. Reminiscent of the 1970s, faculty and staff are helping doctoral students consider options for using their skills in nonacademic careers. These differ by field, of course: biotechnology expertise has clear applications in industry, whereas historians turn to nonprofits rather than to the private sector for work in public history—for example, in museums, libraries, foundations, and government agencies. All of this prompts universities to consider once again adjusting doctoral admissions to match fluctuations in demand and in the flow of research funds available to support graduate students.

As for American graduate education's standing worldwide, roughly one-quarter of U.S. graduate enrollment is international, having risen since the decline that immediately followed the terror attacks of September 11, 2001. By 2007, foreign students accounted for a significant proportion of the degrees in science and engineering, receiving one in four master's degrees and one in three doctorates. The top countries of origin for international graduate students are China, India, South Korea, and Taiwan; together, they account for 20 percent of all doctorates in the United States. Historically, the infusion of foreign-born talent has reached well beyond graduate education and university research, bringing significant innovations into the economy, especially in those areas that draw on engineering expertise. Indeed, the United States has grown so dependent on international talent that analysts are concerned that the United States is losing its market share in the global pool of mobile students, with it having already declined from 25 to 20 percent of the total in 2006. Although some of that decline is attributed to an increase in sheer numbers, other countries are more aggressive in attracting talented students from abroad, and the United States lacks an overall strategy in this arena.[79]

As these varied changes and open questions reveal, the direction—and even the changing structures—of graduate education and research are by no means assured. Yet despite the tensions inherent in these interdependencies and the frustrations often expressed over a lack of progress on resolving some persistent issues, the continued success of the U.S. arrangements is undisputed. Visitors from around the world continue to regard ours as exemplary practices, because of America's impressive track record of producing highly skilled and thoughtful leaders while making dramatic advances in knowledge and technologies for the new economy.

Conclusion: Changing Conduct in Changing Contexts

The trajectory of historical development in the United States is clear: graduate education has become so intertwined with sponsored research that the two have emerged as the foremost raison d'être for universities in the top tier, as an increasingly noble aim for lower tiers to emulate, and as an implicit professional imperative for research university faculty. Historical scholarship reveals that obtaining research funds from the federal government and other patrons has been a requirement for university expansion and competitive advancement. As universities have aggressively vied for talented faculty and graduate students, they have sought to preserve their autonomy by stabilizing a support base from a plurality of sources—including a range of external sponsors and internal revenue sources. Over time, at their own initiative, universities have engaged in fundraising to amass significant endowments, knowing that these would yield discretionary resources and thereby minimize the skewing of institutional priorities toward the incentives of short-term R&D sponsors, as well as buffer them from changes in the external revenue sources on which they have come to depend.

Nonetheless, recent decades show that universities have been continually challenged, because the federal government is an inherently uncertain funding base. The flow of federal funds has left support for doctoral education concentrated in the physical and life sciences, less evident in the social sciences, and virtually nonexistent in the humanities. Over the past four decades, tension has heightened as the federal government provided less support for fellowships and traineeships, leaving individual students to rely on loans and university resources. The bulk of federal support has become indirect—through research assistantships on short-term R&D projects that strain the ideals of the mentor-apprentice relationship. Academic ideals are at times challenged by research training activities that create finer status distinctions among students to secure support from "the right" principal investigators on "cutting-edge" and well-funded research projects. To the extent that doctoral education functions as professional socialization, a distinctive portrait of very demanding and competitive professional work is the model for students in fields relying on sponsored research. Research, and hence research training, has been defined by increased competition for peer-reviewed research grants, a situation where faculty are driven to submit many more proposals than are awarded, where research is conducted on faster clocks with higher stakes, and where sponsors' agendas are magnets for faculty and student engagement that may or may not reflect their passionate interests nor advance them in their fields per se. This raises the question, for what kind of profession are graduate students being prepared?

The aim of this analysis has been to identify the structural foundations in the interdependence of graduate education and research, and to show some of the developments over recent decades and the effects therein. While the tone may not sound optimistic, the long view of this enterprise clearly underscores the remarkable resilience demonstrated by universities, their faculty, and the generations of graduate students who have proceeded with groundbreaking research and research training despite fluctuating resources and uncertain futures. Of course, the future organization and sponsorship of graduate education requires careful collective deliberation. A host of issues must be addressed about the conduct and operation of the enterprise, beyond decisions as to which graduate degree programs a campus should offer. These include the adequacy of financial aid mechanisms, the demographic characteristics of incoming students, the adequacy of advising and mentoring for academic and nonacademic careers, the expectations for research and teaching assistantships across the disciplines, the factors contributing to attrition and a lengthening time to degree, the neglect of humanities and nonscience fields by external funders, the appropriateness of industrial sponsorship that is explicitly for profit, and the ownership of intellectual property. The issues are not strictly about efficient means, but also about desirable ends.

Admittedly, to identify graduate education as paying a price for its linkage to the university research enterprise marks a distinctive shift in scholarly attention away from highlighting what accounts for the remarkable success of this enterprise. Usually, among the inseparable interdependencies within universities, undergraduate education is often characterized as diminished, given all the time and resources focused on faculty research.[80] In truth, an argument can be made that each of the components is suffering. With greater frequency, scholars critically examine other costs and potential tradeoffs in the academic sciences, with crucial consequences for the vitality of the academic profession.[81] Efforts to pursue these and related lines of inquiry in graduate education have been hampered by incomplete historical data, or by work that is in-depth but provides only a snapshot of a point in time. Over the past few decades, national data are collected more consistently and thus lend themselves to trend analyses.[82] However, such databases have substantial limitations for addressing qualitative concerns, let alone for longitudinal analyses that can bring to light changes in the character of the enterprise. Fortunately, some major foundations have supported initiatives that include interventions, in the hope of improving the quality of doctoral education and reducing attrition, as well as diversifying the pipeline for STEM fields.[83]

Moreover, posing perhaps a more formidable obstacle than data availability, deliberation on these high-stakes issues is undermined by the complex and problematic interdependence between graduate education and sponsored research at the national level. There is no clear leverage point for change. Analytically, we can see how the wider society's demands on the social functions of higher education have been changing: graduate education is immersed in an institutional enterprise that produces goods and services, determines expertise, distributes resources, and regulates the uses of and access to knowledge and power. At the center of this enterprise, faculty and their universities continue to carry out their multiple roles while preparing the next generation for the academic profession, among other careers, and conveying to them—either explicitly or implicitly— what is taken for granted about the tensions they experience on a daily basis. They display a remarkable resilience and ingenuity to stay the course, often leveraging limited resources, including their own time and energy, over decades. Nonetheless, it is clear that economic and political challenges will continue to fuel internal tensions in universities, and thus risk dismantling the longstanding humanistic ideals of knowledge creation in favor of purposes that, at their worst, resemble a shortsighted opportunism. Too much is at stake in the years to come— the education of the next generation, the trajectory of faculty careers, the infrastructure of universities, the advancement of knowledge—for us to forego further analyses of these issues. Higher education researchers can play a central role in promoting such informed and thoughtful deliberation.

NOTES

Chris Gonzalez Clarke, Chris M. Golde, and Mary Kay Martin provided valuable assistance in revising this chapter.

1. Examples are drawn from the *Chronicle of Higher Education* archives, 2005–10.

2. As to the question of universities retaining autonomy amid a plurality of sponsors, for celebratory and critical interpretations, respectively, see Roger L. Geiger, *To Advance Knowledge: The Growth of American Research Universities, 1900–1940* (New York: Oxford University Press, 1986); and David F. Noble, *America by Design: Science, Technology, and the Rise of Corporate Capitalism* (New York: Alfred Knopf, 1977). Scholars have separately documented the rise of modern American science—Robert V. Bruce, *The Launching of Modern American Science: 1846–1876* (New York: Alfred Knopf, 1987); the emergence of the American research university—Geiger, *To Advance Knowledge*, and Laurence Veysey, *The Emergence of the American University* (Chicago: University of Chicago Press, 1965); the emergence of graduate education— Richard J. Storr, *The Beginnings of Graduate Education in America* (Chicago: University of Chicago Press, 1953), and Bernard Berelson, *Graduate Education in the United States* (New York: McGraw-Hill, 1960); and postwar changes in federal support of academic science—John T. Wilson, *Academic Science, Higher Education, and the Federal Government, 1950–1983* (Chicago: University of Chicago Press, 1983).

3. The shift is evident beyond research universities; see Françoise A. Quéval, "The Evolution toward Research Orientation and Capability in Comprehensive Universities," PhD diss., University of California, Los Angeles, 1990.

4. Patricia J. Gumport, "Learning Academic Labor," *Comparative Social Research* 19 (2000): 1–23.

5. Little scholarly work has been done at the intersection of these arenas to examine their interrelationship. The major exceptions are Joseph Ben-David, *Centers of Learning: Britain, France, Germany, United States* (New York: McGraw-Hill, 1977); and Burton R. Clark, *Places of Inquiry* (Berkeley: University of California Press, 1995). For a review essay, see Gary D. Malaney, "Graduate Education as an Area of Research in the Field of Higher Education," in *Higher Education: Handbook of Theory and Research*, vols. 1–, ed. John C. Smart (New York: Agathon Press, 1988), vol. 4, 397–454. Most research since then has focused on doctoral students, drawing on national data or retrospective accounts. See, for example, William G. Bowen and Neil L. Rudenstine, *In Pursuit of the PhD* (Princeton, NJ: Princeton University Press, 1992); Michael T. Nettles and Catherine M. Millet, *Three Magic Letters; Getting to PhD* (Baltimore: Johns Hopkins University Press, 2006); Barbara E. Lovitts, *Leaving the Ivory Tower: The Causes and Consequences of Departure from Doctoral Study* (Lanham, MD: Rowman and Littlefield, 2001); George E. Walker, Chris M. Golde, Laura Jones, Andrea Conklin Bueschel, and Pat Hutchings, *The Formation of Scholars: Rethinking Doctoral Education for the Twenty-First Century* (San Francisco: Jossey-Bass, 2008); and reports on PhD career paths and outcomes from the Center for Innovation in Research in Graduate Education. The graduate education–research nexus is undertheorized in higher education literature, except as it is defined by the political economy; see Sheila A. Slaughter and Gary Rhoades, *Academic Capitalism and the New Economy* (Baltimore: Johns Hopkins University Press, 2004).

6. Degree data is from the National Science Foundation [NSF], *Doctorate Recipients from U.S. Universities: Summary Report 2007–08*, NSF 10–309, Dec. (Arlington, VA: National Science Foundation, 2009); the National Center for Educational Statistics, *Digest of Educational Statistics 2008* (Washington, DC: National Center for Education Statistics, 2009). R&D data is from NSF, Division of Science Resource Statistics [NSF/SRS], *Academic Research and Development Expenditures: Fiscal Year 2007*, NSF 09-303, Mar. (Arlington, VA: National Science Foundation, 2008). Institutional data is from the Carnegie Classification Web site, http://classifications.carnegiefoundation.org/ [accessed Feb. 22, 2010].

7. Clark, *Places of Inquiry*. The term "elbow learning" refers to students and faculty working side by side in labs, dating back to G. Stanley Hall, Clark University's first president and himself a well-regarded mentor; see Walker et al., *Formation of Scholars*, 117.

8. Charles P. Snow, *The Two Cultures* (New York: Cambridge University Press, 1959); Tony Becher, "The Cultural View," in *Perspectives on Higher Education: Eight Disciplinary and Comparative Views*, ed. Burton R. Clark (Berkeley: University of California Press, 1984), 165–98; Walter P. Metzger, "The Academic Profession in the United States," in *The Academic Profession: National, Disciplinary, and Institutional Settings*, ed. Burton R. Clark (Berkeley: University of California Press, 1987), 123–208.

9. Nevitt Sanford, "Graduate Education: Then and Now," in *Scholars in the Making*, ed. Joseph Katz and Rodney T. Harnett (Lexington, MA: Ballinger, 1976), 250–51.

10. NSF/SRS, *Academic Research & Development Expenditures: FY 2007*; NSF/SRS, *Academic Research & Development Expenditures: FY 2000*, NSF 02-308 (Arlington, VA: National Science Foundation, 2002).

11. The earliest signs of doctoral education in the United States were the first PhD, awarded in 1861 by Yale's Sheffield Scientific School; the second PhD, by the University of Pennsylvania in 1871; and the third, by Harvard a year later. Perhaps more significant was the explicit organizational mission of graduate education in the founding of Johns Hopkins University in 1876 and of Clark University in 1889. See Bruce, *Launching of Modern American Science*, 335–37.

12. Dael Lee Wolfle, *The Home of Science: The Role of the University* (New York: McGraw-Hill, 1972), 4.

13. Veysey, *Emergence of the American University*, 149, 168, 318–19; see also note 8 above.

14. Richard Hofstadter and C. DeWitt Hardy, *The Development and Scope of Higher Education in the United States* (New York: Columbia University Press, 1952), 44–45; Berelson, *Graduate Education*, 33.

15. Lewis B. Mayhew, *Reform in Graduate Education*, SREB Research Monograph No. 18 (Atlanta: Southern Regional Education Board, 1972), 6; Ben-David, *Centers of Learning*, 61. See also Burton R. Clark, *The Higher Education System* (Berkeley: University of California Press, 1983).

16. Geiger, *To Advance Knowledge*, 37; Ben-David, *Centers of Learning*, 61.

17. Veysey, *Emergence of the American University*, 177.

18. Geiger, *To Advance Knowledge*, 19.

19. Robert K. Merton, "The Matthew Effect in Science," *Science* 159 (Jan. 1968): 56–63.

20. Martin Trow, "The Analysis of Status," in Clark, *Perspectives on Higher Education*, 134; see also Veysey, *Emergence of the American University*, 312.

21. Bruce, *Launching of Modern American Science*, 329–34; Fredrick Rudolph, *The American College and University: A History* (New York: Vintage / Random House, 1962), 425–27.

22. Berelson, *Graduate Education*; Geiger, *To Advance Knowledge*, esp. 166.

23. Undertaking applied research activity also became incorporated into the ideal of service, especially for faculty in public universities. See Noble, *America by Design*; Gary Rhoades and Sheila A. Slaughter, "The Public Interest and Professional Labor," in *Culture and Ideology in Higher Education*, ed. William G. Tierney (New York: Praeger, 1991).

24. Geiger, *To Advance Knowledge*, 174–225.

25. Ibid., 262.

26. Over the next decade, NAS became the site of severe conflicts over membership—which was limited to fifty—and mission, as American scientists from

different fields vied for control of the scientific community; see Bruce, *Launching of Modern American Science*, 301–5, 315–17.

27. Geiger, *To Advance Knowledge*, 13, 100, 165, 256.

28. Paul Starr, *The Social Transformation of American Medicine* (New York: Basic Books, 1982), 193.

29. Wolfle, *Home of Science*, 110; David Dickson, *The New Politics of Science* (Chicago: University of Chicago Press, 1984); Alice M. Rivlin, *The Role of the Federal Government in Financing Higher Education* (Washington, DC: Brookings Institution, 1961), 31.

30. Martin J. Finkelstein, *The American Academic Profession* (Columbus: Ohio State University Press, 1984), 24.

31. Geiger, *To Advance Knowledge*, 220.

32. Rivlin, *Role of the Federal Government*, 47.

33. Dickson, *New Politics of Science*; Government-University-Industry Research Roundtable, *Science and Technology in the Academic Enterprise* (Washington, DC: National Academy Press, 1989).

34. Government-University-Industry Research Roundtable, *Science and Technology*; Ben-David, *Centers of Learning*, 119.

35. Douglas M. Knight, ed., *The Federal Government and Higher Education* (Englewood Cliffs, NJ: Prentice Hall, 1960), 135–37.

36. Estimate is by Porter E. Coggeshall and Prudence W. Brown, *The Career Achievements of NIH Postdoctoral Trainees and Fellows*; NIH program evaluation report is by the Commission on National Needs for Biomedical and Behavioral Research Personnel, Institute of Medicine, NIH 85-2744 (Washington, DC: National Academy Press, 1984).

37. Berelson, *Graduate Education*; National Research Council [NRC], *Summary Report 1986: Doctorate Recipients from United States Universities* (Washington, DC: National Academy Press, 1987); U.S. Department of Education, *Digest of Education Statistics 1989* (Washington, DC: National Center for Education Statistics, 1989); Judith S. Glazer, *The Master's Degree: Tradition, Diversity, Innovation*, ASHE-ERIC Higher Education Report No. 6 (Washington, DC: Association for the Study of Higher Education, 1986).

38. NRC, *Summary Report 1986*; Berelson, *Graduate Education*, 35; Glazer, *Master's Degree*. Education and business remained the largest fields: 29 and 23 percent, respectively, in 2007–8; see Nathan E. Bell, *Graduate Enrollment and Degrees: 1998 to 2008* (Washington, DC: Council of Graduate Schools, 2009).

39. Rudolph, *American College and University*, 239; see also Patricia J. Gumport, "The Research Imperative," in Tierney, *Culture and Ideology*, 87–106.

40. Ben-David, *Centers of Learning*, 124.

41. Government-University-Industry Research Roundtable, *Science and Technology*.

42. Charles V. Kidd, "Graduate Education: The New Debate," *Change* 6 (May 1974): 43; Wolfle, *Home of Science*, 256; Frederick E. Balderston, "Organization, Funding, Incentives, and Initiatives for University Research," in *The Economics of American Universities*, ed. Stephen A. Hoenack and Eileen L. Collins (Albany: State University of New

York Press, 1990), 40; Arthur M. Hauptman, *Students in Graduate and Professional Education* (Washington, DC: Association of American Universities, 1986); Sheila A. Slaughter, "The Official Ideology of Higher Education," in Tierney, *Culture and Ideology*, 59–86.

43. Balderston, "Organization, Funding, Incentives, and Initiatives," 40.

44. Kidd, "Graduate Education"; Hauptman, *Students in Graduate and Professional Education*.

45. They succeeded in an exemption for direct educational expenses—for tuition, books, materials, and equipment used in pursuit of an academic degree; see "Tax Law Shrinks Stipends," *Scientist*, 1, no. 23 (Oct. 18, 1987): 1.

46. NSF/SRS, *Doctorate Recipients from U.S. Universities: Summary Report 2007–08*; Mark K. Feigener, *Numbers of U.S. Doctorates Awarded Rise for Sixth Year, but Growth Slower*, Science Resource Statistics Info Brief, NSF 10-308, Nov. (Arlington, VA: National Science Foundation, 2009); NSF/SRS, *Doctorate Recipients from U.S. Universities: Summary Report 1999*, SRS 01-339 (Chicago: National Opinion Research Center); NRC, *Summary Report 1986*.

47. Data from "Survey of Earned Doctorates," reported in Lori Thurgood, Mary J. Golladay, and Susan Hill, *U.S. Doctorates in the 20th Century*, NSF 06-319, June (Washington, DC: National Science Foundation, Division of Science Resource Statistics, 2006).

48. Catherine Hill, Christianne Corbett, and Andresse St. Rose, *Why So Few? Women in Science, Technology, Engineering, and Mathematics* (Washington, DC: American Association of University Women, 2010).

49. National Science Board [NSB], *Science and Engineering Indicators 2010*, NSB 10-01 (Arlington, VA: National Science Foundation, 2010).

50. NSF/SRS, *Doctorate Recipients from U.S. Universities: Summary Report 2007–08*; NSF/SRS, *Academic Research & Development Expenditures: FY 2007*, NSF 09-303, Mar. (Arlington, VA: National Science Foundation, 2009).

51. National data on postdocs are estimates that understate the totals, since only those with doctorates from U.S. universities are counted. Nonetheless, this total doubled, from 18,000 in 1981 to 39,000 in 1998; within that total, about 75 percent worked in educational institutions, 12 percent in government, and 11 percent in industry. Fifty percent were foreign-born, most on temporary visas. See Thomas B. Hoffer, Karen Grigorian, and Eric Hedberg, *Postdoc Participation of Science, Engineering, and Health Doctorate Recipients*, Science Resource Statistics Info Brief, NSF 08-307, Mar. (Arlington, VA: National Science Foundation, 2008); Committee on Science, Engineering, and Public Policy, *Enhancing the Postdoctoral Experience for Scientists and Engineers* (Washington, DC: National Academy Press, 2000).

52. Data from NSB, *Science and Engineering Indicators 2008*, 2 vols., NSB 08-01 (vol. 1) and NSB 08-01A (vol. 2: Appendix Tables), Jan. (Arlington, VA: National Science Foundation, 2008); Jaquelina C. Falkenheim and Mark K. Fiegener, *2007 Records Fifth Consecutive Annual Increase in U.S. Doctoral Awards*, Science Resource Statistics Info Brief, NSF 09-307, Nov. (Arlington, VA: National Science Foundation, 2008).

53. NSF/SRS, *Academic Research & Development Expenditures: FY 2007*; NSB, *Science and Engineering Indicators 2008*.

54. NSF/SRS, *Federal Science and Engineering Support to Universities, Colleges, and Nonprofit Institutions: FY 2007*, NSF 09-315 (Arlington, VA: National Science Foundation, 2007).

55. Disaggregating the data by field of study reveals major differences in the experiences of graduate students. Assistantships (research or teaching) are overwhelmingly the most common form of support in the physical sciences (74%) and engineering (70%). In contrast, less than half of doctoral graduates in the life sciences (44%), social sciences (42%), and humanities (37%)—and even fewer in education (18%)—report assistantships as their primary source of support. Fellowships are most common in the life sciences (42%), humanities (38%), and social sciences (28%), followed by engineering (21%), physical sciences (19%) and education (11%). Personal sources (including loans) are the dominant form of support for education graduates (60%), and such sources are also relied upon by graduates in the humanities (23%) and social sciences (27%). In contrast, none of the science and engineering fields report higher than small proportions of graduates who rely on personal sources of financial support. All data from NSF/SRS, *Doctorate Recipients from U.S. Universities: Summary Report 2007–08*.

56. Council for Aid to Education, press release, Feb. 3, 2010.

57. Roger L. Geiger, "Organized Research Units: Their Role in the Development of University Research," *Journal of Higher Education* 61 (Jan./Feb. 1990): 1–19. See also Gerald J. Stahler and William R. Tash, "Centers and Institutes in the Research University," *Journal of Higher Education* 65 (Sept./Oct. 1994): 540–54.

58. In fact, over the past four decades, ORUs were viewed as a way to replace federal support with industrial sponsorship. Several federal initiatives were launched to encourage industry's contributions to campus-based, larger-scale operations. Beginning in the mid-1970s, NSF established Industry-University Cooperative Research Projects. In the late 1980s, NSF promoted proposals for university-based Engineering Research Centers, as well as Science and Technology Centers. These programs were to be funded initially by congressional appropriations, and then to be gradually weaned from NSF funds through industry's support.

59. Martin Kenney, *Biotechnology: The University-Industrial Complex* (New Haven, CT: Yale University Press, 1986), 118–21.

60. Robert S. Friedman and Renee C. Friedman, "Organized Research Units in Academe Revisited," in *Managing High Technology: An Interdisciplinary Perspective*, ed. Brian W. Mar, William T. Newell, and Börje Saxberg (Amsterdam, Netherlands: Elsevier Science, 1985), 75–91.

61. See Clark Kerr, *The Uses of the University* (New York: Harper and Row, 1963). Estimates of nonfaculty researchers in universities ranged from 5,000 to over 30,000. See Charles V. Kidd, "New Academic Positions: The Outlook in Europe and North America," in *The Research System in the 1980s: Public Policy Issues*, ed. John M. Logsdon (Philadelphia: Franklin Institute Press, 1982), 83–96; Carlos E. Kruytbosch,

"The Organization of Research in the University: The Case of Research Personnel," PhD diss., University of California, Berkeley, 1970; Albert H. Teich, "Research Centers and Non-Faculty Researchers: A New Academic Role," in *Research in the Age of the Steady-State University*, ed. Don I. Phillips and Benjamin Shih Ping Shen, AAAS Selected Symposium Series No. 60 (Washington, DC: American Association for the Advancement of Science, 1982), 91–108; Government-University-Industry Research Roundtable, *Science and Technology*; Irwin Feller, "University-Industry Research and Development Relationships," paper presented at the Woodlands Center for Growth Studies' conference on "Growth Policy in the Age of High Technology: The Role of Regions and States," 1988.

62. Private universities have had a higher indirect cost rate than publics for several decades. In 1997, the average indirect cost rate was 56 percent for privates and 47 percent for publics. More than a decade later, each was about 10 percent higher. For example, Harvard's rate was 67 percent, MIT's 65 percent, and Johns Hopkins' 63 percent, compared with the University of California, Berkeley, at 53 percent and the University of Michigan at 54 percent. A gap between publics and privates persists, although the size of the gap has varied in recent decades. For a discussion of the rationale, see Roger G. Noll and William P. Rogerson, "The Economics of University Indirect Cost Reimbursement in Federal Research Grants," in *Challenges to Research Universities*, ed. Roger G. Noll (Washington, DC: Brookings Institute, 1998), 105–46.

63. Arthur Bienenstock, "Administrative Burdens Stifle Faculty and Erode University Resources," *American Physical Society Newsletter* 18, no. 7 (July 2009): 8, www .aps.org/publications/apsnews/20090/backpage.cfm [accessed Mar. 23, 2010].

64. Carol Frances, "1984: The Outlook for Higher Education," *AAHE Bulletin* 37, no. 6 (Feb. 1985): 3–7; Kenneth Hoving, "Interdisciplinary Programs, Centers, and Institutes: Academic and Administrative Issues," paper presented at the Twenty-Seventh Annual Meeting of the Council of Graduate Schools, Washington, D.C., Dec. 1–4, 1987; Carlos E. Kruytbosch, "The Future Flow of Graduate Students into Scientific Research," paper presented at the Annual Meeting of the Council of Graduate Schools, Orlando, Florida, Dec. 1979; Bruce L. R. Smith, "Graduate Education in the United States," in *The State of Graduate Education*, ed. Bruce L. R. Smith (Washington, DC: Brookings Institution, 1985).

65. The best national source for such data is the National Postsecondary Student Aid Survey, administered in 1986–87, 1989–90, 1992–93, 1995–96, 1999–2000, and 2003–4; however, some survey items were modified from one administration to the next, thereby thwarting longitudinal analyses. See Susan P. Choy and Emily Forrest Cataldi, *Student Financing of Graduate and First-Professional Education, 2003–04: Profiles of Students in Selected Degree Programs and Part-Time Students*, NCES 2006-185 (Washington, DC: National Center for Educational Statistics, 2006); Susan P. Choy and Sonya Geis, *Student Financing of Graduate and First-Professional Education, 1999–2000: Profiles of Students in Selected Degree Programs and Their Use of Assistantships*, NCES 2002-166 (Washington, DC: National Center for Education Statistics, 2002).

66. Daniel Denecke and Helen Frasier, "PhD Completion Project: Preliminary Results from Baseline Data," *Council of Graduate Schools Communicator* 38, no. 9 (Nov. 2005): 1–2, 7.

67. NSF/SRS, *Doctorate Recipients from U.S. Universities: Summary Report 2007–08*; Robert O. SImmons and Delores H. Thurgood, *Doctorate Recipients from U.S. Universities: Summary Report 1994*, SRS 95-334 (Washington, DC: National Academy Press, 1995).

68. University of Chicago, "Report of the Commission on Graduate Education," *University of Chicago Record* 16, no. 2 (May 3, 1982): 67–180. Two decades later, the university requires "continuous registration" for doctoral students, where they must be enrolled and pay the requisite tuition and fees, thereby creating a financial incentive that is thought to speed up time to degree.

69. Barbara E. Lovitts, *Making the Implicit Explicit* (Sterling, VA: Sylus, 2007); Brian Paltridge, "Thesis and Dissertation Writing," *English for Specific Purposes* 21 (2002): 125–43.

70. Joseph Berger, "Slow Pace toward Doctorates Prompts Fear of Unfilled Jobs," *New York Times*, May 3, 1989, A1. At that time, one study estimated a 22 percent overproduction of science and engineering doctorates—see William F. Massy and Charles A. Goldman, *The Production and Utilization of Science and Engineering Doctorates in the United States* (Stanford, CA: Stanford Institute for Higher Education Research, 1995)—but it was later critiqued for methodological flaws, another sign to be skeptical even of data-based forecasts.

71. Edward J. Hackett, "Science as a Vocation in the 1990s," *Journal of Higher Education* 61 (May/June 1990): 267. Stated more dramatically, the climate has been characterized as a factory floor—or a "quasi firm"—rather than a center of learning. See Henry Etzkowitz, "Entrepreneurial Scientists and Entrepreneurial Universities in American Academic Science," *Minerva* 21 (1983): 198–233.

72. However, structural and normative barriers are major obstacles to these organizing efforts, impeding construction of a collective identity, and thus a basis for solidarity, among graduate students. See Patricia J. Gumport and John Jennings, "Graduate Student Employees: Unresolved Challenges," *CUPA (College and University Personnel Association) Journal* 48, no. 3/4 (Fall/Winter 1997–98): 33–37. For discussion of the contextual shift to a more corporate model of the academy, see Robert A. Rhoads and Gary Rhoades, "Graduate Employee Unionization as Symbol of and Challenge to the Corporatization of U.S. Research Universities," *Journal of Higher Education* 76, no. 3 (2005): 243–275.

73. Chris M. Golde and Timothy M. Dore, *At Cross Purposes: What the Experiences of Doctoral Students Reveal about Doctoral Education* (Philadelphia: Pew Charitable Trusts, 2001); see also Patricia J. Gumport, "Learning Academic Labor."

74. Daniel J. Julius and Patricia J. Gumport, "Graduate Student Unionization: Catalysts and Consequences," *Review of Higher Education* 26 (Winter 2002): 187–216; see also Scott Smallwood, "United Auto (or Is that 'Academic'?) Workers," *Chronicle of Higher Education*, Jan. 17, 2003.

75. *Brown University v. NLRB*, 342 U.S. 402, 483–500 (2004).

76. Parbudyal Singh, Deborah M. Zinni, and Anne F. MacLennan, "Graduate Student Unions in the United States," *Journal of Labor Research* 27, no. 1 (Winter 2006): 55–75.

77. Catharine Stimpson, "A Dean's Skepticism about a Graduate-Student Union," *Chronicle of Higher Education*, May 5, 2000.

78. The American Recovery and Reinvestment Act of 2009 included $10 billion for health research and the construction of National Institutes of Health facilities; and another $9 billion for scientific research, channeled (in part) as follows: $3 billion to the National Science Foundation, $2 billion to the U.S. Department of Energy, and $1.3 billion for university research facilities. Another $50 billion went to a State Fiscal Stabilization Fund, with the stipulation that governors had to spend 80 percent on education, which includes higher education.

79. John Aubrey Douglass and Richard Edelstein, "Whither the Global Talent Pool?" *Change: The Magazine of Higher Learning* 41, no. 4 (July/Aug. 2009): 36–44. The international graduate student "stay rate" in the United States remains strong, rising from 50 to 70 percent in the last decade of the twentieth century.

80. Alexander Astin, "Moral Messages of the University," *Educational Record* 70 (Spring 1989): 22–25.

81. Sheila A. Slaughter, *The Higher Learning and High Technology* (Albany: State University of New York Press, 1990); Hackett, "Science as a Vocation"; Etzkowitz, "Entrepreneurial Scientists."

82. See NSF's *Survey of Earned Doctorates* (www.nsf.gov/statistics/srvydoctorates/), conducted by the National Opinion Research Center, which accumulates longitudinal data in the Doctorate Record File, as well as their *Academic Science/Engineering Graduate Enrollment and Support, Federal Obligations to Universities and Colleges*, and *National Patterns of Science and Technology Resources*; see also the National Center for Education Statistics' *Integrated Postsecondary Education Data System* (http://nces.ed .gov/ipeds/), with institution-level data on enrollment and degrees awarded, as well as their *Digest of Educational Statistics* (http://nces.ed.gov/programs/digest/) for national trend data. See NSF's data on *Science and Engineering Indicators* (www.nsf.gov/ statistics/seind/). See also the Council of Graduate Schools' policy studies (www .cgsnet.org).

83. In 1991 the Andrew W. Mellon Foundation funded a ten-year Graduate Education Initiative, focused on the humanities and social sciences, at ten universities. In 2001 Atlantic Philanthropies, Inc., funded a five-year study by the Carnegie Foundation for the Advancement of Teaching to create local solutions to major challenges in doctoral education, working with eighty-four departments across six disciplines in forty-four universities. In 2004 the Ford Foundation and Pfizer, Inc., supported the Council of Graduate Schools' PhD Completion Project, focusing on science, engineering, and mathematics at more than twenty-nine universities. As for diversifying STEM fields, intervention programs by the federal and state governments, foundations, nonprofits, universities, and scholars have proliferated over the past two decades, but they

often lack comprehensive evaluation, not to mention having an absence of measurable gains. As a sign of the magnitude of this investment, one estimate is that federal agencies alone spent close to $3 billion on over two hundred programs in fiscal year 2004; see Cheryl Leggon and Willie Pearson, Jr., "Assessing Programs to Improve Minority Participation in the STEM Fields," in *Doctoral Education and the Faculty of the Future*, ed. Ronald G. Ehrenberg and Charlotte V. Kuh (Ithaca, NY: Cornell University Press, 2009), 160–71.

CHAPTER FIFTEEN

Curriculum in Higher Education

The Organizational Dynamics of Academic Reform

Michael N. Bastedo

The curriculum in American higher education is often characterized as a pendulum swinging from one extreme to another: from religion to secular science, from prescribed study of the classics to curricular pluralism, and from tradition and conservatism to experimentation and growth. Indeed, these have been some of the major tensions in the American higher education curriculum over the past three centuries, and conflict over these issues has often been intense within academic communities. The need for curriculum reform can be understood as emanating from changes in the broader society, such as scientific advancement, evolving conceptions of knowledge, changing student demographics, and, more recently, labor market demands. These have often provided compelling rationales for some forms of curricular change.

We must also recognize, however, that these explanations have often been egregiously simplified. Over thirty years ago, Douglas Sloan accused historians of treating the higher education curriculum as a "morality play," where the forces of science, growth, and *Lernfreiheit* (student freedom to learn) fought the good battle against the forces of religion, stagnation, and prescription.[1] In reality, those who fought for a prescribed curriculum often struggled with how to provide some

form of academic freedom to students; those who were fervent and pious followers of the Christian faith were often equal believers in the need for education in
the basic sciences; and those who believed that knowledge must be conserved
were also committed to change and innovation. There are identifiable tensions in
the curriculum, but they are not simplistic dichotomies.

In short, we must come to a more nuanced understanding of the reciprocal
relationship between the curriculum and society. While the curriculum can be
seen as a lens for social change, it can also serve society by defining the boundaries of knowledge and thus serve as a force for social change itself, as we will see
in the development of technology and the study of women and minorities. And
while societal forces undoubtedly influence the curriculum, a full understanding
is only possible when we understand how those changes have unfolded over time.
Toward that end, we must identify the agents of change, the ways in which they
organized for social action, and the dynamic relationship between actors in the
university and organizations and leaders in society at large.

With these aims in mind, this chapter provides a broad overview of the organizational dynamics of curriculum reform since the early days of the American college. Using three major tensions in curriculum reform—prescription and election,
stability and growth, and conservation and innovation—historical developments
are considered analytically to understand how early reforms have influenced contemporary debates. In the final section, I briefly consider some conceptual frameworks for understanding the dynamics of curriculum reform, as well as some
emerging policy issues for the coming decade.

Prescription and Election

The curriculum of the early American college was strongly influenced by the
medieval English university, which trained the Calvinist ministers who founded
early American colleges in the seventeenth century. There was one curriculum
for all students, designed to prepare them for a career in law or the clergy. Incoming classes were quite small; until the 1760s, all of the colonial colleges combined
did not yield more than one hundred graduates per year.[2] Students themselves
were generally only fourteen to eighteen years old and were often taught by the
college president himself. In later years, recent graduates, themselves only eighteen or nineteen years old, assisted him as tutors.[3]

Training for the Protestant ministry required learning the major languages of
biblical texts—Latin, Greek, and Hebrew—so that students could understand them

in the original. Study of the classical languages was also highly valued for its perceived ability to shape the human mind; the complexity of the grammatical structures of ancient languages was believed to train students to think at a more advanced level than was possible in the vernacular or other modern languages. Although a basic knowledge of Latin and Greek was often required for admission, teaching in these languages comprised much of the first two years of study, with the addition of logic, grammar, and some rhetoric. Logic was highly valued for its usefulness in teaching students to think rationally and critically, as it had been in the English university. In the final two years, a greater portion of the curriculum consisted of rhetoric, poetry, literature, ethics, arithmetic, and philosophy. Teaching itself consisted of lectures, verbatim recitations, and public disputations.

Emerging topics that did not fit into the ordinary curriculum were covered in weekly "extracurricular" lectures to the student body. Extracurricular topics were also occasionally taught in courses that were stated to be Latin or logic. Student literary societies served an important curricular role, promoting the reading of poetry, literature, science, and other topics that were not a priority in the standard curriculum.[4] Beyond simply reading the works, debates on these subjects were often organized by competing societies for the benefit of the campus. As is often true today, a great deal of learning in the early American college took place outside of the classroom.

As students and faculty became excited by new knowledge, they made extensive efforts to incorporate new materials into the curriculum, both formally and informally. After Timothy Dwight was hired by Yale, the senior class successfully petitioned the trustees to allow students to take lectures from him in rhetoric, history, poetry, and literature.[5] The evolution of the Scientific Revolution in European universities also could not be ignored; American faculty returned from Europe fired up to teach these new and daring subjects to eager students. Gradually, courses in physics, anatomy, chemistry, and more advanced mathematics were added to the final two years of the college curriculum.

With new topics emerging at a rapid pace, many openly considered allowing students to select the courses of their choosing. At the turn of the nineteenth century, the American college curriculum was in a state of conflict over the knowledge and skills necessary for a liberal education in contemporary society. As the interests and career goals of incoming students became more catholic, as society expected higher education to cover an increasing number of subjects, and as faculty grew restive, the curriculum came under attack from progressives for its intensive focus on ancient languages and theology. The result was an unplanned growth of subjects in the curriculum without an overarching philosophy, which to some meant chaos and confusion. According to historian Frederick Rudolph, "higher education behaved in harmony with a culture that built canals and railroads in seemingly endless number and for reasons that were often more consistent with the national psychology than with sound economic and engineering practice."[6] Students were also getting older; the age of the average college student rose throughout the nineteenth century, making the idea of an elective curriculum increasingly acceptable as students grew from boys to men.

Yet there were many who were opposed to such changes, for reasons both traditional and contemporary. The defense of the classical curriculum by the president and faculty of Yale College in 1828 was often seen as the last bulwark against the radical changes being proposed by students and society. The Yale Report famously defined the purpose of liberal education as providing "the *discipline* and *furniture* of the mind."[7] Intensive study of Latin and Greek, they argued, was necessary for students to expand their memory; logic and scientific experiments were required to teach students to think through complex problems. Ordinary Americans could be trained on the job for careers in "subordinate" positions. Yale's purpose, they argued, was to train young men from the upper classes who would serve as society's enlightened leaders and decision makers.[8]

Despite widespread acceptance of the report, Yale and the other elite colleges could not single-handedly resist the demands of a changing society and the propulsion of increasingly rapid knowledge change. As state, community, and denominational competition drove the creation of hundreds of colleges throughout the nineteenth century, those states, communities, and denominations expected college curricula consonant with their needs and interests. Advanced education was increasingly necessary for professions outside of the law and the clergy, and students expected a more rational connection between their course work and future career opportunities. Faculty and students, seeing emerging knowledge being created in new academic fields such as science, economics, and sociology, expected to find that knowledge reflected in the curriculum. The complexity of these demands by college constituents made reform virtually irresistible.

Once the classical curriculum was dismantled, it happened with remarkable speed. Although Frances Wayland had instituted an elective curriculum at Brown University by 1850—and, as a result, increased enrollment by 40 percent—Harvard president Charles Eliot, in embracing reform, popularized the new curriculum throughout higher education, despite being appointed nearly twenty years after Wayland inaugurated changes at Brown.[9] By 1879, only the freshman year was prescribed for Harvard undergraduates, but there was still intense conflict over the elective reforms. Numerous public debates among high-ranking college presidents were conducted throughout the late nineteenth century. Indeed, presidents and faculty were often conflicted within themselves about the choice between prescription and election.

The changes at Brown and Harvard led to similar moves throughout higher education, part of what David Riesman has described as a "meandering snake-like procession" of ideas through colleges and universities.[10] Nevertheless, there was widespread unhappiness with the rapid decline in standards that accompanied the adoption of the elective system; students increasingly enrolled in entry-level courses and abandoned logic and languages in droves, leading to charges that universities were educating a generation of sophists and dilettantes. The appointment of A. Lawrence Lowell to the Harvard presidency in 1909 was, in large degree, a response to Eliot's radical overhaul of undergraduate education. Lowell's mandate was to institute a set of distribution requirements to ensure that all students received a liberal education, a plan he outlined at his inauguration, with Eliot sitting next to him on the dais.

An idea that worked in theory never seemed to work well in practice. Distribution requirements forced students to select courses from particular categories, but there was still no common curriculum for all undergraduates. Proponents of a rigorous liberal education were still around to make plenty of trouble for the new system. Dissent crystallized around Robert M. Hutchins, who took over the University of Chicago in 1919, at the age of twenty-nine. Hutchins was driven by a desire to elevate the common man through standards of culture, thought, and morality, and thus to elevate society as well. The only way to accomplish these goals, Hutchins believed, was a prescribed program of general education.

The development of general education programs would be facilitated by institutional changes in the disciplines. Historians, who needed to introduce students to their rapidly developing field, shaped broad courses that covered Western history from Greece to the present.[11] These courses were the basis for War Issues courses developed during World War I, whose purpose was to create solidarity between future American soldiers and their European counterparts by educating them on their common heritage.[12] These courses, in turn, led to the "Great Books" movement launched in the 1940s and 1950s and discussed later in this chapter.

The response to the concerns of Hutchins and his sympathizers within higher education was exemplified by Harvard's famous Red Book.[13] The Red Book was a report written by a committee of Harvard faculty charged with evaluating the state of general education for undergraduates. The committee did not go as far as Hutchins or Mortimer J. Adler might have hoped, but they did acknowledge that distribution requirements were inadequate and recommended that all students be exposed to the major areas of knowledge. Tension between prescription and election is evident throughout the monograph, an artifact not only of the prevailing views of the country, but also of the conflicting views of the faculty on the committee.[14] Once again, the Harvard plan proved to be popular, and it became a model for general education programs throughout the country.

Twenty years later, Columbia University faced concerns about its general education program, but from the opposite direction. Columbia's Contemporary Civilization program required a single course sequence in the classics for the entire first-year class, leading to attacks claiming that it restricted the academic freedom of students and consisted of works largely irrelevant to contemporary social concerns. Daniel Bell, a prominent sociologist at the university, was asked to write a report on the subject for the consideration of the faculty. His 1966 book, *The Reforming of General Education*, was a thoughtful, pragmatic approach to the problem of general education. Bell argued that since college takes its place between secondary school, which emphasizes facts, and graduate school, which emphasizes specialization, "the distinctive function of the college must be to teach modes of conceptualization, explanation, and verification of knowledge."[15] The selection of canonical texts included in Columbia's program broadened the mind, he said, because the works were presented as contingent, allowing the reader to draw conclusions that differed from those of the professor. Material presented merely as fact or dogma, Bell argued, would lead only to specialization and vocationalism, thereby undermining the goals of general education.

Despite his defense of Columbia's core curriculum, Bell's pragmatic argument provoked those who believed that the classics were worthwhile in and of themselves. This view was most clearly expressed by Leo Strauss, a political philosopher at the University of Chicago. "Liberal education is education in culture or toward culture . . . The finished product of a liberal education is a cultured human being," Strauss wrote. "We are compelled to live with books. But life is too short to live with any but the greatest books."[16] Robert Belknap and Richard Kuhns later took an even more reactionary stance, arguing that contemporary students were ignorant, and that universities had failed to integrate the disciplines by instead placing a premium on specialization. "Universities and schools," they said, "have lost their common sense of what kind of ignorance is unacceptable."[17]

Allan Bloom extended this argument in 1987 in *The Closing of the American Mind*. Bloom derided the culture of American college students and the curriculum of American colleges, both of which, he believed, encouraged an unhealthy cultural pluralism. Teaching students merely to be open to new cultures was wrongheaded, he said, because it is natural to prefer your own culture, just as it is natural to prefer your own child over another's. Without this proprietorship of culture, students were left in a "no man's land between the goodness of knowing and the goodness of culture, where they have been placed by their teachers who no longer have the resources to guide them."[18] Students, Bloom argued, no longer had a cultural orientation with which to organize the world around them, leaving them unable to construct meaning from a stream of facts and opinions. In a society characterized by torrents of information, Bloom said, colleges have abandoned students by their ideology of openness.

Bloom's tract led to a flood of books on the state of the American college generally and liberal education specifically. In 1991, Dinesh D'Souza, in *Illiberal Education*, argued that the problem was not that colleges taught non-Western culture, but that it was taught ignorantly. Instead of teaching classic non-Western texts such as the *Analects* of Confucius or the *Ramayana*, he said, faculty taught explicitly political works like *I, Rigoberta Menchu* and *The Wretched of the Earth*, books that were written by Westerners and served merely to reflect liberal Western conceptions of non-Western peoples.[19] Thus D'Souza advocated a prescriptive but not ethnocentric curriculum that identified essential texts from multiple traditions. D'Souza strongly supported *50 Hours*, a similar curriculum published in 1989 during the Reagan administration, under the auspices of the National Endowment for the Humanities.[20]

In the 1990s, a few scholars emerged to defend the university against these often vituperative critiques.[21] They were united in their opinion that most discussion of liberal education was oblivious to its history, and they emphasized how the curriculum has always been a contested area full of controversy and disagreement. The curriculum, even in its classical period, was never entirely static—new books gained entrance (for example, Austen, Twain, James, Freud) and old books were discarded. In this way, the curriculum has always responded to changing fashions in scholarship, taste, and the demands of an evolving society.

They said further that the new demographics of higher education mandated the inclusion of new authors in general education programs that reflected an increasingly multicultural society. University of Chicago philosopher Martha Nussbaum, for example, has argued that shaping citizens remains a vital function of higher education. Students must be prepared for a culturally diverse and international world, she said, and doing so requires understanding the perspectives of a wide variety of cultures. Nevertheless, she saw the Western tradition as remarkably consonant with emerging demands for pluralism. Books in the Western tradition can help students with the critical examination of people and cultures, including one's own, and develop the ability to think about the emotions and values of people in other cultures. This ability "to step out of your own shoes," she concluded, was key to living in a world marked by people's diversity in race, class, gender, and sexual orientation.[22]

Debate over the nature and necessity of the prescribed college curriculum continues to this day, although it has abated substantially in the wake of concerns about access, funding, and accountability. Most recently, the burden of defending the case for a prescribed curriculum has fallen to the American Council of Trustees and Alumni (ACTA), which has issued a series of reports alleging the failures of American higher education to hold students to rigorous academic standards. By their criteria, in 2009 only eleven of the top one hundred undergraduate programs require an acceptable course in U.S. government, just seventeen require an acceptable course in literature, and only fifty-six require two years of a foreign language.[23] The ACTA standards themselves are controversial—the University of Notre Dame's literature requirement is deemed unacceptable because it permits a theme course in Migration and Identity—but it is fair to say that for many people, the American university curriculum remains one of "chaos and confusion."

There are remarkable parallels between debates over the elective system in the 1880s and 1890s and more recent debates over general education since the 1980s. In both cases, the degree to which knowledge evolution and changing student demographics demand curricular reform are key points of contention. Both sides have engaged in significant debates on the utility of more traditional curricula compared with emerging subjects. The primary question is always, what do college students need to learn to be educated members of society? Ultimately, general education does not exist in a vacuum, and it must be as dynamic as the rest of the curriculum.

Stability and Growth

Persistent debates on the state of general education have occurred amid the massive expansion of knowledge and the development of organizational structures to support them. During the 1880s and 1890s, as the implementation of the elective system was negotiated in colleges across the country, the modern disciplines were also beginning to emerge. In a process that Walter Metzger has called *subject parturition*, the disciplines that we have come to understand as the foundation of the modern university were organized into distinctive and recognizable units.[24] As knowledge created in the university became increasingly complex and differentiated, new subjects emerged to help define the boundaries of that knowledge. In their early days, professors in these fields often struggled for legitimacy with professors in more established areas of knowledge. Over the years, through a process Metzger termed *subject dignification*, these fields gradually gained legitimacy through the creation of scholarly societies, academic journals, and distinctive and rigorous methodologies.

Subject parturition was led in the nineteenth century by the sciences, which began to break out from the more general and humanistic approach taught in the colonial and antebellum colleges under the rubric "natural philosophy." As scientific modes of investigation were incorporated and PhDs returned from advanced study in Germany, the study of science seemed increasingly differentiated from other subjects. Before the widespread adoption of the elective system, chemistry, geology, astronomy, physics, and biology were already recognized as distinct subjects at most colleges.[25] The social sciences quickly followed, with economics emerging from political economy, and sociology emerging from economics. These new fields were supported by scholarly societies like the American Anthropological Association, founded in 1802, and journals such as the *American Journal of Sociology*, founded in 1895.[26]

New forms of knowledge and methodologies for their investigation led to new forms of classroom pedagogy. The lectures and recitations of the early American colleges were simply ineffective methods for science education or for advanced students at the graduate level. Laboratory sections were added to courses to facilitate the empirical investigation of scientific phenomena. While the lecture would remain the primary mode of instruction for most of the twentieth century, the seminar was implemented for graduate students and then gradually diffused to advanced undergraduates.[27] Having learned the basic foundations of their field, graduate students and advanced undergraduates were deemed capable of engaging in direct dialogue with professors and colleagues.

The disciplines became increasingly specialized over the course of the twentieth century. Universities helped to define what forms of knowledge were worth knowing by the disciplines' placement in the curriculum, and researchers themselves established new modes of inquiry. These changes were then diffused throughout the academic community through scholarly societies and journals, and transmitted to society by graduating students and faculty who interacted with people outside the university. The curriculum was transformed further as faculty sought to teach more specialized courses, resulting in a greater differentiation of courses and degrees. The professional self-identification of faculty changed concurrently. Whereas once faculty members might call themselves psychologists or biologists, later they would declare themselves to be Jungians or neuroendocrinologists.[28]

Subjects outside of the traditional disciplines have also been accommodated, particularly in fields that are closer to the economy. Schools in medicine, law, education, social work, and public health emerged to meet the needs of an increasingly professionalized society, and to certify and elaborate professional knowledge.[29] Academic work in these schools was often a laboratory for increasing specialization and the interdisciplinarity of knowledge. Technical and vocational subjects have become a core mission for the community colleges, ranging from automobile repair to medical technology and radiation therapy. This is not to say that vocational subjects were solely the realm of community colleges; on the contrary, students across the spectrum of both public and private colleges became increasingly vocational in their orientation and demanded curricula relevant to their needs.[30]

In recent years, the humanities have been an increasingly fertile field for the development of new programs and departments within the university. Unlike those founded in earlier periods, these programs were often explicitly connected to organized social movements led by students.[31] The civil rights movement of the 1950s and 1960s inspired student groups to demand black studies programs at more than eight hundred colleges and universities. Black faculty worked in concert with the students, making strenuous efforts to increase scholarship in the emerging field. Funding was often provided by the Ford Foundation, whose grants helped to establish many black studies programs across the country.[32]

Over the course of the 1960s, however, black students increasingly associated themselves with the Black Power movement, a more militant attempt to force society to recognize the rights of black Americans. Students inspired by the Black Power movement often thought black faculty, tainted by their socialization in the academy, were "too white" to reflect an authentic black culture, and they demanded programs that explicitly rejected the involvement of the traditional disciplines and incorporated community members into the curriculum.[33] Their goal was not simply to establish a separate curriculum, but to transform the curriculum of the university as a whole and to address racism in society more broadly.

Women's studies programs followed a similar path in the early 1970s.[34] Feminism was a powerful influence on young women entering the university, who demanded that the study of women and women's issues be incorporated into the curriculum. Female faculty who pursued graduate work during the 1960s often risked their careers by writing dissertations in women's studies and, once they were hired, faced sharp critiques from their disciplinary colleagues that their work was methodologically weak or "too political." Women's studies faculty and students, like those in black studies, explicitly sought to change the curriculum of the university and to rectify institutionalized sexism and misogyny in society. Similar identity-based movements can be seen today in efforts to promote Chicano studies, Asian American studies, and Queer studies in the curriculum.[35]

Further growth in the higher education curriculum has resulted from interdisciplinarity, the integration of two or more disciplines to form a new content area or mode of inquiry.[36] Interdisciplinarity creates fundamental tensions as new organizational spaces are created in the university. Many will advocate for an entirely new interdisciplinary program to establish a foothold in the curriculum and, not incidentally, to make a permanent claim in the university budget. Inevitably, another faction will argue that interdisciplinary programs should exist only across the existing departments, so as to wait until the field matures, retain disciplinary legitimacy for scholars, and maintain faculty hires in the departments.

Interdisciplinary inquiry has occurred almost since the foundation of the disciplines; recently, however, there have been movements to organize new subjects in separate departments and programs. Interdisciplinary programs are in evidence across the fields of knowledge, from biostatistics and biopsychology to area studies of Latin America, Eastern Europe, and Africa. The disciplines themselves have also become increasingly interdisciplinary, as subfields of the disciplines have grown ever closer to their neighbors. Thus we see areas of study such as economic sociology, where sociologists have directed their energies into areas previously claimed by economists, and behavioral economics, where economists have taken on insights from psychology to paint a more realistic picture of economic behavior. Growth in the disciplines is therefore increasingly fractal, as each discipline differentiates within itself into smaller and smaller parts, but in ways that are highly and predictably patterned through social, philosophical, and methodological lenses.[37]

Finally, growth in the curriculum can be seen in areas that serve to segregate students and academic programs within colleges and universities.[38] In the past, the differentiation of students generally occurred among colleges; increasingly, this separation also occurs *within* individual colleges, particularly at public universities.[39] Separate admissions standards are often established for popular academic programs, especially at community colleges, forcing some students into less-lucrative or less-popular fields. Honors colleges, which provide special sections and other benefits to enrolled students, are a rapid growth industry in higher education; fully one-quarter of all honors programs were established at public colleges in the decade from 1989 to 1999.[40] On the other side of the academic spectrum, state officials are concerned that remedial education is increasingly provided to underprepared students, resulting in lower academic standards and persistence rates. Each of these trends has significant implications for equitable access to higher education, particularly within the public sector.

Amid all the talk of growth, there are fields in sharp decline. Those associated with agriculture—botany, horticulture, veterinary medicine, and animal science—have declined sharply since 1975. Home economics programs have fallen nearly 40 percent, and most of those programs were eliminated before 1975. Programs such as journalism, library science, and speech have been systematically eliminated across the country, and romance languages like French and German have been hard hit. These trends have been summarized by sociologist Steven Brint and his colleagues as "Old Economy," "Old Media," and "Old Culture/Identity."[41]

Despite all of these pressures toward change and differentiation, impressive stability has accompanied this tremendous growth. Disciplines established over a century ago—and some longer than that—remain at the core of the academic enterprise today. If anything, there is greater consensus within the disciplines on appropriate modes of inquiry and the established domains of content. Societal demands on the university and on knowledge construction have certainly become more complex over time, but the university has often adapted by accommodating those changes within its existing organizational structures. Despite seemingly unending specialization, conflict, and change, the university curriculum is a recognizably stable entity that has adapted remarkably to social, economic, and political demands.

Conservation and Innovation

One of the main forces of stability in the curriculum has been academic culture. Scholars have been trained to believe that one of the core missions of the university is to preserve the knowledge of past generations. The classical curriculum, while dynamic in some ways—through extracurricular lectures, literary societies, and the gradual adoption of new subjects—remained remarkably consistent for most of the colonial period and well into the nineteenth century. In an era when it was plausible to believe that Latin and Greek were essential for any man who considered himself liberally educated, the forces of stability were a powerful influence in the American college.

The effect of Christianity on the college curriculum cannot be underestimated. Although the central role of colleges in the preparation of ministers gradually declined, Christianity nevertheless remained infused throughout student life and the curriculum. Protestant revivalism, as expressed through the Great Awakenings of the 1740s and the early 1800s, found fertile ground in the American college. Indeed, one of the major sources of the Second Great Awakening was Yale University, and one historian has described colleges during this period as "revival camps."[42] The curriculum and Christianity were thus mutually reinforcing; faculty concern for the salvation of their students was paramount, and it was transmitted to students in courses such as ethics, literature, and theology.

Although science was certainly on the rise throughout the nineteenth century, there was not as sharp a divide between science and religion as is often perceived today. After the *Summa Theologica* of Thomas Aquinas, the major intellectual project of the Middle Ages was the resolution of biblical revelation with classical science and philosophy. Thus the people who were founding new colleges as an expression of religious faith were also the same people establishing science departments in these colleges, and they saw no contradiction in those two actions. The scientific method, far from undermining religion, was, rather, an instrument for the revelation of sacred truth.

Nonetheless, a gradual secularization of the Protestant university took hold over the course of the nineteenth and twentieth centuries. As new subjects were added to the curriculum at a rapid pace, their connection to the religious mission of the college was often increasingly tenuous. Protestant leaders, for their part, valued religious tolerance and a unified American culture, making it difficult to retain denominational separatism and distinctive religious missions.[43] As the nature of the multiversity became the secular pursuit of knowledge, religion was increasingly unimportant to the college mission, and leaders of the academy themselves were drawn from prominent academics rather than ministers. The declining influence of Christianity was quite gradual; Wellesley College, for example, did not eliminate required chapel until 1968.[44]

The secularization of the university was not entirely welcomed, and neither was the liberalization of academic requirements. Robert M. Hutchins, the University of Chicago president who led the attack on distribution requirements during the 1930s and 1940s, began to think about resurrecting more traditional curricula that would meet the standards of an earlier era. He was encouraged by John Erskine's General Honors course at Columbia University, which was an extension of the War Issues course developed by Erskine for outgoing American soldiers during World War I. Erskine designed the course in response to what he saw as the increasing specialization and vocationalism in college education, and his students read fifty-two classics—from Homer to William James—in a single year.[45] Hutchins soon taught a course of his own, first to high school students, and then as a Great Books course at the University of Chicago, limited to twenty students by invitation.

The Great Books idea was highly influential both inside and outside of the university, leading to a small industry of book publishing and discussion groups during the 1940s and 1950s. This was initiated by the publication of Hutchins's caustic *The Higher Learning in America* in 1936, which derided the vocationalism and intellectual content of higher education and prescribed a new course centered on the classics.[46] His book was an instant bestseller despite—or perhaps because of—its rather elitist attitude toward college education. Ten years later, Hutchins left the Chicago presidency to assist the Great Books movement, which had inspired a charitable foundation, discussion groups throughout the country, and a rather lucrative company that published approved selections as *The Great Books of the Western World*.[47]

Adherents of the Great Books method were so pleased with the results of the courses at Columbia, Chicago, and elsewhere that they were eager to revamp an entire college based on the premise. The opportunity presented itself when two-hundred-year-old St. John's College announced that it would close, due to budget problems.[48] Stringfellow Barr and Scott Buchanan, Great Books adherents at the University of Virginia, decided to try and save the college by instituting a four-year prescribed course in the classics. The "New Program" curriculum that they developed, based on the Chicago and Columbia models but with the addition of a substantial amount of science and mathematics, has remained largely as it was since its creation in 1939.[49]

St. John's College was only one of many experimental colleges founded during the postwar period, with the 1950s and 1960s being a particularly fertile time. In its willingness to upend the foundations of the college curriculum, this period is virtually unmatched in American history. Prominent examples include the University of California at Santa Cruz (UCSC), whose cluster colleges tried to break down the multiversity into manageable organizational units, each with its own distinctive character. As one example, UCSC's Kresge College experimented with using t-groups in courses inspired by the 1960s encounter movement, founded by Carl Rogers.[50] Another example is Black Mountain College, which attracted famous writers and artists from across the country to its utopian community in North Carolina until its collapse in 1956.[51]

The 1960s served as a period of experimentation even within traditional colleges. The emergence of national student movements and the breakdown of social conformity that characterized the post–World War II era pressured colleges to alter traditional curricular and pedagogical practices. For student activists, the curriculum had become far too abstracted from relevant political and social concerns. The best-known group was Students for a Democratic Society (SDS), which formed in 1960 to organize students around the social concerns of the period, primarily social justice issues and the Vietnam War.[52] Because the university graduated the future leaders of the country, the SDS viewed reforming the university as essential to promoting social change.

Resistance to the idea of "politicizing" the university curriculum was strong, so SDS members moved to create "free universities" where any student could study or teach, and where individuals in the university community, regardless of academic qualifications, were welcome to participate. In free universities, the political neutrality of courses and instructors was explicitly rejected, because the mission was to encourage political activism to improve society. Any form of grading was often eliminated as irrelevant to the learning process. Over time, free universities were widely accepted at colleges across the country. Indeed, they were so successful that militant students, seeing that free universities were peacefully coexisting with the traditional curriculum, became disenchanted with their ability to transform the university and eventually abandoned them.[53]

As the 1960s came to a close, many students and faculty became cynical about the ability of universities to inspire social change. The persistence of the Vietnam War and the student killings at Kent State and Jackson State universities in 1970 coincided with an overall contraction in university growth. Student activism declined dramatically, reaching record lows in the 1980s and 1990s. The major curricular experiments in higher education had, one by one, failed to achieve their goals, leading to further cynicism and apathy. In future decades, curricular reforms would be significantly less ambitious, but would nevertheless influence the core of the educational enterprise. In an incremental manner, these changes would ultimately have more impact on the curriculum than the most ambitious experimental colleges.

The influence of technology on the modern curriculum is undeniable.[54] The information technology revolution of the 1970s and 1980s has transformed how students conduct their work and how they expect to obtain and transmit information. Improving a student's ability to use technology is often explicitly stated as part of the core educational mission of undergraduate education, and the "digital divide" is a key issue among those concerned with equity and access. The widespread adoption of the Internet by colleges and universities during the 1980s and 1990s has revolutionized our ability to obtain vast quantities of information and synthesize it in a short time. Classroom teaching itself has been changed through the use of computer laboratories, educational software, and sophisticated presentation techniques.

New forms of learning have emerged to take advantage of new technologies. Distance education, which allows instructors and students to connect visually across multiple classroom locations, has expanded access to higher education for those who live vast distances from a university or who are determined to seek out programs that are outside their local communities. The Internet has created innumerable opportunities for online education, where students communicate solely by discussion groups, e-mail, video chat rooms, podcasts, and instant messaging. More recently, even mainstream programs have begun to experiment with combining both traditional and virtual modes of instruction as the needs of students, faculty, and the subject dictate. Many institutions now require students to purchase laptop computers, and they include the cost in financial aid packages; for a few years, Duke University famously gave iPods to the entire freshman class. Although proclamations of the death of the traditional university have proved to be premature, there has been an undeniable change in the nature of academic work for many students and faculty.

Other forms of curricular experimentation are making their claims on the university as well, often with remarkable success. One prominent example is the development of experiential education and service-learning programs. Service learning emerged in the experimental fervor of the 1960s from the same social movements that led to the creation of the SDS and the free universities.[55] Consonant with the ideals of the time, service learning was a means for students to engage and transform society through efforts that were rewarded with academic credit by the university. At first, service learning was simply a loosely defined group of internships and volunteer activities, many with a political or nonprofit bent. As notions of community service expanded into society throughout the 1980s and 1990s, service-learning programs grew in importance and were co-opted, becoming increasingly apolitical. Over time, service learning has emerged as an identifiable and legitimate mode of inquiry, with applications across the fields of study, and it serves as a demonstration of the university's commitment to public service.

Curriculum reform has also been aimed at improving student persistence and graduation rates, particularly at community colleges and public comprehensive universities. In "learning communities," groups of students enroll simultaneously in a sequence of courses, or even an entire academic program, instead of choosing those courses separately. These courses often have a unifying theme that draws students and faculty together to study one topic intensively. Although research in this area remains embryonic, learning communities seem to promote student persistence by providing classroom experiences that are more meaningful for students, and by building support structures among the students themselves.[56] Another effort to address dropout rates has been to use "supplemental instruction" in the classroom, which provides coursework in basic skills for underprepared students enrolled in traditional credit-bearing courses, rather than segregating them into separate remedial courses. Data on these programs suggests that students in supplemental instruction earn higher grades and are more likely to persist than their peers.[57]

Understanding Curriculum Change

For many observers, the curriculum is an "academic graveyard" where ideas for educational reform go to die. It is widely believed that the curriculum simply does not change, and that reforms never move forward, but merely swing from one extreme to the other over the course of time. On the contrary, significant changes in the curriculum have occurred in American higher education throughout its history. Although revolutionary change in the curriculum has been rare, incremental changes have often accumulated over time to create significant and lasting impacts.[58] By using the curriculum as a lens for social change, we can see the effect of society's demands on higher education, and how universities have sought to define the boundaries of knowledge and thereby influence how the public views social issues.

Knowledge differentiation is certainly a key factor in curricular change. For some, knowledge is the prime unit of analysis, putting constant pressure on the university organization to adapt to its increasing complexity.[59] To cope with these unrelenting pressures, the curriculum must accommodate them by altering the content and form of courses, as well as the requirements and organization of programs and departments. Unending differentiation thus yields an organization that is remarkably adaptable to the range of demands placed upon it, but it faces increasing problems of integration, since students and faculty have less in common when they move further and further apart. In this perspective, general education for all students can never be resurrected, because it is impossible to build a consensus across the university on which types of knowledge are most valuable to undergraduates.[60]

Curricular change can also be understood as an inhabitant of the organizational culture that supports it.[61] In this view, the curriculum is socially constructed among the constituents of the university, who interact with one another to create meaning. The curriculum itself signifies changes in the faculty's underlying assumptions about what counts as knowledge, what knowledge is most worthy of transmission, and what organizational forms are most appropriate. The curriculum also serves as a form of organizational culture for students, socializing them into the content and skills needed to navigate the world of the university. From this perspective, in order to understand curricular change, we must first understand the organizational culture of the university, and then identify the mechanisms by which faculty and students interact within the curriculum to construct the meaning of knowledge.

Social movements can also be a key motivator for curricular change.[62] Traditional accounts of curricular change have often cited changing student demographics—increasing numbers of racial and ethnic minorities, women, and sexual minorities in the university—as the main causal factor behind change in the curriculum. With this explanation, there has been little understanding of how these demographics have led to actual change in the curriculum. One answer is social movements, which have organized students and faculty around political and identity-based causes so as to make demands for new programs and departments in the curriculum. Earlier, we saw how the Black Power movement, leftist movements, and feminists have marshaled themselves to create new content and produce new organizational structures in the curriculum.

The construction of the curriculum can also be connected to powerful politi-cal and economic actors in society.[63] As both the government and profit-seeking corporations have become increasingly involved in the funding of university re-search activities, their influence on the curriculum in departments and programs closely connected to those agencies has become apparent. For-profit corporations make grants to science departments and business schools; the government pours substantial funds into medical schools, science departments, and schools of edu-cation. In addition, nonprofit foundations are often significant providers of funds in the humanities and the social sciences. Although it is not yet clear how these connections yield specific changes in coursework or organizational structures, these actors are undoubtedly powerful resource providers exerting a marked in-fluence on research-oriented faculty.

Finally, we must consider efforts to influence undergraduate education through state policy. Nonpartisan organizations, including the Education Com-mission of the States and the National Center for Public Policy and Higher Edu-cation, have been sharply critical of the inability of states and colleges to im-prove teaching or monitor progress on student learning.[64] State policymakers in Ohio and Massachusetts have been equally disparaging about faculty productiv-ity and about more time being spent on research and service than on teaching.[65] Increasingly, states are considering the use of measures such as Graduate Record Exam scores, critical-thinking inventories, and even high-stakes graduation ex-ams to improve and assess undergraduate instruction. Regional accreditation agencies now routinely require institutions to use assessment instruments that evaluate student learning outcomes. Although these ideas are still in their early stages, policy makers expect this to be a major policy issue throughout the next decade.

NOTES

1. Douglas Sloan, "Harmony, Chaos, and Consensus: The American College Cur-riculum," *Teachers College Record* 73 (1971): 221–51.

2. Frederick Rudolph, *Curriculum: A History of the Undergraduate Course of Study since 1636* (San Francisco: Jossey-Bass, 1977). Rudolph's work is still the standard for historical examination of the college curriculum, and his influence can be seen throughout this chapter.

3. John D. Burton, "The Harvard Tutors: The Beginning of the Academic Profes-sion, 1690–1825," *History of Higher Education Annual* 16 (1996): 1–17.

4. James McLachlan, "The 'Choice of Hercules': American Student Societies in the Early 19th Century," in *The University in Society*, ed. Lawrence Stone (Princeton, NJ: Princeton University Press, 1974), vol. 2, 449–94; Rudolph, *Curriculum*, 95–98.

5. Although this effort was successful, the lectures were not incorporated into the standard curriculum, and attending students were required to get permission from their parents. See Rudolph, *Curriculum*, 39.

6. Ibid., 55.

7. "The Yale Report of 1828," in *American Higher Education: A Documentary History*, ed. Richard Hofstadter and Wilson Smith (Chicago: University of Chicago Press, 1961), vol. 1, 275–91 (emphasis in the original).

8. For extensive discussion of the Yale Report, see Jack C. Lane, "The Yale Report of 1828 and Liberal Education: A Neorepublican Manifesto," *History of Education Quarterly* 27 (1987): 325–38; Melvin I. Usofsky, "Reforms and Response: The Yale Report of 1828," *History of Education Quarterly* 5 (1965): 53–67; Rudolph, *Curriculum*. Rudolph has been strongly criticized for overestimating the effect of the Yale Report. See David B. Potts, "Curriculum and Enrollments: Some Thoughts on Assessing the Popularity of Antebellum Colleges," in *The American College in the Nineteenth Century*, ed. Roger Geiger (Nashville. TN: Vanderbilt University Press, 2000).

9. Hugh Hawkins, *Between Harvard and America: The Educational Leadership of Charles W. Eliot* (New York: Oxford University Press, 1972); Phyllis Keller, *Getting at the Core: Curricular Reform at Harvard* (Cambridge, MA: Harvard University Press, 1982).

10. David Riesman, *Constraint and Variety in American Education* (Garden City, NY: Doubleday, 1958).

11. Gilbert Allardyce, "The Rise and Fall of the Western Civilization Course," *American Historical Review* 87 (1982): 695–725.

12. Carol S. Gruber, *Mars and Minerva: World War I and the Uses of the Higher Learning in America* (Baton Rouge: Louisiana State University Press, 1975).

13. Paul H. Buck et al., *General Education in a Free Society: A Report of the Harvard Committee* (Cambridge, MA: Harvard University Press, 1945).

14. Ironically, the Harvard faculty never formally adopted the report, and it had far more influence outside of Harvard than within it. See Bruce A. Kimball, *Orators and Philosophers: A History of the Idea of Liberal Education* (New York: College Entrance Examination Board, 1995).

15. Daniel Bell, *The Reforming of General Education: The Columbia College Experience in Its National Setting* (New York: Columbia University Press, 1966), 8.

16. Leo Strauss, *Liberalism Ancient and Modern* (New York: Basic Books, 1968), 3, 7.

17. Robert L. Belknap and Richard Kuhns, *Tradition and Innovation* (New York: Columbia University Press, 1977), 23.

18. Allan Bloom, *The Closing of the American Mind* (New York: Simon and Schuster, 1987), 37.

19. Dinesh D'Souza, *Illiberal Education* (New York: Free Press, 1991).

20. Lynne V. Cheney, *50 Hours: A Core Curriculum for College Students* (Washington, DC: National Endowment for the Humanities, 1989).

21. W. B. Carnochan, *The Battleground of the Curriculum: Liberal Education and the American Experience* (Stanford, CA: Stanford University Press, 1993); Lawrence W. Levine, *The Opening of the American Mind* (Boston: Beacon Press, 1996); John K. Wilson, *The Myth of Political Correctness: The Conservative Attack on Higher Education* (Durham, NC: Duke University Press, 1995).

22. Martha Nussbaum, *Cultivating Humanity: A Classical Defense of Reform in Liberal Education* (Cambridge, MA: Harvard University Press, 1997).

23. American Council of Trustees and Alumni, *What Will They Learn? A Report on General Education Requirements at 100 of the Nation's Leading Colleges and Universities* (Washington, DC: American Council of Trustees and Alumni, 2009).

24. Walter P. Metzger, "The Academic Profession in the United States," in *The Academic Profession*, ed. Burton R. Clark (Berkeley: University of California Press, 1987), 123–208. See also Laurence R. Veysey, *The Emergence of the American University* (Chicago: University of Chicago Press, 1965), 121–70.

25. Metzger, "Academic Profession," 128.

26. On the beginnings of the social sciences, see Dorothy Ross, *The Origins of American Social Science* (Cambridge: Cambridge University Press, 1991); Thomas Haskell, *The Emergence of Professional Social Science* (Urbana: University of Illinois Press, 1977).

27. For a brilliant discussion of the origins of the research seminar and the fall of the disputation, see William Clark, *Academic Charisma and the Origins of the Research University* (Chicago: University of Chicago Press, 2006).

28. For more on the differentiation of knowledge, see Burton R. Clark, *The Higher Education System* (Berkeley: University of California Press, 1983); Patricia J. Gumport and Stuart K. Snydman, "The Formal Organization of Knowledge: An Analysis of Academic Structure," *Journal of Higher Education* 73 (2002): 375–408.

29. The definitive statement on professions is by Andrew Abbott, *The System of Professions: An Essay on the Expert Division of Labor* (Chicago: University of Chicago Press, 1988).

30. Steven Brint, "The Rise of the Practical Arts," in *The Future of the City of Intellect: The Changing American University*, ed. Steven Brint (Stanford, CA: Stanford University Press, 2002), 231–59. For an empirical analysis, see Steven Brint, Mark Riddle, Lori Turk-Bicakci, and Charles S. Levy, "From the Liberal to the Practical Arts in American Colleges and Universities: Organizational Analysis and Curricular Change," *Journal of Higher Education* 76 (2005): 151–80. On the increasing vocational orientation of traditional liberal arts colleges, see Matthew S. Kraatz and Edward J. Zajac, "Exploring the Limits of the New Institutionalism: The Causes and Consequences of Illegitimate Organizational Change," *American Sociological Review* 61 (1996): 812–36.

31. Philip G. Altbach, *Student Politics in America: A Historical Analysis* (New York: McGraw-Hill, 1974); Sheila A. Slaughter, "Class, Race, and Gender and the Construction

of Post-Secondary Curricula in the United States," *Journal of Curriculum Studies* 29 (1997): 1–30; Julie A. Reuben, "Reforming the University: Student Protests and the Demand for a Relevant Curriculum," in *Student Protest: The Sixties and After*, ed. Gerard De Groot (New York: Longman, 1998), 153–68.

32. Fabio Rojas, *From Black Power to Black Studies: How a Radical Social Movement Became an Academic Discipline* (Baltimore: Johns Hopkins University Press, 2007).

33. Joy Ann Williamson, *Black Power on Campus: The University of Illinois, 1965–1975* (Urbana: University of Illinois Press, 2003).

34. Marilyn J. Boxer, *When Women Ask the Questions: Creating Women's Studies in America* (Baltimore: Johns Hopkins University Press, 1998); Patricia J. Gumport, *Academic Pathfinders: Knowledge Creation and Feminist Scholarship* (Westport, CT: Greenwood Press, 2002).

35. Thomas J. La Belle and Christopher R. Ward, *Ethnic Studies and Multiculturalism* (Albany: State University of New York Press, 1996); Janice L. Ristock and Catherine G. Taylor, *Inside the Academy and Out: Queer Studies and Social Action* (Toronto: University of Toronto Press, 1998). Growth in these fields is demonstrated in Steven Brint, Lori Turk-Bicakci, Kristopher Proctor, Scott Patrick Murphy, and Robert A. Hanneman, "The Market Model and the Growth and Decline of Academic Fields in U.S. Colleges and Universities, 1975–2000," working paper, University of California at Riverside.

36. Lisa R. Lattuca, *Creating Interdisciplinarity* (Nashville, TN: Vanderbilt University Press, 2001). For a longitudinal examination of the growth of interdisciplinary programs and fields, see Steven Brint, Lori Turk-Bicakci, Kristopher Proctor, and Scott Patrick Murphy, "Expanding the Social Frame of Knowledge: Interdisciplinary, Degree-Granting Fields in American Colleges and Universities, 1975–2000," *Review of Higher Education* 32 (2009): 155–83.

37. Andrew Abbott, *Chaos of Disciplines* (Chicago: University of Chicago Press, 2001). For a compressed version of the argument, see Andrew Abbott, "The Disciplines and the Future," in Brint, *Future of the City of Intellect*, 205–30.

38. Michael N. Bastedo and Patricia J. Gumport, "Access to What? Mission Differentiation and Academic Stratification in U.S. Public Higher Education," *Higher Education* 46 (2003): 341–59; Patricia J. Gumport and Michael N. Bastedo, "Academic Stratification and Endemic Conflict: Remedial Education Policy at the City University of New York," *Review of Higher Education* 24 (2001): 333–49.

39. See Michael N. Bastedo, "Convergent Institutional Logics in Public Higher Education: State Policymaking and Governing Board Activism," *Review of Higher Education* 32 (2009): 209–34.

40. At private colleges, the figure is 39 percent. See Bridget Terry Long, "Attracting the Best: The Use of Honors Programs and Colleges to Compete for Students," working paper, Harvard University.

41. Brint et al., "Market Model," 55.

42. Sloan, "Harmony, Chaos, and Consensus," 227–32.

43. George M. Marsden, "The Soul of the American University: A Historical Overview," in *The Secularization of the Academy*, ed. George M. Marsden and Bradley J. Longfield (New York: Oxford University Press, 1992).

44. Ibid.

45. James Sloan Allen, *The Romance of Commerce and Culture* (Chicago: University of Chicago Press, 1983); Joan Shelley Rubin, *The Making of Middlebrow Culture* (Chapel Hill: University of North Carolina Press, 1992).

46. Robert M. Hutchins, *The Higher Learning in America* (New Haven, CT: Yale University Press, 1936).

47. Allen, *Romance of Commerce and Culture*; Robert M. Hutchins, ed., *The Great Books of the Western World* (Chicago: Encyclopedia Britannica, 1952). See also Alex Beam, *A Great Idea at the Time: The Rise, Fall, and Curious Afterlife of the Great Books* (New York: PublicAffairs, 2008).

48. Gerald Grant and David Riesman, *The Perpetual Dream: Reform and Experiment in the American College* (Chicago: University of Chicago Press, 1978).

49. Ibid., 40–76. Outside of St. John's, very few Great Books programs exist today. Prominent holdouts are the general education programs at Columbia University and the University of Chicago, and Stanford's Structured Liberal Education option.

50. Grant and Riesman, *Perpetual Dream*, 77–134.

51. Martin Duberman, *Black Mountain: An Exploration in Community* (New York: E. P. Dutton, 1972).

52. Altbach, *Student Politics in America*, 221–26; Reuben, "Reforming the University."

53. Reuben, "Reforming the University," 156. Few of the free universities exist today. At Oberlin, the Experimental College (ExCo) sponsors dozens of student-taught courses every year, and students may earn up to five ExCo credits toward graduation either by teaching or by enrolling in these courses.

54. Robert C. Heterick, Jr., *Reengineering Teaching and Learning in Higher Education: Sheltered Groves, Camelot, Windmills, and Malls* (Boulder: CAUSE, 1993); Martin J. Finkelstein, *Dollars, Distance, and Online Education: The New Economics of College Teaching and Learning* (Phoenix: Oryx Press, 2000). For a more critical perspective, see David F. Noble, *Digital Diploma Mills: The Automation of Higher Education* (New York: Monthly Review Press, 2001).

55. Timothy K. Stanton, Dwight E. Giles, Jr., and Nadine I. Cruz, *Service-Learning: A Movement's Pioneers Reflect on Its Origins, Practice, and Future* (San Francisco: Jossey-Bass, 1999); Janet Eyler and Dwight E. Giles, Jr., *Where's the Learning in Service Learning?* (San Francisco: Jossey-Bass, 1999).

56. Vincent Tinto, "Classrooms as Communities: Exploring the Educational Character of Student Persistence," *Journal of Higher Education* 68 (1997): 599–623; Faith Gabelnick, Jean MacGregor, Roberta S. Matthews, and Barbara Leigh Smith, *Learning Communities: Creating Connections among Students, Faculty, and Disciplines* (San Francisco: Jossey-Bass, 1990).

57. Deanna C. Martin and David R. Arendale, *Supplemental Instruction: Increasing Achievement and Retention* (San Francisco: Jossey-Bass, 1994).

58. For a framework for understanding incremental change in the curriculum, see Larry Cuban, *How Scholars Trumped Teachers: Change Without Reform in University Curriculum, Teaching, and Research, 1890–1990* (New York: Teachers College Press, 1999); see also David Tyack and Larry Cuban, *Tinkering Toward Utopia: A Century of Public School Reform* (Cambridge, MA: Harvard University Press, 1995), esp. 60–109.

59. Clark, *Higher Education System*.

60. Burton R. Clark, "The Problem of Complexity in Modern Higher Education," in *The European and American University since 1800*, ed. Sheldon Rothblatt and Björn Wittrock (Cambridge: Cambridge University Press, 1993), 263–79.

61. William G. Tierney, *Curricular Landscapes, Democratic Vistas* (New York: Praeger, 1989); Patricia J. Gumport, "Curricula as Signposts of Cultural Change," *Review of Higher Education* 12 (1988): 49–62.

62. See, for example, Scott Frickel and Neil Gross, "A General Theory of Scientific/Intellectual Movements," *American Sociological Review* 70 (2005): 204–32; Rojas, *Black Power to Black Studies*; Fabio Rojas, "Social Movement Tactics, Organizational Change, and the Spread of African-American Studies," *Social Forces* 84 (2006): 2147–66.

63. Sheila A. Slaughter, "The Political Economy of Curriculum-Making in the United States," in Brint, *Future of the City of Intellect*; Slaughter, "Class, Race, and Gender."

64. Dennis P. Jones and Peter Ewell, *The Effect of State Policy on Undergraduate Education* (Denver: National Center for Higher Education Management Systems, 1993); National Center for Public Policy and Higher Education, *Measuring Up 2008* (San Jose, CA: National Center for Public Policy and Higher Education, 2008).

65. Michael N. Bastedo, "The Making of an Activist Governing Board," *Review of Higher Education* 28 (2005): 551–70; Carol L. Colbeck, "State Policies to Improve Undergraduate Teaching: Administrator and Faculty Responses," *Journal of Higher Education* 73 (2002): 3–25.

CHAPTER SIXTEEN

Markets in Higher Education

Trends in Academic Capitalism

Sheila Slaughter and Gary Rhoades

A n *academic capitalist knowledge-learning regime* is characterized by the increased commercialization of colleges and universities.[1] On the administrative side, commercialism pervades growing numbers of offices and services, ranging from enrollment management offices in student personnel services that "market" institutions to student consumers, to creative products offices that manage faculty copyrights in intellectual property departments. On the academic side, commercialization spreads across the curriculum: from science and engineering, where discoveries are patented and marketed, to a variety of other fields that market courseware and other instructional materials. The entrepreneurial initiatives do not benefit all students equally, nor do they necessarily generate large amounts of external revenue for institutions, although they sometimes cause them to incur serious costs. Commercialization is instituted by many actors, internal and external to colleges and universities, who seek to take advantages of the new opportunities created by the neoliberal state.

Numerous federal and state initiatives provide a policy framework for what we call an academic capitalist knowledge-learning regime. Among these initiatives are competitiveness-coalition legislation such as the America COMPETES Act

(2007), which provides new and generous funding to science, technology, engineering, and mathematics fields to enhance economic development, innovation, and the United States' ability to compete in the global economy.[2] In this chapter, we focus on three broad federal initiatives: a federal student financial aid policy that gives money to students rather than institutions (student as consumer); patent law and policies that marketize segments of the sciences and engineering; and copyright law and policies, along with information technology law and policies, that provide opportunities for colleges and universities to market curricula. The period in which the academic capitalist knowledge-learning regime developed is approximately from 1980 to 2000. It continues to accelerate in the twenty-first century.

Within sections, we first describe the federal policy sets that we see as supporting academic capitalism, and then examine the way institutions intersect these initiatives. The presentation of laws and policies is followed by selected examples that illustrate the academic capitalist knowledge-learning regime. We conclude each section by looking at various data sets that allow us to use financial indicators (tuition, income from patents, income from distance education) to track changes. On the whole, we see the academic capitalism knowledge-learning regime as intensifying in the 2000s.

Although we begin with the federal government, we do not see the federal government as the sole policy driver for the academic capitalist knowledge-learning regime. Federal and state laws and policies, as well as institutional rules and policies, interact in complex ways to produce knowledge-learning regimes.[3] States have an array of initiatives that promote economic development. Many of these initiatives, ranging from preparing students for the workforce to fostering industries that contribute to the states' economic base, feature the participation of colleges and universities.[4] Indeed, several states frequently devise innovative solutions to pressing national problems before the federal government does.[5] Moreover, colleges and universities are not simply acted upon, or *corporatized*. Actors within colleges and universities participate in creating new knowledge-learning regimes by networking and partnering with an array of external actors. Segments of the administration and the faculty work to shape the politico-legal climate that fosters an academic capitalist knowledge-learning regime, and segments of the faculty and administration actively and ardently engage in commercialization. They are reinforced by judicial decisions, administrative law, executive orders, bureaucratic procedures, and institutional policies at both the state and federal levels.

Because this chapter focuses on policy, we want to clarify the theory of the state that informs our work. We see the academic capitalist knowledge-learning regime and the three policy sets on which we focus as tied to the rise of the *neoliberal state*.[6] The neoliberal state focuses not on social welfare for the citizenry as a whole, but on enabling individuals and corporations (which, in the United States, are legally considered as individual persons who are economic actors). The neoliberal state concentrates its funding in state agencies that contribute to economic growth—for example, research funding for corporations and academic fields that produce exploitable intellectual property. The neoliberal state works to build the "new" economy, which is a knowledge, or information, economy. The neoliberal state attempts to articulate national economies with global economies. To provide funds to reshape the economy, the neoliberal state often institutes processes of deregulation, commercialization, and privatization, re-regulating in order to create a state that no longer provides "entitlements" such as welfare. Instead, the neoliberal state often restructures and reduces general services such as health care, social security and education. The benefits of the neoliberal state tend be distributed somewhat differently from those of the welfare state. They do not accrue to the citizenry as a whole; instead, they are acquired unevenly by various groups, often by the upper-middle-class closely associated with the growth of the new economy, and by the rich. Because higher education is simultaneously a welfare function of the state and a contributor to economic growth, the policy process often plays out in ironic, contradictory, and perhaps unintended ways, which we describe below.

Student Financial Aid

Despite the rhetoric of student as consumer, which implies that all students are able to make informed choices among the many U.S. institutions of higher education, federal student financial aid legislation segments the student markets in higher education, directing different types of aid to very different kinds of students. Some programs and appropriation patterns encourage upper-middle-class as well as knowledgeable, able students from other social strata to attend costly elite, (increasingly) private institutions.[7] Other programs and appropriation patterns encourage large numbers of adult learners to upgrade their education to master skills appropriate to the new economy through two-year and four-year programs, sometimes with substantial distance-education components, and increasingly through for-profit higher education institutions.

In the early 1970s, federal legislation shifted from institutional to student aid, making students consumers.[8] The Committee on Economic Development, together with a number of foundations, particularly the Carnegie Foundation for the Advancement of Teaching, worked assiduously for the *marketization* of higher education. The mechanism of marketization was federal financial aid placed in the hands of students. When students were able to spend their grants at the institution of their choice, proponents of what was perhaps the first educational voucher program argued that they were introducing market discipline to institutions of higher education, forcing colleges and universities to provide better services at lower costs to attract students. The Committee on Economic Development and Carnegie also pushed strongly for all postsecondary students, whether enrolled in public or private institutions, to pay for one-third to one-half of the costs of their education, a not unrealistic expectation in what was then a low-tuition era.[9]

Student choice in this context preferred the private colleges and universities, because the (public) grants for students attending private nonprofit schools were larger than those for students attending publics. In other words, students received a greater amount of government assistance to attend more costly private institutions, while students who attended public institutions had to pay more out of their own pockets as the cost of tuition gradually rose to one-third to one-half of the total cost of an education. The market model of higher education encouraged competition, but it did not reduce costs, a phenomenon that was in keeping with the philosophy of the neoliberal state, which sought to reduce programs for all citizens and shift costs to users. Of course, increasing tuition so that students bore a greater share of the cost of public higher education reduced the cost to the state, always an interest of taxpaying businesses. By the 1980s and 1990s, higher education was construed less as a necessary public or social good and more as an individual or private good, justifying "user pays" policies.[10]

Federal policy supported quasi-market competition for students among institutions of higher education, on the grounds of greater efficiencies that would lead to cost reductions. Ironically, as the market model became entrenched, costs escalated.[11] Although costs went up in all market segments, niche markets developed in which a relatively small number of (largely upper- and upper-middle-class) students competed nationally for ever-more-expensive places at a relatively small number of (elite and increasingly private) institutions. Federal loan programs enabled middle- and upper-middle-class students, especially those attending high-cost elite private institutions, to meet higher tuition costs. In effect, federal loans subsidized markets for students by providing some students with the funds to choose high-tuition institutions.[12]

As the shift from grants to loans benefited those families and students with the ability to repay the loans, so some programs in the Taxpayer Relief Act of 1997 benefited families with money to protect. The Taxpayer Relief Act included several programs: Hope scholarships, penalty-free individual retirement account (IRA) withdrawals for college expenses, tax-sheltered college savings accounts, and a tax credit for lifelong learning. Hope scholarships provided a $1,500 nonrefundable tax credit for the first two years of college, which phased out for individuals earning $40,000–$50,000 per year or couples earning $80,000–$100,000 per year. Penalty-free IRA withdrawals would not count as gross income, so long as they paid for college expenses. Additionally, families could shelter up to $500 per year for each child in the same way as contributions to an IRA; these savings would be taxed as an IRA, so long as the funds were spent on college expenses. This program was capped for families earning $150,000–$160,000 per year. The subsidies provided by tax credits are not trivial. "The package of tax credits and tax deductions has been estimated to cost $39 billion in the first five years [of the Taxpayer Relief Act], making it slightly larger than the Pell Grant program, the primary federal grant program for low income youth."[13] The increased ability of these well-to-do or market-knowledgeable and academically able students to pay for their postsecondary education makes them preferred customers for elite institutions.

Although the 1997 Taxpayer Relief Act applied primarily to nonprofit institutions of higher education, whether public or private, some programs within the act benefited working adults seeking further education to better compete in the new economy. The tax credit for lifelong learning offered a nonrefundable tax credit for undergraduate and graduate education that was worth up to 29 percent of up to $5,000 per year spent on tuition and fees through 2002, and 20 percent of up to $10,000 per year after that, with the same income caps as the Hope scholarships. The tax credit for lifelong learning expanded markets for for-profits, such as the University of Phoenix, which for a number of years required its attending students to have jobs. The tax credit also created opportunities for increasing numbers of public institutions, such as the University of Maryland University College, that emulated for-profits by serving working adults retooling for the new economy. As all students paid a greater share of the cost of their tuition and fees, the costs to working adults who returned to school to improve their position in the new economy were normalized, even though those students paid a greater share of their income for tuition than did well-to-do, traditional-age students.[14]

The 1998 Higher Education Act further contributed to marketization, through new provisions that encouraged profit taking in higher education by creating a number of special provisions to aid for-profit postsecondary education. The law made it easier for for-profit higher education to appeal federal penalties stemming from their students' defaults on loans. Given that for-profits have an excessively high default rate, this was an important provision. Additionally, the law no longer required unannounced accreditation visits, allowing for-profit postsecondary educational institutions to prepare for inspections, making sure students were in class. Most importantly, the law no longer treated for-profits as a separate category; they were redefined as institutions of higher education. This allowed for-profits to share in federal aid. Their students were twice as likely to receive federal aid as students at nonprofits, and at the two-year level, their students received more federal aid than comparable students in public institutions. The 1998 Higher Education Act further signaled federal governmental support for for-profits by creating a special liaison within the U.S. Department of Education for proprietary schools, a privilege previously held only by historically black tertiary educational institutions and community colleges.[15]

Changes in student aid legislation over the past thirty years contributed to the academic capitalist knowledge-learning regime by marketizing higher education. The legislation made students (partially) state-subsidized consumers in quasi markets for higher education.[16] According to the rhetoric surrounding marketization, markets empowered students by making them consumers, allowing them to use their grant or loan to discipline markets to better serve them. However, markets in higher education seem to work like all other markets. Far from being perfectly competitive, offering goods and services at the lowest price to any buyer, (deregulated and re-regulated) markets tend to favor the middle and upper-middle class.[17] Just as housing markets prefer middle-class customers with high credit ratings who are unlikely to be loan risks, and then indirectly subsidize them through mortgage tax deductions, so markets in higher education prefer students (and families) who are confident they can repay loans and are indirectly subsidized through parental tax relief and the higher grant or loan aid attached to private institutions. Ironically, market legislation, which defined higher education as a private benefit captured by individuals, prefers the middle and upper-middle classes.

Student aid legislation also contributed to market segmentation. While middle- and upper-middle-class students became preferred customers, lower-middle-class students and working adults entered two-year colleges, four-year college programs with substantial distance-education components, and for-profit institutions of higher education. Given that many do not complete a degree at two-year colleges, they receive just-in-time education that channels them, with only a modicum of skills, into entry-level jobs in the new economy. Working adults in four-year programs often receive college degrees for what amounts to retraining or professional development, allowing them to upgrade their skills to better serve the needs of the new-economy corporations where they are already employed. Although these students do not receive dramatic returns on their investment in human capital, they are often satisfied with their education, because they do better than if they had not acquired some college education or a degree.

Since the early 1980s, the cost of college has risen steadily. In constant (1996) dollars, the average tuition at U.S. four-year public institutions has increased by nearly 128 percent between 1980 and 2002. Private four-year institutions' tuitions have increased more rapidly, over 130 percent in constant dollars over this twenty-two-year period.[18] In 2002, tuition and fees at four-year private institutions averaged $18,273 and room and board averaged $6,779; when tuition and fees and room and board are combined, the average cost of attending a private college or university was $25,052. For a four-year public college or university, the average 2002 costs were $4,081 for tuition and fees and $5,327 for room and board; combined, the average cost was $9,408.[19] According to the College Board, by 2009–10, before discounts based on individual student characteristics, the average costs for tuition, room, board, and books were as follows: for public universities, $19,388, up 5.8 percent from the previous year; and for private universities, $39,028, up 4.4 percent from the previous year.[20] Although tuition at community colleges is much lower, with an average published cost of $2,544 in 2009–10, federal student financial aid is often difficult for students to secure.[21] Nearly one in ten community college students are unable to apply for student federal financial aid, because their schools do not participate in the program. This forces many community college students—who are more likely to be first generation, nonwhite, and women—to drop out, take fewer classes, work more hours for pay, or turn to more expensive private loans.[22]

As the costs of higher education increased, federal financial aid in the form of grants lagged behind, and the share of family income required to pay for college tuition increased for most families. The percentage of family income, after financial aid, needed to pay for public four-year schools has risen in all but two states since 2000. In 2008, "on average, students from working and poor families must pay 40% of family income to enroll in public four-year colleges. Students from middle-income families and upper-income families must pay 25% and 13% of family income, respectively, to enroll in public four-year colleges."[23] However, federal grants to pay students' tuition have decreased since the early 1980s, while loans have increased. In 1981, loans accounted for 45 percent of student federal financial aid, and grants for 52 percent. In 2000, loans represented 58 percent of federal student financial aid, and grants 41 percent.[24] This change, which accelerated dramatically in the 1990s, shifted costs from the state to the student. At the same time, student debt rose rapidly. The "average debt levels for graduating seniors with student loans rose to $23,200 in 2008—a 24% increase from $18,650 in 2004." For public universities, the average debt was $20,200, 20 percent higher than in 2004. At private nonprofit universities, it was $27,650, 29 percent higher than in 2004. For graduating seniors with Pell Grants, 87 percent had student loans, with an average debt load of $24,800—almost $2,000 more than the average for all seniors graduating with loans.[25]

Market practices are increasingly incorporated into the recruitment of students at four-year nonprofit institutions. It is not just highly able students that colleges and universities are targeting, but well-to-do students whose parents can afford to pay full tuition with no financial aid. As Michael McPherson and Morton Shapiro put it with regard to private colleges and universities, "the simplest way to describe the change over the past decade in the way private colleges and universities approach student aid is to say that, rather than viewing student aid as a kind of charitable operation the college runs on the side, most private colleges and universities—and increasing numbers of public institutions—now regard student aid as a vital revenue management and enrollment management tool."[26]

As one commentator has suggested, "in some ways, American colleges and universities have become like airlines and hotels, practicing 'yield management' to try to maximize the revenue generated by every seat or bed. But in most cases, unlike hotels and airlines, colleges also care about who is in those seats and beds."[27] To that end, institutions develop early-decision admissions policies, no-test admission policies, and on-site admissions policies, all of which are aimed at increasing their *yield rates*, or the ratio of students who apply to those that accept. The higher the ratio, the higher the institution's rating in publications such as *U.S. News and World Report*, and, hence, the higher the market value of the institution.

Early-decision admissions processes are employed by highly selective private colleges and universities. Students commit to enrolling in an institution if they are accepted, in return for which they are notified earlier than those who apply to the regular process. Such a practice increases the institution's yield rate, ensuring an almost one-to-one ratio of admitted students to those who will enroll. That enables the institution to increase its yield, and thereby enhance its market position. Yet early-decision programs may not serve the interests of prospective students, or of society. In forcing earlier and earlier decisions that may not be freely informed by a range of options, these programs represent a case of inherent market inefficiency, what Alvin Roth and Xiaolin Xing have referred to as "unraveling."[28] Such a system may tend to disadvantage students who have less access to good counseling and less knowledge of the admissions process, characteristics that disproportionately describe students from lower socioeconomic backgrounds. Indeed, these programs tend to undermine efforts to enhance the demographic diversity of entering classes, a fact that led the University of North Carolina, Chapel Hill, to eliminate its program, and Richard Levin, president of Yale, to call for the collective abandonment of such programs among selective institutions. This call, issued in 2001, has gone unheeded at Yale, though Harvard and Princeton dropped their early admissions programs in 2006.[29]

A second example of institutions seeking to manipulate their selectivity scores in ways that do not serve consumer interests is the recent practice of several selective colleges, making SAT scores optional for applicants. The strategy's effectiveness has been documented by Marcia Yablon in an article entitled "Test Flight: The Scam behind SAT Bashing."[30] The aim is to enhance a school's acceptance rate and average SAT score by not requiring these scores for admission. Less-qualified students are encouraged apply, but only high-scoring students are likely to submit their test scores to these institutions, raising the overall selectivity profile of the institution.

"Snap apps" are another marketing tool of enrollment management offices seeking to achieve high yields. On-site admissions are an in-person, instant-admissions-decision program, often made during a prospective student's campus visit. In contrast to the early-decision process, these decisions are not binding; the student may later choose not to attend the institution. Advocates of the process see it as "a service to students and a savvy marketing tool."[31] Instant admissions benefits students, reducing the paperwork, time, and anxiety of the admissions process, as well as humanizing it. However, this type of admissions program is more typically found at less-selective institutions (for example, at the California State University System versus the University of California System, at Virginia Tech and Radford University versus the University of Virginia, and at many community colleges). By employing this process, such institutions are more likely to gain access to higher-achieving students, who are more likely to apply for instant admissions. Therein lies part of the problem, say critics of snap apps. Accelerated admissions encourage students to make decisions on the spur of the moment. Making the choice easier and more immediate for prospective students in some sense restricts their choice (though not in a legal sense), as it reduces their likelihood of shopping for colleges and exploring options that might prove to be a better fit. On-site admissions can be seen as a "hard sell" approach to recruiting students, leading students to make their decisions during their campus visit, rather than encouraging them to reflect on and deliberate about their options over time.

Although the majority of for-profits do not compete directly with two- and four-year nonprofit institutions of higher education for the "market" in students, the rapid increase in for-profit higher education is a marker of the commercialization of higher education. At the same time that nonprofit higher education institutions raised their tuition, targeting student niche markets, for-profit institutions multiplied, the number of students enrolled in them rose, and their costs went up. Between 1989 and 1999, enrollment in for-profit, degree-granting institutions increased 59 percent, totaling about 365,000 students.[32] For 2009–10, the cost of private universities rose to $39,028, and for-profit colleges saw the largest recent increase in the proportion of their students graduating with debt. In 2008, the average student debt at for-profit universities was $33,050, 23 percent higher than 2004, and substantially higher than the debt load at public and private nonprofit universities.[33] For-profit schools also have the highest federal student loan default rate. For the cohort who entered repayment in 2007, 400,000 had defaulted by 2009, representing 12 percent of all students who had entered repayment in that year. Nearly half of these borrowers (44%) attended for-profits, even though only one in fourteen students (7%) overall attend such schools.[34]

The federal student aid legislation was the first federal legislation to explicitly use market discourse. In some ways the market rhetoric was a trope for partial privatization, in that the neoliberal state effectively moved to a high tuition–low aid policy.[35] In other ways, the market rhetoric masked the continued and rising contribution by the state. Although federal financial aid has shifted from grants to loans, the amount of grant money available (although not the amount of the grant per individual) has risen every year, and many loans are publicly subsidized. At the state level, support for higher education increased 13 percent (in constant dollars) from 1980 to 1998, but tuition increased faster. In other words, the student markets for nonprofits and for-profits are heavily subsidized at both the state and federal levels.

Federal and state student financial aid policy thus followed the general direction of neoliberal policy, moving away from treating public benefits as social goods for the citizenry as a whole and toward requiring the user to pay more. Public funds were shifted toward production functions by making aid available for working adults re-educating themselves for knowledge-economy jobs. That well-to-do users paid (relatively) less than other users also reflected trends characteristic of the new economy and the neoliberal state.

Patents

Before the 1980 Bayh-Dole Act, federal policy placed discoveries made with federal grant funds in the public domain. Universities were able to secure patents on federally funded research only when the federal government, through a long and cumbersome application process, granted special approval. Few universities engaged in patenting before 1980.[36] The Bayh-Dole Act directly signaled the inclusion of universities in profit taking. It allowed universities and small businesses to retain title to inventions made with federal R&D monies. In the words of the act, "it is the policy and objective of the Congress . . . to promote collaboration between commercial concerns and nonprofit organizations, including universities."[37] Bayh-Dole "explicitly recognized technology transfer to the private sector as a desirable outcome of federally financed research, and endorsed the principle that exclusive licensing of publicly funded technology was sometimes necessary to achieve that objective."[38]

Bayh-Dole shifted the relationship between university managers and faculty in several important ways. As potential patent holders, university trustees and administrators could see all research generated by faculty as relatively easily protected intellectual property. Faculty, too, could better conceptualize their discoveries as products or processes—private, valuable, and licensable—not necessarily as knowledge to share publicly with a community of scholars.[39] The Bayh-Dole Act gave new and concrete meaning to the phrase "commodification of knowledge." The act streamlined universities' participation in the marketplace.

Bayh-Dole was presented as a support for small businesses, which the Reagan administration had deemed as engines of economic growth. In 1983, however, Reagan extended Bayh-Dole's coverage to large corporations through executive order. After 1983, any entity performing federal research and development (R&D) could patent and own discoveries made in the course of research, a shift that contributed to the privatization and commercialization of research across all categories of performers, including large corporations.

The Federal Courts Improvements Act of 1982 created a new Court of Appeals for the Federal Circuit (CAFC), which handled patent appeals from district courts, thereby ending "forum shopping" in intellectual property cases, creating a more uniform approach to patents. The new court led the way for a greatly strengthened approach to intellectual property. "Before 1980, a district court finding that a patent was valid and infringed was upheld on appeal 62% of the time; between 1982 and 1990 this percentage rose to 90%."[40] The CAFC led the patent office to offer broader protections through patents. "There are now patents for genetically engineered bacteria, genetically altered mice, particular gene sequences, surgical methods, computer software, financial products, and methods for conducting auctions on the World Wide Web. For each of these, there would have been before 1980 at least serious doubt as to whether or not they would be deemed by the PTO [U.S. Patent and Trademark Office] and the courts to fall within the realm of patentable subject matter."[41]

University administrators and faculty members were well aware that strengthened intellectual property protection made patentable knowledge more valuable. The Small Business Innovation Development Act of 1982 mandated that federal agencies with annual expenditures of more than $100 million devote 1.25 percent of their budgets to research performed by small businesses, on the grounds that they were crucial to economic recovery. Universities strongly opposed this legislation, making the case that it diverted the mission agencies from funding university research.[42] Ironically, as universities became more deeply involved in academic capitalism, they increasingly took equity positions in small enterprises started by their faculty, often with funding provided by the Small Business Innovation Development Act.[43]

Equity deals did not occur frequently among research universities until the 1980s. The number of equity deals spread among research universities, slowly at first, and then, starting in the 1990s, quite rapidly. Taking equity positions rather than licensing intellectual property and receiving royalties became a market strategy for research universities. According to Feldman, Feller, Bercovitz, and Burton, equity provides three advantages over licensing: first, equity gives universities options or financial claims on companies' future income; second, equity deals align the interests of the university and the firm with regard to the rapid commercialization of technology; and third, equity signals interested investors about the worth of the technology.[44] These scholars attribute the rapid growth of universities taking equity positions to organizational learning through technology transfer offices.

In 2002, Feldman, Feller, Bercovitz, and Burton surveyed sixty-seven Carnegie I and II research universities that had active technology transfer operations. Of these institutions, 76 percent had taken equity in a company; altogether, they had participated in 679 equity deals. Public universities took more equity in companies than private universities, even though thirteen of the public universities (19% of the total sample) were prohibited by state laws from holding equity in companies. Ten of these public universities were able to circumvent state statutes by forming independent entities, or 501(c)(3)s—usually research foundations or other intermediary institutions—that were able to take equity in corporations based on faculty intellectual property. Although the study does not deal with which set of universities, public or private, initiated the first equity deals, this market strategy spread rapidly between both sets of universities, and even more rapidly among the publics than the privates, despite the barriers to public institutions taking equity. Both sets of institutions adopted similar strategies, geared to increasing their external revenue streams.

During the 1980s, as universities' intellectual property activity and potential grew, state systems and universities and colleges initiated or began to develop and change their patent property policies. They moved from minimal policies to more expansive ones, some of which dramatically changed the way intellectual property is handled. The following data, which illustrates current practices, is drawn from a study of eighteen colleges and universities, both public and private, in six states, and it addresses royalty splits, categories of persons covered by policies, exceptions to the policies, and conflicts of interest.[45]

Royalties

The various patent policies offered a wide range of royalty splits among faculty, department or college, and university. All were sufficient to provide strong incentives to patent. The greatest incentives were for the faculty, who were able to put the income in their bank accounts, as compared with all others, who had to use the revenue stream generated by patents for institutional purposes. The policies that were most generous to faculty split royalties fifty-fifty with faculty. At the bottom of the range of royalty splits, faculty received one-third of the royalty income. Private universities tended to be less generous than public ones, with many offering faculty one-third of the income from their licenses. When policies were changed over time, they usually gave faculty a lower percentage of royalties.

Personnel Coverage

Categories of persons covered by patent policies were elaborated on by many state system or college and university policies over the years. In the 1970s and 1980s, a number of patent policies covered only "inventors." By the mid-1990s, they included faculty, staff, graduate students, postdoctoral fellows, nonemployees who participate in university research projects, visiting faculty and, in a very few policies, undergraduates.

Exceptions

Universities had long claimed ownership of discoveries made by faculty; the decisive court cases were heard in the 1950s. Initially, however, there were exceptions to universities' ownership claims to intellectual property patented by faculty. If faculty made the discoveries on their own time, using their own resources, and not availing themselves of university facilities, they could claim a patent for themselves—for example, if they invented something in the summer, in their garage workroom. As the academic capitalist knowledge-learning regime developed, definitions of time, resources, and facilities uses were specified to the point where it was very difficult for faculty to assert any claims. For example, several policies had guidelines that indicated that if researchers depended on anything other than routinely available office equipment and commercially available software, or library materials generally available in nonuniversity locations, they were making substantial use of university resources.

Initially, state system and institutional policies addressed only patents. Over the years, the forms of intellectual property that were covered multiplied. Among those included were licensing income, milestone payments, equity interest, mask work (which charted the topography of a semiconductor chip product), material transfer agreements, tangible property (cell lines, software, compositions of matter), and trade secrets.

Managerial Capacity

System and institutional patent policies delineated academic capitalism practices that greatly expanded market managerial capacity in colleges and universities. The new functions were many: surveilling institutional employees' intellectual property activity to ensure capture by the system or institution; reviewing and evaluating faculty disclosures; licensing technology; supervising royalty flows, including the distribution of funds within institutions; reinvesting funds in new market activities; litigating to defend intellectual property; evaluating intellectual property for institutional equity investments; monitoring and occasionally administering corporations in which the institution held equity; overseeing initial public offerings (IPOs); and developing and monitoring market activity for conflict-of-interest issues. As colleges and universities become more involved in academic capitalism, they hired more managerial professional staff. Expanded managerial capacity institutionalized business activity in colleges and universities by allowing segments of institutions to directly engage the market.

The multiple forms of market activity pursued by universities, together with the faculty's close involvement in them, created many opportunities for conflicts of interest. Factors that expanded the possibilities of conflicts of interest for faculty were increased magnitude of personal compensation; growing numbers of financial relationships between a creator and a company; greater commitment of a faculty's time to a company; faculty or administrators holding equity in a company; the involvement of trainees or students in a company; and the involvement of patients or human subjects in company research trials. In other words, the risk of conflicts of interest increased the more closely faculty members or creators participated in market activity, yet intellectual property policies continue to aggressively promote this close involvement.

A dramatic example of university patenting and licensing is provided by Onco-Mouse, a genetically engineered animal that reliably reproduces characteristics of various human cancers. It was created in Harvard Medical School laboratories in the early 1980s through the manipulation of cancer-causing genes. OncoMouse was patented by Harvard and licensed by DuPont for sale as a research tool. The patent was contested by a number of groups opposed to the patenting of living organisms, but it was upheld by the Canadian Supreme Court.[46]

The mouse research tool quickly became the standard in global cancer research that focused on the ways in which cancers develop and that tested new treatments for breast, prostate, and other forms of cancer. The cost of the mouse created access problems for some researchers. In 2001, DuPont, Harvard, and the National Institutes of Health signed an agreement that made the mouse more readily available to university researchers. However, DuPont will not allow the mouse research tool to breed, nor to be used in industry-supported research. Many groups, for example breast-cancer activists, think these restraints retard the development of a broad understanding of cancers and treatments for them.

They argue that the mouse tool was developed in large part with public research funds and should not be privately owned. Rather, it should be freely available to all researchers.[47]

Although patents are concentrated in biology and engineering fields, they are increasingly being granted in other areas. For example, Carnegie Mellon University developed a series of Cognitive Tutor products that were licensed to Carnegie Learning, a company which spun out of the university in 1998. This instructional math software is based on artificial intelligence, integrating technology and print curricula into realistic problem situations. The company has claimed that minority and nonminority students using the program perform at a much higher level in classes, as well as improve their SAT scores.[48] However, Math Curriculum Kits— which cover Bridge to Algebra, Algebra I, Geometry, Algebra II, and Integrated Math for home users—cost $99 each, prices sufficient to deter many users.[49]

Before 1981, fewer than 250 patents per year were issued to universities. Between fiscal year (FY) 1991 and FY 1999, annual college and university invention disclosures increased by 63 percent (to 12,324); new patents filed grew by 77 percent (to 5,545); and new licenses and options executed by universities increased by 129 percent (to 3,914).[50] Since 1980, at least 3,807 new companies have been formed that were based on a license from an academic institution, including the 494 established in FY 2001. Colleges and universities received an equity interest in 70 percent of their startups in FY 2001, compared with 56 percent in FY 2000. At the end of 2001, 159 institutions reported that 2,514 startups were still operating. When similar statistics are reviewed in the National Science Foundation's *Science and Engineering Indicators 2010*, invention disclosures grew from 13,700 in 2003 to 17,700 in 2007. Patent applications increased from 7,200 in 2003 to 10,900 in 2007. Startup companies based on university inventions rose from 348 in 2003 to 510 in 2007. By 2009, there were 3,148 cumulative operating startups associated with U.S. university patenting and licensing activities.[51]

While technology transfer brings external revenue to colleges and universities, it also takes funds from them. In FY 2001, colleges' and universities' adjusted gross license income was $1.071 billion, and running royalties on product sales were $845 million.[52] However, the median net royalty per university has only climbed from $440,00 in 1996 to $950,000 in 2005. In 2007, 161 universities received $1.9 billion from net royalties. In other words, there are winners and losers. Most royalties accrue to a few patents and the universities that hold them. In 2007, many university technology transfer offices reported negative incomes. Colleges and universities or state systems had to pay for legal fees and for their technology transfer offices. In 2001, legal fees were $161 million. The magnitude of nonreimbursed legal fees has increased about 250 percent over the eleven years that the Association of University Technology Managers (AUTM) has surveyed technology transfer activities. AUTM makes the case that about 40 percent of these costs are reimbursed through the legal process. However, these costs could be substantially higher, since AUTM explicitly modified its definition of legal fees in 1999, omitting major litigation to better focus on benchmarking patent prosecution costs.

In the 1980s, many smaller universities and colleges received patents; the one hundred largest universities held only 82 percent of all patents. However, that trend was reversed in the 1990s, and the one hundred largest universities received more than 90 percent of all patents awarded. Income from patents was also concentrated in the top one hundred.[53] In 2005, the top R&D-performing universities continued to dominate, accounting for 95 percent of patents.

Patents dramatically illustrate the growth of the academic capitalist knowledge-learning regime. Patents, licensing and running royalties, startup companies, and universities holding equity positions in corporations built on faculty patents are not *market-like* behaviors; they are *true* market behaviors that involve nonprofit institutions in profit taking. Yet colleges and universities are not market entities, because they are chartered differently from corporations and do not disburse profits to shareholders. Instead, funds from external market revenues are put back into the institutions. In some ways, colleges and universities that patent are able to cross the traditional borders between public and private, engaging in practices that best meet their needs for generating external revenues. If patenting, which is expensive, fails to lead to licenses and royalties, the state bears the cost in the case of public institutions. Similarly, the startup corporations initiated by universities are in many ways a form of state-subsidized capitalism, although there are few penalties for failure. The income from royalties and licenses is tax free, so long as the profits are returned to the university, even if the profits are earmarked for the further development of technology transfer. Public universities try to defend their patents by invoking the Eleventh Amendment. Although patenting and technology transfer is generally portrayed as a win-win endeavor, a relatively small number of large research universities are the only ones to generate substantial external revenues. For many smaller colleges and universities, the cost of maintaining a technology transfer office exceeds any revenues.[54]

Copyrights

In the 1980s, many universities became involved in patenting; in the late 1980s and 1990s, a substantial number of them developed copyright policies. In the 1990s, new copyright legislation was enacted as digital technologies and telecommunications grew rapidly. The new laws strongly emphasized the protection of digital forms of creative expression, including new forms of intellectual property such as courseware, multimedia, electronic databases, and tele-immersion. Changes in the copyright law opened up opportunities for academic capitalism in areas other than the physical and life sciences, which had been the primary fields participating in the patent phase of the academic capitalism knowledge regime. Faculty from all fields were involved with copyrights, because copyright applied to student instructional materials, thus making academic capitalism not just a knowledge regime, but also a knowledge-learning regime.

The Telecommunications Act of 1996 dramatically altered the industry's regulatory framework. Before 1996, the 1934 Communications Act, as implemented through the Federal Communications Commission, authorized separate monopolies: broadcast, cable, wire, wireless, and satellite. The 1996 Telecommunications Act deregulated these various industries, creating a competitive climate that favored growth of the Internet, the World Wide Web, and e-business, all of which utilized previously separated communications media in new patterns. The deregulation of telecommunications created numerous possibilities for an academic capitalism knowledge-learning regime, ranging from software to distance education.

The Digital Millennium Copyright Act (DMCA) of 1998 protects digital property by prohibiting unauthorized access to a copyrighted work, as well as unauthorized copying of a copyrighted work. The DMCA is far reaching and covers an array of technologies, from Web casting to hyperlinks, online directories, search engines, and the content of the materials made available by these technologies. Not only are citizens (and students) penalized for unauthorized access, but devices and services that circumvent copyrights are also prohibited. The law very deliberately seeks to develop electronic commerce and its associated technologies by strengthening protections for all forms of digital property. There are some exceptions, the broadest being for law enforcement and intelligence. The other exceptions are quite narrow.

The DMCA has a special section on distance education. Generally, the DMCA seems to take the position that purchasing or licensing digital materials should be a cost born by distance educators, as is the case with hardware and software. Currently, exemptions for the educational use of digital products are only for traditional classrooms that offer "systematic instructional activity by a nonprofit educational institution or governmental body," or for students who are in situations that make them unable to access such classrooms.[55] In other words, there is no exemption for distance-education networks not tied into conventional instruction. Fair use offers an exemption that might apply to distance education, but there is not yet a body of case law that clarifies how this would work. Moreover, if a U.S. educational institution transmits courses to students in other countries, the law is not clear as to which will apply, U.S. law or the law of the country receiving the transmission.

As it currently stands, the DMCA offers traditional colleges and universities an advantage in developing distance education. For the time being, they are best able to make use of such educational exemptions as exist, because of the physical classroom requirement. They also benefit because for-profit distance-education organizations are currently unable to access federal financial aid for their students. (However, the Department of Education has provisionally agreed to a change in these regulations, which will provide federal aid for students taking for-profit distance-education courses.) Traditional colleges and universities have every incentive to try to capture a sizable market share of distance education before for-profit competition explodes.

The Technology, Education and Copyright Harmonization (TEACH) Act was passed in 2002. TEACH attempted to modify provisions of the DMCA that constrained the delivery of distance education. TEACH allows educators greater freedom than that provided by the DMCA with regard to copyrighted materials. For example, the new law allows the display and performance of most works, unlike the DMCA, which limited broad classes of work, particularly those that had entertainment as well as instructional value. The DMCA confined free use of copyrighted materials to classrooms; TEACH allows institutions to reach students through distance education at any location. Unlike the DMCA, TEACH also lets students retain material for a short time. Further, TEACH permits digitization of analog works, but only if the work is not available in digital form.[56]

However, TEACH also has many restrictions. Copyrighted material used in distance education must be part of "systematic mediated instructional activity"; be supervised by an instructor; be directly related to the teaching plan; be technologically limited (protected) to enrolled students; and provide information about copyright protections attached to the works. The works may not be retained by students, and dissemination cannot interfere with the technological protections embedded in the works. TEACH assigns the responsibility for monitoring and policing copyrights to universities, steering universities in the direction of developing copyright policies, disseminating them, and staffing copyright offices. The act applies only to accredited nonprofit institutions, which must institute copyright policies that provide informational materials about copyrights to faculty, students, and staff. Generally, the TEACH provisions are designed to permit the use of digitized products and processes in distance education, but they are also framed to protect the material and property of copyright holders, especially for commercial developers of educational materials.

As was the case with patent policies, copyright policies moved from minimal policies to more expansive policies, some of which dramatically changed the way intellectual property is handled. The following data, which illustrates current copyright practices, is drawn from the same study of eighteen colleges and universities, both public and private, in the same six states that we used for the patent policies. As with patents, we look at the way copyright policies address royalty splits, categories of persons covered by policies, and exceptions to the policies.[57]

Institutional claims to their faculty's copyrighted materials are different from institutional claims to patents. Historically, many faculty published and held copyrights to scholarly and artistic materials, including instructional materials, that they created in the course of their employment at colleges and universities. They contracted with a variety of commercial publishing houses to produce and distribute their works. However, the stakes in scholarly publishing, with the exception of textbooks, were relatively small, and institutions were not interested in them. As our analysis of copyright policies demonstrates, this seems to be changing as the increased use of information technology mediates instruction. Institutions are aggressively advancing claims to shares of faculty intellectual property in copyrights, beginning with technology-mediated products. This is a sharp break with the past and potentially affects all faculty, regardless of field or institutional type.

Generally, our argument is that universities and colleges have initiated an aggressive pursuit of external revenues based on instruction and curriculum, and a number of faculty have cooperated, participating in the commercialization of instructional materials. State system and institutional copyright policies were very often introduced after patent policies, and they are substantively different from patent policies, following their own legal and product trajectories. We make the argument that knowledge in the public domain is increasingly being treated as raw material, which can be transformed into products sold for (potential) private profit or generate external revenues for colleges and universities. Over time, there is no case in which the intellectual products covered in the policies became less restrictive. Instead, the most comprehensive coverage is found in the most recent policies, providing evidence of institutions' increasingly expansive claims to copyrightable works.

Royalties

There is substantial variation among institutions on copyright royalties, with the faculty's share of royalties ranging from a high of 75 percent to a low of 33 percent. Still, the shares accorded to faculty at all institutions are generous. In contrast, none of the institutions give the growing numbers of nonfaculty employees involved in creating educational materials—for example, managerial professionals who create Web pages or course materials—any shares in royalties.

Personnel Coverage

As with patent policies, the categories of coverage in copyright policies also expanded over time. Copyright policies cover not only full-time and part-time faculty, but also a wide range of other categories of people: classified staff, student employees, appointed personnel, graduate assistants and teaching associates, persons with "no-salary" appointments, and visiting faculty and managerial professionals. Even faculty who are employed at other institutions but who work on research projects at institutions with aggressive patent policies are included in the coverage. However, there are a few cases in which coverage has not expanded. For example, only faculty are covered by the copyright and computer-software policies at several institutions. There are also cases in which the expansiveness of policies is extraordinary with regard to students. For example, one institution's policy stated that not only were students who were using substantial university resources or who were employed by the university covered by the policy, but also any student not employed by the university who created copyrightable intellectual property. Faculty using such volunteer, nonemployed students in their scholarly work projects were requested to have students sign a form that gave ownership of the property to this university.[58]

Exceptions

Historically, universities and colleges excepted faculty creative works from institutional ownership, and advanced claims to faculty members' copyrightable intellectual products only under certain conditions. One condition was when a work produced by faculty was specified as "work for hire." The other was when faculty work that was copyrighted was specified as "within the scope of employment." This language reversed the universities' traditional position with regard to their faculty's copyrightable intellectual property and enables colleges and universities to claim the material created by faculty. In their separate studies of research universities, Laura Lape and Ashley Packard both noted the greatly increased number of college and university intellectual property policies that have work-for-hire and within-the-scope-of-employment language, giving institutions a broader claim to property.[59]

Examples of introducing and expanding work-for-hire and within-the-scope-of-employment language are provided by some universities in our sample. Perhaps the most extreme example comes from the University of Utah. In 1970, this university's policy held that their faculty owned almost all of their copyrighted material, with one important exception: "Notwithstanding any other university policy provision, unless other arrangements are made in writing, all rights to copyrightable material (except material which is placed on videotape using university facilities, supplies, and/or equipment) and all financial and other benefits accruing by reason of said copyrightable material shall be reserved to the author, even though employed by the university." The university only claimed rights to ownership when there was a specific contract between the university and a third party, or when the author was specifically hired to do the work. (In the case of videotapes, the university also claimed ownership when its "facilities, supplies, and/or equipment" had been used, a point we will subsequently explore in discussing "substantial use" language.) In their 2001 revised policy, all intellectual work of University of Utah faculty is declared as work for hire: "Works created by University staff and student employees within the scope of their University employment are considered to be works made for hire, and thus are Works as to which the University is the Owner and controls all legal rights in the work." In the revisions, the university agreed to transfer rights to their faculty in some instances, such as in the case of "traditional scholarly work," but it still claimed ownership if the materials were produced with the "substantial use" of university resources.

In many cases, faculty work for hire is defined fairly narrowly. For example, the University of Miami's policy refers only to "a project assigned to members of the faculty" that will be owned by the institution "only if so specified at the time of assignment by an instrument of specific detail and agreement." Similarly, in the State University of New York System's policy, "[faculty] Work for Hire shall mean work done . . . under campus consulting, extra service, or technical assistance arrangements either through contract, consultancy, or purchase order, but not within the Scope of Employment."[60]

Although work for hire is sometimes defined narrowly for faculty, this is generally not the case for managerial professionals. As greater numbers of managerial professionals are employed within colleges and universities, and as they become more involved in "production" activities—such as the development of copyrightable educational products—institutions not only expand the personnel covered by their policies, but they also define the intellectual products of these personnel as works for hire. For example, the policy of the University of North Texas reads: "Electronically published course materials created jointly by faculty authors and others, whose contributions would be works for hire, will be jointly owned by the faculty author and the University." In short, managerial professionals have no property rights, and by virtue of their involvement in the educational production processes, universities have expanded their ownership claims.

While many faculty may be excepted from college and university copyright polices with regard to their creative work, they frequently lose that exception if they make significant use of institutional resources in the creative process. Most policies in the eighteen institutions we studied had language about "use of institutional resources" or "substantial use of institutional resources." As with patents, universities and colleges made the case that faculty use of institutional resources entitled institutional claims to intellectual property. Ironically, the institutional resources used by copyrighting faculty were often information technologies which patenting faculty may have developed, and which the institution owned.

Expanded Managerial Capacity

Most of the college and university policies we studied did not develop the equivalent managerial capacity for copyrighted materials as they had for patented discoveries—for example, taking an equity position in corporations based on faculty intellectual property. However, some universities were moving in that direction with regard to copyrights. The case of Brigham Young University (BYU) points to a growing internal capacity to commodify education on the part of universities. At BYU, "the Technology Transfer and Creative Works Offices have the responsibility to license or sell the technology or work; or they may sell university developed products to end users when sales and support do not interfere with the normal activities of campus personnel, and when the sale is consistent with the educational mission of the university." If they "deem" the action "consistent with the educational mission and academic purposes of the university," they can approve the creation of an "enterprise center" that will pursue such activity. BYU has a Center for Instructional Design for producing copyrightable works, a Creative Works Office to oversee "the business aspects of commercializing intellectual properties and [managing] copyright issues," and the potential of enterprise centers that will further develop and market copyrightable educational materials.

The policies of other institutions are not so elaborate, but they point to some development of managerial capacity for the pursuit of academic capitalism in the realm of educational materials. Overall, it is evident that universities are developing internal managerial capacity to create and commodify copyrightable educational materials. Such capacity and investment has not only been used to justify institutions' more aggressive ownership claims to such products, but it has also enabled the organizational production of materials independent of faculty. In contrast to patenting and technology transfer, colleges and universities can develop and produce copyrightable educational materials without the direct involvement of full-time faculty. Staff who are hired to participate in these production and commercialization activities, whether they are full-time managerial professionals or part-time faculty, generally have no claims to the proceeds of their labors, since their directed labor is regarded as work for hire, entirely within the scope of their employment.

Under many of the copyright policies we have considered, colleges and universities could hire managerial professionals to develop curricular materials and part-time faculty to deliver them, and the institution would own the courses. These policies often cover distance-education efforts on the part of colleges and universities, as copyrights became a significant source of possible institutional revenues as colleges and universities pursued distance education. An example of the success that colleges and universities look to achieve through the management of copyrights is provided by WEB-CT. A computer science professor at the University of British Columbia developed WEB-CT, educational Web site software that serves as a platform for colleges and universities. The University of British Columbia spun it off as a private corporation, which "entered into production and distribution relationships with Silicon Graphics and Prentice-Hall and fast became a major player in the American as well as the Canadian higher educational market. By the beginning fall term of 1997, WEB-CT licensees included, in addition to the University of California, Los Angeles, and the California State University System, the public universities of Georgia, Minnesota, Illinois, North Carolina, and Indiana, and such private universities as Syracuse, Brandeis, and Duquesne."[61]

Although for-profits lobbied to change financial aid requirements that call for institutions to register their students for at least twelve hours of instruction, to offer less than 50 percent of their courses via distance education, and to prohibit bonuses or incentives to admissions officers for enrolling students, through 2009 the for-profits were unsuccessful in changing legislation. However, during the George W. Bush administration, rules about compensating recruiters for the numbers of students admitted were relaxed. Indeed, colleges and universities can now reward recruiters for the number of students that are admitted, although factors such as retention must also be considered. For-profits were also able to win exceptions and to modify or reinterpret various restrictions with regard to federal student financial aid. For example, the Distance Education Demonstration Program, started in 1999 in response to these restrictions, waived requirements for 15 schools, and, in the ensuing years, the quantity of waivers rose, including for a number of for-profits. Moreover, the 50 percent rule does not apply to many vocational education, job-training, or professional programs.[62] As one financial aid site, displaying ads for the University of Phoenix and the American Public University (ironically, a for-profit distance learning institution), puts it, "as long as you are attending a nationally accredited program . . . you are eligible for the same federal and state financial aid as a student attending a brick and mortar school."[63]

The University of Maryland University College (UMUC) provides a distance-education story with an interesting twist with regard to the source of profits from academic capitalism. Although UMUC was designed as a for-profit venture based on private monies, it has succeeded by tapping into state monies from Maryland and federal contracts with the military. UMUC was created with private-sector investment, although in recent years it has received tens of millions of dollars in state appropriations—about $10 million in both 1999 and 2000, $15 million in 2001, and $20 million in 2002.[64] Its greatest success has been in securing military funding to provide education to servicemen and -women around the globe. More recently, UMUC was awarded a Tri-Services Education contract from the U.S. Army, at a value of $350 million over 10 years. By its own accounts, members of the military accounted for 47,000 UMUC enrollments in 2002, out of a total of 87,000 for all of UMUC.[65]

UMUC was initially conceived as a profit center for the University of Maryland. It was expected to bring in external revenues for the system as a whole by expanding enrollments, and by saving through both economies of scale and reduced instructional costs, the latter made possible by using digitized materials rather than live faculty. When UMUC's costs remained high, the state of Maryland increased its contributions, perhaps because clicks and mortar were cheaper than bricks and mortar. However, the largest external revenue stream has been from the federal government, in the form of funding for the education of those in the military services. As in several of the other examples we have considered, the state—at the level of the several states and the federal government—supplies the lion's share of external revenue for a system designed to tap private external revenue streams.

In recent years, however, for-profit distance-education providers have eclipsed UMUC's military contracts. For-profits account for 29 percent of active-duty students and 40 percent of the half-billion-dollar annual tab in federal tuition for all students in the military. The cost for attending for-profits (such as the University of Phoenix) is $250 per credit, as compared with $50 per credit at community colleges. Federal student financial aid was $478 million in 2008, more than triple the spending of a decade earlier. Military personnel are eager to enroll, because courses taken count toward promotion. Critics claim that for-profit courses are faster and easier than those offered by nonprofit or public colleges and universities, and they compare the University of Phoenix, which allows some students to earn an associate's degree in five weeks, with community colleges, where an associate's degree usually takes two years. Large for-profits seek out students in the military because they do not count with regard to the Department of Education's 10 percent rule, which requires 10 percent of for-profits' revenues to be other than federal aid. Indeed, the University of Phoenix derived 86 percent of its $3.77 billion in revenues in 2009 from the Department of Education, up from 48 percent in 2001. Even though for-profits have not yet been able to change the 10 percent rule, they are close to running on students' Pell grants and loans alone.

The networks involved in academic capitalism are extraordinarily complex. In exploring business–higher education connections, most scholars have focused on research activities and on universities.[66] Yet the commodification of education involves a wider range of higher education institutions, and activities other than patenting. Copyrighting occurs not only in the sciences and engineering, but across all fields in higher education, and it holds out the possibility of generating new sources and forms of higher education revenue.

Conclusion

Over the past thirty-five years, the academic capitalist knowledge-learning regime was instantiated in higher education. It is not the only knowledge-learning regime, however. It coexists uneasily with, for example, both the military-industrial-academic knowledge regime and the liberal education learning regime. While the academic capitalist knowledge-learning regime did not replace these other regimes, considerable space was created for it within colleges and universities.

The academic capitalist knowledge-learning regime was not unilaterally imposed on universities by external forces. Actors within colleges and universities worked to intersect opportunities created by the new economy. For example, the states have created an array of new opportunities. Many states have adjusted their conflict-of-interest laws so that universities (as represented by administrators) and faculty (as inventors and advisers) can hold equity positions in private corporations, even when those corporations do business with universities. Again, these laws were not imposed on passive institutions. Universities often lobbied their state legislators to ensure that the conflict-of-interest laws were changed, as did, for example, Texas A&M University.[67] The changing politico-legal climate provided new opportunities for faculty and administrators in an uncertain resource environment.

Federal and state policies enabled colleges and universities to treat students as consumers, stimulated civilian technology policy, and created and (re)regulated the telecommunications infrastructure and product development. Only the 1972 amendments to the Higher Education Act, which created what came to be known as Pell grants, were directed toward postsecondary education. The other legislative initiatives were developed primarily to transform the industrial economy to an information economy, and to connect the national economy with global markets. Nonetheless, actors in and segments of postsecondary institutions, ranging from research universities to community colleges, worked to articulate their departments, programs, and offices with the new economy. Generally, the research and educational products, processes, and programs that they created did not contribute to the welfare of their institutions as a whole, but they expanded the opportunities for the actors and segments of institutions able and willing to intersect with the new economy. As a result, some portions of colleges and universities—enrollment management offices within student personnel services, programs within the life sciences and engineering that patent, and departments and programs throughout the university that manage copyrights that intersect with educational initiatives in telecommunications—are prospering, while many others are not. Finally, large numbers of students served by or enrolled in departments or colleges and schools do not necessarily relate to how units fare within postsecondary institutions.

NOTES

1. Sheila A. Slaughter and Gary Rhoades, *Academic Capitalism and the New Economy* (Baltimore: Johns Hopkins University Press, 2004).

2. Deborah D. Stine, *America COMPETES Act: Programs, Funding, and Selected Issues* (Apr. 17, 2009), Congressional Research Service Report RL34328, http://opencrs .com/document/RL34328/ [accessed Aug.19, 2010].

3. Sheila A. Slaughter and Gary Rhoades, "Changes in Intellectual Property Statutes and Policies at a Public University: Revising the Terms of Professional Labor," *Higher Education* 26 (1993): 287–312; Sheila A. Slaughter and Gary Rhoades, "The Emergence of a Competitiveness Research and Development Policy Coalition and the Commercialization of Academic Science and Technology," *Science, Technology, and Human Values* 21, no. 3 (Summer 1996): 303–39.

4. Andrew M. Isserman, "State Economic Development Policy and Practice in the United States: A Survey Article," *International Regional Science Review* 16, no. 1–2 (1994): 49–110; Peter K. Essinger, *The Rise of the Entrepreneurial State: State and Local Economic Development Policy in the United States* (Madison: University of Wisconsin Press, 1988).

5. David E. Osborne, *Laboratories of Democracy* (Boston: Harvard Business School Press, 1988).

6. David Harvey, *A Brief History of Neoliberalism* (New York: Oxford University Press, 2005).

7. The same applies at the state level. States that have greatly increased their student aid programs usually have also increased merit scholarships, which tend to benefit the well-to-do. In other words, state policies have generally followed in much the same direction as federal ones. See Donald E. Heller, *The States and Public Higher Education Policy: Affordability, Access, and Accountability* (Baltimore: Johns Hopkins University Press, 2000).

8. Lawrence E. Gladieux and Thomas R. Wolanin, *Congress and the Colleges: The National Politics of Higher Education* (Lexington, MA: Lexington Books, 1976).

9. Committee for Economic Development, "A Strategy for Better-Targeted and Increased Financial Support," in *ASHE Reader on Finance in Higher Education*, ed. David W. Breneman, Larry L. Leslie, and Richard E. Anderson (Needham, MA: Simon and Schuster, 1996), 61–68.

10. Larry L. Leslie and Paul Brinkman, *The Economic Value of Higher Education* (New York: ACE/Macmillan, 1988). For a more current discussion of higher eco-

nomic development country (HED) markets and public versus private good, see Brian Pusser, "Higher Education, the Emerging Market, and the Public Good," in *The Knowledge Economy and Postsecondary Education,* ed. Patricia Albjerg Graham and Nevzer Stacey (Washington, DC: National Academy Press, 2002).

11. Ronald G. Ehrenberg, *Tuition Rising: Why College Costs So Much* (Cambridge, MA: Harvard University Press, 2000).

12. The Middle Income Assistance Act of 1978 provided grant aid to a greater number of middle-income students and took the $25,000 limit off the Guaranteed Student Loans. The Middle Income Assistance Act was an anomalous moment in student financial aid's movement toward a greater reliance on loans, and by the 1980s it proved too broad a welfare benefit for the neoliberal state. For details, see James C. Hearn, "The Growing Loan Orientation in Federal Financial Aid Policy," in *ASHE Reader on Finance in Higher Education,* ed. John L. Yeager, Glenn M. Nelson, Eugenia A. Potter, John C. Weidman, and Thomas G. Zullo (Boston: Pearson, 1998).

13. Thomas Kane, *How We Pay for College in the Price of Admission* (Washington, DC: Brookings Institution Press, 1999), 11.

14. Donald E. Heller, *The States and Public Higher Education Policy: Affordability, Access, and Accountability* (Baltimore: Johns Hopkins University Press, 2000).

15. *1998 Amendments to the Higher Education Act of 1965,* Public Law 105–244, Part F, Sec. 961—Liaison for Proprietary Institutions of Higher Education, 112 Stat. 1836–37.

16. Ehrenberg, *Tuition Rising.*

17. Larry L. Leslie and Gary Johnson, "The Market Model and Higher Education," *Journal of Higher Education* 45 (1974): 1–20.

18. DePaul University, *National and Regional Trends in College Tuition,* http://oipr.depaul.edu/TuitionReport/2002/surveyrep.asp.

19. College Board, "$90 Billion Available in Student Financial Aid, with Scholarship Growth Outpacing Loan Growth," press release, Oct. 24, 2002, www.collegeboard.com/press/releases/18420.html.

20. College Board, *Trends in College Pricing 2009,* www.trends-collegeboard.com/college_pricing/.

21. Ibid.

22. Project on Student Debt, an Initiative of the Institute for College Access & Success, "Getting With the Program," *Issue Brief* (Oct. 2009), http://projectonstudentdebt.org/files/pub/getting_with_the_program.pdf.

23. National Center for Public Policy and Higher Education [NCPPHE], *Measuring Up 2008* (San Jose, CA: National Center for Public Policy and Higher Education, 2008), http://measuringup2008.highereducation.org, quotation on p. 15.

24. NCPPHE, *Losing Ground: A National Status Report on the Affordability of American Higher Education,* 2002, www.highereducation.org/reports/losing_ground/ar.shtml.

25. Project on Student Debt, *Quick Facts About Student Debt* (updated Jan. 2010), http://projectonstudentdebt.org/files/File/Debt_Facts_and_Sources.pdf.

26. McPherson and Shapiro, *Student Aid Game*, 15–16.

27. Albert B. Crenshaw, "Price Wars on Campus: Colleges Use Discounts to Draw Best Mix of Top Students, Paying Customers," *Washington Post*, Oct. 5, 2002, A1.

28. Alvin E. Roth and Xiaolin Xing, "Jumping the Gun: Imperfections and Institutions Relating to the Timing of Market Transactions," *American Economic Review* 84 (1994): 992–1044.

29. Christopher Flores, "U. of North Carolina at Chapel Hill Drops Early-Decision Admissions," *Chronicle of Higher Education*, May 3, 2002, A38; "Harvard to Eliminate Early Admission," *Harvard University Gazette*, Sept. 12, 2006; "Princeton to End Early Admission," *News at Princeton*, Sept. 18, 2006.

30. Marcia Yablon, "Test Flight: The Scam Behind SAT Bashing," *New Republic*, Oct. 30, 2001, 24–25.

31. Eric Hoover, "Instant Gratification: On-Site Admissions Programs Let Applicants Know Immediately Whether They Have Been Accepted," *Chronicle of Higher Education*, Apr. 12, 2002, A39.

32. Kathleen F. Kelly, *Meeting Needs and Making Profits: The Rise of For-Profit Degree-Granting Institutions* (Denver: Education Commission of the States, 2001).

33. Project on Student Debt, *Quick Facts*.

34. Project on Student Debt, "New Default Rate Data for Federal Student Loans: 44% of Defaulters Attended For-Profit Institutions," press release, Dec. 15, 2009.

35. Carolyn P. Griswold and Ginger M. Marine, "Political Influences on State Policy: Higher-Tuition, Higher-Aid, and the Real World," *Review of Higher Education* 19, no. 4 (1996): 361–89.

36. David C. Mowery and Arvids Ziedonis, "Academic Patent Quality and Quantity Before and After the Bayh-Dole Act in the United States," *Research Policy* 31 (2002): 399–418.

37. *Bayh-Dole Act 1980*, Public Law 96–517, 94 Stat. 3019.

38. Adam B. Jaffe, "The U.S. Patent System in Transition: Policy Innovation and the Innovation Process," *Research Policy* 29, no. 4–5 (2000): 531–57.

39. Gary Rhoades and Sheila A. Slaughter, "Professors, Administrators, and Patents: The Negotiation of Technology Transfer," *Sociology of Education* 64, no. 2 (1991): 65–77; Gary Rhoades and Sheila A. Slaughter, "The Public Interest and Professional Labor: Research Universities," in *Culture and Ideology in Higher Education: Advancing a Critical Agenda*, ed. William G. Tierney (New York: Praeger, 1991), 187–211.

40. Jaffe, "U.S. Patent System."

41. Ibid.

42. Sheila A. Slaughter, *Higher Learning and High Technology: Dynamics of Higher Education Policy Formation* (Albany: State University of New York Press, 1990).

43. Henry Etzkowitz and Magnus Gulbrandsen, "Public Entrepreneur: The Trajectory of United States Science, Technology, and Industrial Policy," *Science and Public Policy* 26, no. 1 (1999): 53–62.

44. Maryann Feldman, Irwin Feller, Janet Bercovitz, and Richard Burton, "Equity and the Technology Transfer Strategies of American Research Universities," *Management Science* 48, no. 1 (2002): 105–21.

45. Slaughter and Rhoades, *Academic Capitalism.*

46. Harvard Medical School, "Statement Regarding Canadian Supreme Court 5–4 Decision Dec. 5, 2002 Denying the Patentability of OncoMouse in Canada," www.geometry.net/detail/basic_c/canadian_supreme_court.html.

47. Dorsey Griffith, "Researchers Roar over OncoMouse Restrictions," *Sacramento Bee*, Nov. 2, 2003.

48. Association of University Technology Managers [AUTM], *AUTM Licensing Survey: FY 2001* (Deerfield, IL: Association of University Technology Managers, 2003).

49. Carnegie Learning, math curriculum kits, https://store.carnegielearning.com/.

50. Council on Governmental Relations, *A Tutorial on Technology Transfer in U.S. Colleges and Universities* (Washington, DC: Council on Governmental Relations, 2003), www.cogr.edu/viewDoc.cfm?DocID=151742/.

51. National Science Foundation, *Science and Engineering Indicators 2010*, NSB 10-01 (Arlington, VA: National Science Foundation, 2010).

52. AUTM, *AUTM Licensing Survey*, 11–12.

53. National Science Board, *Science and Engineering Indicators 2002*, NSB 02-1 (Arlington, VA: National Science Foundation, 2002).

54. Slaughter and Rhoades, *Academic Capitalism.*

55. Senate Committee on the Judiciary, *Statement of Marybeth Peters, the Register of Copyrights, before the Senate Committee on the Judiciary*, on Technology, Education and Copyright Harmonization (TEACH) Act (S. 487), 107th Cong., 1st sess., Mar. 13, 2001, www.copyright.gov/docs/regstat031301.html.

56. Kenneth D. Crews, *New Copyright Law for Distance Education: The Meaning and Importance of the TEACH Act*, 2002, http://www.ala.org/Template.cfm?Section= Distance_Education_and_the_TEACH_Act&Template=/ContentManagement/ ContentDisplay.cfm&ContentID=25939#/ [accessed Aug. 19, 2010].

57. Slaughter and Rhoades, *Academic Capitalism.*

58. Ibid.

59. Laura Lape, "Ownership of Copyrightable Works of University Professors: The Interplay between the Copyright Act and University Copyright Policies," *Villanova Law Review* 37 (1992): 223–71; Ashley Packard, "Copyright or Copy Wrong: An Analysis of University Claims to Faculty Work," *Communication Law and Policy* 7 (2002): 275–315.

60. Slaughter and Rhoades, *Academic Capitalism*, 143.

61. David F. Noble, *Digital Diploma Mills: The Automation of Higher Education* (New York: Monthly Review Press, 2001), 31.

62. U.S. Department of Education, Office of Postsecondary Education, "Distance Education Demonstration Program: Selected Waivers Granted" (Apr. 16, 2007), www2.ed.gov/programs/disted/waivers.html.

63. Jobmonkey, "Distance Learning, Part 3: Financial Aid," www.jobmonkey .com/blog/distance-learning-part-3-financial-aid.html [accessed Aug. 19, 2010].

64. G. A. Heeger, "President's Testimony to the Maryland General Assembly, February 8–9, 2001," online archives of presidential addresses, www.umuc.edu/presi dent/testimony/2001/testimony.html [accessed Mar. 1, 2003].

65. University of Maryland University College [UMUC], "The UMUC News Page: UMUC Awarded Tri-Services Education Contract for Europe," 2003, www.umuc .edu/events/press/news143.html [accessed Feb. 28, 2003]; UMUC, "About Us," University of Maryland University College home page, 2003, www.umuc.edu/gen/about .html [accessed Feb. 28, 2003].

66. Norman E. Bowie, *University-Business Partnerships: An Assessment* (Lanham, MD: Rowman and Littlefield, 1994); Henry Etzkowitz, Andrew Webster, and Peter Healey, *Capitalizing Knowledge: New Interactions of Industry and Academe* (Albany: State University of New York Press, 1998).

67. Peter Schmidt, "States Push Public Universities to Commercialize Research," *Chronicle of Higher Education*, Mar. 29, 2002, A26–A27.

CHAPTER SEVENTEEN

The Diversity Imperative

Moving to the Next Generation

Daryl G. Smith

D iversity represents one of the most dramatic societal changes in the twenty-first century, with significant implications for American higher education.[1] It is not only shaping higher education, but also higher education's role in society. Today, diversity is no longer a projection—it is a reality. The challenge, however, is that while the historic issues of diversity, which have occupied many in U.S. higher education over the last forty years, have grown in their urgency, new issues are developing. The breadth of concerns related to diversity on campuses throughout the United States include not only race, ethnicity, gender, and class, but religion, sexual orientation, gender identity, and disability, among others. The combination of shifting demographics and the increasing visibility of issues related to numerous identity groups indicates that the context for diversity is expanding. The new context suggests that higher education's role in achieving the promise of democracy—developing a pluralistic society that works—could emerge as even more central than when the Truman Commission or the GI Bill articulated the link between higher education and a healthy democracy.

This chapter will briefly look at the status and the evolution of diversity efforts. It will then explore how diversity is being reframed, building on decades of research in a number of domains. The final section will examine some of the key themes from research and practice.

The Status of Diversity

It is not possible, in this limited space, to provide an adequate overview of the development of diversity in higher education over time, nor of the current status of diversity, given its many dimensions. There are many resources available for a more in-depth look.[2] A quick overview, however, is necessary to provide a context for the rest of the chapter and for understanding the roots of diversity, along with its future.

Demographics

The changing demographic context, from a racial and ethnic point of view, not only anchors the work on diversity in higher education, but it increasingly frames the context for the nation as well. These changes tell a powerful story, creating conditions for change that have not been seen before. Most projections suggest that by 2050 the United States will be a majority minority nation. Higher education's overall enrollment, which is now one-third "minority" (13% black, 12% Latino, 7% Asian American / Pacific Islander, 1% American Indian / Alaska Native) and 3 percent international will, as early as 2018, be only about 59 percent white (non-Hispanic). Historically underrepresented minorities (black, Latino, American Indian / Alaska Native) will comprise about 30 percent, Asian Americans (and Pacific Islanders) about 8 percent, and American Indians / Alaska Natives just over 1 percent. Significantly, while the *percentages* of white students will continue to decline, the increases in enrollment overall in higher education mean that the *numbers* of white students, as well as the numbers for every racial and ethnic group, have and will continue to increase.[3]

While higher education will necessarily continue to address historically underrepresented groups of African American, Latino, American Indian, and low-income students, the dramatic shifts in immigration mean that other ethnicities are also emerging as underrepresented. Vietnamese and Hmong students are just two groups for whom access will be an issue. Class—often an invisible category, or one with limited data—is also reappearing as critically important.

The shifting demographics of undergraduates, in particular, are not synonymous with the deep overall changes that many scholars suggest will be needed in terms of diversity: in leadership, faculty, centrality to the institution's core mission, research contributions, the graduate population, and the reduction of continuing gaps in student achievement. Indeed, scholars have expressed concern that diversity in undergraduate enrollments may camouflage the lack of diversity elsewhere on campus.

Faculty diversity, for example, has grown only marginally in the last twenty years. Since 1993, the percentage of black, Latino, and American Indian faculty combined has gone from 5 percent to 7 percent of full-time faculty nationally. Asian American faculty has gone from 5 percent to 7 percent as well. International faculty has more than doubled as a percentage (from 2% to 4%). As with enrollment, even as the percentage of white faculty has declined, the numbers of white faculty, both male and female, continue to grow, with the largest expansion occurring among white women. This is in part because full-time and tenured or tenure-track faculty have grown significantly in size during this period.

Indeed, higher education has been in the midst of hiring the next generation of faculty. On a large number of campuses, that hiring has been robust. Many campuses have already replaced one-third to one-half of their faculty in the last eight to ten years.[4] At this rate, the next generation will have been hired in the next ten years. However, a change in the nature of academic appointments, more part-time staff, and pressures on salaries will create problems.

Nevertheless, despite new hiring patterns that are slightly more diverse than the faculty composition overall, turnover rates now indicate that retention of faculty is slowing the rate of change. On some campuses, 60 percent of new hires go to replace people who leave, rather than enlarging the existing faculty.[5] On other campuses this percentage is even higher. Also, because federal data now make it possible to separate domestic numbers from international, we can see that the international component of faculty has grown faster than any racial and ethnic group since 1993. This suggests that campuses may understand the need to globalize their faculty for the sake of their own legitimacy more than they sense the urgency of increasing their faculty to include more members from historically underrepresented groups.

The Evolution of Diversity

The central work of diversity, especially with respect to historically underrepresented minorities (URM)—African Americans, Latinos, and American Indians— and white women in STEM fields (science, technology, engineering, and math), began over fifty years ago. The struggle for access focused not only on student admissions, but also on hiring. Legislation, legal challenges, and executive orders, along with campus activism, pushed higher education institutions to change. Economic access has been a factor from early on. For example, the Higher Education Act of 1965 established need-based financial aid for the first time and created programs designed to support students from disadvantaged backgrounds. Through the early 1970s, other important steps were taken to address access: the establishment of Pell grants, a long overdue fulfillment of the Truman Commission's report of 1947; and the passage of Title IX in 1972, mandating access for women.

While early research and policy work focused on access, the next generation recognized that opening doors would not be enough, and that student success would also need to be examined. Research done in the 1970s and 1980s began to focus on the institution, and explored whether institutions were prepared to educate a diversity of students for success. This period represents an important shift by not only addressing pipeline concerns, but also by considering the climate, culture, curriculum, research, and institutional ethos of higher education institutions more generally. During that time, important intellectual and academic developments, along with student and faculty activism, led to the creation of ethnic studies and women's studies programs. These efforts were largely compensatory, showing what was missing in the traditional curriculum. But at their core they represented fundamental critiques of generic approaches to knowledge and to how knowledge, rather than being neutral and objective, reflected existing power and social structures.[6]

Historically, the primary domain of diversity has been directed to underrepresented communities and white women, although legislation and academic work has also addressed disability rights and struggles concerning equity and access for all communities of color, including Asian Americans, as well as LGBTQ (lesbian, gay, bisexual, transgender, and questioning) and working-class communities. Within each of these efforts, there have been calls for institutional change and attempts to make diversity central to that change. While one could argue that change has occurred—and somewhat dramatically—making diversity central has challenged practitioners and researchers alike.

Since the 1980s, the legal challenges to affirmative action have occupied a central place in the diversity literature. Important court battles, from the Bakke case in 1978 to the University of Michigan cases in 2002, have succeeded in narrowing the use of race and gender in admissions criteria, especially in public institutions. In addition, several public initiatives, such as Proposition 209 in California and Proposition 2 in Michigan, have curtailed the explicit use of race and gender not only in admissions, but presumably in other domains as well. The challenges to affirmative action have centered on definitions of merit and whether race and gender should be considered a compelling national interest that would warrant different admissions and hiring criteria. In most of the litigation involving student challenges, merit has been defined as test scores, and the affirmative action disputes have relied on differences in test scores. Another argument posits that admitting students to selective institutions under affirmative action did not serve them well.[7] While the resulting court decisions have suggested that race, in particular, could be one of many factors to be considered, these decisions have virtually eliminated parallel admissions processes.

The impact of these rulings, by basically doing away with higher education's parallel access systems, have, in some respects, forced institutions to return to basic principles about the role of diversity in their educational and institutional missions. Redefining excellence in ways that consider diversity is now emerging as being critically important. Furthermore, while legal challenges remain, the communication challenge of educating the public, as well as constituencies within higher education, about the role of diversity in the well-being of society is beginning to shift conversations to higher education's role in creating the capacity needed for a pluralistic society.[8] Educational disparities—in graduation rates, teacher production, workforce capacity, and diversity in STEM fields—and health-related disparities, for example, are placing pressure on higher education to increase quality and reduce these differentiations. In addition, the research that documented the limited role of standardized tests in identifying talent, especially in "nontraditional" groups, has prompted institutions to consider other ways to identify talent and merit.

A great deal of work continues on access, student success and support, campus climate, curricular and pedagogical transformation, and the diversification of faculty and staff. The intellectual agenda begun over forty years ago is more likely to be reflected in the contemporary curriculum, and (though not without its challenges) it is also part of many, though not all, mainstream academic disciplines. Thus, even with all the legal and other challenges to affirmative action and diversity, it is reasonably clear that diversity is being engaged.

At the same time, the domains of diversity have increased to address the differences within the major ethnic categories; the intersections of race, class, gender, sexuality, and disability; and growing immigrant populations. Globalization presents an interesting case in point. It is clear that on many campuses, internationalization has achieved a kind of centrality not always seen with domestic areas of diversity. And, for many, international diversity is clearly seen as part of diversity. The increasing interest in globalization could develop in ways that are compatible with diversity efforts, or in ways that overshadow issues of equity dealing with race, class, and gender from a domestic perspective. Current data suggest that international diversity may, to some degree, be being substituted for domestic diversity. International issues, while clearly bringing "diverse" perspectives that challenge a U.S.-centric approach, may well need to be tracked separately, especially in terms of graduate education and faculty hiring.

Reframing Diversity: The Research Base for the Future

The next generation of work on diversity is being built on decades of significant research. There are at least eight bodies of research that are critically important to building higher education's capacity for diversity, and, while they have been well described in depth elsewhere, they are briefly summarized here.[9]

Effective Educational Practices

Research looking at effective educational practices for URM students and for white women in STEM fields provides a strong and growing body of knowledge about what works and about the conditions under which students succeed. In addition, the findings on student success more generally, and on what can be learned in particular from special-purpose institutions such as historically black colleges and universities, tribal colleges, and women's colleges, lays an important foundation for the institutional elements that facilitate or hinder student success. Research suggests that good educational practices matter, and the following are just some of the themes that have emerged: the capacity of an institution to place student learning and student success at the center of its culture, with high expectations and the necessary support; faculty-student engagement in educationally purposeful activities; the creation of clear pathways to success; assurances that gateway courses are not barriers to a discipline; and attention to advising, mentoring, and pedagogy.

Experiencing Higher Education

There is a rich body of literature that addresses diversity in higher education from a number of perspectives, including historical, organizational, legal, developmental, and cultural ones. Some of the literature focuses on students and their experiences. Other segments more broadly discuss the experience of Latinos, African

Americans, American Indians, Asian Americans, undocumented immigrants, LG-BTQ peoples, those with disabilities, religious minorities, women, and the increasing diversity within each of these communities. Each of these literatures illuminates the ways in which institutional cultures inhibit diversity and change. While it is hard to summarize it adequately, this body of literature not only highlights the saliency of identity in institutional cultures and groups, but also underscores the diversity within groups (such as race, class, and sexual orientation).

Educational Benefits of Diversity

The research on the educational benefits of diversity for all students has provided both legal and educational grounds for the positive implications of building diversity into educational programs. As that body of research has developed, it has become clearer that to achieve optimum results, appropriate conditions must also be created. Significantly, research has demonstrated the benefits of diversity to learning (such as cognitive complexity), to retention, and to satisfaction. This body of research has also explored the powerful role that identity groups play on campus; while this aspect is quite complex, there are a few conclusions that may be drawn. In the context of an institutional ethos committed to diversity and community, identity groups can play a positive role in student success. Furthermore, in contrast to the literature that challenged the balkanization of campuses because of ethnic identity groups, the research is reasonably clear that, on predominantly white campuses, it is the white student who is likely to be segregated. This body of research demonstrates the positive impact of experiencing a diverse curriculum and diversity programs.

Faculty Diversity

This literature focuses both on the hiring and retention of a diverse faculty, and on the difference that a diverse faculty makes in terms of research and teaching. The hiring and retention literature stresses the barriers to hiring, including the myths given for limited hiring, the passive nature of searches, biases in how excellence is defined and sought, and embedded cultures that privilege existing norms over change. This research also records a similar set of challenges for the retention and success of diverse faculty. The research on the impact of a diverse faculty documents contributions not only in terms of teaching and learning, but also in terms of scholarship, community engagement, and leadership at all institutional levels.

Emerging Conceptualizations of Identity

A growing body of literature underscores the complexity of identity. While identity research is often introduced in higher education studies in the context of student development theory, this literature has important implications for the study of institutions as well. The new research facilitates the ways in which diversity must be understood as inclusive and differentiated. Three important concepts about identity have appeared in the literature: the multiplicity of identity, the ways in which identity intersects, and the contextual factors that underline how identity emerges in individuals, groups, and institutions. While this might suggest that any single identity is less important, or that studying identity at all is too complex, the literature strongly emphasizes that the significant role of identity in historical and social contexts is critically important in order to build institutions and societies that can function, creating the conditions for people to interact across boundaries.

Focusing on the ways in which identity is not about a single salient factor, but instead is inevitably about multiple characteristics (of individuals or institutions), creates conditions in which diversity within and across groups can be addressed. Furthermore, the robust body of scholarship that underscores how these intersect provides a more adequate approach to identity. More recent research on college students demonstrates how important it can be to look at race, class, and gender together, rather than singly. While it is appealing to examine one identity group at a time, the resulting picture is not adequate. If we study women and minority faculty separately, for example, the data on women will inevitably be about white women, just as the data on minorities will hide patterns concerning gender.

Intergroup Research

In addition, there is a core group of studies in the organizational literature that demonstrates that simply bringing diverse groups together does not automatically create healthy institutional or educational environments, especially for those who are in the minority. This research highlights the important role played by the design of interventions and the culture of institutions, which impact the ways in which people participate. Asymmetry in intergroup relations is a consistent theme in the literature on diversity in groups and on intergroup dynamics, particularly in organizational and societal contexts. For example, the literature in social psychology dealing with ethnic conflict throughout the world and intergroup relations demonstrates that intergroup teamwork can be experienced quite differently, depending on the position of and the context for individuals. Indeed, this research suggests that for groups in less-powerful positions, trying to downplay identity will only enhance its significance. The management literature also suggests that placing diversity at the center of an institution's mission will be crucial in establishing the conditions in which diversity is positive.

Asymmetry in power and position and the role of institutional commitment are just two of the concepts that are important in understanding intergroup relations. The research literature is rather clear, however, in noting that this is not a function of the people who represent diversity, but rather of the capacity of institutions to create healthy conditions *for* diversity. While much of the intergroup research in higher education has focused on students, there is a large group of studies that looks at institutional capacity and conditions that create positive environments for all participants.

Educational Competencies for a Global Society

There is increasing attention to the educational implications of a pluralistic society and a very interconnected world. A number of scholarly domains have paid attention to these educational implications in terms of outcomes and competencies. Some of this work emerges out of the intercultural literature that examined cultural knowledge and the ways in which students will need to build their competencies to cross cultures. Another body primarily focuses on the competencies required for addressing the inequity and power issues that emerge more from structural concerns than cultural ones. Recent work has attempted to provide frameworks that bring these two domains together, so that the outcomes of education enable students to cross boundaries of both culture and power.

Levers for Change

Finally, there is a growing body of literature that has begun to illuminate the levers for change in higher education, both broadly and for those dealing with diversity. When combined with other literature in the social sciences on change, this has produced increasing knowledge about the transformational process and the means by which capacity can be built. Emerging themes include the significance of institutional mission and culture, intentionality, commitment, leadership at all levels, change agents, critical incidents, social movements, and the role of outside agencies.

Reframing Diversity to Include Building Capacity

Some important directions for the next generation begin to emerge from the efforts to date. One of the important shifts appears to be the question of diversity's relationship to the institution. Conceptualizing diversity, and the identities associated with it, as not only being about individuals and groups, but also as embedded in institutions, is emerging as central. In other words, diversity is being framed *institutionally*, not only in the ways institutions educate a diverse group of students, but also in the ways that institutions do or do not create healthy pluralistic communities and fulfill their mission for a pluralistic society.

Building both on the work that has come before and on dramatic changes in demography, it is reasonably clear that diversity, as with technology before it, is likely to be central to higher education's mission and excellence in the twenty-first century. While legal challenges to efforts that seem to target particular groups will probably persist, the overwhelming shifts in demography and the need to appear equitable will increase the pressures on institutions to "diversify." How this will be done, and which institutions will reflect the most change, will need to be studied in the coming years. This, however, does represent a shift from having to defend diversity as if it were optional. While the value of diversity may need to be demonstrated for communications purposes or in response to legal challenges, the reality of diversity is likely to become embedded in at least some parts of institutional practice. Diversity will have implications for how to build the capacity of institutions to be effective and high performing in an increasingly pluralistic society, forming an arena in which diversity thrives and also where conditions are created to make sure diversity works. Some of these changes may emerge from the necessity of appealing to diverse groups, or from incidents that require institutions to act, or from political pressures.

The Technology Analogy

Reframing diversity as addressing institutional capacity, and locating diversity as central to the institution, is not an easy transition conceptually. Understanding the notion of "building capacity" requires a clear picture of the stakes for *institutions* concerning diversity. Here I want to suggest a useful parallel, aligning diversity with campus efforts to build capacity for technology.

Several decades ago, as technological shifts began, campuses all across the country understood that their viability as institutions would rest on building capacity for technology. Technology was understood to be central, not marginal, to teaching and research. Most critically, technology was also seen as central to the viability of every institution, that is, to how the institution communicated, built infrastructure, spent money, and went about hiring. The absence of technology was seen as a threat to the attractiveness of campuses and their ability to function. Moreover, because technology is continually changing, institutions, almost without question, have adapted as new technologies have been introduced. A redesign of all institutional domains—from the curriculum to hiring to infrastructure—has occurred. Technology, being at its core, is now a part of everyday life and of every corner of institutional life. And, on many campuses, a position has been created for a Chief Information Officer whose task is to develop strategies for the future, for allocating resources, and for coordinating campus efforts.

Building technological capacity has required that institutions develop the human, physical, fiscal, knowledge, and cultural resources to respond effectively in a technological society. The technology imperative required institutions to change in order to be excellent; it was not about changing just so students would be competent. Significantly, there was and has been skepticism, and even hostility, regarding the impact of technology on society and institutions. While much of the fears that were generated have not come to pass, it was also true that no one waited for the skeptics to be satisfied. Rather, technology was understood to be a given, and institutions realized that engaging technology was imperative for their viability.

Higher Education and Diversity Today

We are now at a time when diversity, like technology, is a powerful presence. Current work suggests that increasing numbers of institutions will need to address diversity to be credible or, indeed, viable. An understanding of the role of diversity for institutional viability and vitality is emerging in business and other sectors of society. It is already fundamental to urban planning and the language of community building. Reframing diversity as central to institutional effectiveness, excellence, and viability will no doubt be a requisite for higher education. For example, enrollment-dependent institutions in the Midwest are already working to become more attractive to Latino and Asian communities in the Southwest.

One way to think about diversity in the twenty-first century is to begin with a scan of many compelling issues in society that are linked to diversity and higher education. Changing demographics, increasing demands for equity from many groups, immigration, health disparities, educational disparities, inequities, civil rights, nation states and ethnic identity, the strengthening of indigenous communities, acknowledgment of histories of injustice, equity in the workplace, and the business interest of appealing to diverse markets are among the larger topics with implications for higher education and diversity.

A fundamental question emerging in the literature is how society goes about building its capacity to harness the talent and full participation of its citizens in order to address the compelling challenges it faces. Indeed, almost every report that explores the political and economic future of society begins by discussing education and its role. For example, in its 2005 report, *Now Is the Time*, the American Association of State Colleges and Universities and the National Association of State Universities and Land-Grant Colleges declare that "the promise of a truly just and truly multicultural democracy made possible through a more diverse academy cannot wait for another generation. The challenge for change within higher education must be taken up and addressed boldly. And it must be addressed today."[10]

What, then, is higher education's role? The tendency in much of the literature is to imagine education as a linear path in which higher education is the elite end of the pipeline, with K–12 as the place to begin. At one point, the notion was that if K–12 were fixed, the problem would be fixed. Increasingly, however, higher education is understood as crucial to educational reform. Teacher training, workforce development, knowledge creation, and student success are just a few of the mandates linked to higher education. Yet, despite improvements in the pipeline, there is evidence that higher education is not prepared to educate the diverse students who come to its institutions. More critically, it is not well-enough prepared to identify talent and excellence in students, in staff, or in faculty to take full advantage of the talent and excellence that currently exists.

In this next generation of diversity work, student success is a necessary but not always sufficient indicator of institutional effectiveness. Judging from the literature, the next generation will need to take a systems approach to diversity, focusing on building capacity in all sectors: identifying talent, expanding the knowledge and research base, and even engaging in difficult dialogues. The literature strongly suggests that developing capacity for diversity will require, among other things, engaging more deeply with mission, including being able to link diversity with excellence; framing diversity in ways that are both inclusive and differentiated; building human capacity; and mounting an intentional effort to monitor progress.[11]

Mission

The role of institutional mission is emerging as central to much of the writing and research on diversity seen from an institutional perspective. It has become clear that a key lever for change is the degree to which diversity is understood to be an imperative for the institution—an imperative that goes beyond simply serving students. A mission that places diversity at its center has implications for student success, for creating inclusive environments, and for fostering the benefits of diversity.

On many campuses, diversity efforts focus on undergraduate students and on admissions criteria. As important as these are, they are issues for only a small set of institutions. Even as diversity in admissions has been a central topic for selective institutions, increasing numbers of campuses are beginning to ask how and in what ways diversity is relevant to a university's *research* mission. Why is diversity in STEM fields important—not only at the undergraduate level, but at the field level? Why is diversity vital to a high-quality medical education in the twenty-first century? These questions were previously answered with regard to technology, and the answers helped instigate fundamental changes in institutions. The same now applies to diversity. Framing diversity as central, rather than parallel, to the core mission of a campus or a field requires a deep understanding of the institution, its history, its position, and the imperatives that motivate it.

Operationalizing Diversity as Inclusive and Differentiated

The definition of diversity is a challenging one these days. Indeed, on many campuses, diversity committees begin with the question, how will we define diversity? The subtext asks, are we to be inclusive or should we focus only on the historic issues of racial (or gender) inequities on campus? The reality is that there is a growing list of questions to be considered, with a growing set of projects and programs designed to provide support and promote institutional change. Historic and largely unfinished efforts related to race, class, and gender are being addressed. Other concerns—applying to disability, sexual orientation, gender identity, immigration, and religion, among others—are also pressing topics. This has led to strong criticism of many diversity efforts, seeing them as losing a crucial focus on historic issues of inequity in favor of a laundry list of concerns. At the same time, how can a campus choose among legitimate concerns expressed by diverse groups?

The evolution of diversity, as described earlier, shows how it can be understood to be both inclusive and differentiated. With careful articulation, it would seem possible to move forward on multiple fronts. In this conceptualization, access and the success of historically underrepresented populations remain the legacy and the soul of diversity. Moreover, the research on both diversity and identity makes it clear that intersections of identities and the multiplicity of identities will need to be addressed, even for traditionally underrepresented populations; these are places where gender and class, as well as other identities, are gaining in significance. Linking diversity to this multiplicity of identities, to the intersections of identities, and to their institutional and societal contexts is conceptually and analytically important.

Figure 17.1 presents a conceptual framework to reflect one way of capturing diversity across four institutional dimensions. Each engages different aspects of the university and encompasses much of the diversity work that is occurring. Each dimension is also clearly connected to the others. Together, they frame a way to think about an operational approach to diversity that is both inclusive and differentiated. While this figure was designed to foster thought about diversity institutionally, these four dimensions may also be useful in thinking about the larger task of systemic change. Moreover, because institutions (either within or outside of higher education) are centers for much of this effort, the institutional and societal connections are important and, hence, are reflected in the figure. Finally, if we think of the framework as holistically reflecting the mission and

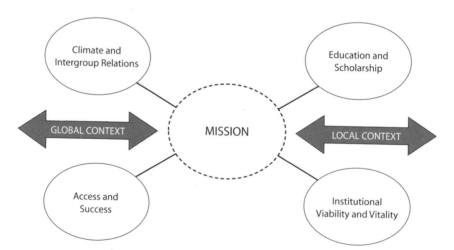

Figure 17.1 Framework for diversity

domains of an institution of higher education, it is not difficult to see how diversity efforts and excellence are linked.

The *institutional viability and vitality* domain, in particular, addresses institutional-level concerns about capacity. How does the mission engage diversity? How are the core indicators of excellence and the priorities for strategic planning directly linked to diversity? For example, if we were to read a strategic plan for a research university, is diversity central in that document? This domain also includes how the institution is viewed from the perspective of diverse communities: whether it is seen as having a commitment to diversity, and whether it has the leadership capacity with the requisite expertise to meet the demands of diversity. Moreover, because institutions are also employers and organizations, excellence will include understanding whether the institution is inclusive, and whether it creates an environment in which all of its members can thrive.

The second domain for diversity reflects what diversity is in the academic core of higher education—*education and scholarship*. What is the knowledge that *all* students (including graduate and professional students) and professionals need to have in a pluralistic society, and what is the capacity of faculty to provide the necessary research and curricular base? In a research university, this dimension might also emphasize graduate education and scholarly contributions. In a community college, attention to success with respect to developmental education is important. This domain focuses not only on what is offered and what students take, but also on what students learn. Thus the educational domain goes directly to learning outcomes, so central to higher education today. What are the core competencies essential to a twenty-first-century education? Do these competencies address both global and domestic sets of issues? Excellence, then, as a twenty-first-century mandate, would be connected to how research, scholarship, teaching, and learning all relate to diversity.

The third dimension focuses on *climate and intergroup relations* on the campus as they apply to students, staff, and faculty. What is the climate, culture, and ultimate attractiveness of the institution, or what is it in a given area, such as STEM? This dimension is often the focus of concern for groups that have experienced marginalization. For all communities of color on predominantly white campuses, campus climate emerges as an essential topic. Climate has also been an important point of departure with respect to women's issues, as well as to those regarding sexual orientation and sexual identity. In the years following 9/11, climate has been a concern for Muslim faculty, staff, and students, along with curricular concerns about whether enough is done to educate all about Islam. Some of the research today suggests that if campuses and departments don't deal with the issue of climate, and don't examine their attractiveness and capacity for people to thrive, pipeline efforts will reach a dead end. Excellence, then, would rest on whether an inclusive environment for diverse groups of faculty, staff, and students has been established.

This dimension also includes a concern for intergroup relationships. How do groups engage across differences? While higher education has begun to address, quite formally, intergroup relationships among students, there has been less engagement of intergroup relationships among faculty and staff. While the higher education literature has focused on the conditions for bringing students together in order to realize the benefits of diversity, applying what has been learned to creating the conditions necessary for bringing people from diverse backgrounds together at every level on a campus—from the president's cabinet, to decision-making bodies, to administrative units, to women's studies departments—is becoming increasingly important.

The literature clearly suggests that one area in which too few institutions have capacity is in that of engaging difficult issues. Even diversity task forces are challenged to talk through the topic of how to be both inclusive and differentiated with regard to diversity. The lack of capacity for such engagement is a powerful and negative model for students, and it also makes campuses increasingly vulnerable to incidents when such issues explode. Moreover, an inability to have difficult dialogues makes it hard to truly use all of the talent available to address the critical challenges of society. A Ford Foundation program recently identified this area as one of the most urgent ones on increasingly diverse campuses.[12] Significantly, the concerns expressed were not just about students. They touched on dealing with conflict in the classroom, decision making on the campus, and community relations.

The last of the four dimensions is really the soul and heritage of diversity in higher education—*access and success of historically underrepresented students.* Here one is asking not just about admissions (who has access?), but also, who succeeds? While graduation rates are often the starting point, increasingly campuses are asking how different groups are thriving. The movement out of STEM fields by many white women and underrepresented groups is taking center stage in current discussions about the human capital needs in STEM and the health professions. Of those who begin with an interest in science, which groups persist and why? For whom is higher education not successful, and what should be done about it?

Indeed, if we map much of the diversity work to date onto these dimensions, we would see that the bulk of it has been focused on improvement in the access and success dimension. Inevitably, however, institutional changes in each of the other dimensions emerge—climate, curriculum, faculty diversity, and so forth. Fortunately, the results of research and the evolution of promising practices in each of these domains are fairly well aligned. Moreover, because of the lack of adequate institutional capacity, focused efforts to support historically underrepresented groups so they can succeed will likely remain a critical priority, requiring strategic programmatic approaches. Excellence will be very much connected to the institution's success in educating diverse populations. This requirement is increasingly central to emerging accreditation practices, as well as federal and state discussions of effectiveness.

Developing Human Capacity: The Rationale for Leadership Diversity

The important role of leadership at all institutional levels in building capacity for diversity is discussed in virtually all of the research and field work in higher education. It focuses not only on the critical role of leaders who may be presidents, but also on faculty, staff, administrators, and even students. While virtually all diversity work emphasizes diversity in leadership, the rationale is often implicit. As such, it deserves some elaboration here. These rationales apply to all the identities reflected in diversity efforts. However, because most of the attention in the leadership arena has been on the continuing inadequate representation of communities of color, they are the focus here.

In the literature on faculty diversity, for example, the rationale for diversity in hiring has relied on an assumption (one that has merit) that student success will be impacted by faculty diversity. The mismatch here is that faculty hiring is rarely determined by student demographics. Thus, while changing institutions for the sake of students is compelling to some, it is but one of the reasons that make diversity compelling for institutional success and excellence.

From both an institutional perspective and the perspective of the field, the central question is, what expertise and talent will be needed for institutions, in order for them to be credible, effective, and viable in a pluralistic society? When technology became central, this was clearly described. What, then, are the reasons that can be identified for diversity in leadership?

—Diversity in leadership represents values concerning equity in both hiring and retention. Any institution that simultaneously describes itself as open and committed to diversity, yet has the faculty or leadership demographic common today, could be seen as disingenuous and hypocritical.

—Diversity is also a central component in the academy's ability to develop newer forms of knowledge. The consistent findings from numerous studies demonstrate the role of diverse faculty in bringing diversity themes to scholarship, in increasing diversity in the curriculum, and in introducing more and different patterns of pedagogy, including upping the engagement of students in the community. The likelihood of framing new questions and approaches is greater when diversity is increased. The result for the institution is better knowledge and more credible applications of it.

—Another way in which leadership diversity contributes is in developing vital relationships with diverse communities. There are few campuses in the United States that have not begun to formulate relationships with communities off campus, many of which are very diverse. Moreover, some funding agencies are requiring campuses to demonstrate relationships with such communities for clinical purposes or educational efforts. At such times, campuses look to demonstrate their capacity with respect to diversity by highlighting key people on campus who can bring legitimacy to those community relationships. Community connections and credibility are compromised without diversity in leadership.

—Faculty and staff from diverse racial and ethnic backgrounds are also essential to the capacity of institutions and policy groups to make fully informed decisions at all levels—what has been called the demography of decision making. Such participation not only increases the likelihood of more informed perspectives, but also increases the credibility of decision making.

—These rationales are implicitly understood with respect to globalization (or technology, for that matter)—where an interest in furthering internationalization as part of an institution's mission almost inevitably involves hiring international faculty who bring educational and scholarly expertise. Moreover, it is clear that having people from international backgrounds represented on the faculty will enhance an institution's credibility and its ability to connect to an increasingly globalized society. While these arguments commonly inform global discussions, they are not always applied when hiring faculty from diverse domestic racial and ethnic backgrounds.

—Faculty and staff diversity is also essential for creating an environment that will be attractive to persons from diverse backgrounds as a good place to work and to develop. Increasing numbers of faculty and administrators (of all backgrounds) are basing their decisions about where to work on the diversity of students and the diversity of faculty and staff on the campus. Until there is sufficient diversity in campus departments and divisions, members of underrepresented groups will struggle to be seen as individuals, rather than as tokens. Environmental appeal appears to be well understood as a critical factor for white women in science. It remains underappreciated as it pertains to URM faculty and students, where the pipeline explanations are dominant.

—Perhaps the most overlooked rationale is the relationship between the current demographics of faculty and staff and the future leadership pipeline. Since most academic administrators come from faculty ranks, a relatively homogenous faculty clearly limits the future development of diversity in leadership—something that is cause for great concern in a number of sectors in higher education.

—Finally, the most frequently mentioned rationale is to provide role models for all. While the empirical literature is mixed, it seems reasonably clear that seeing individuals from diverse backgrounds function in faculty and other leadership roles in all areas provides ways of envisioning oneself (whether as an undergraduate, graduate, or faculty member) in that role or experiencing others there. While less often mentioned or studied, it is likely that the *absence* of diversity in so many departments and fields is what sends strong signals about what is possible and about the degree to which talent from diverse groups is valued. Recent research in STEM fields highlights the number of os and 1s in the count of URM and white women in many science and medical school departments.[13]

These reasons are both broad and deep in their implications for diversifying leadership—the core strategy for building capacity. A review of current research and emerging literature on promising practices suggest that higher education will have to "interrupt the usual" to build its potential to identify talent and excellence in hiring and promotion.

Monitoring Progress

A number of different initiatives have all concluded that monitoring progress will be essential for change.[14] The reality on many campuses is that perceptions of progress toward diversity are very much influenced by individual perspectives. Leaders often need to highlight positive changes, even as many in the institution see little or no change in other domains. Talking past one another is common, but it is an impediment to change.

The literature also recognizes that using data for decision making, especially in higher education, is difficult. This is not about compliance. Indeed, most of this literature frames its emphasis on the role of data in terms of organizational learning—that is, using data to assist in making decisions or evaluating progress. On too many campuses, diversity task forces are spinning their wheels or generating programs that the same few people have to oversee. Moreover, because creating programs does not require *addressing* institutional change, the proliferation of programs is leading to "projectitis" rather than change.[15] The guiding question now is, how can an institution know if it is making progress, and in what areas, so that resources can be strategically applied?

While the following paragraphs focus on key indicators that are often quantitative, qualitative assessments are also important. The quantitative indicators, however, serve as ways of seeing directions for change from an institutional or unit perspective. In fact, key indicators associated with each of the dimensions of diversity in figure 17.1 are beginning to be identified.

To date, the most common of these have to do with the access and success demographics of underrepresented students, disaggregated by race intersected with gender. Because patterns for African American, Latino, and American Indian men and women often differ, today's disaggregation among URM as well as Asian groups is providing more complete data. Work in the access and success dimension is now focusing on indicators of success and institutional practices that facilitate success. Persistence and graduation rates are the most common, again disaggregated at least by race and gender. While graduation rates have been controversial—because of differences in institutional selectivity, federal reliance just on statistics for full-time students, and the fact that the information only reveals the graduation rate from a particular institution—these data provide powerful descriptions of an institution's success with the students it admits. Indeed, the cost of dropouts, both to society and to fields such as science and health, is now being documented. On campuses with high graduation rates, another key

indicator being proposed is the diversity in STEM graduates or honors graduates. Moreover, there are data that suggest that many URM students enter
higher education interested in STEM fields but leave during their undergraduate
years, indicating that an emphasis merely on the pipeline may not be altogether
appropriate.

Key indicators emerging in the viability and vitality dimension are faculty,
staff, and board diversity. Because faculty diversity that moves beyond token
representation is connected to every element of capacity building—research,
clinical practice, teaching, decision making, external credibility, and so forth—it
is located in the dimension related to institutional viability. Historically, the diversity of the graduate and professional school population was considered part of
the analysis of student demographics. It is becoming increasingly clear that graduate student and professional school diversity instead needs to be linked to the
pipeline for faculty. Indeed, on many campuses the graduate students are not
much more diverse than the faculty. Higher education produces its own labor
market, so concerns about faculty diversity involve monitoring graduate student
populations as well.

What might indicators in the educational and scholarship domain be—at
least, indicators that can be monitored?[16] For example, in medicine, to what degree does a medical education include cultural competency? Who is exposed to
such a curriculum? What about the content of continuing education for physi-
cians? Where and how much research is addressing diversity in health care, medicine, pharmacology, and the like? In the study of higher education, to what degree does the literature on organizational culture or leadership deeply engage the
ways in which diversity influences and informs both theory and practice? A review of these areas suggests that a deep engagement with diversity is largely absent from the classical study of leadership and organizational culture, while there
is a rich literature on that topic emanating from the study of diversity in higher
education.

In the climate domain, there are a number of key indicators that are used. A
powerful one for campuses has been the perception of an institution's commitment to diversity, disaggregated by constituency and identity groups. Single questions on overall satisfaction, and whether one would choose the institution (or
field) again, can be very illuminating when disaggregated. While invisible forms
of identity have often rendered some communities "silent" in official data, more
and more campuses are asking about the campus climate for the LGBTQ community as well.

Implications for Higher Education as a Field of Study

Just as diversity has often functioned parallel to core institutional domains, parallelism is also true in some areas in the study of higher education. While there is a substantial body of literature on college students that addresses diversity, less has been done on how diversity perspectives impact the study of organizations, especially in the context of higher education. Moreover, where diversity and organizational theory and practice are linked, the research and theory are often located in a larger body of literature connected to diversity, rather than to the study of higher education organizations.

Adrianna Kezar, Rozana Carducci, and Melissa Contreras-McGavin note that while literatures exist that do study, for example, leadership in cross-cultural contexts, little of that has impacted the core study of leadership in higher education.[17] Though there is considerable research on institutional change, Anthony Antonio and Marcela Muñiz suggest that work on the intersection of diversity and transformation has only begun.[18] Further, many scholars of color have observed that observations on how institutions are racialized or gendered are largely absent from the study of organizations within or outside of higher education.[19] Marta Calás and Linda Smircich describe it this way:

> The organizational literature that supposedly considers gender has been labeled women-in-management literature. The . . . label reveals that gender is important to organizational theorizing only because the biological entities— women—suddenly arrived in management, changing the nature of the situation. Prior to the entrance of women, there was (apparently) no "gender" in management.[20]

The significance of this quotation is that diversity, and the identities associated with diversity, are not only about individuals and groups. Rather, they are embedded in institutions—and, indeed, in the study of institutions—in ways that are more often ignored than addressed. While the literature on organizational culture often includes some reference to diversity, it is the literature on diversity that highlights the ways in which culture reflects the stratification and values of higher education and society. It is in that literature where what is often described generically as "institutional culture" is uncovered to show the ways in which culture is racialized, gendered, classed, and so on. If the study of culture is to be robust, the processes of how culture is shaped and changed by the dynamics of power and the asymmetry of power in institutions will need to be engaged.[21]

Indeed, Frances Maher and Mary Kay Tetrault, in their study of three universities in transition, found that an important element in institutional transformation, and therefore in the study of institutions, consisted of taking into account
forms of privilege that are embedded in institutional norms and practices—forms
of privilege that may be invisible to some, but are certainly very visible to those
on the margins of that experience.[22] White privilege. Class privilege. Gender
privilege. Heterosexual privilege. Additionally, Robert Merton's concept of cumulative advantage is applicable to the study of higher education, as an aid to
understanding how privilege accrues in institutions.[23]

Just as the scholarship in ethnic studies and women's studies has ultimately
informed many of the disciplines, the field of organizational studies in higher
education is now positioned to benefit from decades of conceptual, theoretical,
and practical work on diversity in higher education.

Conclusion

Diversity as transformation has been apparent in the literature for decades. However, a changing societal context in the United States creates the likelihood that
diversity, like technology, will take its place as more of an imperative, one that
may lead to greater institutional change. And the pressure for change, as in the
past, will most likely come from a variety of external entities. By framing diversity
as central to the institution and to society, and emphasizing it as an imperative,
campuses may be positioned to positively address contemporary challenges.

The emerging research suggests some important elements for building capacity: establishing links to mission and excellence; framing diversity as inclusive
and differentiated; increasing diversity in leadership; and monitoring progress. It
is clear from the literature that building institutional capacity so that individuals
and groups can thrive will not be easy, but it is a critical component. Intentionality, rather than myths and excuses to explain a lack of progress, and the fostering
of synergy among the many creative efforts and talented people already working
in the area both appear to provide proactive and inclusive ways to create change.
Finally, identifying key indicators and monitoring progress on a regular basis,
with some form of accountability, is emerging in the literature as vital for institutions, in order to see where progress is being made and where more work is
needed.

Higher education's crucial role in building a thriving pluralistic and equitable
society is now being established. Reorienting diversity to an institutional level

488   *Daryl G. Smith*

will be necessary if real progress is to be made. Diversity is no longer an option. Calls for accountability, and concerns about society, will make this agenda more and more urgent, and they are likely to determine higher education's role as a public good for a healthy democracy.

NOTES

1. For a more complete and extensive analysis see Daryl G. Smith, *Diversity's Promise for Higher Education: Making it Work* (Baltimore: Johns Hopkins University Press, 2009).

2. See, for example, Bryan J. Cook and Diana. I. Córdova, *Minorities in Higher Education: Twenty-Second Annual Status Report* (Washington, DC: American Council on Education, 2006); Michael J. Cuyjet, "African American College Men," in *African American Men in College*, ed. Michael J. Cuyjet (San Francisco: Jossey-Bass, 2006), 3–23; Catherine E. Freeman, *Trends in Educational Equity of Girls and Women: 2004*, NCES 2005-016 (Washington, DC: U.S. Department of Education, Institute of Education Sciences, 2005); Jacqueline E. King, *Gender Equity in Higher Education: 2006* (Washington DC: American Council on Education, Center for Policy Analysis, 2006); National Research Council, *Hispanics and the Future of America* (Washington, DC: National Academy Press, 2006).

3. National Center for Educational Statistics, *Projections of Education Statistics to 2018* (2009), table 22, http://nces.ed.gov/pubsearch/pubsinfo.asp?pubid=2009062.

4. José F. Moreno, Daryl G. Smith, Alma R. Clayton-Pedersen, Sharon Parker, and Daniel H. Teraguchi, *The Revolving Door for Underrepresented Minority Faculty in Higher Education* (San Francisco: James Irvine Foundation, 2006), www.irvine.org/assets/pdf/pubs/education/insight_Revolving_Door.pdf; see also Smith, *Diversity's Promise*.

5. Alma R. Clayton-Pedersen, Sharon Parker, Daryl G. Smith, José. F. Moreno, and Daniel H. Teraguchi, *Making a Real Difference with Diversity: A Guide to Institutional Change* (Washington, DC: Association of American Colleges and Universities, 2007); see also Moreno et al., *Revolving Door*; Smith, *Diversity's Promise*.

6. See, for example, Elizabeth K. Minnich, *Transforming Knowledge*, 2nd ed. (Philadelphia: Temple University Press, 2005); Fabio Rojas, *From Black Power to Black Studies: How a Radical Social Movement Became an Academic Discipline* (Baltimore: Johns Hopkins University Press, 2007); Linda T. Smith, *Decolonizing Methodologies: Research and Indigenous Peoples* (London: Zed Books, 1999).

7. Carl Cohen and James P. Sterba, *Affirmative Action and Racial Preference: A Debate* (New York: Oxford University Press, 2003); Shelby Steele, *A Dream Deferred* (New York: HarperCollins, 1999); Richard H. Sander, "A Systemic Analysis of Affirmative Action in American Law Schools," *Stanford Law Review* 57, no. 2 (2004): 367–484; Mark A. Chesler, Amanda E. Lewis, and James E. Crowfoot, *Challenging Racism in Higher Education: Promoting Justice* (Oxford: Rowman and Littlefield, 2005).

8. There is a tendency to assume that only publics external to higher education need to be engaged. Instead, several of the movements against affirmative action in higher education began with internal constituencies of faculty and/or alumni.

9. Smith, *Diversity's Promise*.

10. American Association of State Colleges and Universities and National Association of State Universities and Land-Grant Colleges, *Now Is the Time: Meeting the Challenge for a Diverse Academy* (Washington, DC: American Association of State Colleges and Universities and National Association of State Universities and Land-Grant Colleges, 2005), 3.

11. See, for example, Estela M. Bensimon, "The Diversity Scorecard: A Learning Approach to Institutional Change," *Change* 36, no. 1 (2004): 45–52; Clayton-Pedersen et al., *Making a Real Difference*; Smith, *Diversity's Promise*.

12. Ford Foundation, *Difficult Dialogues: Promoting Pluralism and Academic Freedom*, http://fordfound.org/news/more/dialogues/05_difficult_dialogues_letter.pdf [accessed June 20, 2005].

13. Donna J. Nelson and Diana C. Rogers, *A National Analysis of Diversity in Science and Engineering Faculties at Research Universities*, www.now.org/issues/diverse/diversity_report.pdf [accessed June 15, 2007].

14. See, for example, Susan P. Sturm, "The Architecture of Inclusion: Advancing Workplace Equity in Higher Education," Columbia Public Law Research Paper No. 06-114 and *Harvard Journal of Law & Gender* 29, no. 2 (June 2006), http://ssrn.com/abstract=901992; Clayton-Pedersen et al., *Making a Real Difference*; Peter D. Eckel, Madeleine F. Green, and Barbara Hill, *On Change V: Riding the Waves of Change; Insights from Transforming Institutions* (Washington, DC: American Council on Education, 2001); Adrianna J. Kezar and Peter D. Eckel, *Leadership Strategies for Advancing Campus Diversity: Advice from Experienced Presidents* (Washington, DC: American Council on Education, 2005). Also see note 11.

15. Robert Shireman, "10 Questions College Officials Should Ask about Diversity," *Chronicle Review*, Aug. 15, 2003, http://chronicle.com/article/10-Questions-College-Offici/22781/.

16. More information about key indicators can be found in Smith, *Diversity's Promise*.

17. Adrianna J. Kezar, Rozana Carducci, and Melissa Contreras-McGavin, *Rethinking the "L" Word in Higher Education*, ASHE Higher Education Report, vol. 31, no 6 (San Francisco: Jossey-Bass, 2006).

18. Anthony L. Antonio and Marcela M. Muñiz, "The Sociology of Diversity," in *Sociology of Higher Education: Contributions and Their Context*, ed. Patricia J. Gumport (Baltimore: Johns Hopkins University Press, 2007), 266–94.

19. See, for example, Stella M. Nkomo and Taylor Cox, Jr., "Diverse Identities in Organizations," in *Handbook of Organization Studies*, ed. Stewart Clegg, Cynthia Hardy, and Walter R. Nord (Thousand Oaks, CA: Sage, 1996), 338–56.

20. Marta B. Calás and Linda Smircich, "Re-Writing Gender into Organizational Theorizing: Directions from Feminist Perspectives," in *Rethinking Organization: New*

Directions in Organization Theory and Analysis, ed. Michael I. Reed and Michael Hughes (London: Sage, 1992), 229.

21. See, for example, Regina D. Langhout, Francine Rosselli, and Jonathan Feinstein, "Assessing Classism in Academic Settings," *Review of Higher Education* 30, no. 2 (2006): 145–84.

22. Frances A. Maher and Mary Kay Tetrault, *Privilege and Diversity in the Academy* (New York: Routledge, 2007).

23. Robert K. Merton, "The Matthew Effect in Science, II: Cumulative Advantage and the Symbolism of Intellectual Property," *ISIS* 79 (1988): 606–23.

Contributors

Philip G. Altbach is the Monan University Professor and director of the Center for International Higher Education at Boston College. He served as editor of the *Review of Higher Education.* He is author of *Tradition and Transition: The International Imperative in Higher Education, Comparative Higher Education, The Knowledge Context,* and other books. He coedited *World-Class Worldwide: Research Universities in Developing and Middle-Income Countries* and *Asian Universities: Historical Perspectives and Contemporary Challenges,* both published by the Johns Hopkins University Press. He served as Distinguished Scholar Leader of the Fulbright New Century Scholars program.

Benjamin Baez is an associate professor of higher education in the Department of Leadership and Professional Studies at Florida International University (FIU). He received his law degree in 1988 and his doctorate in higher education in 1997, both from Syracuse University. Baez is also the vice president of the FIU chapter of the United Faculty of Florida. He recently published two books, *The Politics of Inquiry: Education Research and the "Culture of Science"* (with Deron Boyles) and *Understanding Minority-Serving Institutions: Interdisciplinary Perspectives* (with Marybeth Gasman and Caroline Turner), both from the State University of New York Press (2009). He also published *Affirmative Action, Hate Speech, and Tenure: Narratives About Race, Law, and the Academy* (Routledge, 2002).

Michael N. Bastedo is an associate professor in the Center for the Study of Higher and Postsecondary Education at the University of Michigan. His expertise is in the governance and politics of higher education in the United States and abroad. His work has been published in the *American Educational Research Journal, Review of Higher Education, Higher Education,* and *Research in Higher Education.* He has been a Fulbright New Century Scholar in the Netherlands, research director of the Institutes on Public University Governance, and a Ford Foundation Global Policy Fellow at the Institute for Higher Education Policy.

Robert O. Berdahl is a professor emeritus of higher education in the College of Education at the University of Maryland, College Park. He has written extensively on governance issues and on statewide coordination in higher education.

Marjorie A. E. Cook is a doctoral candidate in the Educational Leadership and Policy Analysis program in the School of Education at the University of Wisconsin–Madison.

Melanie E. Corrigan is the assistant director of the Center for Policy Analysis at the American Council on Education (ACE). Prior to joining ACE, she conducted federal policy analysis and research for the National Association of Independent Colleges and Universities.

Judith S. Eaton is the president of the Council for Higher Education Accreditation (CHEA), an institutional membership organization of degree-granting colleges and universities based in Washington, D.C. Prior to joining CHEA, she served as chancellor of the Minnesota State Colleges and Universities, president of the Community College of Philadelphia, and president of the Community College of Southern Nevada.

Peter D. Eckel is the director of programs and initiatives in the American Council on Education's Center for Effective Leadership. His portfolio includes the *ACE Institute for New CAOs*; *Advancing to the Presidency: A Workshop on Successful Presidential Search and Transition*; and the ACE Presidential Roundtable series. His latest two books are *Changing Course: Making the Hard Decisions to Eliminate Academic Programs* (2nd ed., Rowman and Littlefield) and *Privatizing the Public University*, with Christopher Morphew (Johns Hopkins University Press).

Gustavo Fischman is an associate professor in the Division of Advanced Studies in Educational Policy, Leadership, & Curriculum in the Mary Lou Fulton Institute & Graduate School of Education at Arizona State University. His research background is in comparative education and critical policy studies. He is the editor of *Educational Policy Analysis Archives / Archivos Análiticos de Políticas Educativas* and *Education Review / Reseñas Educativas*, and the author of four books and numerous articles on higher education, teacher education, and gender issues in education.

Roger L. Geiger is the Distinguished Professor of Higher Education at the Pennsylvania State University. He is the author of *Research and Relevant Knowledge:*

American Research Universities since World War II (Oxford University Press) and the editor of the *History of Higher Education Annual.*

Lawrence E. Gladieux is an independent consultant. Among his clients are the U.S. Department of Education, the Gates Foundation, and others. He is former executive director of the Washington office of the College Board.

Sara Goldrick-Rab is an assistant professor of educational policy studies and sociology at the University of Wisconsin–Madison. She is also a Senior Scholar at the Wisconsin Center for the Advancement of Postsecondary Education and an affiliate of the Institute for Research on Poverty, the LaFollette School of Public Affairs, and the Consortium for Chicago School Research. Dr. Goldrick-Rab was named a Rising Scholar in Higher Education in 2004 by the National Forum on Higher Education for the Public Good, received a Spencer Foundation / National Academy of Education postdoctoral fellowship in 2006, and in 2010 was awarded the William T. Grant Foundation's Faculty Scholars Award.

Patricia J. Gumport serves concurrently as the vice-provost for graduate education, a professor of education, and the director of the Stanford Institute for Higher Education Research at Stanford University. Her most recent book is an edited volume, *Sociology of Higher Education: Contributions and Their Contexts,* also published by the Johns Hopkins University Press (2007).

Fred F. Harcleroad is a professor emeritus of higher education at the University of Arizona and the founding director of the Center for the Study of Higher Education there. Previously, he served as the founding president of the California State University, East Bay, and as president of the American College Testing Program.

D. Bruce Johnstone is the Distinguished Service Professor of Higher and Comparative Education Emeritus at the State University of New York at Buffalo and director of the International Comparative Higher Education Finance and Accessibility Project. His principal scholarship is in international comparative higher education, higher education finance, governance, and policy formation, and he is the author of many books, monographs, articles, and chapters on these topics. His project has conducted conferences and workshops in Dar es Salaam, Arusha, Nairobi, Prague, Moscow, and Wuhan. He has been a speaker at many international conferences and a World Bank consultant on higher education reform projects in Morocco, Romania, and Kenya. Prior to the

University at Buffalo, he held the posts of vice president for administration at the University of Pennsylvania, president of the State University College of Buffalo, and chancellor of the State University of New York System.

Adrianna Kezar is an associate professor for higher education at the University of Southern California. She has published over seventy-five journal articles, fifty book chapters, and twelve books. She authored two new books in 2009: *Organizing for Collaboration* (Jossey-Bass) and *Rethinking Leadership Practices in a Complex, Multicultural, and Global World* (Stylus Press).

Jacqueline E. King is the founding director of the Center for Policy Analysis at the American Council on Education (ACE). Prior to assuming this role in October 2000, she served for four years as the director of federal policy in the ACE division of government and public affairs and for two years as the associate director for policy analysis at the College Board. She is the editor of *Financing a College Education: How It Works, How It's Changing* (Oryx Press).

Aims C. McGuinness, Jr., is a senior associate with the National Center for Higher Education Management Systems, Boulder, Colorado. He was previously at the Education Commission of the States. He has advised many of the states on major higher education reforms and also has been involved in international projects of the World Bank and the Organisation for Economic Co-operation and Development

Amy Scott Metcalfe is an assistant professor of higher education in the Department of Educational Studies at the University of British Columbia. The focus of her work is research policy, and the theoretical basis for her scholarship stems from critiques of capital formation in the public sphere, feminism, and the sociology of science and organizations. Her publications have appeared in *Higher Education*, the *Journal of Higher Education*, and the *Canadian Journal of Higher Education*, and she has recently coauthored (with Matthew M. Mars) an Association for the Study of Higher Education (ASHE) Higher Education Report, *The Entrepreneurial Domains of American Higher Education* (Jossey-Bass, 2009).

Michael Mumper is a professor of government and provost at Adams State College in Colorado. Previously, he served as the chair of the Political Science Department and associate provost for graduate studies at Ohio University. His area of specialization is higher education policy and finance. He is the author of *Removing*

College Price Barriers: What Government Has Done and Why It Hasn't Worked (State University of New York Press, 1996).

Michael A. Olivas is the William B. Bates Distinguished Chair in Law at the University of Houston Law Center and director of the Institute for Higher Education Law and Governance at the University of Houston. He has been elected to membership in the American Law Institute and the National Academy of Education, the only person to have been selected to both honor academies. He served as general counsel to the American Association of University Professors (AAUP) from 1994 to 1998. He is president of the Association of American Law Schools.

Robert M. O'Neil is a professor of law and director of the Thomas Jefferson Center for the Protection of Free Expression at the University of Virginia. He served as president of the University of Wisconsin System from 1980 to 1985 and of the University of Virginia from 1985 to 1990. He has also served as a trustee of several corporations and nonprofit agencies, including the Carnegie Foundation for the Advancement of Teaching and the Educational Testing Service.

Gary Rhoades is on leave as professor of higher education at the University of Arizona, where he served for eleven years as the director of the Center for the Study of Higher Education. He is currently the general secretary of the American Association of University Professors, trying to further translate into practice the focus of his scholarly work of twenty-five years on the restructuring of academic institutions and professions. Two books in particular capture his work in this realm, *Academic Capitalism and the New Economy* (coauthored with Sheila Slaughter, Johns Hopkins University Press, 2004) and *Managed Professionals* (State University of New York Press, 1998).

Frank A. Schmidtlein is an associate professor emeritus in the Department of Education Policy and Leadership at the University of Maryland, College Park. He serves as an associate editor of *Higher Education Planning* and is on the editorial board of *Tertiary Education and Management*.

Sheila Slaughter is the Louise McBee Professor of Higher Education in the Institute of Higher Education at the University of Georgia. Her research areas are the political economy of higher education, with an emphasis on marketization; science and technology policy; academic freedom; and women in higher education.

Daryl G. Smith is a professor of education and psychology at the Claremont Graduate University. Prior to her faculty position, she was a college administrator for twenty-two years. Her research and writing have focused extensively on diversity issues in higher education, and she is the author of *Diversity's Promise for Higher Education: Making It Work* (Johns Hopkins University Press, 2009).

John Willinsky is the Khosla Family Professor of Education at Stanford University and director of the Public Knowledge Project (PKP) at Stanford, the University of British Columbia, and Simon Fraser University. Much of his work, including his book, *The Access Principle: The Case for Open Access to Research and Scholarship* (MIT Press, 2006), the winner of two outstanding book awards, as well as PKP's open-source software for journals and conferences, is free to download through the project's Web site (http://pkp. sfu.ca).

Index